A TEXT BOOK OF

# BASIC ELECTRICAL DRIVES AND CONTROLS

FOR

Second Year Degree Course in
Mechanical and Automobile Engineering

As Per Syllabus of North Maharashtra University, Jalgaon

**B. P. PATIL**
'Best Teacher Award Winner',
Government of Maharashtra,
Formerly Head, Deptt. of Electrical Engg.,
Government Polytechnic Jalgaon & Aurangabad.

**K. R. PATIL**
Head, Electrical Engg. Deptt.
K.C.E.'s College of Engg., Jalgaon,
Formerly Head, Deptt. of Electrical Engg.,
Government Polytechnic, Jalgaon.

# NIRALI PRAKASHAN

**BASIC ELECTRICAL DRIVES AND CONTROLS (NMU) Sem. - II**

**First Edition** : March, 2014

**ISBN 978-93-5164-000-4**

© : **Authors**

The text of this publication, or any part thereof, should not be reproduced or transmitted in any form or stored in any computer storage system or device for distribution including photocopy, recording, taping or information retrieval system or reproduced on any disc, tape, perforated media or other information storage device etc., without the written permission of Authors with whom the rights are reserved. Breach of this condition is liable for legal action.

Every effort has been made to avoid errors or omissions in this publication. In spite of this, errors may have crept in. Any mistake, error or discrepancy so noted and shall be brought to our notice shall be taken care of in the next edition. It is notified that neither the publisher nor the authors or seller shall be responsible for any damage or loss of action to any one, of any kind, in any manner, therefrom.

**Published By :**
**NIRALI PRAKASHAN**
Abhyudaya Pragati, 1312, Shivaji Nagar,
Off J.M. Road, PUNE – 411005
Tel - (020) 25512336/37/39, Fax - (020) 25511379
Email : niralipune@pragationline.com

**Printed at**
**Repro Knowledgecast Limited**
**India**

## DISTRIBUTION CENTRES
### PUNE

*Nirali Prakashan*
119, Budhwar Peth, Jogeshwari Mandir Lane
Pune 411002, Maharashtra
Tel : (020) 2445 2044, 66022708, Fax : (020) 2445 1538
Email : bookorder@pragationline.com

*Nirali Prakashan*
S. No. 28/25, Dhyari,
Near Pari Company, Pune 411041
Tel : (022) 24690204 Fax : (020) 24690316
Email : dhyari@pragationline.com
            bookorder@pragationline.com

### MUMBAI
*Nirali Prakashan*
385, S.V.P. Road, Rasdhara Co-op. Hsg. Society Ltd.,
Girgaum, Mumbai 400004, Maharashtra
Tel : (022) 2385 6339 / 2386 9976, Fax : (022) 2386 9976
Email : niralimumbai@pragationline.com

## DISTRIBUTION BRANCHES

**NAGPUR**
*Pratibha Book Distributors*
Above Maratha Mandir, Shop No. 3, First Floor,
Rani Jhanshi Square, Sitabuldi, Nagpur 440012,
Maharashtra, Tel : (0712) 254 7129

**BENGALURU**
*Pragati Book House*
House No. 1, Sanjeevappa Lane, Avenue Road Cross,
Opp. Rice Church, Bengaluru – 560002.
Tel : (080) 64513344, 64513355,
Mob : 9880582331, 9845021552
Email:bharatsavla@yahoo.com

**JALGAON**
*Nirali Prakashan*
34, V. V. Golani Market, Navi Peth, Jalgaon 425001,
Maharashtra, Tel : (0257) 222 0395
Mob : 94234 91860

**KOLHAPUR**
*Nirali Prakashan*
New Mahadvar Road,
Kedar Plaza, 1st Floor Opp. IDBI Bank
Kolhapur 416 012, Maharashtra. Mob : 9855046155

### CHENNAI
*Pragati Books*
9/1, Montieth Road, Behind Taas Mahal, Egmore,
Chennai 600008 Tamil Nadu, Tel : (044) 6518 3535,
Mob : 94440 01782 / 98450 21552 / 98805 82331, Email : bharatsavla@yahoo.com

## RETAIL OUTLETS
### PUNE

*Pragati Book Centre*
157, Budhwar Peth, Opp. Ratan Talkies,
Pune 411002, Maharashtra
Tel : (020) 2445 8887 / 6602 2707, Fax : (020) 2445 8887
*Pragati Book Centre*
Amber Chamber, 28/A, Budhwar Peth,
Appa Balwant Chowk, Pune : 411002, Maharashtra,
Tel : (020) 20240335 / 66281669
Email : pbcpune@pragationline.com

*Pragati Book Centre*
676/B, Budhwar Peth, Opp. Jogeshwari Mandir,
Pune 411002, Maharashtra
Tel : (020) 6601 7784 / 6602 0855
*PBC Book Sellers & Stationers*
152, Budhwar Peth, Pune 411002, Maharashtra
Tel : (020) 2445 2254 / 6609 2463

### MUMBAI
*Pragati Book Corner*
Indira Niwas, 111 - A, Bhavani Shankar Road, Dadar (W), Mumbai 400028, Maharashtra
Tel : (022) 2422 3526 / 6662 5254, Email : pbcmumbai@pragationline.com

# Preface

We are glad to present the text book on **'Basic Electrical Drives and Controls'** written as per the syllabus of North Maharashtra University, Jalgaon, for the students of Second Year Degree Course in Mechanical and Automobile Engineering.

This book contains number of figures, sketches, circuit diagrams with the help of which the subject matter is explained in simple language, so that students and teachers will understand the subject with ease. At the end of each chapter number of examples with solutions solved steps by step wherever required are added. At the same time questions which may occur in examination papers are given.

We hope that this book will receive good response from students and teachers community, and we are confident that it will fulfill all their requirements in connection with the subject.

Our special appreciation goes to Shri Dineshbhai Furia, Shri Jigneshbhai Furia, Mr. M. P. Munde of Nirali Prakashan, for publishing this book. We are also thankful to Mr. Ilyas Shaikh, Mrs. Roshan Khan and Ms. Chaitali Takle for preparing this book within a very short span of time.

Authors will be glad to receive feedback from students, teachers and practicing engineers for any correction, addition etc.

**27th February 2014**                                                          **B. P. Patil**
**Pune**                                                                                       **K. R. Patil**

# SYLLABUS

1. **Electric Power Measurement, Electric Energy Measurement, Illumination** (Marks 16)
   (a) Three-phase power measurement by single wattmeter method, two wattmeter method, three wattmeter method.
   (b) Effect of load power factor on wattmeter reading. Measurement of reactive power by one wattmeter method.
   (c) Single phase energy meter (construction and working).
   (d) Various term related to illumination types.
   (e) Requirement of good lighting scheme, special purpose lighting.

2. **D.C. Machines, Special Purpose Machines** (Marks 16)
   (a) Constructional, Working principle of D.C. generator, Types of D.C. generator, e.m.f. equation of D.C. generator (Theoretical concept only).
   (b) Working principle of D.C. motor, back e.mf., e.m.f. equation, types of D.C. motor and torque equation for D.C. motor.
   (c) Characteristics of shunt, series, compound motors, methods for speed control of D.C. shunt and series motor and applications of D.C. motor.
   (d) Explain the necessity of starter and types.
   (e) Principle, working and application of stepper motor, servomotor.

3. **Single Phase and Three Phase Transformers and Three Phase Induction Motor** (Marks 16)
   (a) Working principle and Constructional of Single phase transformer and derive e.m.f. equation. Efficiency of transformers and condition for maximum efficiency of transformer.
   (b) Types of transformer connection star/star, delta/delta, star/delta, delta/star connections, V-V and Scott connections.
   (c) Constructional features of induction motor and working principle of three phase induction motor types.
   (d) Define slip and derive torque equation, explain torque slip characteristics, power stages.
   (e) Explain different types of starters and applications of induction motors.

4. **Single Phase Induction Motors and Synchronous Generator** (Marks 16)
   (a) Principle of operation, types and applications.
   (b) Constructional features (Salient and non-salient) of alternators and principle of operation.
   (c) Pitch factor or chording factor and Distribution factor or winding factors, e.m.f. equation.
   (d) Alternator on load, concept of synchronous reactance and impedance, Phaser diagram of loaded alternator.
   (e) Voltage regulation of alternator by direct loading method and synchronous impedance method.

5. **Sensors, Robotics, DAS and Relays** (Marks 16)
   (a) Proximity sensors, Light sensors.
   (b) Hall effect sensors, Ultrasonic sensors.
   (c) Robotics, Block diagram and operation of Data acquisition system.
   (d) Electromechanical control relays, solid state relays, Timing and latching relays.

# CONTENTS

1. **Measurement of Electrical Power and Electric Energy Measurement, Illumination**  1.1 – 1.86

2. **D.C. Machines and Special Purpose Machines**  2.1 – 2.108

3. **Single Phase and Three Phase Transformers And Three Phase Induction Motor**  3.1 – 3.164

4. **Single Phase Induction Motors and Synchronous Generator**  4.1 – 4.64

5. **Sensors, Robotics, DAS and Relays**  5.1 – 5.54

# Chapter 1

# MEASUREMENT OF ELECTRIC POWER AND ELECTRIC ENERGY MEASUREMENT, ILLUMINATION

## 1.1 CONCEPT OF POEWR IN A.C. CURRENT

### 1.1.1 Active Power

Instantaneous power drawn by an A.C. circuit is equal to the product of instantaneous values of voltage and current.

Thus, instantaneous power = $v \times i$ where, v and i are instantaneous values of voltage and current respectively.

Let the instantaneous value of voltage applied to a circuit be given by:

$$v = V_m \sin \omega t \qquad \ldots (1.1)$$

For a general case, the current flowing in a A.C. circuit is assumed to lag applied voltage by an angle $\phi$.

Then the instantaneous value of current is given by,

$$i = I_m \sin(\omega t - \phi) \qquad \ldots (1.2)$$

$\therefore$ Instantaneous power = $V_m \sin \omega t \times I_m \sin(\omega t - \phi)$

$$= \frac{1}{2} V_m I_m [\cos \phi - \cos(2\omega t - \phi)]$$

$$= \frac{1}{2} V_m I_m \cos \phi - \frac{1}{2} V_m I_m \cos(2\omega t - \phi) \qquad \ldots (1.3)$$

Equation (1.3) consists of two components:

1. $\frac{1}{2} V_m I_m \cos \phi$, which remains constant irrespective of time, and

2. $\frac{1}{2} V_m I_m \cos(2\omega t - \phi)$, indicating the variation of this component of power at twice the supply frequency.

The average value of this component over one complete cycle is zero and hence it does not contribute towards average value of power drawn from supply.

Hence, average power over one cycle is given by:

$$P = \frac{1}{2} V_m I_m \cos\phi \quad \ldots (1.4)$$

$$= \frac{V_m}{\sqrt{2}} \times \frac{I_m}{\sqrt{2}} \times \cos\phi$$

$$= VI \cos\phi \quad \ldots (1.5)$$

where, V and I are the r.m.s. values of applied voltage and current flowing in the circuit and $\cos\phi$ is the power factor of the circuit. The average power is also termed as active power taken by the circuit and is measured in watts.

## 1.1.2 Apparent Power

The product of r.m.s. value of voltage and current in A.C. circuit is normally greater than the active power drawn by the circuit, such a product is termed as apparent power and is measured in volt-ampere (VA).

Thus, Apparent power = $V \times I$ ... (1.6)

## 1.1.3 Reactive Power

In A.C. circuits, current lags or leads the applied voltage by an angle $\phi$. As such current can be resolved into its active and reactive components, the reactive component of current is equal to $I \sin\phi$. Power drawn by circuit due to reactive component of current is called reactive power, and it is given by,

Reactive power = $VI \sin\phi$

## 1.1.4 Principle of Power Measurement

Instruments designed for measurement of power passing in a electrical circuit are called as wattmeters.

In case of D.C. circuits, if the applied voltage remains constant, the reading of ammeter will give indication of power supplied to a circuit, as in this case power is equal to VI watts; hence wattmeters are not so necessary for measurement of power. But in case of A.C. circuits power is given by $VI \cos\phi$ where $\cos\phi$ is the p.f. of the circuit, for measurement of which a third instrument called as p.f. meter is required, hence we have to record the reading of voltmeter, ammeter and p.f. meter and the product of these readings will give the power supplied to a circuit. Instead of that, a wattmeter will directly record the power supplied to a circuit.

## 1.1.5 Wattmeters

Common forms of wattmeters as installed on switch-boards or as portable instruments are of the direct indicating type with pivoted moving elements. Since their modes of operation are basically the same as certain types of ammeters and voltmeters, it is only to be expected that their individual mechanical and electrical component parts are identical with or bear a close resemblance to those already discussed.

There are two types of wattmeters. They are:
1. Dynamometer type
2. Induction type.

The third type i.e. electrostatic type is not used commercially. However, it is very useful for the measurement of small amount of power particularly when the voltage is high and power factor is low. We will now study them separately.

A wattmeter essentially consists of a current coil which carries the load current and a voltage coil (pressure coil) which carries a current proportional to and in phase with the voltage. The fluxes produced by these currents set up a torque on the moving system, making it to deflect.

We will now discuss the working principle of the following types of wattmeters.
(a) Dynamometer type
(b) Induction type
(c) Electrostatic type.

## 1.1.6 Dynamometer Wattmeter (Principle and Construction)

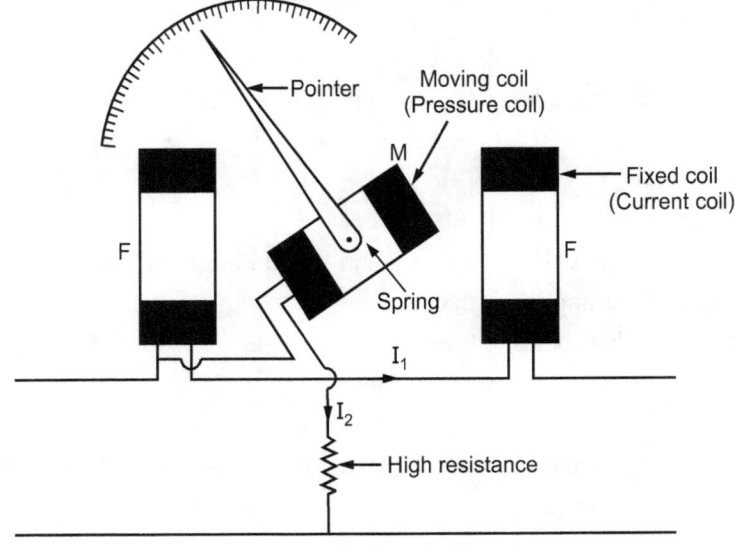

**Fig. 1.1**

The construction of a dynamometer wattmeter is just similar to a dynamometer type ammeter or voltmeter. The internal arrangement and connections are shown in Fig. 1.1. It consists of two fixed coils wound from a thick wire and of few number of turns, they are connected in series and are used for conduction of load current and are called as 'current coil'. It also consists of a moving coil which has large number of turns in comparison to current coil, and is wound from a fine wire. A non-inductive high resistance is connected in series with it. It is connected across supply voltage and is called as 'pressure coil'. The current passing through it is proportional to line voltage. The interaction between the magnetic field produced by the fixed coils and the moving coil produces a torque on the moving coil, making it to move around it's axis. Generally, two springs are used to produce controlling torque. The deflecting torque is proportional to power, which is also proportional to angle of deflection, hence power is proportional to angle of deflection. Hence, the scale is uniform. Here Prisition type air friction damping is generally used.

The average torque in this type of instruments is proportional to power. We will consider the D.C. circuit first.

The flux density produced by current flowing through current coils is directly proportional to current $I_c$ flowing through them.

$$\therefore \quad B \propto I_c \quad \ldots (1.7)$$

If the current flowing through pressure coil is $I_p$
then,
$$I_p \propto V \quad \ldots (1.8)$$

Then deflecting torque $\quad T_d \propto BI_p$

but $B \propto I_c$ and $I_p \propto V$

$$\therefore \quad T_d \propto I_c V$$

But in D.C. circuit, $I_c V$ represents power supplied to a circuit.

$$\therefore \quad T_d \propto \text{Power}$$

In case of A.C. circuit,

Average power, $\quad P = VI \cos \phi$

Where $\phi$ is phase angle between V and I, and V and I are r.m.s. values of voltage applied to a circuit and current flowing through it.

Let instantaneous values be as follows:

$$v = V_m \sin \omega t$$
$$i = I_m \sin (\omega t - \phi)$$

The instantaneous torque produced by them will be proportional to product of instantaneous values of V and I

$$\therefore \quad T \propto v\,i$$

As the inertia of the instrument makes it to record average value of power.

Hence, average power is proportional to average value of v i

and $\quad$ Torque, $T = \int_0^{2\pi} v i \, dt$

$$= \frac{1}{2\pi} \int_0^{2\pi} V_m \sin \omega t \cdot I_m \sin(\omega t - \phi)\, dt$$

$$= \frac{V_m I_m}{2} \cos \phi = \frac{V_m}{\sqrt{2}} \cdot \frac{I_m}{\sqrt{2}} \cdot \cos \phi$$

$$\therefore \quad T = VI \cos \phi$$

where V and I are the r.m.s. values of applied voltage and current flowing through a circuit and, VI cos $\phi$ represents the average value of power supplied to a circuit.

**Advantages:**
1. It is free from eddy current and hysteresis losses.
2. It can be used for measurement of A.C. or D.C. power, without any modification.
3. Scale on dial is uniform.
4. Gives fairly high degree of accuracy in readings.

**Disadvantages:**
1. As air cored coils are used more e.m.f. is required for producing necessary flux, hence number of turns of coils used are large in comparison to iron cored instrument.
2. Heavy moving element makes the torque to weight ratio small, hence the frictional loss is high.
3. Cost of instrument is more.
4. Instrument operates with weak magnetic field because coils are air cored and not wound on any iron core.

### 1.1.6.1 Errors and Their Compensation

**(a) Pressure Coil Inductance:** The pressure coil has inductance effect. For lagging p.f. of load, the angle between current in the current coil circuit and the current in the pressure coil circuit is less than $\phi$, the p.f. angle, hence the wattmeter reading will be higher than the actual, the reverse will be the case in case of leading p.f. loads.

**Compensation for inductance of pressure coil:** Most of the wattmeters are compensated for errors caused by inductance of pressure coil by means of a capacitor connected in parallel with a portion of multiplier (series resistance) as shown in Fig. 1.2.

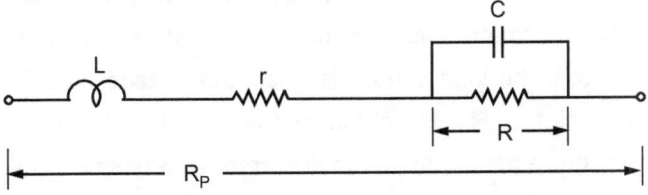

**Fig. 1.2**

**(b) Pressure Coil Capacitance:** The pressure coil may have certain capacitance also. It is mainly due to interturn capacitance of series resistance. The effect of capacitance is opposite to that produced by inductance, hence the wattmeter reads high on lagging p.f. of load.

The phase angle between pressure coil current and the applied voltage depends upon the reactance of the pressure coil circuit. The inductive reactance is generally greater than the capacitive reactance and therefore, the phase angle varies with frequency.

**(c) Error Due to Mutual Inductance Effects:** Errors are caused due to mutual inductance between current and pressure coils of wattmeter. These errors are quite low at power frequencies but they increase and become more important as the frequency is increased.

Instruments have been developed whose coil systems are so arranged that they are always in a zero position of mutual inductance and thus are free from errors caused by mutual inductance effects.

**(d) Errors Caused Because of Connections:** There are two alternate methods of connecting a wattmeter in a circuit, which are shown in Fig. 1.3 (a) and 1.3 (b). Errors are introduced in the measurement owing to power loss in the current and pressure coils.

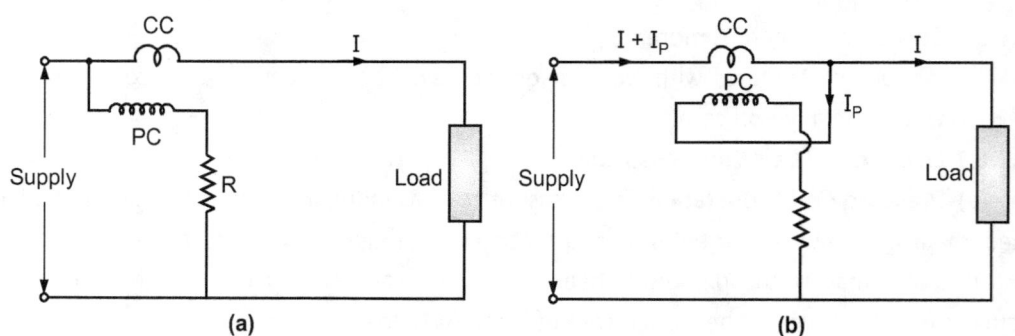

**Fig. 1.3**

In Fig. 1.3 (a), the pressure coil is connected on the supply side and therefore the voltage applied to the pressure coil is the voltage across the load plus voltage drop across the current coil. Hence, the wattmeter measures the power loss in its current coil in addition to power supplied to load. If the load current is small, the voltage drop in the current coil is small, hence the connection of Fig. 1.3 (a) induces very small error. On the other hand if the load current is large, the value of pressure coil current is very small in comparison to load current, hence power loss in the pressure coil will be very small, as compared with load power and therefore connection of Fig. 1.3 (b) is preferred.

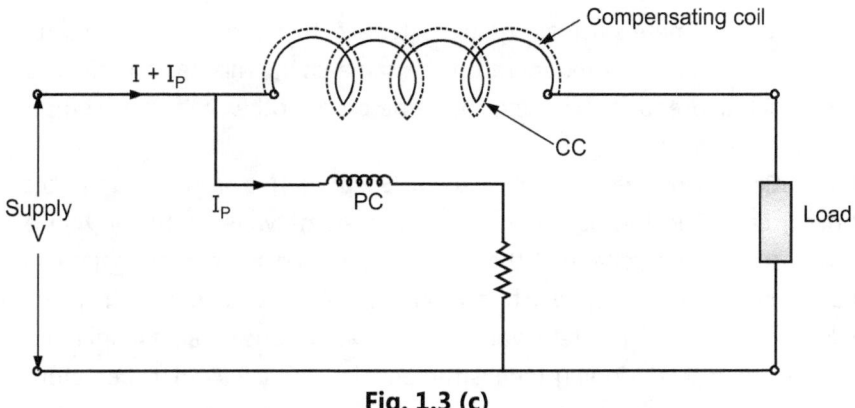

**Fig. 1.3 (c)**

It should be noted that in an uncompensated wattmeter, the reading of wattmeter includes the power loss in the coil connected on the load side. The use of above connections for different applications holds good only if the power loss in the instruments is to be neglected. However, if accuracy requires that power loss in the instrument be taken into account connection of Fig. 1.3 (b) is preferred. However in cases, where the load current is large and p.f. is low, connection of Fig. 1.3 (b) will result in large error since total power measured is small. Hence, in wattmeters which are designed for low p.f. measurement a compensating coil may be used in the instrument for compensating the error caused by power loss in pressure coil circuit. Such a circuit is shown in Fig. 1.3 (c).

**(e) Eddy Current Errors:** Eddy currents are induced in the solid metal parts and in conductor itself by alternating magnetic fields of current coil. These currents produce a field of their own and change the magnitude and phase of the current coil field causing errors.

This error is similar in principal to the error caused by the inductance of pressure coil, except that the sign of error is opposite. The wattmeter will read low for lagging p.f. and high for leading power factors.

Solid metal parts should be avoided as far as possible. Stranded conductors should be used for current coil if the current carried is large which will reduce eddy currents induced within the thickness of the coil.

**(f) Stray Magnetic Field Errors:** The electrodynamometer wattmeter has a relatively weak operating field and therefore it is particularly effected by stray magnetic fields resulting in the serious errors.

Shielding is provided in such instruments to avoid the effects of stray magnetic fields. Laminated iron shields are used in portable laboratory instruments, while steel cases are used for switch-board instruments.

Precision type wattmeters use an astatic system i.e. they are constructed with two similar sets of fixed and moving coils mounted on the same shaft. This has an effect of increasing torque in one half and equally reducing the same on the other half, thus compensating the stray magnetic field effects.

**(g) Errors Caused by Vibration of Moving System:** This error is found occasionally on alternating currents. The torque on the moving systems varies critically with a frequency which is twice that of the voltage. If the pointer, spring or some other parts of the moving system has a natural frequency which is in approximate resonance with the frequency of torque pulsation, the moving system would vibrate with a considerable amplitude.

They are avoided by designing the instruments in such a way that the natural frequency of the moving system is very much away from twice the frequency of the system on which the wattmeter is intended to be used.

**(h) Temperature Error:** Reading of wattmeter is affected by changes in room temperature, it is due to changes in the resistance of the pressure coil and stiffness of springs. These effects are opposite in nature and would nearly neutralize each other, if the pressure coil circuit was composed of copper and of a resistance alloy having a negligible resistance temperature coefficient in the ratio of 1 : 10.

## 1.1.7 Polyphase Wattmeter

A dynamometer type three phase wattmeter consists of two separate wattmeter movements mounted together in one case with the two moving coils mounted on the same spindle. The arrangement is as shown in Fig. 1.4 (a).

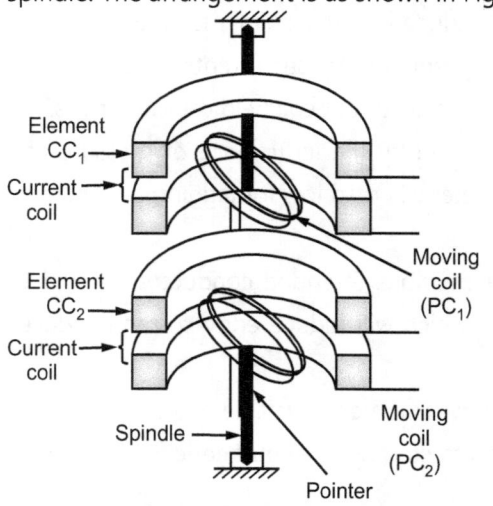

(a) Three phase two elements wattmeter

(b) Compensation for mutual effects between two elements of a three phase wattmeter

**Fig. 1.4**

There are two current coils ($CC_1$ and $CC_2$) and two pressure coils ($PC_1$ and $PC_2$).

A current coil together with its pressure coil is known as an element. Therefore, a three phase wattmeter has two elements.

The connections of two elements of a three phase wattmeter are the same as that for two wattmeters method using two single phase wattmeters.

The torque developed on each element is proportional to the power being measured by it. The total deflecting torque on the moving system is equal to sum of the deflecting torques of the two elements.

i.e. say

Deflecting torque of element $1 \propto P_1$

Deflecting torque of element $2 \propto P_2$

∴ Total deflecting torque $\propto P_1 + P_2 \propto P$ (i.e. Total three phase power)

Hence, total deflecting torque on moving system is proportional to the total power.

For correct reading of a three phase wattmeter, there should not be any mutual interference between the two elements. A laminated iron sheild may be provided between the two elements to eliminate the mutual effects.

Compensation for mutual effects can be done by using Weston's method. The arrangement of which is shown in Fig. 1.4 (b). Resistance R' may be adjusted to compensate the errors caused by mutual interference.

## 1.1.8 Multiplying Factor of Wattmeter

When large power is to be measured by small range wattmeters, its range is increased by using C.T. and P.T. in case of A.C. circuits and by using shunts and multipliers in case of D.C. supply systems.

The connection diagram for extension of range in case of A.C. system i.e. single phase and three phase wattmeters and D.C. system are represented in Article 1.1.8.1 and method of calculating total power supplied to the load is also explained there. The necessary circuits are shown in Fig. 1.5 (a), (b), (c) and (d) respectively.

### 1.1.8.1 Extension of Wattmeter Range

The range of wattmeters can be extended to measure power of A.C. circuit having high voltage and large current, when we make the use of potential transformer and current transformers, which reduce the voltage applied across the wattmeter and current flowing through the instrument, in such case the actual power = recorded power of wattmeter × P.T. ratio × C.T. ratio.

Similarly, the range of wattmeter in D.C. circuits can be extended by using the multiplier resistance in series with potential coil and shunt resistance in parallel with current coil of the wattmeter.

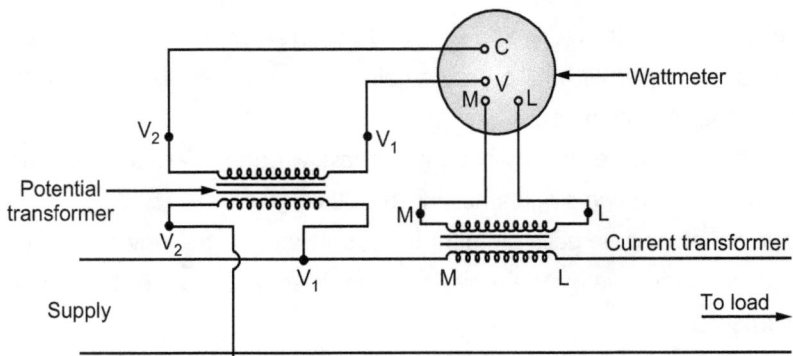

**Fig. 1.5 (a)**

Fig. 1.5 (a) shows the diagram of connections of a wattmeter for measuring power in a single phase circuit, where both voltage and current are greater than the wattmeter ranges.

Fig. 1.5 (b) shows a similar circuit for measuring the power in a three phase, three wire, unbalanced load using a double element wattmeter.

Fig. 1.5 (a) and 1.5 (b) not only illustrate the way in which instrument transformers are connected in circuit but also serve to illustrate the manner in which the terminals of wattmeters, and their associated transformers are given distinctive markings as an aid to the correct installation of such equipment.

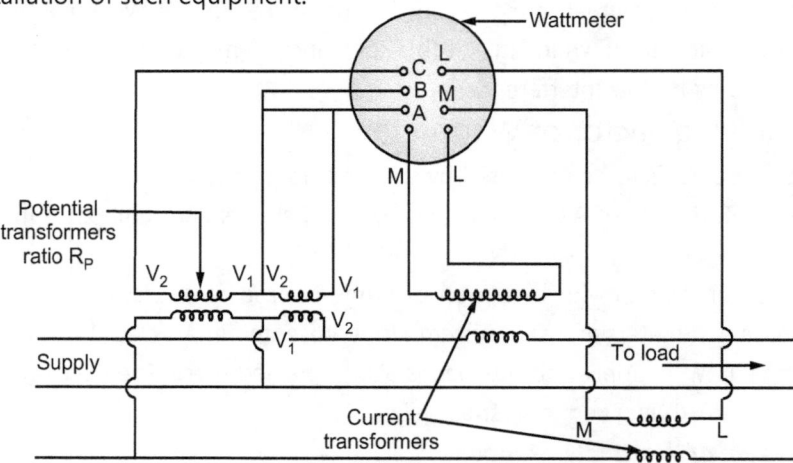

**Fig. 1.5 (b)**

The total power flowing in the circuit of Fig. 1.5 (a) and (b) is in both cases, given by total power in watts = wattmeter reading × $R_c$ × $R_p$ where $R_c$ is the ratio of the current transformers, assuming the current transformer ratios are identical where more than one is used and $R_p$ is the ratio of the potential transformers, again identical transformers being used where there is more than one.

The appropriate diagram of connection for installing wattmeters for power measurement of D.C. systems are given in Fig. 1.5 (c) and Fig. 1.5 (d). The wattmeter range is extended by using shunts and multipliers.

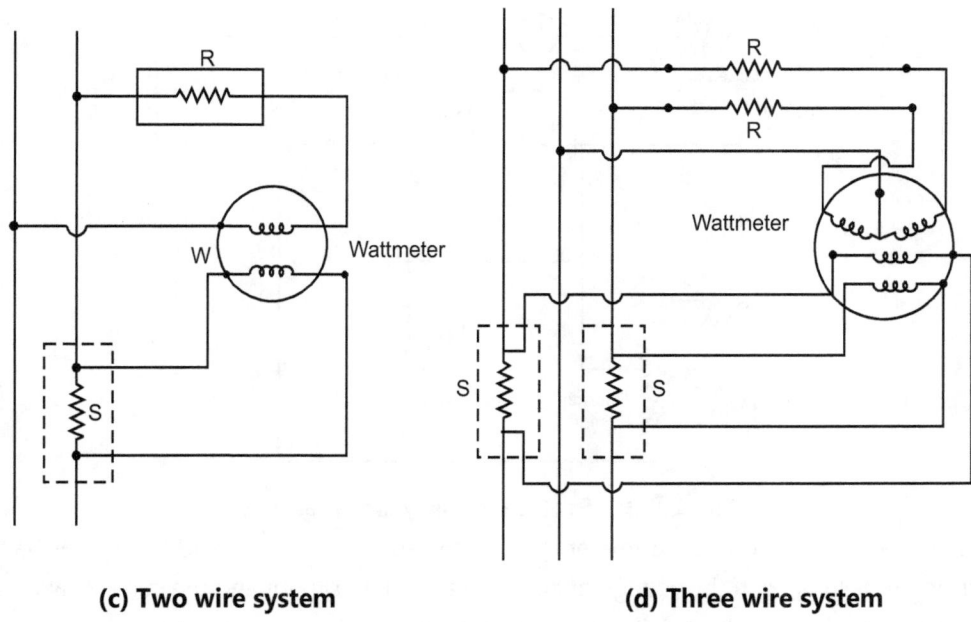

**(c) Two wire system**  **(d) Three wire system**

**Fig. 1.5**

## 1.1.9 Calibration of Wattmeter

**Single-element Industrial Grade Instruments:**

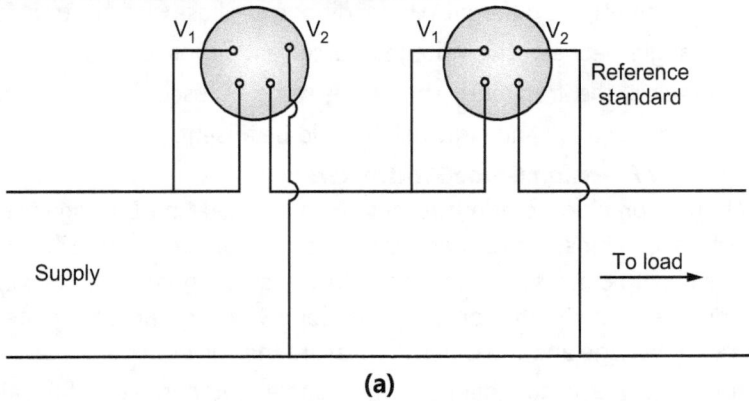

**(a)**

The wattmeter under test and reference standard (precision grade instrument) are connected adjacent to each other as shown in Fig. 1.6 (a). When a wattmeter of rating say 440 V and current rating of 100 A is to be tested, a power loss of 440 × 100 watt will take place if the test is to be made at unity p.f. only. The circuit of Fig. 1.6 (a) may be used for current coil connections to supply the desired voltage and a circuit of Fig. 1.6 (b) may be used to produce a artificial load current, and the power required for the test may be reduced to losses taking place in both the instruments.

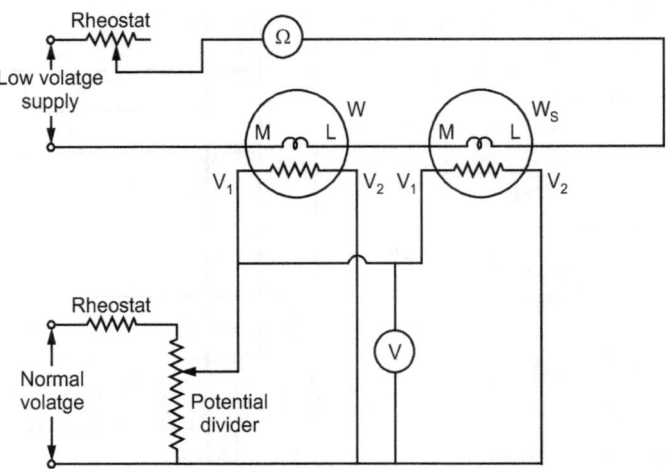

**Fig. 1.6 (b): Fantum loading arrangement**

When a industrial grade wattmeter is to be tested, the meter should be run for half an hour before testing, with the voltage at 80% of its rated maximum and the current two thirds of its rated maximum value, multi-range wattmeters must be given a pre-testing run. In the test, the current in the two meters is kept same, at a fixed scale marking of one under test, and reading is taken of true watts from the reference standard.

For testing of wattmeter at different p.f. conditions, a phase shifting transformer is used to create a phase angle between the voltage and current supplied to a circuit. In testing of high grade instruments, the frequency should be same as used for normal use of meter, temperature should not change and stray field should be absent.

### 1.1.9.1 Calibration of Precision Grade Wattmeters

The calibration of precision grade wattmeter can be made on D.C. against the standard cell, and involves a combined measurement of voltage and current. The actual value of voltage and current can be measured with the help of a single potentiometer with the help of a double pole double throw switch or it can be done with two potentiometers, one being used to measure the voltage and the other to measure the current.

Fig. 1.7 represents the circuit diagram with single potentiometer for calibration of a precision grade wattmeter. The current coil of wattmeter is supplied from a low voltage supply and a series rheostat is inserted to adjust the value of current.

The potential circuit is supplied from a high voltage supply, which can be varied at will, with the help of a potentiometer. A volt ratio box is used to step down the voltage for the potentiometer to read. This type of arrangement of loading is known as Phantom loading.

The voltage V and the current I are measured in turn with the potentiometer employing a double pole double throw switch. The true power is then VI watts; and the wattmeter reading may be compared with this value to determine the error.

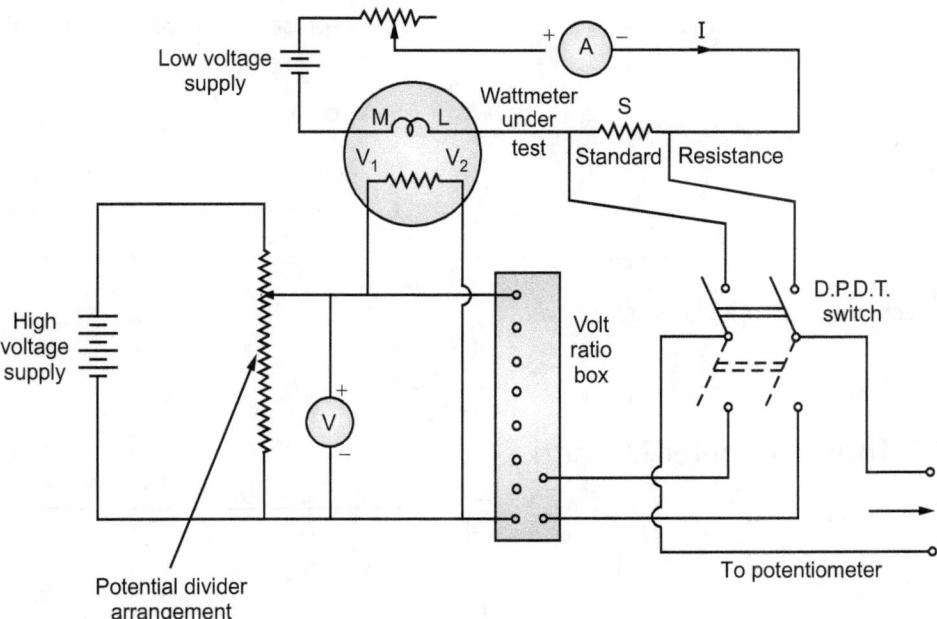

**Fig. 1.7**

## 1.1.10 Measurement of Power

A.C. power in a circuit may be measured without using a wattmeter either by using :
(i) Three voltmeter method or
(ii) Three ammeter method.

### 1.1.10.1 Three Voltmeter Method

Three voltmeters $V_T$, $V_R$ and $V_L$ are connected in the circuit with load as shown in Fig. 1.8 (a).

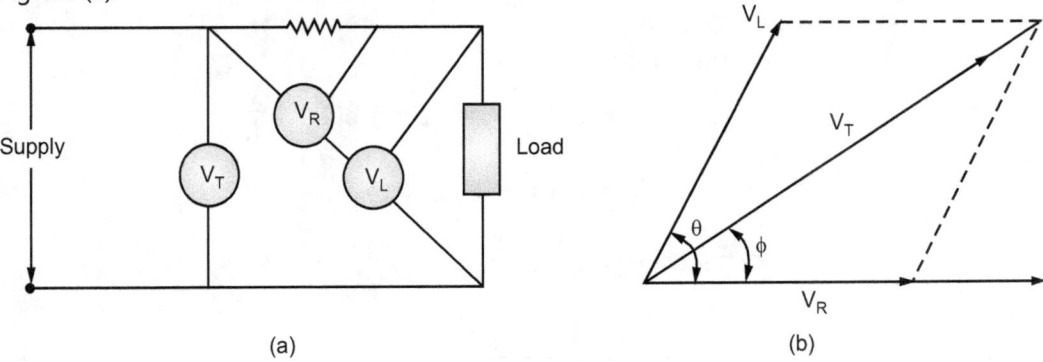

**Fig. 1.8**

R is the known non-inductive resistance which is connected in series with the load, $V_L$ is the voltage drop across the load, the load current I lags behind $V_L$ by an angle $\phi$. $V_R$ is the voltage drop across resistance R and $V_R = I \times R$ and is in phase with I. $V_T$ is the supply voltage which is equal to vector sum of $V_R$ and $V_L$. Fig. 1.8 (b) represents the vector diagram from which we get,

$$V_T^2 = V_R^2 + V_L^2 + 2V_R V_L \cos\phi$$

or

$$V_T^2 = V_R^2 + V_L^2 + 2IR V_L \cos\phi$$

or

$$V_L I \cos\phi = \frac{V_T^2 - V_R^2 - V_L^2}{2R} \quad \ldots(1.9)$$

Which is equal to power used by load,

p.f. of load,

$$\cos\phi = \frac{V_T^2 - V_R^2 - V_L^2}{2V_R V_L} \quad \ldots(1.10)$$

## 1.1.11 Three Ammeter Method

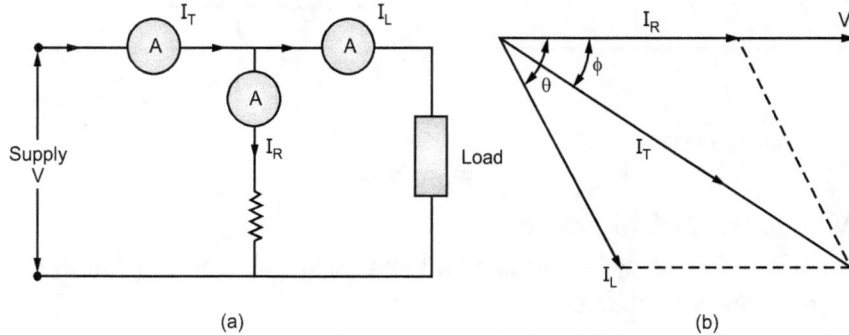

(a)　　　　　　　　　　　　　(b)

**Fig. 1.9**

In this method, three ammeters are used and a known non-inductive resistance. Fig. 1.9 represents the connection diagram. Let $I_T$ be the total current supplied, $I_R$ be the current flowing through known resistance and $I_L$ be the current flowing through the load, of which power consumed is to be calculated.

From vector diagram of Fig. 1.9 (b).

$$I_T^2 = I_R^2 + I_L^2 + 2I_R I_L \cos\phi, \text{ but } IR = \frac{V}{R}$$

∴

$$I_T^2 = I_R^2 + I_L^2 + 2\frac{V}{R}I_L \cos\phi$$

or

$$2\frac{V}{R}I_L \cos\phi = I_T^2 - I_R^2 - I_L^2$$

or

$$V I_L \cos\phi = \frac{R\left(I_T^2 - I_R^2 - I_L^2\right)}{2} \quad \ldots(1.11)$$

which is equal to power used by load.

Load p.f.

$$\cos\phi = \frac{R\left(I_T^2 - I_R^2 - I_L^2\right)}{2 V I_L} \quad \ldots(1.12)$$

## 1.1.12 Measurement of Three Phase Power

Power in a three phase system can be measured by using the following methods:
(i) Two single phase wattmeters.
(ii) One single phase wattmeter.
(iii) Three single phase wattmeters.
(iv) One three phase wattmeter.

## 1.1.13 Two-Wattmeter Method

This method of measuring power is mostly used. This is applicable to delta as well as star connected systems, balanced or unbalanced loads, but it is not applicable to three phase, four wire system.

## 1.1.14 Star Connected Load

Let $i_a$, $i_b$ and $i_c$ be the three currents in lines $L_1$, $L_2$ and $L_3$ respectively at any instant. Then current through $W_1 = i_a$.

e.m.f. across the pressure coil of $W_1 = e_{ac} = e_a - e_c$

∴ Instantaneous power recorded by $W_1$ at that instant $= i_a (e_a - e_c)$.

Similarly, current through $W_2 = i_b$ and e.m.f. across its pressure coil $= e_{bc} = e_b - e_c$.

∴ Power read by $W_2$ at that instant $= i_b (e_b - e_c)$.

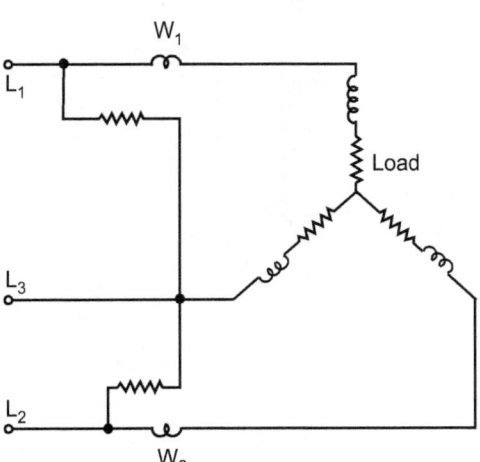
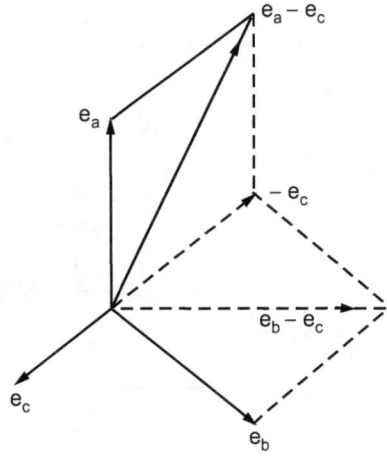

**Fig. 1.10**

If $P_1$ and $P_2$ are the readings of two wattmeters $W_1$ and $W_2$ respectively, then

$$P_1 + P_2 = i_a (e_a - e_c) + i_b (e_b - e_c)$$
$$= i_a e_a + i_b e_b - e_c (i_a + i_b)$$

Some of current at a point is zero,
i.e. $\quad i_a + i_b + i_c = 0$
or $\quad i_a + i_b = -i_c$

$$\therefore \quad P_1 + P_2 = i_a e_a + i_b e_b - e_c(-i_c)$$
$$= i_a e_a + i_b e_b + i_c e_c$$
$$= P_1 + P_2 + P_3$$

where, $P_1$, $P_2$ and $P_3$ are the instantaneous powers in the three loads connected in star.

Therefore, at any instant, sum of two wattmeter readings is the total power supplied to a star connected load.

As the wattmeter records average power instead of instantaneous power, total power P in watts supplied to a three phase star connected load is,

$$P = P_1 + P_2$$

In case of 3-phase, 4-wire system if the load is balanced, then $i_a + i_b + i_c$ will be equal to zero, in that case two wattmeters can give the correct value of power. Otherwise this method cannot be used for 3-phase, 4-wire system.

## 1.1.15 Delta - Connected Load

When the load is delta connected the connection of two wattmeters to measure the power is as shown in Fig. 1.11 (a). We will see now whether the two wattmeters connected in this fashion give the total power supplied to the circuit.

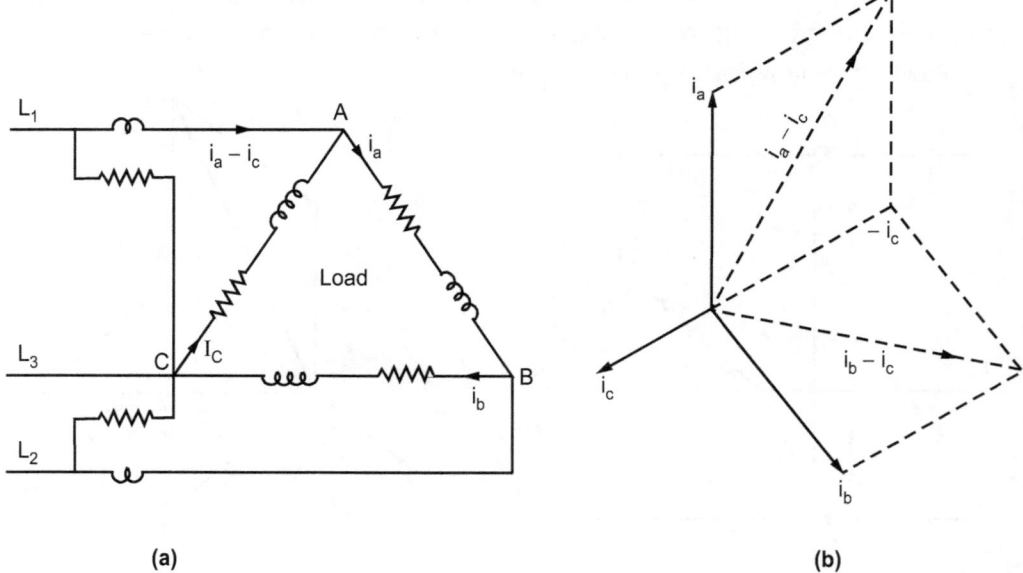

**Fig. 1.11**

Let $i_a$, $i_b$ and $i_c$ be the three phase currents at any instant respectively.
Then current through $W_1 = i_a - i_c$ and through $W_2 = i_b - i_c$
e.m.f. across $W_1 = e_{ac}$ and
e.m.f. across $W_2 = e_{bc}$
if $P_1$ and $P_2$ be the readings of $W_1$ and $W_2$ respectively, then

$$P_1 = e_{ac}(i_a - i_c)$$
$$P_2 = e_{bc}(i_b - i_c)$$

∴  $P_1 + P_2 = e_{ac}(i_a - i_c) + e_{bc}(i_b - i_c)$
$= e_{ac} i_a + e_{bc} i_b - i_c(e_{ac} + e_{bc})$

For a closed loop, as per Kirchhoff's law

$e_{ab} + e_{bc} + e_{ca} = 0$

or $e_{bc} + e_{ca} = -e_{ab}$

∴ $P_1 + P_2 = e_{ac} i_a + e_{bc} i_b + e_{ab} i_c$

which represents instantaneous powers in the three phases.

∴ $P_1 + P_2 = p_1 + p_2 + p_3$

Since the wattmeters always read the average power, therefore the sum of two wattmeter readings always will give the total average power supplied to the load.

## 1.1.16 One Wattmeter Method of Measuring Power of Three Phase Circuit

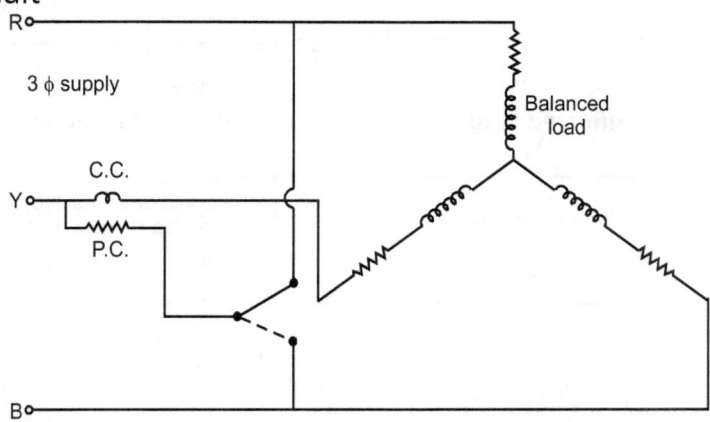

**Fig. 1.12**

This method is to be used for balanced loads only, and it is a modification of two wattmeter method of measuring the power. The wattmeter current coil is connected in one line and the readings of wattmeter are taken by connecting its pressure coil alternately across the line voltages with the help of a change over switch and values of $P_1$ and $P_2$ are obtained. Adding $P_1$ and $P_2$ total power supplied to the circuit is determined.

p.f. angle can be calculated by using same relations which are derived for two wattmeter method.

## 1.1.17 Measurement of Three Phase Power Using Three Single Phase Wattmeters

Measurement of power in three phase circuit using three single phase wattmeters is used in case of three phase star or delta connected, balanced or unbalanced loads. In case of a three phase, four wire system the three wattmeter method is essential. The connection diagrams to measure the three phase power in delta, star and three phase, four wire system with the help of three single phase wattmeter are shown in Fig. 1.13 (a), (b) and (c) respectively. Separate wattmeters read the power supplied by each phase to load, and the total power supplied from mains, in this case, is given by $P = P_1 + P_2 + P_3$ where $P_1$, $P_2$ and $P_3$ are the readings of wattmeters $W_1$, $W_2$ and $W_3$ respectively.

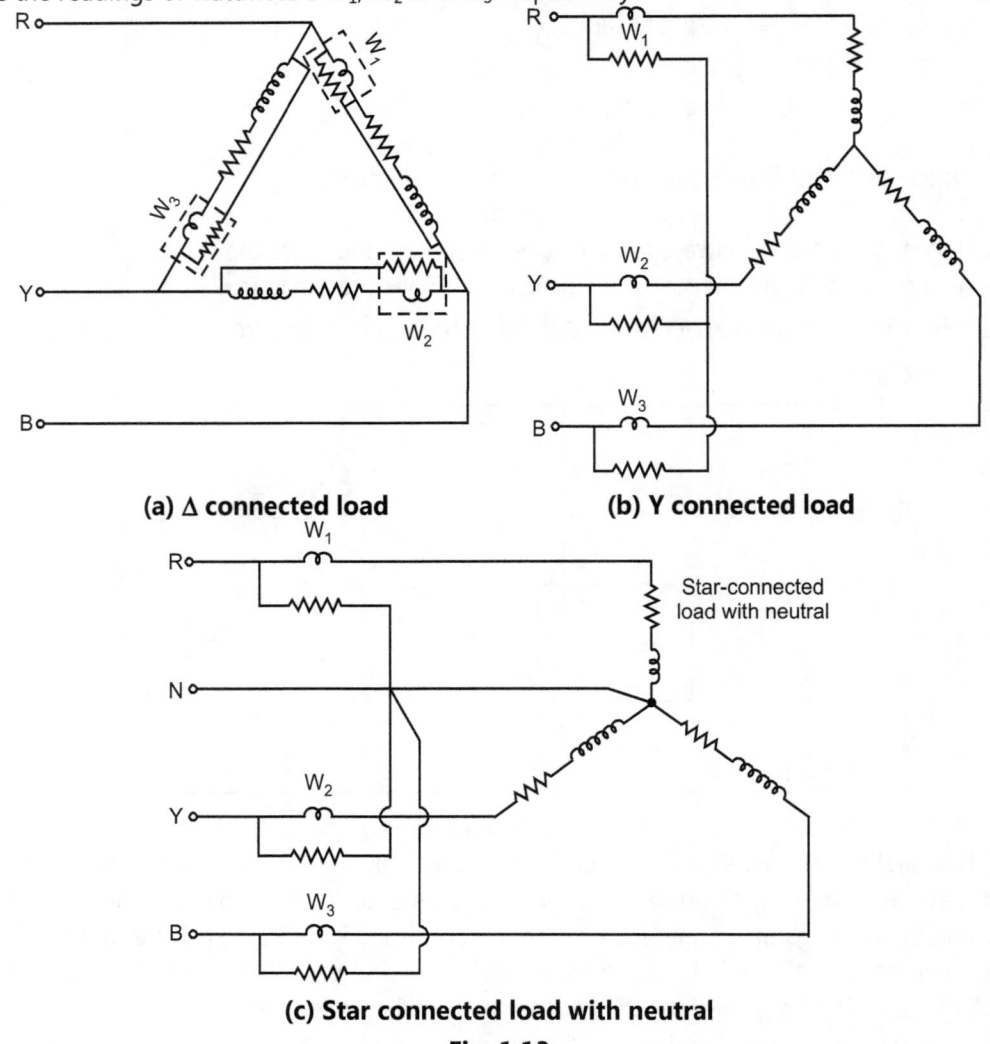

(a) Δ connected load

(b) Y connected load

(c) Star connected load with neutral

Fig. 1.13

## 1.1.18 By Using a Three Phase Wattmeter

A dynamometer type three phase wattmeter will consists of two separate wattmeters mounted on each other in one case, with the two moving coils mounted on the same spindle. It consists of two current coils and two pressure coils. One current coil with its corresponding pressure coil is termed as 'an element' i.e. three phase wattmeter consists of two elements. The connections of the two elements of the wattmeter are just similar to that of two wattmeter method using two single phase wattmeters. The torque on each element is proportional to power being measured by it. The total torque deflecting the system is equal to sum of torques on the two elements.

Therefore, total torque ∝ ($P_1 + P_2$) ∝ P the power to be measured. There should not be any interference between the two elements other wise the reading will not be correct, hence a laminated iron shield may be provided between the two elements.

## 1.2 EFFECT OF P.F. VARIATION ON WATTMETER READINGS IN TWO WATTMETER METHOD

p.f. and wattmeter readings when power is measured by two wattmeters of a balanced load system:

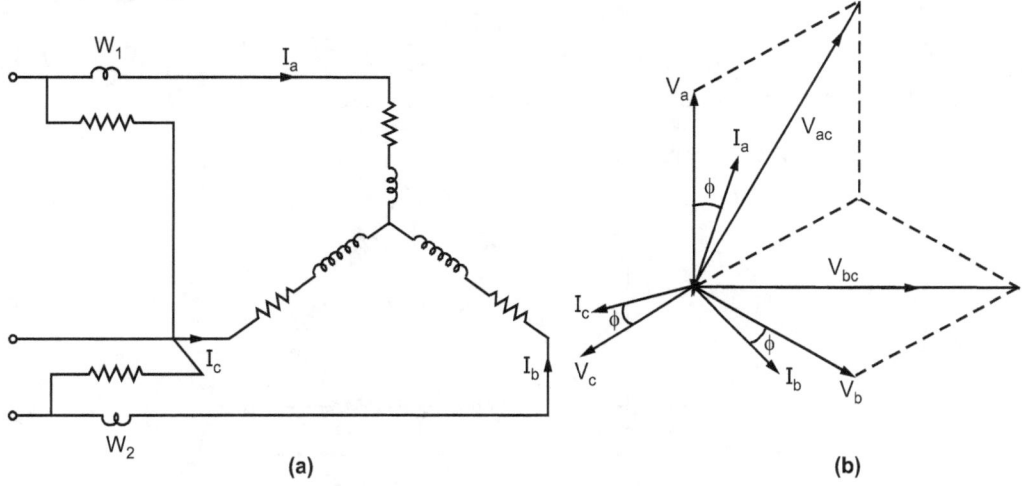

**Fig. 1.14**

We will consider a star connected inductive balance load i.e. impedance of all three branches is same and their values of resistances and reactances are also equal. Fig. 1.14 (b) represents the vector diagram of such a load. $V_a$, $V_b$ and $V_c$ are the three phase voltages and $I_a$, $I_b$ and $I_c$ are the three phase currents, φ represents the p.f. angle of load given by $\phi = \tan^{-1}\frac{X}{R}$ connections are shown in Fig. 1.14 (a), the current flowing through current coil of wattmeter $W_1$ is $I_a$, and voltage across its pressure coil is vector difference of $V_a$ and $V_c$ i.e. $V_{ac}$. The angle of phase difference between $V_{ac}$ and $I_a$ is (30° − φ). Similarly current flowing through $W_2$ is $I_b$ and voltage across it is $V_{bc}$, and the angle between $I_{bc}$ and $V_{bc}$ is (30° + φ).

If the readings of $W_1$ and $W_2$ are $P_1$ and $P_2$ respectively,

$$P_1 = V_{ac} I_a \cos(30° - \phi) \quad \ldots (1.13)$$

and

$$P_2 = V_{bc} I_b \cos(30° + \phi) \quad \ldots (1.14)$$

As the load is balanced,

$$V_{ac} = V_{bc} = V, \text{ the line voltage}$$

and

$$I_a = I_b = I_c = I, \text{ the line current}$$

∴

$$P_1 = VI \cos(30° - \phi) \quad \ldots (1.15)$$

$$P_2 = VI \cos(30° + \phi) \qquad \ldots (1.16)$$

a similar relation can also be determined when the load is delta connected.

For this purpose, consider the Fig. 1.14 (c) and vector diagram Fig. 1.14 (d).

The voltage across $W_1$ is $V_{ca}$ and across $W_2$ is $V_{bc}$. Vector diagram indicates that the current through $W_1$ is $(I_c - I_a)$ and that through $W_2$ is $(I_b - I_a)$, $\phi$ is the power factor angle of the load, therefore power recorded by $W_1$ i.e. $P_1 = V_{ca}(I_c - I_a)\cos(30° - \phi)$ and by $W_2$ i.e. $P_2 = V_{bc}(I_b - I_a)\cos(30 + \phi)$ for balance load condition.

$$V_{ca} = V_{ab} = V_{bc} = V \text{ volts}$$

and
$$(I_c - I_a) = (I_b - I_a) = I \text{ ampere}$$

∴
$$P_1 = VI \cos(30° - \phi) \qquad \ldots (1.17)$$

and
$$P_2 = VI \cos(30° + \phi) \qquad \ldots (1.18)$$

It is just similar to that calculated for a star connected load.

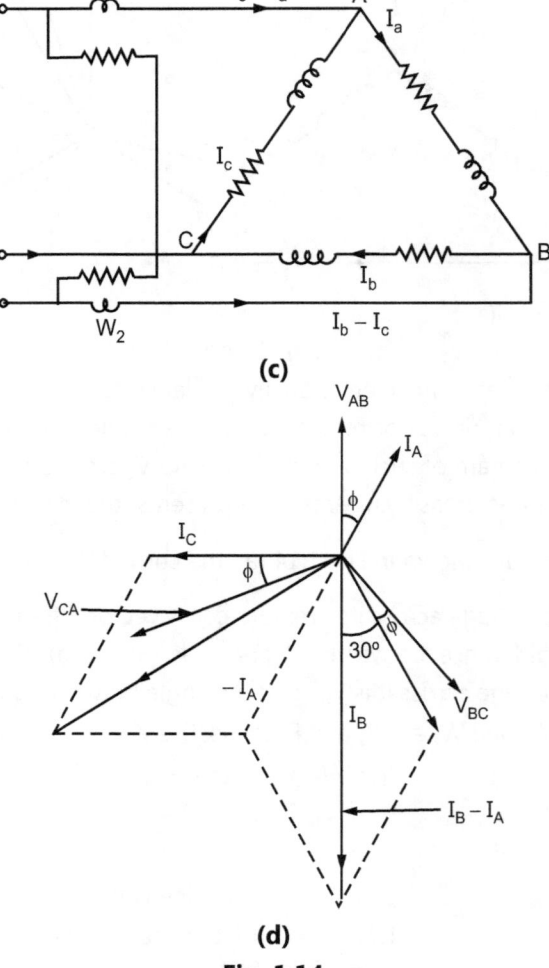

**Fig. 1.14**

$$\therefore \quad P_1 + P_2 = VI \cos(30° - \phi) + VI \cos(30° + \phi)$$
$$= VI (\cos 30° \cos \phi + \sin 30° \sin \phi + \cos 30° \cos \phi - \sin 30° \sin \phi)$$
$$= VI (2 \cos 30° \cos \phi)$$
$$= \sqrt{3} \, VI \cos \phi$$

Hence, the readings of the two wattmeters record the total power of three phase load.

1. When the p.f. is unity, $\phi = 0°$  $P_1 = VI \cos \phi$, $P_2 = VI \cos \phi$
   and  $P_1 + P_2 = 2 VI \cos 30°$
   i.e. both wattmeters give equal positive readings.

2. When $\phi = 60°$, i.e. load p.f. 0.5 lag
   $$P_1 = VI \cos(30° - 60°)$$
   $$= VI \cos 30°$$
   and  $$P_2 = VI \cos(30° + 60°)$$
   $$= VI \cos 90° = 0$$
   i.e. wattmeter $W_1$ will record total power and $W_2$ will read zero.

3. When $\phi$ is greater than 60° and less than 90° i.e. p.f. is between 0.5 and 0, $W_1$ will be positive and $W_2$ will be negative. Hence for taking readings of $W_2$, its pressure coil connection or current coil connection is to be changed, and total power $P = P_1 - P_2$.

4. When $\phi = 90°$
   $$P_1 = VI \cos(30° - 90°)$$
   $$= VI \cos(90° - 30°) \qquad [\because \cos(-\phi) = \cos \phi]$$
   $$P_1 = - VI \sin 30°$$
   and  $$P_2 = VI \cos(30° + 90°)$$
   $$= VI \sin 30°$$
   $\therefore \quad P_1 + P_2 = 0$

5. When p.f. is leading,
   $$P_1 = VI \cos(30° + \phi)$$
   $$P_2 = VI \cos(30° - \phi)$$
   i.e. the readings of the two wattmeters will only interchange.

   Calculation of p.f. of load from the wattmeter readings:
   $$P_1 + P_2 = \sqrt{3} \, VI \cos \phi$$
   and  $$P_1 - P_2 = VI \{\cos(30° - \phi) - \cos(30° + \phi)\}$$
   $$= VI \{\cos 30° \cos \phi + \sin 30° \sin \phi - \cos 30° \cos \phi + \sin 30° \sin \phi\}$$
   $$= VI \{2 \sin 30° \sin \phi\}$$
   $$= VI \sin \phi$$

$$\therefore \quad \frac{P_1 - P_2}{P_1 + P_2} = \frac{VI \sin \phi}{\sqrt{3} \, VI \cos \phi} = \frac{\tan \phi}{\sqrt{3}}$$

or
$$\tan \phi = \sqrt{3} \, \frac{P_1 - P_2}{P_1 + P_2}$$

If the reading of $W_2$ is obtained by reversing the connection i.e. load p.f. less than 0.5 or $\phi$ between 60° and 90°.

$$\tan \phi = \sqrt{3} \, \frac{P_1 - (-P_2)}{P_1 + (-P_2)} = \sqrt{3} \, \frac{P_1 + P_2}{P_1 - P_2}$$

## 1.2.1 Measurement of Reactive Power

### 1.2.1.1 Measurement of Reactive Power in Three Phase Balanced Load by Two Wattmeter Method

Reactive power of a three phase balanced load using two wattmeters can be calculated by using two wattmeter method of measuring power. In the circuit are also inserted a voltmeter for measuring line voltage and a ammeter to measure the line current.

The circuit used is as follows:

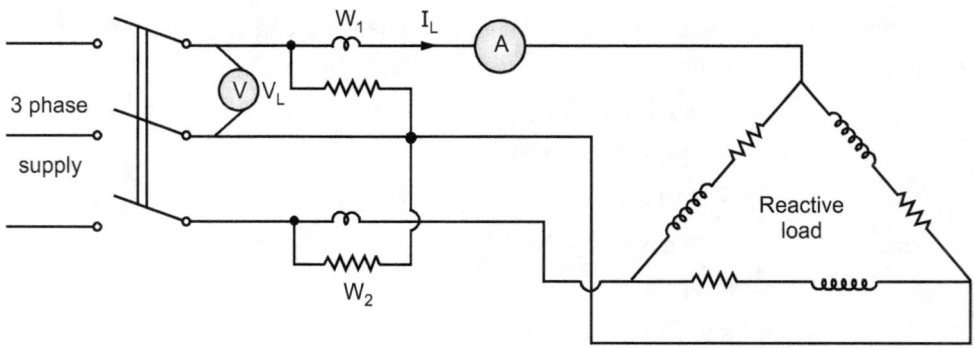

**Fig. 1.15**

Total power supplied to the circuit
$$P = W_1 + W_2 \quad \ldots (1.19)$$

P is also equal to $\sqrt{3} \, V_L I_L \cos \phi$ ... (1.20)

Equating (1.19) and (1.20)
$$P = \sqrt{3} \, V_L I_L \cos \phi$$

As values of P, $V_L$ and $I_L$ are recorded $\cos \phi$ is determined; from the value of which $\sin \phi$ is calculated, and the total reactive power of the three phase circuit under test can be calculated as,

Total reactive power = $\sqrt{3} \, V_L I_L \sin \phi$

## 1.2.2 Measurement of Reactive Power in a Three Phase Circuit

**One wattmeter method:** The reactive power of a balanced three phase circuit can be easily measured with the help of a single phase wattmeter. The circuit used for this purpose is shown in Fig. 1.16 (a). The current coil of the wattmeter is connected in one of the phase while the pressure coils is connected across the remaining two phases as shown in Fig. 1.16 (a) with reference to the circuit diagram. The vector diagram for the circuit is shown in Fig. 1.16 (b).

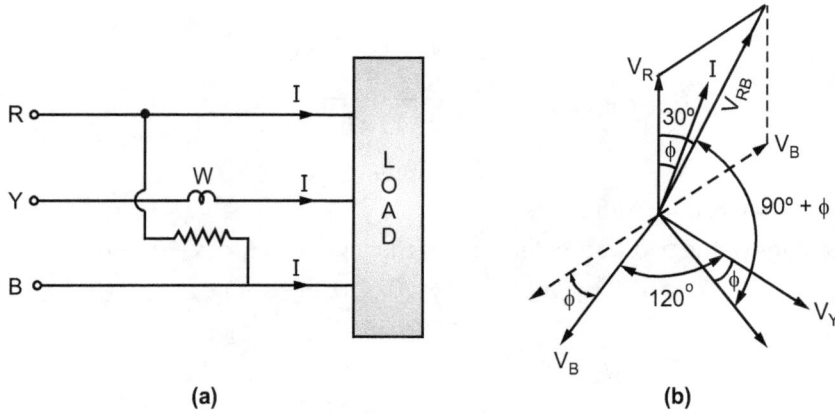

**Fig. 1.16**

Current through current coil of wattmeter = I amperes.

Voltage across the pressure coil = V

∴ Wattmeter will record power

$$= V_{RB} \, I \cos (90° + \phi)$$
$$= \sqrt{3} \, VI \cos (90° + \phi) \text{ as } V_{RB} = \sqrt{3} \, V$$

i.e. $V_{RB} = \sqrt{3}$ phase voltage

∴ Power recorded $= -\sqrt{3} \, VI \sin \phi$

Total reactive VA of the circuit (load)

$$= 3 \, VI \sin \phi$$

where,

V = Phase voltage

I = Phase current

$\phi$ = p.f. angle of load

∴ Q = 3 VI sin $\phi$

$= (-\sqrt{3} \times$ Reading of wattmeter)

and p.f. angle $\phi = \tan^{-1}\left(\dfrac{Q}{P}\right)$

# ILLUSTRATIVE EXAMPLES

**Example 1.1:** A 440 V, 3 phase motor has an output of 80 H.P. and an efficiency of 90% at p.f. 0.8 lag. Find the readings on each of the two wattmeters connected to measure the output.

**Solution:** 
$$\text{Input on full load} = \frac{\text{H.P.} \times 735.5}{0.9}$$
$$= \frac{80 \times 735.5}{0.9} = 65377.77 \text{ watts}$$
$$\text{Power} = \sqrt{3} \, V_L \, I_L \cos\phi$$
$$\text{Line current, } I_L = \frac{65377.77}{\sqrt{3} \times 440 \times 0.8}$$
$$= 107.2 \text{ Amp.}$$

From $\cos\phi = 0.8$, $\phi = 36.86°$

The readings of the two wattmeters are given by $W_1 = V_L \, I_L \cos(30° - \phi)$

or
$$W_1 = 440 \times 107.2 \cos(-6.86)$$
$$= 47168 \text{ watt}$$

But $W_1 + W_2 = W$

$\therefore$
$$W_2 = 65377.77 - 47168 \text{ watt}$$
$$W_2 = 18209.77 \text{ watt}$$

Using relation of $W_2$,
$$W_2 = V_L \, I_L \cos(30° + \phi)$$
$$= 440 \times 107.2 \times \cos 66.86$$
$$= 18536 \text{ watt}$$

---

**Example 1.2:** A three phase star connected load consist of three similar coils. Each coil has a resistance of 12 ohms and reactance of 16 ohms. It is supplied from 440 V, three phase mains. Find the readings on each of the two wattmeters connected to measure the input to the load.

**Solution:** 
$$\text{Impedance per phase} = \sqrt{R^2 + X_L^2}$$
$$= \sqrt{(12)^2 + (16)^2} = 20 \text{ ohms}$$
$$\text{Voltage/phase} = \frac{V_L}{\sqrt{3}} = \frac{440}{\sqrt{3}} = 254 \text{ volt}$$

$\therefore$
$$\text{Current/phase} = \frac{V_p}{Z_p} = \frac{254}{20} = 12.7 \text{ A}$$
$$\text{Power factor of load} = \frac{R}{Z} = \frac{12}{20}$$
$$= 0.6 \text{ lag}$$

$\therefore$
$$\phi = 53.13°$$

Reading of first wattmeter, $W_1 = V_L I_L \cos(30 - \phi)$
or
$$W_1 = 440 \times 12.7 \cos 23.13°$$
$$W_1 = 5138.81 \text{ watt}$$

Reading of second wattmeter,
$$W_2 = V_L I_L \cos(30 + \phi)$$
$$= 440 \times 12.7 \cos 83.10°$$
$$= 668.41 \text{ watt}$$

**Example 1.3:** The readings of two wattmeters connected to measure the total power in a three phase 3 wire circuit are 10 kW and 1 kW, the latter reading being obtained after reversal of the current coil connections. Calculate the total power and p.f. of the load.

**Solution:** Here, $W_1 = 10$ kW

$W_2 = 1$ kW as the reading is obtained after reversal of current coil connections

∴ Total power, $W = W_1 + W_2$
$$= 10 + (-1) = 9 \text{ kW}$$

From
$$\tan \phi = \frac{\sqrt{3}(W_1 - W_2)}{(W_1 + W_2)}$$
$$= \sqrt{3} \frac{[10 - (-1)]}{10 + (-1)} = \sqrt{3} \times \frac{11}{9}$$

or $\tan \phi = 2.117$

∴ $\cos \phi = 0.4273$

**Example 1.4:** The readings of the two wattmeters connected in R and B phase are 10 kW and 1 kW respectively. The latter being obtained after reversing the connections of current coil. Calculate the real and reactive power of the load and state whether the p.f. leading or lagging the phase sequence is RYB.

**Solution:** $W_1 = 10$ kW
$$W_2 = -1 \text{ kW}$$

∴ Total power $= W_1 + W_2$
$$= 10 + (-1) = 9 \text{ kW}$$

Reactive power $= \sqrt{3} V_L I_L \sin \phi$

but $W_1 - W_2 = V_L I_L \sin \phi$

∴ Reactive power $= \sqrt{3}(W_1 - W_2)$
$$= \sqrt{3}[10 - (-1)]$$
$$= \sqrt{3} \times 11 = 19.05 \text{ RkVA}$$

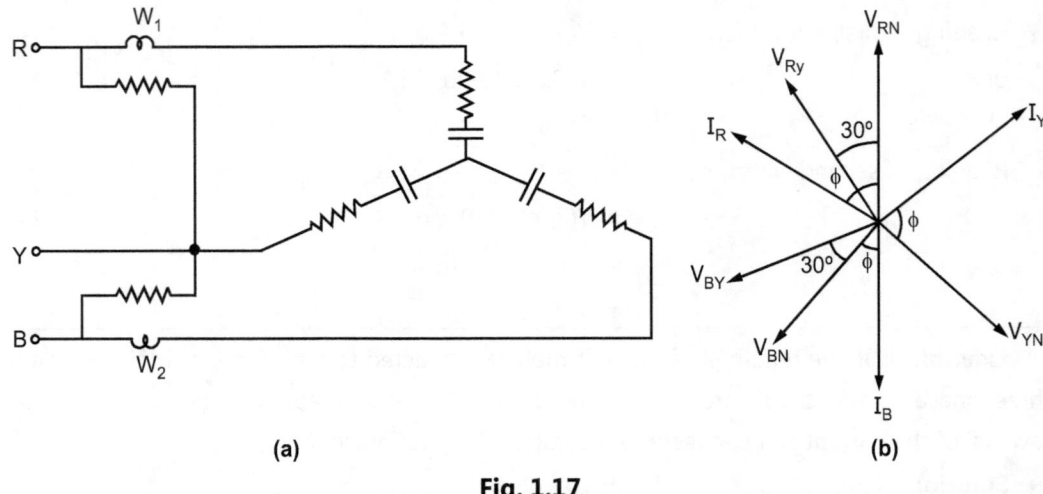

(a)            (b)

**Fig. 1.17**

**Example 1.5:** Draw the connection diagram of two element wattmeter with C.T. and P.T. in high tension circuit. If C.T. and P.T. ratios are 100 : 5 and 11000 : 110 V respectively, state the multiplying factor to be used.

**Solution:**

$$\text{Ratio of P.T.} = \frac{11000}{110} = 100$$

$$\text{Ratio of current transformer} = \frac{100}{5} = 20$$

∴ Multiplying factor = Ratio of P.T. × Ratio of C.T.
= 100 × 20 = 2000

∴ Total power = Reading of wattmeter × 2000

**Example 1.6:** Power input to a 150 kW, 440 V, 3-phase induction motor is measured by two-wattmeter method. The wattmeter readings are 115 kW and 50 kW. Calculate (i) The input to the motor, (ii) Power factor of the motor, (iii) Line current drawn by the motor, (iv) Efficiency of the motor.

**Solution:**

(i)      Total input to the motor = $W_1 + W_2$
                             = 115 + 50 = 165 kW

(ii) Power factor of a motor will be determined as follows:

$$\tan \phi = \sqrt{3}\,\frac{W_1 - W_2}{W_1 + W_2} = \sqrt{3}\,\frac{115 - 50}{115 + 50}$$

$$\tan \phi = 0.6823$$

∴           $\phi = 34.3°$

∴    Power factor, $\cos \phi = 0.826$

(iii) Power input to the motor = $\sqrt{3}\, V_L\, I_L\, \cos \phi$
                                  = $\sqrt{3} \times 440 \times I_L \times \cos \phi$

$$165 \times 10^3 = \sqrt{3} \times 440 \times I_L \times 0.826$$

$$\therefore \quad I_L = \frac{165 \times 10^3}{\sqrt{3} \times 440 \times 0.826}$$

$$= 262.1 \text{ A}$$

i.e. Line current drawn by the motor

$$= 262.1 \text{ A}$$

(iv) Efficiency of the motor $= \dfrac{\text{Output}}{\text{Input}}$

$$= \frac{150 \times 10^3}{165 \times 10^3}$$

$$= 0.909 \text{ or } 90.9\%$$

**Example 1.7:** A balanced star-connected load is supplied from a 3-phase, 440 V, 50 Hz supply system. The current in each phase is 20 amperes and lags behind its phase voltage by 40°. Calculate (i) phase voltage, (ii) load impedance, (iii) load parameters, (iv) readings of two wattmeters, connected in the load circuit to measure the power.

**Solution:**

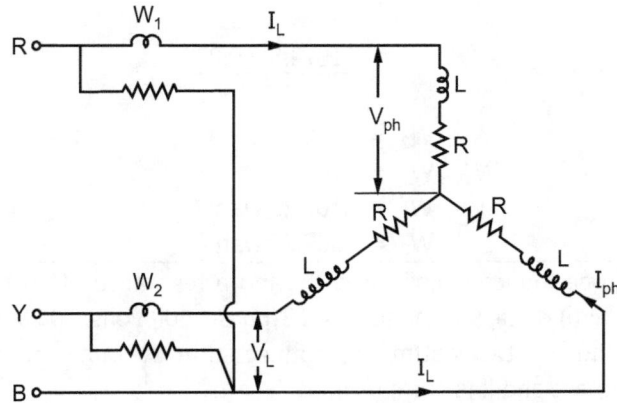

**Fig. 1.18: Representing method**

(i) Line voltage = 440 V

$$\therefore \quad \text{Phase voltage} = \frac{440}{\sqrt{3}} = 254 \text{ V}$$

(ii) Current in each phase = 20 A

Impedance of load per phase $= \dfrac{V_{ph}}{I_{ph}}$

$$= \frac{254}{20} = 12.7 \, \Omega$$

As current lags the voltage by 40°, p.f. cos φ = cos 40° = 0.766 lag

$$\cos\phi = \frac{R}{Z}$$

$$0.766 = \frac{R}{12.7}$$

∴ $\quad R = 9.728\ \Omega$

$$X = \sqrt{Z^2 - R^2}$$
$$= \sqrt{(12.7)^2 - (9.728)^2}$$

or $\quad X = 8.16\ \Omega$

(iii) Total power consumed = 3 × Power consumed by each phase
$$= 3 \times V_{ph} I_{ph} \cos\phi$$
$$= 3 \times 254 \times 20 \times 0.766$$
$$= 11674.5\ \text{watts}$$

(iv) Total power = $W_1 + W_2$

i.e. $\quad W_1 + W_2 = 11674.5\ W$

Using relation $\quad \tan\phi = \sqrt{3}\,\dfrac{W_1 - W_2}{W_1 + W_2}$

or $\quad W_1 - W_2 = \dfrac{\tan 40° \times (W_1 + W_2)}{\sqrt{3}}$

$$= \frac{11674.5 \times 0.839}{\sqrt{3}}$$

or $\quad W_1 - W_2 = 5656$

$\quad W_1 + W_2 = 11674.5$

∴ $\quad W_1 = 8665.25\ \text{watts}$
$\quad W_2 = 3009.25\ \text{watts}$

**Example 1.8:** Three inductive coils, each having a resistance of 20 Ω and reactance of 15 Ω are connected in (i) delta, (ii) star, across a 3-phase, 400 volts, 50 Hz supply. Calculate in each case, the readings on two wattmeters connected in the circuit to measure the input. Also determine the phase and line currents in each case.

**Solution:** (i) Consider the coils connected in delta

∴ $\quad V_L = V_{ph} = 400\ \text{volts}$

$\quad \text{Impedance/phase} = \sqrt{(20)^2 + (15)^2}$
$$= 25\ \Omega$$

∴ $\quad \text{Phase current, } I_{ph} = \dfrac{V_{ph}}{Z} = \dfrac{400}{25}$
$$= 16\ A$$

$\quad \text{Line current} = \sqrt{3}\ I_{ph} = \sqrt{3} \times 16 = 27.72\ A$

$\quad \text{Power factor of load} = \dfrac{R}{Z} = \dfrac{20}{25} = 0.8$

$$\text{Power input} = \sqrt{3}\, V_L I_L \cos\phi$$
$$= \sqrt{3} \times 400 \times 27.72 \times 0.8$$
$$= 15362 \text{ watts} = W_1 + W_2 \qquad \ldots (1)$$
$$\tan\phi = \tan\cos^{-1} 0.8 = 0.75$$

Also
$$\tan\phi = \sqrt{3}\,\frac{W_1 - W_2}{W_1 + W_2}$$

or
$$0.75 = \sqrt{3}\,\frac{W_1 - W_2}{15362}$$

∴
$$W_1 - W_2 = \frac{15362 \times 0.75}{\sqrt{3}} = 6652.5 \text{ watts} \qquad \ldots (2)$$

From equations (1) and (2),
$$W_1 = 11007.75 \text{ watts}$$
$$W_2 = 4315.25 \text{ watts}$$

(ii) Same three coils are now star connected.

∴
$$Z = 25\,\Omega$$
$$V_{ph} = \frac{V_L}{\sqrt{3}} = \frac{400}{\sqrt{3}} = 231 \text{ V}$$
$$I_{ph} = \frac{231}{25} = 9.24 \text{ A}$$
$$I_L = I_{ph} = 9.24 \text{ A}$$
$$\cos\phi = \frac{R}{Z} = \frac{20}{25} = 0.8$$
$$\text{Total power input} = \sqrt{3}\, V_L I_L \cos\phi = W_1 + W_2 \qquad \ldots (1)$$
$$= \sqrt{3} \times 400 \times 9.24 \times 0.8 = 5121 \text{ watts}$$
$$\tan\phi = 0.75$$

∴
$$0.75 = \sqrt{3}\,\frac{W_1 - W_2}{W_1 + W_2}$$
$$= \sqrt{3}\,\frac{W_1 - W_2}{5121}$$

or
$$W_1 - W_2 = \frac{5121 \times 0.75}{\sqrt{3}} = 2217.5 \qquad \ldots (2)$$

From equations (1) and (2),
$$W_1 = 3669.25 \text{ watts}$$
$$W_2 = 1451.75 \text{ watts}$$

**Example 1.9:** The readings of two wattmeters connected for measurement of three-phase power are 5000 watts and 500 watts respectively. The latter reading is obtained after reversal of current coil connection. Find the total power and power factor of the load.

**Solution:**

$$W_1 = 5000 \text{ watts}$$
$$W_2 = -500 \text{ watts}$$
$$\therefore \text{Total power} = W_1 + W_2$$
$$= 5000 - 500 = 4500 \text{ W}$$

Using the relation
$$\tan \phi = \sqrt{3} \frac{W_1 - W_2}{W_1 + W_2}$$

or
$$\tan \phi = \sqrt{3} \times \frac{5000 - (-500)}{5000 + (-500)}$$

or
$$\tan \phi = \sqrt{3} \times \frac{5500}{4500} = 2.127$$

$$\therefore \phi = \tan^{-1}(2.127) = 64.8°$$

Hence, $\cos \phi = 0.426$

i.e. p.f. of circuit = 0.426

**Example 1.10:** The readings of the two wattmeters used for measuring power of a three-phase balanced load by two wattmeter method were 5000 W and 1000 W respectively. Calculate the power and power factor if:

(i) Connection of one wattmeter current coil is reserved.

(ii) Both meters record without any change.

**Solution:** (i) When current coil connection of wattmeter is changed, power recorded by it is negative. Hence, $W_1 = 5000$ W and $W_2 = -1000$ W.

$$\therefore \text{Total power} = 5000 - 1000 = 4000 \text{ W}$$

$$\tan \phi = \sqrt{3} \frac{W_1 - W_2}{W_1 + W_2}$$

$$\tan \phi = \sqrt{3} \frac{(5000) - (-1000)}{(5000) + (-1000)}$$

or
$$\tan \phi = \sqrt{3} \frac{6000}{4000}$$

or
$$\phi = \tan^{-1}(\sqrt{3} \times 1.5) = 69°$$

$$\therefore \cos \phi = 0.358$$

Hence, p.f. = 0.358

(ii) Total power of circuit = $W_1 + W_2$
$$= 5000 + 1000 = 6000 \text{ W}$$

$$\tan \phi = \sqrt{3} \frac{W_1 - W_2}{W_1 + W_2}$$

or $\quad \tan\phi = \sqrt{3}\,\dfrac{5000 - 1000}{5000 + 1000}$

$\quad\quad\quad = \sqrt{3} \times \dfrac{4000}{6000}$

$\quad\quad\quad = \sqrt{3} \times \dfrac{2}{3} = \dfrac{2}{\sqrt{3}}$

$\text{p.f.} = \cos\left(\tan^{-1}\dfrac{2}{\sqrt{3}}\right)$

$\quad\quad = 0.565$

**Example 1.11:** One wattmeter method is used for measuring reactive power of a three-phase balanced load. Total reactive power measured is 0.346 kVAR. Find the reading on the wattmeter.

**Solution:** Total reactive power = 0.346 kVAR

$\text{kVAR} = \sqrt{3} \times \text{Reading of wattmeter}$

$0.346 \times 1000 = \sqrt{3} \times \text{Reading of wattmeter}$

$\therefore\quad$ Reading of wattmeter $= \dfrac{0.346 \times 1000}{\sqrt{3}}$

$\quad\quad\quad\quad\quad\quad\quad\quad\quad = 199.76$

**Example 1.12:** One wattmeter method is used to determine the reactive power of a three-phase circuit. Reading of wattmeter when its current coil is connected in one phase and pressure coil between same phase and neutral is 5540 W. The balanced load is connected across symmetrical, 3-phase system and draws 30 amperes at 400 volts. Determine the reading of wattmeter, if the current coil connection remains unchanged, while the potential coil is connected across the remaining two phases of the supply system.

**Solution:** In the first case i.e. when current coil is connected in one phase and pressure coil is connected between same phase and neutral, the reading of the wattmeter is the power supplied per phase.

$\therefore\quad$ Total three-phase power = 3 × Reading of wattmeter

$\quad\quad\quad\quad\quad\quad\quad\quad\quad = 3 \times 5540 = 16620\ \text{W}$

Also power per phase = $V_{ph}\,I_{ph}\cos\phi$

where $V_{ph}$ is phase voltage and $I_{ph}$ is phase current and $\cos\phi$ = p.f. of load

$\therefore\quad 5540 = \dfrac{400}{\sqrt{3}} \times 30 \times \cos\phi$

$\therefore\quad \cos\phi = \dfrac{5540 \times \sqrt{3}}{400 \times 30}$

or $\quad \cos\phi = 0.7996$ say $0.8$

$\therefore\quad \sin\phi = 0.6$

When the current coil connection remaining unchanged, pressure coil connected between other two phases, the wattmeter reads $\sqrt{3}$ times the reactive power per phase.

$$= \sqrt{3} \times VI \sin \phi = \sqrt{3} \times 231 \times 30 \times 0.6$$
$$= 7200 \text{ VAR or } 7.2 \text{ kVAR}$$

**Example 1.13:** A 250 V, 10 amperes dynamometer type wattmeter has resistance of current coil as 0.5 Ω and that of pressure coil is 12000 Ω. Find the percentage error due to each of the two methods of connection when unity p.f. load of 8 A is supplied at 250 V.

**Solution:** (i) We will consider first method of connection as shown in Fig. 1.19.

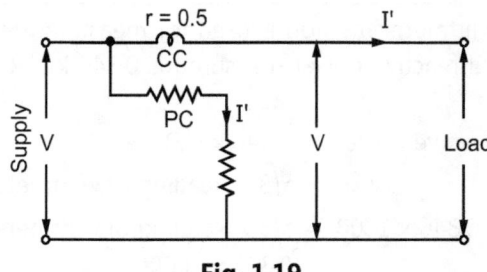

**Fig. 1.19**

Power loss in current coil $= I^2 r = 8^2 \times 0.5 = 32$ watts

Power supplied to load $= 250 \times 8 = 2000$ W

∴ Wattmeter reading $= 2000 + 32 = 2032$ W

∴ % error $= \dfrac{32}{2032} \times 100 = 1.574\%$

(ii) Power loss in pressure coil resistance

$$= \dfrac{V^2}{R}$$
$$= \dfrac{(250)^2}{12000} = \dfrac{62500}{12000} = 5.2 \text{ W}$$

∴ Total power taken $= 2000 + 5.2 = 2005.2$ W

∴ % error $= \dfrac{5.2}{2005.2} \times 100 = 0.259\%$

**Example 1.14:** Two wattmeters are used to measure power input to a synchronous motor. Each of them indicate 50 kW. If the power factor is to be changed to 0.9 leading, determine the reading of the two wattmeters, total input power remaining the same.

**Solution:** As power recorded by both the wattmeters are equal, the synchronous motor must be working at unity p.f. condition.

Hence $W_1 = 30$ kW and $W_2 = 50$ kW.

In second case, p.f. is 0.9 leading

In this case,

$$W_1 = VI \cos(30° + \phi)$$

$$W_2 = VI \cos(30° - \phi)$$

and
$$\tan\phi = \frac{\sqrt{3}(W_1 - W_2)}{(W_1 + W_2)}$$

As $\cos\phi = 0.9$,
$$\phi = \cos^{-1} 0.9$$
$$= 25.84°$$

$\therefore \quad \tan\phi = \tan 25.84°$
$$= 0.4842$$

$\therefore \quad 0.4842 = \dfrac{\sqrt{3}(W_1 - W_2)}{W_1 + W_2}$

But $W_1 + W_2 = 100$ kW

$\therefore \quad 0.4842 = \sqrt{3}\dfrac{W_1 - W_2}{100}$

$\therefore \quad \dfrac{0.4842 \times 100}{\sqrt{3}} = W_1 - W_2 = 27.95$ kW

$\therefore \quad 2W_1 = 127.95$ or $W_1 = 63.97$ kW

$\therefore \quad W_2 = 100 - 63.97 = 36.03$ kW

# 1.3 MEASUREMENT OF ELECTRICAL ENERGY

## 1.3.1 Concept of Electrical Energy

Energy is the total power delivered or consumed over a time interval, that is

$$\text{Energy} = \text{Power} \times \text{Time}$$

Electrical energy developed as work or dissipated as heat over an interval of time t may be expressed as

$$W = \int_0^t Vi\, dt$$

When V is expressed as voltage in volts, i as current in amperes, t is the time expressed in seconds, the energy so obtained is expressed in joules or watt seconds i.e. one watt of power used for a period of one second. When the unit, of time is taken as one hour, energy is expressed in watt-hours. This being a small unit a bigger unit of measuring energy is used mostly, which is a kilowatt hour i.e. energy consumed when power is delivered at an average rate of 1000 watts (1 kW) for one hour. Thus, 1 unit = 1 kWh.

## 1.3.2 Induction Type Watt-Hour Meter

These are the energy meters widely used for the purpose of measuring electrical energy in A.C. circuits. Fig. 1.20 represents the simple construction diagram of a induction type watt hour meter.

The pressure coil is wound on the central limb of upper E shaped electromagnet, while the current coil is wound on the lower 'U' shaped electromagnet. The lower end of E type electromagnet is encircled by a fixed pole-shading copper band. Another adjustable copper band is placed parallel to the face of the central-limb.

The pole shading band produces phase difference of 90° between the applied voltage across the pressure coil and the flux that it produces. The adjustable band produces two torques on the disc for compensating the frictional error.

On the lower electromagnet the current coil is wound, and in addition a auxiliary coil is provided, which has a adjustable slider, by which a correct phase difference of (90 + $\phi$) is obtained between pressure coil flux and the current coil flux.

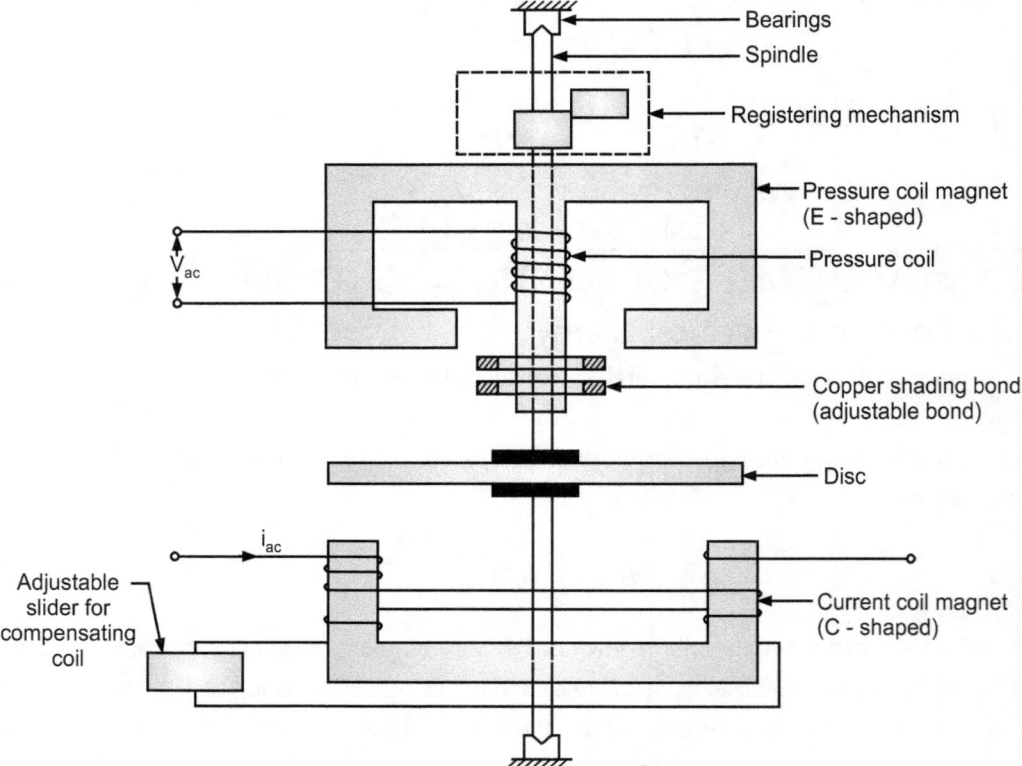

**Fig. 1.20: Induction watt-hour meter**

As the disc is placed between the two electro-magnets, eddy currents will be induced on the disc by the two fluxes i.e. flux due to pressure coil and flux due to current coil, which will set up a torque on the disc, which is proportional to power i.e. VI cos $\phi$, causing the disc to rotate. The torque is produced because of interaction of two fluxes and induced eddy currents. The vertical spindle is supported between bearings and carries a worm and gear arrangement, which drives the counting gear.

Braking torque is provided by means of a permanent magnet used for braking, and eddy currents are induced in the disc due to flux of this permanent magnet.

As the disc start rotating, the spindle also rotates. On upperside, the spindle is connected to registering mechanism through small gears. This registering mechanism counts the rotation of disc over a period of time. Thus, energy is quantified. The numbering system is operated by gears and these numbers directly display the number of units (kWh) consumed.

The vector diagram for different fluxes, voltages and currents can be drawn as follows :

Let 'V' represents the applied voltage and I be the load current lagging V at an angle $\phi$. The current flowing through pressure coil produces a flux $\phi_v$; as this current is proportional to V, $\phi_v \propto V$; but it is made to lag V by 90°. Let $\phi_c$ be the flux produced by current coil, when load current I flows through it, and it will be in phase with I. $e_v$ be the induced e.m.f. (eddy) in the disc, by the flux $\phi_v$, and $e_c$ be the induced e.m.f. by $\phi_c$.

Hence, $e_v$ lags $\phi_v$ by 90°. As the inductance of eddy current is negligible, eddy current will be in phase with their respective induced e.m.fs. Let $i_v$ and $i_c$ be the magnitudes of the two eddy currents.

$i_c$ will have a component $I_c \cos \phi$ in phase with $\phi_v$ and produces a

$$\text{torque} \propto i_c \cos \phi \qquad \ldots (1.21)$$

Similarly, $i_v$ has a component $i_v \cos (180 - \phi)$ in direction of $\phi_c$ and it will produce a torque proportional to $\phi_c i_v \cos (180 - \phi)$ ... (1.22)

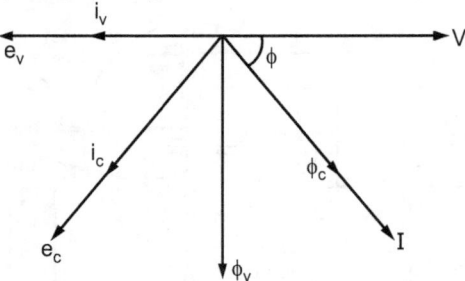

**Fig. 1.21**

But the two torques act in opposition. Hence, average torque is

$$T_a \propto \{\phi_v i_c \cos \phi - \phi_c i_v \cos (180 - \phi)\}$$

∴ $$T_a \propto (\phi_v i_c \cos \phi + \phi_c i_v \cos \phi\}$$

But $\phi_v \propto v$, and $i_c \propto \phi_c \propto I$

∴ $$\phi_c I_c \propto VI \quad \text{and}$$

$$\theta_c i_v \propto VI$$

or $$T_{av} \propto VI \cos \phi$$

The speed of the disc will be proportional to $T_{av}$. Hence, in a given time number of revolutions will be proportional to $T_{av} \times$ time.

i.e.                      VI cos φ × Time

i.e.                      Power in watt × Time

The counting arrangement can be so arranged that it will register the energy directly in kWh.

### 1.3.3 Three Phase Energy Meters

The three phase energy meters are:

(a) Two element energy meters for a three phase, three wire system and

(b) Three element energy meters for a three phase, four wire system.

The arrangement and connection of these meters are just similar to three phase watt meters. We will study two element, three phase energy meter.

### 1.3.4 Two Element Energy Meters

Fig. 1.22 represents the constructional details of a two element energy meter. It consists of two discs one for each element. The two elements should read equal when equal amount of energy passes through them. The two discs are mounted on the same spindle and the torque produced on it at any time is proportional to the power supplied to the circuit.

The worm and gear arrangement is used to engage the counting mechanism which will record directly the energy in kWh.

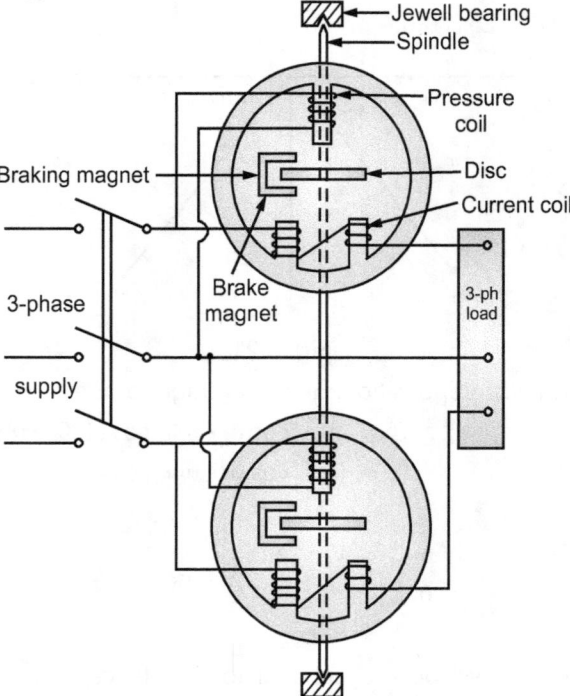

**Fig. 1.22: Two element energy**

## 1.3.5 Three Element Energy Meter

This is used on 3 phases, 4 wire system of supply.

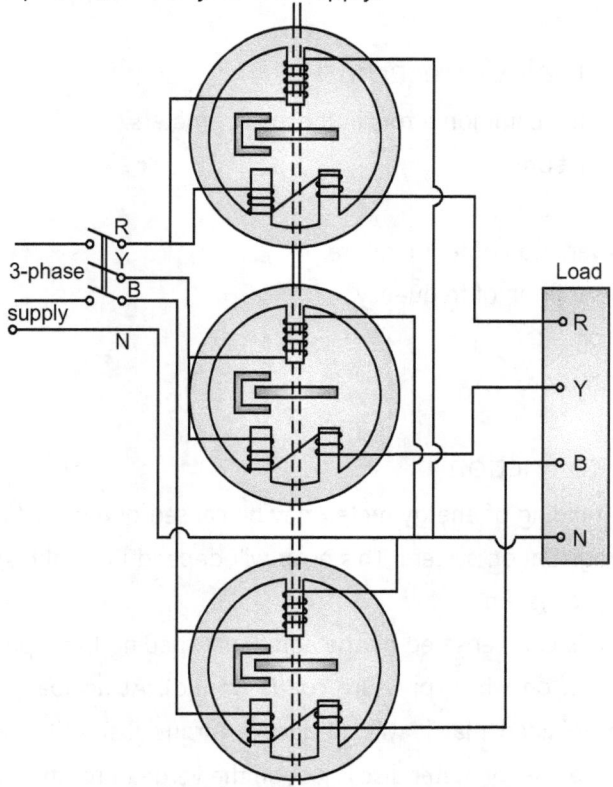

**Fig. 1.23: Three element energy meter**

Fig. 1.24 represent its circuit connection diagram with C.T. and P.T.

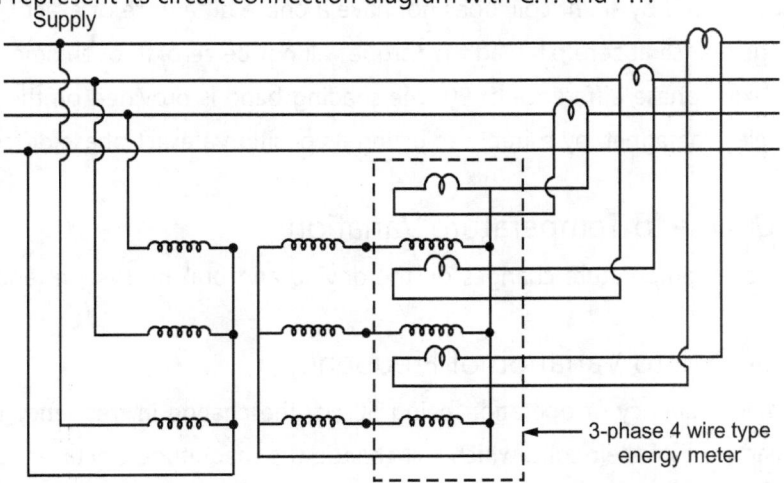

**Fig. 1.24: Circuit connections for three-element induction wattmeter**

## 1.3.6 Extension of Range of Energy Meters

Extension of range of energy meters can be carried in a similar manner as is used for wattmeters.

## 1.3.7 Errors and Their Correction

The following are the common errors in the energy meters:

(a) Error due to friction.

(b) Phase or low p.f. error.

(c) Error due to variation of temperature.

(d) Error due to variation of frequency.

(e) Creeping error.

(f) Error in registration.

(g) Speed error.

## 1.3.8 Error Due to Friction

The error in the reading of energy meter may be caused due to friction at bearing of the spindle and in the registration system. This error will depend upon the speed of the spindle or upon the load of the system.

This type of error is compensated by the additional shading band provided on the shunt electromagnet (magnet on which pressure coil is wound). At no load, the position of this shading band is so adjusted that it will produce a torque just sufficient to overcome the frictional torque i.e. the energy meter disc is just on the verge of rotation.

## 1.3.9 Phase or Low p.f. Error

The flux produced by shunt coil, does not have a phase difference of exact 90° due to its applied voltage; hence at zero p.f. load the torque will not be zero, to overcome this error, or to achieve a exact phase difference of 90° the shading band is provided on the central limb of the shunt electromagnet, by suitably adjusting its position a exact phase difference of 90° is achieved.

## 1.3.10 Error Due to Temperature Variation

The effects of temperature changes on the driving and braking system tend to balance each other.

## 1.3.11 Error Due to Variation of Frequency

The normal frequency of operation being 50 Hz, the change in frequency will result in change of reactance of their coils, which will change the magnitude of current and also the flux due to it causing a small error.

## 1.3.12 Creeping Error

In this type of error, the energy meter disc will rotate even at no load. This may be due to overvoltage applied across the meter or over compensation of frictional error; stray magnetic field etc.

For overcoming this type of error two small holes are drilled on the disc diametrically opposite side, when the hole will come under the pole of a shunt magnet it will stop running.

## 1.3.13 Error in Registration

The number of revolution per kWh of the meter are designed under normal condition, but there may be error in revolution made by energy meter under working condition, which may be due to weakening of strength of permanent magnet if used, wrong adjustment of compensating mechanism. This error can be compensated by adjusting, braking magnet or by adjustment of compensating arrangement or even by changing the registering system.

## 1.3.14 Speed Error

The speed of the disc is proportional to current in A.h. (Ampere hour) meters and to power in case of W.h. (Watt hour) meters. The braking torque is produced by permanent magnets, if its strength is weakened then the braking torque will be less than deflecting torque, and the disc will run fast, but at the same time a increase in the frictional torque will take place which will compensate slightly the error. Complete compensation can be obtained by readjusting the compensating mechanisms.

## 1.3.15 Calibration of Energy Meter

The calibration of energy meter means its testing with the help of sub-standard equipment or with the help of rotary sub-standard energy meter to determine its % error.

The energy meters are tested under the following conditions and if its registration system show error in recording, the adjustments can be carried out to bring its error within permissible limits.

(a) At 5% of rated full-load current with unity p.f. load.
(b) At 100% or 125% of marked full load with unity p.f. load.
(c) Any suitable load between above two, with unity p.f. load.
(d) At rated current with 0.5 lagging p.f. condition.

In addition to above tests on each, the following tests are essential :

(e) **Creap Test:** This test is carried out by applying 110% rated voltage at no load, the disc should not complete more than one revolution under this condition.
(f) **Starting Test:** At rated voltage 0.5% rated current is made to flow through the current coil, the disc of the meter must start rotating.

## 1.3.16 Testing Methods

Following are the main methods of testing motor energy meters :

(a) Long-period dial test.

(b) Using rotary sub-standard meter.

(c) Using precision grade instruments.

## 1.3.17 Long-Period Dial Test

A rotating sub-standard meter is used to measure the correct amount of energy passing through the energy meter being tested in a given time.

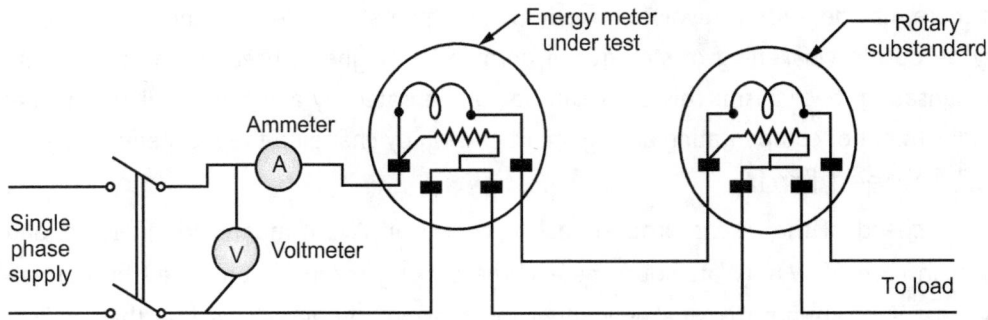

**Fig. 1.25**

The current coils of the two meters are connected in series hence they carry same current; and the pressure coils or shunt coils are connected in parallel so that same voltage is applied across them. The meters are started and stopped simultaneously. The energy recorded by the two meters are compared at the end of the period which may be one hour or even more, the error is calculated as follows :

Let,
$D$ = Registration of meter under test in kWh

$D_s$ = Registration of sub-standard in kWh

$$\% \text{ error} = \frac{D - D_s}{D_s} \times 100$$

## 1.3.18 Using Rotary Sub-Standard Meter

For carrying out testing by this method, a rotary sub-standard meter is used. The current coil of the meter under test and rotary sub-standard are connected in series as shown in Fig. 1.25 and the pressure coils are connected in parallel. Arrangement is made to start and stop the two meters simultaneously. For a particular short interval of time, the revolutions made by the two discs are compared or the speed of the two discs are compared.

Let,
$K$ = Number of revolutions/kWh of the meter under test.

$K_s$ = Number of revolutions made by the meter under test during above period.

R = Number of revolutions made by the meter under test during above period.

$R_s$ = Number of revolutions made by sub-standard during the test period.

N = Speed of disc of meter under test.

$N_s$ = Speed of disc of sub-standard.

t = Time interval in hours.

### (a) When revolutions are compared:

Energy recorded by meter under test during test period R/K

Energy recorded by sub-standard meter $R_s/K_s$.

$$\therefore \quad \% \text{ Error} = \frac{R/K - R_s/K_s}{R_s/K_s} \times 100$$

### (b) When speeds are compared:

Energy recorded by meter under test = $N_r\, t/K$

Energy measured by sub-standard = $N_s \cdot t/K_s$

$$\therefore \quad \% \text{ Error} = \left(\frac{N_r \cdot K_s}{N_s \cdot K} - 1\right) \times 100$$

For this test long period dial test is required.

## 1.3.19 Using Precision Grade Instruments

In this method of testing, a energy meter precision grade instruments are used i.e. wattmeter, ammeter and voltmeter used for the testing purpose will be precision grade, also a clock having start and stop switch and recording correct value of short times is also used. The current flowing through the precision instruments and the meter under test will be kept constant and a rated (constant) voltage is applied across the instruments and energy meter, the test circuit will be similar to that shown in Fig. 1.26. The number of revolutions made by the meter disc during the test are recorded, and time required for it is also correctly measured.

Then energy recorded by meter under test = $R/K_s$ kWh.

Energy calculated from the readings of precision instruments = kW.t kWh.

Where,  R = Number of revolution made by disc of energy meter under test.

$K_s$ = Number of revolutions per kWh for meter under test.

kW = Power in kilo-watt, as calculated from readings of instruments.

T = Time in hours.

$$\therefore \quad \% \text{ error} = \left(\frac{\frac{R}{K_s} - kW \times t}{kW \times t}\right) \times 100$$

## 1.3.20 Meter Testing Circuit

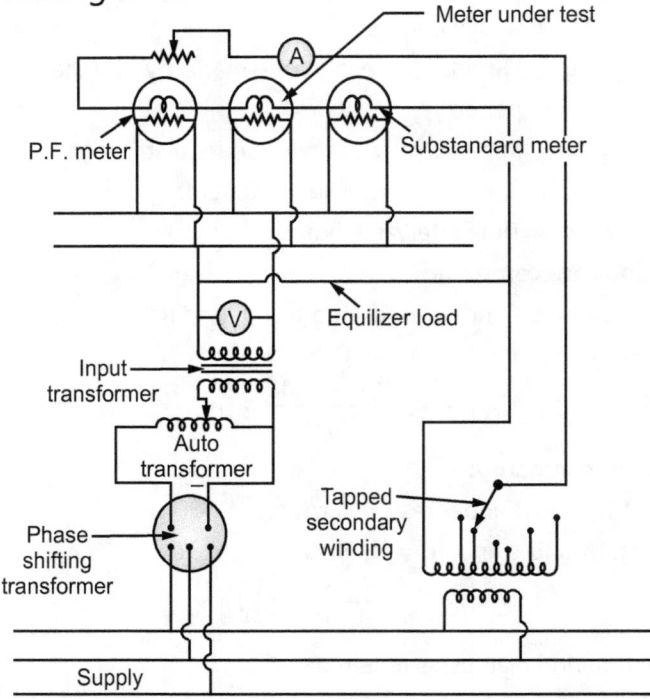

**Fig. 1.26: Testing of A.C. meters with phantom loading and phase-shifting device**

Such circuits make use of phantom loading arrangements. Therefore, separate supply sources are used for voltage and current supplied. Also the arrangement for phase shifting is used in such circuits hence a phase shifting transformer is used here Fig. 1.26 represents a simple circuit used for meter testing at desired load condition.

## ILLUSTRATIVE EXAMPLES

**Example 1.15:** A single-phase energy meter has a constant of 6000 rev./kWh. A test was carried out with a resistive load for one minute, during which the meter made 21 revolutions. The voltage was 110 volts and current 2 A. Calculate the % error.

**Solution**

$$1 \text{ kWh} = 1 \text{ kW} \times 1 \text{ hour}$$
$$= 1 \text{ kW} \times 3600 \text{ sec.}$$
$$= 3600 \text{ kW sec.}$$

Meter makes 6000 rev./kWh $= \dfrac{6000}{3600}$

or $K = \dfrac{3600}{6000}$

$= 0.6$

∴ Meter testing constant    K = 0.6 kW sec./rev.

$$\text{Energy consumed during the test} = \frac{VI}{1000} \times \text{sec.}$$

$$= \frac{110 \times 2 \times 60}{1000}$$

$$= 13.2 \text{ kW sec.}$$

Number of revolutions made by the meter = 21

∴ Actual kW sec. per revolution,

$$K' = \frac{13.2}{21}$$

$$= 0.628$$

∴ $$\% \text{ error} = \left(\frac{K - K'}{K'}\right) \times 100$$

∴ $$= \frac{0.6 - 0.628}{0.628} \times 100$$

$$= -4.46\%$$

**Example 1.16:** The constant of a 3-phase, 2 element induction energy meter is 0.12 revolutions of disc per kWh. If the meter is normally used with a potential transformer of ratio 22000/110 V and current transformer of ratio 500/5, determine the error, expressed as the percentage of the correct reading from the following test figures, for the instrument only.

Line voltage = 110 V, line current = 5.25, power factor = 1, time to complete 40 revolutions = 61 seconds.

**Solution :**

$$\text{Ratio of P.T.} = \frac{22000}{110} = 200$$

$$\text{Ratio of C.T.} = \frac{500}{5} = 100$$

∴ Multiplying factor of meter = 200 × 100 = 20,000

Constant of meter without C.T. and P.T.

$$= 0.12 \times 20000$$
$$= 2400 \text{ rev. / kWh}$$

1 kWh = 3600 kW sec.

$$\text{Testing constant, } K = \frac{3600}{2400} = 1.5$$

$$\text{Energy consumed during test} = \frac{\sqrt{3} \times 110 \times 5.25 \times 1}{1000} \times 61 \text{ kW sec.}$$

$$= 61 \text{ kW sec.}$$

As the meter makes 40 revolutions

∴ Actual kW sec. per revolution K',

$$K' = \frac{61}{40}$$

$$= 1.525 \text{ kW sec./rev.}$$

∴ 
$$\text{Error} = \left[\frac{K - K'}{K'}\right] \times 100$$

$$= \left[\frac{1.5 - 1.525}{1.525}\right] \times 100 = 1.639\%$$

**Example 1.17:** A three-phase energy meter has a constant of 0.2 revolutions of disc per kWh. The meter is connected with a P.T. of ratio 22000/220 volts and a C.T. of ratio 1000/5 amperes.

It is recorded at the time of testing that, line voltage = 220 volts, line current = 10 amperes, p.f. of load unity and time required for 120 revolutions of the disc was 30 seconds. Determine the percentage error in the reading of the meter and state whether it is fast or slow.

**Solution:** Actual energy supplied during the period of test

$$= \text{Actual power} \times \text{Time}$$

$$= \sqrt{3} \, V_L \, I_L \cos\phi \times \text{Time in hours}$$

$$= \sqrt{3} \times 220 \times 10 \times 1 \times \frac{30}{3600}$$

$$= 31.75 \text{ watt hrs.}$$

Energy recorded by energy meter in watt hours

$$= \frac{\text{Number of revolutions of disc}}{\text{Revolutions per kWh}} \times \text{P.T. ratio} \times \text{C.T. ratio}$$

$$= \frac{120}{0.2} \times \frac{220}{22000} \times \frac{5}{1000} = 0.03 \text{ kWh}$$

or
$$= 0.03 \times 1000 = 30 \text{ watt hrs.}$$

$$\% \text{ error} = \frac{\text{True reading} - \text{Recorded reading}}{\text{True reading}} \times 100$$

$$= \frac{31.75 - 30}{31.75} \times 100$$

$$= 5.51\%$$

As recorded energy is less than the actual, the meter is slow.

**Example 1.18:** A 230 V single-phase energy meter has a constant load current of 4 amperes passing through it for 5 hours at unity p.f. If the meter disc makes 1104 revolutions during this time, determine the meter constant. If the load p.f. changes to 0.8, calculate the number of revolutions of the disc during this period.

**Solution:** Energy used during period of 5 hours, for unity p.f. load

$$= VI \cos \phi \times Time$$
$$= 230 \times 4 \times 1 \times 5 = 4600 \text{ watt hrs.}$$
$$= \frac{4600}{1000} = 4.6 \text{ kWh}$$

Total number of revolutions of the disc for recording this energy = 1104

∴ Energy meter constant $= \frac{1104}{4.6} = 240$ rev./kWh

When load p.f. is 0.8, energy used

$$= 230 \times 4 \times 0.8 \times 5$$
$$= 3680 \text{ watt hrs. or } 3.68 \text{ kWh}$$

∴ Total revolutions $= 3.68 \times 240$
$$= 883.2 \text{ say } 883 \text{ rev.}$$

**Example 1.19:** A lamp load of 2000 watts was connected for a period of 6 hours, through a energy meter, it has a constant of 600 revolutions per kWh. It was recorded that the disc of energy meter rotate at 20.2 r.p.m. Determine the % error of the meter and state whether the meter is fast or slow.

**Solution:** Actual energy supplied to the load

$$= W \times t$$
$$= 2000 \times 6 = 12000 \text{ watt hrs.}$$
$$= \frac{12000}{1000} = 12 \text{ kWh}$$

As the energy is used for 6 hours, total energy recorded

$$= \frac{\text{Revolutions of disc/minute} \times \text{Time}}{\text{Meter constant}}$$

$$= \frac{20.2 \times 6 \times 60}{600} = 12.12 \text{ kWh}$$

∴ % Error $= \frac{\text{Actual} - \text{Recorded}}{\text{Actual}} \times 100$

$$= \frac{12 - 12.12}{12} \times 100 = -1\%$$

As recorded energy is more than the actual energy used, the meter is fast.

**Example 1.20:** A constant for a three-phase, three element wattmeter is 0.12 revolutions of disc per kWh. The meter is normally used with a potential transformer of ratio 22000/110 V and a current transformer of ratio 500/5 A. Find the percentage error in terms of correct reading, from the following test result.

Line voltage = 110 volts, current = 5 amperes, Power factor of load = one.

Time required to complete 40 revolutions = 60 seconds.

**Solution:** Actual energy used during testing period

$$= \sqrt{3} \, V_L \, I_L \cos\phi \times \text{time}$$
$$= \sqrt{3} \times (M.F.) \times V_L \, I_L \cos\phi \times \text{Time}$$
$$= \sqrt{3} \times \left(\frac{22000}{110} \times \frac{500}{5}\right) \times 110 \times 5 \times 1 \times \frac{60}{3600}$$
$$= 339 \times 10^3 \text{ watt hours or } 339 \text{ kWh}$$

Energy recorded by the energy meter during the test period

$$= \frac{\text{Number of revolutions recorded}}{\text{Number of revolutions per kWh}}$$
$$= \frac{40}{0.12} = 333.3 \text{ kWh}$$

∴ % error $= \dfrac{339 - 333.3}{339} \times 100$

$$= \frac{5.7}{339} = 0.0168 \text{ or } 1.68\%$$

The meter records less than actual, hence it is slow.

**Example 1.21:** An energy meter makes 100 revolutions of the disc for one unit of energy. Calculate the number of revolutions made by it when connected to a load carrying 20 A at 230 volts and 0.8 p.f. for one hour. If it actually makes 360 revolutions, find the percentage error.

**Solution:** Energy consumed by load in one hour

$$= VI \cos\phi \times \text{time watt hour}$$
$$= 230 \times 20 \times 0.8 \times 1$$
$$= 3680 \text{ watt hour}$$
$$\text{or } \frac{3680}{1000} = 3.68 \text{ kWh}$$

As the disc makes 100 revolutions for one unit i.e. one kWh, the revolutions that it should make for energy of 3.68 kWh

$$= 3.68 \times 100 = 368 \text{ revolutions}$$

Actual revolutions made = 360

∴ % error $= \dfrac{368 - 360}{360} = 2.22\%$

As it records less than required, the meter is slow.

**Example 1.22:** The constant of a 3-phase, 2 element energy meter is 0.24 revolutions of disc per hour. If the meter is normally used with P.T. of ratio 22 kV/220 volts and C.T. of ratio 500/5 A, determine the error expressed as a percentage of correct reading, from the following test results.

Line voltage = 220 V, current = 5.25 A, power factor = 1, time to complete 80 revolutions = 61 seconds.

**Solution:**

$$\text{P.T. ratio} = \frac{22 \times 10^3}{220} = 100$$

$$\text{C.T. ratio} = \frac{500}{5} = 100$$

∴ Wattmeter multiplying factor $= 100 \times 100 = 10 \times 10^3$

Actual energy supplied during test period

$$= \sqrt{3} \, V_L I_L \cos\phi \times \text{Time in hours}$$

$$= \sqrt{3} \times 220 \times 5.25 \times 1 \times \frac{61}{3600}$$

$$= 33.89 \text{ watt hour}$$

Energy recorded by energy meter in watt hours

$$= \frac{\text{Number of revolutions of disc}}{\text{Revolutions per kWh}} \times \text{P.T. ratio} \times \text{C.T. ratio}$$

$$= \frac{80}{0.24} \times \frac{220}{22000} \times \frac{5}{500} = 0.033 \text{ kWh}$$

or  $0.033 \times 1000 = 33$ watt hours

∴

$$\% \text{ error} = \frac{\text{True reading} - \text{Recorded reading}}{\text{True reading}} \times 100$$

$$= \frac{33.89 - 33}{33.89} \times 100 = 2.626\%$$

The meter is slow as recorded reading is less than the actual energy used.

**Example 1.23:** A watt-hour meter is calibrated to measure energy on a 250 V supply. On test a steady current of 15 amperes is passed through it for 5 hours at unity power factor. If the meter readings before and after the test are 6234.21 kWh and 6253.13 kWh respectively, calculate the percentage error.

If the spindle turns through 290 revolutions in 5 minutes, when a current of 20 A is passing through the meter at 250 volts and 0.87 power factor, calculate the meter constant.

**Solution:** Energy recorded by energy meter

$$= 6253.13 - 6234.21$$

$$= 18.92 \text{ kWh}$$

Actual energy used $= \dfrac{VI \cos \phi}{1000} \times$ Time in hours

$= \dfrac{250 \times 15 \times 1 \times 5}{1000} = 18.75$ kWh

$\therefore$ % error $= \dfrac{\text{Actual} - \text{Recorded}}{\text{Actual}} \times 100$

$= \dfrac{18.75 - 18.92}{18.75} \times 100 = -0.906\%$

$\therefore$ The meter is fast.

Energy used $= \dfrac{250 \times 20 \times 0.87}{1000} \times \dfrac{5}{60}$

$= 0.3625$ kWh

Meter makes 290 revolutions for 0.362 kWh

$\therefore$ Revolutions/kWh $= \dfrac{290}{0.362} = 801$

$\therefore$ Meter constant $= 800$ rev./kWh

**Example 1.24:** A meter recorded 0.5 kWh, in a test of 30 minutes duration with a constant current of 5 A. If now the same meter is used on a 200 V supply, determine its error, and state whether the meter is fast or slow.

**Solution:** Energy recorded $= V \times I \times \cos \phi \times$ Time

$0.5 \times 1000 = V \times 5 \times 1 \times \dfrac{30}{60}$

$500 = 2.5\ V$

$\therefore$ $V = \dfrac{500}{2.5} = 200$ volts

As the voltage applied during the test is 200 volts, the same meter when will be used on 200 volts will have no error in recording.

**Example 1.25:** Following is the electricity consumption for the office:
(i) 10 tubes each of 40 watts working 8 hours/day.
(ii) 4 fans each of 60 watts working 8 hours/day.
(iii) 2 coolers each of 100 watts working 4 hours/day.
(iv) 5 lamps each of 40 watts working 2 hours/day.

Calculate electricity bill for the month of April at the rate of ₹ 0.75 per unit.

**Solution:** First of all we calculate the total energy in watt-hours consumed by all types of loads in one day.

Total wattage × time
(i) Energy consumed by tubes = 10 × 40 × 8 = 3200 Wh
(ii) Energy consumed by fans = 4 × 60 × 8 = 1920 Wh
(iii) Energy consumed by coolers = 2 × 100 × 4 = 800 Wh
(iv) Energy consumed by lamps = 5 × 40 × 2 = 400 Wh
Total energy consumed/day in Wh = 6320 watt-hours

or     Energy consumed/day = $\dfrac{6320}{1000}$ = 6.32 kWh

which is the unit of energy for which bills are charge.
Number of days in the month of April = 30
Total energy consumption in April = 6.32 × 30 = 189.6 kWh or units.
Monthly energy charges at the rate of ₹ 0.75/ unit.
= 189.6 × 0.75 = 142.2 Rupees

**Example 1.26:** A bungalow has the following electrical load:
(i) A T.V. set - 60 watt working 6 hours/day.
(ii) 6 tubes each - 40 watt working 8 hours/day.
(iii) 4 fans - 60 watts working 4 hours/day.
(iv) A heater – 1000 W working 2 hours/day.
(v) A cooler - 100 watt working 4 hours/day.

Find the electricity bill for the month of April at the rate of ₹ 0.5 kWh

Total energy consumed by each type of load in watt-hours can be calculated as follows.

| Sr. No. | Appliances | Total connected load in watts | Duration in hours/day | Energy consumed during a day watt-hours |
|---|---|---|---|---|
| 1. | T.V. Set | 60 | 6 | 360 |
| 2. | Tubes | 40 × 6 | 8 | 1920 |
| 3. | Heater | 1000 | 2 | 2000 |
| 4. | Cooler | 100 | 4 | 400 |
| 5. | Fans | 60 × 4 | 4 | 960 |
|  |  |  | **Total** | **5640** |

**Solution:** ∴ Energy consumed per day in kWh = $\dfrac{\text{Watt hour}}{1000}$ = $\dfrac{5640}{1000}$ = 5.64 kWh or unit

Number of days in the months of April being 30
Total units consumed = 5.64 × 30 = 169.2
Energy bill @ ₹ 0.50 per unit = 169.2 × 0.5 = ₹ 84.6

**Example 1.27:** A bungalow consists of the following loads, which are used for the duration shown against them:
(i) Heater load of 2 kW used for 4 hours/day.
(ii) Pump load of 1 H.P. used for 2 hours/days
(iii) Freeze load of 100 watts used for 24 hours/day.
(iv) Lighting load of 250 watts used for 4 hours/day.
(v) Cooler load of 200 watts used for 6 hours/day.
(vi) Other domestic appliances 200 watts, 1 hour/day.

Find out the monthly electricity bill for the month of May, when the electricity is charged at ₹ 1.5 / unit.

We will prepare the table for finding out total units consumed/day.

| Sr. No. | Types of load | Load in kW | Time for which used | Energy in kWh |
|---|---|---|---|---|
| 1. | Heater | 2 | 4 | 8 |
| 2. | Pump Load | $1 \times 735.5/1000$ | 2 | 1.471 |
| 3. | Freeze | 100/1000 | 24 | 2.4 |
| 4. | Lighting Load | 250/1000 | 4 | 1.00 |
| 5. | Cooler | 200/1000 | 6 | 1.200 |
| 6. | Other Appliances | 200/1000 | 1 | 0.20 |

**Solution:** Energy consumed in month of May = $14.27 \times 31$ = 442.40 units.

Energy bill for the month of May

$$442.40 \times 1.5 = 663.60 \text{ Rupees}$$

# 1.4 VARIOUS TERMS RELATED TO ILLUMINATION

## 1.4.1 Luminaries

For illumination (Luminous output) following types of electric lamps are used:
(i) Incandescent lamp.
(ii) Arc lamps.
(iii) Electric discharge lamps.

### 1.4.1.1 Incandescent Lamp

When an electric current is passed through a fine metallic wire it raises temperature, of the wire and heat energy will be radiated out at low temperature. At high temperature, heat as well as light energy will be radiated. The wire used in such type of lamps must have the following properties:
(i) Its melting point must be high so that it can work at very high temperature.
(ii) It must have low temperature coefficient of expansion.
(iii) It must be ductile.

(iv) It must be very strong mechanically so as to withstand any vibrations during normal use.

(v) It must have low vapour pressure. Tungsten is the most common material used as filament, however carbon and tantalum can also be used.

**Construction:** The lamps which work at incandescence of filament metal are called as incandescent lamps. The details of construction are as shown in Fig. 1.27.

It consists of a glass bulb. At the centre there is a glass stem through which two lead wires are run. To the lead wires is connected the tungsten filament. Which may be either coil, or coil type coil, with the help of support. The bulb is sealed by means of a cap having two pins and lead contacts.

The lamps are manufactured either vacuum type or gas filled type. In case of vacuum type lamps, air is removed from the glass bulb, while in case of gas filled lamps nearly 90% of nitrogen and 5 to 10% argon gas is filled, which improve the efficiency of lamp and blackening effect is also eliminated.

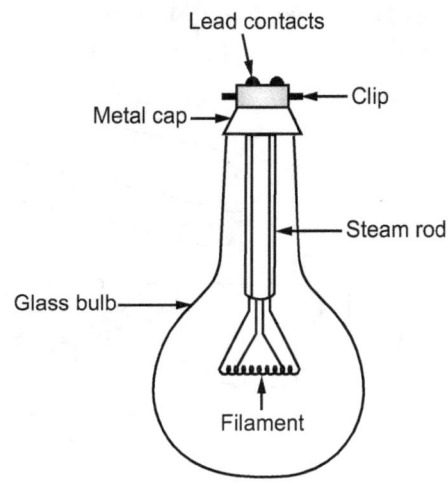

**Fig. 1.27**

The efficiency is nearly 10 to 20 lumens/watt. Tungsten filament is generally used because it has high melting point nearly 3500°C, high resistivity and low rate of evaporation, good mechanical strength.

These lamps are manufactured in different sizes varying from 5 watts to 500 watts. They are generally used for residential buildings, offices, roads etc.

### 1.4.1.2 Arc Lamps

These lamps are sometimes used for obtaining extreme brightness. Following types of arc lamps are usually used.

**(a) Carbon arc lamp:** In this type, two carbon electrodes are used, which are brought together for a moment and as soon as arc is struck, these are separated by manual operation or by some automatic mechanism. The arc has a negative volt ampere characteristic and so it is necessary to insert ballast in series with it to obtain stable performance. Resistance and inductance ballasts are used for D.C. arcs respectively.

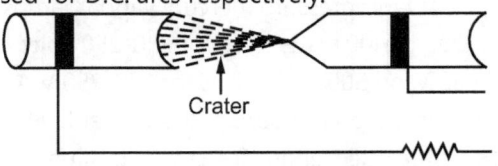

**Fig. 1.28 (a)**

In low intensity D.C. arc lamps (operating at 30 A and 55 volts) the positive electrode is heated to a very high temperature due to concentration of high amount of discharged electrical energy in small area. Due to this, a crater is formed on the positive electrode. This crator acts as a concentrated source of high luminious intensity and emits approximately 80% of light.

For maintaining arc, the minimum voltage required is given by
$V = (39 + 28l)$ where $l$ is length in cm.

**(b) Flame arc lamp:** The principle of operation is similar to carbon arc lamps. The electrodes in this type have 5 to 15% fluoride (flame material) and 85 to 95% carbon.

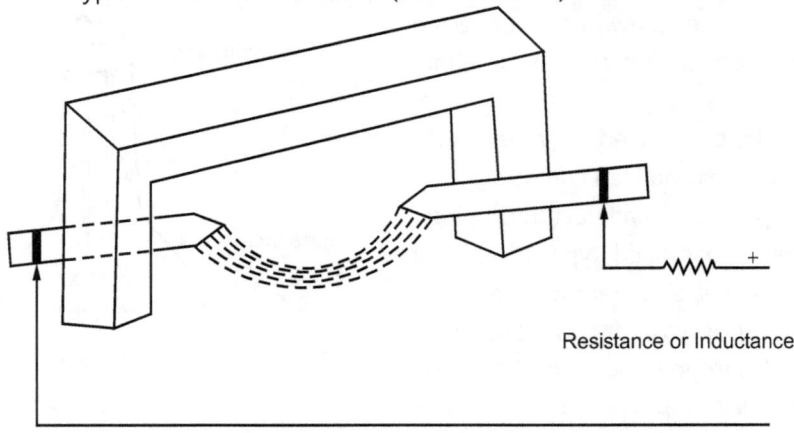

**Fig. 1.28 (b)**

Generally, core type carbon electrodes are used and the cavities are filled with fluoride. The fluoride has a characteristic which radiates light energy efficiently from a very high heated arc stream. Fluoride turns into vapour along with the carbon and these fluoride vapours produce a very high luminous intensities. In addition to fluoride, there are also other flame materials. Different flame materials will produce different colours. Most of these colours do not appeal to eyes and at the same time they produce strain on them. With the help of magnets as shown in Fig. 1.28 (b) the arc can be turned to one side, it has a efficiency of about 8 lumens per watt.

**(c) Magnetic arc lamp:** In this case, positive electrode is of copper and negative electrode is of magnetic oxide of iron. The arc is struck in similar manner as in case of carbon lamps.

### 1.4.1.3 High Pressure Mercury Vapour Lamps

There are different types of high pressure mercury vapour lamps. They are:
(a) M.A. Type made in 250 to 400 watts sizes for 230-250 volts A.C. Supply.
(b) M.A. Type made in 300 and 500 watts sizes for 230-250 V A.C. supply.
(c) M.B. Type working at very high pressure and is available in 80 and 125 W sizes.

The high pressure lamps are used either for street lighting or for industrial purposes if there is no objection for the greenish light produced by them.

**M.A. Type Mercury Vapour Lamps:** It consists of a glass tube of borosilicate. At the two ends of the tube are provided two electrodes of wire having a special coating. Near the upper electrode is a auxiliary starting electrode which is connected to the bottom electrode through a high resistance. The tube is sealed by inserting mercury and a small quantity of argon gas keeping inside pressure of 1.5 atmosphere. It is further enveloped by another tube, the advantage of which is that the heat of the inner tube is prohibited to dissipate to atmosphere.

The lamp has a screwed cap and is connected to the supply mains through a choke. To improve the p.f. of the tube a condenser is connected across the mains.

When the tube is switched on, the arc starts between an auxiliary electrode and the main electrode. At this instant, the discharge is in argon gas controlled by high resistance, due to this discharge the whole of the argon gas becomes conducting and a discharge starts between the two main electrodes. Due to the high resistance in auxiliary anode circuit the discharge shifts in between the main electrodes.

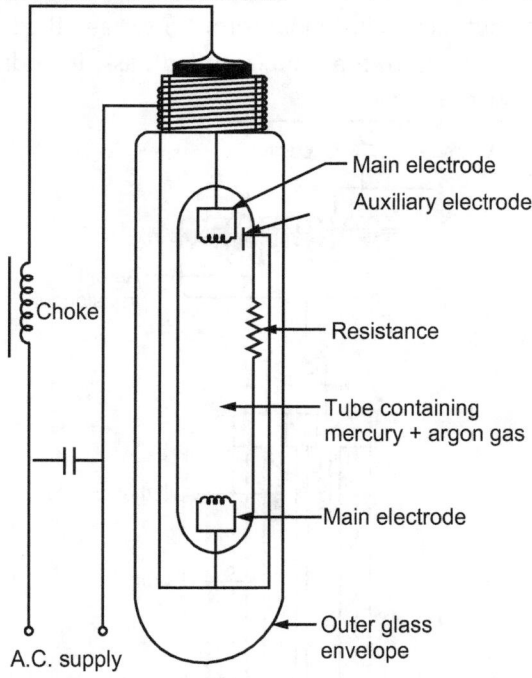

**Fig. 1.29**

The discharge is of pale blue glow controlled by the choke. Due to the heat produced during discharge, the tube gets heated up and the mercury get evaporated developing the pressure inside the tube. The discharge then takes up a shape of intense arc. After about 5 minutes the lamp starts giving full output.

Following points should be remembered in case of M.V. lamps.
(i) The lamp is not operative when cold, so it takes some time for running up which may be about 5 to six minutes.
(ii) If lamp is switched off, it will not restart again until and unless the pressure developed inside the tube subsides.
(iii) The lamp should always be hung vertically, otherwise the arc will burn the inner tube.

Construction and working of (b) type lamps is similar to (a), while high pressure M.V. lamps used high pressure mercury discharge due to which its proportion of radiations in visible spectrum is increased and we get light having bluish finge.

### 1.4.1.4 Sodium Vapour Gas Discharge Lamp

It is in the form of a 'U' tube as shown in Fig. 1.30. A special type of glass (sintered aluminium oxide arc tube) is used which will not get blackened due to effect of sodium vapours. The lamp is quite sensitive to temperature. When the temperature is above normal working temperature the velocity attained by the colliding electrons becomes excessive and they excite the electrons to second energy level. The radiations from second energy level of 3.61 V is of wavelength lies in the ultraviolet region. If its temperature lowers below the normal, the sodium does not remain in vapour form. So to keep the temperature of the lamp within working range it is enclosed in a double-walled flask. In addition to sodium a small quantity of inert gas is also inserted.

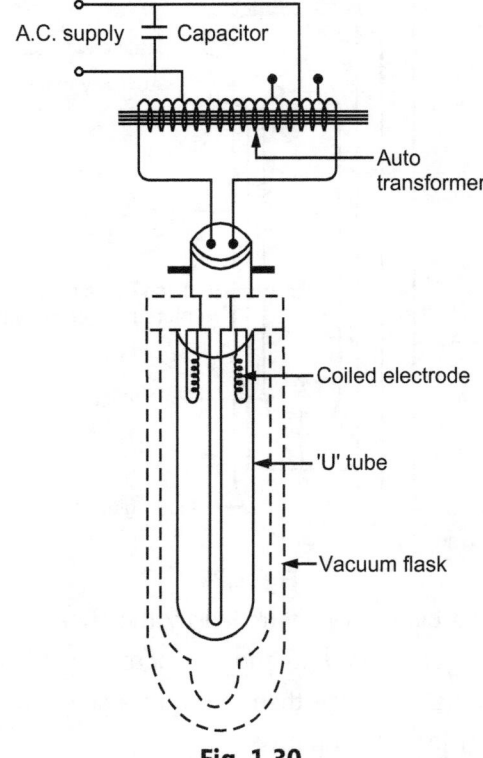

**Fig. 1.30**

## Operation:

In cold condition, sodium is in the form of solid deposit on the sides of the tube walls. When the switch is made on, it will work as a low pressure neon lamp with pink colour. But as the lamp get heated up sodium gets vapourised and slightly it will start radiating out yellow light and after about twenty minutes the lamp starts giving full output.

## 1.4.2 Electric Lighting

Electric lighting is the modern method of lighting. Electric lighting system produces an artificial light, which should resemble day light if it is to be used for carrying out work even during night. Good electric light enables man to distinguish between colours and shapes of things. Protect his eyes from becoming untimely tired, and will also help in preventing accidents.

Before going to different lighting schemes and design of illumination scheme we will first of all define and understand the meaning of the terms used in illumination scheme.

## 1.4.3 Radiant Energy

The body which is at a higher temperature than its surrounding medium radiates out energy into the medium. At low temperatures the radiation is in the form of heat waves, but when it becomes red-hot it emits light waves in addition to heat-waves. At about 3000° C, (working temperature of filament lamp) the wavelength of radiation is $0.4 \times 10^{-6}$ m to $0.7 \times 10^{-6}$ m. The wavelengths between $4000 \times 10^{-8}$ cm to $7500 \times 10^{-8}$ cm can produce the sensation of sight.

The wavelength is usually represented in the following units,

$$1 \text{ micron} = 10^{-6} \text{ meter}$$
$$1 \text{ A}° = 10^{-8} \text{ cm}$$

**Colour:** When a body is heated and if it radiates out only one wavelength, then the colour of radiation will be as below for different wavelengths.

| Wavelength $\overset{\circ}{A}$ | Colour |
|---|---|
| 4000 | Violet |
| 4750 | Blue |
| 5500 | Green |
| 6000 | Yellow |
| 7000 | Red |

### 1.4.3.1 Radiant Efficiency

A body when heated to a temperature, of incandescent, radiates out light energy as well as heat energy. Hence, radiant efficiency is defined as

$$\text{Radiant efficiency} = \frac{\text{Energy radiated in the form of light}}{\text{Total energy radiated by body}}$$

## 1.4.3.2 Light Energy

It is the radiant energy in the form of waves which produce a sensation of vision upon the human eye. It is expressed as "Lumen-Seconds" or "Lumen-hours".

## 1.4.3.3 Luminous Flux ($\phi$):

It is defined as the illumination in the form of light waves radiated per second from the luminous body. Its unit is "Lumens".

## 1.4.3.4 Lumen

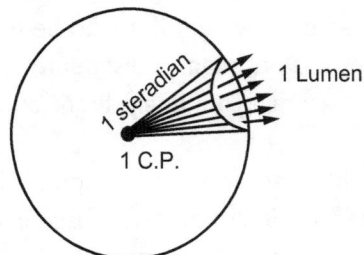

**Fig. 1.31**

It is a unit of flux, and may be defined as 'the Luminous flux per unit solid angle from a source of one candle power'.

or  Lumens = Candle power × Solid angle
or  Lumens = C.P. × ω

The total flux emitted by a source of 1 C.P. is $4\pi$ lumens.

## 1.4.3.5 Plane Angle

When two straight lines lying in the same plane meet at a point. They make an angle at the meeting point. This angle (θ) is termed as plane angle. This angle in radians is given by

$$(\theta)_{Radians} = \frac{Arc}{Radius}$$

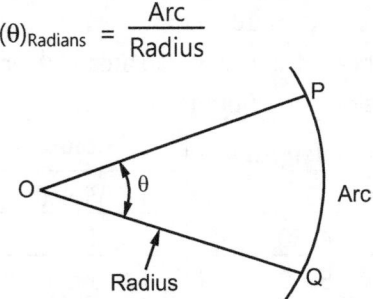

**Fig. 1.32**

## 1.4.3.6 Solid Angle

The angle substended at a point 'O' in space by an area say A is termed as solid angle. In case of solid angle, the volume is enclosed by numerous lines lying on the surface and meeting at a point. It is represented by letter ω, and is measured in streadian; where solid angle ω is equal $= \dfrac{\text{Area subtended}}{(\text{Radius})^2} = \dfrac{A}{R^2}$.

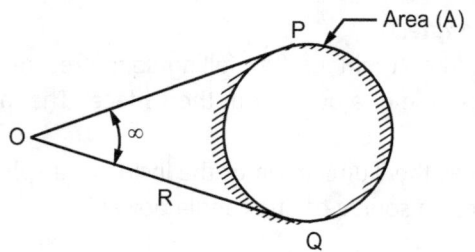

**Fig. 1.33**

In case of a sphere, $\omega = \dfrac{4\pi R^2}{R^2} = 4\pi$

∴ Solid angle of a sphere = $4\pi$ steradian

### 1.4.3.7 Candle Power

It can be defined as 'the number of lumens emitted in a unit solid angle in a given direction'.

or Candle power = $\dfrac{\text{Lumens}}{\text{Solid angle}}$

### 1.4.3.8 Luminous Intensity (I)

Luminous intensity, in a given direction can be defined as 'Luminous flux per unit solid angle in that direction'. Its unit is candela or lumens/steradian.

i.e. Luminous intensity = $\dfrac{\text{Flux in lumens}}{\text{Solid angles}}$

### 1.4.3.9 Illuminance or Illumination or Degree of Illumination

When the light falls on a surface it is said to be illuminated. The illuminance is defined as 'the luminous flux received per unit area'.

If a light flux dF falls on area dA, then the illuminance = $\dfrac{dF}{dA} = \dfrac{\text{Lumens}}{\text{Area}}$.

or illuminance from a source placed at the centre of a sphere = $\dfrac{C.P. \times \omega}{\text{Area}}$

Where W represents solid angle subtended by the area illuminated, and C.P. the candle power of source.

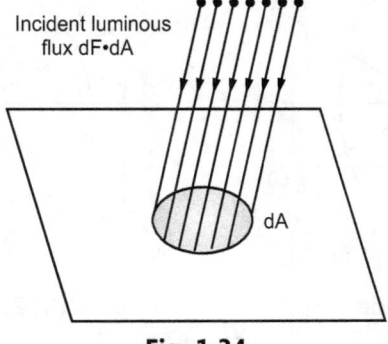

**Fig. 1.34**

### 1.4.3.10 Lux OR Metre Candle:

It can be defined as 'the Luminous flux falling/sq.metre area from the source of one candle power and placed one metre away from the surface'. The rays being perpendicular to the surface.

It can also be defined as the illumination of the inside of a sphere of radius one metre at the centre of which is placed a source of one candle power.

### 1.4.3.11 Candela

It is the unit of Luminous intensity. It is equal to $\dfrac{1}{60}^{th}$ of the luminous intensity per square cm, radiated by a black body radiator kept at the temperature of solidification of platinum i.e. 2043 K.

### 1.4.3.12 Brightness

It is defined as 'the luminous intensity per unit projected area of the surface in the given direction'.

$\therefore$ Brightness or Illuminance = $\dfrac{\text{Luminous intensity}}{\text{Area}}$    It is measured in candela/sq.metre.

### 1.4.3.13 Nit

It is unit of illuminance, and can be defined as 'illumination of one candle per square metre'.

### 1.4.3.14 Stilb

It is bigger MKS unit of illuminance, and is equal to 'illumination of one candle/sq.cm'.

### 1.4.3.15 Polar Curves

In most sources of light (lamps) the luminous intensity is not same in all directions. If we measure the candle power in horizontal plane about a vertical axis and plot a curve between candle power and the angular position, a horizontal polar curve is obtained.

If the candle power is measured at angular positions in a vertical plane a polar curve in the vertical plane is obtained. The two types of polar curves for a filament lamp are shown in Fig 1.35 below.

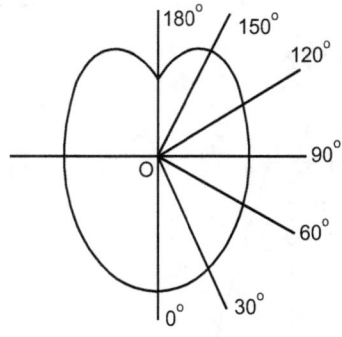    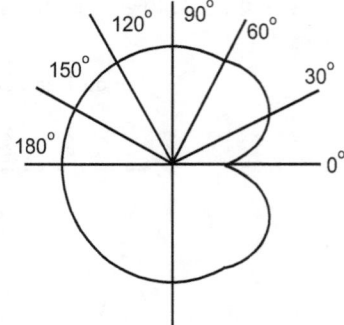

(a) For vertical plane                    (b) For horizontal plane

**Fig. 1.35**

## 1.4.3.16 Mean Horizontal Candle Power

The mean of candle powers in all directions in a horizontal plane passing through the source of light is called as "Mean Horizontal Candle Power (M.H.C.P.)" of the source.

## 1.4.3.17 Mean Spherical Candle Power

If the mean of candle powers is taken in all planes in all directions it will give the Mean-Spherical Candle Power (M.S.C.P.) of the source.

$$\text{M.S.C.P.} = \frac{\text{Luminous flux } (\phi)}{\text{Solid angle } (4\pi)} \text{ in lumens.}$$

## 1.4.3.18 Mean Hemi-Spherical Candle Power

It is the mean of the candle powers below a horizontal plane passing through the light source (M.H.C.P.).

## 1.4.3.19 Reduction Factor

It is the ratio of M.S.C.P. to M.H.C.P.

i.e. $\quad\quad$ Reduction factor $= \dfrac{\text{M.S.C.P.}}{\text{M.H.C.P.}}$

# 1.4.4 Laws of Illumination

The illumination of a surface due to point sources is governed by the following two laws of illumination:

(i) Inverse-square law.

(ii) Lambert's cosine law OR $\cos^3 \theta$ law.

## 1.4.4.1 Inverse-square Law

For understanding this law, we will consider a point source of light 'S'. Area $A_1$ and $A_2$ placed at distances h and 2h make same solid angle $\omega$ with the point source 'S'. Let I be the intensity of illumination of the source in the direction of area $A_1$ and $A_2$.

∴ Total flux ($\phi$) falling on area $A_1$ and $A_2$ = $I\omega$ Lumens. $\quad\quad\quad$ ... (1.23)

from solid angle, $\omega = \dfrac{\text{Area}}{h^2}$

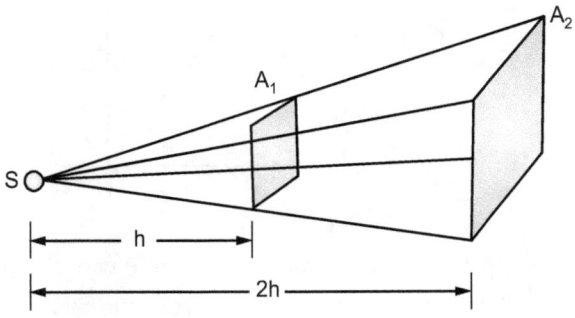

**Fig. 1.36**

for area $A_1$, $\omega = \dfrac{A_1}{h^2}$ ... (1.24)

for area $A_2$, $\omega = \dfrac{A_2}{(2h)^2}$ ... (1.25)

Total flux for area $A_1$ from equations (1.23) and (1.24),

$$\phi = I \times \dfrac{A_1}{h^2} = \dfrac{IA_1}{h^2}$$ ... (1.26)

Total flux for area $A_2$ from equations (1.23) and (1.25),

$$\phi = I \times \dfrac{A_2}{(2h)^2} = \dfrac{IA^2}{(2h^2)}$$ ... (1.27)

∴ Illumination of area $A_1 = \dfrac{IA_1}{h^2} \times \dfrac{1}{A_1} = \dfrac{1}{h^2}$ ... (1.28)

Similarly, illumination of area $A_2 = \dfrac{IA_2}{(2h)^2} \times \dfrac{1}{A_2} = \dfrac{1}{(2h)^2}$ ... (1.29)

From equations (1.28) and (1.29) it is seen that illumination due to a point source at a point is proportional to $\dfrac{1}{h^2}$ i.e. inversely proportional to square of distance from the source of the point. Hence, it is termed as a inverse-square law of illumination. It is directly proportional to intensity of illumination.

### 1.4.4.2 Lambert's Cosine Law

When the ray of light is perpendicular to the surface on which it is falling then as per inverse square law,

$$\text{Illumination} \propto \dfrac{1}{d^2}$$ ... (1.30)

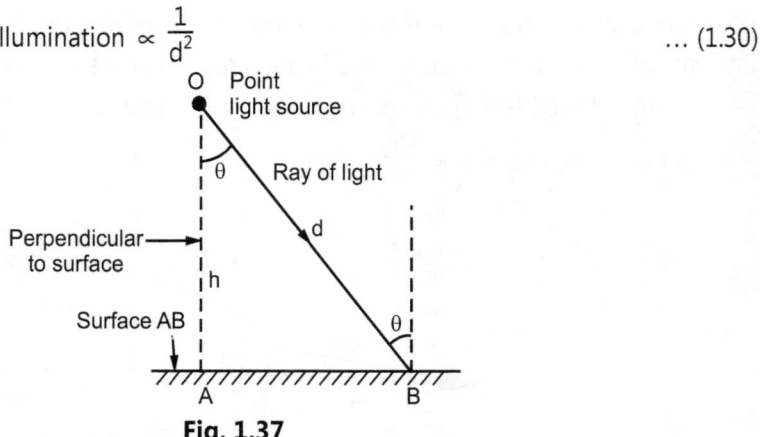

Fig. 1.37

But when the light falling on the plane makes an angle θ with the perpendicular to plane from the source, then the illumination on the plane is proportional to cosine of angle θ, or

$$\text{Illumination} \propto \cos\theta$$ ... (1.31)

Therefore, illumination at point B due to light falling from point source at O can be obtained by adding equations (1.30) and (1.31).

Illumination at point B due to light source,

$$O = \frac{1}{d^2} \cos \theta \qquad \ldots (1.32)$$

Where, d is the distance of point B from O, and the constant of proportionality taken as one.

Equation (1.32) can be modified as illumination at $B = \frac{I}{h^2} \times \frac{h^2}{d^2} \times \cos \theta$.

or illumination at $B = \frac{I}{h^2} \times \cos^3 \theta$ ... (1.33)

i.e. illumination at B = illumination at A $\times \cos^3 \theta$

Hence, this law is also termed as $\cos^3 \theta$ law.

## 1.5 FACTORS ON WHICH QUALITY OF LIGHTING SYSTEM DEPENDS

The quality of lighting system depends upon so many factors, but the following can be considered as most important.

(i) The distribution of light.
(ii) The degree of diffusion.
(iii) The amount of glare.
(iv) Colour of the light.
(v) The steadiness of the light sources.
(vi) Uniform distribution of light.

**(i) Distribution of light:** The general appearance by light of any room, work-shop etc. is greatly affected by the way in which light is distributed among the different parts of the room. For example, if all the light is concentrated on the working plane leaving the ceiling and upper parts of the walls in relatively darkness, the effect will be most depressing and uncomfortable. Hence, it is expected that every part of the room should receive enough light to make its general features easily and clearly distinguishable. Also the higher the illumination provided for the work, the higher should be the general brightness of the surroundings.

**(ii) Degree of diffusion:** The degree of diffusion desirable depends upon the purpose for which the lighting is required. For example, for work in which discrimination of the detail depends almost entirely upon shadows, for example, needle work on self-coloured materials, the stronger the shadows the better, so that too much diffusion is a disadvantage. The example of the opposite extreme is work on the drawing board for which shadows are most undesirable.

In the great majority of cases it is best to have some direct and some diffused light.

**(iii) Glare:** When rays from a highly illuminated surface or from a very bright source enter the eye of a human being it produces glare. The glare on eye causes fatigue and in some cases may cause the accident also. Hence, as far as possible it should be avoided. The glare is of two types.

- **(a) Direct glare:** When lamps are mounted at low height without reflector, the rays of light directly strike the human eyes causing glare. Hence, mounting height of lamps should be proper.
- **(b) Indirect glare or glare by reflection:** When light rays strike a shining object, such as nickel or cromium plated parts of machine or equipment, it will reflect almost all incident light which when strikes the eyes of a human being a glare on eyes is caused. This can be avoided by fixing lamps at such positions that no direct light falls on shining surfaces.

**(iv) Colour of light:** For most lighting purposes any form of "white light" is satisfactory. So the sources which gives this light i.e. filament lamp and fluorescent lamp should be used.

If it is desired to mix artificial light with daylight, for example, in parts of a room in adequately delighted, the artificial light must be of day light colour as far as concerns the visual sensation it produces.

**(v) Steadiness of the light:** Flickering of light should not be there, such that is produced by a low frequency A.C. supply used for filament lamps. Cyclic variations of frequency is not less than 100 per second as with the lamps operated on a 50 Hz supply are generally unnoticeable, but precautions should be taken to avoid stroboscopic effects where these are likely to produce trouble.

**(vi) Uniform distribution of light:** Non-uniform distribution of light causes, glare and fatigue to the eye and is responsible for reduction in productivity and causing accidents. Uniform light distribution can be achieved by using sufficiently large number of lamps spaced at equal distance with proper reflectors. Also the mounting height should be adequate. For uniform distribution of light, a ratio of spacing between two lamps to its mounting height should be between 1 to 1.5.

## 1.5.1 Lighting Schemes

The lighting schemes are as follows and are used depending upon the requirement for a particular purpose. (i) Direct lighting (ii) Indirect lighting (iii) Semi-direct lighting (iv) Semi-indirect lighting.

**(i) Direct lighting:** In this system, the light falls directly on the object to the illuminated. While designing this scheme the possibility of glare is eliminated. A correct size of lamp with suitable shades is selected. The shades used are opaque on upperside as shown in Fig. 1.38 (a) and reflect all light in downward direction, dust collected on lamps and shades in such type of system will decrease the luminous intensity and hence require regular cleaning.

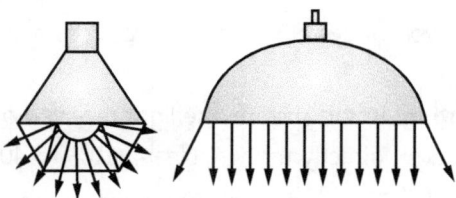

**Fig. 1.38 (a)**

Working constantly under a direct lighting causes strain on eyes. These schemes are comparatively economical and efficient. It is used in industries, residential lighting. Its uitlisation factor is between 0.25 to 0.5.

**(ii) Indirect lighting:** This type of lighting system is used where the shadows are to be eliminated; the examples being drawing offices and workshops etc. The light in this system of lighting does not fall on the objects directly. In this case, the lamps are placed in opaque type bowls which throw the light on ceiling or walls, from where it reaches the object by diffusion or reflection.

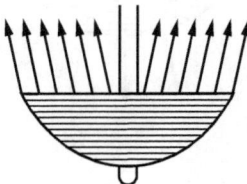

**Fig. 1.38 (b)**

If the bowls are not properly cleaned then the illumination is greatly reduced. The requirement of light in this case is more, hence costly, and produces a dull-effect. Its utilisation factor is between 0.1 to 0.3.

**(iii) Semi-direct lighting:** This system is having high efficiency and it reduces the chances of glare on eye as is developed in direct lighting system. The shades used in this type of lighting system are such that 60% of the light is directed downward and 40% is projected upwards on the walls and ceiling.

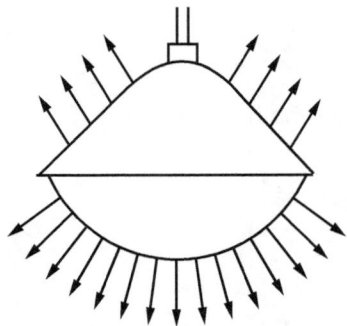

**Fig. 1.38 (c)**

The advantage of this type of system is that it produces a uniform distribution of light with higher efficiency.

**(iv) Semi-indirect lighting:** In this system, the light received on the working plane is due to (i) diffused reflection and (ii) directly thrown. Nearly 10% to 40% light from the source is directly thrown and about 60% to 90% is projected upwards which is received by the object due to defused reflection from walls and ceiling, such type of lighting scheme is useful for indoor lighting. It is free from glare and is pleasing the eye.

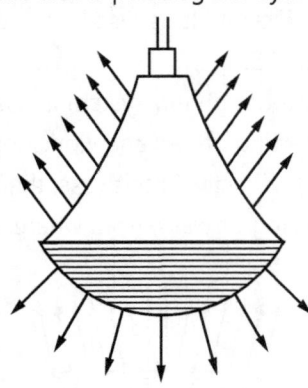

Fig. 1.38 (d)

## 1.5.2 Illumination Level

The requirement of lumens/sq.m for particular purposes depends upon the type of work to be carried out, as the visibility of objects depends upon the magnitude of light falling over them. It also depends upon other factors such as size of object, its distance from source, colour of object etc. The illumination levels for different purposes are different, the recommended levels as per standard practice and experience are given in the table below, which can be used for design of illumination schemes.

**RECOMMENDED LEVELS OF ILLUMINATION**

1. **Residential place:**      **Lux**
    - (i) Living room, General      150
       Locally for reading, writing      500 – 1000
    - (ii) Kitchens, bed rooms, stairs, bath rooms etc.
       General      150
       Locally for mirrors, ranges, readings etc.      250 – 500
2. **Schools:**
    - (i) Nursery schools      150
    - (ii) Other schools, class rooms, work-shops etc.      250 – 500
    - (iii) Class-room for drawing      500 – 1000

3. **Hospitals:**
    - (i) General — 150
    - (ii) Working place-first aid etc. — 500 – 1000
    - (iii) Operating table — 20000 – 40000
    - (iv) Operating theatre-general — 500 – 1000
4. **Offices:**
    - (i) Drawing offices, Mapping rooms — Over 2000
    - (ii) Machine engineering architecture — 1000 – 2000
    - (iii) Drawing and sketching — 500 – 1000
    - (iv) Conference rooms — 250 – 500
    - (v) Typing rooms — 500 – 1000
    - (vi) Minor clerical jobs — 250 – 500
5. **Shops:**
    - (i) Shops interior in multiple stores — 500 – 1000
    - (ii) Show windows — 1000 – 2000
    - (iii) Other places — 250 – 500
6. **Hotels and Restaurants**
    - (i) General bath rooms stairs, conference room — 150
    - (ii) Lounge restaurant-bar — 150
    - (iii) Bed-rooms General — 150
    - (iv) Writing desks dressing table — 250 – 500
7. **Factories and Work-shops:**
    - (i) Rough machining and fitters job — 250 – 500
    - (ii) Precision machining, rough grinding — 500 – 1000
    - (iii) High precision machining, grinding, polishing etc. — 1000 – 2000
    - (iv) Welding General — 250 – 500
        - Supplementary lighting on job for precision arc welding — Over 2000
    - (v) Wood Working
        - General-sawing and machining, non-precision — 250 – 500
        - Planning-course sanding, gluing etc. — 250 – 500
        - Precision machining, fine sanding and finishing — 500 – 1000
    - (vi) Textile Industry:
        - General-bale breaking, mixing, sorting — 150
        - Carding, drawing, sizing, bobbin winding, spool winding — 250 – 500
        - Weaving-inspection — 500 – 1000

8. **Power Houses:**
   (i) Blower plants, boiler and boiler accessories, turbine room, coal handling plant, water treatment plant etc.  150
   (ii) Large control room  500 – 1000
   (iii) Small simple control rooms  250 – 500
9. **Storage Places:**
   (i) Loading and unloading  20 – 40
   (ii) General stores  50 – 100
   (iii) Factory stores for storing small items (use frequently)  100 – 200
10. **Surveyance Lighting:**  5 – 10
11. **Tunnels:**
    (i) Day time lighting  100 – 200
    (ii) Threshold lighting  1000 – 2000
12. **Railway Yards:**
    (i) Heavy  10 – 20
    (ii) Light  5 – 10
13. **Sports Grounds:**
    (i) Stadium  200 – 400
    (ii) Foot ball field  100 – 200
    (iii) Hockey field  150 – 400
    (iv) Tennis court  250 – 500
14. **Canteens:**  150 – 300

## 1.5.3 Design of Lighting Scheme

In the design of lighting scheme, we are required to find out number of light fittings, with their spacing and height of mounting so that desired level of illumination can be obtained on the working plane without any glare or shadows.

At the time of designing a lighting scheme we are supposed to take into account the following factors.

**(i) Space height ratio:** It is the ratio of horizontal distance between the two adjacent lamps and their mounting height from the working plane.

OR  $\text{Space height ratio} = \dfrac{\text{Horizontal distance between lamps}}{\text{Mounting height from working plane}}$.

For obtaining uniform illumination on the working plane it is necessary to use proper value of this ratio. When reflectors are used, the value of this ratio should be between 1 and 2.

**(ii) Utilisation factor:** All the light emitted by a source does not fall on the working plane as some of it will be reduced due to the colour of surrounding walls, ceilings, type of fitting used. It also depends upon the type of lighting systems used. Hence, a factor called as utilisation factor is to be taken into account, which is stated as follows:

$$\text{Utilisation factor} = \frac{\text{Total lumens utilised working plane}}{\text{Total lumens given out by lamp}}$$

This factor also depends upon, the area to be illuminated and the height of lamps from the working plane. The value of this factor varies between 0.5 to 0.8.

**(iii) Depreciation factor OR Maintenance factor:** We know that the flux given out by lamps is reduced, when they are covered with dirt, dust and smoke. Also after some time the walls, ceilings and surroundings are covered with dirt and dust, hence the light received from them by reflection is reduced. Hence, a depreciation factor is to be taken into account at the time of designing an illumination scheme.

This factor is defined as,

$$\text{Depreciation factor} = \frac{\text{Illumination under normal working condition}}{\text{Illumination when every thing is clean}}$$

Its average value is nearly 0.8.

Sometimes the depreciation factor is also defined as,

$$\text{D.F.} = \frac{\text{Illumination when every thing is clean}}{\text{Illumination under normal working condition}}$$

In this case, the value of depreciation factor lies between 1.3 to 1.4.

**(iv) Waste light factor:** When a surface is illuminated by number of lamps, there is certain amount of wastage of light flux, due to overlapping of certain flux on certain area due to adjacent lamps. Hence, a waste light factor has to be taken into account. In order to determine the gross lumens required, the theoretical lumens required must be multiplied by waste light factor. Its value for rectangular area is nearly 1.2 and for irregular shaped area is nearly 1.5.

## 1.5.4 Total (Gross) Lumens Required

The gross lumens output of a lighting scheme can be calculated if we know the following factors:

(i) Illumination (metre-candle).
(ii) Area of surface to be illuminated in $m^2$.
(iii) Waste light factor.
(iv) Utilisation factor.
(v) Depreciation factor.

$$\text{Gross Lumens required} = \frac{\text{Illumination (metre-candle)} \times \text{Area in m}^2 \times \text{Waste light factor}}{\text{Utilisation factor} \times \text{Deprecation factor}}$$

When Depreciation factor is less than 1.

OR

$$\text{Gross lumens required} = \frac{\text{Illumination} \times \text{Area in m}^2 \times \text{Waste light factor} \times \text{Depreciation factor}}{\text{Utilisation factor}}$$

When depreciation factor is more than 1.

## 1.5.5 Requirement of Light for Various Places

### 1.5.5.1 Factory Lighting

The planning of a factory lighting installation takes into account the factors discussed above. The illumination required is determined by the nature of the work and the installation is planned to give this illumination with fittings which provide the desirable light distribution, the necessary degree of diffusion etc.

The value of illumination prescribed for the whole of the working area is in general 60-70 lumens/m$^2$ measured at a level of 1 metre above the floor. We may require to make provision of additional illumination required to render the lighting sufficient and suitable for the nature of work. The general illumination of passages etc. should not be less than 5-6 lumens/m$^2$, at floor level. When any additional or local lighting in the factory is used, it is to be observed that it should not produce a glare.

### 1.5.5.2 Office Lighting

Office buildings are different in lay-out, in size and also the nature of work carried out in them. In case of small offices illumination can be 150 lux or an illumination of 100 lux supplemented by local lighting. In case of book keeping office, typing, filing and similar work the illumination should be 200 lux. Bad seeing conditions, such as use of blue or green papers against which pencil marks or type script or shiny papers and indelible pencil should be avoided.

The glare can be avoided by the choice of suitable light-toned decoration for the walls and by the use of light toned furniture, so that excessive contrasts in the field of view can be avoided. But the uniformity of tone can be very dull hence moderate contrast give pleasant working condition.

General or Semi-direct lighting can be suitably used; the fittings should be mounted as high as possible.

### 1.5.5.3 Shop Lighting

Shops are having larger variations in their purpose and manner of arrangements. The lighting should be as unobtrusive as possible, generally a concealed lighting should be preferred. However diffused lighting becomes dull and lifeless for the shops of glass-ware and polished metals, hence for such shops direct lighting is essential.

High value of illumination should be provided on counters. A reflector spot light is best suited for the purpose. The illumination may be between 300 to 500 lux. While the general illumination of the shop may be 150 to 200 lux.

In lighting a shop-windows, which is used to advertise the shop, and to attract the attention of the passerby, as forcibly as possible, to indicate that the shop is of such and such a kind and that it is necessary to have a closer inspection. Generally, the lighting should provide a high illumination over the whole of the window space, but the lamps should be completely concealed. The common practice is to use about 300 watts/metre run of window.

### 1.5.5.4 Street Lighting

The main object of street lighting is to enable traffic, both vehicular and pedestrian to move about easily and with safety.

The level of illumination is low for economic reasons and the colour of objects is not important. The height of lamps should be such that they should not produce any glare on eyes as far as possible.

The design of street light installations is based upon two principles:

**(i) The diffusion principle:** In this system, the lamps are fitted with suitable reflectors, which spread the light uniformly over the surface of rod, so that it appears bright to the observer. In this, suitable reflectors are used for avoiding the glare.

**(ii) Specular reflection principle:** In this type of system, light from the sources fall on the object at a very large angle of incidence and is therefore reflected at a correspondingly large angle.

It is seen from Fig. 1.39 that the object will appear silhouetted against the bright road surface on account of light from lamps $L_2$ and $L_3$ rather than $L_1$. In this case, the reflectors are so selected that they throw light on road surface at very large angle of incidence. This system produce glare and is suitable only for straight run of roads.

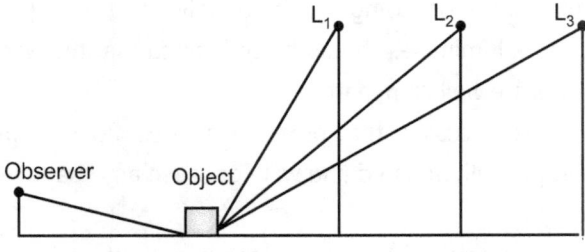

**Fig. 1.39**

Satisfactory results are obtained in case of traffic routes of medium width, when lamps are fitted at 8 m height and spacing between poles being 40 to 50 metres, the luminous output of source being between 3000 lm to 8000 lm.

### 1.5.5.5 Petrochemical Industry Lighting

In petrochemical industry, which consists of oil and petro-chemical products manufacturing plants different types of lighting arrangements are used to provide the necessary illumination for different purposes.

The oil and petroleum manufacturing plant consists of so many locations which may be called as hazardous or very sensitive. NEC (National Electrical Code) has classified and grouped the common dangerous materials found in the manufacturing process of such industries. Hence, specially designed and non-explosion proof flood lights should be provided at hazardous locations. Also the factors such as corrosive vapours, moisture, temperature etc. are to be taken into account in the design of lighting scheme for such industries. Here we may require to use general lighting and local lighting for panels and other activities etc.

### 1.5.5.6 Chemical Industry Lighting

In a chemical industry mostly the following operations are to be carried out. The requirements of illumination for these operations are also specified below, hence depending upon the requirement of each type of work, we are required to provide the necessary level of illumination on the planes.

The processes are as follows:

| Sr. No. | Process | Level of illumination required |
|---|---|---|
| 1. | Boiling tanks, stationary driers, crystallizers, hand furnaces etc. | 300 lux |
| 2. | Mechanical furnaces, mechanical driers, evaporators, filtration, mechanical crystallizers bleaching. | 300 lux |
| 3. | Tanks for cooking, extractors, percolator, nitrates etc. | 300 lux |

In the dry cleaning process using naphtha solvent, the explosion proof lighting equipment is a must. These luminaries should be so located that the washer's, extractor's and drying-fumbler's interiors are well illuminated.

The light should be so focussed that pressure gauges, flow gauges and temperature, indicators should be properly illuminated and will not cause any shadows on it.

### 1.5.5.7 Flood Lighting

Flood lighting may be employed to enhance the beauty of ancient monuments by night or for commercial advertisement, industrial purposes such as the illumination of railway yards. It may be carried out by means of projectors. The different equipments giving suitable beam spread suitable for various conditions are available. The beam-spread is defined as 'the total angle between the directions at which the luminous intensity is one-tenth of maximum'. This may be from 12° to 25° in case of narrow beam projector, which is used for long throws.

$$\text{The Beam factor} = \frac{\text{Flux obtained within the limits of beam-spread}}{\text{Flux emitted from lamp}}$$

Its value may lie between 0.3 to 0.4. When wider spread of 40° to 60° are used the beam factor is between 0.4 to 0.5.

The illumination required depends upon (i) Reflection-factor of building (ii) completion from lighting in the neighbourhood. The illuminance required may be from 20 lux to 200 lux in most favourable conditions. While calculating total flux, a waste-light factor has to be taken into account.

Projectors are fitted in such a way that lighting falls from an angle on objects, because surface illuminated from front and viewed from front has un-natural appearance. Shadow texture is very necessary, but the shadows must not be too dense and some times addition to main lighting will be good.

The lighting of large areas, such as sports grounds arenas, swimming pools etc. is in many respects similar to flood-lighting, but with added complication that the players must not suffer from glare. The projectors are mounted in banks high up at the sides of the arena and behind the spectators. Each unit is carefully focused and trained onto its own portion of the arena, and shields are used to prevent the spill of light.

## 1.5.6 The Fluorescent Lamp (Tube)

The fluorescent tube is actually a discharge lamp, in which radiation from the gas or vapour excite the fluorescent materials so that light emitted by the lamp is that given by the material.

In the fluorescent material, most of the useful radiation emitted is the ultra-violet by mercury vapour at low pressure, although the tube also contains argon at about 2-5 mm pressure to assist starting. Even with argon the discharge does not take place at supply voltage, hence a starter switch is used to give a momentary high voltage across the tube and so start the discharge.

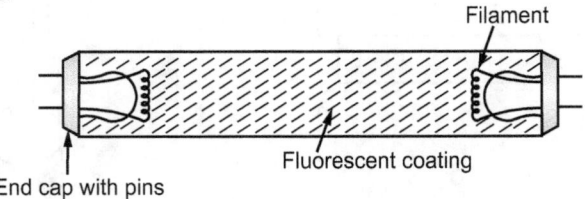

**Fig. 1.40: Fluorescent tube**

In Fig. 1.40, a 40 W, 4 feet tube is shown. Each electrode consists of two parts electrically connected. One is a tungsten coiled coil filament coated with a mixture of alkaline earth oxides, the other (not shown) a metal strip or pin. The latter serves as anode during one half cycle of the current, since the coating on the filament can function only as a cathode. The two ends of the filament at each end of the tube are brought out to a special type of cap. The electrical circuit is shown in Fig. 1.40. The desired voltage for gas discharge is developed by the choke when the starter suddenly breaks the established circuit, which may be of the order of 1000 V or so. The voltage across the lamp when running, is about half the supply voltage. The condenser corrects the power factor.

### 1.5.6.1 Starter Switch

There are two types of starter in use i.e. the glow discharge type and the thermal type. The former consists of two metal strips, one or both bimetallic mounted in a bulb, and carrying two contacts which are normally held apart as shown in Fig. 1.41 (a). When the supply is made on, a glow discharge is started between the bimetal strips, which will get heated up and bend so as to bring the contracts together. This short-circuits the glow discharge and allows the heating current to flow through the electrodes of the lamp. At the same time the bimetal strips begins to cool and cause contacts to open. At this moment a high voltage kick developed by choke, causes to take place a gas discharge between electrodes. The voltage across the after this discharge is only about 50% of supply voltage, which is not sufficient to re-start the glow in the switch, hence it remains out of order until the next time the lamp is started.

The circuit of the thermal starter is shown in Fig. 1.41 (b), in this case, the contacts are normally closed. One is carried on a bimetal strip, which can be heated by means of a heater coil in series with the lamp, when the supply is made on, the electrode heating current also passes through this coil, the bimetal strip is heated and bends so as to separate the contacts. This causes the discharges to pass, and normal lamp current flowing through the heater coil is sufficient to keep the contacts apart. A small capacitor (0.02 µF) is fitted across the starter contacts to suppress radio interference. Fig. 1.41 (c) represent a starterless circuit for fluorescent tube.

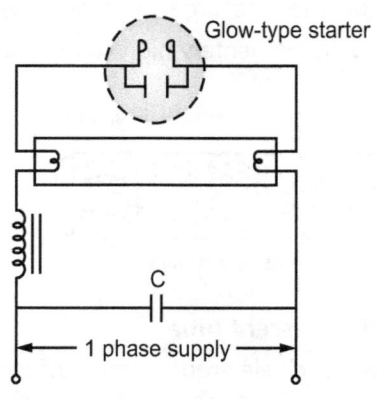

(i) Circuit with glow type starter

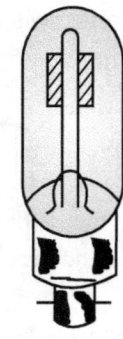

(ii) Glow starter switch

(a)

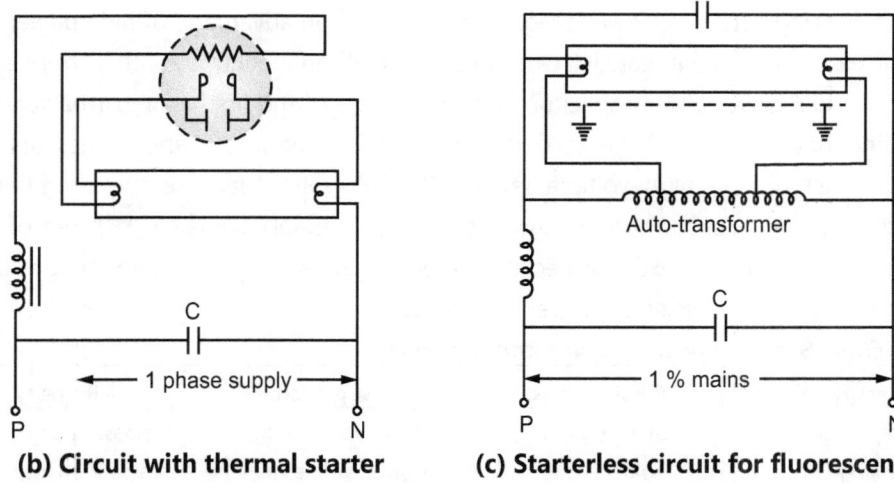

**(b) Circuit with thermal starter**  **(c) Starterless circuit for fluorescent lamp**

Fig. 1.41

A high reactance Auto-transformer is connected across the lamp when the supply is made on, almost full mains voltage is applied across the lamp and transformer. The electrodes are rapidly heated and then applied voltage is sufficient to start the discharge, especially there is an earthen metallic strip running from one end of lamp to other as shown. As soon as discharge has been started, the lamp voltage falls to its normal operating value. The reduced voltage on the transformer causes a reduction in the current through the electrodes, which are then maintained at their proper operating temperature, by the discharge. A circuit of this kind is often called an 'instant start' circuit.

### 1.5.6.2 Twin Lamp Circuits

Some times a slight stroboscopic effect is noticed with fluorescent lamps due to the light being extinguished every half cycle. In some circumstances, it may prove troublesome. In large installations, the effect may be neutralized by connecting successive lamps to different phases; by using fluorescent and incandescent lamps in conjunction, by balancing capacitive and inductive lamp circuits or by using twin lamp circuit. This method can be employed for any size of installation.

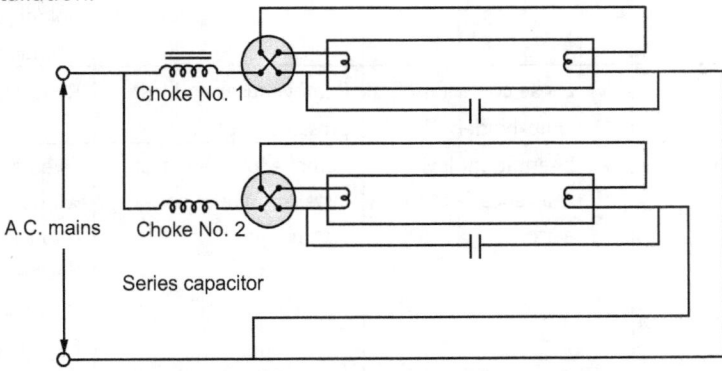

**Fig. 1.42: Twin circuit of fluorescent tubes**

The twin lamp circuit is shown in Fig. 1.42. It has also an advantage of high power factor. Two lamps are connected in parallel. One circuit is stabilized inductively with a choke and the other contains a choke and a capacitor. The lagging p.f. of the first is almost balanced with the leading power factor of the second, and so the resulting p.f. approaches unity. The capacitor must have a high voltage rating (400/500 volts), because the conditions are approaching resonance. The currents in the two lamps are approximately 120° out of phase, so that when one lamp is extinguished the other is approaching its maximum light output. Consequently stroboscopic effect is greatly reduced.

### 1.5.6.3 Fluorescent Lamps: Troubles and Remedies

| Symptom | Possible causes | Test procedure | Remedy |
|---|---|---|---|
| (1) Lamp A light but 'blinking' Intermittently | (i) Sparking at fuse holders | Whole groups of fittings involved visible sparking at fuse holder contacts or alternately sounds of sparking. | Increase spring pressure on fuse-holder blades, if contacts badly pitted replace parts. Usually due to over loading split up circuits. |
| | (ii) Sparking at switch | Localised group of fittings. Sparking at switch contacts or terminals. | Increase spring pressure. If badly pitted replace parts. Due to over-loaded switches split up circuits. |
| | (iii) Intermittent open circuit. | Remove fuses and test wiring with 'megger'. If in order remove lamps and test fittings. | Faulty wiring rewire; faulty fittings, check terminals and wires if in order check choke, starter switch, and lamp holder, usually due to vibration. |
| | (iv) Loose contact in lamp-holder | Remove fuses and test pressure of plungers | Renew lamp holders. |
| | (v) Intermittent low resistance fault to earth | Remove fuses and test installation resistance with megger. | Overhaul earth on wiring, if wiring is good, look for loose flexible strand, if wiring is sound check starter switch, choke and p.f. capacitor. |

| | | | |
|---|---|---|---|
| | (vi) Missing pin of cap or loose pin | Visual inspection | Renew lamp. |
| | (viii) Varying supply voltage | Check for intermittent fault on heavy current equipment low mains voltage | Overhaul defective equipment report to local electricity board. |
| (2) Lamp attempts to start | (i) Low mains voltage. Low fitting voltage | Check with voltmeter Check with voltmeter | Mains volts should be within ± 6% of declared volts. Circuits over-loaded, reduce load or increase cable capacity. |
| | (ii) Wrong choke impedance | Check against makers data. For tapped choke check size and tappings against makers data. | Wrong markings, change choke wrong tappings, adjust. |
| | (iii) Wrong capacitor (Twin tube circuit) | Check against makers data. | Change capacitor. |
| | (iv) Faulty starter switch | Test in a sound fitting. | Replace. |
| | (v) Wrong starter switch | Check rating and voltage | Replace. |
| | (vi) Faulty lamp (damaged or at the end of life) | Test in a sound fitting | Renew lamp. |
| (3) Both filaments glow, lamp does not light | (i) Starter switch contacts welded | Test in a sound fitting | Replace starter switch. |
| | (ii) Short circuit or earth inside fitting | Test for 1 (iii) and (v); no obvious fault, test choke starter switch and p.f. capacitor for earth or short circuit. | Renew defective component. |
| | (iii) Faulty radio suppress or capacitor | Disconnect capacitor and check if fault clears. | Replace starter |
| | (iv) Faulty lamp or lamp at end of life. | Test in sound fitting. | Renew lamp. |

| | | | |
|---|---|---|---|
| (4) One filament of lamp only glows (lamp fails to light) | (i) Short inside cap; lamp holder or of lamp holder leads. | Test leads: Test for internal short. Test lamp in sound circuit. | Rewire lamp-holder, clear short replace lamp. |
| | (ii) Lamp-holder wiring, earth to frame. | Check wiring with megger after disconnecting fuses | Rewire. |
| | (iii) Earth in starter component | Check in a sound fitting with control gear connected in line and not neutral, insert suspected starter and test. | Replace starter. |
| (5) Lamp fails to start. | (i) No volts at fittings. | Supply failure, blown fuses open circuit in wiring test with "megger" tester or bell and battery after removing fuse. | Check other lights. Check fuses rewire. |
| | (ii) Open circuit inside fitting. | Check terminal connections. | Tighten terminal screws and ensure all wires making good contact. |
| | (iii) Bad contact at starter switch | Check starter switch contacts for dirt check socket contacts for dirt and springingness | Clean or increase pressure. |
| | (iv) Open circuit in heater coil of thermal starter or insufficient volts for glow starter | Test in sound fitting, if same result switch is defective | Renew starter switch. |
| | (v) Open circuit in one filament or glass envelope cracked. | Test in a sound fitting, fault persists. | Renew lamp. |
| | (vi) Choke open circuited | Remove choke, Test continuity. | Renew choke. |

|   | (vii) Earth to frame between choke and lamp. | Remove fuses and test with "megger". | Rewire fitting. |
|---|---|---|---|
|   | (viii) Cap with pins incorrectly assembled and contacts rotated 90°. | Check position of slots and pins. | Reassemble lamp holder. |

## ILLUSTRATIVE EXAMPLES

**Example 1.28:** A lamp giving 300 candle power in all directions is suspended 2 metres above the centre of a square table of one metre each side. Calculate maximum and minimum illumination on the surface of table.

**Solution:**

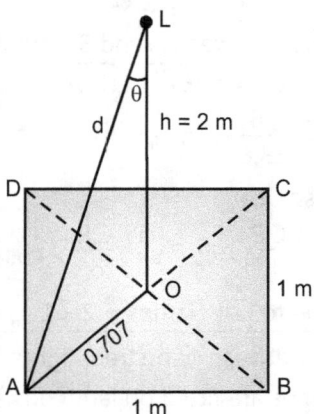

**Fig. 1.43**

Diagonal length AB of table = $\sqrt{1^2 + 1^2}$ = 1.41 m.

∴ Length AO = 0.707 m, Height of lamp, OL = 2 m.
Length of all corners from L = $\sqrt{(0.707)^2 + (2)^2}$
AL or d = 2.12 m.

∴ $\cos\theta = \dfrac{22}{2.12} = 0.94$

Illumination just below the lamp i.e. at

$$O = \dfrac{C.P.}{h^2} = \dfrac{300}{(22)^2} = 75 \text{ lux}$$

Illumination at all corners = $\dfrac{C.P.}{d^2} \times \cos\theta$

Or
$$= \frac{C.P.}{h^2} \times \cos^3 \theta$$
$$= 75 \times (0.94)^3 = 75 \times 0.83 = 62.29 \text{ lux}$$

Hence, maximum illumination is at the centre of table and is equal to 75 lux while minimum illumination is at the corners of table and is equal to 62.29 lux.

**Example 1.29:** Two light sources each having an intensity of 600 cd are mounted 6 m high and 25 m apart. Determine the illumination at a distance mid-way between lamps; will you suggest this system for room lighting?

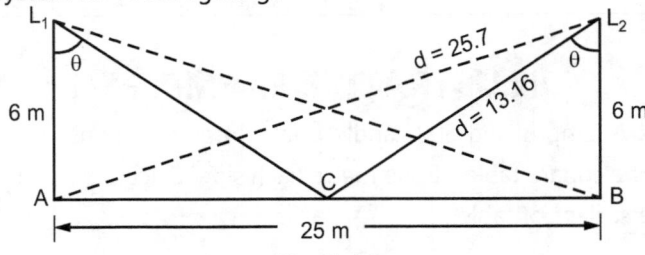

Fig. 1.44

**Solution:** Distance of mid-point between A and B from the lamps $L_1$ and $L_2 = \sqrt{(6)^2 + (12.5)^2}$ or d = 13.86 m.

$$\cos \theta = \frac{6}{13.86} = 0.441$$

Illumination at C due to one source

$$= \frac{C.P.}{h^2} \times \cos^3 \theta \text{ or } \frac{C.P.}{d^2} \times \cos \theta = \frac{600}{(6)^2} \times (0.441)^3 = 1.43 \text{ lux}$$

∴ Illumination at point C due to both lamps = 2 × 1.43 = 2.86 lux.

**Example 1.30:** The distance between two street lights is 20 metres along the road, the width of road is 5 metres. The lamps are fitted on lamp posts of 7 metres height. 200 W lamp is fitted on each pole giving individual 2800 lumens output. Taking coefficient of utilisation as 0.5, calculate level of illumination at the centre of lamps and also just beneath the lamp.

**Solution:** The luminous output of each lamp = 2800 lumens, as coefficient of utilisation is 0.5 lumens actually utilised will be = 2800 × 0.5 = 1400 lumens.

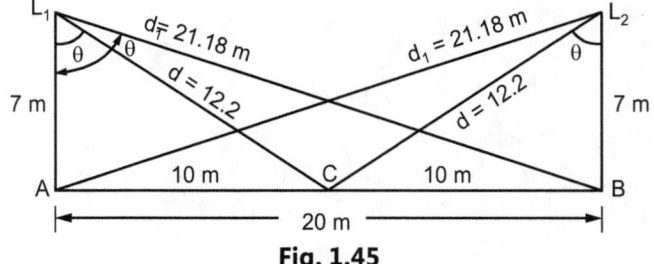

Fig. 1.45

BASIC ELECTRICAL DRIVES & CONTROLS                    MEASUREMENT OF ELECTRIC POWER & .....

The candela power available from each lamp = $\dfrac{1400}{4\pi}$ = 111.46 C.P.

or
$$d = \sqrt{7^2 + 10^2}$$
$$d = 12.2 \text{ m}$$
$$d_1 = \sqrt{(7)^2 + (20)^2}$$
or
$$d_1 = 21.18 \text{ m}$$
$$\cos\theta = \dfrac{7}{12.2} = 0.573$$
$$\cos\theta_1 = \dfrac{7}{21.18} = 0.33$$

Illumination at mid-point between poles = Illumination at point C due to one lamp × 2

$$= \dfrac{C.P.}{h^2} \times \cos^3\theta \times 2 = \dfrac{111.46}{(7)^2} \times (0.573)^3 \times 2 = 0.855 \text{ lux}$$

Illumination just beneath the lamps = $\begin{bmatrix}\text{Illumination due to}\\ \text{the lamp itself}\end{bmatrix} + \begin{bmatrix}\text{Illumination due}\\ \text{to other lamp}\end{bmatrix}$.

Hence, illumination either at point A or B

$$= \dfrac{C.P.}{h^2} + \dfrac{C.P.}{h^2} \times \cos^3\theta_1$$

$$= \dfrac{111.46}{(7)^2} + \dfrac{111.46}{(7)^2} \times (0.33)^3$$

$$= 2.27 + 0.08 = 2.35 \text{ lux}$$

**Example 1.31:** A small assembling shop 15 m × 9 m having height of trusses 4 metres is to be illuminated to a level of 200 lux. The coefficient of utilisation is 0.75 and depreciation factor is 0.8. Assume working plane at a height of 1 metre from floor. The whole area is to be illuminated by lamps having individual output as 3000 lumens. Calculate number of lamps required. Show the disposition of lamps on plan. Determine space-height ratio along with length of the shop.

**Solution:** Gross lumens required = $\dfrac{\text{Intensity of illumination} \times \text{Area}}{\text{Utilisation factor} \times \text{Depreciation factor}}$

$$= \dfrac{200 \times (15 \times 9)}{0.75 \times 0.8}$$

$$= 45000 \text{ lumens.}$$

As output of one lamp = 3000 lumens, Total number of lamp required = $\dfrac{45000}{3000}$ = 15 nos.

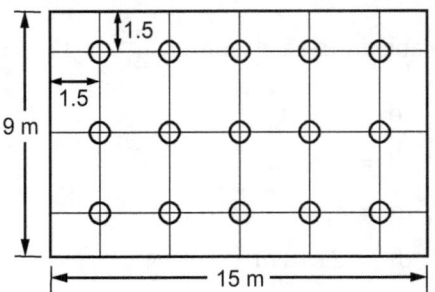

**Fig. 1.46**

Now, we will arrange these lamps suitably. As the working plane is 1 metre above floor and assuming that lamps will be fixed on trusses height of lamps above working plane = 3 m. Assuming space height ratio widthwise as one. Three lamps will be arranged widthwise with a spacing of 1.5 m on each side as shown in Fig. 1.46. Similarly same space height ratio will be used lengthwise so that 5 lamps with a clearance of 1.5 m at each end as shown in Fig. 1.46 will be arranged lengthwise.

∴ Total lamps arranged = 15 nos.

**Example 1.32:** A fitting shop 16 m × 10 m is illuminated by 200 W incandescent lamps. Take coefficient of utilisation as 0.68 and depreciation factor as 0.75. An illumination of 260 lux is required to be maintained. Calculate number of luminaries required. Show the arrangement of luminaries required. Calculate space-height ratio along width and length of the shop. Assume height of mounting as 3 m from floor and working plane height from floor as one metre, lumens output per 200 W lamp is 2950 lumens.

**Solution:**

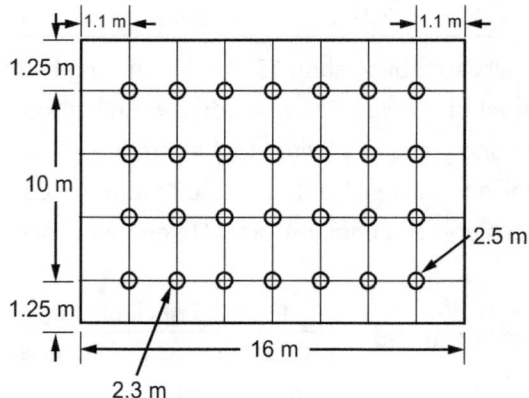

**Fig. 1.47**

$$\text{Gross lumens required} = \frac{\text{Intensity of illumination} \times \text{Area}}{\text{Utilisation factor} \times \text{Depreciation factor}}$$

$$= \frac{260 \times (16 \times 10)}{0.68 \times 0.75} = 81568.627 \text{ lumens}$$

∴ Number of lamps = $\dfrac{81568.627}{2950}$ = 27.65 Nos. say 28 Nos.

As the mounting height is 3 m, from floor and working plane 1 m above floor, the height of lamps from working plane = 2 m, we will assume a space height ratio of 1.25 widthwise so that, spacing between lamps widthwise = 2.5 m, so that 4 lamps will be arranged widthwise with a spacing of 1.25 metres at each end as shown in Fig. 1.47.

For lengthwise arrangement we will use a space/height ratio = 1.15, therefore spacing between two adjacent lamps length-wise will be 2.30 m, we will arrange 7 lamps lengthwise with a side clearance of 1.1 m at each end, so that total lamps = 7 × 4 = 28 Nos.

**Example 1.33:** A factory hall 80 m × 25 m is to be illuminated by assuming the following data: (i) Total illumination = 15 lux, (ii) Depreciation factor = 0.7, (iii) Utilisation factor = 0.4. Space height ratio = 1.33.

Assuming efficiency of each lamp 15 lumen watt. Find out the number of lamps and C.P. of each. Propose the arrangement of lamps. Find out the load current if the total load of lamps is connected to 3 phase, 4 wire, 400 V, supply.

**Solution:**

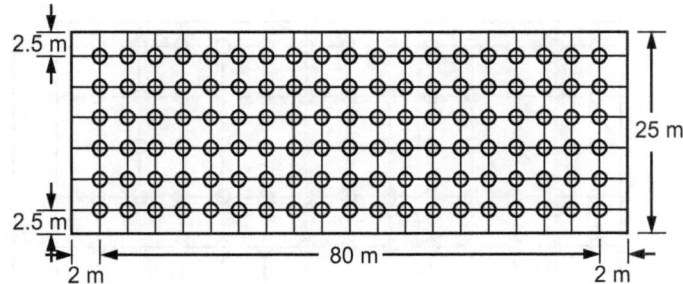

**Fig. 1.48**

Gross lumens required = $\dfrac{15 \times (80 \times 25)}{0.4 \times 0.7}$

Or Gross lumens = 107142.86 lumens

Total wattage of lamps = $\dfrac{107142.86}{15}$ = 7142.85 W

Assuming height of factory = 4 m and working plane 1 m, above floor, the lamps being fixed to ceiling so that height of lamps from working plane = 3 m.

As space/height = 1.33

Space between lamps = 1.33 × 3 = 4 m.

∴ Number of lamps lengthwise = 20

Number of lamps widthwise = 6

The arrangement is shown in Fig. 1.48 with side clearances.

Wattage of each lamp = $\dfrac{7142.85}{20 \times 6}$ = 59.52 say 60 watts.

∴ Total load = 60 × 120 = 7200 watts

$$I_L = \dfrac{W}{\sqrt{3}\, V_L \times \cos\phi} = \dfrac{7200}{1.732 \times 400 \times 1} = 10.39 \text{ Amps.}$$

**Example 1.34:** A hall 30 m × 40 m × height 4 m requires on an average illumination of 110 lux on the working plane which is 1 m above the floor. Two types of filament lamps are available.
  (i) 200 W lamps, with luminous efficiency = 18 lumens/Watt.
  (ii) 500 W lamps with luminous efficiency = 22 lumens/Watt.
Coefficient of utilisation is 0.4 and depreciation factor is 0.8.
Which lamps you will select? why? Justify your answer.
For your choice of lamps, find the number of lamps and total electrical load, show on a plan the disposition of these lamps.

**Solution:**

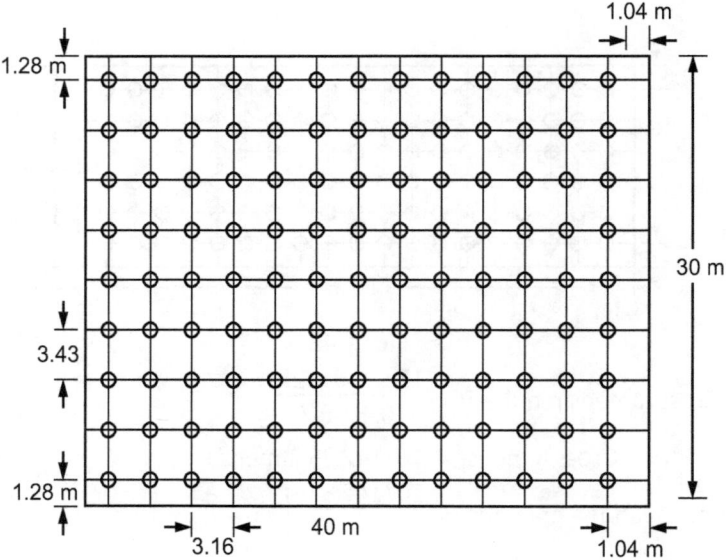

**Fig. 1.49**

Gross lumens required = $\dfrac{110 \times (30 \times 40)}{0.4 \times 0.8}$ = 412500 lumens

Output of 200 W lamp = 18 × 200 = 3600 lumens

and   Out put of, 500 W lamp = 22 × 500 = 11000 lumens

∴ No. of 200 W lamps required = $\dfrac{412500}{3600}$ = 114.58 say 115 Nos.

No. of 500 W lamps required = $\dfrac{412500}{11000}$ = 37.5 say 38 Nos.

Working plane is 1 m above floor. Let the lamps be suspended at 0.25 m from ceiling. Therefore, height of lamps from working plane = 4 − 1.25 = 2.75 metres for proper and uniform illumination the space/height ratio should be between 1 to 1.5.

We will assume space/height ratio = 1.25.

∴ Spacing between lamps widthwise = 3.43 m.

Hence, we will arrange 9 No. of lamps widthwise with a spacing between lamps = 3.43 m and clearance at sides = 1.28 metres as shown in Fig. 1.49.

For arranging lamps lengthwise we will assume a space/height ratio of 1.15.

∴ Spacing between the lamps = 2.75 × 1.15 = 3.16 m.

Hence, we will arrange 13 lamps lengthwise with a spacing of 3.16 m, with a side clearance of 1.04 m as shown in Fig. 1.49.

Total number of lamps required = 13 × 9 = 117 Nos.

We have calculated that we need 115 lamps of 200 watts to provide the necessary level of illumination, which is just near to 117 Nos. As this arrangement will provide uniform and glare free illumination we will select 117 lamps of 200 W with arrangement shown in Fig. 1.49.

The total electrical load = 117 × 200 = 23400 watts
= 23.4 kW

**Example 1.35:** An automobile showroom measuring 36 m × 13.5 m × 5.5 m high is divided into square sections of side 4.5 m by beams and columns. If the minimum desired illumination is 90 lux, estimate the number, location, and wattage of lighting units required. Also suggest suitable type of unit from the following:

| Units available | Wattage | Lumens/Unit |
|---|---|---|
| Filament lamps | 200 | 2880 |
|  | 300 | 4650 |
| Fluorescent tube | 40 | 2000 |
|  | 80 | 2880 |

**Solution:**

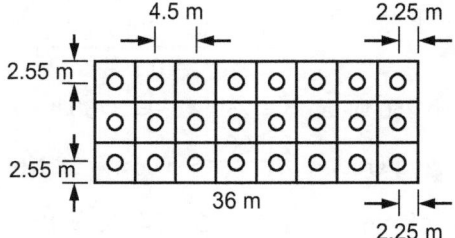

**Fig. 1.50**

For calculating gross-lumens required, we will assume, utilisation factor = 0.5 and depreciation factor = 0.8.

$$\therefore \text{Gross lumens required} = \frac{\text{Intensity} \times \text{Area}}{\text{U.F.} \times \text{D.F.}}$$

$$= \frac{90 \times (36 \times 13.5)}{0.5 \times 0.8} = 109350 \text{ lumens}$$

$$\text{No. of 80 watt tubes or 200 W lamps} = \frac{109350}{2880} = 37.96 \text{ say 38 Nos.}$$

$$\text{No. of 300 W bulbs required} = \frac{109350}{2000} = 54.67 \text{ say 55 Nos.}$$

The plane of showroom is shown with the squares of 4.5 × 4.5 m formed by beams and columns.

Assuming the working plane as 1 m above floor and light fittings fixed to the ceiling, the height of lamps from working plane = 4.5 metre (5.5 – 1)

Taking a space/height ratio = 1

The spacing between lamps = 4.5 m.

Hence, with a spacing of 4.5 m between the lamps and fixing each lamp at the centre of the squares so formed we will need 24 lamps.

As the 300 watt-lamps, 24 in number give the desired illumination, we will select 300 watt lamps, and they will be arranged as shown in Fig. 1.50.

**Example 1.36:** Design a flood lighting installation with incandescent lamps for the frontage of the building having dimensions 50 m × 20 m. The approximate level of illumination is 120 lumen/m². Assume depreciation factor as 1.5, utilisation factor 0.5. Find the number of lamps if 250 W lamps is to be used for flooding. Find also, current per phase when 400 V, 3 phase supply is used. Efficiency of lamp is 15 lumens/watt.

**Solution:**

As the flood lighting is to be provided for the frontage of a building, we will assume a waste light factor = 1.2, it is 1.5 for irregular surfaces.

$$\therefore \text{Gross lumens required} = \frac{\text{Inensity of illumination} \times \text{Area} \times \text{Waste light factor} \times \text{D.F.}}{\text{Utilisation factor}}$$

$$= \frac{120 \times (50 \times 20) \times 1.2 \times 1.5}{0.5} = 216000 \text{ lumens}$$

Luminous output of each 250 W lamp = 250 × 15 = 3750 lumens

$$\therefore \text{Number of lamps required} = \frac{216000}{3750} = 57.6 \text{ say 58 Nos.}$$

Total load of lamps = 250 × 58 = 14500 watts

Assuming p.f. = 1 for lamp load

From

$$W = \sqrt{3} V_L I_L \cos\phi$$
$$I_L = \frac{W}{\sqrt{3} V_L} = \frac{14500}{\sqrt{3} \times 400} \text{ OR } I_L = 20.92 \text{ amps.}$$

## THEORY QUESTIONS

1. Define the following terms.
   (a) Luminous flux
   (b) Lumen
   (c) Luminous-intensity
   (d) Lux or metre - candle.
2. State and explain laws of illumination.
3. State and explain the factors on which quality of lighting system depends.
4. State and explain the different systems of lighting, with their advantages and disadvantages in brief.
5. What do you mean by lighting scheme?
6. What are the factors to be taken into account at the time of designing a lighting scheme.
7. Define and explain the following factors:
   (a) Space height ratio.
   (b) Utilisation factor.
   (c) Depreciation factor.
   (d) Waste light factor.
8. Tube light fails to light. Give probable reasons and give remedies.
9. What do you mean by flood lighting ? Where it is provided ? Why ?
10. Define beam factor.
11. Draw circuit of tubes to eliminate stroboscopic effect.

## UNSOLVED EXMPLES

1. An office 30 m × 15 m is illuminated by twin 40 W fluorescent luminaries of lumen out put 5600 lumens. The lamps being mounted at a height of 3 in from working plane, the average illumination required is 240 lux. Calculate the number of lamps required to be fitted in the office, assuming coefficient of utilisation to be 0.6 and depreciation factor to be 0.8. Also estimate the quantity of material required for the above installation and disposition of lamps on plan. Assume any additional data required.

2. A hall measuring 12 m × 30 m is to be illuminated by 80 watts each of 1.5 metre long and the efficiency 40 lumens/watt. An illumination of 40 lux is required on the working plane. Assuming maintenance factor 0.75 and utilisation factor 0.66, estimate number of lamps required, sketch the layout plan of hall indicating thereon the position of tube lights.

3. A hall 20 m × 30 m × 5 m is to be illuminated by direct lighting. An average illumination of 120 lux is to be provided on a horizontal plane parallel to the floor and one metre above it. Design a suitable scheme of illumination using filament lamps. Coefficient of utilisation is 0.4 and depreciation factor is 0.8. Efficiency of 100 W lamp = 16 lumens / watt.

4. A room 20 m × 10 m is to be illuminated by 8 lamps and average illumination is to be 50 lumens/m². If the utilisation factor is 0.48 and depreciation factor 1.2. Calculate mean spherical candle power of each lamp.

# Chapter 2

# D.C. MACHINES AND SPECIAL PURPOSE MACHINES

## 2.1 D.C. GENERATOR

### 2.1.1 General

D.C. machines are those machines which are either used for generating D.C. voltages, or used on D.C. supply to run as motor. Same machine can work as generator or a motor depending up on the nature of use, when a D.C. machine is moved by source of mechanical energy to generate electrical energy it is called a D.C. generator, while when the same D.C. machine is connected to a source of D.C. supply it works as motor, developing mechanical energy.

Now a days D.C. supply is not used for distribution purpose, still D.C. machines are used in Industry, Railways etc. as they are having suitable characteristics for specific works. Hence, it becomes essential to study the D.C. machines in regards with their construction, operation, characteristics and uses. The performance characteristics of these machines becomes a base to study the characteristics and uses of other electrical machines.

### 2.1.2 Principal of Generator Action

Faraday was the first scientist who established certain relation between the magnitude of the induced e.m.f. and the flux linkages (Product of flux and number of turns of a coil). He made the invention in this regard and stated two laws which are known as Faradays's laws of magnetic induction. These laws are as stated below.

**Faraday's First Law :**

Whenever the flux linking with a coil or closed electric circuit changes an electro-motive force (e.m.f.) is induced in it, and such an e.m.f. last only for the time the change is taking place. Such type of e.m.f. is called as statically induced e.m.f., as in this case the conductor (coil) in which e.m.f. is induced is stationary and their takes place a change in the magnitude of flux linking with conductor. This principal is used in case of transformer.

**The other way of defining the same law is as follows:**

When a conductor (coil) moving in the magnetic field, cut the magnetic field (lines of force) an e.m.f is induced in it, which is called as dynamically induced e.m.f. This principal is used in generators.

From this law it is seen that if an e.m.f is to be induced in a conductor (coil), there should be a magnetic field or a system that produce magnetic field and a system on which conductors are housed to rotate them inside the magnetic field so as to cut the magnetic lines of force, i.e. a field system and armature system are essential for a generator.

**Faraday's Second Law:**

This law states about the magnitude of the induced e.m.f. it is stated as follows:

The magnitude of the induced e.m.f. is proportional to the rate of change of flux linkages.

The magnitude of the dynamically induced e.m.f. is given by the following relation:

$$E = Blv \sin \theta \text{ Volts}$$

Where,
- $E$ = Induced e.m.f. in volts
- $B$ = Flux density in Tesla (wb/m$^2$)
- $l$ = Length of conductor in m
- $v$ = Velocity of conductor in m/s
- $\theta$ = Angle in degrees, which a conductor makes with lines of force

**Right Hand Rule:**

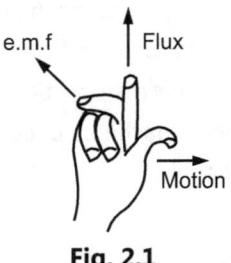

Fig. 2.1

This rule is used to determine the direction of the induced current.

It is stated as follows :

If the thumb, fore-finger and middle-finger of right-hand are at right angles to each other, and thumb gives the direction of motion, fore finger direction of magnetic field, then the middle finger will give the direction of induced current or induced e.m.f.

## 2.1.3 Principle of Motor Action

The working principle of motor action is that when a current carrying conductor is placed in the magnetic field it experiences a force.

Instead of a single conductor a coil carrying electric current is placed in the magnetic field the forces exerted on the two sides of the coil are equal in magnitude and act in opposite direction forming a couple of forces, which set up a torque on the coil making it to rotate. The value of the force exerted on a conductor is given by the relation.

$$F = BIl \sin \theta$$

Where,
- $B$ = Flux density in Tesla (wb/m$^2$)
- $I$ = Current in amps. flowing through the conductor
- $l$ = Length of conductor in m

θ = Angle in degrees which the conductor makes with magnetic lines of force

If only one coil is used the torque developed is not uniform and is zero at some position. Hence, we need number of coils distributed, for which an armature is required, in the slots of which such number of coils can be distributed and also to produced a magnetic flux, the field is also essential.

It can therefore be stated that for a motor also a armature system and field system is required.

## 2.1.4 Fleming's Left hand Rule

To determine the direction of force exerted on a current carrying conductor placed in the magnetic field Fleming's left hand rule is used. It is stated as follows :

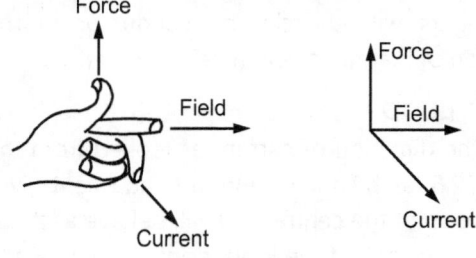

Fig. 2.2

If the three fingers i.e. the thumb, fore finger and middle finger of our left hand are held mutually at right angles to each other, and if the fore finger represents direction of magnetic lines of force, the middle finger represents the direction of current flow through the conductor, then the thumb will represent the direction of motion of the conductor.

## 2.1.5 Cork - Screw Rule

This rule is used to determine the direction of the magnetic flux produced by a current flowing through a conductor, students have studied it in their previous study, it will be better for them to recollect their memory, hence it is repeated here.

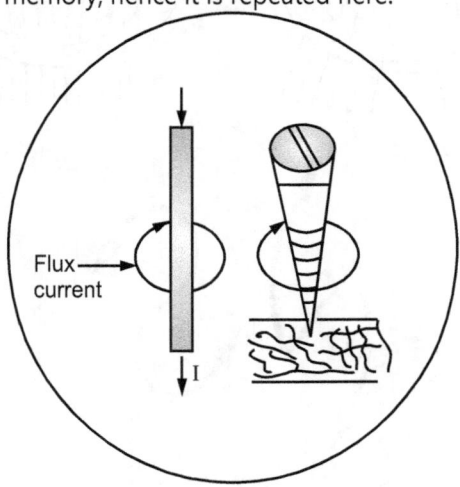

Fig. 2.3

If we imagine the right handed cork screw to be along the wire carrying the electric current, the current flowing from the top to bottom of the conductor, then the flux surrounding the conductor bears the same relation to the flow of current as the direction of rotation of a right handed screw bears to the direction of advancement of its point.

## 2.1.6 Hand Rule

This rule is also used to determine the direction of the magnetic flux produced by flow of electric current through a conductor. It is stated as :

If a observer holds the current carrying conductor in his right hand with the thumb pointing in the direction of flow of current, then the fingers will encircle the conductor in the direction of magnetic field (lines of force).

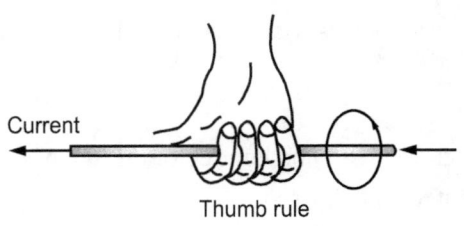

Thumb rule

**Fig. 2.4**

## 2.1.7 Magnetic Field Due to a Circular Loop

If a circular conductor carries current, and if the direction of current as looked from the top of the conductor is clockwise as shown in Fig. 2.5 (a), by application of hand rule it gives a resultant flux at right angles to the plane of the loop at the centre, and will behave as if it is a south pole. If the current in the loop looking from the top of the loop is anti-clockwise, the flux will be emerging out of plane of loop thus will form a north pole.

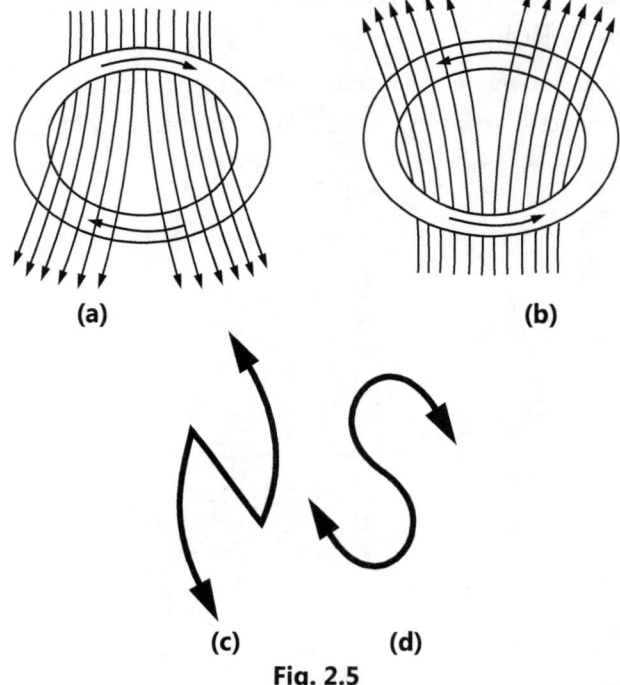

**Fig. 2.5**

The simple way of understanding the polarity formed by flow of current through a coil is as represented in Fig. 2.5 (c) and 2.5 (d) i.e. if the current flows in anti-clockwise direction through a coil it will produce north polarity and if the current flows in clock-wise direction through a coil it will produce south polarity.

## 2.1.8 Necessity of Commutating System

For understanding the need of a commutator in case of a D.C. machine, we will study first the elementary generator.

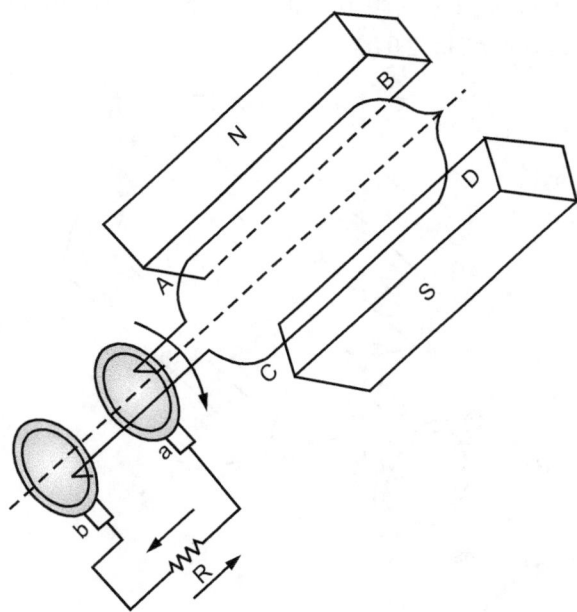

**Fig. 2.6 (a)**

Fig. 2.6 (a) represents a elementary generator, consisting of a coil, which form two coil sides AB and CD, placed inside the magnetic field, produced by two magnet poles N and S, and the ends being connected to two rings, on which two brushes a and b respectively rest The magnitude of induced e.m.f. in side AB and CD will be equal but opposite in direction, hence the resultant voltage available at any time is equal to sum of e.m.f. in the two coil sides. In one coil side it is equal to $Blv \sin A$.

Therefore, e.m.f. in the coil is equal to $2 Blv \sin \theta$, where B, $l$, v and $\theta$ have their usual meaning. Hence, this type of voltage wave will represent sinusoidal variation of voltage with a maximum of $2 Blv$ volts. Such a wave is represented in Fig 2.6 (b).

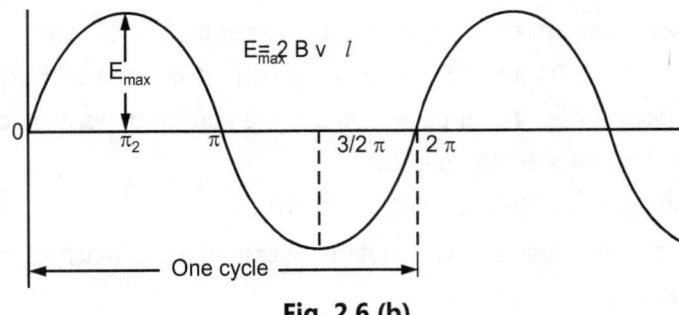

**Fig. 2.6 (b)**

To obtain a unidirection a simple modification in the construction of a elementary generator is made as shown in Fig. 2.6 (c).

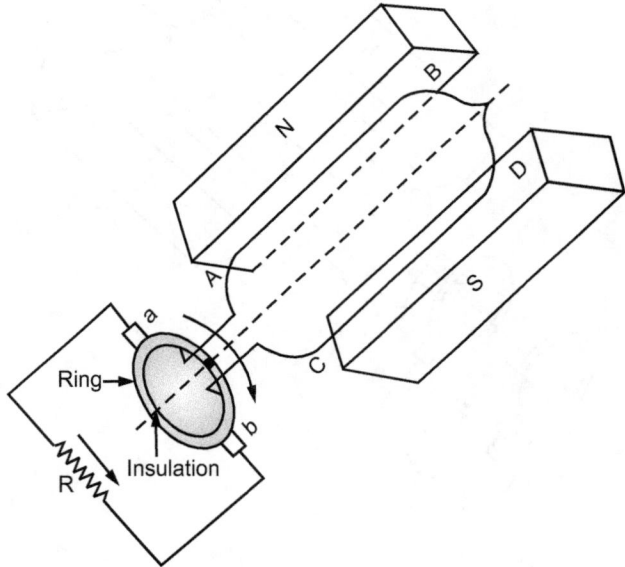

**Fig. 2.6 (c)**

In this generator instead of two rings only one ring with two halves and insulated at two points as shown in Fig. 2.6 (c) is used. In this case, the e.m.f. wave obtained is as shown in Fig. 2.6 (d) and the current in the external circuit will flow from brush a to brush b i.e. unidirectional as shown by arrow across resistance R. Hence, it will be understood that instead of two rings only one ring with two insulated halves is used we get unidirectional e.m.f., with a changing magnitude from instant to instant. Instead of one coil, two coils placed on the same shaft at right angles to each other and the ends of which are connected four insulated segments of a ring. The variation of the resultant voltage available across brushes a and b will be as shown in Fig. 2.6 (e) by dark line.

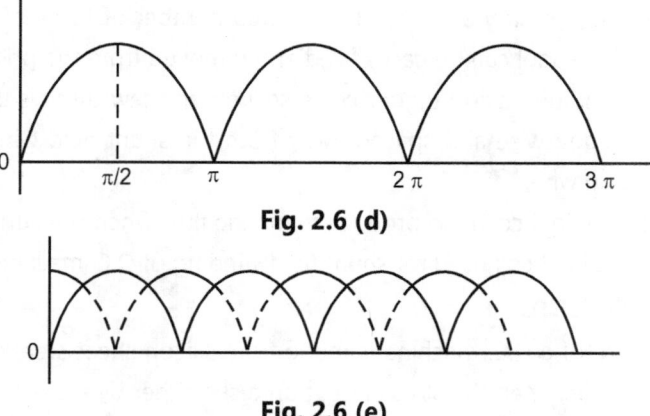

**Fig. 2.6 (d)**

**Fig. 2.6 (e)**

If the number of coils is made four and ring is divided into eight sections, the unidirectional voltage wave form will be further smoothened. Instead of that if 16 coils equally spaced and connected to 32 insulated sections of a ring a closely straight line voltage in one direction can be obtained.

From the above discussion one can understand the number of sections insulated from each other and each section connected to the end of coil to obtain a unidirectional voltage with very small (negligible) ripple. Such a ring in case of a D.C. generator is called as commutator.

The need of a commutator in case of D.C. motor will be explained at the time of studying the working principle of a D.C. motor.

## 2.1.9 Field Coils

Feild coils are usually prepared from insulated wires. If they are manufactured by using cotton insulated wires, these coils are dried in a vacuum before they are impregnated with an insulating varnish. The outer cotton insulation is generally protected by cotton tape or cord.

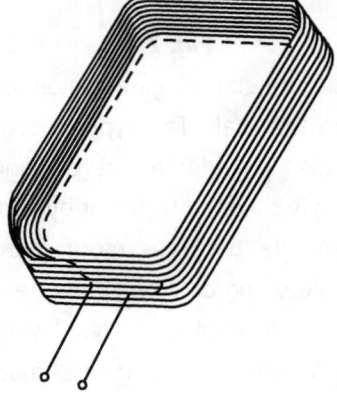

**Fig. 2.7**

Another method of forming a field coil is to wind number of turns of insulated wire on the metal spool. Such a spool can be easily fixed and removed from the pole core.

The series field winding having bigger cross-section and few turns is usually made from copper-strip wound edge-wise and spaced away from the shunt field winding having large number of turns of thin wire.

The function of the field coil is to produce magnetic flux, when the current flows through it. Fig. 2.7 represents a field coil used for shunt field winding of D.C. machine.

## 2.1.10 Armature Core

The armature core of a D.C. machine is made from silicon sheet steel disks punched out in circular shape by a die. Then the slots are cut on disks either by a die or they are punched by a slotting machine. In case of small machines the circular stampings are keyed directly to the shaft. Axial wholes are provided to permit the air to pass through for cooling purpose.

Fig. 2.8 represents such an assembled armature. Each stamping is insulated from other by means of insulating varnish etc. to minimise the eddy current losses.

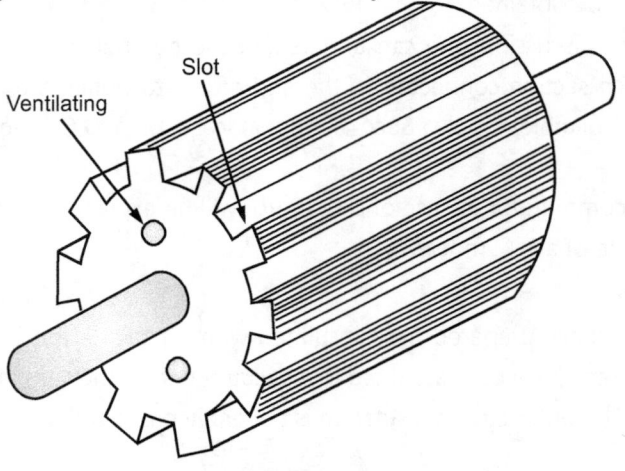

**Fig. 2.8**

In machines of medium size, the stampings are assembled and keyed to an armature spider, which is in turn keyed to the shaft. This type of construction is used to reduce the amount of steel required and also provides a free passage of air through the centre of armature. The stampings are usually clamped together by end plates held by through bolts.

When the diameter of armature becomes more then 100 cm or 50 cm it is not economical to punch out a complete ring of laminations, hence such armatures are made up of segments, each segment lapping the joint in the next layer.

The slots are generally straight sided in case of small machines, the armature conductors are held in slots by binding wire while in case of large machines the conductors are held in slots by hard-fibre strip wages. The slots are well insulated by a layer of hard substance, such as fibre or press board just near the laminations, it should then be next insulated by providing a liner (slot liner) prepared from varnished cambric.

The conductors which are housed in the armature slots may be single cotton covered, double cotton covered or enamel insulated. Fibre glass, treated with organic varnishes and silicone are also used for the conductors which are used for machines operating at higher temperature such as traction motors. Sometimes a mica tape insulation is also used.

The function of the armature core is to provide space for armature conductors and to provide a low reluctance path to the magnetic flux.

## 2.1.11 Armature Conductors and Armature Winding

In the slots of the armature are housed insulated copper wires and are connected in a particular way to the commutator. The length of copper wire housed in the armature slot and lying in the magnetic field is called as conductor, while the number of such armature conductors connected in a particular fashion to close on it self, the ends of the coils being connected to commutator is called as armature winding. The purpose of armature winding in case of generators is to develope a induced e.m.f. In case of motor, the same are used to circulate current for developing the torque.

All modern windings are called as lap and wave windings or modifications of these. The difference between the two windings lies merely in arrangement of the end connections at the front of the armature.

Before going into details of the two types of windings generally used in D.C. machines, we will study the meaning of the terms used in these windings.

**(a) Conductor:** The length of wire which lies in the field and when rotated there is a induced e.m.f. in it is called as a conductor. Length AB and CD shown in the Fig. 2.9 (a) are called as conductors.

**(b) Turn:** When two conductors are joined at their back, they form a turn in Fig. 2.9 (a) AB and CD are joined at their back and form a turn.

**(c) Coil Side and Coil:** When number of turns are connected in series, it forms a multiturn coil AB and CD are the two coil sides forming a coil. (Fig. 2.9 (b)).

**(d) Coil Span or Coil Pitch:** Fig. 2.9 (c) represents a developed surface of the armature. Here the coil sides of one coil have been placed in slots no. 1 and slot no. 5 while of the other they are placed in slot no. 2 and slot no. 6.

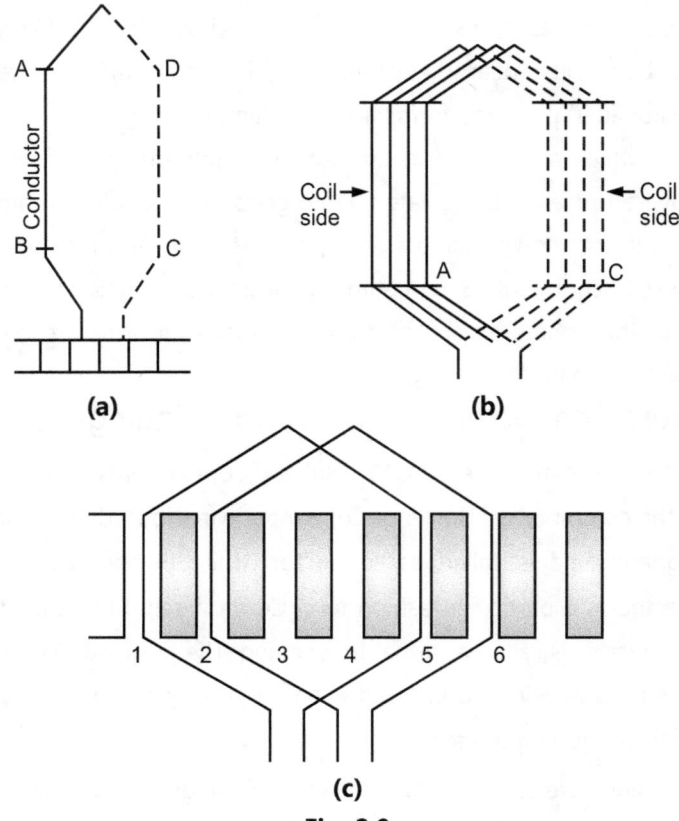

**Fig. 2.9**

The coil span or coil pitch is defined as the distance measured between the two sides of a coil in terms of armature slots.

**(e) Pole Pitch:** If a armature of a machine is having 16 no. of slots, and is to be used for a 4 pole machine. Then the pole pitch is equal to 16/4 i.e. 4 slots. Hence, a pole pitch is defined as total no. of armature slots per pole.

It is also defined as periphery of armature divided by no. of poles, measured in length i.e. $\pi D/4$.

**(f) Full Pitch:** When the two sides of a coil are housed in the armature slots with a distance equal to pole pitch, then such type of winding is termed as full-pitch winding. If pole pitch is equal to 4 slots, then Fig. 2.9 (c) will represents coils used for a full-pitch winding.

In this case, the two sides of the coil will lie under opposite poles and the resultant e.m.f. in the coil is equal to sum of e.m.fs. in the two coil sides and its value will be maximum.

**(g) Fractional Pitch:** If the coil span is less than a pole pitch, then the winding is termed as fractional pitch winding. In this case, there is a phase difference between the e.m.fs. in the two sides of the coil and the total e.m.f. around the coil is the vector sum of the e.m.fs. in the two coil sides, and is less than that in the full pitched coils. The advantage of using fractional pitch windings is the substantial saving in the copper of the end connection and it helps in improving commutation, owing to the lesser mutual inductance between coils; and lesser magnitude of reactance voltage being induced in the coil undergoing commutation.

**(h) Pitch of Winding:** It is defined as the distance around the armature between two successive conductors which are directly connected together or it may also be defined as the distance between the beginning of two consecutive turns measured in terms of armature slots.

**(i) Front Pitch:** The number of elements (coil sides) spanned by a coil on the front i.e. commutator end of armature is called as the front pitch and is represented by letter $Y_F$.

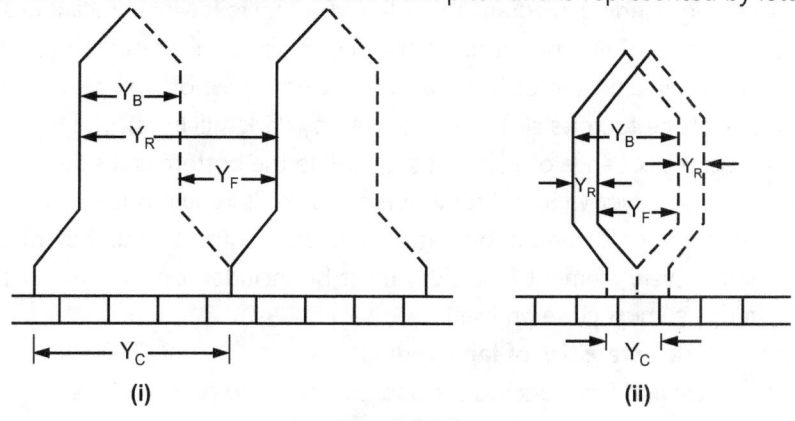

**Fig. 2.9 (d)**

**(j) Back-Pitch:** The distance measured in terms of armature conductors (coil sides) which a coil advances on the back of the armature is called as back pitch and it is represented by letter $Y_B$.

**(k) Commutator Pitch:** It is the distance measured in terms of commutator bars or segments between the segments to which the two ends of the coil are connected.

**(l) Resultant Pitch:** It is the distance measured in terms of coil sides, between the beginning of the one coil and the beginning of the next coil to which it is connected.

All these pitches in case of lap and wave windings are represented in Fig. 2.9 (d) (i) and (ii) for clear understanding.

**(m) Single Layer Winding:** When one conductor or one coil side occupies one slot of armature at the time of carrying out the winding. Such type of windings are very rarely used in practice.

**(n) Double Layer Winding or Two Layer Winding:** In this type of winding, there are two conductors or coil sides per slot arranged two layers. Usually they are so arranged to obtain a proper shape and ease in connection, that one side of every coil lies in the upper half of one slot and other side of that coil lies in the lower half of some other slot at a distance of winding pitch.

**(o) Progressive Winding:** It is that type of winding which advance or progresses in clockwise direction. In case of lap winding when $Y_B > Y_F$ we get a progressive winding.

**(p) Retrogressive Winding:** It is that winding which progresses or advances in anti-clockwise direction. In case of lap winding when $Y_F > Y_B$ we get a retrogressive winding.

**(q) Lap Winding:** Lap winding is that winding, in which the finishing end of one coil connected to the starting end of the adjacent coil the joint being connected to the same commutator segment. This process is continued till all the coils are connected to the commutator segments. The winding is known as lap winding because the sides of successive coils overlap each other.

While developing winding diagram for a lap winding following precautions are taken. Though the coil consists of number of turns, their coil sides are represented by single line. In case of double layer winding the coil side at the bottom of a slot is shown by dotted lines. While the coil side at the top of a slot is represented by dark (full lines). The top coil sides are given odd numbers in sequence of adjacent slots, while the bottom coil sides are given even numbers. For a double layer winding, total number of coils required is equal to number of slots, and the number of commutator segment is also equal to number of coils. While developing winding every element (coil-side) must be included only once and the winding must be re-entrant, i.e. must close on itself.

**Following are the characteristics of lap winding:**
  (i) The back pitch and front pitches are odd numbers and of opposite sign.
      They can not be equal and should differ by two in case of simple lap winding.
  (ii) Both $Y_B$ and $Y_F$ should be nearly equal to a pole pitch.
  (iii) The average pitch = $\dfrac{Y_B + Y_F}{2}$ will be a even number.
  (iv) Commutator pitch $Y_C = \pm 1$.
  (v) Resultant pitch $Y_R$ is even number being the difference of $Y_B$ and $Y_F$.
  (vi) Number of slots is equal to number of coil for a double layer winding and is also equal to number of commutator segments.
  (vii) When $Y_B = Y_F - 2$, we get a retrogressive winding, here $Y_C = -1$.
  (viii) When $Y_B = Y_F + 2$, we get a progressive winding, here $Y_C = +1$.
  (ix) Number of parallel paths in a lap winding is equal to number of poles.

## 2.1.12 Equalizing Rings

In case of a multipolar lap-wound armature circulating currents will flow if the value of induced e.m.f. in each armature circuit is not the same. These circulating currents will have to flow through the brushes, and at the time of load, it will cause certain brushes to overload. This may happen in practice due to the fact that e.m.f. induced in each circuit of a multipolar machine may not be same, it may be due to the fact that values of reactance of the different circuits may not be the same, the parts may have considerable variation. The unequal loading of the circuits will result in increased armature reaction by the more loaded circuits, which tend to reduce the flux linked with the circuits concerned and so tending to unequalise the e.m.fs.

For preventing this circulating current flowing through brushes a provision is made by providing the other permanent paths for the circulation of such currents, by connecting together certain points of the same potential these points are generally connected to rings fixed at the back of armature called as equalising rings.

**Dummy Coils:** Sometimes we are required to make the use of a standard armature punching, to be employed for a wave winding. The number of slots of above armature does not confirm to the required number of slots for a wave winding. Hence, we use generally a armature in which one coil more than actually required for a wave winding is provided. This extra coil is called as dummy coil and is put in position to maintain the mechanical balance of the armature but it is not connected in circuit and kept completely insulated from the remainder of the winding.

## 2.1.13 Comparison of Lap and Wave Windings

| Sr. No. | Lap Winding | Wave Winding |
|---|---|---|
| 1. | Coil span = $\frac{Z}{P}$ (appr.) | Coil span = $\frac{Z}{P}$ (appr.) |
| 2. | Number of commutator segments is equal to number of coils | Number of commutator segments is equal to number of coils. |
| 3. | Average $Y_A = \frac{Z}{P} = \frac{Y_B + Y_F}{2}$ | $\frac{Y_B + Y_F}{2} = \frac{Z \pm 2}{P} = Y_{av}$ and must be a whole number. |
| 4. | Both $Y_B$ and $Y_F$ must be odd number and nearly equal to Z/P and should differ by two. | Both must be odd, may differ by two or may be equal. |
| 5. | Commutator pitch $Y_C = \pm 1$ | Commutator pitch $Y_C = \frac{C \pm 1}{P/2}$ where, C = number of coils and P/2 = number of pairs of poles or $Y_C = \frac{Z \pm 2}{P} = Y_A$ and must be integral. |
| 6. | $Y_C = +1$ gives progressive windings and $Y_C = -1$ gives retrogressive winding. | Positive sign gives progressive winding and negative sign gives retrogressive winding. |
| 7. | Parallel paths A = P | Parallel paths A = 2 |

| 8. | Number of brushes = A or P | Number of brushes = 2 (in case of large machines we may provide equal to P) |
|---|---|---|
| 9. | Current flowing through each conductor $I_c = I_a/A$ | It is equal to $I_c = I_a/2$ |
| 10. | No dummy coil is required. | Dummy coil is required. |
| 11. | Equalizer rings are required. | Equalizer rings are not required. |

## 2.1.14 Uses of Lap and Wave Windings

A lap winding has large number of parallel paths, which is equal to number of poles of machine, hence it is more suitable for generating large currents and low voltages. If we desire large voltage to be developed in a lap-winding. We will need large number of conductors, which will result in high winding cost, and lower efficiency for the utilisation of the space in slots.

While the wave winding has an advantage of giving more e.m.f. than the lap winding for the given number of poles and armature conductors. Hence wave winding is suitable for small generators, required for voltages of 500-600 volts circuits. In wave winding equalizing connections are not required, while in lap - winding they are definitely required.

Hence, lap-winding is suitable for comparatively small voltages but high current generators, while wave windings are used for high voltage, low current machines.

## 2.1.15 Commutator

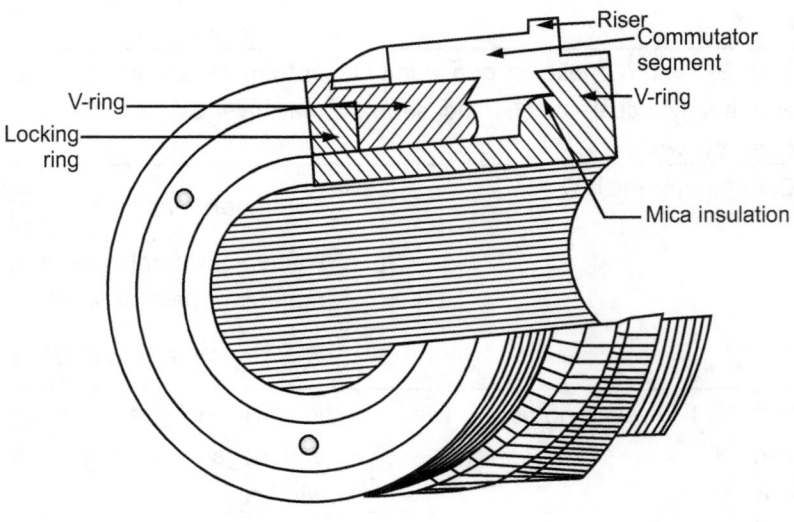

**Fig. 2.10 (a)**

Commutator is made from wedge-shaped segments as shown in Fig. 2.10 (b), of hard drawn or drop forged copper. These segments are arranged in circular shape with a separation of built up mica cut in same shape as that of copper segments. These segments are held together by locking rings which pull segments inward. The locking rings and V rings are prevented from short circuiting the segments by two rings of built up mica. The details of this type of construction is shown in Fig. 2.10 (a). The leads from the armature coil are soldered into small longitudinal slits in the end of the segments or the slits provided in the riser portion of the commutator segments.

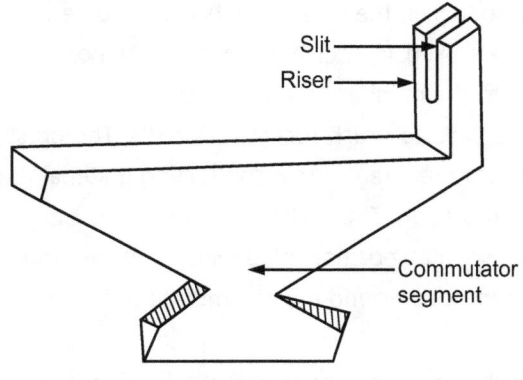

**Fig. 2.10 (b)**

## 2.1.16 Brushes and Brush Holder

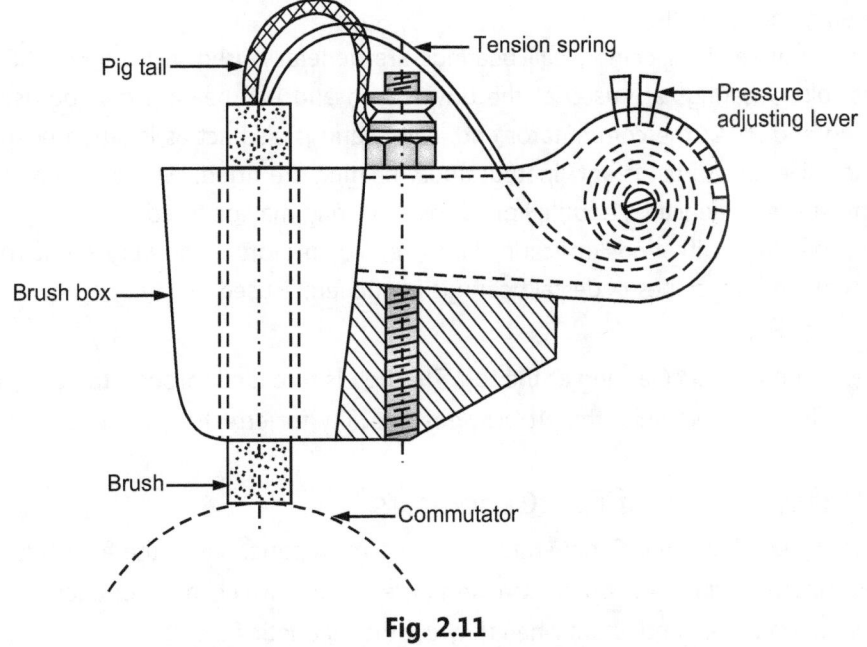

**Fig. 2.11**

Brushes are needed to collect the current from the armature winding in case of generators, while they are required to supply current to the armature in case of motors. Normally, brushes are made up of carbon and graphite; so that while in contact with the commutatuor, the commutator surface is not weared out, instead the brushes become uneven or wear out after a particular period of use, when they are replaced.

Fig. 2.11 shows the details of the brush and brush holder, the brush is accommodated in the brush holder where a spring presses it against the commutator, with a pressure of 1.5 to 2 N/cm$^2$. A twisted flexible copper conductor called as pigtail securely fixed into the brush is used to make connection between the brush and its brush holder.

Normally brush holders used in D.C. machines are of box type. The number of brush holders are usually equal to the number of main poles.

The brush holders are fixed to brush rocker with bolts. The brush rocker may be of non-conducting material or if it is prepared from a conducting material then the brush holders are fixed to it with a proper insulation. The rocker arm is fixed to the yoke and have a provision of changing its position, so that position of brushes can be adjusted in magnetic neutral plane. It is arranged concentrically round the commutator.

## 2.1.17 Shaft

It is that part on which armature is built, make it fixed in bearings and armature free to rotate. The diameter of the shaft should be able to withstand the turning moment of the load and it should also be not affected by the bending action due to weight of armature and any unbalanced magnetic pulls.

**Bearings:** In small machines, ball bearings are generally used at both ends. For larger machines roller bearings are used at the driving end and ball bearing may be used at the non-driving end i.e. at the commutator end. Ball bearings also act as location bearings, but where excessive end thrust is anticipated, thrust bearing are fitted. Where a limited amount of end thrust is experienced a double lipped roller bearing may be fitted.

Sleeve bearings with ring lubrication are used for motors when very silent running is required. For large machines pedestal bearings are generally used.

## 2.1.18 Eye-Bolt

This is a bolt with circular ring at the top. This bolt is threaded through the body of frame of the machine. Its function is that, it provides a facility for errection, transport or handling etc.

## 2.1.19 Classification of D.C. Generators

We have seen that the D.C. generator have two main parts, one is the field system which produces magnetic flux and other is a armature system which has conductors. E.M.F. is developed in armature conductors when they cut the magnetic flux.

Depending up on the method of exciting the field system (circulating D.C. current) generators are divided into the following two categories:

(a) Separately excited generators, (b) Self excited generators.

**(a) Separately excited generators:** These are the D.C. generators, in which the field coils are connected to a separate source of D.C. voltage, so as to cause a circulating current through field coils, which produces the required magnetic flux.

**(b) Self excited generators:** in these types of generators, the field coils receive a circulating current from the armature of the generator itself, no external source is required.

**Classification based on field connection:**

In the construction of field coils we have seen that two types of coils are generally manufactured. One type of coil consists of large number of turns of a thin wire, and number of such coils are connected in series to form a field winding, this type of winding is connected in parallel with the armature and is called as shunt field winding.

The type of coil which consists few turns of thick wire and (equal to number of poles) are connected in series, is termed a series field winding.

The coil of shunt field or series field are so corrected that adjacent coils will form alternate north and south polarity.

Depending up on the type of connection of these windings and which type of winding is used the generators are classified as :

(1) Series Generator,

(2) Shunt Generator,

(3) Compound Generator.

Compound generators are those generators which consists of shunt as well as series field winding. These generators are further classified as long shunt or short shunt depending upon whether the shunt field winding is connected in parallel to armature and series field winding or only the armature.

The compound generator can further be classified depending up on the action of the flux produced by the field coil, i.e. whether the flux produced by the series field winding helps the flux produced by the shunt field winding or it weakens the flux produced by the shunt field winding. In this case, it may be called as cumulative compound generator or differential compound generator.

Series field winding ends are represented by letters S, SS or Y, YY. Shunt field winding terminals are represented by letters F, FF or $Sh_1$, $Sh_2$.

The classification of generators is represented in the following chart.

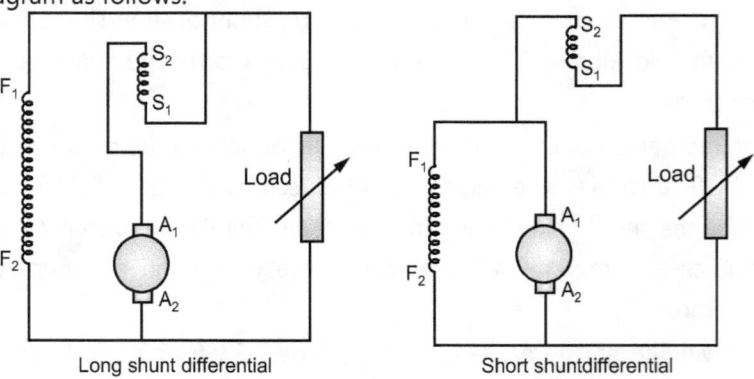

Fig. 2.12 (a)

When the series field winding connection is reversed the flux produced by it opposes the main flux, such compound generators are called as long shunt differential compound generators and short shunt differential compound generators, they are represented by schematic diagram as follows.

Fig. 2.12 (b)

D.C. compound generators are some times classified from the nature of the characteristic, such as when the terminal voltage of the generator at no load and full load is the same then it is termed as level compound generator.

When the terminal voltage of the generator is greater than its T.V. at no load, such a compound generator is termed as over compounded compound generator and if the generator T.V. on load is less than its T.V. at no load then such compound generator is called as under compounded compound generator.

## 2.1.20 Materials Used in Construction of D.C. Machines

The materials used in construction of D.C. machines can be divided into the following categories :
(i) Magnetic.
(ii) Conducting.
(iii) Insulating.

## 2.1.21 Magnetic Materials

Soft magnetic materials come under the following categories :
(a) Solid core materials, (b) Electrical sheet steel, (c) Special purpose alloys.

**(a) Solid core materials:** These materials are generally used for parts of magnetic circuit carrying steady flux, such as cores of field poles and field frames. It is used because of high permeability particularly at high flux density. It should also have low hysteresis loss. The materials can be as soft iron, cast steel, cast iron, and ferro-cobalt (cobalt 35%, iron 65%).

**(b) Sheet Steel:** In early days iron with low content of carbon and the impurities was used for the magnetic circuits of electrical machines. It has a drawback that due to 'Ageing' effect the co-ercive force and hysteresis increases, causing over heating and break down. In present century it is discovered that when silicon is added to iron, the magnetic properties of the alloy are much improved. The laminations now used in electrical machines are made of silicon steel in which the content of silicon lies between 0.3% to 4.5%.

When silicon is added to steel it eliminates the problem of ageing, reduces hysteresis loss and increases resistivity of the material there by reducing the eddy current loss also. If the percentage of silicon is made more than 5% it has a drawback that the permeability at high flux density is reduced and it looses ductility hence the materials becomes brittle and cannot be punched or sheared. Hence, in case of D.C. machines the core laminations are punched out from a sheet steel containing a low silicon, which permits higher values of flux density and higher ratio of output to weight can be achieved. The sheet steels used in rotating machine is termed as 'Dynamo grade steel'.

In small machines where least importance is given to iron losses magnetic materials with 0.5 silicon or even less are employed. While in case of very high capacity machines, such as turbo generators iron losses play an important role to bring their value to a minimum, high silicon content laminations, containing silicon upto 4.5% are used.

**(c) Special purpose alloy:** Special alloys, which gives high flux density in weak magnetic field are generally used in say instrument transformers etc. The important alloys in this category are permalloy and mumetal.

### 2.1.22 Conductive Materials

Generally, the following materials are used as conducting materials in D.C. machines :

(a) Copper, (b) Aluminium.

**(a) Copper:** Copper is widely used as conducting material in electrical machines, as it has high electrical conductivity, good mechanical properties and it is less affected by atmospheric conditions. It can be cast, forged, rolled, drawn, and machined, its softness is achieved by annealing.

D.C. machines (almost all machines) use windings of annealed high conductivity copper wire. It has a resistivity of $0.017241 \times 10^{-6}$ ohm.m and resistance temperature coefficient 0.00393 per °C. Hard drawn copper wires are used in electrical machines.

**(b) Aluminium :** Aluminium is the conductor material next to copper, which is used in electrical machines. It is softer than copper it can be drawn in thin sheets but cannot be drawn into very fine wires on account of its low mechanical strength, when we want to replace copper conductors by aluminium conductors in electrical machines we have to take into account, the difference in their resistivity, density and mechanical strength, when we will be using aluminium conductors for winding wire, we have to design electrical machines for larger slots. It can also be used for field coil.

Aluminium conductors are generally used for stator windings of induction motors, cage windings of motor and also the transformer windings of small transformers.

### 2.1.23 Insulating Materials

**(a) Insulating materials for wires:** The materials in general use are enamel, cotton, rayon, silk and fibrous glass.

**(i) Enamel Covering:** This consists of a thin film of oil base or synthetic base varnish applied by drawing the wire through a tough of varnish and then through a heated chamber so as to bake the varnish covering into a tough elastic film of high dielectric strength. Such enamelled wires are used for armature winding of generators and motors, following enamels are used for different machines.

Refrigerator Motors — Polyvinyl formal, Polyesterimide.

Generator, Motor — Polyesterimide.

**(ii) Cotton Covering :** It consists of number of cotton thread wound helically on the wire in a lapping machine. They are either single covered or double covered. The D.C.C. wires are largely used for field coils, and armature windings. They withstand rougher handling than enamel covered wires. The coils are impregnated with varnish to improve dielectric strength and heat dissipating qualities.

**(iii) Fibrous Glass Covering :** It consists of a double lapping of threads of continuous glass fibres on the conductors. The thickness for round wire is about 0.15 to 0.2 mm. Varnishing of such wires is essential. They are used for windings which are required to operate in class B temperature range.

**(b) Insulating materials for laminations:**

**(i) Insuline:** This is a kaolin (china) mixture which sprayed on to one or both sides of the lamination. The total thickness of insulation coating may vary from 0.01 to 0.025 mm.

**(ii) Oxide:** A natural oxide coating is formed on the sheets during the hot rolling process. Extra oxide coating is applied to obtain reliability of insulation.

**(iii) Varnish:** Varnish is applied to both sides of lamination to a thickness of about 0.006 mm. It makes laminations rust proof and is not affected by temperature produced in electrical machines.

**(c) Insulating materials for machines:**

**(i) Class A materials:** They include tapes and flexible sheet materials, tapes used for taping of rectangular conductors.

**(ii) Cotton and oiled cambric tapes:** Cotton tapes are impregnated to prevent absorption of moisture. Oiled cambric tapes (Empire cloth) is prepared from a roll of cotton fabric which have been treated with linseed oil and oxidised.

**(iii) Tough fibrous materials:** They are used for slot linings of low voltage machines. The thickness may be from 0.25 mm. to 0.5 mm. The examples of such materials are latheriod paper, press-board, harb fibre treated with oil.

**(iv) Nylon and terylene:** These materials have high tensile strength and good dielectric strength and are used as tapes.

**Class B meterials:** Typical materials are fibrous glass, asbestos and mica.

**(i) Fibrous glass tape:** It is prepared by wovening continuous filament yarn and is impregnated in varnish before use. It is generally used as tape, sleeve, cord etc.

**(ii) Asbestos tape:** Asbestos in the form of paper finds limited applications. It is used for providing inter-turn insulation in case of inter pole windings of large D.C. machines. The field of application is limitted due to superiority of fibre glass.

**(iii) Mica :** Mica is used in form of built up mica sheets, rings and cones and tapes.

Mica is used in the form of splittings or flakes. They are fixed on a paper with help of shellac or synthetic resign to a desired thickness and are hot pressed to form a hard solid plate, such a formed mica can be used for making slot liners commutator insulation strips, 'V' rings etc.

Mica tape is used for taping armature and field coils.

**(iv) Varnishes:** Formerly varnishes were prepared from natural gums or resins with suitable solvents and oxidizing oils say linseed oil. Such varnishes are still used for repair works, large manufacturers use synthetic varnishes of the phenol-formaldehyde type, because during baking the polymerization taking place, produces uniform hardening through out, while in case of oxidising varnishes the hardening takes place on the surface only.

New silicon varnishes being more resistant to heat and water proof than other varnishes makes the machines with fibrous glass and other inorganic insulation to operate at a tempreture of 200°C to 250°C ; such type of insulation is used in traction motors having class H insulation.

## 2.1.24 E.M.F. Equation of a D.C. Generator

Let a D.C. generator have P = Number of poles. Z = Total number of armature conductors, A = Number of parallel paths of armature winding.

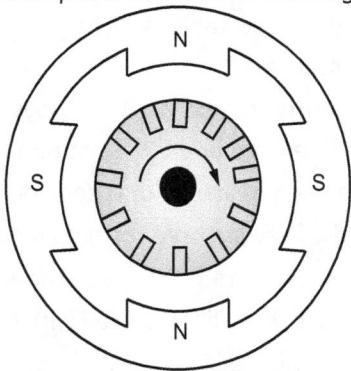

**Fig. 2.13**

∴ Number of conductors per parallel path = Z/A Nos. N = speed in r.p.m. at which armature is rotating.

$\phi$ = flux per pole in wb.

Then from average induced e.m.f. per conductor = flux cut per second.

or from Faraday's law of electromagnetic induction.

$e = \dfrac{d\phi}{dt}$ when N = 1, $e_{av} = \dfrac{d\phi}{dt}$ i.e. rate of cutting the flux

where N = Number of conductors.

When one conductor is completing one revolution it cuts a total flux due to all the P poles = $P\phi$ webers.

When N is the speed in r.p.m., time required in seconds to complete one revolution of armature = $\dfrac{60}{N}$ sec.

Then putting the values of $d\phi$ and dt in equation (i) we get average e.m.f.,

$$e_{av} = \dfrac{P\phi}{60/N} = \dfrac{P\phi N}{60} \text{ volts.}$$

As Z/A number of armature conductors which are connected in series per path of armature winding and e.m.f. induced in armature winding being equal to e.m.f. per parallel path.

Generated e.m.f. Eg = e.m.f./Conductor X number of conductors per parallel path.

OR Generation e.m.f., $\quad Eg = \dfrac{P\phi N}{60} \times \dfrac{Z}{A} = \dfrac{\phi Z N P}{60 A}$ Volts.

The value of A for wave winding being equal to two, and for a lap winding being equal to number of poles.

## 2.1.25 Building up of Voltage in Case of Separately Excited Generators

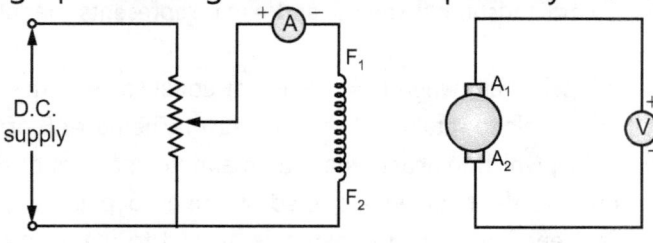

**Fig. 2.14 (a)**

In separately excited generators the field winding is connected to a separate source of D.C. supply, as shown in Fig. 2.14 (a). Generally, the supply is connected by a potential divider arrangement so that current flowing in the field circuit can be varied from zero. For determining the voltage built up characteristic of such a generator a voltmeter is connected across the armature terminals and the armature is made to rotate at a constant rated speed with the help of a prime mover. Then the field current is increased in steps from zero and corresponding values of induced e.m.f. are recorded.

At constant speed from $E = \dfrac{\phi Z N P}{60 \, A}$ volts

induced e.m.f $E \propto \phi$ other factor being constant, flux $\phi$ produced is proportional to e.m.f. which is equal to number of turns of field. Winding multiplied by field current in amps. number of turns being constant, flux will be proportional to field current till saturation. Hence, if we plot the graph between field current and induced e.m.f. its nature will be as shown in Fig. 2.14 (b) which represents building up of voltage in case of separately excited generator.

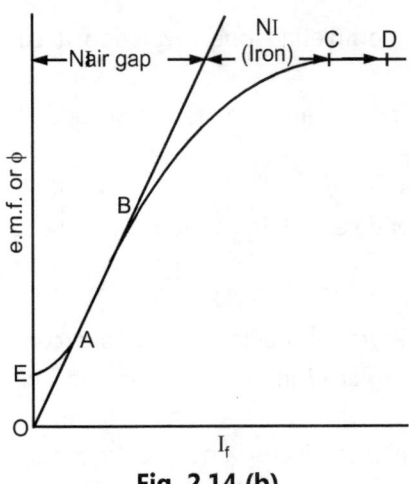

**Fig. 2.14 (b)**

Fig. 2.14 (b) is also called as a magnetisation characteristic of D.C. machine i.e. a characteristic which represents relation between or a graph between magnetisation and magnetising force. The magnetisation i.e. flux produced is indirectly measured in terms of induce e.m.f. as $E \propto \phi$ and the magnetising force is measured in terms of field current as m.m.f. $\propto I_F$. Hence, a characteristic between $I_F$ and e.m.f. represents magnetisation curve to some other scale.

From the curve, it is seen that when $I_F = 0$, E is not equal to zero, this is because of the property of magnetic materials to retain certain magnetism. The part AB of the curve is more or less than a straight line, which indicates that, the magnetic material of the field system is unsaturated during this part, the reluctance offered by the air gap is the greater percentage of the total reluctance, Hence, most of the m.m.f. is utilised to maintain the flux in airgap. Beyond this the reluctance of the iron increases which causes saturation in the magnetic material. Finally, the curve takes the form as shown by the path CD, point - D representing the final saturation of magnetic circuit. EA represents bottom knee portion which is due to high permeability of magnetic material at start of magnetisation.

## 2.1.26 Building up of Voltage in Self Excited Shunt Generator

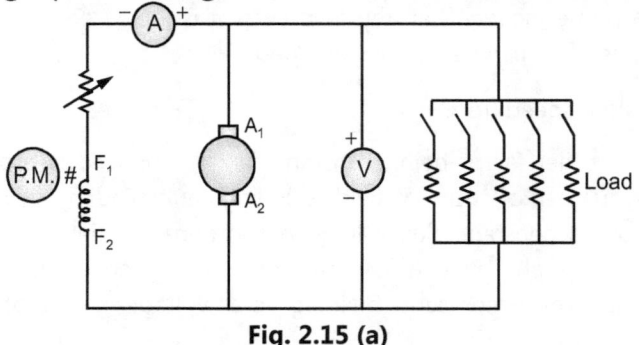

**Fig. 2.15 (a)**

Fig. 2.15 (a) represents the circuit diagram for a self excited shunt generator. In which a voltmeter V is connected across the armature terminals and the load is open circuited. A field winding $F_1F_2$ is connected across $A_1A_2$ through a variable resistance and a ammeter is inserted in the circuit to measure the field current.

When the generator is at rest the induced e.m.f is zero, but when its armature is made to rotate with constant speed with the help of a prime mover, the e.m.f generated by this type of generator is very small, may be 10 to 20 volts, as represented by Oa in Fig. 2.15 (b). As the load circuit is not connected it causes a circulating current in the field circuit, hence m.m.f. of the field circuit increases, which will increase (produce) some flux, this flux should be such as to increase the residual flux, due to which e.m.f. of 10 or 20 volts (Oa) is induced, will increase to the value of induced e.m.f. to say 50 volts. These 50 volts will cause a further increase in circulating current in the field circuit causing a further increase in flux per pole and a subsequent increase in induced e.m.f. thus the process of building up will continue final steady voltage depending up on the field circuit resistance is developed.

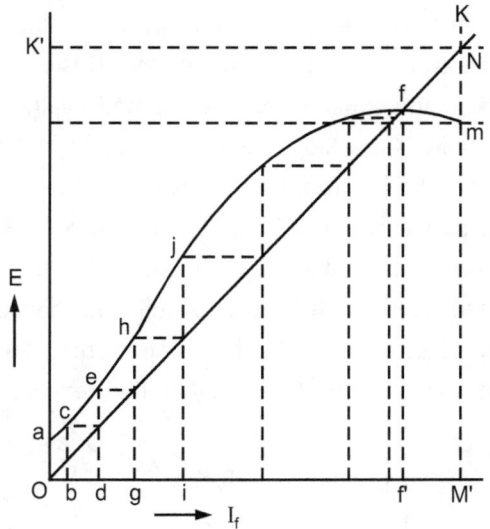

**Fig. 2.15 (b)**

The building up of voltage in a self excited shunt generator can also be explained with the help of Fig. 2.15 (b). In this 'Of' represents the shunt field resistance line, i.e. a line of which every point will have a value equal to field circuit resistance or $E/I_{sh} = R_{sh}$ ; and 'af' represents the induced e.m.f. against field current characteristic, which can also be called as magnetisation characteristic. When Oa is the induced e.m.f. due to residual flux, it causes a circulating current of Ob in the field, this field current will induce a voltage equal to bc. e.m.f. of bc volts causes a further increased current to flow in field circuit; it will increase the e.m.f. to de; and so on till point f is reached on the curve. The generator can not build up beyond this point for the following reasons :

Consider a point K above f on the field resistance line, it will cause a field current of OM amps. To produce this field current, is required a voltage NM volts, but it produces a e.m.f. of Mm only. As the e.m.f. required to produce a field current of OM is MK and it produces a e.m.f. of Mm only it is obvious that the generator can not build up to point K. Hence, the voltage to which a shunt generator will build is dependent up on the field circuit resistance and for a machine having, field resistance represented by line Of, the final voltage developed will be only equal to f f' volts.

The generator will not build up in large discrete increments as shown by the dotted lines in Fig. 2.15 (b). The flux can not change instantly, so that the indications of the voltmeter connected across the generator terminals will increase gradually and smoothly.

## 2.1.27 Critical Field Resistance

In Fig. 2.16, is represent a magnetisation curve AD, the stable voltage developed, when the field circuit resistance is equal to that represented by OD is equal to DG. If the field circuit resistance is increased and made equal to that represented by line OC, then the stable e.m.f. developed (induced) is equal to CC' which is less than DG. When the field circuit resistance is increased in such a way that the line represented by it becomes tangent to the straight line portion of the magnetisation curve (e.m.f. curve) as shown in Fig. 2.16 by line OB. The generator will stop building up the voltage. If the resistance of the field circuit is made more than the value represented by line OB it fails to build up, hence the value of resistance represented by line OB is called as critical field resistance and if the generator is to build up the voltage its field circuit resistance must be less than that represented by line OB.

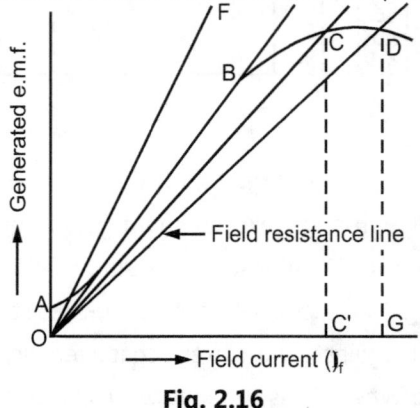

**Fig. 2.16**

## 2.1.28 Building up of Voltage in Series Generators

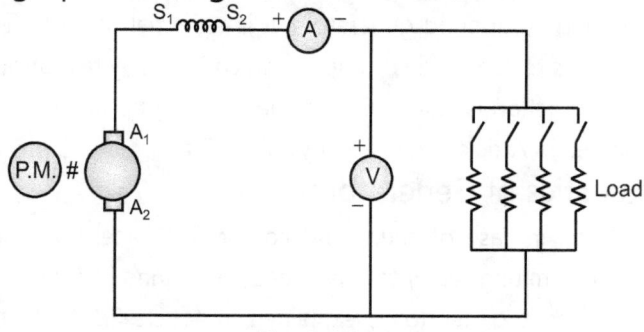

**Fig. 2.17 (a)**

D.C. series generators are the generators in which a field winding represented by letters $S_1$ and $S_2$, consisting of few turns of thick wire connected in series with armature w.r.t. load. In such generators, the field current, load current (current supplied to load and recorded by ammeter in this circuit) and armature current are same. It means unless there is load current there will be no field current.

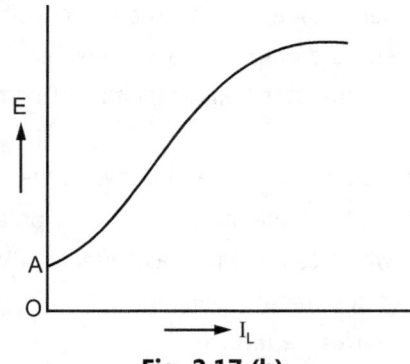

**Fig. 2.17 (b)**

The building up of voltage in this type of generator can be explained as follows :

When the armature is rotated at rated speed, there is a voltage induced in (equal to OA) armature this is due to residual magnetism of the field system, which may be 10 to 20 volts. Now when we connected some load by closing a switch, the electric circuit will be complete and the armature e.m.f will cause some current to flow through load, the same current passes through the field winding, which will produce some flux, the direction of the current through series field should be such as to produce a magnetic flux which will strengthen the residual flux. This increased flux increases the e.m.f. in the armature if the load resistance is further reduced by closing one more branch of load, the load current and hence the field current increases the flux, and further increase in the induced e.m.f. The process can be repeated, and when we plot a curve of $I_L$ or $I_F$ versus e.m.f., the shape of this characteristic is as shown in Fig. 2.17 (b), which is just similar to magnetisation characteristic of D.C. machine.

## 2.1.29 Building up of Voltage in D.C. Compound Generator

In case of self excited compound generators, it is essential that the field system should have residual flux, and it is the shunt field winding which is mainly responsible to build up the voltage. The building up action is just similar to the building up action of self excited shunt generates, as is explained in Article 2.1.26 and by Fig. 2.15 (b).

## 2.1.30 Characteristics of Generators

At no load condition in case of shunt and compound generators, how is the voltage buildup and which is the limiting factor to it is already explained in Article 2.1.26 similarly the building process for a series generator is explained in Article 2.1.27. In this article we will study about the nature of their characteristics. The different types of characteristics are

(i) External or load characteristic
(ii) Internal characteristic
(iii) Total characteristic.

(i) **External characeristic :** It is the graph or curve, that represents relation between the load current and terminal voltage, the speed being constant.

(ii) The internal characteristic is a graph or curve between the load current and induced e.m.f. the speed of the generator being maintained constant. The e.m.f. is equal to T.V. + $I_a R_a$ drop.

(iii) The total characteristic is a curve or graph between the load current and the flux per pole at constant speed of the generator. The flux per pole can be indirectly measured in terms of total e.m.f. which can be taken as equal to (T.V. + $I_a R_a$) + voltage drop due to demagnetising effect of armature reaction.

### 2.1.30.1 Characteristics of a Series Generator

In case of a series generator the armature, and field winding are connected in series w.r.t. load. The circuit diagram for determining the characteristics is shown in Fig. 2.18 (a), while the nature of the characteristics is shown in Fig. 2.18 (b).

When the armature of the generator is made to rotate at its rated speed, there is some voltage (equal to OA) developed in the armature of the generator due to residual magnetism, which will appear across $A_2 S_2$ and will be recorded by the voltmeter. When load is taken by closing one switch from the load circuit, this e.m.f. will circulate small current, which increase the field current and which in turn should produce a flux strengthening the residual flux, and so increases the induced e.m.f. in turn. Therefore, there is increase in field current which in turn increases flux and e.m.f. In this way, the field system build up its own magnetism. If the flux per pole is plotted against load current, the curve obtained is known as magnetisation curve (Total characteristic) as shown by curve No. 1. The curve starts at A,

OA represents residual magnetism. Due to the demagnetising effect of armature reaction actual curve obtained is not 1 but No. 2. The e.m.f. induced is proportional to flux at constant speed, so the curve represents to some other scale the e.m.f. induced it is also called as internal characteristic. The terminal voltage of the generator is e.m.f. Generated minus the drop of voltage in series field and armature of the generator.

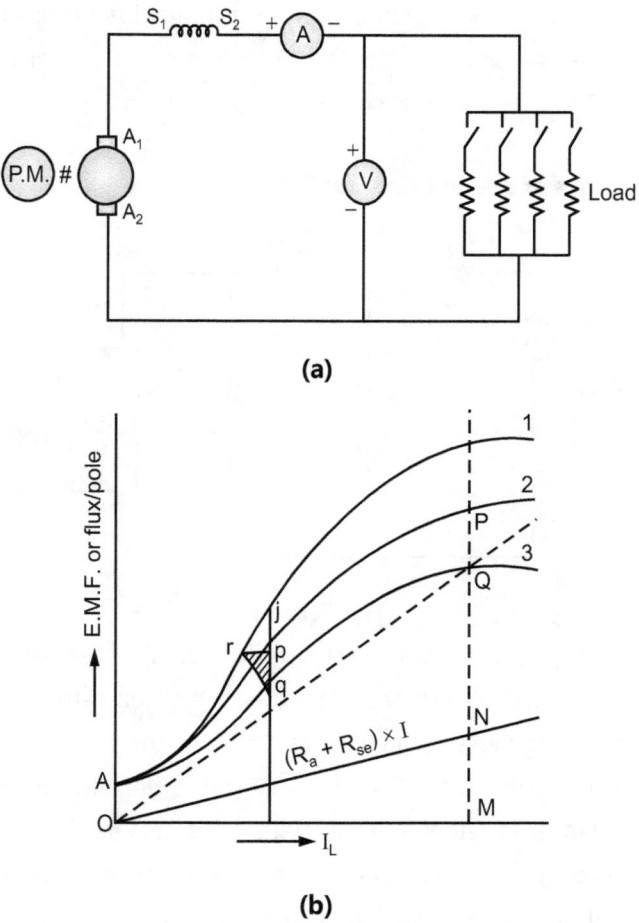

Fig. 2.18

At point M if load current is $I_L$, the e.m.f. induced $E_o$, the drop in resistance (Armature + field) = $I_L (R_a + R_{se})$.

The graph of $I_L$ V/s $I_L (R_a + R_{se})$ is a straight line, called as voltage drop line.

$$\text{Terminal voltage} = E_O - I_L (R_a + R_{se})$$
$$= MP - MN \text{ or } MP - PQ = MQ$$

Where PQ is equal to MN = $I_L (R_a + R_{se})$. Therefore, Q is a point on external characteristic represented by curve 3.

For any load current om, mp is the e.m.f. induced, pq = mn = $I_L (R_a + R_{se})$ then rp = extra field current required to neutralise demagnetising effect of armature reaction. For load current OM

$$\frac{MQ}{OM} = \frac{\text{Voltage across load}}{\text{Load current}} = \text{Load resistance in ohms.}$$

Hence, the slope of the line OQ represents the external load resistance, if OL is drawn tangential to the curve, the slope of this line will represent a critical resistance i.e. if the resistance of the load is more than this critical resistance the generator will not develop the voltage.

### 2.1.30.2 Characteristics of a Shunt Generator

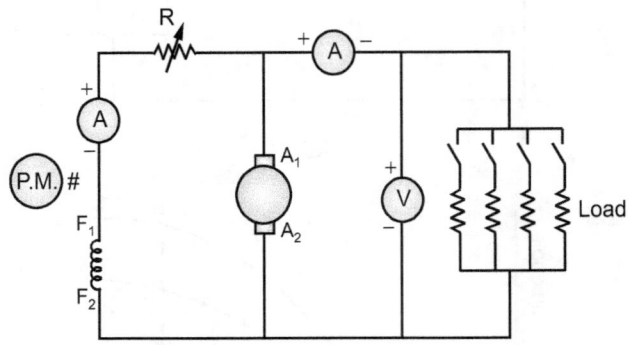

**Fig. 2.19 (a)**

For determining the characteristics of shunt (self excited) generator a circuit diagram as shown in Fig. 2.19 (a) is used. When the armature of the generator is rotated at its rated speed it build up the voltage as explained in Article 2.1.26, the value depends up on its field resistance. Let it be represented by OA (Fig. 2.19 (b)). When the generator is loaded by reducing load resistance in steps, the current supplied its load increases but the corresponding values of voltage across the terminals go on decreasing. The terminal voltage is stable up to normal load current, the field current is kept constant by changing resistance R in field circuit. The conditions are stable up to point C represented on the external or load characteristic. After point C, if the load current is further increased by decreasing the load resistance, the demagnetising effect of armature reaction and internal voltage drop ($I_a R_a$) becomes so important that a further decrease resistance causes a decrease in load current and the characteristic turns back, if we go on reducing the load resistance, at one instant the armature is short circuited and the external characteristic cut the current axis at point B as shown Fig. 2.19 (b).

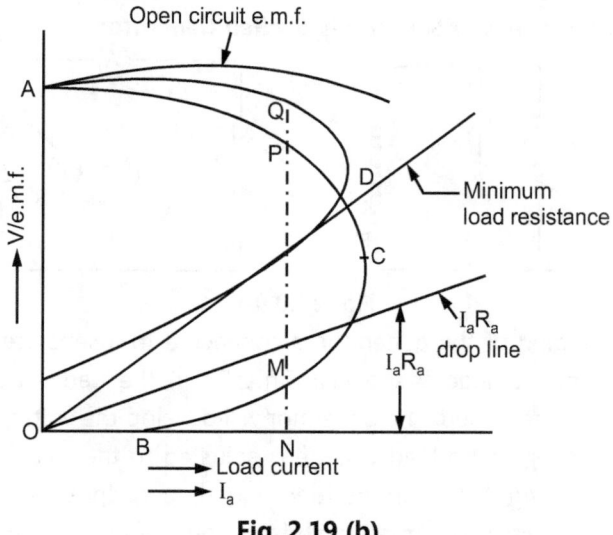

**Fig. 2.19 (b)**

If $I_aR_a$ drop as represented by $I_aR_a$ drop line is added at all points to the external characteristics we will get a characteristic representing $I_L$ V/s E called as internal characteristic. If to this internal characteristic a voltage drop equal to armature reaction is added we will get a total characteristic of self excited shunt generator.

If a line OD is drawn touching to internal characteristic as shown in Fig. 2.19 (b), it represents the minimum value of load resistance and hence is called as critical load resistance line. The meaning is that if the load resistance is less than the value represented by this line, the shunt generator will fail to develope the voltage i.e. load resistance value should be always more than the value represented by critical load resistance line for developing the voltage in a shunt generator.

In case of external characteristic, as the load current is increased, the terminal voltage of the shunt generator drops, following are the reasons responsible :

(i) As the load current increases, the voltage drop in armature also increases because $I_a = I_L + I_{sh}$.

(ii) As the load current increases, armature current also increases, because it is supplied by armature, the armature reaction, which is the effect produced by armature current on the main flux (flux produced by field) weaken the field, which reduce the generated e.m.f. itself.

(iii) The drop of volts due to (i) and (ii) above result in a decreased value of field current because T.V. across field winding is reduced, which further reduces the flux per pole, which in turn decreases the induced e.m.f. and hence the terminal voltage.

## 2.1.30.3 Load Characteristics of Separately Excited Generator

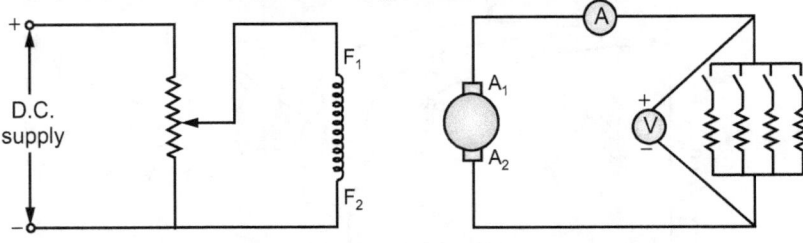

**Fig. 2.20 (a)**

When the field winding of the generator is connected to a separate D.C. supply source and armature is connected to load as shown in Fig. 2.20 (a), the load or external characteristic for such a generator is determined. The generator will develop the voltage when its armature is rotated by prime-mover, its no load voltage is adjusted to the value of induced e.m.f. at rated speed. Then keeping field current (unchanged) and speed constant. The load is connected across the terminals of armature and the corresponding readings of load current and terminal voltage are used to plot an external characteristic. To this when added $I_a R_a$ drop we get the internal characteristic. To the internal characteristic when a effect of armature reaction is added we get the total characteristic for separately excited generator.

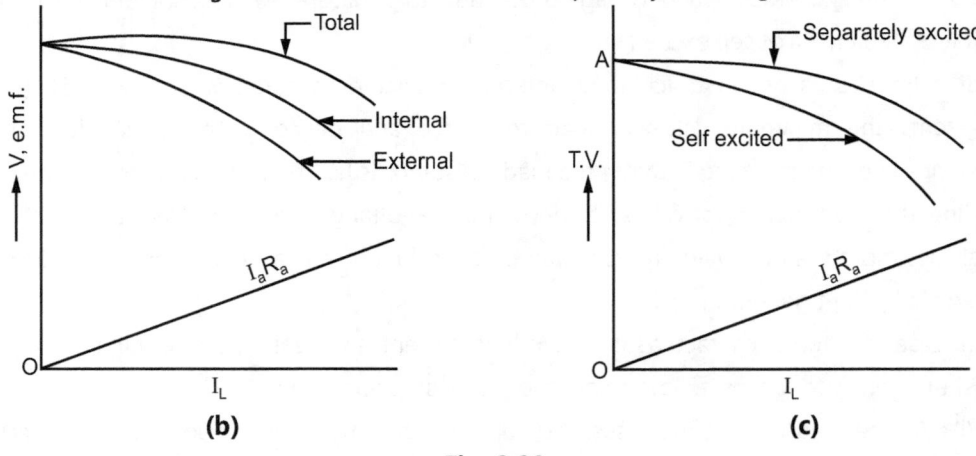

**Fig. 2.20**

To understand the difference in the characteristics of a self excited and separately excited generator. Two characteristics obtained on the same generator with their no load voltage equal to Oa are shown with the same scale in Fig. 2.20 (c); in which it is observed that the load characteristic for a self excited shunt generator is more dropping than the separately excited generator. The reason being that for self excited generator the voltage drop is due to the three reasons as explain in Article 2.1.31.2, while in case of separately excited generator only first two reasons are responsible for voltage drop and the third one is absent, because flux produced by field winding remains constant through out the experiment.

## 2.1.30.4 Characteristics of Compound Generator

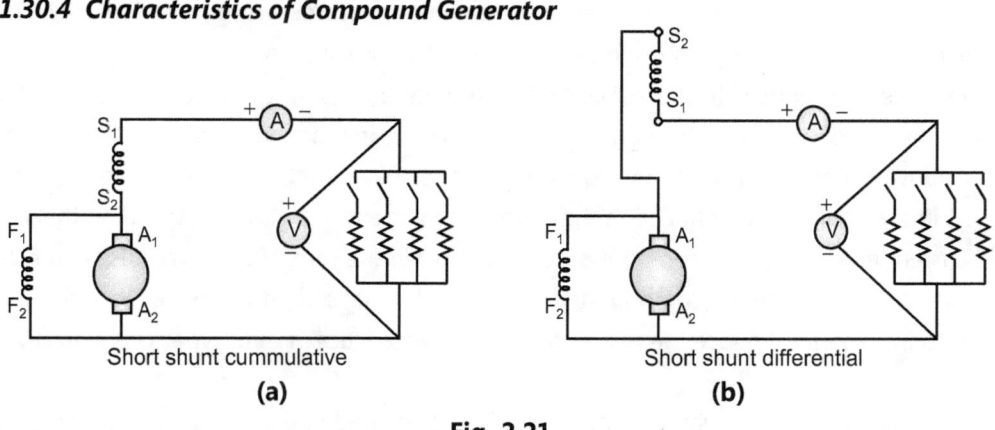

Fig. 2.21

In case of shunt generator the T.V. reduces as the load is increased, due to this, shunt generators are not suitable for electric circuits which need constant voltage. Lamps are much affected by reduction in applied voltage. Hence, we need a generator that will produce constant voltage. It can be made possible by placing on the field core a few turns which are connected in series with either the load or the armature. The direction of current through them is made such as to produce a flux aiding the main flux, when the generator is delivering load current. The flux produced by these turns will depend up on the load current (or armature current) by proper design of turns the flux produced by series turns can be made such as to cause a additional induced e.m.f. to be developed in armature winding which will compensate the voltage drop due to armature resistance and due to armature reaction effect. Due to this the T.V. will remain constant at load, hence the value of the field current will not decrease and it will not reduce the flux causing cause any further decrease in e.m.f. due to this reason. Hence, the terminal voltage remains substantially constant from no load to full load or even it may rise in some cases as the load increases.

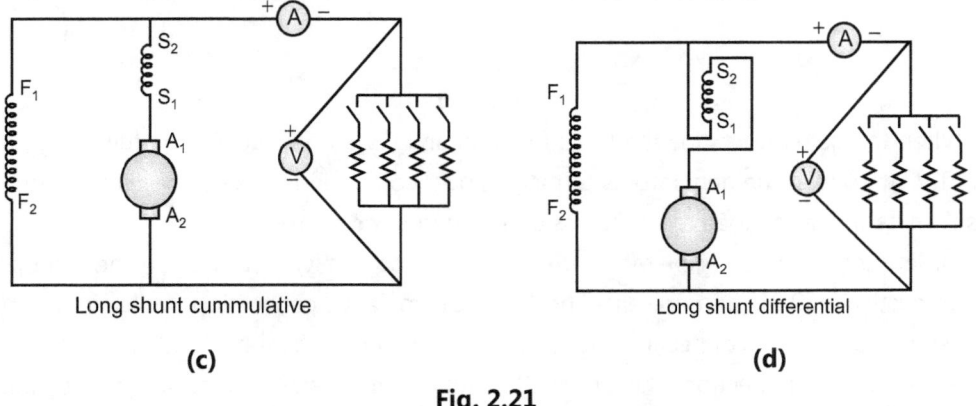

Fig. 2.21

The shunt field be connected directly across the armature as shown in Fig. 2.21 (a) in which case it is called as short shunt. If the shunt field winding is connected across the generator terminal out side the series field, the generator is long shunt. With short shunt connection, current flowing through series field winding is the load current, while in case of long shunt connection current flowing through series field winding is the armature current. Hence, in the short shunt connection the shunt field current is slightly greater than the shunt field current in a long-shunt compound generator, while the series field current is slightly less in short (equal to $I_L$ shunt compound generator, while it is slightly greater in long shunt (equal to $I_L$) generator, hence the nature of load characteristics in both types is practically the same.

By providing series turns if we obtain the T.V. at no load equal to T.V. at full-load of the generator, then the machine is called as flat compounded. It is seen that first the voltage increases as load is increased, and then it starts decreasing, reaching the same value of voltage on full-load as that at no load, it is due to the saturation of the field system, the series m.m.f. (amp, turns) do not increase the same amount of flux as it increases at lower load currents.

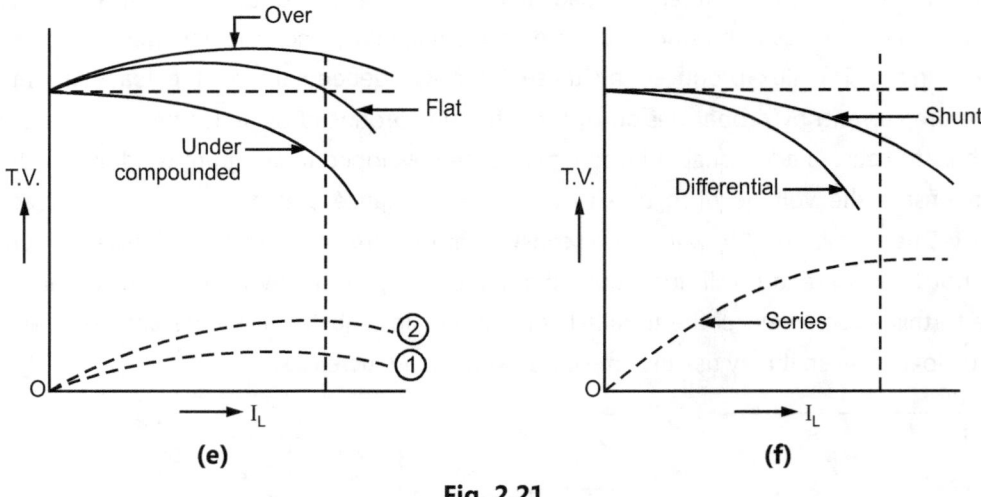

**Fig. 2.21**

When the generator is loaded to its full-load and if we obtained T.V. on full-load greater than T.V. at no load the generator is termed as over compounded. When the voltage on f.l. is less than its T.V. at no load it is called as under compound generator.

Under compounded generator are not used generally; because of their dropping characteristic Fig. 2.21 (a) represents short shunt cumulative connection; while Fig. 2.21 (c) a long shunt cumulative connection, Fig. 2.21 (b) short shunt differential and Fig. 2.21 (d) long shunt differential connection while in Fig. 2.21 (e) are the characteristics obtained by adding shunt and series characteristic, the nature depends up on the m.m.f. (or flux produced) developed by series field, so that we can obtain level compounded, over compounded or under compounded characteristic.

In Fig. 2.21 (f) the resultant characteristics is obtained by subtracting series characteristics and is called as differential characteristic.

### 2.1.30.5 Generator Fails to Develop the Voltage

If a generator fails to develop the voltage it may be due to one or more reasons as listed below :

(i) In case of self excited generators, there may not be residual flux present in the field system. The remedy is to pass a D.C. current through the field system (flushing action) for some time so as to develop the residual flux.

(ii) The direction of the current flowing through the field may be such as to buck-up the residual flux.

The remedy is to change the direction of the current flowing through the field circuit so that the flux produced by it strengthen the residual flux.

(iii) Total resistance of the field circuit may be greater than the critical field resistance. In this case, reduce the field circuit resistance till the generator developes the voltage is the remedy.

(iv) The load resistance may be less than the value represented by critical load resistance line. Increase the load resistance till the generator developes the voltage is the remedy.

(v) The brushes may not be making contact with the commutator resulting in to high resistance from commutator to brush.

Adjust the tension (spring) on the brushes so that they make the contact with the commutator, check for the seating of brushes, and make it proper.

(vi) The speed at which the armature is rotated may be less than the critical speed for the generator.

Increase the speed of the prime-mover and make it equal to the rated speed so that the generator will develop the voltage.

(vii) In case of series generator if the load resistance is greater than the critical load resistance value it will fail to develope the voltage.

In this case, reduce the load resistance till the generator developes the voltage is the remedy.

(viii) In case of separately excited generators or self excited generators the field circuit or rheostat in the field circuit may be open.

Checking of field circuit continuity and rheostat continuity and making proper repair is the remedy.

## 2.1.31 Losses in D.C. Machine

D.C. machines are used for converting one form of energy in to other form i.e. D.C. motors convert electrical energy into mechanical energy and D.C. Generators convert mechanical energy into electrical energy. This conversion of energy does not take place at 100 per cent efficiency. Some part of energy is utilised by the machine itself as losses and is converted into heat. The loss of energy in D.C. machines will take place in

(i) Electric circuit carrying current

(ii) Magnetic circuit experiencing alternating magnetisation.

(iii) Friction between different parts.

## 2.1.32 Classification of Losses in D.C. Machines

The different types of losses taking place in a D.C. machine can be classified as follows:

**(a) Copper losses:** These are the losses taking place, when the current flow through electrical circuit i.e. windings which have their own resistance, it is equal to product of square of current and resistance of that electrical circuit. They can be further divided as:

(i) Armature copper loss

(ii) Series field copper loss

(iii) Shunt field copper loss

(iv) Commutating and compensating winding copper loss

(v) Loss taking place due to brush-resistance.

**(b) Iron losses:** These are the losses taking place in armature core, armature slots, field core etc. due to the varying magnetisation and called as

(i) Eddy current losses and

(ii) Hysteresis losses.

**(c) Mechanical losses:** These losses are developed, when the armature starts rotating; they will take place due to (i) bearing friction, (ii) brush friction, (iii) air friction, to the rotation of armature. These losses are also called as friction and windage losses.

**(d) Stray-load losses:** These losses consists of (i) increased iron-losses on load. (ii) development of eddy current losses in copper conductors, (iii) when the armature coil undergoes commutation, the effect is to cause additional losses in armature teeth, armature core and armature winding.

These losses are negligible in case of small machines but for large machines or uncompensated machine the stray losses are taken as one percent of the output rating of the machine.

Of these losses, the copper losses depend up on the current and resistance, the current flowing through armature and series field, compensating winding inter pole winding varies in accordance with the load condition, hence the copper losses taking place in these windings are called as variable losses. The copper losses taking place in the shunt field winding remains almost constant from no load to full-load and hence is called as a constant loss.

The armature Cu loss is given by $I_a^2 R_a$ where $I_a$ is armature current and $R_a$ is the armature resistance. The series field Cu loss = $I_{se}^2 R_{se}$ where $I_{se}$ is series field current and $R_{se}$ is it's resistance in ohms.

Copper loss in interpole winding = $I_a^2 R_i$ and copper loss in compensating winding = $I_a^2 R_c$

Where $R_i$ and $R_c$ are resistances of interpole winding and compensating winding.

The shunt field copper loss = $I_{sh}^2 R_{sh}$ or it is equal to $V \times I_{sh}$

Where $I_{sh}$ is shunt field current, and $R_{sh}$ is shunt field resistance.

The brush contact loss is equal to the product of voltage drop in brushes multiplied by current flowing through them. When brush drop is given as volts / brush, then total voltage drop for two brushes is to be considered.

The iron losses are constant losses when the load on machine is constant. When iron losses are added to mechanical losses they are called as stray-losses.

To the stray-losses when shunt field copper loss of a shunt machine or compound machine is added, it is called as constant losses for that machine.

**(b) Iron losses:** When the armature of a D.C. machine is made to rotate inside the flux produced by field system, core material being a conducting material, there will be induced e.m.f. in the armature core it-self, also the armature core is subjected to magnetic reversal after passing one pair of poles, the frequency of magnetic flux reversal is given by $f = \dfrac{PN}{120}$ where P = Number of poles of the machine, N = speed of the machine in r.p.m. i.e. the eddy current and hysteresis loss takes place in the armature core.

**(i) Hysteresis loss:** For understanding how a hysteresis loss is developed in the armature, consider a magnetic material wound with a coil connected to a source of alternating e.m.f. as shown in Fig. 2.22 the molecules of magnetic material can be assumed as tiny magnets, arranged in arbitrary maner, when magnetising force is applied, in half cycle they orient in North-South direction while in the next half cycle they will orient in South-North direction, while orienting there takes place a inter-molecular friction, and some energy is wasted in this process which is converted into heat and the loss of power taking place in this process is termed as hysteresis loss.

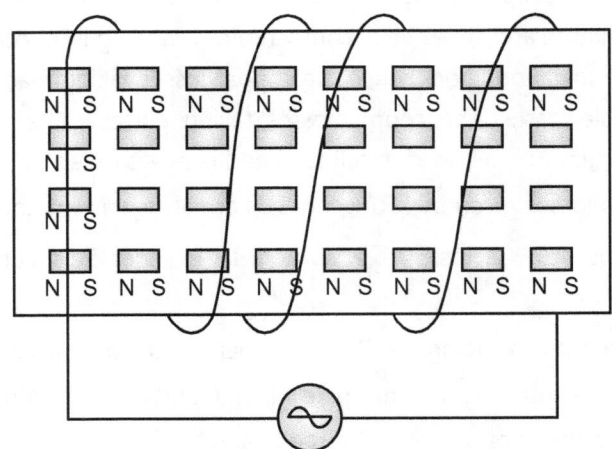

**Fig. 2.22**

It depends up on the volume of the core, the frequency of magnetic flux reversal, the flux density, Dr. Charles Steinmetz suggested an empirical formulae based on his test results as,

$$\text{Hysteresis loss} = \eta \, v \, f \, (B_{max})^{1.6} \text{ watts}$$

Where $\eta$ = constant, known as steinmetz coefficient, or hysterisis coefficient, or hysterisis coefficient for that material.

$$V = \text{Volume of material in m}^3,$$

$B_{max}$ is maximum flux density in wb/m² or Tesla.

Value of $\eta$ for silicon steel (4 % silicon) = 275

Value of $\eta$ for sheet steel = 500

**(ii) Eddy current loss:** As the armature core rotates in the magnetic field produced by field system, e.m.f. is induced in it, as it is a conductor of electricity. If the core would have been a solid mass (Fig. 2.23 (a)) the current paths would be short and of large cross-section, hence large amount of current would be induced in the armature iron, this will cause a large power loss, resulting in to over heating of armature, though the machine may not be loaded. By laminating the armature core (Fig. 2.23 (b)) the paths of these currents are broken up by the insulating effects of the oxides on the surface of laminations, which results in to reduced magnitudes of eddy currents Fig. 2.23 (b) shows that the length of the path for eddy current is in direction of the laminations, while cross-section is limited to the thickness of lamination. Hence, the resistance of the path is also increased. Hence, the eddy currents are reduced due to which power loss due to its effect also greatly reduced.

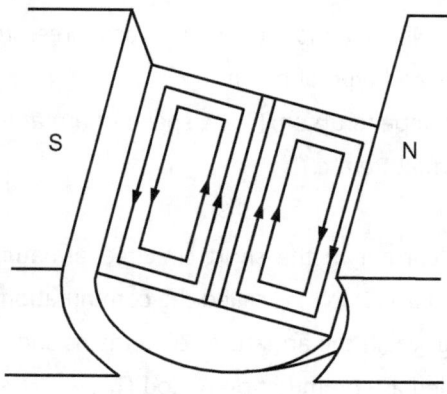

**Fig. 2.23 (a)**

The eddy current losses taking place in a D.C. machine are given by

Eddy current loss = $KB_{max} f^2 t^2 v$ watts

where,
$B_{max}$ = Maximum flux density in tesla
$f$ = frequency of flux reversal
$t$ = thickness of lamination in m
$V$ = volume of core material $m^3$

They are further reduced by using high resistivity material such as silicon steel.

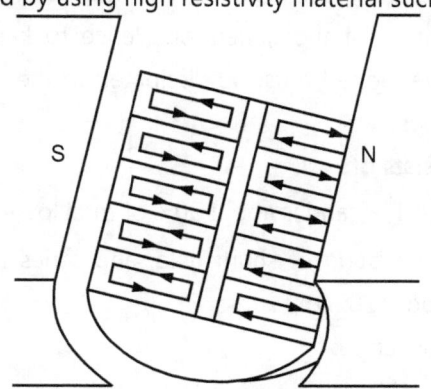

Armature with insulated laminations
**Fig. 2.23 (b)**

(c) **Mechanical losses** : These losses are developed due to rotation of armature and called as friction and windage losses, and consist of power loss due to :

1. Friction in bearings when the armature rotates.
2. Friction of brush on the commutator.
3. Opposition of air in the gap between field and armature to the rotation of armature.

The bearing friction losses depend upon (i) the thrust on bearing, (ii) speed of shaft, (iii) coefficient of friction between bearing and shaft.

The brush friction loss will depend up on (i) brush pressure, (ii) peripheral speed of commutator, and (iii) quality and type of brush.

The windage losses will depend up on, (i) the speed of armature (peripheral), (ii) diameter of armature (iii) length of armature etc.

### 2.1.33 Commutation

The process by which current in the short circuited armature coil is reversed while it crosses the magnetic neutral axis (MNA) is called the commutation.

The short period during which the armature coil remains short-circuited and this reversal of current takes place is called as commutation period ($T_C$).

### 2.1.34 Losses in D.C. Generators

The losses taking place in a D.C. generator are classified as :

(i) Copper losses.

(ii) Iron losses.

(iii) Mechanical losses.

(iv) Stray load losses.

The energy wasted as losses in the machine is converted into heat, which is responsible for increasing the temperature of the generator. Hence to keep the temperature, within permissible limit the heat developed must be dissipated to the surrounding atmosphere by radiation, convection methods.

**(i) The copper losses consists of:**

(a) Armature copper loss $I_a^2 R_a$ and is about 30% of total losses at full load.

(b) Field copper loss, consisting of shunt field, and series field Cu-loss, the total field copper losses are about 20% of f.l. loss.

**(ii) Iron losses:** They are divided as:

(a) Hysteresis loss $\propto B_m^{1.6} f V$ watts

(b) Eddy current loss $\propto B_m^2 f^2 t^2 V$ watts

The total amount of iron losses is nearly 30 to 35% of total loss.

**(iii) Mechanical losses consists of:**

(a) Frictional losses

(b) Windage loss

The total mechanical losses are nearly 10 to 20% of total losses.

**(iv)** The stray load losses are nearly 1% of rated out put in case of uncompensated machines, and large size machines.

## Scheme of losses in D.C. Generator:

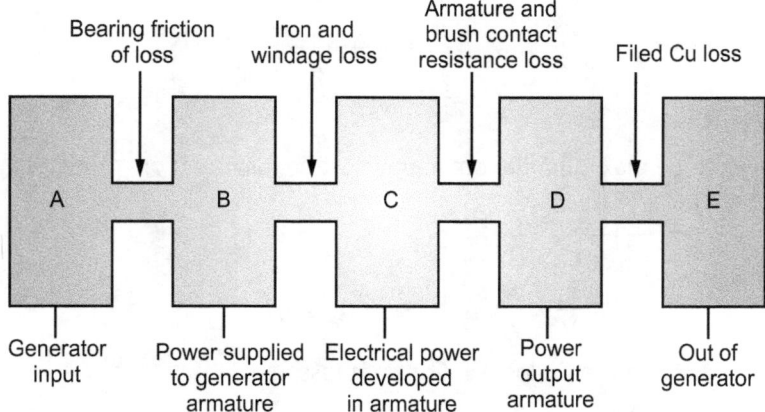

**Fig. 2.24**

### Efficiency of Generator:

(1) Commercial efficiency = E/A = $\dfrac{\text{Generator output in watts}}{\text{Generator input in watts}}$

(2) Electrical efficiency = E/C = $\dfrac{\text{Generator output in watts}}{\text{Electrical power developed by armature in watts}}$

(3) Mechanical efficiency = C/A = $\dfrac{\text{Electrical power developed by armature in watts}}{\text{Generator input in watts}}$

## 2.1.35 Condition for Maximum Efficiency of a Generator

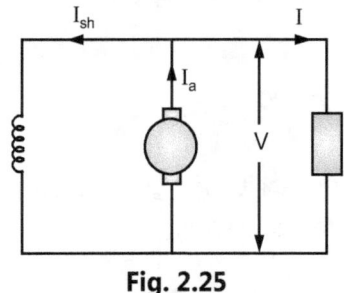

**Fig. 2.25**

For finding condition of maximum efficiency, we will consider a D.C. shunt generator for simplicity. Let I amps. be the load current supplied by it at a T.V. of V volts.

Then generator output = VI watts.

If $I_a$ = Armature current and $I_{sh}$ = shunt field current,

then $I_a = I + I_{sh}$

The generator input = Output + Losses

= $VI + I_a^2 R_a$ + Constant losses

Let $W_c$ = Constant losses

and $I_a \cong I$ because $I_{sh}$ is negligible in comparison to I

∴ Generator input = $VI + I^2 R_a + W_c$.

and efficiency, $\eta = \dfrac{\text{Output}}{\text{Input}}$

or
$$\eta = \frac{VI}{VI + I^2 R_a + W_c}$$

or
$$\eta = \frac{I}{I + \left(\frac{I^2 R_a}{VI} + \frac{W_c}{VI}\right)}$$

for efficiency to be maximum denominator must be minimum or $\frac{d\eta}{dI}$ must be = 0

i.e.
$$\frac{d}{dI}\left(\frac{I^2 R_a}{VI} + \frac{W_c}{VI}\right) = 0$$

or
$$\frac{R_a}{V} - \frac{W_c}{VI^2} = 0 \quad \text{or} \quad I^2 R_a = W_c$$

i.e. Armature Cu loss = Constant loss.

or
$$I = \sqrt{\frac{W_c}{R_a}} \text{ for maximum efficiency}$$

## 2.1.36 Generator Regulation

The regulation of a direct current generator is the change in voltage when the load is reduced from rated load to zero, expressed in percentage of rated load voltage. For separately excited generators, the excitation shall remain constant during the test and for self excited generators the resistance in the field circuit shall remain constant.

In brief, the regulation of a generator can be defined as the change in terminal voltage, when its full load is thrown off, keeping excitation and speed constant.

If      V = T.V. on full load (Rated T.V.)
       E = No load voltage.
Then,    Regulation = E − V
and    % Regulation = $\frac{E - V}{V} \times 100$

From regulation we are in a position to determine, the ability of a generator to maintain its voltage, under load, and its suitability for constant potential service.

## 2.1.37 Applications of D.C. Generators

As the characteristics of different types of generator are different, their field of applications depending up on their characteristics are also different.

**(a) Series Generators:**

In case of series generators, the terminal voltage rises as the load current is increased i.e. they have a rising characteristic. Due to this rising characteristic series generators can not be used to supply power load. They can be used as boosters to maintain line voltage constant. They are also used for arc-lamps. It can also be used as a constant current generator and used for charging batteries by constant current method.

## (b) Shunt Generators:

As the terminal voltage of shunt generators remain almost constant from no load to full load, they can be used for ordinary lighting and power supply They can be used for charging, batteries by constant voltage method. Separately excited shunt generators are generally used for electroplating, electro-refining of metals, they are also used as boosters and for lighting purposes.

## (c) Compound Generators:

Compound generators can be so designed, that they can maintain almost constant voltage over a large range of load, hence they are used where large fluctuations are there in the load system. They are also used for power supply. They are also used as compensators of line drop in electric traction. Over compounded compound generators are used where load is located at a considerable (long) distance from the generator. As the load increases the rise in induced e.m.f. compensates the voltage drop in line, maintaining the T.V. at load constant.

Flat compounded (level compounded) generators are generally used in isolated plants such as hotels and office buildings.

# 2.2 D.C. MOTOR

D.C. motors are the electrical machines which when connected to D.C. supply, convert electrical energy into mechanical energy. The basic principle of any motor is that when a current carrying conductor is placed in magnetic field it will experience a force. Instead of one conductor a turn or coil is placed in magnetic field and if it carries the current, equal and opposite forces will be exerted on the two sides of the coil. This couple of forces cause a torque on the coil making it to move. The torque developed on a coil is not constant at all positions, it may be zero at some positions also as explained below. To avoid such zero torque positions if number of coils distributed uniformly and carrying the current are placed in magnetic field, we get almost constant torque. Hence, the construction of armature of a D.C. motor and generator are identical or we can say that actually a D.C. generator when connected across a D.C. supply will work as a D.C. motor.

## 2.2.1 Principle of Working

For understanding the principle of working of a D.C. motor, we will consider a two pole field system, which produces uniform flux in the air gap. In the air gap, a coil consisting of single turn mounted on the shaft, free to rotate inside the flux is placed. Let the direction of the current flowing through the coil be such, that it is into plane of paper in the conductor under the influence of N pole and it is up the plane of paper into the conductor under the influence of S pole. In Fig. 2.26 (a) is the direction of the magnetic flux when conductors carrying current are not placed in it. Fig. 2.26 (b) and Fig. 2.26 (c) represent the direction of the magnetic flux when current flows in to the plane and when current flows up the plane of paper. Fig. 2.26 (d) represents the combined effect when a coil carrying current is placed in magnetic field, here it is observed that two equal and opposite forces each equal to BIL Nw are developed on the two conductors of the coil, these two forces form a couple of forces, as there is a perpendicular distance between them a torque equal to BIL X perpendicular distance is set up on the coil and it will be maximum.

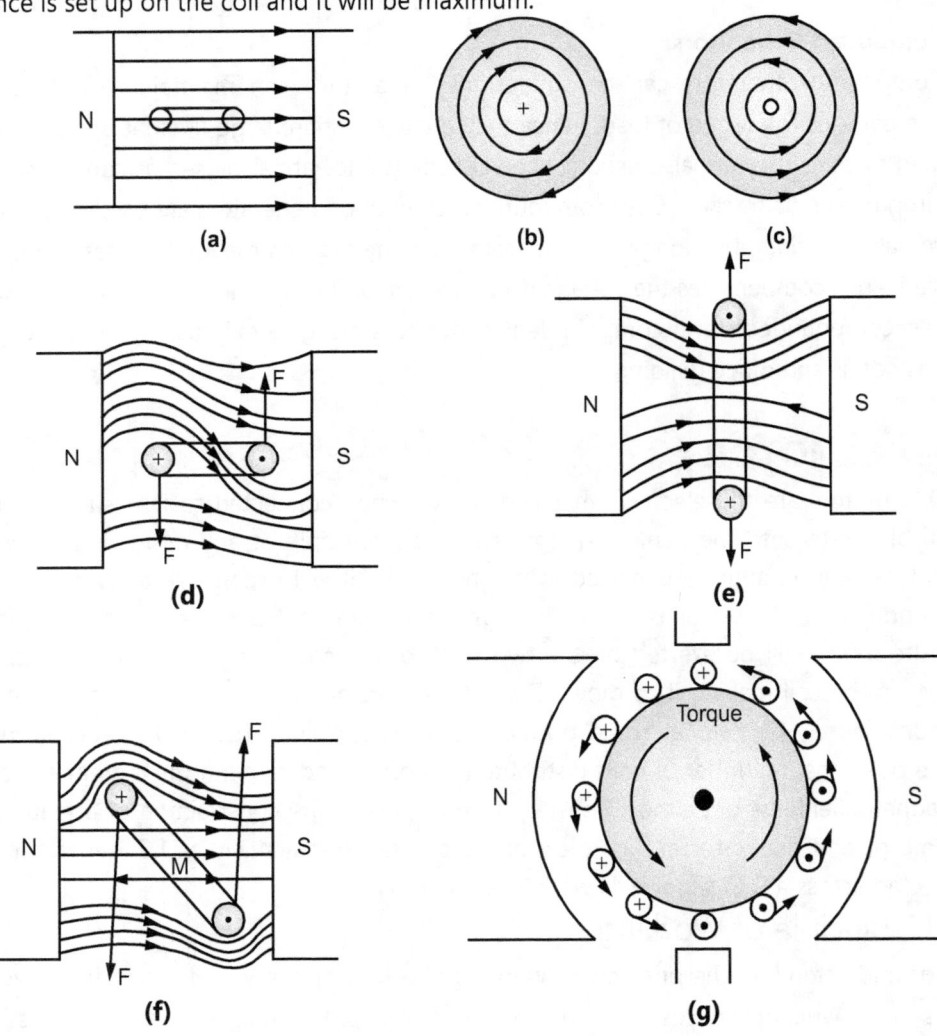

**Fig. 2.26**

Let the coil have attained a position as shown in Fig. 2.26 (e), the magnitude of the forces exerted is again equal, but as they act in same line, the perpendicular distance between them is zero hence the torque produced is zero, and the coil will not move further from this position. Now if the direction of current flowing through the coil is changed, and the coil is moved beyond this dead centre (zero torque position) as in Fig. 2.26 (f) a torque is again developed due to the two forces acting at a perpendicular distance equal to M; which tends to continue to turn the coil in the anti-clockwise direction till again a dead centre is reached. Hence, we can conclude that the torque produced by a single coil is not continuous. The dead centres can be eliminated by providing say two coils at right angles to each other, but still the torque produced will not be uniform. To develop uniform and constant torque in one direction, we need number of coils uniformly distributed and carrying current in the magnetic field, free to rotate, and there should take place a change of direction of current flowing through each coil when it passes dead centres; This is achieved with help of armature which consists of number of coils uniformly distributed, and the commutator serves the purpose of changing the direction of flow of current when a coil passes from dead centre.

In Fig. 2.26 (g) number of coils placed on the armature and carrying current are shown. The torque developed due to flow of current through these coil is anticlock-wise and will have no dead centres, hence the armature will continue to rotate till there is flow of current through the coils, and they are in magnetic field. This is the principle of working of a D.C. motor.

## 2.2.2 Back e.m.f

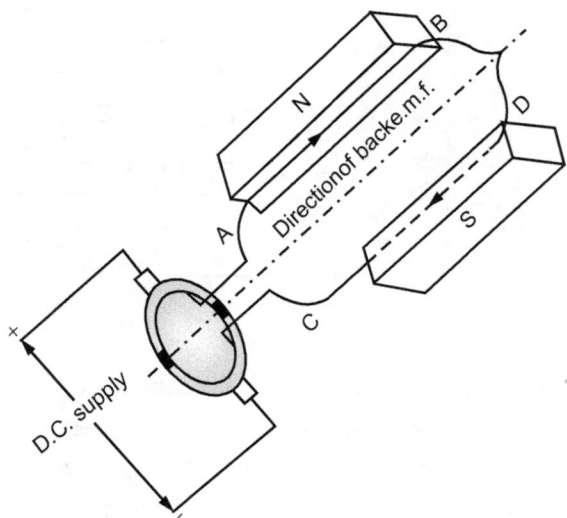

**Fig. 2.27 (a)**

To understand the meaning of back e.m.f. a two pole machine (poles being shown as permanent magnet for simplicity) with only one coil on its armature consisting of two armature conductors AB and CD is shown to be connected from a D.C. supply, At the instant represented, let the current in conductor AB be from A to B and in conductor CD it will be D to C or we can say in conductor AB into the plane of paper while in conductor CD up the plane of paper. The magnitude of current flowing through each conductor being the same and as they are placed in the same magnetic field, equal and opposite forces will be exerted (F = BIL Nw) on the conductors AB and CD, the direction of which can be determined by application of Faraday's left hand rule. The forces form a couple developing the torque on the coil and will make it to rotate in anti-clockwise direction. When the coil moves in the magnetic field it will cut the flux produced by field system, hence there will be induced e.m.f. developed in the conductors AB and CD. The magnitude of the induced e.m.f. will be same as we determine for a generator, as it is the generator action that will cause the induced e.m.f. in the conductors hence its value will be given by

$$E = \frac{\phi ZNP}{60A} \text{ volts,}$$

where $\phi$, Z, N, P and A have the same meanings as that is for a generator. The direction of this induced e.m.f. can be determined by application of Fleming's right hand rule. By application of this rule to conductors AB and CD it is seen that direction of induced e.m.f. or induced current in conductor AB is up the plane or from B to A, and in conductor CD it is in to the plane or from C to D, which is just reverse to the supply conditions. As this e.m.f acts in opposition to supply voltage it is termed as 'back e.m.f.'

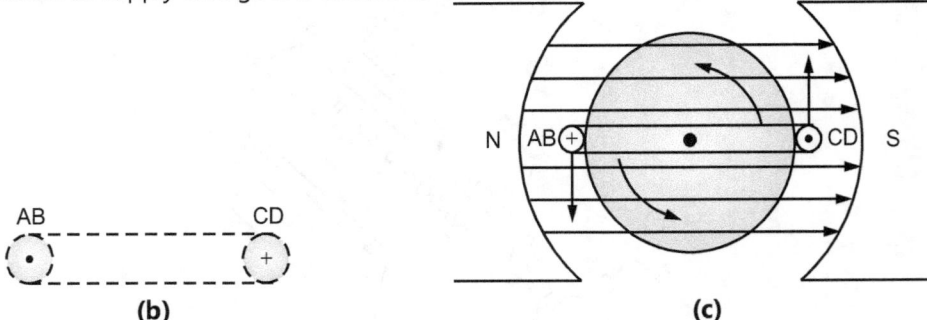

Fig. 2.27

Hence, the resultant voltage acting across the armature in case of a D.C. motor is always equal to supply voltage minus back e.m.f. The back e.m.f. is represented by letter $E_b$.

∴ V – $E_b$ = resultant voltage across armature terminals. As the resultant voltage is utilised as voltage drop in armature resistance it is represented by $I_a R_a$.

∴ V – $E_b$ = $I_a R_a$, $I_a$ being armature current and $R_a$ its resistance in ohms. Fig. 2.27 (a) represents the direction of current flowing through the armature conductors Fig. 2.27 (b), represents the direction of force or torque developed on the coil causing to rotate in anticlockwise direction Fig. 2.27 (e) represents the direction of the induced current. The direction of the induced current is also represented by an arrow in Fig 2.27 (a), which shows that direction of back e.m.f. or induced current is in opposition to supply voltage.

## 2.2.3 Difference in Working of a D.C. Machine as Generator and as a Motor

For understanding the difference in working first of all, we will consider, the case when a D.C. machine is working as a generator. In Fig. 2.28 (a) one pole (N) of the D.C. machine is shown, the armature conductors lying-under this pole are shown.

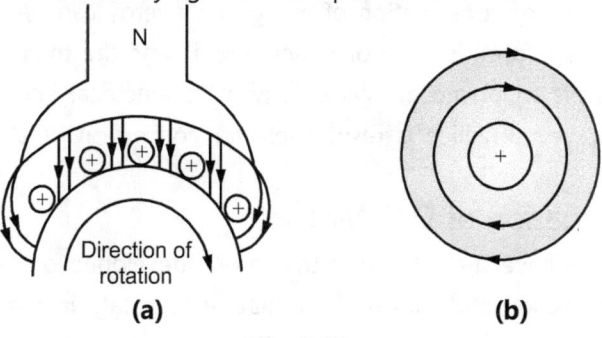

**Fig. 2.28**

Let now the armature be rotated in clock-wise direction by application of mechanical energy to its shaft, it will cause a induced e.m.f. to be developed in armature conductors, the direction of this induced e.m.f. is determined by application of Fleming's right hand rule, it is found to be as into the plane of paper. Fig. 2.28 (b) represents the direction of the field produced by flow of current in conductors under the N pole. When the generator is loaded the current flowing through the armature conductors set up there own field as shown in Fig. 2.28 (b). The combined action of the two fluxes will be as shown in Fig. 2.29 (a) in which it is seen that the flux is crowded on the right side of every conductor lying under the N pole. The effect is to set up a force on the conductors in an anti-clockwise direction, this force is called as a backward force or magnetic drag. The prime mover has to work against this drag, in case of generators the work done by prime mover in over coming this opposition and maintaining the speed is converted into electrical energy.

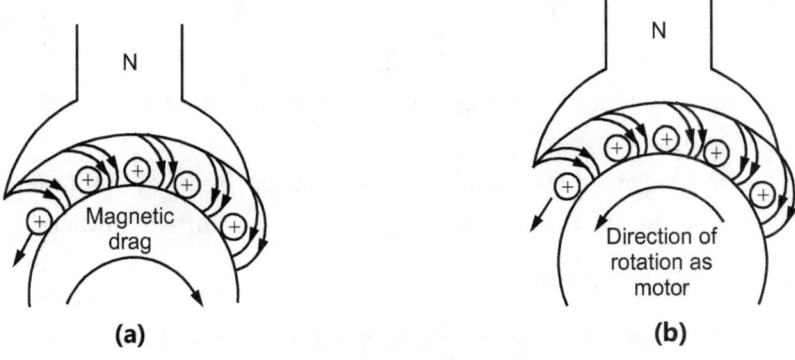

**Fig. 2.29**

Now suppose that the prime mover is disconnected, but the current flowing through the armature conductors is maintained the same as it was when the machine was working as generator. The conductors will experience a force again causing the machine to rotate in anti-clockwise direction, developing a torque, which will produce a mechanical power output at the shaft. In this case, the electrical energy fed to the motor is converted in to mechanical energy. As per principle of conservation of energy no energy can be destroyed, it can be converted in to another form. In case of generators, it was the magnetic drag which was responsible for conversion of mechanical energy in to electrical energy, while in case of motors it is the back e.m.f. which is responsible for conversion of electrical energy in to mechanical energy.

## 2.2.4 Torque Equation of D.C. Motor

**(a)** In Article 2.2.1, we have seen that it is the torque developed on armature conductors, which acts in one direction and makes the armature to rotate in the direction of torque developed. For finding the torque equation of a D.C. motor we will assume that the motor is having P = Number of poles, Z = Number of total armature conductors, $\phi$ = Total flux per pole, L = Length of each armature conductors in m, $I_a$ = Total armature current, A = Number of parallel paths of armature winding.

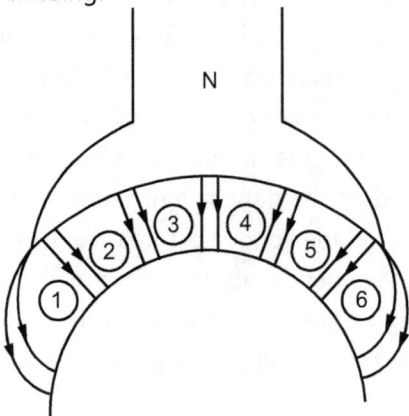

**Fig. 2.30**

Let the armature conductors be equally spaced on armature with a spacing between adjustment conductors = X m.

The total flux $\phi$ be divided into number of fluxes $\phi_1, \phi_2, \phi_3, \ldots \phi_6$ embracing conductors number 1, 2, 3 ... 6 under the N pole, respectively. The current flowing through each conductor will be equal to $\frac{I_a}{A}$ amps.

The force acting on each armature conductors is given by F = BIL Nw.

Hence, force acting on conductor No. 1 = $B_1 \times \dfrac{I_a}{A} \times LN_w$

where, $B_1$ is the flux density across conductor number 1 and its value will be = $\dfrac{\phi I}{x \times L}$.

∴ Force on conductor No. 1 = $\dfrac{\phi_1}{xL} \times \dfrac{I_a}{A} \times L = \dfrac{\phi_1 I_A}{x A}$ Nw ... (2.1)

Similarly force acting on conductor No. 2

$$= \dfrac{\phi_2 \times I_a}{x A} \quad \text{... (2.2)}$$

Force on conductor No. 3 = $\dfrac{\phi_3 I_a}{x A}$ ... (2.3)

∴ Total tangential force on all the conductors lying under one pole

$$= \dfrac{\phi_1 I_a}{x A} + \dfrac{\phi_2 I_a}{x A} + \dfrac{\phi_3 I_a}{x A}$$

$$= \dfrac{I_a}{x A} [\phi_1 + \phi_2 + \phi_3 \ldots] \text{ but } \phi_1 + \phi_2 + \phi_3 + \ldots = \phi$$

Hence, total force on all conductors under one pole

$$= \dfrac{\phi I_a}{x A} \text{ Newtons}$$

If     r = Radius of armature, the torque due to this force

$$= F \times r$$

$$= \dfrac{\phi I_a}{x A} \times r$$

The value of     $x = \dfrac{2\pi r}{Z}$

∴     Torque = $\dfrac{\phi I_a}{\dfrac{2\pi r}{Z} \times A} \times r$

or     Torque = $\dfrac{\phi Z I_a}{2\pi \times A}$

∴ Torque due to all conductors lying under all the P poles = $\dfrac{\phi Z I_a}{2\pi A} \times P$ mN.

or Torque developed by a D.C. motor = $0.159 \dfrac{\phi Z I_a P}{A}$ mN

or     Torque developed = $\dfrac{0.159}{9.81} \dfrac{\phi Z I_a P}{A}$ mkg

$$= 0.0162 - \dfrac{\phi Z I_a P}{A} \text{ mkg}$$

## (b) Alternative Method:

We know that the back e.m.f. developed in the armature of a D.C. motor is equal to $V - I_a R_a$

i.e. 
$$E_b = V - I_a R_a \qquad \ldots (2.4)$$

Where $V$ = Supply voltage and

$I_a R_a$ = Voltage drop in armature

Multiplying equation (2.4) by $I_a$

$$E_b I_a = V I_a - I_a^2 R_a \qquad \ldots (2.5)$$

where, $VI_a$ represents total electrical power supplied to the armature.

$I_a^2 R_a$ = Power wasted in armature or is called as armature Cu loss. From the power input to the armature when armature copper losses are subtracted, we get mechanical power developed in the armature.

$\therefore$ Mechanical power developed = $E_b I_a$ watts $\qquad \ldots (2.6)$

If $T_g$ is the gross torque developed by the armature of motor, running at speed of N r.p.m.

Then mechanical power developed = $\dfrac{2\pi N T_g}{60}$ Nm/sec. or watts $\qquad \ldots (2.7)$

Equating equations (2.6) and (2.7),

$$E_b I_a = \dfrac{2\pi N T_g}{60} \qquad \ldots (2.8)$$

$\therefore$ Gross torque $T_g = \dfrac{60}{2\pi} \times \dfrac{E_b I_a}{N}$ mN

or $\qquad T_g = 9.552 \dfrac{E_b I_a}{N}$ Nm $\qquad \ldots (2.9)$

or $\qquad T_g = \dfrac{9.552}{9.81} \dfrac{E_b I_a}{N} = 0.9738 \dfrac{E_b I_a}{N}$ kg.m

Substituting, $\qquad E_b = \dfrac{\phi ZNP}{60A}$ Volts in equation (2.9)

Gross torque, $T_g = \dfrac{9.552 \times \phi ZNP \times I_s}{60 \times A \times N}$

or $\qquad T_g = 0.159 \dfrac{\phi Z I_a P}{A}$ Nm $\qquad \ldots (2.10)$

where, $\phi$, $Z$, $I_a$, $P$ and $A$ have usual meanings.

### 2.2.4.1 Shaft Torque

We have seen that the gross torque developed by the motor is given by

$$T_g = 9.552 \dfrac{E_b I_a}{N} \text{ Nm}$$

or
$$T_g = 0.9738 \frac{E_b I_a}{N} \text{ kg m}$$

Whole of this torque developed is not available at the shaft or pulley of the motor as certain quantity of torque is utilised in over coming the torque due to friction and windage losses. The frictional torque can be written in view of equation (2.9) above as

$$T_f = \frac{9.552 \times \text{Iron, friction and windage loss}}{N} \text{ in Nm}$$

or
$$T_f = \frac{0.9738 \times \text{Iron, friction and windage loss}}{N} \text{ kg m}$$

The torque available at the shaft is called as shaft torque and is equal to the gross torque minus frictional torque or shaft torque,

$$T_{sh} = T_g - T_f \text{ and the output of motor}$$
$$= \frac{2\pi N T_{sh}}{60} \text{ Nm/sec. or watts.}$$

if value of $T_{sh}$ is used in Nm. and HP developed

$$= \frac{2\pi N T_{sh}}{60 \times 735.5}$$

The kW output $= \dfrac{2\pi N T_{sh}}{60 \times 1000}$ kW

## 2.3 NECESSITY OF STARTER, STARTING TORQUE AND CURRENT

As is shown in Article 2.2.4 the torque developed by a D.C. motor is given by

$$T_g = 0.159 \frac{\phi Z I_a P}{A} \text{ Nm. or } T_g \propto \phi I_a \text{ other factors being constant.}$$

This torque is party utilized in over coming the frictional torque and partly it is utilized to accelerate the armature from rest; and some part of it is also utilized in accelerating the load connected across the shaft. Hence, the value of starting current depends up on the nature of duty expected from the motor. At starting if the motor shaft is subjected to a torque equal to full load torque, motor has to develop a torque at starting which will be more than full load torque, to provide the extra torque necessary to accelerate the armature (i.e. motor itself) and the load connected to its shaft. If it is a shunt motor in which the flux produced is almost constant, then the torque produced at starting will be directly proportional to armature current, as is seen from $T \propto \phi I_a$ but $\phi$ = constant

$\therefore \quad T \propto I_a$ only.

The starting torque varies, depending up on the duty to be performed by the motor, it varies from about 50 per cent to about 200 per cent in special cases or more, of the normal full load current; and in the particular case of a motor starting up against full load will be nearly 150 per cent of full load current.

When the motor is at rest i.e. in stand still condition, there will be no back e.m.f. in the armature conductors, hence for circulating 1.5 times full load current through the armature a very small voltage is required as this voltage will be equal to $I_a R_a$ only. If we are having a system of supply whose voltage can be changed from zero volts as is possible in case of ward-Leonard system or grid controlled rectifiers, we will not need any starting equipment.

As we use a constant voltage source for running the motors, which when connected directly across the motor terminals when the motor is at rest will cause very large. Current to flow in the armature circuit, being equal to $\frac{V}{R_a}$, generally V may be equal to 230 volts and $R_a$ may be 0.5 or 1.0 ohm. Hence, $I_a = \frac{230}{0.5}$ = 460 amperes, such a huge current at starting will damage the armature winding and if fuses are sensitive they will blow off. To avoid this very large current from flowing in the armature of D.C. motor and restrict it to nearly 1.5 times its full load value, we are required to connect a variable resistance in series with the armature, so that a maximum voltage will appear across the variable resistance connected in series with armature, and will cause a current to flow in armature (nearly 1.5 time full load) being sufficient to develop the necessary starting torque. As the motor will gain the speed, the back e.m.f. is generated in armature conductors which will reduce the armature current. If the same value of resistance is kept constant in armature circuit, the torque developed will be less and it will be sufficient to over come the friction and windage loss but will not be able to accelerate the armature and the load and will run at low speed. To maintain the rate of acceleration constant, the current flowing through armature circuit is kept almost constant by reducing the resistance from the armature circuit, this will help in accelerating the motor armature at constant speed and the load, at the same time the power loss in the variable resistance is also minimised. The processes of cutting down the resistance from the armature is continued till all the resistance is cut out.

In case of D.C. motor starters, instead of using a variable resistance in series with the armature a graded resistance is used, so that the current flowing in the armature circuit varies between minimum and maximum range of current when the handle is moved from one stud to other (At the time of notching) or when we cut down certain section resistance by notching the handle from one stud to other stud.

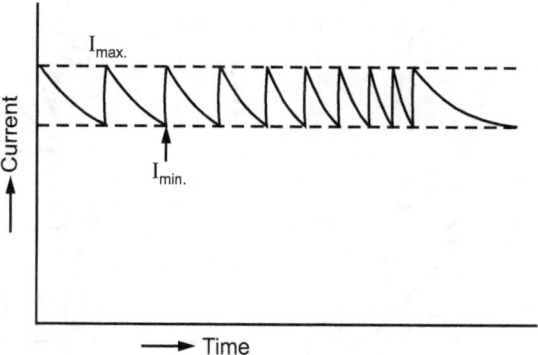

**Fig. 2.31**

Variation of starting current with time, when using a resistance graded starter is shown in Fig. 2.31.

## 2.3.1 D.C. Shunt Motor Starter

Fig. 2.32 (a) shows the schematic representation of a three point starter used for D.C. shunt motor. It is provided with five resistance sections or six number of studs. A provision of no volt release and over load release is also made which serve the purpose of protection to the motor. The three terminals A, B, C are connected respectively to positive terminals of line, shunt field and armature. The other terminals of field and armature are connected to negative of the line. A rheostat is added in the field circuit of the motor so that the speed of the motor can be adjusted, to its rated value. The handle lies in the off position when the motor is at rest.

The motor is started, by making the supply switch on and moving the handle to stud no. 1, at this position all the resistance of the starter is included in the armature circuit and the motor draws its permissible maximum limit of current or the starting current $I_{st} = \dfrac{V}{R_a + R_a}$

Where $R_s$ is total resistance of starter when handle is on stud No. 1.

The shunt field winding of motor is connected to brass segment s, and hence full voltage is connected across the field winding, and it will remain the same inspite of the position of handle.

When the motor gains sufficient speed on first stud the handle is moved to stud No. 2, 3, 4 etc. up to stud No. 6 at this position the electromagnet of no volt coil will keep attracted the iron-strip on the handle so that handle will remain in this position till it is in a magnetised condition.

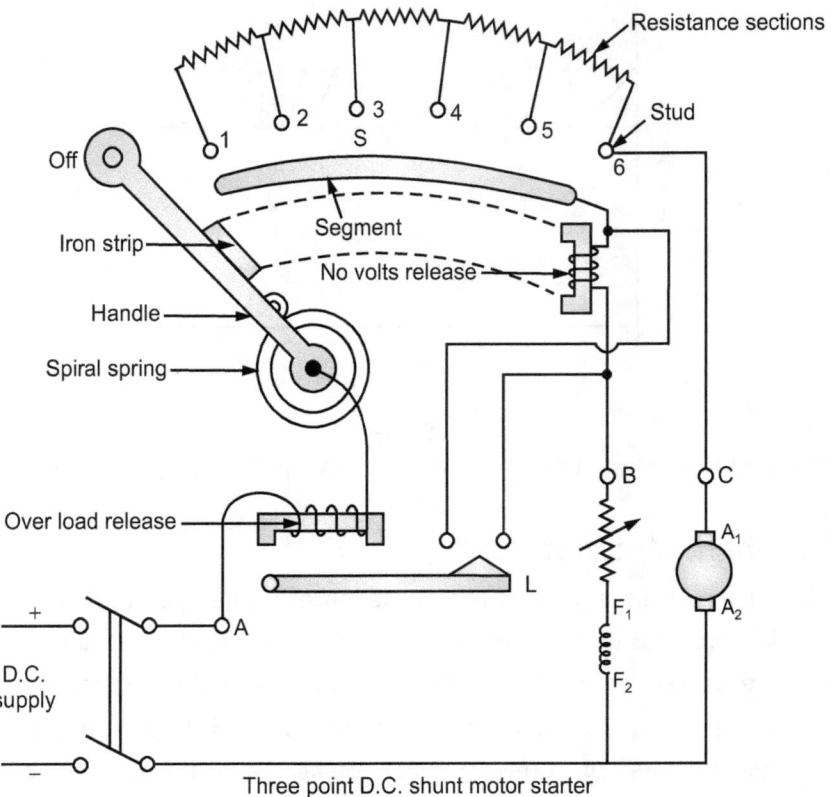

**Fig. 2.32 (a)**

The no volt coil consisting of large number of turns of thin wire and its ohmic resistance being high, is connected in series with a field coil as shown in Fig. 2.32 (a). When the supply fails the current flow through this coil becomes zero, hence the handle goes to off position by the force of the spring. If the handle remained there on stud No. 6, and the supply resumes again, the back e.m.f. of the motor being zero, in this condition, it will draw very large current which will damage the motor hence purpose of using the starter will not be served. Also the no volt coil serves the function of disconnecting the motor from mains when there is open in the field circuit, field current being zero in this condition, if the handle does not go to off position the motor will attain a tremendously high speed. Hence, the no volt coil provides protection from these factors and hold on the handle in position when the condition of motor is normal.

The over load release consists of an electromagnet, having few turns, of thick wire and connected in line, so that total current drawn by the motor flows through it.

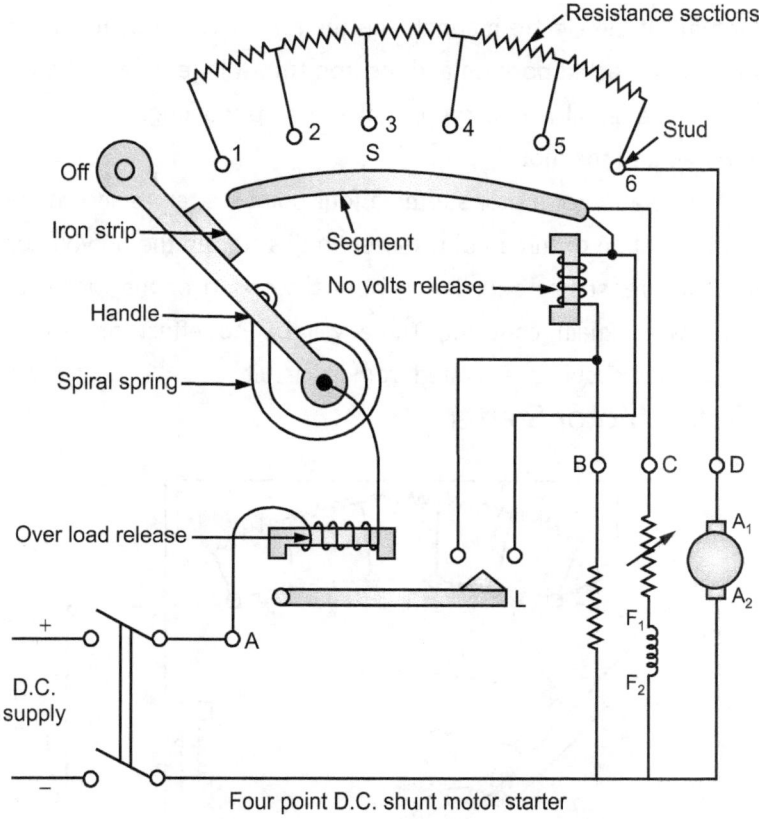

Four point D.C. shunt motor starter

**Fig. 2.32 (b)**

When the motor becomes over loaded, current drawn by the motor flows through this relay, under this condition the electro-magnetic force set up by this relay is more, so that the attractive force set up by it attracts the lever L which touches the two contacts brought out from the no volt coil i.e. the no volt coil gets short circuited hence no current passes through it, and it gets demagnetised so that the attractive force set up on the iron strip of handle becomes zero and the handle goes to off position due the tension of the spiral spring.

When the motor is to be stopped, it should be stopped by opening the main switch, which will cause the current in the no volt coil to die down and the electro magnet will have no magnetic strength and it will release the starter arm to come back to its off position.

The three point starter described above has a drawback that, when it is used for starting of D.C. shunt motors which are used for large variation of speed by varying its field current or flux control method; in such cases it may be required to reduce the field current for maintaining the speed constant, under such circumstances the field current may become very very low. A very low field current also passes through the no volt coil of the starter, which will weaken the strength of the electro magnet, and the force exerted by it will not be sufficient to hold the handle in attracted position and the iron strip will get released due to the greater back ward force of the spiral spring the motor will stop working. This should not happen during normal working of the motor.

To avoid such operation of motor starter, a four point starter, as shown in Fig. 2.32 (b) is used. This is a modification of three point starter. In this starter, the no volt coil is connected in series with a fixed resistance and during normal working of the motor current flowing through this coil will remain constant. There will be no effect of field current on its performance as the field circuit is separated from its circuits.

## 2.3.2 D.C. Series Motor Starter

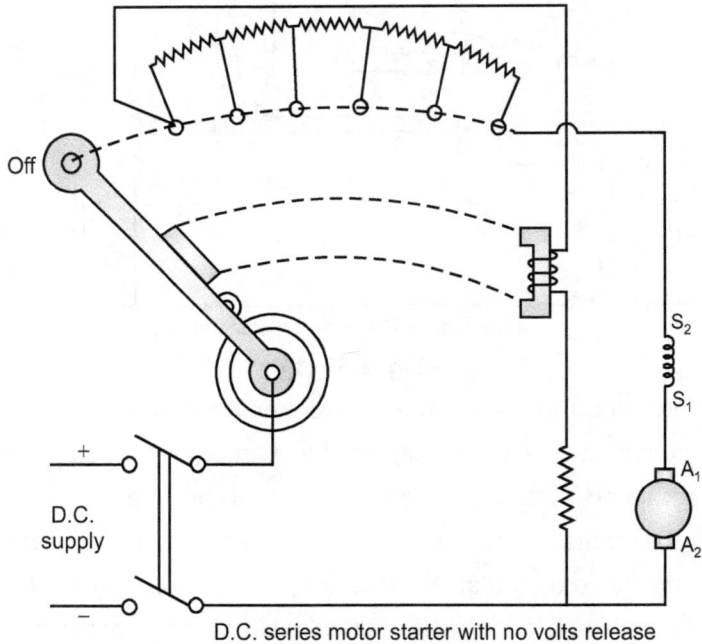

D.C. series motor starter with no volts release

**Fig. 2.33 (a)**

Fig. 2.33 (a) represents one type of starter used for D.C. series motors. Series motor starters also consists of starting resistance gragded in steps. This resistance is included in series with the motor at the time of starting. In the no volt release type of starter as shown in Fig 2.33 (a) the coil of no volt release is connected separately across the supply with a current limiting resistance. If the supply fails this coil will get demagnetised and the handle will go to off position by the back ward force of spiral spring.

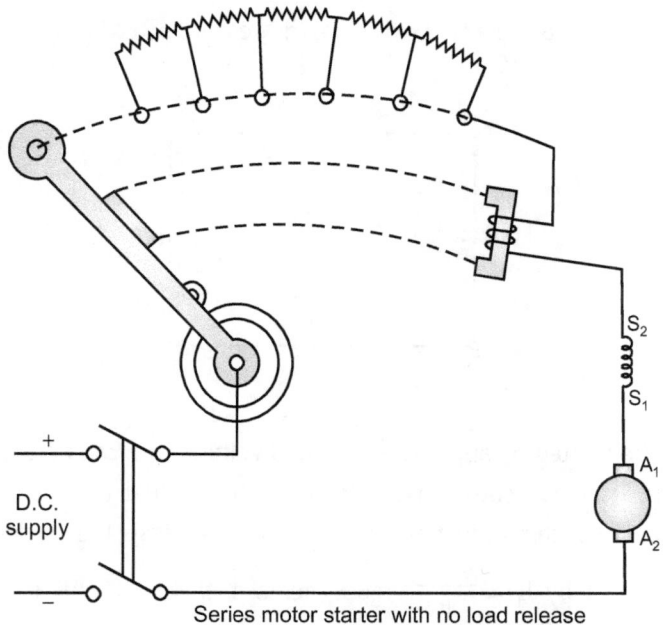

Series motor starter with no load release

**Fig. 2.33 (b)**

Fig. 2.33 (b) shows another type of starter used for series motors. This type of starter is having a advantage that when the load on the series motor reduces to zero, its speed will go high up tremendously, to avoid this the relay coil is connected in series with motor and when the load reduces below set value, the electromagnetic force of the hold on coil will be less than the back ward pull of the spring tension and it will come back to the off position disconnecting the supply to the motor.

## 2.3.3 Characteristic of D.C. Motors

The characteristics of D.C. motors are the curves drawn to represent relation ship between the two quantities of the motor, the different types of such characteristics obtained from the performance of D.C. motors make them to be selected for variety of purposes and find a vast field of application even now. There are mainly the following three characteristics of each type of motor, which decide the suitability of a particular motor for a particular job.

They are :

(i) Torque versus armature current

(ii) Speed versus armature current, and

(iii) Speed versus torque.

We will now discuss about the nature of these characteristics for each type of D.C. motor.

### 2.3.3.1 Shunt Motor

In this motor, the armature and field winding are connected in parallel w.r.t. supply as shown in Fig. 2.34.

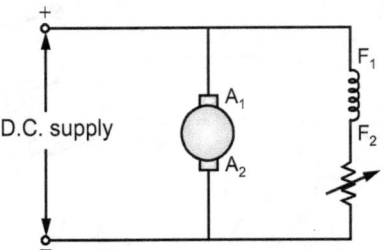

**Fig. 2.34**

Let the motor be started by application of rated voltage with the help of starter and it be running at its rated no load speed. If the load is now applied to its shaft, the motor will immediately slow down, this reduction in speed will decrease the back e.m.f., hence the armature current given by $I_a = \dfrac{V - E_b}{R_a}$ must increase, this will continue till the increased armature current produces a torque which will balance the increased load on the shaft. Hence, a D.C. shunt motor is always in a condition of stable equilibrium, as always the change of load is overcomed by additional power input to armature.

From the torque equation of a D.C. motor

$$T = 0.159 \dfrac{\phi Z I_a P}{A}$$

in case of a shunt motor the flux is almost constant.

Hence $\quad\quad\quad\quad T \propto I_a$ ... (2.11)

The speed can be determined from the relation

$$E_b = V - I_a R_a = \dfrac{\phi Z N P}{60 A}$$

or $\quad\quad\quad\quad N \propto \dfrac{V - I_a R_a}{\phi}$

or $\quad\quad\quad\quad N = K \dfrac{V - I_a R_a}{\phi}$ ... (2.12)

In case of shunt motor K, V, $R_a$ and $\phi$ are substantially constant, therefore the only variable is $I_a$ (armature current).

As the load on the motor is increased $I_a$ increases hence numerator of equation (2.12) will reduce, and the denominator remains almost constant, hence the speed of the motor will drop with increase in load, as $I_a R_a$ for a shunt motor varies from 2 to 6 per cent of rated voltage, the percentage drop in speed from no load to full load is of the same order of magnitude. Hence, a shunt motor can be considered as a constant speed motor; there is a slight reduction in flux $\phi$ due to armature reaction, when the load increases, which helps in maintaining the speed constant.

### (a) Armature Current Versus Speed Characteristic:

If the no load speed of motor is equal to $N_1$ and $I_1$ is the no load armature current and $N_2$ and $I_2$ be the values of speed and armature current on load then from $N \propto \dfrac{V - I_a R_a}{\phi}$

$N_1 \propto V - I_1 R_a$ and $N_2 \propto V - I_2 R_a$, $\phi$ being constant.

or
$$\frac{N_2}{N_1} = \frac{V - I_2 R_a}{V - I_1 R_a}$$

or
$$\frac{N_1 - N_2}{N_1} = \frac{R_a (I_2 - I_1)}{V - I_1 R_a}$$

Neglecting voltage drop in armature at no load.

$$\frac{N_1 - N_2}{N_1} = \frac{R_a (I_2 - I_1)}{V}$$

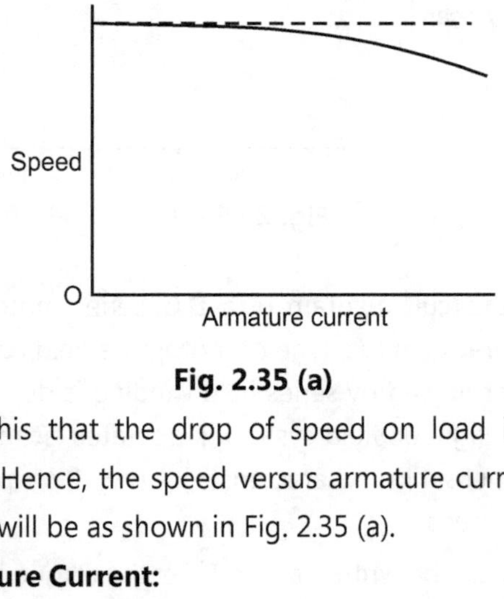

*Speed* vs *Armature current*

**Fig. 2.35 (a)**

It is observed from this that the drop of speed on load is directly proportional to armature resistance drop. Hence, the speed versus armature current characteristic will drop slightly on load. Its nature will be as shown in Fig. 2.35 (a).

### (b) Torque Versus Armature Current:

From the equation of torque produced by a D.C. motor, Torque $T \propto \phi I_a$ but $\phi$ being almost constant in case of a shunt motor, the Torque $T \propto I_a$.

As $T \propto I_a$ i.e. armature current it represents almost a straight line passing from origin.

If OA represents the no load current then the shaft torque characteristic will start from A and will also be a straight line as represented in Fig. 2.35 (b) the value of shaft torque at all points will be equal to total torque minus fictional torque.

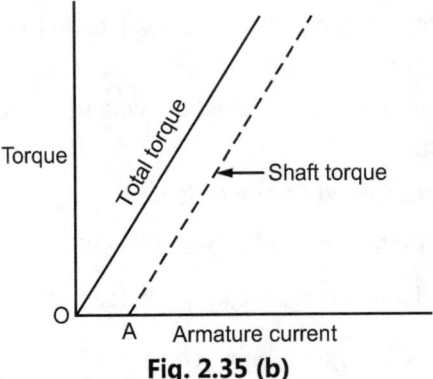

Fig. 2.35 (b)

### (c) Torque Versus Speed Characteristics:

The torque of a D.C. shunt motor is directly proportional to armature current, as is seen from $T \propto \phi I_a$, $\phi$ being almost constant hence the nature of the torque speed characteristic will be the same as that of the armature current speed characteristic.

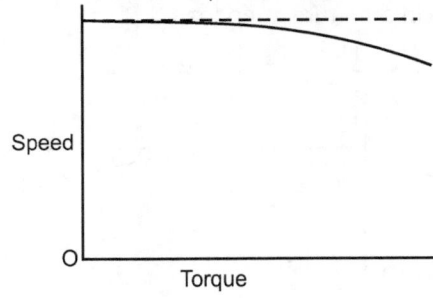

Fig. 2.35 (c)

### D.C. Series Motors:

Fig. 2.36 represents the circuit diagram of a D.C. series motor. The construction is just similar to a d. c. series generator. In this type of motor, the field current and armature current being the same the flux $\phi$ produced by series field winding is dependent up on the armature current, if the iron of the magnetic field system is operated at moderate saturation (on the straight portion of magnetisation characteristic). The flux produced will be directly proportional to armature current.

∴ The torque $T \propto \phi\, I_a$ can be written as $T \propto I_a^2$ i.e. the torque is proportional to square of armature current. Hence, series motors can be used for purposes where a small change in armature current will be able to supply a large torque.

From the relation of speed $N \propto \dfrac{V - I_a(R_a)}{\phi}$, in case of series motor total armature circuit resistance is $(R_a + R_{se})$ where $R_{se}$ is the series field winding resistance hence $N \propto \dfrac{V - I_a(R_a + R_{se})}{\phi}$ as the load on the motor is increased $I_a$ increases and flux $\phi$ will also increase

($\phi \propto I_a$) the effect will be that numerator will reduce and denominator will increase hence the speed of the motor will decrease with increase of load on the motor. The resistance drop is nearly 3 to 8 per cent of T.V. in case of series motors, hence the drop in speed by this effect is also of this magnitude. But speed being inversely proportional to flux a given change in flux produces the same proportionate change in speed.

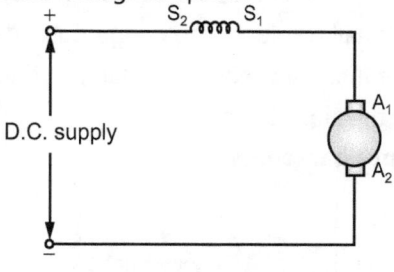

**Fig. 2.36 (a)**

**Operation of Motor on Load :**

When the torque at the shaft of the motor is increased, the reactions set up in the motor are as follows:

The speed will drop momentarily, it will reduce the back e.m.f., hence $I_a (R_a + R_{se})$ will increase hence $I_a$ must increase, hence flux $\phi$ increases, increasing torque $\alpha\ \phi I_a$. The speed and current will adjust themselves till torque developed is equal to load torque and frictional torque and the equilibrium is reached.

When the load torque (Shaft torque) is decreased, the armature will accelerate, increasing the back e.m.f. (momentarily), which will reduce the armature current and flux and hence the developed torque will also reduce, the speed and current will adjust themselves until equilibrium is reached.

If suppose the total load is removed, the armature current will be greatly reduced, $\phi$ will become tremendously small, resulting in a very high speed. Hence, it is dangerous to remove the load from the series motor, otherwise the armature of the motor attains, such a high speed, due to the centrifugal action of which the machine may work.

**(a) Speed Versus Armature Current Characteristic :**

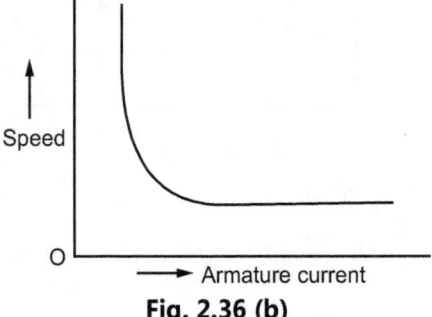

**Fig. 2.36 (b)**

From $N \propto \dfrac{V - I_a(R_a + R_{se})}{\phi}$ as the armature resistance are small, $I_a(R_a + R_{se})$ is small and hence $E_b$ is atmost constant. When the motor is lightly loaded, $I_a$ is small hence $\phi$ is small and the speed of the motor will be very high as it is inversely proportional to $\phi$.

When the load is increased, $I_a$ increases hence flux increases due which speed will fall. However at no load $I_a$ is very small resulting into dangerously high speed. When the motor is highly loaded, $I_a$ is large hence flux will become constant, so the speed of the motor becomes constant as is represented by the Fig. 2.36 (b).

**(b) Torque Armature Current Characteristic:**

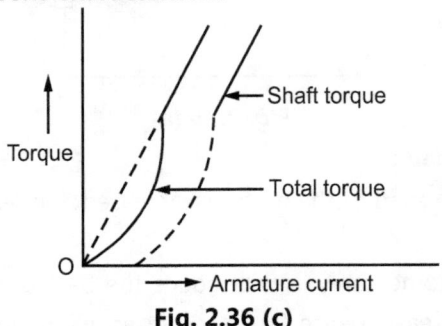

**Fig. 2.36 (c)**

From $T \propto \phi I_a$ and $\phi \propto I_a$ at light loads $T \propto I_a^2$ hence the torque characteristic will represent a parabola in the starting. When the motor is loaded, flux $\phi$ becomes constant due to magnetic saturation, hence $T \propto I_a$ only hence at higher load, the characteristic will be a straight line. The characteristic is represented in Fig. 2.36 (b). The nature of shaft characteristic can be obtained by deducting frictional torque from the gross-torque as shown by dotted curve.

**(c) Speed Torque Characteristic :**

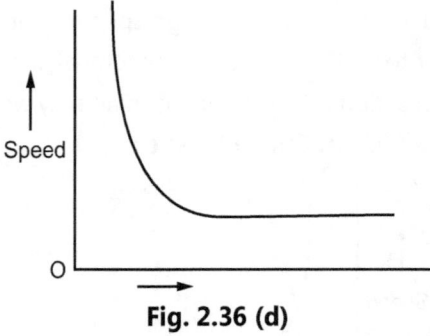

**Fig. 2.36 (d)**

For determining the nature of the torque speed characteristic, we will consider the following relations $N \propto \dfrac{E_b}{\phi}$ or $\dfrac{E_b}{I_a}$ till $\phi \propto I_a$ and $T \propto I_a^2$ upto magnetic saturation and $T \propto I_a$ after magnetic saturation.

When motor is at no load or lightly loaded $I_a$ is very small, hence T is also small, $E_b$ is almost equal to V means constant, $\phi \propto I_a$ is very small hence the speed will be tremendously high. At full load, the value of Torque is large being proportional to $I_a^2$ and $I_a$ being sufficiently large; the value of flux $\phi$ is also large, hence for this condition we get a moderate speed. When the load on the motor is increased beyond full load, so that magnetic field gets saturated, Torque T though is more than f.l. will not increase in same proportion as that increased up to say f.l., $\phi$ becomes atmost constant, hence to supply additional current, $E_b$ must reduce or N must reduce. At very high torque the speed becomes almost constant as is represented by Fig. 2.36 (d). From which it is seen that, when torque is high the speed is low and when torque is low, speed is very high.

### 2.3.3.2 Compound Motor Characteristics

Similar to a compound generator depending up on the series field flux helps the shunt field winding flux or oppose the shunt field flux, the D.C. motor may be called as cumulative compound or differential compound motor.

The characteristics of cumulative compound motor are combination of shunt motor and series motor characteristics. When the motor is loaded, the current flowing through the series field winding increases the flux, causing the torque to increase which will be more than the torque produced by a shunt motor for the same current but as the flux increases the speed will reduce more rapidly, than in a shunt motor. The cumulative compound motor developer a high torque with sudden increase of load, and also at no load it will have a definite speed and hence does not run away. When a load is suddenly applied to the motor it undergoes a substantial drop in speed, when the load is applied. Accordingly much of its stored kinetic energy becomes available for supplying a part of the increased load, hence electrical load of the motor is also reduced.

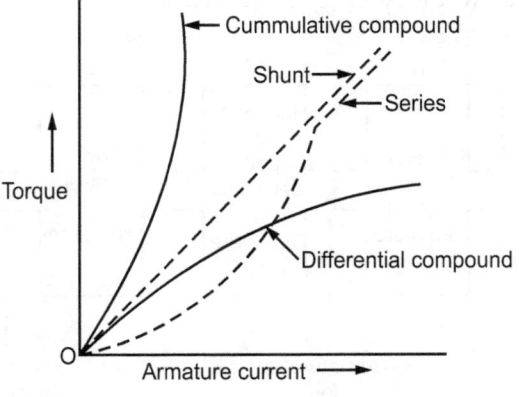

**Fig. 2.37 (a)**

In differential compound motor the series field opposes the shunt field hence on load the resultant flux reduces resulting in to speed increasing with load or remaining almost constant.

As this type of characteristic is available with a shunt motor, this type of motors are rarely used, because it has a drawback that when the load goes on increasing it may weaken the field to such an value that, it may produce instability and the motor may run away.

In starting differential compound motors, series field should be short circuited, as the large starting current in series field will be sufficient to over balance the shunt field ampere turns and to cause the motor to start in wrong direction.

The nature of different characteristics can be obtained by adding or subtracting the shunt and series motor characteristics, and are shown in Fig. 2.37 (a), (b) and (c)

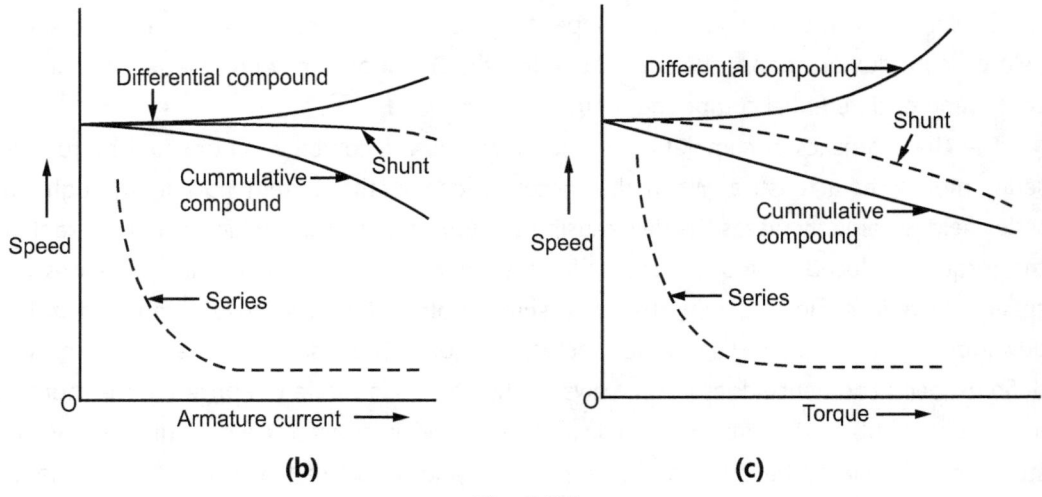

Fig. 2.37

## 2.3.4 Losses and Efficiency of a D.C. Motor

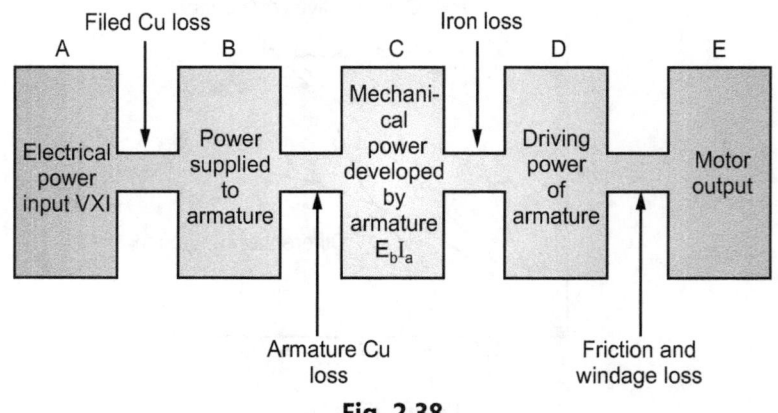

Fig. 2.38

Fig. 2.38 represents the different power stages of a D.C. motor, with the different types of losses taking place at each stage. From this power flow diagram, we are in a position to determine the different types of efficiencies of the motor as stated below.

(1) Commercial efficiency = E/A = $\dfrac{\text{Motor B.H.P.} \times 735.5}{\text{Electrical Power input}}$

(2) Electrical efficiency = C/A = $\dfrac{\text{Mechanical power developed}}{\text{Electrical power input}}$

(3) Mechanical efficiency = E/C = $\dfrac{\text{Motor output}}{\text{Mechanical Power developed}}$

$$\text{Total Cu losses} = V \times I - E_b I_a \qquad \ldots(2.13)$$

$$\text{Iron and friction losses} = E_b I_a - \text{B.H.P.} \times 735.5 \qquad \ldots(2.14)$$

$$\therefore \quad \text{Electrical efficiency} = \dfrac{E_b I_a}{VI} \qquad \ldots(2.15)$$

$$\text{Mechanical efficiency} = \dfrac{\text{B.H.P.} \times 735.5}{E_b I_a} \qquad \ldots(2.16)$$

## 2.3.5 Condition for Maximum Power Output

We know that the back e.m.f. of a motor is given as $E_b = V - I_a R_a$, where V is the supply voltage and $I_a R_a$ represents the armature voltage drop

or $\qquad V = E_b + I_a R_a \qquad \ldots(2.17)$

Multiplying by $I_a$ on both sides,

$$VI_a = E_b I_a + I_a^2 R_a \qquad \ldots(2.18)$$

$VI_a$ represents electrical power supplied to armature.

$E_b I_a$ represents mechanical power developed by the armature of motor, and $I_a^2 R_a$ represents the armature Cu loss.

$\therefore$ Mechanical power developed = $VI_a - I_a^2 R_a \qquad \ldots(2.19)$

If the power developed is to be maximum the differential coefficient of (2.19) must be zero.

$$\therefore \quad \dfrac{W_m}{dI_a} = V - 2 I_a R_a = 0 \text{ or } I_a R_a = \dfrac{V}{2}$$

i.e. armature voltage drop must be equal to $\dfrac{V}{2}$ or back e.m.f. should also be equal to $\dfrac{V}{2}$.

Hence, a D.C. motor will develop maximum power when $E_b = \dfrac{V}{2} = I_a R_a$.

## 2.3.6 Speed Control of D.C. Motors

When the speed of a motor is changed in accordance with the requirement of load connected to its shaft, it is called as speed control. The speed of D.C. motors can be suitably controlled by electrical means D.C. motors offer easy speed control that is why they are preferred over other types of motors for many applications.

The back e.m.f. of D.C. motor is given as $E_b = \dfrac{\phi ZNP}{60A}$ volts, but

P, Z, A and 60 are constant for a particular motor

Hence, $E_b \propto \phi N$ or $N \propto \dfrac{E_b}{\phi}$ but $E_b = V - I_a R_a$

$$N = K \dfrac{V - I_a R_a}{\phi} \text{ r.p.m.,}$$

where,
- $N$ = Speed in r.p.m.
- $V$ = Supply voltage in volts
- $I_a$ = Armature current in amps
- $R$ = Armature resistance in ohms
- $\phi$ = Flux per pole in weber.

From the above equation, speed is dependent up on supply voltage. It will change if armature resistance is changed. It will also change, if flux $\phi$ is changed.

Hence, it can be stated that by controlling the following factors, the speed of D.C. motor can be controlled :

(i) Supply voltage, (ii) Armature resistance, (iii) Flux per pole.

## 2.3.7 Speed Control of D.C. Shunt Motor

### (a) Flux Control Method:

The circuit diagram for this method is shown in Fig. 2.39 (a). A rheostat is connected in the field circuit of the motor, so that the current flowing in the field circuit can be changed, by changing the resistance of the rheostat (variable resistance). The flux per pole produced by the field winding is directly proportional to field current because in such machines the field is not operated at saturation. In case of machines using interpoles, the maximum to minimum speed ratio of 6 : 1 can be obtained, but in case of non-interpolar machines the ratio of 2 : 1 can only be achieved as the reduction in flux affects adversely on commutation. In this method of speed control, we obtain speed above normal. In this case, we can take normal speed as the speed of the motor when there is no external resistance in field circuit.

### (b) Armature Resistance Control:

Fig. 2.39 (b) represents the circuit diagram for this method. In this case, a variable resistance is connected in series with the armature. When we insert some resistance in armature circuit the voltage across the armature terminals will be less than supply voltage; or the back e.m.f. $E = v - I_a (R_a + R)$ is reduced hence the speed will be less than the speed without resistance. Hence by this method of speed control we obtain speed below normal.

If $I_{a1}$ is the armature current without resistance and $I_{a2}$ is the armature current when resistance is added in armature circuit and $N_1$ and $N_2$ are the speeds for same load conditions.

Then
$$\frac{E_{b2}}{E_{b1}} = \frac{N_2}{N_1}$$

or
$$\frac{V - I_{a2}(R_a + R)}{V - I_{a1}(R_a)} = \frac{N_2}{N_1}$$

In this method, the armature current flows through the control resistance, hence large power loss will take place. This method is also not giving a stable operation of the motor because the speed will change with the load. For obtaining a stable operation a diverter across the armature as shown in Fig. 2.39 (d) is used in addition to control resistance, due to this voltage across armature does not vary in same proportion as that in the previous case.

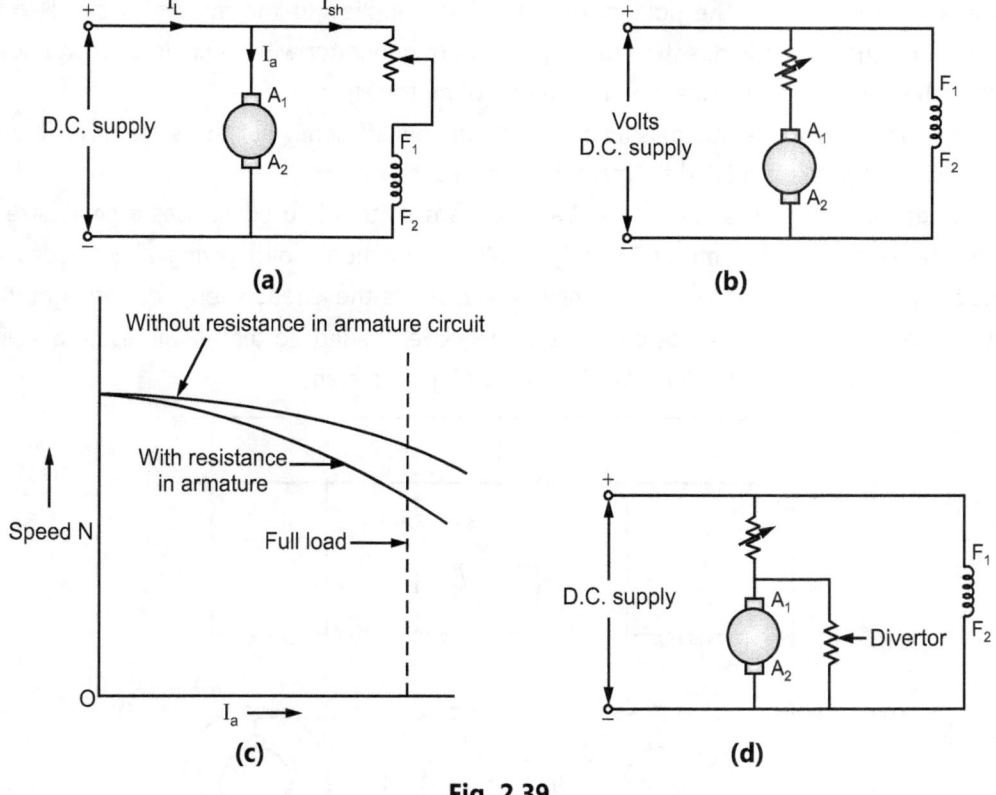

Fig. 2.39

### (c) Voltage Control Method:

**(i) Multiple voltage Control:** In this type of speed control method, the field winding of the motor is connected to a separate source, D.C. voltage with a regulator in series. While the armature of the motor is connected to a source of D.C. voltage from which different voltages can be applied across the armature terminals by using suitable switch-gear. The speed of the motor will vary in accordance with the applied voltage. The speed between any two steps of voltages can be achieved by changing the field excitation.

**(ii) Ward-Leonard System :** This method of speed control is used, when wide range and very sensitive speed control is required. It is represented by a schematic diagram in Fig. 2.40. The motor $M_2$ is separately excited and its armature terminals are connected to a constant voltage, hence it runs at almost constant speed and drives the armature of generator G. Its field winding is separately excited and the excitation to its field winding can be controlled by the field regulator. Hence, the magnitude of induced e.m.f. in the armature of generator can be controlled. The same voltage being applied to the armature of motor $M_1$, its field being separately excited, hence the speed of motor $M_1$ can be controlled by application of variable voltage from generator. The polarity of the voltage applied to the motor $M_1$ can also be changed by changing the direction of field current of generator with the help of change over switch; this will change the direction of rotation of motor $M_1$.

The drawback of the system is its high cost and low efficiency but this system is still used for elevators, hoist control and for main drive in steel mills.

Sometimes a modification of the Ward-Leonard system is used. It uses a small size of motor generator set. The motor $M_2$ is generally a induction motor giving almost constant speed. This set is provided with a fly-wheel, which stores the kinetic energy during light load and the same is used when motor $M_1$ is suddenly over loaded, so that it will result in saving of energy this system is called as 'Ward - Leonard Ilgner' system.

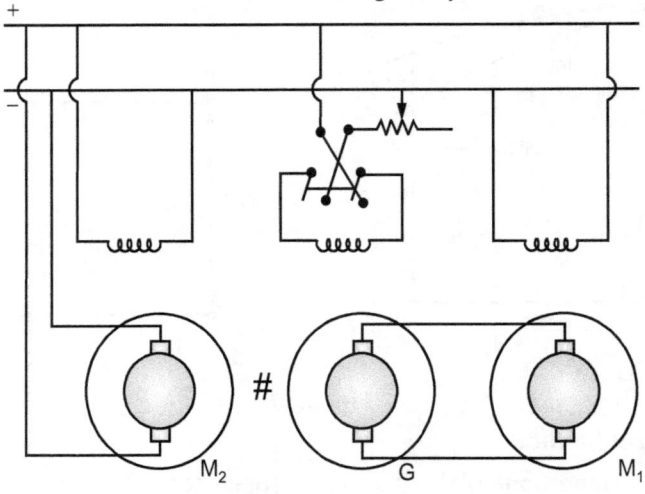

Constant speed   Variable voltage   Variable speed

**Fig. 2.40**

## 3.3.8 Speed Control of D.C. Series Motors

**(1) Flux Control Method:**

In case of series motors the flux can be controlled by various methods we will discuss some of them here.

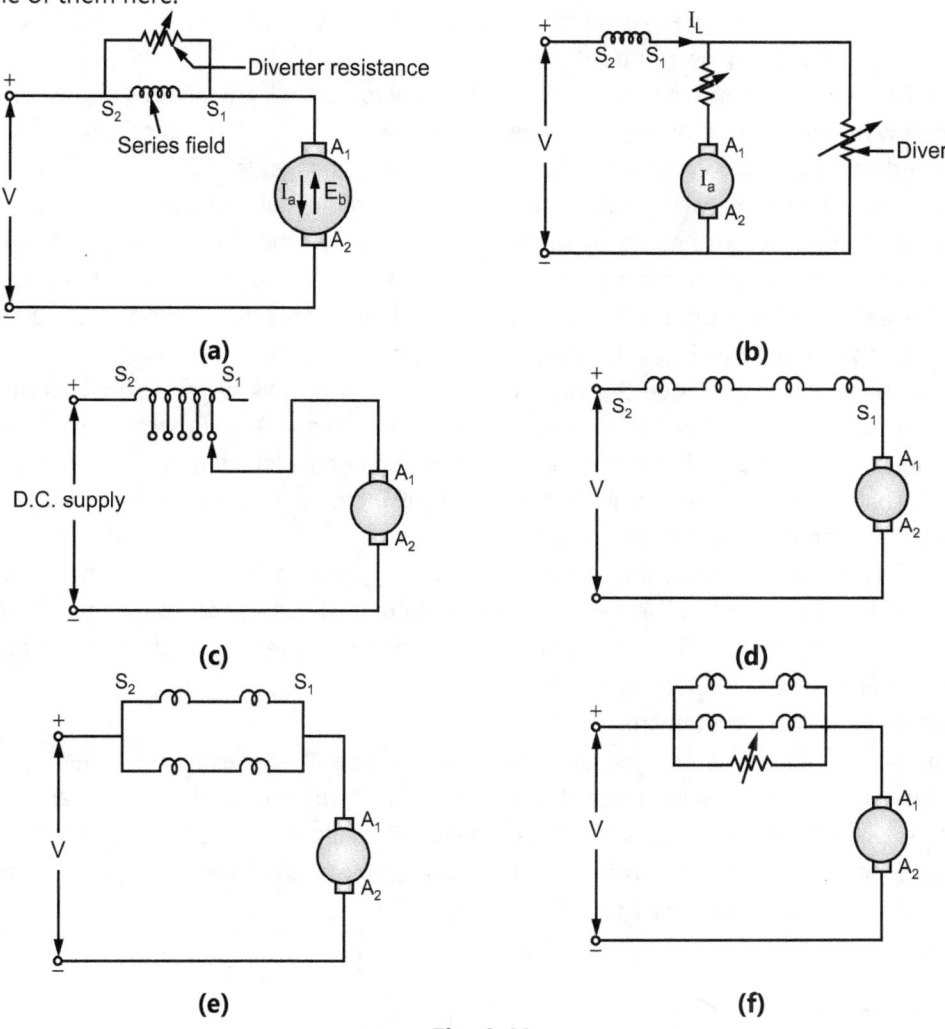

**Fig. 2.41**

**(a) Field Diverter Method:** In this method, a low variable resistance called as diverter is connected in parallel with the series field winding. Hence, the amount of current to be passed through the series field winding can be easily controlled. The armature current being equal to sum of field current and diverter current. Hence, the flux produced can be controlled, actually current flowing through series winding will be always less than when diverter is not used for the same value of $I_a$; hence by this increase in speed only can be achieved.

**(b) Armature Divertor:** In this method of speed control, a low variable resistance is connected across the armature, so that current flowing through the armature can be changed with the help of it. For same value of torque, when the divertor is used the line current ($I_L$) must increase, hence the value of flux $\phi$ increases, which will result into reduction of speed, as speed is inversely proportional to $\phi$. Hence by this method of speed control, speed can be reduced below normal.

**(c) Tapped Field Control:** In this method of speed control, the series field winding is provided with number of taps which can be changed at will. When the motor runs at normal speed and torque, all the turns are included in the circuit hence value of $\phi$ is more and the speed lower. When some of the turns are cut out from the circuit the flux $\phi$ reduces, hence the speed of motor will rise hence by selecting suitable tap of the field winding, suitable rise in speed can be achieved by this method. This type of method is used in electric traction.

**(d) Paralleling Field Coils:** Fig. 2.41 (d), (e) and (f) represents the method of using speed control by this system. In Fig. 2.41 (d). Four coils (for four poles) are shown connected in series for particular load torque the value of flux produced in this system will be maximum, hence the speed will be low. In Fig. 2.41 (e) shown an arrangement in which two coils are connected in series and such two groups are connected in parallel, here the flux produce will be nearly half the previous value hence the speed will increase. A further more speed can be obtained by connecting all the four coils in parallel.

Fig. 2.41 (f) shows an arrangement in which two groups of two coils in series are connected in parallel and a diverter resistance is connected across the combination. By the help of this arrangement a further increase than given by 2.41 (e) in speed can be obtained, but this can be smoothly achieved.

**(2) Armature Resistance Control:**

Fig. 2.42 (a) represents this type of method used in case of a series motor. When the load torque is same and resistance is introduced in series with the motor, the voltage across the armature will reduce, hence $E_b$ will reduce, which will result into reduction in speed of the motor. In Fig. 2.42 (b) are shown the nature of the current versus speed curves, with series resistance and without series resistance.

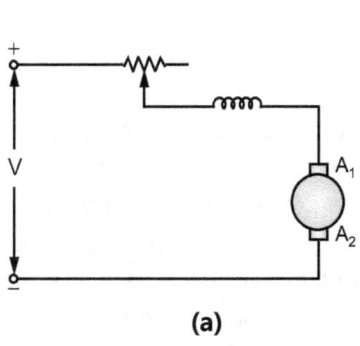
(a)

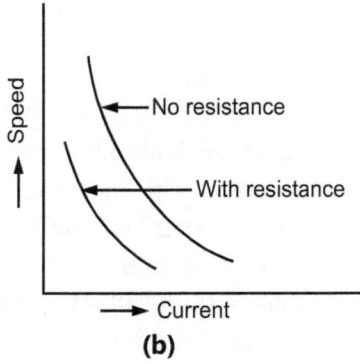
(b)

**Fig. 2.42**

### (3) Series Parallel Control:

This type of speed control is generally used in traction; it is superior to rheostatic method of speed control as far as efficiency is concerned. In this method, motors in multiples of two are required and it is possible to get only two speeds when low speed is required the motors are connected in series as shown in Fig. 2.43 (a) and for high speed they are connected in parallel as shown in Fig. 2.43 (b).

When two motors are in series they have same current passing through them and the voltage across each will be V/2 volts i.e. half the supply voltage. When they are connected in parallel the voltage across each motor is V volts but the current flowing through each of them becomes 1/2 amperes.

When the motors are connected in series voltage across each motor is V/2, Volts.

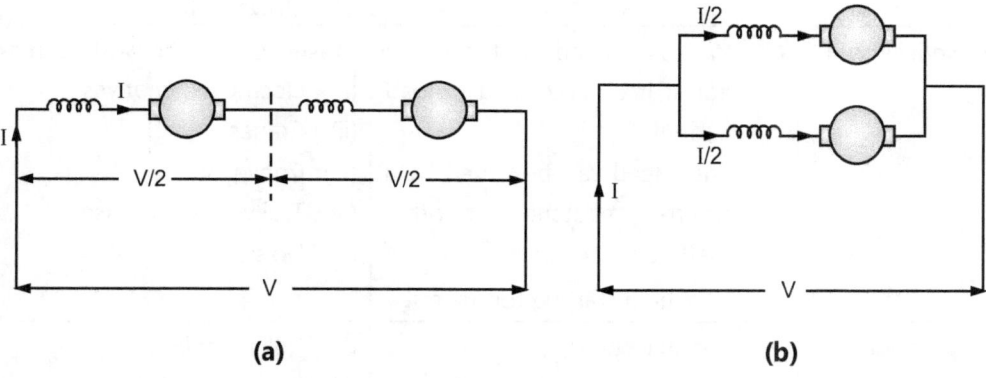

**Fig. 2.43**

From speed $\alpha \dfrac{E_b}{\phi} \cdot E_b \alpha \dfrac{V}{2}$ and $\phi \alpha I$ or

$$N \alpha \dfrac{V}{2}/I \text{ or } \dfrac{V}{2I} \qquad \ldots (2.20)$$

and $\qquad$ Torque $T \alpha \phi I \alpha I^2 \qquad \ldots (2.21)$

When they are connected in parallel from $N \alpha \dfrac{E_b}{\phi} \cdot E_b \alpha V$, and $\phi \alpha I/2$.

$\therefore \qquad$ Speed $N \alpha \dfrac{V}{I/2} = \dfrac{2V}{I} \qquad \ldots (2.22)$

and $\qquad$ Torque $\alpha \phi I \alpha I/2 \times I/2 \alpha \dfrac{I^2}{4} \qquad \ldots (2.23)$

Comparing equations (2.20) and (2.22) it is seen that the speed in parallel connection will be 4 times the speed in series connection while the torque in series connection from equations (2.21) and (2.23) will be 4 times the torque in parallel connection.

This system is used generally in combination with rheostatic control.

## 2.3.9 Applications of D.C. Motors

| Type of Motor | Characteristic | Applications |
|---|---|---|
| (1) Shunt motor | (i) Almost constant speed from no load to full load.<br>(ii) Speed can be regulated.<br>(iii) Starting torque varies from 1.5 to 2 times full load torque. | (i) Machine tools<br>(ii) Wood-working<br>(iii) Paper machine<br>(iv) Printing press<br>(v) Driving line shaft<br>(vi) Pumps<br>(vii) Lathes<br>(viii) Drill machines<br>(ix) Planers<br>(x) Blowers etc. |
| (2) Series motor | (i) Variable speed motor which adjust itself according to load current.<br>(ii) The speed can be varied by a diverter resistance or other methods.<br>(iii) Very high starting torque $\alpha\ I_a^2$ | Mostly for traction work such as:<br>(i) Electric locomotives<br>(ii) Cranes<br>(iii) Conveyors<br>(iv) Trolly cars and buses<br>(v) Hoists |
| (3) Compound motor | (i) Variable speed<br>(ii) High starting torque<br>(iii) Mostly coupled with fly-wheel. | (i) Rolling mills<br>(ii) Punches and shears<br>(iii) Elevators<br>(iv) Conveyors<br>(v) Strokers<br>(vi) Cranes |

## THEORY QUESTIONS

1. Draw the neat sketch of a D.C. machine showing important components; name the parts.
2. Explain in detail the constructional methods used for different parts of the D.C. Machine with their functions.
3. List the main components of a D.C. machine and explain the properties of the materials used for them.
4. Compare a lap and wave winding giving suitable example.
5. What are different methods of excitation?

6. Classify D.C. generators as per their excitation system.
7. Fill in the gaps by selecting suitable words from the given.
    (a) Armature of D.C. machine is laminated to reduce _____ (Armature, Hysteresis loss, eddy current loss)
    (b) Function of a commutator in D.C. generator is _____ (To produce unidirectional current in armature, to convert A.C. into D.C. for external circuit, to reduce sparking at commutator)
    (c) Armature winding is distributed because _____ (To dissipate the heat developed, make the armature dynamically balanced, get maximum generated e.m.f. in the conductors)
    (d) Copper is preferred for carrying out armature winding in comparison to aluminium because _____ (Aluminium has high resistivity, Aluminium needs more space in slots and can not be jointed easily, Thermal conductivity of aluminium is low)
    (e) The power delivered by a D.C. armature whether wave wound or lap wound will be _____ (equal, unequal)
    (f) No. of parallel paths in lap winding are always equal to _____ (two, that in a wave winding, no. of poles)
    (g) Carbon is used for brushes in D.C. machines because _____ (it has low resistance, it has high thermal conductivity, It is softer and having high resistivity).
8. Explain with neat sketches the working principle of D.C. motor.
9. Explain the function of commutator in a D.C. motor.
10. What do you mean by back e.m.f. in case of D.C. motor ? Explain how it is developed and what is its value ?
11. Derive the torque equation for a D.C. motor.
12. How a frictional torque can be determined from iron friction and windage losses?
13. Why a starter is required for starting a D.C. motor ?
14. How will you distinguish between a no volt coil and over load coil of D.C. shunt motor starter by physical observation ?
15. Draw a neat circuit diagram and explain the working of D.C. shunt motor starter (Three point/Four point).
16. Draw the different characteristics of a shunt motor and explain from it its suitability for a particular job.
17. Draw the different characteristics of a series motor and state from it the suitability of this type of motor.
18. Draw different characteristics of compound motor and explain from it its suitability.

19. Derive the condition for maximum output of a D.C. motor.
20. State different types of speed control methods used for a D.C. shunt motor.
21. Draw a neat sketch and explain word Leonard method of speed control.
22. Explain the field diverter method of speed control for series motor, and state whether the speed can be increased or decreased.
23. Which method of speed control can be used to lower the speed of D.C. series motor.
24. Explain how speed can be controlled by connecting field coils in parallel ?
25. Explain the series parallel method of speed control using two series motors.
26. What will happen if the field of D.C. shunt motor is opened while running ?
27. Under constant load condition which factor affects the speed of D.C. motor.
28. State giving reasons, true or false
    (N. B. No marks for merely starting true or false)
    (i) Differentially compounded motor can work well at over loads.
    (ii) The speed control by field current variation gives speeds above normal.
    (iii) Under saturation, the torque of a series motor varies as square of armature current.
    (iv) A four terminal starter protects motor against over loads.
29. State the factors affecting choice of D.C. motors for industrial drives.
30. State the insulating materials used in armature winding and commutator of a D.C. machine.
31. A D.C. series motor is never started on no load. Why ?
32. A D.C. series motor is not preferred for belt drive, why ?
33. Differential compound motor is started by short circuiting the series field winding why?
34. Illustrate any one method of reversing direction of rotation of D.C. motor.
35. Series motor is used for traction work why ?

## ILLUSTRATIVE EXAMPLES

### Shunt - Motors

**Example 2.1:** A four pole motor with a wave wound armature has 180 conductors. The current taken by the armature is 160 Amps, and the flux/pole is 0.028 wb, claculate :

(i) The speed at which the motor will run on a 230 V supply at full load current, the armature resistance is 0.045 ohm and total brush voltage drop 2 volts. (ii) Torque exerted.

**Solution:** (i) The back e.m.f. of the motor when armature current is 160 A, from

$$E_b = V - I_a R_a - \text{Brush drop}$$
$$= 230 - 160 \times 0.045 - 2$$

or $\quad E_b = 230 - 7.2 - 2 = 220.8$

Now, $\quad E_b = \dfrac{\phi ZNP}{60A}$

Substituting the given values.

$$220.8 = \dfrac{0.028 \times 180 \times N \times 4}{60 \times 2}$$

$$\therefore \quad N = \dfrac{220.8 \times 2 \times 60}{0.028 \times 180 \times 4} = 1314.28 \text{ r.p.m.}$$

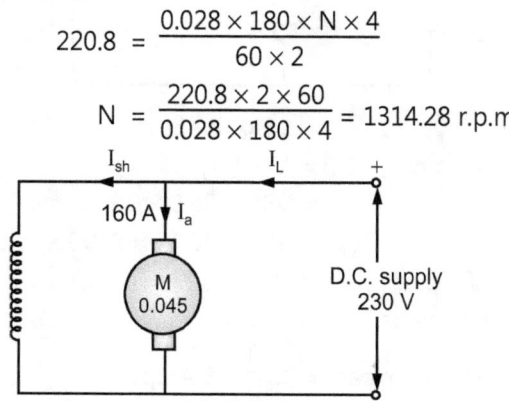

**Fig. 2.44**

(ii) Torque exerted is given by, $T_g = 0.159 \dfrac{\phi Z I_a P}{A}$ mN

$$= \dfrac{0.159 \times 0.028 \times 180 \times 160 \times 4}{2}$$

$$T_g = 256.43 \text{ mN}$$

or $\quad T_g = \dfrac{256.43}{9.81} = 26.14$ mkg

**Example 2.2:** A 10 H.P., 230 V, D.C. shunt motor has a full load efficiency of 86%, while running at a speed of 1200 r.p.m. the armature and field resistance are 0.3 ohm and 180 ohms respectively, calculate :

(i) The no load speed, if under these conditions its total input is 690 watts, and (ii) The value of resistance added to armature circuit to reduce its speed to 900 r.p.m., when giving full load torque with full field current.

**Solution:** (i) Output at full load = $10 \times 735.5 = 7355$ watts. Input at f.l.

$$\dfrac{\text{Output}}{\text{Efficiency}} = \dfrac{7355}{0.86}$$

$$= 8552.32 \text{ watts.}$$

$\therefore \quad$ Motors current on f.l. $= \dfrac{8552.32}{230} = 37.18$ Amps.

$\quad$ Shunt field current $= \dfrac{230}{180} = 1.277$

$\therefore \quad$ Armature current at full load $= 35.90$ Amps.

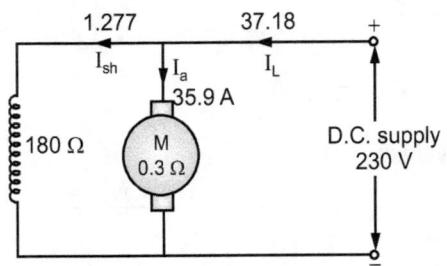

**Fig. 2.45**

∴ Back e.m.f. at f.l., from    $E_b = V - I_a R_a$
$= 230 - 35.9 \times 0.3$
$= 230 - 10.17 = 219.23$ volts ... (1)

Hence, $219.23 \propto 1200$ r.p.m.
At no load input = 690 watts.

∴ Line current at no load $= \dfrac{690}{230} = 3$ Amps.

∴ Armature current at no load $= 3 - 1.277 = 1.723$ amps.

∴ $E_{bo}$ at No load $= 230 - I_{ao} \times R_a$
$E_{bo} = 230 - 1.723 \times 0.3 = 229.48$ volts.

Now $E_{bo} \propto N_o$, No load speed or $229.48 \propto N_o$. ... (2)

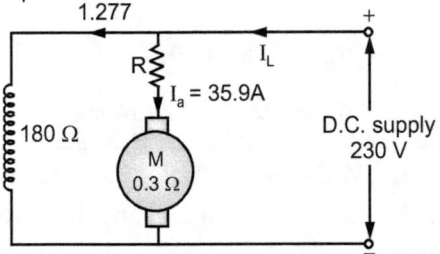

**Fig. 2.46**

Taking ratio of equations (2) and (1).

∴ $N_o = \dfrac{229.48}{219.23} \times 1200$
$= 1256.12$ r.p.m.

Hence, the speed of the motor at no load will be 1256.12 r.p.m.

(ii) Let 'R' ohms be the value of resistance connected in armature circuit to reduce the speed to 900 r.p.m. at full load torque and with full field current.

At full load torque the armature current must be equal to f.l. armature current, as $T \propto \phi I_a$ but $\phi \propto I_{sh}$ and $I_{sh}$ is equal to full field current i.e. 1.277 amps.

∴ $E_{b1}$ at 900 r.p.m. $= V - I_a (R_a + R)$ ... (3)
$E_{b1} \propto 900$ ... (4)

Taking ratio of equations (1) and (4),

$$E_b = 219.23 \times \frac{900}{1200} = 164.42 \text{ volts}$$

Substituting the values in equation (3)

$$164.42 = 230 - 35.9 (R + 0.3)$$
$$35.9 (R + 0.3) = 230 - 164.42 = 65.58$$

or
$$R + 0.3 = \frac{65.58}{35.9} = 1.826$$

or
$$R = 1.826 - 0.3 = 1.526 \text{ ohms}$$

Value of resistance to be connected in series with armature = 1.526 ohms.

**Example 2.3:** A 6 pole, 500 volts, wave connected D.C. motor has 1200 armature conductors and useful flux per pole 0.02 wb. The armature and field resistance are 0.5 ohms and 250 ohms respectively. What will be the speed and torque developed by the motor when it draws 20 amperes from supply ? Neglect armature reaction. If iron and friction losses are 900 watts find the useful torque and output in kW.

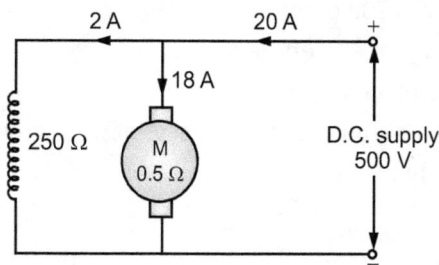

**Fig. 2.47**

**Solution:** When the motor draws 20 amps. from supply,

$$\text{Shunt field current} = \frac{500}{250} = 2 \text{ Amps.}$$

∴ Armature current, $I_a = 20 - 2 = 18$ A

∴ Back e.m.f. of motor at this condition from $E_b = V - I_a R_a$

$$E_b = 500 - 18 \times 0.5 = 491 \text{ volts.}$$

Now $E_b$ is also equal to $\frac{\phi Z N P}{60 A}$

Substituting the known values,

$$491 = \frac{0.02 \times 1200 \times N \times 6}{60 \times 2}$$

or
$$N = \frac{491 \times 60 \times 2}{0.02 \times 1200 \times 6} = 409.16 \text{ r.p.m.}$$

$$\text{Gross torque developed} = 0.159 \times \frac{\phi Z I_a P}{A}$$

$$= 0.159 \times \frac{0.02 \times 1200 \times 18 \times 6}{2}$$

$$\text{Gross torque developed} = 206.06 \text{ mN}$$

$$\text{Frictional torque} = 9.552 \times \frac{\text{Iron friction losses}}{N}$$

$$= 9.552 \times \frac{900}{409.16} = 21.01 \text{ mN}$$

Hence, Shaft torque = Gross torque − Frictional torque

$$= 206.06 - 21.01 = 185.05 \text{ mN}$$

$$\text{Output} = \frac{2\pi N T_{sh}}{60} \text{ mN/sec. or watts}$$

$$= \frac{2 \times 3.14 \times 409.16 \times 185.05}{60} = 7924.84 \text{ W or } 7.9248 \text{ kW}$$

**Example 2.4:** A 5 H.P. (3675 W) shunt motor takes 3 A on no load from 200 V supply mains. Field circuit resistance is 200 ohms and armature circuit resistance is 1 ohm.
(1) Calculate full load current and efficiency.
(2) Enlist the magnitude of various losses.
(3) Estimate the power output and efficiency of the machine while functioning as generator all losses unaltered.

**Solution:** Shunt field current $= \frac{200}{200} = 1$ A

∴ No load armature current = 3 − 1 = 2A. Input at no load

$$= 200 \times 3 = 600 \text{ W}$$

Input to the motor at no load is utilized as losses in the motor at no load; OR Input at no load = Constant losses + $I_a^2 R_a$ loss at no load.

$$200 \times 3 = W_c + (2)^2 \times 1$$

or Constant losses = 600 − 4 = 596 watts.

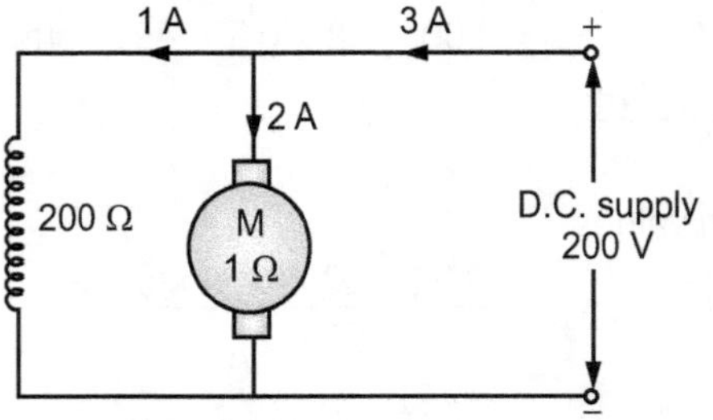

**Fig. 2.48**

Let $I_a$ be the armature current of motor at f.l., then line current is $(I_a + 1)$ A and the input to the motor $= 200 \times (I_a + 1)$.

$$\text{Input} = \text{Output} + W_c + I_a^2 R_a$$

$\therefore \quad 200(I_a + 1) = 3675 + 596 + I_a^2 R_a \quad R_a = 1$

$$I_a^2 - 200 I_a + 4071 = 0$$

Solving quadratic, $\quad I_a = \dfrac{-b \pm \sqrt{b^2 - 4ac}}{2a}$

$I_a = 23$ Amps, neglecting higher value

$\therefore \quad I_a^2 R_a \text{ loss} = (23)^2 \times 1 = 529$ watts.

% full load efficiency $= \dfrac{3675}{3675 + 596 + 529} \times 100 = 76.56\%$

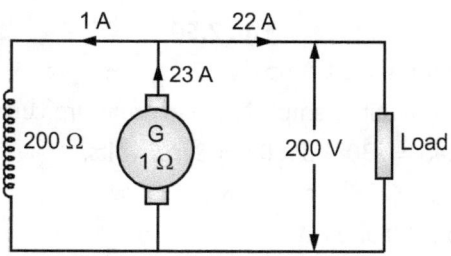

**Fig. 2.49**

When the machine works as a generator, without any change in losses its full load armature current will be 23 A.

$\therefore \quad$ Current supplied to load $= 23 - 1 = 22$ A

Output in watts $= 200 \times 22 = 4400$ watts

Input $= $ Output $+ W_c + I_a^2 R_a$ loss

$= 4400 + 596 + 529 = 5525$ watts

and $\quad$ Efficiency $= \dfrac{4400}{5525} \times 100 = 79.63\%$

**Example 2.5:** A shunt wound D.C. motor runs at 600 r.p.m., when it takes 40 amperes from 230 V supply. The armature and field resistance are 0.5 ohms and 115 ohms resistance respectively, calculate :

(i) No load speed if no load line current is 5 amperes.

(ii) Percentage reduction in the flux per pole in order that speed may be 750 r.p.m., when armature current is 30 amperes.

Neglect the effect of armature reaction and take brush drop as 2 volts.

**Solution:** Shunt field current = $\frac{230}{115} = 2A$

∴ Armature current on f.l. = 40 − 2 = 38A

∴ $E_b$ at f.l. from

$E_b = V - I_a R_a$ − brush drop = 230 − 38 × 0.5 − 2 proportional to speed. Hence, at constant flux 209 α 600 × $I_{sh}$  ... (1)

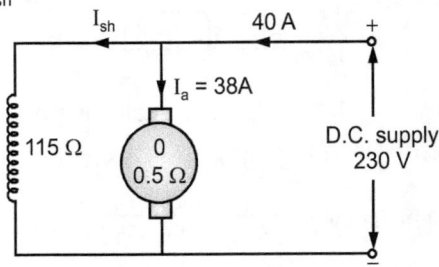

**Fig. 2.50**

When no load line current is = 5A Amps.

Shunt field current being again 2 amps. No load armature current = 5 − 2 = 3 A.

∴ Back e.m.f. at no load = 230 − 3 × 0.5 = 228.5 volts.

$$228.5 \ \alpha \ I_{sh} \times N_o. \quad ...(2)$$

Taking ratio of equations (2) and (1),

$$\frac{N_o \times I_{sh}}{600 \times I_{sh}} = \frac{228.5}{209}$$

or $\quad N_o = 600 \times \frac{228.5}{209} = 655.98$ r.p.m.

That is no load speed will be 656 r.p.m. At 750 r.p.m., let the field current be $I_{sh}$, φ being assumed proportional to field current, as armature current is 30 amps., back e.m.f. $E_{b1}$ at 30 A.

$$E_{b1} = 230 - 30 \times 0.5 - 2 = 213 \text{ volts.}$$

$$213 \ \alpha \ I_{sh1} \times N_1$$

$$213 \ \alpha \ I_{sh1} \times 750 \quad ...(3)$$

Taking ratio of equations (3) and (2),

$$\frac{213}{228.5} = \frac{I_{sh_1} \times 750}{I_{sh} \times 655.98} = \frac{I_{sh_1} \times 750}{2 \times 655.98}$$

∴ $\quad I_{sh1} = \frac{213 \times 2 \times 655.98}{228.5 \times 750} = 1.63$ Amps.

∴ % reduction in flux = $\frac{I_{sh} - I_{sh1}}{I_{sh}} \times 100$

$$= \frac{2 - 1.63}{2} \times 100 = 18.5\%$$

**Example 2.6:** A 250 V shunt motor, running light at 1000 r.p.m. takes a current of 5 A. Its armature and field resistances are 200 mΩ and 0.25 kΩ respectively. Calculate the speed when the motor drawn 50 A, on load, and the armature reaction weakens the field by 3%.

**Solution:** Field resistance = $0.25 \times 1000 = 250\ \Omega$ and Armature resistance

$$= 200 \times \frac{1}{1000} = 0.2\ \Omega$$

Shunt field current at no load $= \dfrac{250}{250} = 1$ Amp.

∴ No load armature current $= 5 - 1 = 4$ A

Back e.m.f. at no load $= 250 - 4 \times 0.2 = 249.2$ volts.

Assuming that flux α field current ($I_{sh}$) from $E_b\ \alpha\ \phi\ N$ for no load condition.

$$249.2\ \alpha\ 1 \times 1000 \qquad \ldots (1)$$

When the motor draws a total current of 50 A,

Armature current $= I_L - I_{sh}$

$= 50 - 1 = 49$ Amps.

∴ $E_{b1}$ at load $= V - I_a R_a$

$= 250 - 49 \times 0.2$

$250 - 9.8 = 240.2$ volts.

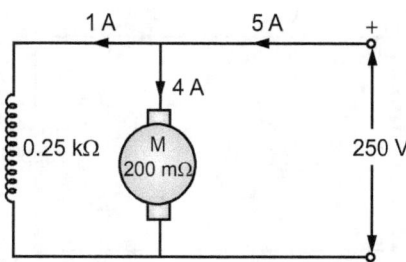

**Fig 2.51**

$E_{b1}\ \alpha\ \phi_1\ N_1$ at load condition $240.2\ \alpha\ (0.97\ I_{sh}) \times N_1$ but $I_{sh} = 1$ as $\phi\ \alpha\ I_{sh}$

$$240.2\ \alpha\ 0.97\ N_1 \qquad \ldots (2)$$

Taking ratio of equations (2) and (1)

$$\frac{0.97\ N_1}{1 \times 1000} = \frac{240.2}{249.2}$$

or $\qquad N_1 = \dfrac{240.2 \times 1000}{249.2 \times 0.97} = 993.69$ r.p.m.

Speed of motor will be 993.69 r.p.m.

**Example 2.7:** (P.S.) A direct current shunt machine generates 250 volts on open circuit at 1000 r.p.m. Armature resistance including brushes 0.5 Ω field resistance, 250 Ω, input to machine running as motor on no load 4 A at 20 V. Calculate the speed and efficiency of the machine as a motor taking 40 A, at 250 V. Armature reaction weakens the field by 4%.

**Solution:** As the generated e.m.f. of the machine is 250 V and its field resistance is 250 Ω, the field current must be 250/250 = 1 Amps. Hence writing the equation for induced e.m.f.

$$E \propto \phi N \text{ where } \phi \propto I_{sh}$$

$$250 \propto (I_{sh}) \times 1000 \text{ or } 250 \propto 1 \times 1000 \quad \ldots (1)$$

When the same machine works as motor on no load, the armature current will be 3 Amps.

∴ 
$$\text{Constant losses} = \text{Input at no load} - I_{ao}^2 R_a$$
$$= 250 \times 4 - (3)^2 \times 0.5$$
$$= 1000 - 4.5 = 995.5 \text{ W}$$

On no load, when line current is 40 A, Armature current will be 39 A.

∴ 
$$I_a^2 R_a \text{ losses} = (39)^2 \times 0.5 = 760.5 \text{ watts}$$

$$\text{Efficiency of motor} = \frac{\text{Input} - \text{Losses}}{\text{Input}} = \frac{\text{I.P.} - W_c - I_a^2 R_a}{\text{I.P.}}$$

$$= \frac{250 \times 40 - 995.5 - 760.5}{10000}$$

or  % Efficiency = 82.44%

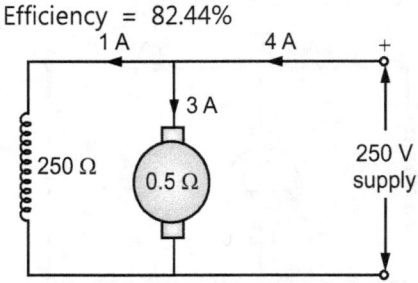

**Fig. 2.52**

$E_{b1}$ at line current of 40 Amps. will be = 250 − 39 × 0.5 = 250 − 19.5

$$E_{b1} = 230.5 \text{ volts}$$

$E_{b1} \propto \phi_1 N_1$, but $\phi_1 = 0.96 \phi$ and $\phi \propto 1$ amp.

∴ $\phi_1 \propto 0.96$, substituting the values $\quad \ldots (2)$

$$230.5 \propto 0.96 \times N_1$$

Taking the ratio of equations (2) and (1),

$$\frac{0.96 N_1}{1 \times 1000} = \frac{230.5}{250}$$

or 
$$N_1 = \frac{230.5 \times 1000}{250 \times 0.96} = 960.41 \text{ r.p.m.}$$

**Example 2.8:** (P.S.) A 220 V shunt motor with an armature resistance of 0.5 ohm is excited to give constant main field. At full load the motor runs at 500 r.p.m. and takes an armature current of 30 A. If a resistance of 1Ω is placed in the armature circuit, find the speed at (a) full load torque, (b) double full load torque, (c) find also the stalling torque.

**Solution:**  Full load $I_a$ = 30 A

∴ $E_b = 220 - I_a R_a$

$= 220 - 30 \times 0.5 = 205$ volts.

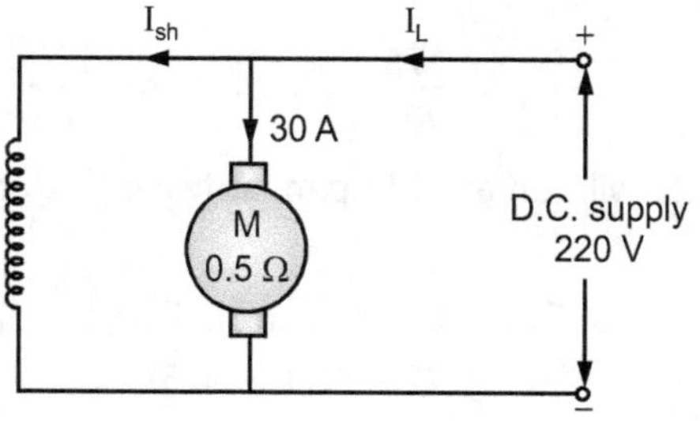

**Fig. 2.53**

As main field is constant, $\phi$ is constant * $E_b \propto N$

or    At full load 205 $\propto$ 500    ... (1)

Now a resistance of 1 ohm is connected in series with armature and

**(a)** The motor is developing full load torque.

From $T \propto \phi I_a$, $\phi$ = constant.

∴ T will be equal to full load torque if $I_a$ is equal to full load current i.e. $I_a$ = 30 A

∴ $E_{b1} = 220 - 30(1 + 0.5) = 175$ volts.

$E_{b1} \propto N_1$ or 175 $\propto N_1$    ... (2)

Taking ratio of equations (2) and (1),

$$\frac{N_1}{500} = \frac{175}{205}$$

or    $N_1 = 500 \times \dfrac{175}{205}$

∴ Speed at full load torque with 1 Ω resistance in armature = 426.82 say 427 r.p.m.

**(b)** Double full load will be developed by the motor when,

$I_a = 2 \times 30 = 60$ A

$E_{b2} = 220 - 60 \times (1 + 0.5) = 130$ V

and    130 $\propto N_2$    ... (3)

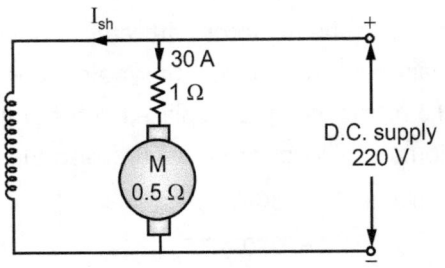

Fig. 2.54

Taking ratio of equations (3) and (1),

$$\frac{N_1}{500} = \frac{175}{205} \text{ or } N_2 = 500 \times \frac{130}{205}$$

$N_2 = 317$ r.p.m. i.e. motor will run at 317 r.p.m. at twice f.l. torque with external resistance of 1 Ω in armature circuit.

**(c)** At stalling, $\quad E_{b3} = 0 \quad \therefore$ from $E_b = V - I_a R_a$

$$0 = 220 - I_a(1 + 0.5)$$

or $\quad I_a = \dfrac{220}{1.5} = 146.66$ amps.

Stalling torque α 146.66 full load torque α 30

∴ $\dfrac{\text{Stalling torque}}{\text{Full load torque}} = \dfrac{146.66}{30} = 0.488$ or 4.88%

### Series - Motors

**Example 2.9:** A 110 V, D.C. series motor when running at 1500 r.p.m. and taking 35 A develops a gross torque of 20 Nw-m. The resistance of the motor is 0.3 ohm. At what speed will the motor run (a) when the developed torque is 14 Nw-m, assuming the flux to the proportional to the current, (b) when the current is doubled, assuming the flux to be increased by 30%.

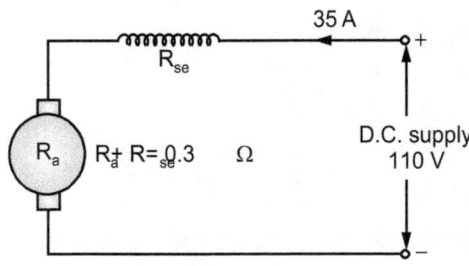

Fig. 2.55

**Solution:** T α φ $I_a$ but φ α I

∴ $\quad T \alpha I_a^2$

$\quad 20 \alpha 35^2 \quad \ldots (1)$

$E_{b1}$ of motor at 35 Amps.

$$V - I_a(R_a + R_{se}) = 110 - 35(0.3) = 99.5$$
$$E_{b1} \propto \phi_1 N_1$$
$\therefore \qquad 99.5 \propto (35) \times 1500 \qquad \ldots (2)$

(i) When developed torque is 14 Nw-m, the armature current is say $I_{a2}$

$\therefore \qquad 14 \propto I_a^2 \qquad \ldots (3)$

Taking ratio of equations (3) and (1)

$$\frac{I_{a2}^2}{35^2} = \frac{14}{20}$$

or
$$I_{a2}^2 = 35^2 \times \frac{14}{20}$$
$$= 857.5$$

$\therefore \qquad I_{a2} = 29.28 \text{ amps.}$

Back e.m.f. at 29.28 amps. = $110 - 29.28 \times 0.3$ or $E_{b2} = 110 - 8.784 = 101.21$ volts.

$$E_{b2} \propto \phi_2 \text{ but } \phi_2 \propto I_{a2} \qquad \ldots (4)$$

$\therefore \qquad 101.21 \propto (29.28) N_2$

Taking ratio of equations (4) and (2),

$$\frac{29.28 N_2}{35 \times 1500} = \frac{101.21}{99.5}$$

or
$$N_2 = \frac{35 \times 1500 \times 101.21}{29.28 \times 99.5}$$
$$= 1823.84 \text{ say } 1824 \text{ r.p.m.}$$

(ii) When the current is doubled i.e. when the current is

$$= 35 \times 2 = 70 \text{ A back e.m.f. at this current}$$
$$E_{b3} = 110 - 70 \times 0.3$$
$$= 89 \text{ volts}$$

Now, $E_{b3} \propto \phi_3 N_3$ but $\phi_3 = 1.3 \phi$ and $\phi \propto 35 \qquad \therefore \phi_3 \propto 1.3 \times 35$

Hence,
$$E_{b3} \propto 1.3 \times 35 \times N_3 \qquad \ldots (5)$$
$$89 \propto 1.3 \times 35 \times N_3$$

Taking the ratio of equations (5) and (2)

$$\frac{29.28 N_2}{35 \times 1500} = \frac{101.21}{99.5}$$

or
$$N_3 = \frac{1500 \times 89 \times 35}{99.5 \times 1.3 \times 35}$$
$$N_3 = 1032.0 \text{ r.p.m.}$$

**Example 2.10:** A 250 volts, 4 pole D.C. series motor with 830 wave connected conductors develops 5 H.P. when taking 20 A. The flux per pole is 27 m-wb. The motor resistance is 1.5 Ω, (i) Estimate the armature torque, (ii) Speed of motor, (iii) Shaft torque.

**Solution:** (i) The gross torque developed by the motor is given by,

$$T_g = 0.159 \frac{\phi Z I_a P}{A} \text{ mN.}$$

Substituting the given values

$$T_g = 0.159 \times \frac{27 \times 10^{-3} \times 830 \times 20 \times 4}{2}$$

or

$$T_g = 142.52 \text{ mN}$$

Back e.m.f., $E_b = V - I_a R_a$

$= 250 - 20 \times 1.5 = 220$ volts.

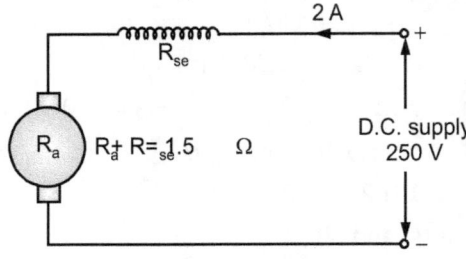

**Fig. 2.56**

(ii) Mechanical power developed $= E_b I_a$ ... (1)

it is also equal to $\frac{2\pi N T_g}{60}$ ... (2)

Equating equations (1) and (2) and substituting the values

$$220 \times 20 = \frac{2 \times 3.14 \times N \times 142.52}{60}$$

∴ Speed, $N = \frac{220 \times 20 \times 60}{2 \times 3.14 \times 142.52}$

$N = 294.96$ say 295 r.p.m.

(iii) Now, Output $= \frac{2\pi N T_{ab}}{60}$ watts. When N is in r.p.m. and $T_{sh}$ is in mN

Output $= 5 \times 735.5 = 3677.5$ watts.

∴ $3677.5 = \frac{2 \times 3.14 \times 295 \times T_{sh}}{60}$

∴ $T_{sh} = \frac{3677.5 \times 60}{2 \times 3.14 \times 295}$

$T_{sh} = 119.1$ mN

**Example 2.11:** A 230 V, D.C. series motor has an armature resistance of 60 m Ω and field resistance of 40 m Ω. It produces full load torque at 500 r.p.m. Calculate its speed at half full load torque. Neglect armature reaction and saturation. Take full load armature current as 40 amperes.

**Solution:** As the motor produces full load torque at 40 A.

From
$$T \propto \phi I_a$$
$$T \text{ f.l.} \propto 40^2 \quad \ldots (1)$$

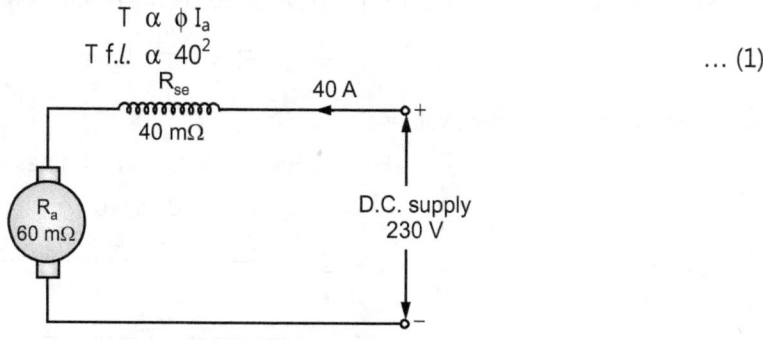

**Fig. 2.57**

Back e.m.f. developed by motor at f.l. from
$$E_b = V - I_a R_a$$
$$= 230 - 40 \times (60 + 40) \times 10^{-3}$$
$$= 226 \text{ volts}$$
$$E_b \propto \phi N \text{ but } \phi \propto I_a.$$
∴
$$226 \propto 40 \times 500 \text{ at full load} \quad \ldots (2)$$

When the torque developed by the motor is half full load torque, let $I_{a1}$ be the armature current then
$$T_1 \propto I_{a1}^2 \quad \ldots (3)$$
but
$$T_1 = 1/2\, T_n$$

Taking ratio of equations (3) and (1)
$$\frac{I_{a1}^2}{40^2} = \frac{1/2\, T_{fl}}{T_{fl}} \text{ or } I_{a1}^2 = \frac{40^2}{2} = 800$$

∴
$$I_{a1} = 28.28 \text{ Amps.}$$

Back e.m.f. at this current
$$E_{b1} = 230 - 28.28 \times 100 \times 10^{-3} = 227.17 \text{ volts}$$
$$E_{b1} \propto \phi_1 N_1 \text{ but } \phi_1 \propto 28.28 \quad \ldots (4)$$

Taking ratio of equations (4) and (2),
$$\frac{28.28\, N_1}{40 \times 500} = \frac{227.17}{226}$$

or
$$N_1 = \frac{227.17 \times 40 \times 500}{226 \times 28.28}$$
$$N_1 = 710.87 \text{ say 711 r.p.m.}$$

**Example 2.12:** A 500 V, series motor has 4 poles, wave wound armature with 948 conductors, and total resistance of 2 ohms. When the total mechanical torque developed is 20 kg m; the flux/pole is 5 mega lines. Calculate the current taken by the motor and its speed.

**Solution:** Total mechanical torque developed by the motor is given by

$$T_g = 0.0162 = \frac{\phi Z I_a P}{A} \text{ kg m}$$

Substituting the known values,

Flux = $5 \times 10^6$ lines and $10^8$ lines is equal to 1 wb.

∴ $\phi = 5 \times 10^{-2} = 0.05$ wb

Hence,

$$20 = \frac{0.0162 \times 0.05 \times 948 \times I_a \times 4}{2}$$

∴ $$I_a = \frac{20 \times 2}{0.0162 \times 0.05 \times 948 \times 4}$$

∴ $I_a = 13.02$ amps.

The gross torque is also given by

$$T_g = 0.9738 \frac{E_b I_a}{N} \text{ kg m} \qquad \ldots (1)$$

$E_b = V - I_a R_a = 500 - 13.02 \times 2 = 473.96$ volts.

$$E_b = \frac{\phi Z N P}{60 A}$$

∴ $$473.96 = \frac{0.05 \times 948 \times N \times 4}{60 \times 2}$$

∴ $$N = \frac{473.96 \times 60 \times 2}{0.05 \times 948 \times 4}$$

$N = 299.97$ r.p.m. say the speed will be 300 r.p.m.

**Example 2.13:** A series motor when operating on unsaturated field and running at certain speed takes 60 A, at 460 volts, if the load torque varies as the cube of the speed, calculate the resistance required to reduce the speed by 25 per cent. Assume that the field and armature resistance is 0.5 ohm.

**Solution:** From $T \propto \phi I_a$, and $\phi \propto I_a$

$T \propto I_a^2$, also $T \propto N^3$

∴ $$\frac{\phi_1 I_1}{\phi_2 I_2} = \frac{I_{a1}^2}{I_{a2}^2} = \frac{N_1^3}{N_2^3}$$

Here $I_{a1} = 60$ A, $N_1 = N$ and $N_2 = 0.75$ N

$$\therefore \quad \frac{(60)^2}{I_{a2}^2} = \frac{(N)^3}{(0.75\,N)^3} \text{ or } \frac{(60)^2}{I_{a2}^2} = \frac{(1)^3}{(0.75)^3}$$

or
$$I_{a2} = \frac{\sqrt{(0.75)^3 \times 60^2}}{(1)^3} = \sqrt{1518.75}$$

or $\quad I_{a2} = 38.97$ Amps.

Now back e.m.f. $E_b \propto \phi N$

$$\therefore \quad \frac{E_{b1}}{E_{b2}} = \frac{\phi_1 N_1}{\phi_2 N_2} = \frac{60 \times N}{38.97 \times 0.75\,N}$$

But
$$E_{b1} = V - I_{a1}(R_a + R_{se})$$
$$= 640 - 60 \times 0.5 = 430$$

$$\therefore \quad \frac{430}{E_{b2}} = \frac{60}{38.97 \times 0.75}$$

$$\therefore \quad E_{b2} = \frac{430 \times 38.97 \times 0.75}{60}$$

$$E_{b2} = 209.46 \text{ volts}$$

Let (R) be the value of external resistance connected in series then total circuit resistance
$$= (0.5 + R) \text{ and } E_{b2} = V - I_{a2}(0.5 + R)$$

or $\quad 209.46 = 460 - 38.97\,(0.5 + R)$

or $\quad 38.97\,(0.5 + R) = 460 - 209.46$

or $\quad 0.5 + R = \dfrac{460 - 209.46}{38.97}$

or $\quad 0.5 + R = 6.42$

or $\quad R = 6.42 - 0.5 = 5.92$ ohm

External resistance required $= 5.92$ ohm

**Example 2.14:** A 220 V, D.C. series motor takes 20 A; when giving its rated out put at 1000 r.p.m. Its total resistance is 1 Ω. Find the value of resistance to be added to obtain rated torque at (i) starting, (ii) at 500 r.p.m.

**Solution:** The motor develops full load torque, when motor current is 20 A.

(1) At starting, back e.m.f. is zero, and to develop full load torque, armature current must be 20 A; therefore total armature circuit resistance can be calculated from

$$I_a = \frac{V - E_b}{(R_m + R)} = \frac{220 - 0}{(R_m + R)}$$

or $\quad (R_m + R) = \dfrac{V}{I_a} = \dfrac{220}{20} = 11\,\Omega$

as $\quad R_m$ i.e. $(R_a + R_{se}) = 1\,\Omega$

$\therefore \quad$ External resistance required $= 11 - 1 = 10\,\Omega$

(2) At full load and 1000 r.p.m. $E_b = 220 - 20 \times 1 = 200$ volts.
and $\quad E_b \; \alpha \; \phi N, \; 200 \; \alpha \; 20 \times 1000 \quad$ ... (1)

At 500 r.p.m. let $E_{b1}$ be the back e.m.f. of motor then

$$E_{b1} \; \alpha \; \phi N_1, \; \phi \; \alpha \; I_a, \text{ or } E_{b1} \; \alpha \; 20 \times 500 \quad ...(2)$$

Taking ratio of equations (2) and (1)

$$\frac{E_{b1}}{200} = \frac{20 \times 500}{20 \times 1000} \text{ or } E_{b1} = 100 \text{ volts.}$$

Now
$$E_{b1} = V - I_a (R_m + R0)$$
$$100 = 220 - 20 (R_m + R)$$
or $\quad 20 (R_m + R) = 120$
or $\quad (R_m + R) = 6\Omega$ as $R_m = 1\Omega$
$$R = 6 - 1 = 5 \text{ ohms.}$$

External resistance to be connected in series to reduce to speed to 500 r.p.m. at f.l. output is 5 volts.

**Example 2.15:** A D.C. series motor driving a fan has armature resistance of 2 ohms and series field resistance of 3 ohms. It takes 5 amps. from 220 V supply and runs at 800 r.p.m. When the regulator resistance of 35 ohms is added in the circuit the current there by is reduced to 2 amps. Find out the speed of the fan. Assume that the flux is reduced to 50 percent.

**Solution:** Back e.m.f. developed by the motor when it drawn 5 amps.

$$E_b = V - I_a (R_a + R_{se})$$
$$= 220 - 5 (2 + 3)$$
$$E_b = 195 \text{ volts}$$
$$E_b \; \alpha \; \phi N \text{ but } \phi \; \alpha \; 5 \text{ amps.}$$
$$195 \; \alpha \; \phi \times 800 \quad ...(1)$$

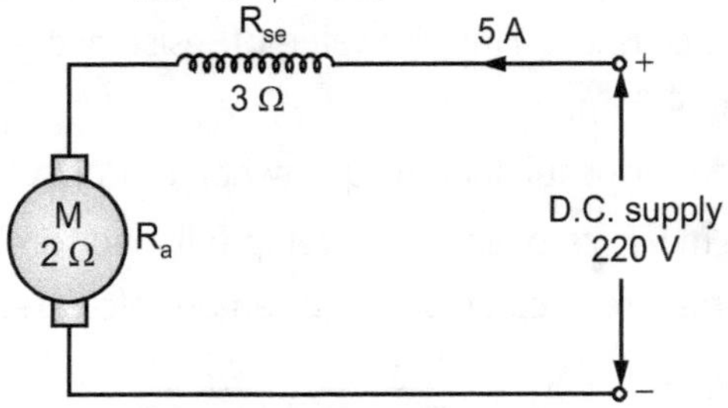

**Fig. 2.58**

When the regulator resistance of 35 ohms is added, the total series resistance will be $(2 + 3 + 35) = 40 \, \Omega$, and the current is reduced to 2 Amps, but the flux produced by this current $= 1/2 \, \phi$ i.e. 50% of flux produced by a current of 5 amps.

∴ New $\quad E_{b1} = 220 - 2 \times 40 = 140$ volts and $140 \; \alpha \; \phi/2 \times N_1 \quad ...(2)$

Taking ratio of equations (2) and (1)

$$\frac{\phi N_1}{2\phi \times 800} = \frac{140}{195}$$

or

$$N_1 = \frac{40 \times 2 \times 800}{195}$$

$N_1$ = 1148.71 r.p.m. speed of the motor will be 1148.71 r.p.m.

**Example 2.16:** A 4 pole 500 V D.C. series motor has total resistance of 4 ohms, the armature is wave wound with 900 conductors. The flux per pole is 2 m-wb per ampere of field current. Calculate the current drawn by motor and its speed when the torque developed is 18.9 kg m.

**Solution:** Torque developed $(T_g)$ = $0.0162 \dfrac{\phi Z I_a P}{A}$ kg m

Substituting the values, $18.9 = 0.0162 \dfrac{\phi \times 900 \times I_a \times 4}{2}$ kg m

But 
$$\phi = (2 \times 10^{-3}) \times I_a \text{ wb.}$$

∴
$$18.9 = 0.0162 \dfrac{2 \times 10^{-3} \times I_a \times 900 \times I_a \times 4}{2}$$

or
$$I_a^2 = \dfrac{18.9 \times 2}{0.0162 \times 2 \times 10^{-3} \times 900 \times 4}$$

$I_a$ = 18 amps.

The motor will draw a current of 18 amps.

$$E_b = V - I_a R_a$$
$$= 500 - 18 \times 4 = 428 \text{ volts.}$$

$$E_b = \dfrac{\phi Z N P}{60 A}$$

$$428 = \dfrac{(2 \times 10^{-3} \times 18) \times 900 \times N \times 4}{60 \times 2}$$

or
$$N = \dfrac{428 \times 60 \times 2}{2 \times 10^{-3} \times 18 \times 900 \times 4} \text{ r.p.m.}$$

N = 396.29 r.p.m.

The motor will run at 396 r.p.m.

**Example 2.17:** A series motor runs at 900 r.p.m. when taking a current of 30 A at 230 volts. The total resistance of the armature and field 0.8 ohm. Calculate the values of the additional resistance required in series with the machine to reduce the speed to 500 r.p.m. if the gross torque is (i) constant (ii) proportional to speed (iii) proportional to the square of speed. Assume the magnetic circuit to be unsaturated.

**Solution:** Back e.m.f. of motor when it runs at 990 r.p.m. taking 30 A from mains.

$$E_b = 230 - 30 \times 0.8 = 206 \text{ volts.}$$

From $E_b \propto \phi N$ and $\phi \propto 30$, $N = 900$

$$206 \propto 30 \times 900 \quad \ldots (1)$$

(1) When gross torque is constant, $I_a = 30$ A, but at this value of current the speed is to be reduced to 500 r.p.m. by inserting resistance in series with motor.

$$\therefore \quad E_{b2} \propto 30 \times 500 \quad \ldots (2)$$

Taking ratio of equations (2) and (1)

$$\therefore \quad \frac{E_{b2}}{206} = \frac{30 \times 500}{30 \times 900}$$

or $\quad E_{b2} = 114.44$ volts

$$E_{b2} = V - I_{a2}(R_a + R) = 230 - 30(R_a + R)$$

Where R is external resistance connected in series.

$$114.44 = 230 - 30(0.8 + R)$$

or $\quad 0.8 + R = \dfrac{230 - 144.4430}{30} = 3.852 \ \Omega$

$\therefore \quad R = 3.052$ ohm

(2) When torque is proportional to speed and the speed is reduced to 500 r.p.m. by adding resistance.

From, $\quad T_1 \propto I_{a1}^2$ and $T_2 \propto I_{a2}^2$

and $\quad T \propto N_1$ and $T_2 \propto N_2$

$\therefore \quad \dfrac{T_1}{T_2} = \dfrac{I_{a1}^2}{I_{a2}^2} = \dfrac{N_1}{N_2}$

or $\quad \dfrac{T_1}{T_2} = \dfrac{(30)^2}{(I_{a2})^2} = \dfrac{900}{500}$

or $\quad I_{a2}^2 = \dfrac{(30)^2}{(900)} \times 500$ or $I_{a2} = 22.36$ A

Now, $\quad E_{b1} \propto \phi_1 N_1$

$\phi_1 \propto 30$ A

$E_{b2} \propto \phi_2 N_2$

$\phi_2 \propto 22.36$ A

or $\quad \dfrac{30 \times 900}{22.36 \times 500} = 206 / E_{b2}$

$\therefore \quad E_{b2} = 85.30$ volts

But $\quad E_{b2} = V - I_{a2}(R_a + R)$ or $85.3 = 230 - 22.36(0.8 + R)$

$R = 5.67$ ohm

(3) Now the torque is proportional to $N^2$

$\therefore$ $\quad T_1 \alpha N_1^2 \alpha I_{a1}^2$

$\quad T_3 \alpha N_3^2 \alpha I_{a3}^2$

or $\quad \dfrac{T_1}{T_2} = \dfrac{(30)^2}{(I_{a3})^2} = \dfrac{(900)^2}{(500)^2}$

$\therefore \quad I_{a3} = 16.6$ amps.

$\therefore \quad E_{b3} = 230 - 16.6\,(0.8 + R)$ ... (3)

and $\quad E_{b3} \alpha \phi_3 N_3$ i.e. $\alpha\ 16.6 \times 500$

$\therefore$ Taking ratio of equations (3) and (1)

$\quad \dfrac{E_{b3}}{206} = \dfrac{16.6 \times 500}{30 \times 900}$ or $E_{b3} = 63.32$ volts.

$\quad 63.32 = 230 - 16.6\,(0.8 + R)$

or $\quad (0.8 + R) = \dfrac{230 - 63.32}{16.6} = 10.08$

$\therefore \quad R = 10.08 - 0.8 = 9.28$ ohms

External resistance required = 9.28 ohms

**Example 2.18:** A 460 volts series motor takes a current of 40 A at certain load. If the load torque varies as cube of speed, find the resistance necessary to reduce the speed to 80% of its original value. Take $(R_a + R_{se}) = 1\,\Omega$.

**Solution:** Torque $T \alpha \phi I_a$ but $\phi \alpha I_a$

$\therefore \quad T \alpha I_a^2$

Also $\quad T \alpha N^3$ for the two conditions

$\quad \dfrac{T_1}{T_2} = \dfrac{\phi_1 I_1}{\phi_2 I_2} = \dfrac{I_1^2}{I_2^2} = \dfrac{N_1^3}{N_2^3}$ ... (1)

We know that, $I_1 = 40$ A and $N_2 = 0.8\, N_1$

Substituting the value, $\quad \dfrac{(40)^2}{I_2^2} = \dfrac{(N_1)^3}{(0.8\, N_1)^3}$ or $I_2^2 = (40)^2 \times 0.512$

or $\quad I_2^2 = 819.2$

$\therefore$ Current drawn by the motor when its speed is reduced to 80% of previous = 28.62 A.

Now, $\quad E_{b1} \alpha \phi_1 N_1$ ... (3)

But $\phi_1 \alpha\ 40$, and $E_{b2} \alpha \phi N_2$

$\phi_2 \alpha\ 28.62$, $N_2 = 0.8\, N_1$ ... (4)

Substituting in equations (3) and (4) above

$\quad \dfrac{E_{b1}}{E_{b2}} = \dfrac{40 \times N}{28.62 \times 0.8\, N_1} = \dfrac{40}{22.89} = 1.747$ ... (5)

Also, $E_b = V - I_a (R_a + R_{se})$
$E_{b1} = 460 - 40 \times 1 = 420$ volts.
$E_{b2} = 460 - 28.62 (1 + R)$

Putting the values in equation (5) above.

$$\frac{420}{460 - 28.62 (1 + R)} = 1.747$$

or $\quad 420 = 803.62 - 50 (1 + R)$

or $\quad 50 (1 + R) = 803.62 - 420$

or $\quad (1 + R) = \dfrac{803.62 - 420}{50} = 7.66 \ \Omega$

$R = 7.66 - 1 = 6.66$ ohms.

## 2.4 STEPPER - MOTORS

These motors work in steps hence they are called as stepper motors, stepping motors or step motors. These motors rotates through a fixed angular step in response to each input current pulse received by its controller, they can be controlled directly by computers, microprocessors and programmable controllers.

In case of stepper motor its output shaft rotates in a series of discrete angular intervals or steps, one step being taken each time a commond pulse is received. When we apply certain number of pulses the shaft will turn through a known definite angle which makes such motors to be used for open loop position control, as there is no need of any feedback.

Such type of motors can develop torques ranging from 1 µN-m up to 40 Nm and power from 1 W to 2500 W. As the moving part i.e. rotor of the motor is not having winding, commutator or brushes etc. this motor is robust and reliable.

**(i) Step-angle:** Before going into construction and operational details of such motor, we will first understand the meaning of step-angle. Step-angle is that angle through which the motor shaft rotates for each command pulse, and is denoted by angle β. When the step angle is small, we get large number of steps per revolution of the shaft, and it offers higher accuracy or resolution. Generally, following step sizes are in use 1.8°, 2.5°, 7.5° and 15°. They may vary from 0.72° to 90°.

The step angle is either expressed in terms of rotor and stator poles say Nr and Ns or in terms of stator phases (m) and number of rotor feeth (poles).

Hence, $\quad \beta = \dfrac{N_s - N_r}{N_s \cdot N_r} \times 360°$

or $\quad \beta = \dfrac{360°}{mN_r}$

$\quad = \dfrac{360°}{\text{Number of stator phases} \times \text{Number of rotor teeth}}$

**(ii) Resolution:** It is the number of steps required to complete one revolution of the rotor-shaft.

**(iii) Stewing:** Stepper motors can operate at very high stepping rates, which may be as high as 20,000 steps per second and remain in synchronism with the command pulses. At such high pulse rate the shaft's rotation seems to be continuous. Operation of stepper motor at high speeds is called slewing. The motor shaft speed is given by,

$$n = \beta \times f/360 \text{ rps.}$$

where f is stepping frequency (pulse rate), P is the step angle.

While in operation if the stepping rate of the motor is increased too quickly, the motor falls out of synchronism and stops, the same thing will take place when motor is slewing and command pulses are suddenly stopped. As these motors can operate for a long period with rotor held in a fixed position with rated current flowing through its stator winding, stalling creates no problem in this type of motors.

## 2.4.1 Types of Stepper Motors

The stepper motors can be divided into the following categories :
(a) Variable reluctance stepper motor.
(b) Permanent magnet stepper motor.
(c) Hybrid stepper motor.

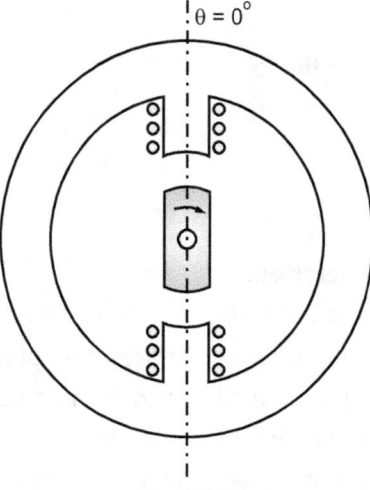

**Fig. 2.59**

**(a) Variable reluctance stepper motors:** A variable reluctance motor is constructed from ferromagnetic material with salient poles. The rotor may be solid or laminated having four projecting feeth of same width as that of a stator teeth (pole). The stator is made from laminations of steel and has six equally spaced projecting teeth (poles), in each pole a exciting coil of equal turn is wound. These coils are so connected as to form three independent stator circuits or phases A, B and C each one can be energised by a direct current pulse from the drive-circuit. The simple way of representing arrangement for supplying current to stator coil in proper sequence is represented in Fig. 2.60.

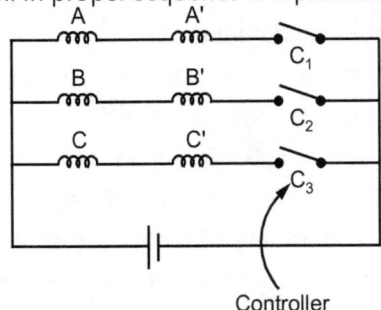

**Fig. 2.60**

These coils called as phases A, B, C have their independent control switch. As is seen from Fig. 2.60 and circuit diagram diametrically opposite coils of stator-poles are connected in series in such a way that they produce opposite polarities when the stator coils carry no current rotor is free to move, but when stator coils are energised, will cause the rotor to step forward (or backward) to a position that will form a path of least reluctance with magnetised stator steeth. The step angle of this type of three phase, four rotor teeth motor is given by,

$$\beta = \frac{360}{4 \times 3} 30°$$

This type of motor operates in the following modes,

(i) 1-phase-ON or Full-step operation.
(ii) 2-phase-ON mode.
(iii) Half step operation.
(iv) Micro stepping.

**(i) 1-Phase-ON or Full-step operation:**

When controller $C_1$ is operated to energise phase A, it produced magnetic field with its axis along stator poles of phase A, which attracts the rotor poles in to the position of minimum reluctance i.e. making rotor teeth 1 and 3 lining up with stator teeth 1 and 4 as shown in Fig. 2.61. Now $C_2$ is closed and $C_1$ is opened which energize phase B causing rotor teeth 2 and 4 to be in line with stator teeth 3 and 6, as shown in Fig. 2.61. Here we see that the rotor advances in clockwise direction by a full-step of 30°. In a similar way if $C_3$ is closed and $C_2$ is opened simultaneously, phase C is energized, which makes rotor teeth 1 and 3 in line with stator teeth 2 and 5 as shown in Fig. 2.61 ($b_1$) X the rotor advances by further 30° in clockwise direction. Now if $C_3$ is opened and $C_1$ is closed simultaneously, the rotor teeth 2 and 4 will align with stator teeth 4 and 1 respectively, which causes movement of rotor in clock-wise direction by further 30°, see Fig. 2.61 (b₁) X (d). Uptill now the rotor has advanced by 90°. We have seen that when we operate (close) one contacter and open the preceding one, the rotor each time advances by 30°, hence by repeating the operation of contacters in sequence 1-2-3-1 i.e. energizing the stator phases in sequence A, B, C, A etc. the rotor will rotate in clock-wise direction in 30° steps. When the sequence of operation is made 3-2-1-3 or phase sequence CBAC etc. the rotor will rotate counter clock-wise.

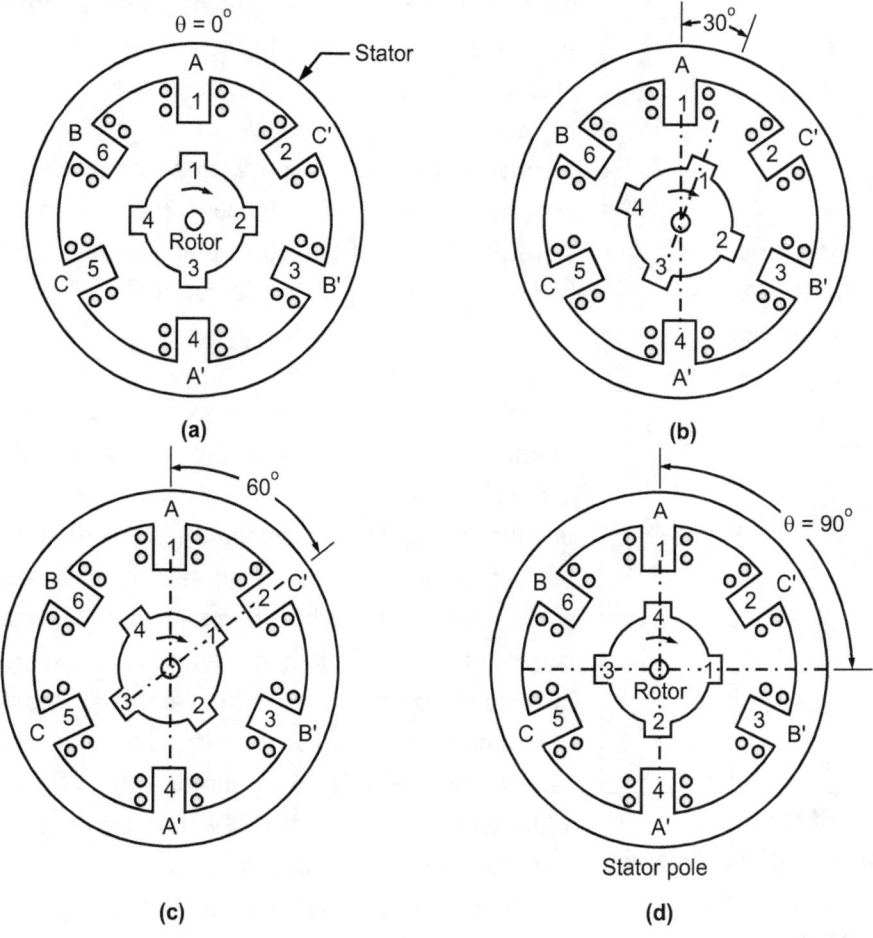

**Fig. 2.61**

This type of most of operation is known as 1-phase-ON mode or full-step operation.

**(ii) 2-Phase-ON mode:**

In this type of mode operation two phases are excited simultaneously. When phase A and phase B are excited together, the rotor experiences two torques from these phases and it comes to rest in a position mid-way between the two adjacent full-step positions. The phase switching truth table for this mode will be as follows.

If the stator phases are switched in sequence AB, BC, CA, AB, etc. the motor takes full-steps of 30° each, but its equilibrium positions will be interlevel) between the full-step positions. This type of mode operation provides greater holding torque and much better damped single-stack response than 1-phase on mode of operation.

### (iii) Half Step-Operation:

Truth Table

| A | B | B | θ |
|---|---|---|---|
| + | + | 0 | 15° |
| 0 | + | + | 45° |
| + | 0 | + | 75° |
| + | + | 0 | 105° |

2-Phase on mode
AB, BC, CA, AB

'Half step' operation or half-stepping is obtained by exciting the three phases in the sequence A, AB, B, BC, C etc., it means we have to excite one phase and two phase in sequence as given above or the motor is operated alternately 1-phase on and 2-phase on modes. It is also known as wave excitation. It causes the rotor to advance in steps of 15° i.e. half the full-step angle. The truth table for half stepping is given below for reference.

### (iv) Microstepping:

Truth Table

| A | B | C | θ |
|---|---|---|---|
| + | 0 | 0 | 0° |
| + | + | 0 | 15° |
| 0 | + | 0 | 30° |
| 0 | + | + | 45° |
| 0 | 0 | + | 60° |
| + | 0 | + | 75° |
| + | 0 | 0 | 90° |

Half stepping
Alternate, 1-phase on and
2-phase on mode
i.e. A, AB, B, BC, C, CA, A.

Microstepping or mini-stepping utilizes two phases simultaneously, similar to a 2-phase on mode but the currents flowing through these two phases are made unequal in magnitude deliberately. The current in phase A held constant while that in phase B is increased in very small steps, till it reaches its maximum. The excitation of current of phase A is then reduced to zero in steps of small increments. By this process the resultant step becomes very small and is called a micro-step. For example, a variable reluctance stepper motor with a resolution of 100 steps/rev., ($\beta$ = 3.6°) can with microstepping have a resolution of 10,000 steps/rev. ($\beta$ = 0.036). Micro-step stepper motors are used in printing and photo type setting where very fine resolution is required.

### Multi-stack VR stepper motor:

We have discussed only single stack VR stepper motors uptill now, multi-stack motors are also available which can provide smaller step angles.

Multi-stack VR motor is divided along its axial length into a number of magnetically isolated sections called as stacks, which are excited by separate windings or phases.

The number of poles on stator and rotor are equal in numbers. The stator have a common frame and rotor have a common shaft. The teeth (poles) of all the rotor are perfectly aligned with respect to themselves but stator teeth of various stacks have a progressive angular displacement.

**(v) Permanent magnet stepper motor:**

The stator of this type of stepper motors is constructed from ferromagnetic material similar to single stack VR motor. The stator has projecting poles while the rotor is cylindrical and has radially magnetised permanent magnets.

For understanding the working principle of such motors consider a stepper motor having two rotor poles and four stator poles, i.e. they are excited by two phases A and B. The step angle being equal to $360°/m \times N_r = 360/2 \times 2 = 90°$ or $\beta = (4-2)\,360°/2 \times 4 = 90°$ stator windings can be excited with either polarity current, (+A refers to positive current + $i_A$, in phase A and –A to negative current –$i_A$) Fig. 2.62 (a) shows the condition when phase A is excited with +$i_A$ in this case $\theta = 0°$, now if excitation is given to phase B and simultaneously disconnected from A as shown in Fig. 2.62 (b) the rotor advances by a full-step of 90° in clock-wise direction. In the next step phase A is excited with –$i_A$ excitation as shown in Fig. 2.63 (c) the rotor advances further by a step i.e. 90° in clockwise direction, in a similar way next the phase B is excited by –$i_B$ excitation, the rotor turns further by 90° in clockwise direction, as represented in Fig. 2.63 (b). Next the excitation of A with + $i_A$ makes the rotor complete one revolution of 360°.

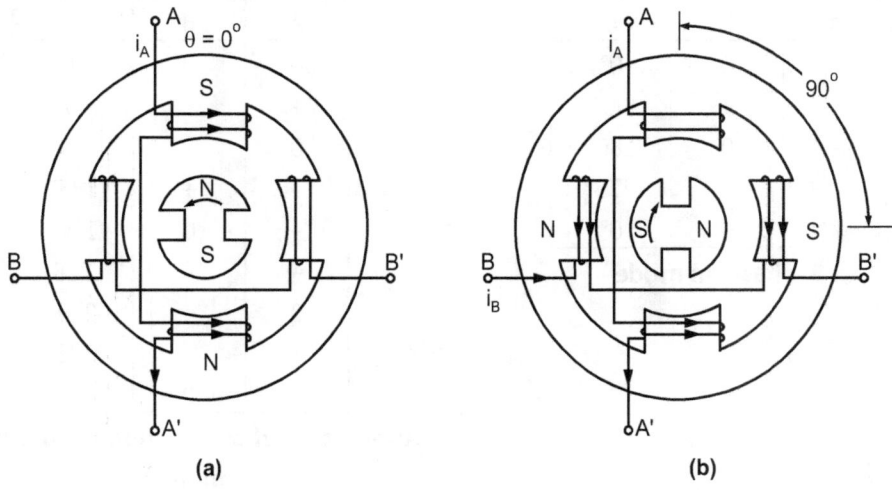

**Fig. 2.62**

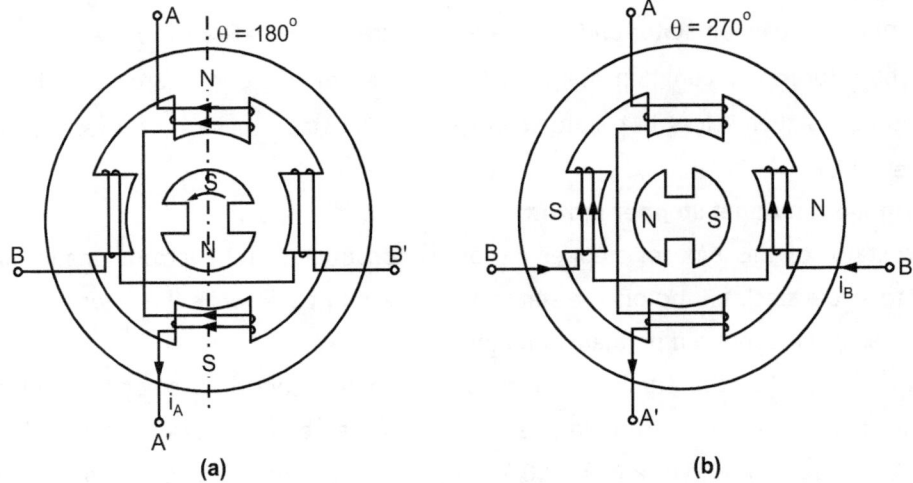

**Fig. 2.63**

The direction of rotation depends upon the direction of current through exciting windings. The sequence of excitation of phases A and B for clock-wise and anti-clockwise direction of rotation of motor is as follows :

$\left.\begin{array}{l} + i_A, + i_B, -i_A, -i_B, + i_A, \ldots \\ + A, + B, -A, -B, + A \ldots \end{array}\right\}$ For clockwise rotation.

$\left.\begin{array}{l} + i_A, - i_B, -i_A, +i_B, + i_A, \ldots \\ + A, - B, -A, + B, + A \ldots \end{array}\right\}$ For clockwise rotation.

Truth tables for one phase one mode and alternate 1-phase on and 2-phase on modes are given below for obtaining clockwise rotation of motor.

| A | B | θ |
|---|---|---|
| + | 0 | 0° |
| 0 | + | 90° |
| − | 0 | 180° |
| 0 | − | 270° |
| + | 0 | 0° |

**1-phase on mode**

| A | B | θ |
|---|---|---|
| + | 0 | 0° |
| + | + | 45° |
| 0 | + | 90° |
| − | + | 135° |
| − | 0 | 180° |
| − | − | 225 |
| 0 | − | 270° |
| + | − | 315 |
| + | 0 | 0° |

**Alternate 1-phase on mode and 2-phase on mode**

Two phase on mode can be obtained by energising two phases simultaneously.

This type do not requires external exciting current, it requires less power but has a high detent torque as compared to VR stepper motor. It has low acceleration due to high inertia. As it is not possible to manufacture small rotor with large number of poles, the step size in such motors is comparatively large which is from 30° to 90°. It produces more torque per ampere stator current as compared to a VR motor. Now-a-days disc rotors are used, which are magnetised axially to give a small step size and low inertia.

**Hybrid Stepper Motor:**

This type of motor combines the features of VR and permanent magnet stepper motor hence called as hybrid-motors. It consists of rotor having the permanent magnets, which are magnetised axially to create pair of poles N and S, Fig. 2.64. Two end caps are fitted at both ends of this axial magnet. These ends caps have equal number of teeth which are magnetised by respective polarities of the axial magnets.

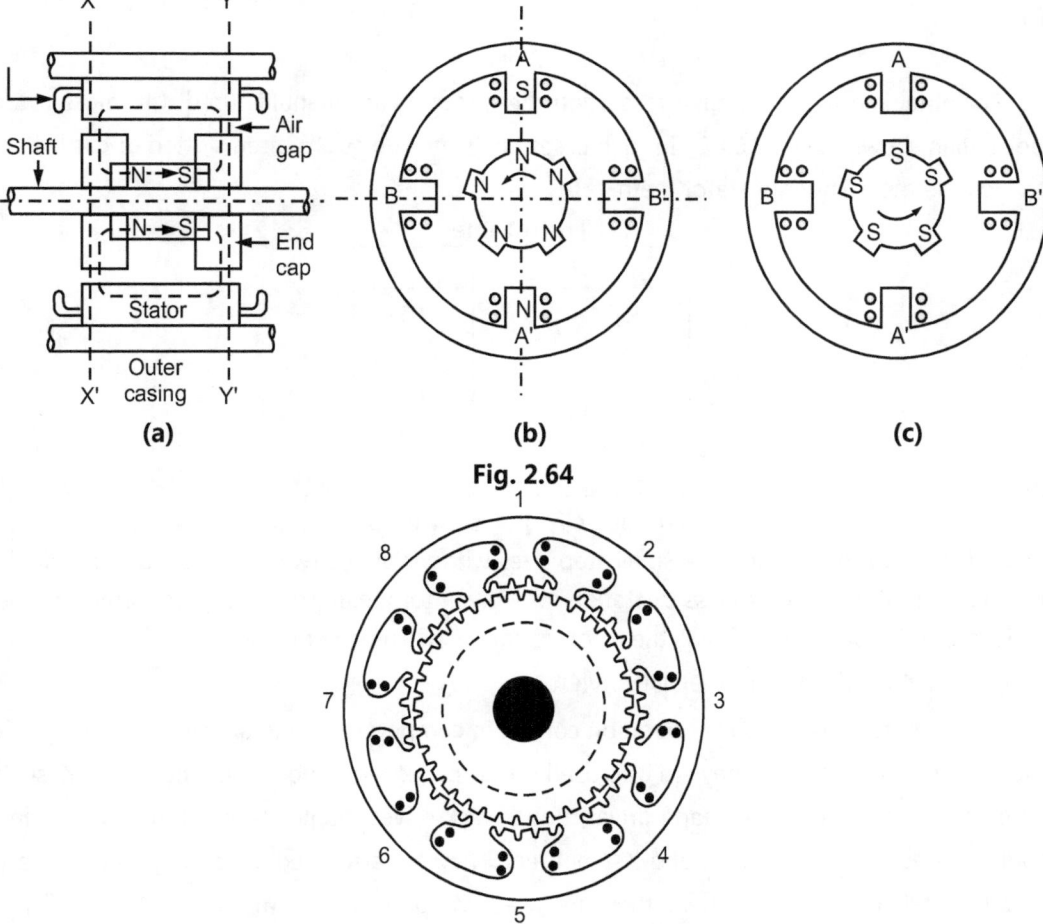

Fig. 2.64

Fig. 2.65: Castleated Stator Construction

The rotor teeth of one end-cap are off-set by a half tooth pitch. So that a tooth at one end-cap co-insides with a slot at the other. The cross-sectional views along $XX^1$ and $YY^1$ are shown in Fig. 2.64 (b) and (c) respectively. It is seen that stator consists of four poles, which are excited by two phases, the rotor has five magnets giving 5, N poles at one end and 5, S poles at the other end, the step angle of such a motor will be

$$= (5 - 4) \times 360 / 5 \times 4 = 18°$$

Consider that phase A is excited in such a way that top stator pole gives S polarity, so counter clockwise that it will attract the N pole of the rotor and brings it in line with $AA^1$ axis. To move the rotor, phase A is de-energised and phase B is energised positively, the rotor turns, in CCW direction by a full-step of 18°. Next phase A and B are energised negatively one after other to produce further rotation of 18' each in counter clockwise, The truth table for obtaining clockwise rotation is given in table below. The sequence of phases should be as follows.

$$+ A, - B, - A, + B, + A, \text{etc.}$$

For obtaining higher angular resolution these motors are manufactured with more rotor poles than shown in Fig. 2.64 $Z_1$. In such cases, the stator poles are often slotted or castleated to increase the number of stator teeth.

**Truth Table**

| A | B | θ |
|---|---|---|
| + | 0 | 0° |
| 0 | + | 18° |
| - | 0 | 36° |
| 0 | - | 54° |
| + | 0 | 72° |

**1-phase-ON, Full step-mode**

This type of motor can have small step sizes without difficulty. In comparison to variable reluctance motor it requires less excitation for a given torque. It provides good detent torque similar to PM motor, which holds the rotor stationary when power is switched off.

## 2.4.2 Application of Stepper Motors

These motors are used for operation control in computer peripherals, textile industry, I.C. fabrications and robotics. They are also used for purposes requiring incremental motion, such as type-writers, line printers, tape drives, floppy disk drives, numerically controlled machine tools, process control systems and X-Y poltters. They are also used for commercial, military and medical applications, where they are used for purposes of mixing, cutting, striking, metering, blending and purging.

## 2.4.3 Servomotors

These motors are also called as control motors and produce high torques. They are used for percise speed and percise position control at high torques. Their power rating vary from a fraction of watt to few 100 watts. They have low inertia, hence they respond at high speed, hence their length is more in comparison to their diameter. They operate at low speed, which may be zero also some times. They are used in radars, tracking and guidance systems, process controllers, computers and machine tools.

**Types of servomotors :**

Following types of servomotors are in use now-a-days.
(i) D.C. Servomotors.    (ii) A.C. Servomotors.

**(i) D.C. Servomotors :**

D.C. Servomotors are either separately excited D.C. motors or permanent magnet D.C. motors. Fig. 2.65 represents the schematic diagram of a separately excited D.C. motor. Fig. 2.66 represents the armature m.m.f. and field m.m.fs. of such a servomotor. The speed of this type of servomotor is generally controlled by varying the armature voltage. The armature of such-motors is purposely designed to have large resistance due to which the torque speed characteristics are linear, and have a large negative slope as shown in Fig. 2.65 (c). The negative slope of the characteristic is used for providing the viscous damping for servo drive system. As the armature m.m.f. and field m.m.fs. are in quadrature, it provides a fast torque response as torque and flux become decoupled. Accordingly a step change in the armature voltage or armature current produces a quick change in the position or speed of the rotor.

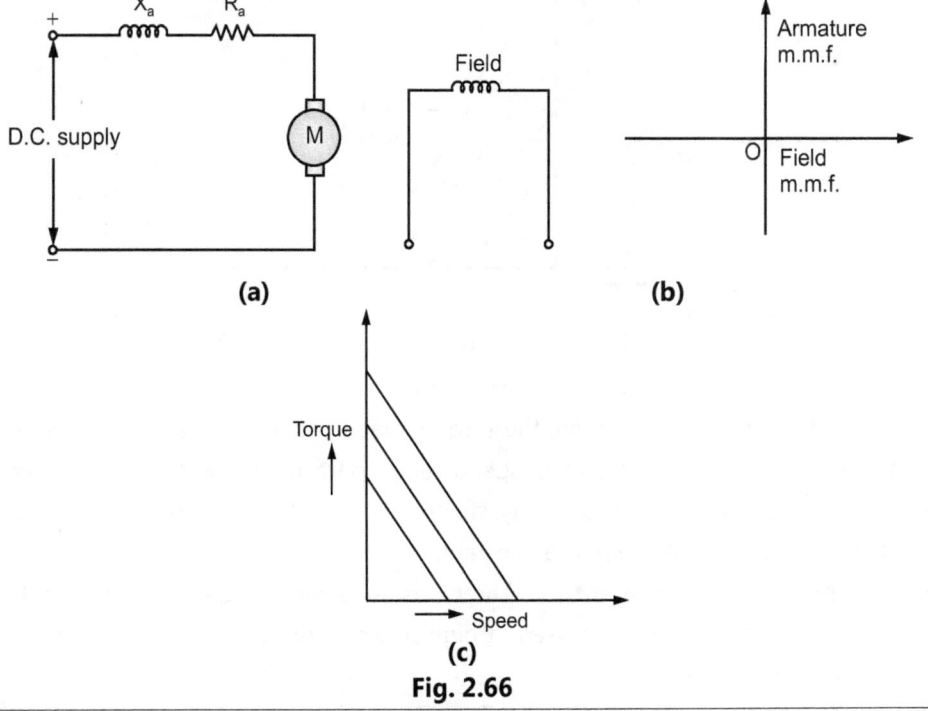

**Fig. 2.66**

## (ii) A.C. Servomotors:

Most of the A.C. servomotors are of the two-phase squirrel-cage induction type or three-phase type.

**(a) Two-phase A.C. servomotor:** The stator of such type of servomotors is similar to induction motors, and it Games two distributed windings, which are displaced from each other by 90° i.e. a two phase winding is carried out on it. The main winding which is also called as fixed phase or reference is supplied from a constant voltage source $V_m < 0$. The other winding which is called as control phase is supplied with a variable voltage of same frequency as that used for reference phase but displaced by 90° (electronic) voltage of the control phase is controlled by electronic controller. The speed and torque of the rotor are controlled by the phase difference between the main and control windings. When the phase difference is reversed the direction of motor reverses.

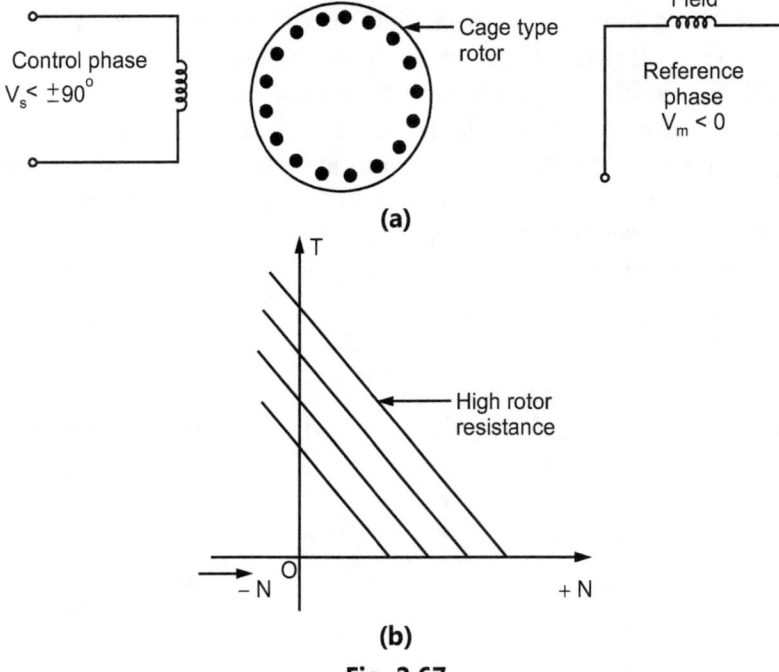

**Fig. 2.67**

As resistance of rotor bars is high, the torque-speed characteristics for various armature voltages are almost linear over a wide speed range particularly near the zero speed. The operation of motor can be controlled by changing the voltage of the main phase, while keeping the voltage of reference phase constant.

**(b) The phase A.C. servomotors:** Three phase squirrel-cage induction motors are modified now-a-days which can be used in high power servo-systems, which can give high speed and a high torque response.

## THEORY QUESTIONS

1. Explain what will happen if a D.C. series motor is connected to A.C., $1\phi$ supply.
2. What modifications are necessary to use a D.C. series motor as $1\phi$, A.C. series motor.
3. Draw the nature of operating characteristics of single phase A.C. series motor and explain in brief
4. What is universal motor?
5. Draw circuit diagram and explain any one method of speed control of universal motor.
6. What is a stepper motor? Explain the following terms in connection with stepper motor:
    (a) Step-angle
    (b) Resolution
    (c) Slewing
7. Draw figure and explain working principle of a VR stepper motor.
8. Draw figure and explain working principle of PM stepper motor
9. What is Hybrid stepper motor? Explain its working principal.
10. State the applications of stepper motors.
11. What are servomotors?
12. Draw circuit diagram and explain how a D.C. Servomotor works.
13. Draw circuit diagram and explain how a two phase A.C. servo-motor works.

## 2.4.4 Motors Selection

Due to the universal adoption of electric drive, it has become necessary for the manufacturer to manufacture motors of various designs according to the suitability and use in various classes of industry. This resulted in to number of types of motors. Hence the selection of the motor has become an important but the tedious process. Considering the conditions under which a motor is required to operate, following factors can be taken into account to decide the type of motor required :

**(1) Electrical Characteristics :** Following electrical characteristics can be considered.
   (a) Starting characteristics
   (b) Running characteristics
   (c) Speed control
   (d) Braking.

**(2) Mechanical characteristics :** These are enclosure and bearing
   (a) Structural features i.e. type of enclosure and bearing etc.
   (b) Method used for transmission of power

(c) Noise

(d) Type of cooling.

**(3) Size and rating of motor:** The following are the sub-heads under this category.

(a) Rating of motor

(b) Suitability of motor for continuous intermittent or variable loads.

(c) Over load capacity.

**(4) Cost :** Following factors should be taken into account

(a) Initial cost

(b) Running cost.

Initially, all these factors are thoroughly studied and the selected are assessed. The final selection made should be economical.

Following table indicates the load characteristics of different motors suitable for various purposes.

### Motor Suitability Table

| Load Characteristic | Type of Equipment | Suitable D.C. Motor | Suitable A.C. Motor |
|---|---|---|---|
| (i) Low torque, nearly constant speed.<br>(ii) Frequent start.<br>(iii) Load duration comparatively small. | Vacuum cleaners | Universal motor | Single phase universal motor capacitor start 1 $\phi$ induction motor |
| (i) Small load<br>(ii) High torque<br>(iii) High output | Small compressors<br>Shoe machinery<br>Wood working machinery<br>Refrigerator | | Repulsion type 1$\phi$ motor.<br>Repulsion start induction motor. |
| (i) Unloaded or loaded start.<br>(ii) Nearly constant speed. | Line shaft conveyors.<br>Grinders (Pulp) | Series motor | (i) Squirrel cage induction motor.<br>(ii) Slip-ring induction motor.<br>(iii) Synchronous motor for line shaft. |

| | | | |
|---|---|---|---|
| (i) Low load requirement.<br>(ii) Intermittent or continuous loads.<br>(iii) Constant speed.<br>(iv) Noiseless requirement. | Electric clocks phonography Instruments<br><br>Hair dryers. | | Shaded pole single phase motor. |
| (i) Constant speed<br>(ii) Load requirement upto 1 kW.<br>(iii) Starting torque between 1.5 to 2 times f.l. torque. | Electric fans<br>Blowers<br>Pumps | Shunt motor | (i) Squirrel cage inductor motor.<br>(ii) Synchronous motors. |
| (i) Variable speed<br>(ii) High starting torque | Conveyors<br>Shear<br>Floor mills | Compound motor coupled with fly wheel. | Squirrel cage inductor motor. |
| (i) Constant speed<br>(ii) High starting torque. | Rolling mill<br>Paper mill<br>Rubber mill | Compound motor coupled with fly-wheel | (i) Squirrel cage induction motor.<br>(ii) Synchronous motor. |
| (i) Frequent starting and reversing<br>(ii) Starting at full load.<br>(iii) Intermittent service. | Elevators small cranes and hoists<br>Large cranes and hoists. | Series motor<br><br>Series motor<br><br>Series motor | Squirrel cage induction motor.<br>Slip-ring I.M.<br><br>Squirrel cage induction motor. |
| (i) High load.<br>(ii) High starting torque.<br>(iii) Capable of with-standing heavy duty of rolling. | Iron and steel works | Specially designed shunt motor | Specially designed induction motor. |

| | | | |
|---|---|---|---|
| (i) Flammable gases surrounding the motor.<br>(ii) Variable load | Mining work | Compound motor | (i) For small load upto 10 h.p. squirrel cage inductor motor.<br>(ii) For high load slip-ring I.M. |
| (i) Variation in speed to a large extent.<br>(ii) High starting torque | Electric trains | Series motor | (i) Single phase series motor.<br>(ii) Three phase induction motor. |
| (i) Accuracy<br>(ii) Constant speed<br>(iii) Low load<br>(iv) Low starting torque. | Lathe milling machines. | Shunt motor | Induction motor with pole changing arrangement. |

# Chapter 3

# SINGLE PHASE AND THREE PHASE TRANSFORMERS AND THREE PHASE INDUCTION MOTOR

## 3.1 TRANSFORMER

### 3.1.1 Introduction

Transformer is a static machine, which transforms electrical energy from one alternating current system to another alternating current system without having electrical connection between them by the process of electromagnetic induction. While doing so there takes place a change in current, voltage i.e. a high voltage can be changed to low voltage with a corresponding change in current so the VA remains the same on both sides. Thus, change takes place without change in frequency. The physical basis of transformer is mutual induction between two circuits linked by a common magnetic flux.

Generally, electrical power is generated by using large capacity generators, which are installed near the fuel sources such as coal mines, oil and gas, resources, large hydro power plants are erected in hilly area, near the big dams, the high pressure water from which is used for generating electrical power. By such means we can not generate D.C. power as it has certain limits to generation voltage. Further this voltage can not be raised to very high value easily for transmission or a high voltage can not be easily lowered to low value; but if we adopt A.C. system, then it is possible by the use of transformer.

Generally in A.C. system, the generation voltage is of the order of 3.3 kV, 6.6 kV, 11 kV which is then raised to transmission voltage of 66 kV, 132 kV, 220 kV or 400 kV with the help of transformer. Hence, electrical power from the generating stations at remote places is transmitted to long distances where it is required at very high voltage and low current, the effect is, size of the transmission line conductors reduces, copper loss in the line reduces, and voltage drop is also less, this increases the transmission efficiency and regulation. At the receiving sub-station, the transmission voltage is reduced to the feeder voltage, subtransmission voltage using step-down transformer. Feeder voltage is then fed to distribution transformer to reduce it to 3 phase 400 volts or single phase 230 V, which can be used by the consumers for their domestic and other purposes. Hence, transformers play a major role in transmission and distribution of A.C. power. Hence, it can be stated that it is the transformer which has made possible the generation and wide spread development of A.C. system. Transformers are also used in rectifier, furnaces, for welding purposes, traction system, testing units, starting device, isolation system, converters, booster etc.

## 3.1.2 Principle of Operation

Transformer mainly consists of two parts (1) The magnetic circuit and (2) the electric circuits. The magnetic circuit is in the rectangular or circular form, in Fig. 3.1 shown a rectangular (laminated) magnetic circuit, which forms a magnetic frame. On this magnetic frame are shown windings primary and secondary separately represented by letters (P) and (S); though in actual transformer, both windings are wound with 50% turns on each limb. These windings are properly insulated from each other and the core (limb).

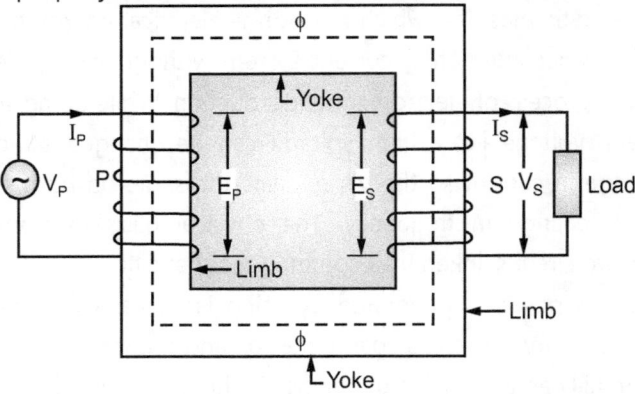

**Fig. 3.1**

The winding which is connected to source of alternating voltage is called as primary winding, while the winding from which voltage is applied to load is called as secondary winding. When a alternating voltage of $V_p$ volts is applied to primary winding, it being a closed electric circuit alternating current flows through it. This current produces a flux proportional to m.m.f., the turns being constant, flux proportional to current is produced, i.e. a flux alternating in nature and proportional to the magnitude of instantaneous value of current is produced by primary winding. The magnetic frame or core provides a low reluctance path to this flux; hence a alternating flux $\phi$ is established in the core. This flux links with the secondary winding, causing an induced e.m.f. to be developed in it. The e.m.f. developed in the secondary winding is due to the changing (alternating) flux produced by primary winding, and the winding being stationary it is called as statically mutual induced e.m.f., and its value as per Faraday's laws of electromagnetic induction is given by

$$E_s = -N_s \frac{d\phi}{dt}$$

where, $N_s$ is the number of turns of secondary winding and $\frac{d\phi}{dt}$ is the rate of change of flux, or

$N\frac{d\phi}{dt}$ Represents the rate of change of flux linkages.

The alternating flux $\phi$ produced by primary winding also links with the turns of primary winding ($N_p$) inducing in it statically self induced e.m.f. its value being $E_p = -N_p \frac{d\phi}{dt}$ as per Faraday's laws of electromagnetic induction. This e.m.f. is nearly equal in magnitude to supply voltage $V_p$ and acts in apposition to it (as per Lenz's law).

Now if load is connected across secondary then it will cause current to flow through it. Means secondary winding will supply electrical energy to load, but it can not generate electrical energy. Hence it is required to be received from some source. In case of transformer it is the primary winding which receives electrical energy and transforms it to secondary through electromagnetic coupling.

Transformers are generally used as step up or step down the voltage in alternating current system. The step up transformer transforms low voltage and high current A.C. in to high voltage low current A.C. while a step down transformer transforms a high voltage, low current A.C. in to low voltage and high current A.C. and if we neglect the losses taking place in transformer the input power is equal to out put power.

It should be noted that transformer will not work on D.C. supply system, because if D.C. is applied to primary winding a steady current flows through it and produces a constant (steady) magnetic flux; as there takes place no change in flux linkage ($N\phi$) there will be no A.C. induced e.m.f. developed either in primary or secondary.

## 3.1.3 (a) Construction of Transformers

Any transformer mainly consists of the following main components:

(i) Magnetic circuit consisting of core and yoke.

(ii) Electric circuit or windings.

The windings are primary, secondary and tertiary (if any).

(iii) The tank and other accessories such as, bushings, conservator, breather, explosion rent, tap changing arrangement, temperature indicators, Buchholz relay, radiator tank etc.

Depending upon construction, transformers can be classified as:

(a) Core type, (b) Shell type, (c) Berry type, (d) Spiral core type.

## (a) Core Type:

Fig. 3.2 (a) and (b) represents the constructional details of a core type single phase transformer.

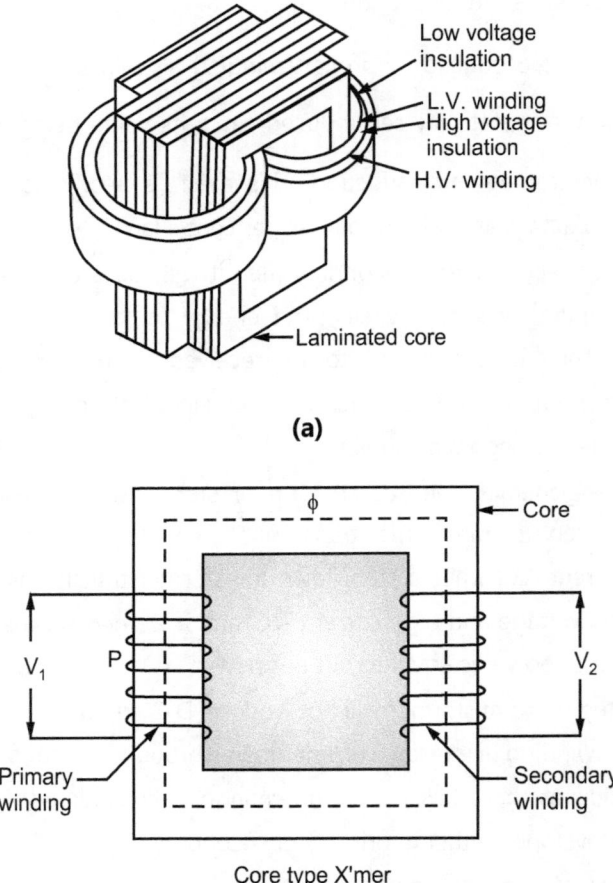

**Fig. 3.2**

In case of very small transformers the complete magnetic circuit can be punched as a whole as shown in Fig. 3.2 (a). In case of large transformer, the same practice can not be adopted because it will cause more wastage of magnetic material and will give trouble in carrying out the windings.

In case of large capacity transformers formed coils are used and are placed on the core after it is assembled.

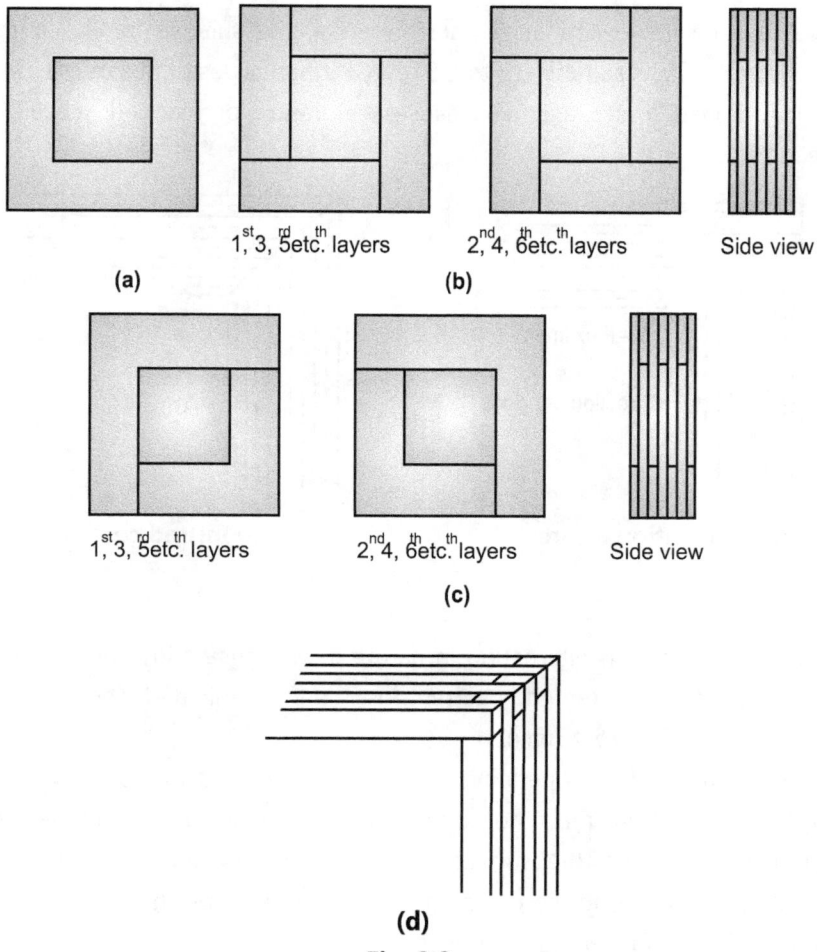

Fig. 3.3

The magnetic circuit of core type transformers is made of different types of laminations to give it a proper shape. In Fig. 3.3 (b) is represented the assembly of core using I shaped laminations. To eliminate the continuous air gap at joints, they are overlapped by the next layer of laminations. Fig. 3.3 (c) represents assembly of magnetic circuit using L-shaped laminations. In case of large core type transformers I type laminations are used and the joints between the limbs (core) and yoke are interleaved, Fig. 3.3 (d). In practice two or three laminations are arranged at a time. Fig. 3.3 (e) represent the difference in conventional and mitred joint which is used for reducing the hysteresis loss further, in case of construction of cores for modern transformers.

Transformer sheet steel consisting of 3% to 5% silica, having high resistivity and low hysteresis loss is used for transformer cores. Two types of such materials called as Hot Rolled Grain Oriented Steel (H.R.G.O.) and Cold Rolled Grain Oriented (C.R.G.O.) Steel are in general use. H.R.G.O. is used for low capacity transformers and is suitable for flux densities upto 1.45 tesla, while C.R.G.O. is suitable up to 1.8 tesla. Higher values of flux density increases no load current, no load losses and also causes saturation of magnetic circuit producing harmonic e.m.f.s.

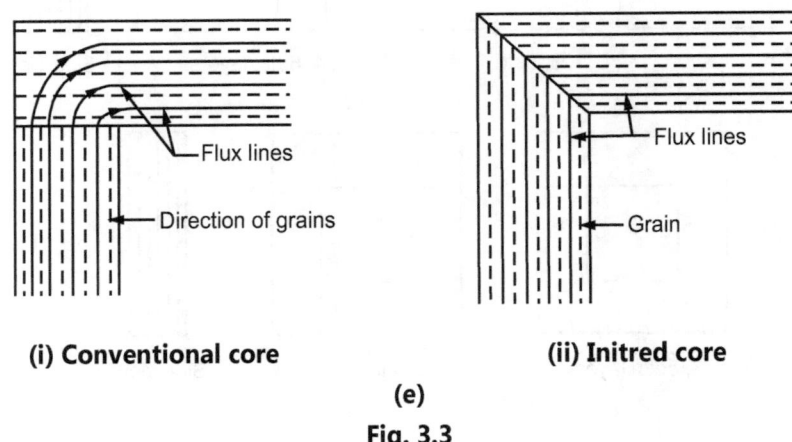

(i) Conventional core          (ii) Initred core

(e)

**Fig. 3.3**

As the flux in the core is alternating in nature it will cause eddy currents in it and the eddy current loss, to reduce the eddy current loss, core is laminated. The thickness of each lamination varies from 0.35 to 0.5 min.

Generally for transformers operating at 50 Hz, a thickness of 0.35 mm is used. Each lamination is insulated from the other, by providing a varnish-layer, a paper insulation or creating an oxide layer on the surface of laminations. At the time of punching the laminations, they are cut along the direction of grains, due to which the material gives high magnetic permeability and low hysteresis loss.

## 3.1.3 (b) Shell Type Transformers

**Core:** Fig. 3.4 (a) represents the details of single phase shell type transformer. The magnetic circuit, that is the core and yoke is built up by using.

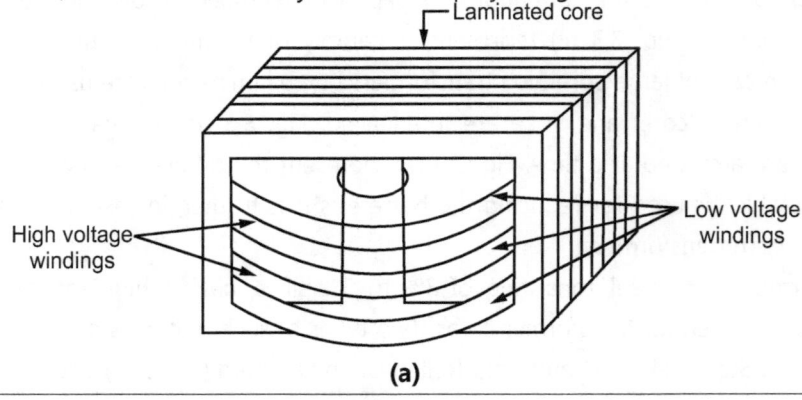

(a)

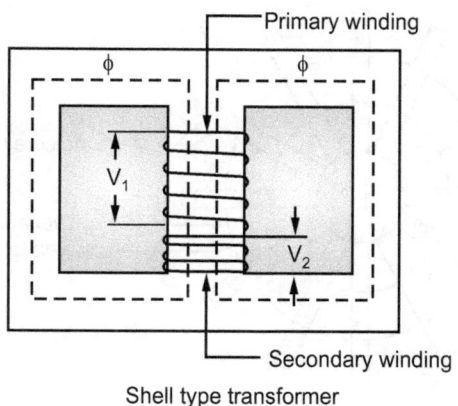
Shell type transformer

**(b)**
**Fig. 3.4**

The I type laminations, the arrangement is made to overlap the butt joints in the next layer the arrangement is shown in Fig. 3.4 (b). The width of central limb is generally twice that of the side limbs (core,) because the windings are carried out on the central limb, and the flux produced by primary winding get divided in to two parallel paths of the magnetic circuit i.e. 1/2 the flux passes through side core. This type of transformers are manufactured for low rating and the material used for core laminations is generally H.R.G.O. silicon steel having high resistivity and low hysteresis loss.

**Windings :** In case of shell type transformers also coils are form - wound but are multi-layer disc type. They are usually wound in the form of pancakes as shown in Fig. 3.4 (a). These pancakes or multi-layer discs are insulated from each other by paper insulation. While placing the disc on the central core, a precaution is to be taken that H.V. disc will be sandwiched between the L.V. disc and there will be L.V. disc at the bottom and top of the core, as shown in Fig. 3.4 (b). In this type of transformers the iron forms a shell for the coils, hence termed as shell type.

### 3.1.3 (c) Berry Type Transformers

Fig. 3.4 (c) represents the arrangement of Berry type transformer. It consists of a distributed magnetic circuit. The number of independent magnetic circuits is more than two. The yokes radiate out from the centre as shown in Fig. 3.4 (c) the arrangement of the L.V. and H.V. windings is as shown. This type of transformer construction is not used now-a-days; due to ease in construction and maintenance core type of transformers are preferred.

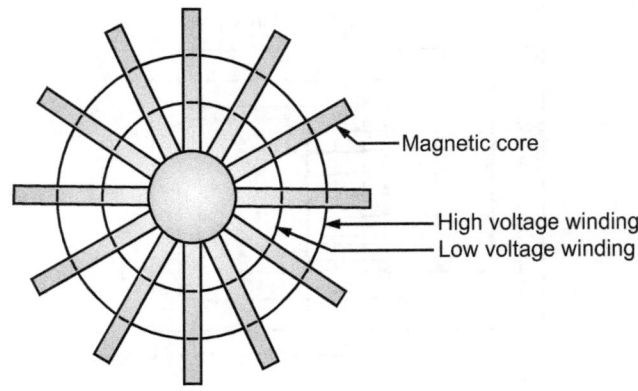

**Fig. 3.4 (c) : Berry type transformer (Plan View)**

## 3.1.3 (d) Spiral - Core Transformers

These type of transformers use the latest development in the core construction of transformers. For construction the core of this type of transformer a continuous strip or ribbon of the grain oriented silicon steel, cut in the direction of grain is used. This strip is wound in the form of a circular cylinder. Such a construction helps the flux to flow in the direction of grains. As C.R.G.O. is used for core, it makes it possible to operate at higher flux densities, and reduces the specific iron loss per kg, it will also reduce the requirement of iron, and also the weight of copper required, hence giving a less weight/KVA output; hence the overall cost will be reduced. At the same time efficiency is increased.

**Comparison of Shell and Core Type Transformers:**

1. In core type, windings surround the cores while in shell type core surrounds the windings.

2. Leakage flux is reduced by placing 1/2 the turns of each winding on each core while insulation cost is reduced by placing L.V. winding nearer to core in case of core type. In case of shell type leakage is reduced by sub-dividing each winding in to sections (pancakes) and inter Leaving L.V. and H.V. windings are as shown. The leakage reactance in case of core type transformer is still more than shell type.

3. Core type construction gives longer mean length of core and shorter mean length of coil turn.

4. Core type is more suitable for E.H.V. and H.V. requirements because insulation can be suitably provided between L.V. and H.V. windings.

5. In shell type construction, the windings are provided with good bracing and mechanical support, hence are less liable to damage due to high electromagnetic forces set up at the time of short circuits.
6. Shell type transformer requires more specialised fabrication facilities.
7. Core type transformer provides ease in fault finding and repairs at the sub-station site, hence now-a-days core type transformers are used in high voltage installations.
8. Regulation of core type transformers is poor in comparison to shell type.

## 3.1.4 Advantages of Transformer

The transformers being a static device it is having the following advantages:
(i) As it has no rotating parts the frictional and winding losses are absent.
(ii) Wear and tear of parts does not take place.
(iii) Efficiency of the order of 95% to 99.5% can be obtained.
(iv) Transformers can be designed and manufactured in a very large capacity and high voltage ratings such as 250 MVA and 400 kV.
(v) Cost of insulation required for the windings bushings etc., it being stationary is low and can be easily provided.
(vi) Effective cooling can be provided by providing separate radiators or air blast by fans etc.
(vii) It can be erected at load centres either by out door sub-station or indoor sub-station means.
(viii) It is possible to generate electricity at voltage such as 11 kV, 6.6 kV near the dams, fuel sources and can be transmitted to long distances at very high voltage and can be stepped down to desired voltage where it is required.

## 3.1.5 Types of Transformers

Transformers are classified in the following ways :
(i) Classification according to the frequency group.
   (a) Power frequency transformers 50 Hz.
   (b) Audio frequency transformers 50 Hz to 20 kHz.
   (c) Radio frequency transformers above 20 kHz.
(ii) The transformers can be classified according to the mode of operation as :
   (a) Voltage transformers used for stepping up or lowering down the voltage.
   (b) Current transformers used for lowering down the current.

(iii) They are also classified according to the type of cooling system used.

| No. | Method of Cooling | Type | Abbreviation |
|---|---|---|---|
| (a) | Natural Cooling | (i) Air natural cooled. | AN |
|  |  | (ii) Oil immersed natural cooled. | ON |
|  |  | (iii) Oil immersed force oil circulation with natural cooling. | OFN |
| (b) | Artificial Cooling (Air) | (i) Air blast cooling. | AB |
|  |  | (ii) Oil immersed air blast cooling. | OB |
|  |  | (iii) Oil immersed force oil circulation with air blast cooling. | OFB |
| (c) | Artificial Cooling (Water) | (i) Oil immersed water cooling. | OW |
|  |  | (ii) Oil immersed forced oil circulation with water cooling. | OFW |
| (d) | According to purpose for which it is used | (i) Power transformers. |  |
|  |  | (ii) Distribution transformers. |  |
|  |  | (iii) Testing transformers. |  |
|  |  | (iv) Instrument transformers. | (C.T. and P.T.) |

## 3.1.6 Constructional Details of a Single Phase Transformer with Different Accessories or Attachments

Fig. 3.5 represents the constructional details of a assembled single phase transformer having rating above 200 kVA. The assemble transformer with windings is housed in a steel tank (leak proof) with cooling tubes as shown in Fig. 3.5. To the tank are fixed other important accessories such as bushings (H.V. and L.V.), a conservator tank to which attached a breather, the oil level indicator so as to maintain minimum oil level required by tapping it from conservator.

In the pipe line connecting tank (main) and conservator tank is fixed a gas actuated Buchholz's relay. The connections of the windings are brought out and insulated from tank by means of conducting rods passed through bushings and used as terminals of transformer. A safety protection in case of heavy faults is provided by means of explosion vent.

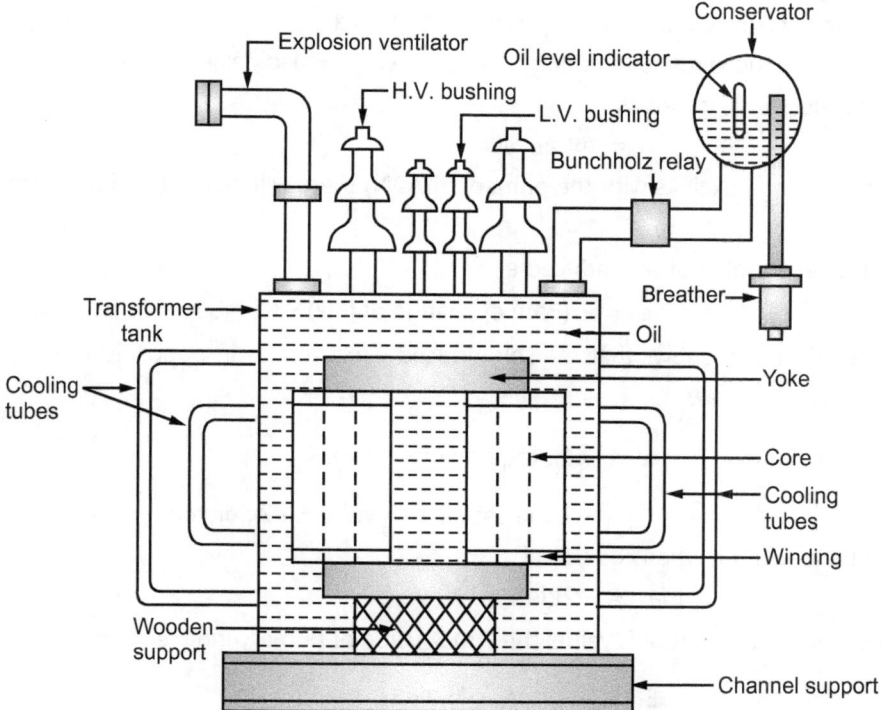

**Fig. 3.5**

## 3.1.7 (a) Transformer e.m.f. Equation

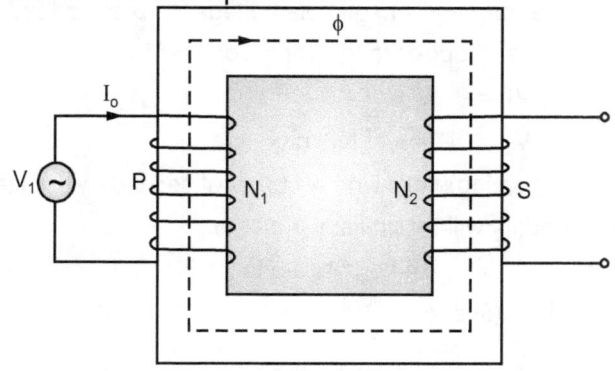

**Fig. 3.6**

Fig. 3.6 represents a core type transformer, with its primary winding (P) connected to a source of alternating voltage $V_1$; it will cause a small current $I_o$ to flow through it. This current produces and establish alternating flux $\phi$ in the transformer core. This alternating (varying) flux links with the secondary (S), having $N_2$ turns and produces an e.m.f. $E_2$ in it by mutual induction. The same flux $\phi$ links with $N_1$ turns of primary (P) and produces an e.m.f. $E_1$ due to self induction.

Let $V_1$ be the sinusoidal voltage applied to the primary.

The flux produced by this voltage will also vary sinusoidally, hence flux at any time (instantaneous) will be given as

$$\phi = \phi_m \sin \omega t \qquad \ldots (3.1)$$

As this varying flux links with the primary turns $N_1$ there will be a self induced e.m.f. in the primary.

Instantaneous value of self induced e.m.f.

$$e = -(\text{Rate of change of flux}) \times \text{Number of turns, volts}$$

The negative sign shows that the self induced e.m.f. will be in opposition to the applied voltage as per Lenz's law.

or
$$e = -\frac{d}{dt}(\phi_m \sin \omega t) \times N_1 \text{ volts} \qquad \ldots (3.2)$$

$$= -\phi_m \omega \cos \omega t \times N_1 \text{ volts} = -2\pi f \phi_m \cos \omega t \times N_1 \text{ volts}$$

e will be maximum when $\cos \omega t = 1$

$\therefore \qquad E_1 \text{ max} = -2\pi f \phi_{max} \times N_1 \text{ volts}$

As we always record R.M.S. value, the R.M.S. value of primary induced e.m.f.

$$E_1 = -\frac{2\pi}{\sqrt{2}} f \phi_{max} N_1 \text{ volts}$$

or
$$E_1 = -4.44 \phi_m f N_1 \text{ volts} \qquad \ldots (3.3)$$

As the resistance of the primary is negligible voltage drop at no load is negligible and $E_1$ will be approximately equal and opposite to supply voltage $V_1$.

or $\qquad V_1 = -E_1$

$\therefore \qquad V_1 = 4.44 \phi_m f N_1 \text{ volts} \qquad \ldots (3.4)$

Now the same flux $\phi$ (varying) links with $N_2$ turns of secondary, hence the induced e.m.f. (R.M.S. value) in the secondary will be similarly equal to

$$E_2 = -4.44 \phi_m f N_2 \text{ volts} \qquad \ldots (3.5)$$

Taking ratio of equations (5) and (3),

$$\frac{E_2}{E_1} = \frac{N_2}{N_1} = \text{Constant say K}$$

Where K is called as transformation ratio of a transformer.

If $B_m$ = flux density in core and $A_i$ = Net iron area of core, then

$$\phi_m = B_m \times A_i$$

and $\qquad A_i \text{ net} = A_i \text{ gross} \times \text{Iron factor (stacking factor)}$

$\therefore \qquad E_1 = 4.44 B_m A_i f N_1$ volts, where $A_i$ = Net iron area

and $\qquad E_2 = 4.44 B_m A_i f N_2$ volts

While comparing equations (3.1) and (3.2) it is observed that equation (3.1) giving flux $\phi$ is sine function while equation (3.2) giving induced e.m.f. is negative cosine function.

The equation (3.2) i.e. $e = -\omega \phi_m \cos \omega t \times N_1$ can be written as

$$e = -\omega \phi_m \sin(\omega t - \pi/2) \times N_1 \text{ volts.} \quad \ldots (3.6)$$

i.e. the instantaneous value of induced e.m.f. lags by 90° to the instantaneous value of flux $\phi$, producing it.

**Second - Method:**

Fig. 3.7 represents, one cycle of sinusoidal flux established in the core of the transformer when a sinusoidal voltage $V_1$ is applied across its primary.

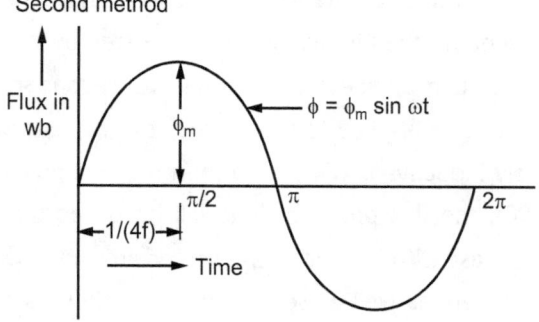

**Fig. 3.7**

It is seen that the flux starts varying from zero value and reaches to its maximum value $\phi_m$ in one quarter of the cycle. The time for completion of 1/4 cycle will be equal to $\frac{1}{4f}$ seconds, as $T = \frac{1}{f}$ i.e. time period of one cycle.

$\therefore$ Average rate of change of flux $= \dfrac{\text{Change in flux}}{\text{Time taken}} = \dfrac{\phi_m}{\frac{1}{4f}} = 4 \phi_m f$ weber/sec.

As per the statement of Faraday's law of electromagnetic induction,

Average rate of change of flux = Average induced e.m.f. per turn.

$\therefore$ Average induced e.m.f. in primary winding $= 4 \phi_m f N_1$ volts. $\quad \ldots (3.7)$

$\therefore$ R.M.S. value of induced e.m.f. = Form factor

× Average value for sinusoidal voltage form factor = 1.11

$\therefore$ Primary induced e.m.f. $= 1.11 \times 4 \phi_m f N_1$ volts or

$$E_2 = 4.44 \phi_m f N_2 \text{ volts} \quad \ldots (3.8)$$

$\therefore \quad \dfrac{E_2}{E_1} = \dfrac{N_2}{N_1} = \text{constant say } K$

which is called as voltage ratio.

## 3.1.7 (b) Ideal Transformer

A transformer can be called as a ideal transformer, if its windings have no ohmic resistance, or there will take place no copper losses in its windings. When the alternating flux is established in core, there will not take place any iron losses (core-losses). There will take place no leakage of flux from its windings. Hence, no voltage drop on load i.e. the voltage of primary and secondary will remain constant; in other words the two windings of the transformer will work as purely inductive coils only.

It is not possible to construct such a ideal transformer in practice, however for clear understanding working principle of transformer it is started with such a imaginary transformer, and then can be reached to actual conditions step by step.

Fig. 3.8 (a) represents such an ideal transformer, its secondary is kept open and an alternating voltage of $V_1$ volts is applied to its primary, it will cause current $I_o$ to flow. As the coils (windings) are purely inductive $I_o$ will set up the magnetic flux $\phi$ in the core, which will lag the voltage $V_1$ by 90°; the flux produce by it will be proportional to its instantaneous value and will be in time phase with it; hence represented in phase with it in Fig. 3.8 (c). As this flux links with the primary as well as secondary turns, there is self induced e.m.f. $E_1$ in primary and mutually induced e.m.f. $E_2$ in secondary. The magnitude of $E_1$ is at every instant equal and opposite to $V_1$ as represented in Fig. 3.8 (b) and is called as counter e.m.f. of primary. The secondary induced e.m.f. is also in antiphase with $V_1$ and its magnitude is shown by vector in Fig. 3.8 (c) and its wave shape in Fig. 3.8 (b). From Fig. 3.8 (b) and Fig. 3.8 (c) it is clear that primary and secondary induced e.m.f.s act in phase and have a phase difference of 180° with supply voltage $V_1$.

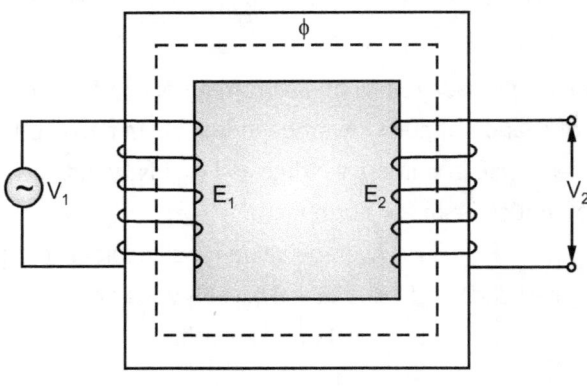

(a)

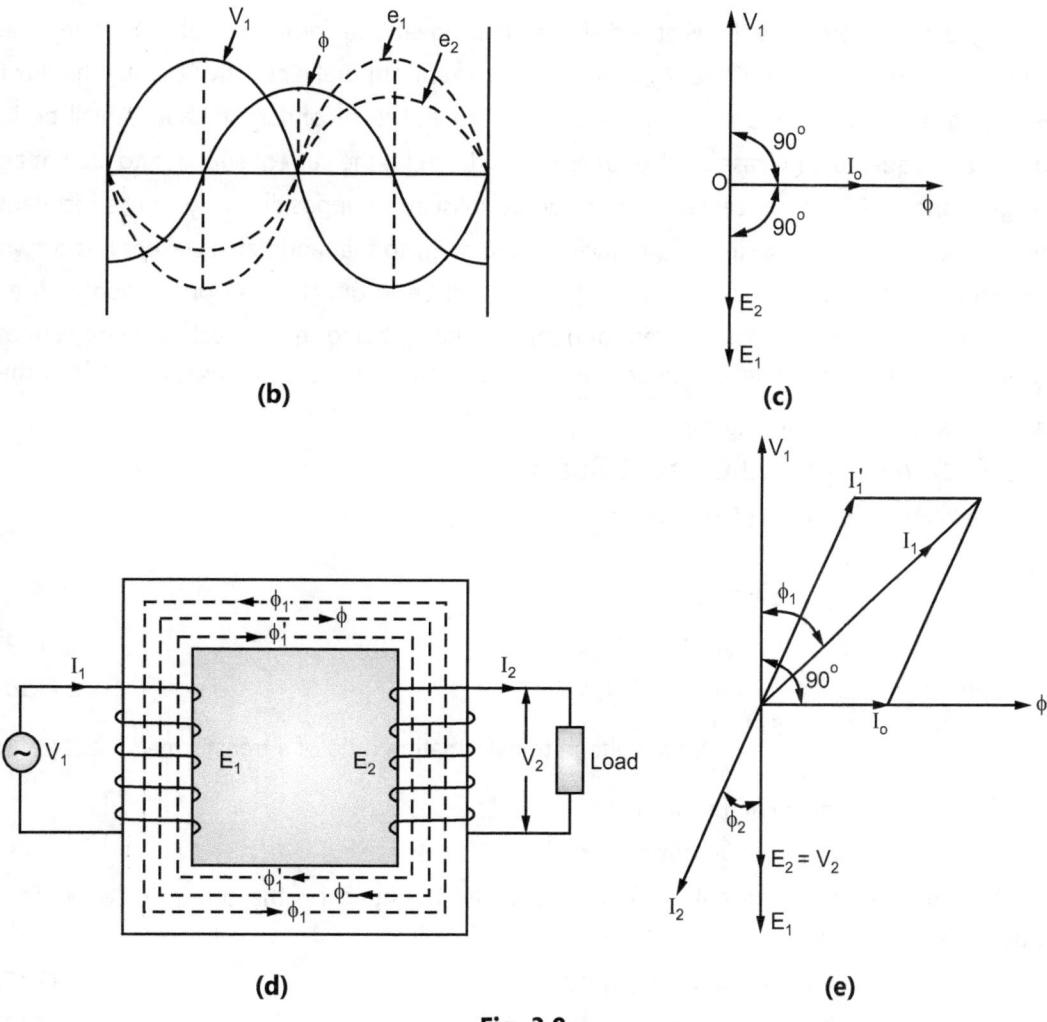

**Fig. 3.8**

Let a load be connected across the secondary terminals, so that it will cause current of $I_2$ amperes to flow from the secondary winding to load. When current of $I_2$ amperes, flow through the secondary winding it will produce its own flux the direction of the flux produced by secondary current will be such as to appose to the flux due to which e.m.f. is induced in secondary (As per Lenz's law), hence a flux $f_1$ as shown in Fig. 3.8 (d) in the opposite direction of flux $\phi$ is produced; the effect is that, resultant flux in the core is now ($\phi - \phi_1$), hence the counter e.m.f. $E_1$ reduces and the difference between $V_1$ and $E_1$ is now a real value, hence it will cause more current to flow through primary, say the additional current be $I_1$ amperes, this will set up a additional flux $\phi_1$ in the core in same direction as that of $\phi$, and will have a value equal and opposite to $\phi_1$. So that again a normal flux $\phi$ is established in the core.

Fig. 3.8 (e) represents the vector diagram of an ideal transformer on load. $V_1$ being the supply voltage, $I_o$ lags by 90° to $V_1$, as it being a current of purely inductive circuit. The flux f is in phase with $I_o$. $E_2$ and $E_1$ are lagging by 90° to $\phi$. The secondary voltage $V_2$ will be in phase and equal to $E_2$ in case of ideal transformer. Let $I_2$ be the current supplied to load at an lagging angle of $\phi_2$. It will cause flux $\phi_1$ to be established in opposition to $\phi$, hence resultant flux in the core reduces to $(\phi - \phi_1)$, reducing value of $E_1$, so that additional current $I_2$ is drawn by primary winding its value being $(K\,I_2)$ amps., will be in direct phase opposition of $I_1$ as shown in Fig. 3.8 (e). The total current of primary winding being then, equal to vector sum of $I_0'$ and $I_1'$ i.e. $I_1$ amperes in magnitude and phase as shown by vector diagram, it lags the applied voltage $V_1$ by an angle $\phi_1$.

## 3.1.7 (c) Voltage and Current Ratio

We know that in case of ideal transformer

$$V_1 = -E_1$$
$$V_2 = -E_2$$

Hence, $\quad E_1 = V_1 = 4.44\,\phi_m\,f\,N_1$ volts  ... (3.9)

and $\quad E_2 = V_2 = 4.44\,\phi_m\,f\,N_2$ volts  ... (3.10)

$\therefore \quad \dfrac{V_2}{V_1} = \dfrac{E_2}{E_1} = \dfrac{N_2}{N_1} = K$, voltage transformation ratio of a transformer  ... (3.11)

Also in case of an ideal transformer

$$\text{Input power} = \text{Output power}$$

If $I_1$ amperes is the current on primary side and $I_2$ amperes is the current on secondary side both at a p.f. $\cos\phi$ then,

$\quad\quad\quad\quad\quad$ Input $= V_1\,I_1\,\cos\phi$ watts  ... (3.12)

and $\quad\quad\quad$ Output $= V_2\,I_2\,\cos\phi$ watts  ... (3.13)

$\therefore \quad \dfrac{V_2}{V_1} = \dfrac{I_1}{I_2} = K$, the current ratio of the transformer,  ... (3.14)

Combining equations (3.11) and (3.14),

$$\dfrac{V_2}{V_1} = \dfrac{E_2}{E_1} = \dfrac{N_2}{N_1} = \dfrac{I_1}{I_2} = K, \text{ for an ideal transformer.}$$

## 3.1.8 (a) Losses in Transformer

In every machine, the output power can not be equal to input power, because some of the power input is lost in the machine as losses in it self, same is the condition of transformer, in no case its output power will be equal to input power. The power lossed by transformer it self is called as its losses.

The losses taking place in the transformer can mainly be divided into the following categories:
(i) Iron losses, taking place in the core of the transformer.
(ii) Copper losses, taking place in the windings of the transformer due to their resistance to flow of current. The other losses which are very low in magnitude and can be neglected are:
  (a) Dielectric losses, take place, due electric field set up between conductors and insulation.
  (b) Stray load losses, these losses are due to eddy currents set up in the conductors, when alternating current flow through them and also due to eddy currents set up in the tank and supporting structure of the transformer.

(i) **Iron losses :** These losses take place in the core of the transformer as it is subjected to an alternating flux. They are classified as
  (a) Eddy current losses
  (b) Hysteresis losses

These losses are independent of load on the transformer, hence are called constant losses and converted in to heat and cause temperature rise.

(ii) **Copper losses :** These losses take place when the current flows through the winding.

Copper loss taking place in primary winding = $I_1^2 R_1$ watts and

Copper loss taking place in secondary winding = $I_2^2 R_2$ watts.

Where $I_1$, $R_1$, $I_2$ and $R_2$ have their usual meanings.

Also total copper losses are equal to $I_1^2 R_1$ or $I_2^2 R_2$ watts, where $I_1$ is the primary current and $R_1$ is equivalent resistance referred to primary.

Similarly $I_2$ and $R_2$ are the secondary current and secondary equivalent resistance respectively.

These losses are proportional to square of current and are converted in to heat, hence are responsible for temperature rise of the transformer.

## 3.1.8 (b) Efficiency of Transformer

Like other machines, the efficiency of transformer can be defined as the ratio of output in watts or kilowatts to its input power in watts or kilo watts.

OR    Mathematically, efficiency = $\dfrac{\text{Output power in watts}}{\text{Input power in watts}}$

Also in case of an ideal transformer

Input power = Output power

If $I_1$ amperes is the current on primary side and $I_2$ amperes is the current on secondary side both at a p.f. $\cos\phi$ then,

$$\text{Input} = V_1 I_1 \cos\phi \text{ watts} \quad \ldots (3.15)$$

and

$$\text{Output} = V_2 I_2 \cos\phi \text{ watts} \quad \ldots (3.16)$$

## 3.1.9 Transformer with Losses Working at no Load

Uptill now we have discussed an ideal transformer. We will now proceed a step ahead, in which we will discuss the operation of transformer at no load. When the transformer primary winding is connected to its rated voltage and secondary winding is kept open circuited. The no load current $I_o$ flows through the primary winding. Under this condition, there takes place a iron loss in the core as the flux established in core is alternating (Pulsating) hysteresis and eddy current loss will take place. Also there will take place a small (negligible) copper loss in primary winding, because $I_o$ is very small and resistance of the winding is also low. There takes place no copper loss in the secondary as in this condition secondary current is nil. Hence the no load current $I_o$ is not wholly reactive i.e. it does make an angle of 90° with $V_1$, is less than 90', hence the power input at no load.

$W_o = V_1 I_o \cos\phi_o$ where $\cos\phi_o$ is the primary power factor under no load conditions. The no load current $I_o$ has to perform two functions:

(i) To supply no load losses of transformer.
(ii) To set up a magnetic flux in the transformer core.

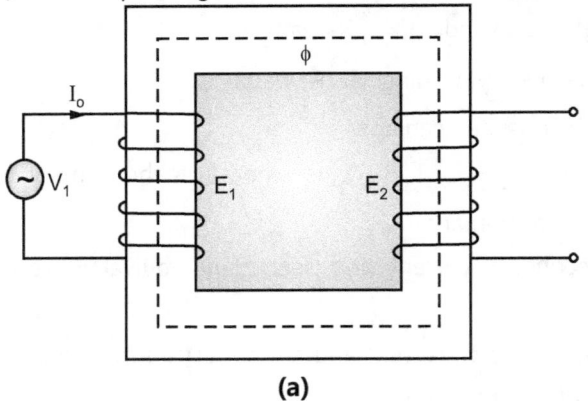
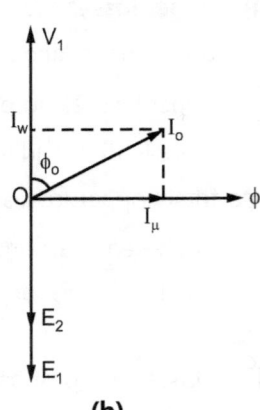

(a)                                            (b)

**Fig. 3.9**

The circuit for no load operation of transformer represented in Fig. 3.9 (a). The vector diagram for the no load condition of the transformer will be as shown in Fig. 3.9 (b), in which $I_o$ is making angle $\phi_o$ with $V_1$. Now $I_o$ can be resolved in to two components one in the direction of flux $\phi$ equal to $I_o \sin\phi_o$ and called as magnetising component of no load current and is represented by letter $I\mu$. While the other component is in the direction of $V_1$ and is equal $I_o \cos\phi_o$ and is used to supply the losses taking place in transformer at no load, and is represented by letter $I_w$.

The vector sum of $I_w$ and $I\mu$ is equal to $I_o$ or

$$I_o = \sqrt{(I_o \cos \phi_o)^2 + (I_o \sin \phi_o)^2}$$

or

$$I_o = \sqrt{I_\omega^2 + I_\mu^2}$$

As the no load current is very small, the no load Cu losses which are proportional to $I_o^2$, will be negligible, hence the power input at no load condition of transformer, when the primary is connected to its rated voltage is taken as the iron losses of transformer. The small amount of copper losses taking place in primary are neglected, and there are no Cu losses in the secondary winding being open circuited.

## 3.1.10 (a) Transformer with Winding Resistance

As the windings of the transformers are carried out of conducting material such as copper or aluminium, it will have resistance. Hence, while approaching a step ahead towards actual transformer, we will discuss now, the effect of winding resistance on the operation of transformer. Let the ohmic value of primary and secondary winding resistances be $r_1$ and $r_2$ ohms respectively. For understanding winding the concept, they are represented out side the winding in Fig. 3.10 (a). $I_2$ amperes be the current supplied to load by secondary winding. $V_2$ be the T.V. (load voltage). This voltage will be less than secondary induced e.m.f. $E_2$ by a value of voltage drop, $I_2\, r_2$ (vectorially) in the secondary winding. When current $I_2$ is supplied by secondary its equivalent $I_1' = K\, I_2$ is drawn by the primary, the total primary current being vector sum of $I_o$ (No load current) and $I_1'$ i.e. $I_1$ amperes flows through the primary winding, it will cause a resistance drop $I_1\, r_1$ in the primary winding resistance. Hence, the supply voltage $V_1$ must be equal to vector sum of $E_1$ (primary induced e.m.f.) and $I_1\, r_1$ (voltage drop in primary winding resistance).

Hence, we can write down the equation for primary and secondary voltages as follows.

$$V_2 = E_2 - I_2\, r_2 \quad \ldots (3.17)$$

and

$$V_1 = E_1 + I_1\, r_1 \quad \ldots (3.18)$$

**Circuit representation:**

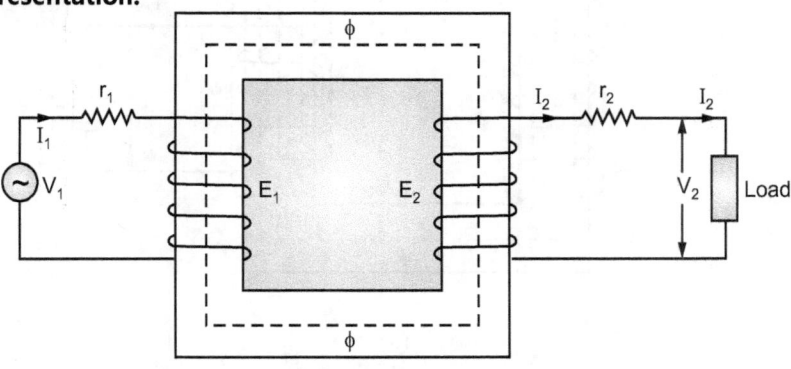

**Fig. 3.10 (a)**

The vector diagrams for resistive load i.e. when $I_2$ is in phase with $V_2$, inductive load or lagging p.f. condition i.e., when $I_2$ lags $V_2$ by angle $\phi_2$ and for capacitive load i.e., leading p.f. load, when $I_2$ leads $V_2$ are drawn in Fig. 3.10 (b), (c) and (d) respectively.

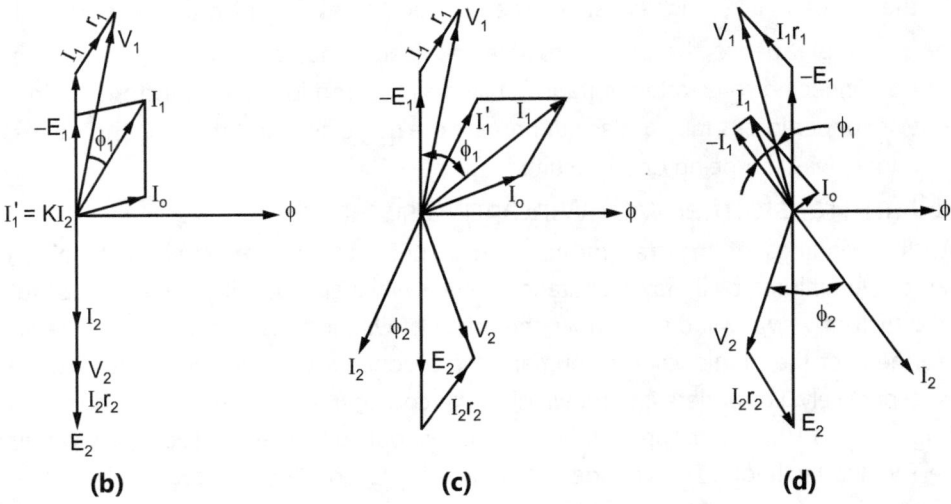

Fig. 3.10

## 3.1.10 (b) Transformer with Leakage Flux

Uptill now we have assumed that all the flux produced by primary or secondary windings is linked with the primary and secondary windings. But in actual practice the total flux produced can be divided into the following.

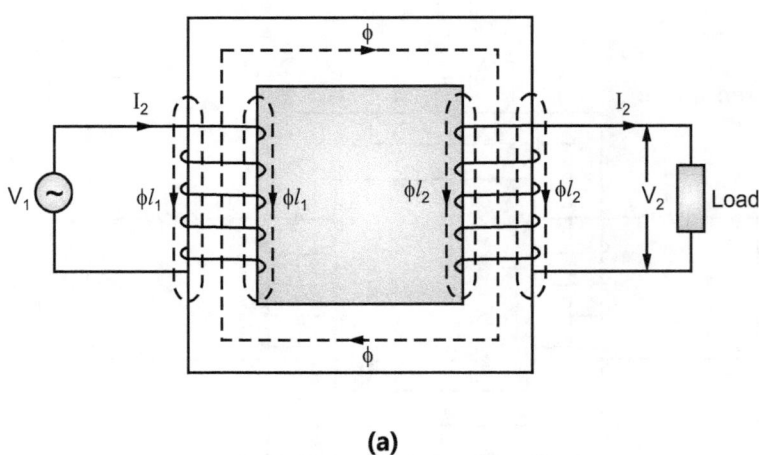

(a)

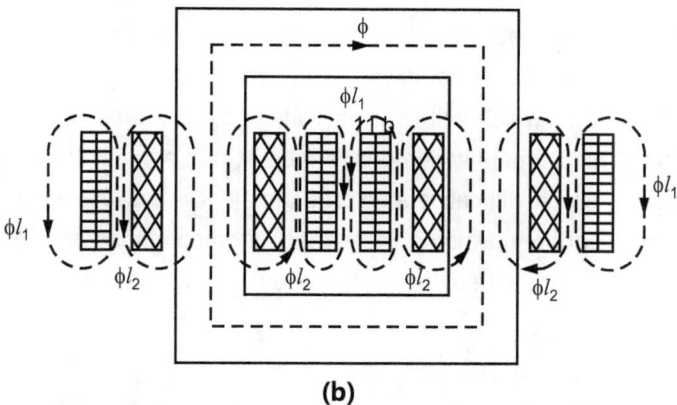

**(b)**
**Fig. 3.11**

(i) The flux which links with both the primary and secondary windings.

(ii) The flux $\phi\, l_1$ which links with primary winding only and completes its path through air.

(iii) The flux $\phi\, l_2$ which links with the secondary winding only, and completes its path through air as shown in Fig. 3.11 (a) and (b).

The fluxes given by (ii) and (iii) above, which are linked by only one winding and leak through air are known as primary and secondary leakage fluxes respectively.

## 3.1.10 (c) Leakage Reactance

$\phi\, l_1$ the leakage flux of primary winding is proportional to primary current $I_1$ as this leakage flux is due to primary winding only and links with the turns of primary winding $N_1$ it will induce an e.m.f. in the primary winding only. The flux $\phi\, l_1$ in time phase with the total primary current $I_1$ amps. The e.m.f. $e_1$ induced by $\phi\, l_1$ must lag $\phi\, l_1$ and $I_1$ by 90°. The e.m.f. is necessary to balance this back (counter) e.m.f. is opposite and equal to it, and therefore leads the current $I_1$ by 90°. As this e.m.f. $e_1$ induced by the primary leakage flux is proportional to current $I_1$ and lags it by 90°, it is similar to a reactance voltage and can be represented by $e_1 = -I_1 X_1$. The component of supply voltage that will balance this e.m.f. must be $+I_1 X_1$. Hence, the effect of the primary leakage flux is to induce an e.m.f. that opposes the current flowing to the transformer.

The leakage flux $\phi\, l_2$ links with the secondary turns $N_2$ only ; induces an e.m.f. $e_2$ in the secondary lagging the current $I_2$ by 90°. This is also similar to a reactance voltage and the component that balances it, must lead the secondary current by 90°. Hence, it can be represented by $e_2 = I_2 X_2$. And the balancing voltage = $I_2 X_2$. The secondary reactance opposes the current flowing out of secondary winding.

In actual transformer, the primary and secondary windings are not placed on separate legs, if they are placed so, large primary and secondary leakage fluxes will take place and the effect will be the poor regulation of transformer. Hence to reduce the leakage flux, the primary and secondary should be interleaved as shown in Fig. 3.11 (b).

The imaginary value $X_1$ which will cause a voltage drop equal to $-I_1 X_1$ balancing e.m.f due to leakage flux $\phi\ l_1$ of primary winding is termed as primary leakage reactance. While the imaginary ray value $X_2$ which will cause a voltage drop equal to $I_2 X_2$, balancing e.m.f. due to leakage flux $\phi\ l_2$ of secondary winding is termed as secondary leakage reactance; these reactance values can be represented in circuit as shown in Fig. 3.11 (c).

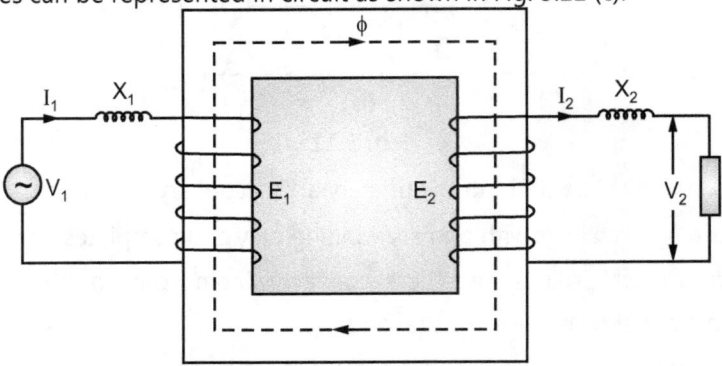

**Fig. 3.11 (c)**

## 3.1.10 (d) Actual Transformer Vector Diagram on Load

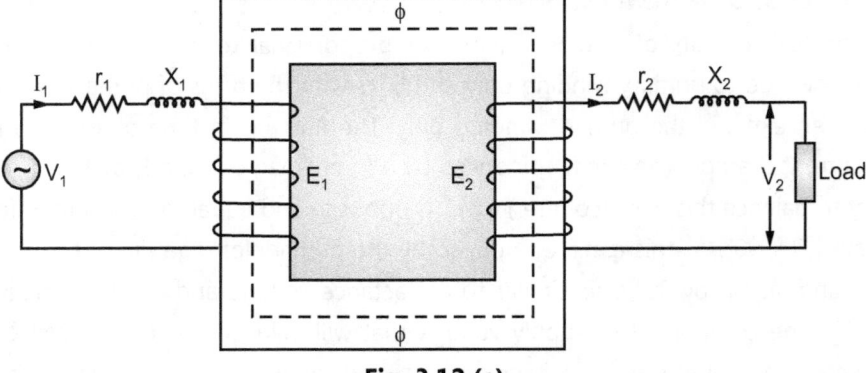

**Fig. 3.12 (a)**

Fig. 3.12 (a) represents the circuit of a actual transformer, when delivering load current $I_2$ amperes at a terminal voltage of $V_2$ volts and load p.f. being cos $\phi_2$ lag. For understanding the primary and secondary resistances and reactances are represented separately out side the windings.

Let $\phi$ be flux set up in the core, it is drawn in magnitude and direction along X axis as shown in Fig. 3.12 (b). The vector for secondary and primary induced e.m.f. $E_2$ and $E_1$ will lag by 90° to $\phi$. Secondary current $I_2$ is drawn lagging $V_2$ by an angle $\phi_2$. Now the secondary resistance drop $I_2\ r_2$ will act in phase with $I_2$ and is added to $V_2$ as shown. The secondary current $I_2$ will set up a leakage flux $\phi\ l_2$, in time phase with $I_2$; and will induce an e.m.f. $e_2$ lagging $\phi\ l_2$ by 90°, this e.m.f. is counter balanced by a component of secondary induced e.m.f. equal and opposite to $e_2$ represented by $I_2 X_2$ leading $I_2$ by an angle of 90°. Hence, secondary induced e.m.f. $E_2$ is now equal to $\bar{V}_2 + \bar{I}_2 r_2 + \bar{I}_2 X_2$.

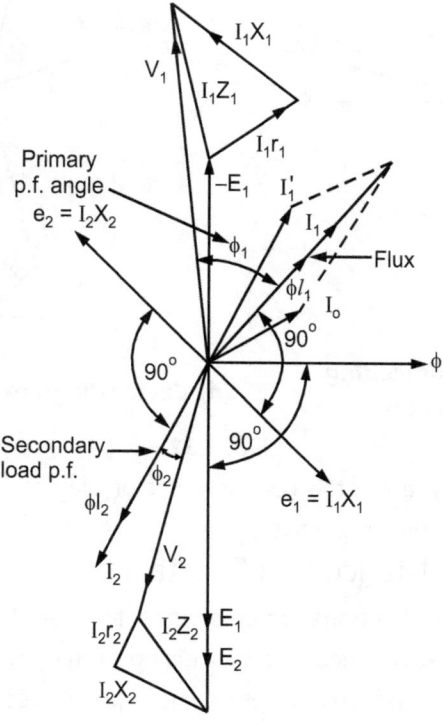

**Fig. 3.12 (b)**

The primary induced e.m.f. $E_1$ also lags the mutual flux $\phi$ by 90° and is in phase with $E_2$. The supply voltage has to over come the counter equal $-E_1$ volts. Now when the transformer is loaded the secondary ampere turns are equal to primary ampere turns (neglecting ampere turns required for no load condition). Hence for a current of $I_2$ amperes on secondary an equivalent current $I_1' = K I_2$ flows in the primary winding. If $I_o$ is the no load current lagging supply voltage V, by $\phi_o$, then total primary current is equal to $I_1$ amperes lagging $V_1$ by $\phi_1$. This current produces a leakage flux of primary equal to $\phi l_1$ in time phase with $I_1$. The leakage flux $\phi l_1$ will induce an e.m.f. $e_1 = -I_1 X_1$, lagging $\phi\ l_1$ by 90°. The supply voltage $V_1$ has to over come now, the counter e.m.f. $E_1$, the primary resistance drop $I_1 r_1$ and $I_1 X_1$ leading $I_1$ by 90° as shown in Fig. 3.12 (b). The total primary current $I_1$ then makes an angle $\phi_1$ with primary supply voltage $V_1$ and is called as primary p.f. angle.

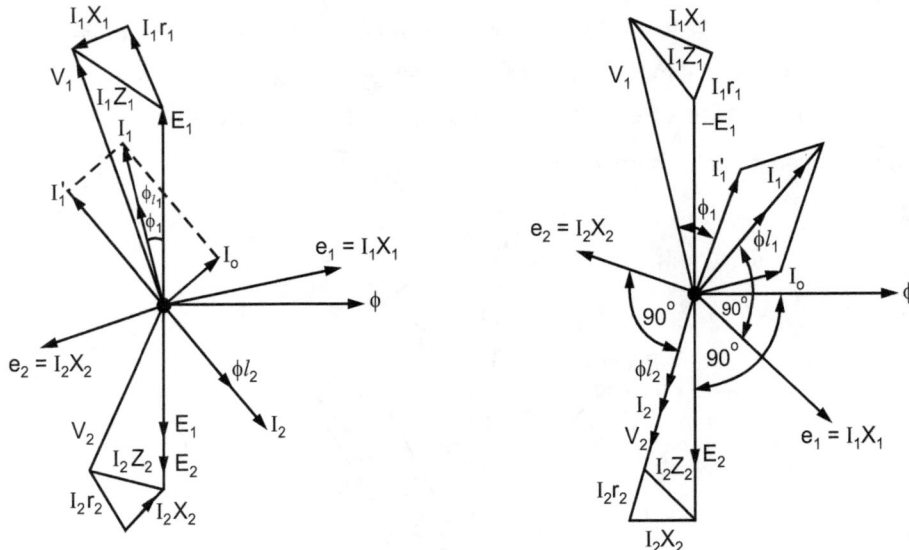

(c) Vector diagram for leading p.f. load connection

(d) Vector diagram u.p.f. road condition

Fig. 3.12

Fig. 3.12 (c) and (d) represent the complete vector diagram of transformer for unit p.f. and leading p.f. load conditions respectively.

## 3.1.11 Equivalent Resistance and Reactance

From the actual circuit of the transformer, on load it is seen that it has primary resistance, primary leakage reactance (combined together giving primary winding impedance), primary current, primary voltage. The primary current being equal to vector sum of primary no load current and equivalent of secondary current drawn by primary winding from supply source. The primary and secondary windings being magnetically coupled. The same quantities are there for the secondary winding, and a load impedance connected across secondary terminals. To make the calculations simpler, it is better to transfer the voltage, current resistance, reactance or impedance to either the primary side of secondary side.

When the resistance or reactance is transferred to either primary side or secondary side its effect should not change. The process of transferring the resistance, reactance or impedance to one side of transformer, so as to work in one winding only is called finding equivalent value referred to that side.

We will now see how the resistance, reactance or impedance can be transferred from one side to other.

Voltage drop in primary resistance = $I_1 r_1$
Voltage drop in secondary resistance = $I_2 r_2$

where,
- $I_1$ = Primary current in amperes
- $r_1$ = Primary resistance in ohms
- $I_2$ = Secondary current in amperes
- $r_2$ = Secondary resistance on ohms

Also we known that $\dfrac{E_2}{E_1} = \dfrac{I_1}{I_2} = K$ or $E_2 = K E_1$ and $I_1 = K I_2$.

Hence, primary resistive drop referred to secondary

$$= I_1 r_1 K \qquad \ldots (3.19)$$

but $\quad I_2 = I_2 K \qquad \ldots (3.20)$

Putting in equation (3.19) value from equation (3.20).

∴ Primary resistive drop referred to secondary

$$= I_2 r_1 K^2 \qquad \ldots (3.21)$$

Total resistive drop referred to secondary

$$= I_2 r_2 + I_2 r_1 K^2 = I_2 (r_2 + r_1 K^2)$$

i.e. the term $(r_2 + r_1 K^2)$ represents the total resistance of the transformer referred to the secondary and let it be equal to $R_2$.

∴ $\quad R_2 = (r_2 + r_1 K^2) \qquad \ldots (3.22)$

in a similar way, equivalent reactance referred to secondary

$$X_2 = (x_2 + x_1 K^2) \qquad \ldots (3.23)$$

Again secondary resistive drop as referred to primary side $= \dfrac{I_2 r_2}{K}$

but $\quad I_2 = \dfrac{I_1}{K}$

Hence, secondary resistive drop referred to primary side

$$= \dfrac{I_1 r_2}{K^2} \qquad \ldots (3.24)$$

The factor $\dfrac{r_2}{K^2}$ is called as secondary resistance referred to primary.

Similarly $r_1 K^2$ is the equivalent resistance of primary referred to secondary. Similarly the reactances can also be referred.

Total resistive drop referred to primary side

$$= I_1 r_1 = \dfrac{I_1 r_2}{K^2}$$

$$= I_1 \left( r_1 + \dfrac{r_2}{K^2} \right) \qquad \ldots (3.25)$$

The term $\left(r_1 + \frac{r_2}{K^2}\right)$ is known as the equivalent resistance of transformer referred to primary side and is represented by letter $R_1$. Hence,

$$R_1 = \left(r_1 + \frac{r_2}{K^2}\right) \qquad \ldots (3.26)$$

Similarly equivalent reactance (leakage) referred to the primary side

$$X_1 = x_1 + \frac{x_2}{K^2} \qquad \ldots (3.27)$$

Hence, primary and secondary resistive drop (equivalent)
$$= I_1 R_1 \text{ and } I_2 R_2 \text{ respectively}$$

$$\% \text{ Resistive drop } v_1 = \frac{I_1 R_1}{V_1} \times 100$$

and $\quad \% \text{ Resistive drop } v_2 = \frac{I_2 R_2}{V_2} \times 100$

$$\% \text{ Reactive drop } = \frac{I_1 X_1}{V_1} \times 100 \text{ or } \frac{I_2 X_2}{V_2} \times 100$$

where $V_2$ is the secondary no load voltage.

## 3.1.12 Equivalent Circuit of Transformer

An equivalent circuit of transformer is that circuit whose behaviour is identical to the behaviour of the transformer. Problem regarding the determination of voltage and current in the secondary side can be solved by means of vector diagram, but this method is quite labourious. Hence, it becomes convenient, if the transformer is replaced by its equivalent circuit and the problems will become easier.

For developing the equivalent circuit of the transformer, we will proceed step by step. Fig. 3.13 (a) represents the circuit diagram of transformer at no load condition, consuming no load losses (core loss + small primary copper loss) and drawing no load current $I_0$ from mains. Which is having two components, $I_\mu$ the component of no load current producing mutual flux $\phi$ in core and acting in phase with it and $I_w$ the working component of no load current supplying no load losses, which act in phase with supply voltage $V_1$. The component $I_\mu$ acts at an angle of 90° lag w.r.t. $V_1$, hence in the equivalent circuit it can be assumed that a imaginary pure reactance of value $X_0$ is connected in parallel with $V_1$, which draws a current $\frac{V_1}{X_0} = I_0 \sin \phi_0$ lagging $V_1$ by 90°. In a similar way $I_w$ acts in phase with $V_1$ and its value is $I_0 \cos \phi_0$, as currents through pure resistance only act is phase, It can be imagined that the loss component of no load current $I_\omega$ flows through a imaginary pure resistance $R_0$ connected in parallel with supply voltage $V_1$, or value of imaginary $R_0 = \frac{V_1}{I_w}$. Hence, the total no load current $I_0$ is divided in a imaginary parallel circuit consisting of $R_0$ and $X_0$ called as shunt circuit; as shown in Fig. 3.13 (b).

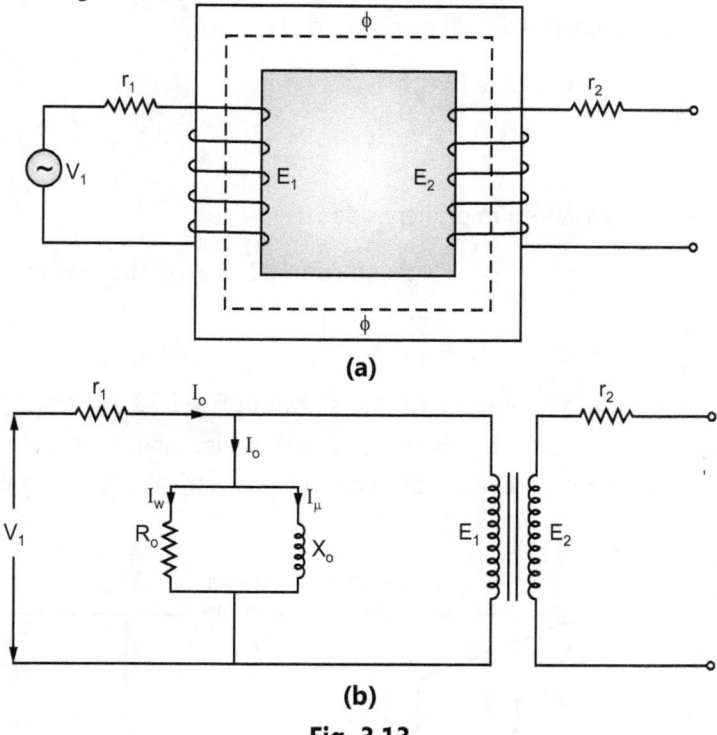

(a)

(b)

Fig. 3.13

In Fig. 3.13 (b) leakage reactance is not represented, because at no load the primary leakage flux will be negligible and there will be no leakage flux of secondary winding.

Consider now the actual conditions of the transformer, in which it is delivering a load current of $I_2$ amperes at a terminal voltage of $V_2$ volts to a load having load impedance $Z_L$. The resistance and reactance values being represented separately outside each winding and the shunt drawing the current $I_0$, being divided into $I_\omega = I_0 \cos \phi_0$ and $I_\mu = I_0 \sin \phi_0$. The windings are drawn to represent the magnetic coupling.

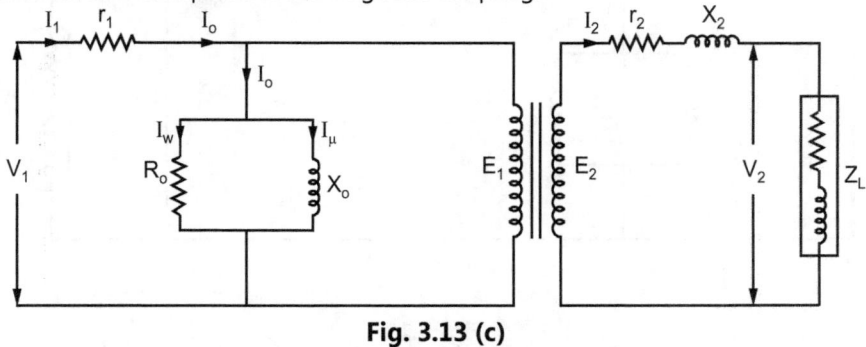

Fig. 3.13 (c)

Now the circuit of 3.13 (c) can be simplified if we transfer the secondary resistance, reactance, load impedance, voltage and currents on primary side. The secondary resistance $r_2$, when transferred to primary side will be equal to say

$$r_2' = \frac{r_2}{K^2}$$

Similarly,
$$x_2' = \frac{x_2}{K^2}$$

Secondary T.V. $V_2$, transferred to primary side,

$$V_2' = \frac{V_2}{K} \text{ and current } I_2' = K I_2. \text{ The load impedance}$$

$$Z_L' = \frac{Z_L}{K^2}, E_2' = \frac{E_2}{k}$$

The equivalent circuit then reduces to that shown in Fig. 3.13 (d) in which all quantities are transferred to primary side by their equivalent values and coils being removed for simplicity, as the above circuit is now the equivalent electrical circuit for the transformer under consideration.

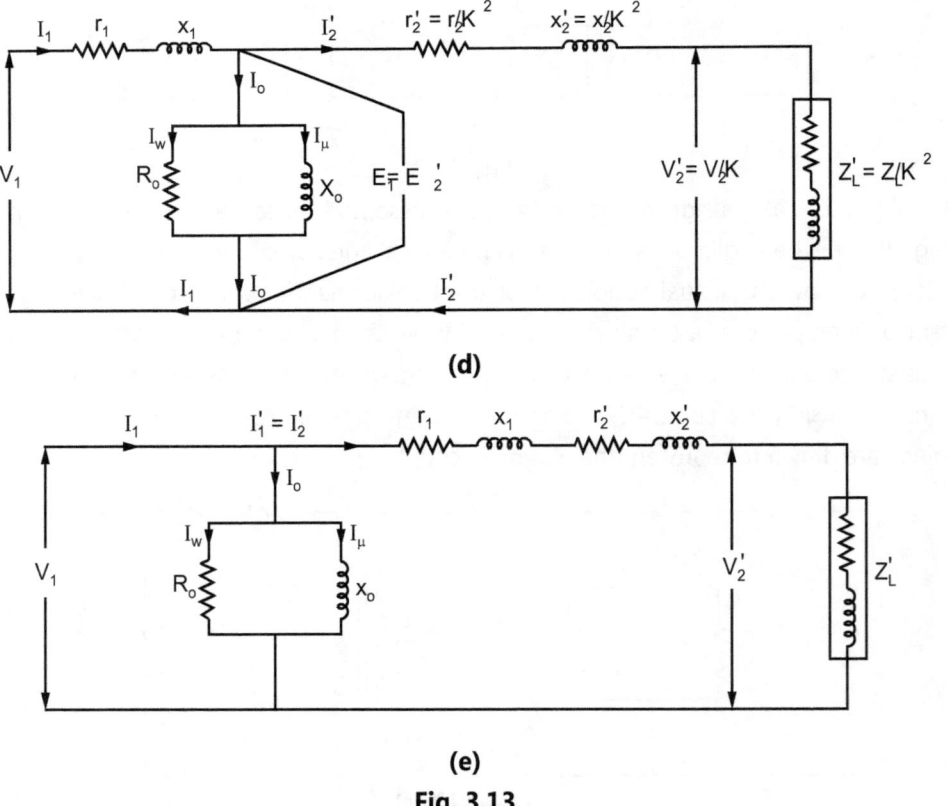

(d)

(e)

**Fig. 3.13**

If we transfer the shunt circuit from its position in Fig. 3.13 (d) to the input terminals as shown in Fig. 3.13 (e). The transformer calculations become much more easy and simplified. While doing so there will be a small (negligible) error in the calculations of no load current and voltage drop in primary winding resistance and leakage reactance.

The equivalent circuit represented in Fig. 3.13 (e) becomes a simple series circuit after the shunt circuit, hence the resistance and reactance values can be added together to get the combined equivalent resistance and reactance referred to primary side; hence the simplified circuit reduces to that shown in Fig. 3.13 (f).

where $R_1 = r_1 + \dfrac{r_2}{K^2}$ and $X_1 = x_1 + \dfrac{x_2}{K^2}$

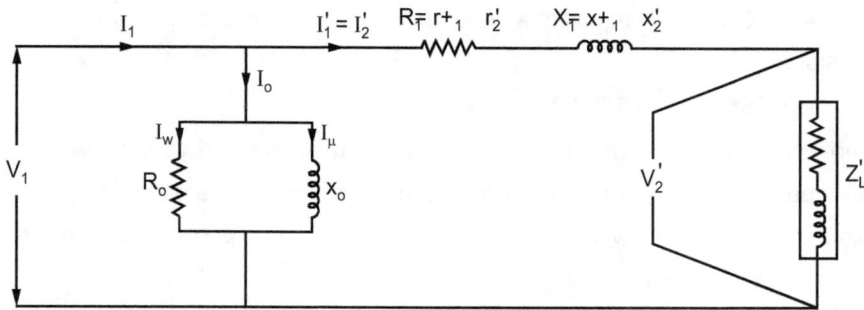

**Fig. 3.13 (f)**

The most simple form of the approximate equivalent circuit can be obtained by completely ignoring the shunt circuit as shown in the equivalent circuits up till now, and substituting primary current $I_1$ for $I_2$ as shown in Fig. 3.13 (g).

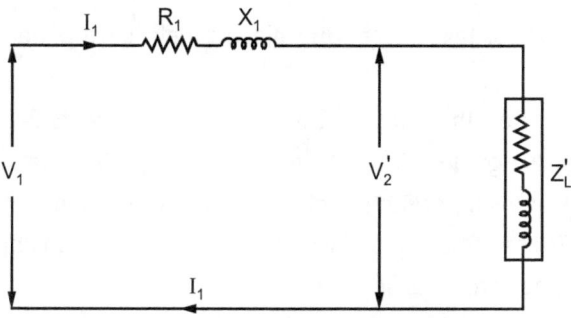

**Fig. 3.13 (g)**

A similar approximate equivalent circuit can be obtained when the quantities are referred to secondary side, it is shown in Fig. 3.13 (h).

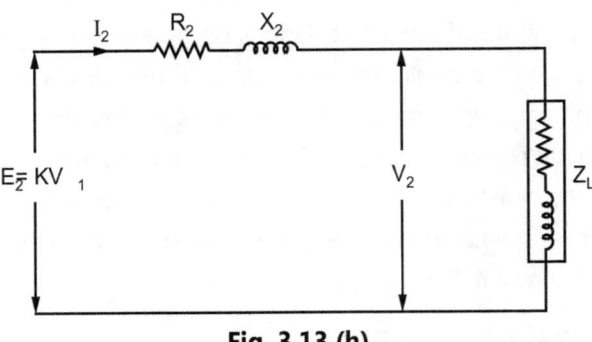

**Fig. 3.13 (h)**

where $R_2 = r_2 + r_1 K^2$ and
$X_2 = x_2 + x_1 K^2$ are the equivalent resistance and reactance of primary referred to the secondary side.

## 3.1.13 (a) Losses in Transformer

In every machine, the output power can not be equal to input power, because some of the power input is lost in the machine as losses in itself, same is the condition of transformer, in no case its output power will be equal to input power. The power lossed by transformer it self are called as its losses.

The losses taking place in the transformer can mainly be divided into the following categories:

(i) Iron losses, taking place in the core of the transformer.

(ii) Copper losses, taking place in the windings of the transformer due to their resistance to flow of current. The other losses which are very low in magnitude and can be neglected are :

(a) Dielectric losses, take place, due electric field set up between conductors and insulation.

(b) Stray load losses, these losses are due to eddy currents set up in the conductors, when alternating current flow through them and also due to eddy currents set up in the tank and supporting structure of the transformer.

**(i) Iron losses :** These losses take place in the core of the transformer as it is subjected to an alternating flux. They are classified as

(a) Eddy current losses

(b) Hysteresis losses

These losses are independent of load on the transformer, hence are called constant losses and are converted in to heat and cause temperature rise.

**(ii) Copper losses :** These losses take place, when the current flows through the winding. Copper loss taking place in primary winding.

$$I_1^2 = r_1 \text{ watts and}$$

copper loss taking place in secondary winding = $I_2^2 r_2$ watts.

where $I_1$, $r_1$, $I_2$ and $r_2$ have their usual meanings.

Also total copper losses are equal to $I_2^2 R_1$ or $I_2^2 R_2$ watts, where $I_1$ is the primary current and $R_1$ is equivalent resistance referred to primary.

Similarly $I_2$ and $R_2$ are the secondary current and secondary equivalent resistance respectively.

These losses are proportional to square of current and are converted in to heat, hence are responsible for temperature rise of the transformer.

## 3.1.13 (b) Efficiency of Transformer

Like other machines the efficiency of transformer can be defined as the ratio of output in watts or kilowatts to its input power in watts or kilo watts.

$$\text{Mathematically Efficiency} = \frac{\text{Output power in watts}}{\text{Input power in watts}}$$

OR

$$\text{Efficiency} = \frac{\text{Output power in watts}}{\text{Output power in watts + Losses in watts}}$$

This efficiency is represented in per unit and represented by letter η (eta).

The general mode of representing efficiency is in percentage which is equal to per unit efficiency multiplied by 100.

i.e.

$$\text{Efficiency} = \frac{\text{Output in watts}}{\text{Input in watts}} \times 100$$

## 3.1.13 (c) Conditions for Maximum Efficiency of a Transformer

At no load, the output is zero, but some power is drawn by the transformer to supply no load losses. Hence, the efficiency is zero. Now as the load on the transformer is increases gradually it is observed that efficiency goes on increasing. It will take place up to the point representing maximum efficiency thereafter if the load on the transformer (output) is increased the efficiency falls. The reason begin that up to maximum efficiency point the losses increase in proportion to output ; but after maximum efficiency point the losses increase in a great proportion than the increase in output.

For determining the condition for maximum efficiency of a transformer, we will consider, that :

$P$ = Full load output of the transformer in watts.

$P_e$ = Its full load copper loss in watts,

$P_i$ = Total iron loss of the transformer when connected to rated voltage at rated frequency, and can be taken as constant.

Let x be the fraction of the full load output at which maximum efficiency of the transformer takes place.

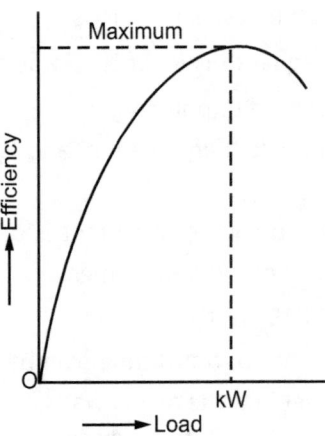

**Fig. 3.14**

∴ Output at maximum efficiency = xp watts. Copper losses which are proportional to square of current are also proportional to square of output, hence will be equal to = $x^2 P_C$ watts.

Hence from,
$$\eta = \frac{\text{Output}}{\text{Output + Losses}}$$

$$\eta = \frac{xp}{xp + x^2 P_C + P_i}$$

if this efficiency is maximum its derivative w.r.t. variable x must be equal to zero.

$$\frac{d\eta}{dx} = \frac{(xp + x^2 P_C + P_i) P - xp (p + 2x P_C)}{(xp + x^2 P_C + P_i)^2}$$

or $\quad 0 = \dfrac{(xp + x^2 P_C + P_i) P - xp (p + 2x P_C)}{(xp + x^2 P_C + P_i)^2}$

or $\quad 0 = (xp + x^2 P_C + P_i) P - xp (p + 2x P_C)$

or $\quad 0 (xp + x^2 P_C + P_i) = xp (p + 2x P_C)$

or $\quad xp + x^2 P_C + P_i = xp + 2x^2 P_C$

or $\quad P = x^2 P_C$

i.e. the efficiency of the transformer will be maximum, when iron loss is equal to copper loss or variable losses are equal to constant losses.

## 3.1.13 (d) Rating of Transformers

The name plate details of a particular single phase transformer may be as follows : 100 kVA, 440 V/220 V, 50 Hz transformer H.V. f.l. current = 22.72 A, and L.V. f.l. current = 45.45 A. maximum temperature = 75°C. In this case, we will receive a continuous output of 100 kVA, or secondary output current of 45.45 A at a terminal voltage of 220 V, with a maximum temperature of windings equal to 75°C.

It is to be noted that the rated output is expressed in kilo-volt amperes. (kVA) and not in kilowatts (kW). It is because of the fact that rated output of the transformer is limited by the heating which is due to losses taking place in the transformer, converted in to heat energy ultimately responsible for the temperature rise. We know that the core losses are dependent up on the voltage applied and the copper losses are dependent up on the square of current and the load p.f. has a negligible effect on the value of these losses. Hence, we can say that at zero p.f. load condition a transformer can be made to operate at rated kVA output, but in this case the power output of the transformer will be zero watts. Hence the transformer output is expressed in kVA and not in kW.

## 3.1.14 (a) Regulation of Transformer

When the transformer is loaded with a constant primary voltage, the voltage available across the secondary winding (or load) will reduce, due to the voltage drop taking place in the resistance and leakage reactance (i.e. impedance) of the transformer windings. The equivalent impedance drop referred to secondary being equal to $I_1 Z_2$ where $I_2$ is the secondary current and $Z_2$ its equivalent impedance referred to secondary. If

$E_2$ = Secondary terminal voltage at no load which is equal to secondary induced e.m.f.

$V_2$ = Secondary terminal voltage at full load. The change in terminal voltage from no load to full load will be $E_2 - V_2$ on secondary side with a constant voltage $V_1$ applied to its primary at constant temperature is known as regulation (inherent) of the transformer. Generally, the regulation of the transformer is expressed in terms of percentage.

When the percentage regulation of the transformer is expressed as,

% Regulation = $\dfrac{E_2 - V_2}{E_2} \times 100$ it is termed as regulation down; because in the method of determining regulation of transformer by this method the primary voltage $V_1$ is kept constant hence $E_2$ remains constant, but $V_2$ will go on falling as the load on the transformer is increased; that is why this method is called as regulation down method. Generally, we follow this method of finding regulation of transformer in the laboratory.

Let at no load $E_2$ be the secondary induced e.m.f., $V_2$ be the no load terminal voltage or voltage across load and $V_1$ be the rated primary supply voltage. When the transformer is loaded the secondary terminal voltage $V_2$ will go on reducing due to resistance and leakage reactance drop. If the load on the transformer is its full load, and the primary supply voltage increased to such a value that secondary terminal voltage is equal to $V_2$ again, i.e. the no load voltage of secondary. Now if the load is suddenly thrown-off keeping primary voltage unchanged, and recording the new no load terminal voltage (induced e.m.f.) of secondary winding; if it is equal to $E_2$, then the % regulation of the transformer is calculated as

% Regulation up $= \dfrac{E_2 - V_2}{E_2} \times 100$.

If the percentage regulation of a transformer is low, it is taken as a sign of good transformer, because in case of such transformers the change in secondary voltage from no load to full load is very low, or such a transformer is capable of delivering output up to full load at a sufficiently constant terminal voltage. The regulation can also be calculated in terms of primary voltages.

## 3.1.14 (b) Mathematical Expression for Regulation of Transformer

When the transformer is on no load its open circuit secondary terminal voltage is $E_2$ volts (equal to secondary induced e.m.f.) when it is loaded its terminal voltage decreases to $V_2$.

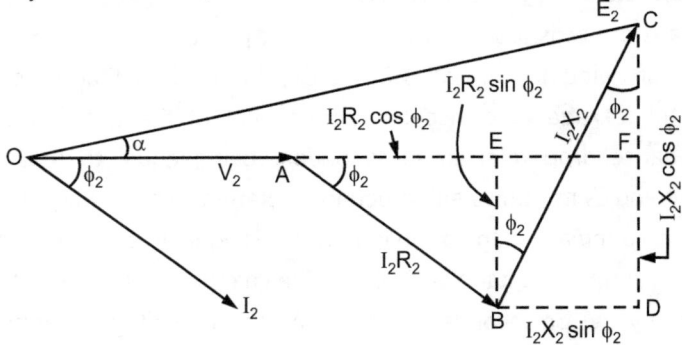

**Fig. 3.15 (a)**

Fig. 3.15 (a) represents the vector diagram of the transformer referred to its secondary side. OA represents its secondary terminal voltage $V_2$ on load. $I_2$ the secondary load current at p.f. angle $\phi_2$. AB is the resistive voltage drop $I_2 R_2$ taking place in secondary equivalent resistance $R_2$, and acting in the direction of current $I_2$. BC represents the reactive drop taking place in equivalent secondary leakage reactance and acting at an angle of 90° to the direction of $I_2$ and leading it by 90°. OC is the induced e.m.f. in the secondary winding equal to $E_2$ volts, making angle $\alpha$ with $V_2$.

For determining mathematical expression, following constructional lines are drawn, OA extended up to E and F. BD drawn parallel to EF and CD drawn perpendicular to BD.

$$OF = V_2 + AE + EF$$

OR $\quad OF = V_2 + I_2 R_2 \cos \phi_2 + I_2 X_2 \sin \phi_2$

An angle $\alpha$ is very small

$\quad OF = OC \cos \alpha = E_2 \cos \alpha$

$\therefore \quad V_2 \cong E_2 \cos \alpha - I_2 R_2 \cos \phi_2 - I_2 X_2 \sin \phi_2$

OR $\quad \dfrac{V_2}{E_2} = \cos \alpha - \dfrac{I_2 R_2 \cos \phi_2}{E_2} - \dfrac{I_2 X_2 \sin \phi_2}{E_2}$ ... (3.28)

OR $\quad \dfrac{V_2}{E_2} = \cos \alpha - V_r' \cos \phi_2 - V_x' \sin \phi_2$ ... (3.29)

Where $V_r'$ and $V_x'$ are the unit resistive and reactive drops.

OR $\quad \dfrac{V_2}{E_2} = 1 - 2 \sin^2 \alpha/2 - V_r' \cos \phi_2 - V_x' \sin \phi_2$ ... (3.30)

Also from Fig. 3.15 (a) $\dfrac{CD - FD}{OC}$ i.e. $\dfrac{CD - EB}{OC} = \sin \alpha$

OR $\quad \dfrac{I_2 X_2 \cos \phi_2 - I_2 R_2 \sin \phi_2}{E_2} = \sin \alpha$

OR $\sin \alpha = V_x' \cos \phi_2 - V_r' \sin \phi_2$

as $\alpha$ is small

$\quad \sin \alpha/2 = 1/2 (V_x' \cos \phi_2 - V_r' \sin \phi_2)$

and $\quad \sin^2 \alpha/2 = 1/4 (V_x' \cos \phi_2 - V_r' \sin \phi_2)^2$ putting in equation (3.30) ... (3.31)

$\therefore \quad \dfrac{V_2}{E_2} = 1 - \dfrac{2}{4} (V_x' \cos \phi_2 - V_r' \sin \phi_2)^2 - V_r' \cos \phi_2 - V_x' \sin \phi_2$

Now, % Regulation $= \dfrac{E_2 - V_2}{E_2} \times 100$

or % Regulation $= \left(1 - \dfrac{V_2}{E_2}\right) \times 100$

Putting value from equation (3.31),

or % Regulation $= \left[1 - 1 + \dfrac{2}{4} (V_x' \cos \phi_2 - V_r' \sin \phi_2)^2 + V_r' \cos \phi_2 - V_x' \sin \phi_2 \right] \times 100$

or % Regulation $= (V_r \cos \phi_2 + V_x \sin \phi_2) + \dfrac{1}{2 \times 100} (V_x' \times 100 \cos \phi_2 - V_r' \times 100 \sin \phi_2)^2$

Where $V_r$ and $V_x$ represent percentage resistive and reactive drops.

OR % Regulation $= (V_r \cos \phi_2 + V_x \sin \phi_2) + \dfrac{1}{200} (V_x \cos \phi_2 - V_r \sin \phi_2)^2$

Since the term $\dfrac{1}{200} (V_x \cos \phi_2 - V_r \sin \phi_2)^2$ is very small it can be neglected and the approximate regulation of the transformer can be calculated from

$\quad$ % Regulation $= V_r \cos \phi \pm V_x \sin \phi$

The positive sign gives regulation for lagging p.f. condition, while the negative sign is used to determine regulation of transformer at leading load power factor.

$V_r$ can be taken as $\dfrac{I_1 R_1}{V_1} \times 100$ or $\dfrac{I_2 R_2}{E_2} \times 100$

and $V_x$ can be taken as $\dfrac{I_1 X_1}{V_1} \times 100$ or $\dfrac{I_2 X_2}{E_2} \times 100$

$\phi$ as the p.f. angle of the side for which calculations are done.

## 3.1.14 (c) Regulation of Transformer by the Method of Determining Induced E.M.F.

### (i) Regulation for Unity p.f. Load Condition:

Fig. 3.16 (a) represents the vector diagram referred to secondary side of transformer delivering load current $I_2$ amperes at unity p.f. condition.

From vector diagram, $E_2^2 = (V_2 + I_2 R_2)^2 + (I_2 X_2)^2$

or $\qquad E_2 = \sqrt{(V_2 + I_2 R_2)^2 + (I_2 X_2)^2}$ volts.

Where $R_2$ = Equivalent resistance of transformer referred to secondary and $X_2$ = Equivalent reactance referred to secondary side.

and $\qquad$ % Regulation = $\dfrac{E_2 - V_2}{E_2} \times 100$

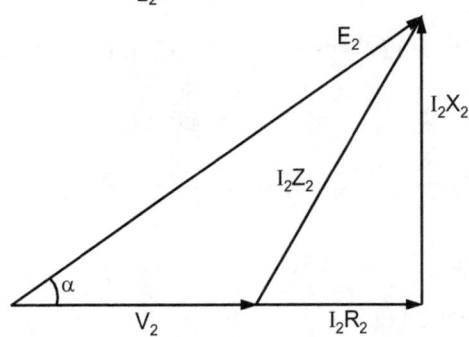

**Fig. 3.16 (a)**

### (ii) Regulation for Lagging p.f. Load Condition :

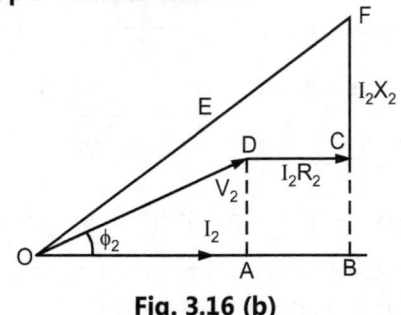

**Fig. 3.16 (b)**

Fig. 3.16 (b) represents vector diagram for a lagging p.f. load condition, in which the transformer is delivering a load current of $I_2$ amperes at a terminal voltage of $V_2$ volts and lagging p.f. $\cos \phi_2$.

From the vector diagram the value of secondary induced e.m.f. can be determined as follows:

$$E_2 = OF \text{ and } OF^2 = OB^2 + BF^2$$

also  $OB = OA + AB = OA + DC$

or  $OB = V_2 \cos \phi_2 + I_2 R_2$

and  $BF = BC + CF = AD + CF$

or  $BF = V_2 \sin \phi_2 + I_2 X_2$

∴  $E_2 = \sqrt{(V_2 \cos \phi_2 + I_2 R_2)^2 + (V_2 \sin \phi_2 + I_2 X_2)^2}$

and  % regulation $= \dfrac{E_2 - V_2}{E_2} \times 100$

### (iii) Regulation for Leading p.f. load Conditions:

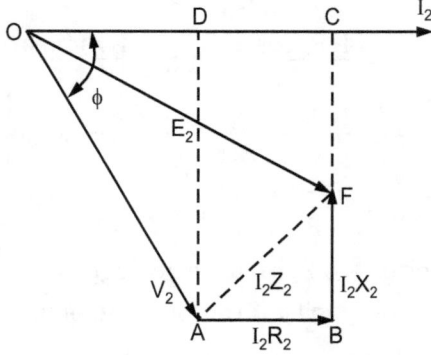

**Fig. 3.16 (c)**

Fig. 3.16 (c) represents the vector diagram for a leading p.f. load condition, in which $V_2$ is the secondary terminal voltage, $I_2$ is the load current supplied by it at a leading p.f. load condition. $R_2$ and $X_2$ are its equivalent resistance and reactances referred to secondary side while $E_2$ is the secondary induced e.m.f.

The value of $E_2$ is obtained as follows:

$$(OF)^2 = (OC)^2 + (CF)^2$$
$$(OF)^2 = (OD + DC)^2 + (CD - BF)^2$$

or  $(OF)^2 = (OD + AB)^2 + (DA - BF)^2$

∴  $OF = E_2 = \sqrt{(V_2 \cos \phi_2 + I_2 R_2)^2 + (V_2 \sin \phi_2 + I_2 X_2)^2}$

and  % Regulation $= \dfrac{E_2 - V_2}{E_2} \times 100$

## 3.1.15 (a) Total Voltage Drop in Terms of Current, Equivalent R, X and p.f.

Referring to Fig. 3.16 (a), the secondary induced e.m.f. can be written as

$$\overline{E}_2 = \overline{V}_2 + I_2 Z_2 \text{ for unity p.f. load}$$

or $$\overline{E}_2 = \overline{V}_2 + \overline{I}_2 (R_2 + j X_2)$$

∴ Voltage drop $\overline{E}_2 - \overline{V}_2 = \overline{I}_2 (R_2 + j X_2)$

where $E_2$, $V_2$, $I_2$, $R_2$ and $X_2$ are the parameters referred to secondary side while the load p.f. is unity i.e. $\phi_2 = 0°$.

A similar expression can be obtained when parameters referred to primary side are known.

Voltage drop $\quad \overline{V}_1 - \overline{E}_1 = \overline{I}_1 (R_1 + j X_1)$

## 3.1.15 (b) Voltage Drop for a Lagging p.f. Load Condition

In article 3.1.14 (b1), we have seen the % regulation, for lagging p.f.

$$= V_r \cos\phi + V_x \sin\phi$$

$$= \frac{I_2 R_2 \cos\phi_2}{E_2} \times 100 + \frac{I_2 X_2 \sin\phi_2}{E_2} \times 100$$

$$\% \text{ Regulation} = \frac{I_2 R_2 \cos\phi_2 + I_2 X_2 \sin\phi_2}{E_2} \times 100$$

But $\quad \% \text{ Regulation} = \frac{E_2 - V_2}{E_2} \times 100$

Hence, $E_2 - V_2 = I_2 R_2 \cos\phi_2 + I_2 X_2 \sin\phi_2$ i.e. for lagging p.f. load condition, the voltage drop = $I_2 R_2 \cos\phi_2 + I_2 X_2 \sin\phi_2$ volts. It can be represented for primary side as voltage drop = $I_1 R_1 \cos\phi_1 + I_1 X_1 \sin\phi_1$ volts.

## 3.1.15 (c) Voltage Drop for a Leading p.f. Load Condition

% Regulation for leading p.f. load condition is given by

$$\% \text{ Regulation} = V_r \cos\phi - V_x \sin\phi$$

$$= \frac{I_2 R_2 \cos\phi_2}{E_2} \times 100 - \frac{I_2 X_2 \sin\phi_2}{E_2} \times 100$$

$$= \frac{I_2 R_2 \cos\phi_2 - I_2 X_2 \sin\phi_2}{E_2} \times 100$$

but $\quad \% \text{ Regulation} = \frac{E_2 - V_2}{E_2} \times 100$

Hence, $\quad E_2 - V_2 = I_2 R_2 \cos\phi_2 - I_2 X_2 \sin\phi_2$ volts.

Similarly voltage drop for primary side

$$= I_1 R_1 \cos\phi_1 - I_1 X_1 \sin\phi_1$$

## 3.1.16 Efficiency and Regulation by Direct Loading Method

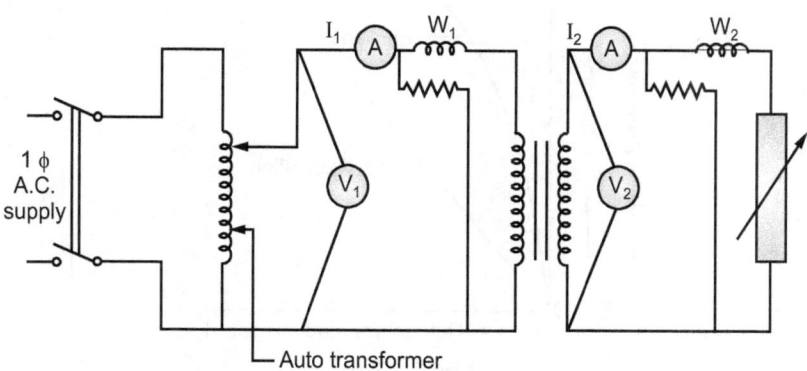

**Fig. 3.17 (a)**

For determining the regulation and efficiency of a transformer by direct loading, the connections are made as shown in Fig. 3.17 (a). The primary is connected to an A.C. supply of rated frequency and the primary (or secondary depending up on suitability) voltage is adjusted to its rated value of $V_1$ volts and maintained constant throughout the experiment with the help of auto transformer. Ammeter, voltmeter and wattmeter ($W_1$) of suitable range are connected on primary side and similarly ammeter, voltmeter and wattmeter are also connected on secondary side.

The readings of primary and secondary instruments are taken, in sequence from zero load condition i.e. when $V_2 = E_2$ up to a load condition of full load or even 1.25 times full load and recorded in the observation table as given below. The readings taken are then used to determine the regulation and efficiency.

**Observation Table**

| Sr. No. | Primary Side | | | Secondary Side | | | % Regulation | % η |
|---|---|---|---|---|---|---|---|---|
| | $V_1$ | $I_1$ | $W_1$ | $V_2$ | $I_2$ | $W_2$ | $\dfrac{E_2 - V_2}{E_2} \times 100$ | $\dfrac{W_2}{W_1} \times 100$ |
| | | | | | | | | |
| | | | | | | | | |
| | | | | | | | | |

**Calculations :** The wattmeter ($W_1$) on the primary side represents total input power and the corresponding reading of ($W_2$) wattmeter on secondary side represents output power in watts of the transformer, hence for every reading.

$$\% \text{ efficiency} = \dfrac{W_2}{W_1} \times 100$$

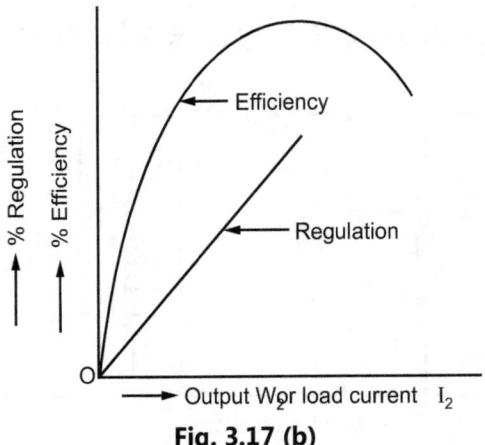

**Fig. 3.17 (b)**

In case of u.p.f. load (resistive load) there is no need of connecting $W_2$, the product of $V_2$ $I_2$ will be equal to $W_2$ as $\cos \phi_2 = 1$.

Efficiency curve starts from zero, because output at no load is zero. The reading of secondary voltmeter at (zero load) no load condition is equal to $E_2$ while its readings at other load conditions are taken as secondary terminal voltage $V_2$. The secondary terminal voltage at no load $V_2 = E_2$ = hence regulation at no load will be zero. The regulation then goes on increasing with load as shown in Fig. 3.17 (b).

### 3.1.17 All Day Efficiency of a Transformer

The distribution transformers (i.e. the transformers which are used for distributing electrical energy to consumers for light and fan load, domestic power etc.) are connected to their rated primary voltage at rated frequency to the supply system for 24 hours of the day so as to provide the electrical energy to the consumer at any instant of the day, during 24 hours. The load that will come on the transformer during 24 hours will not be constant it will vary from instant to instant i.e. during some hours the transformer is lightly loaded, during other it may be highly loaded, and during some hours of the day the load may be negligible. The copper losses taking place in the transformer are proportional to square of current or square of output, will change according to load condition of the transformer. But the iron losses which depend up on the flux density and supply frequency, will remain constant at rated voltage and frequency during 24 hours of the day. Hence, if we want to determine the performance of such a distribution transformer it can be best determined if its efficiency is calculated on the energy basis instead of power basis, taking working of transformer for 24 hours of day into consideration.

When the efficiency of a transformer is calculated on energy basis it is called as all day efficiency or operational efficiency.

It is defined as the ratio of energy output in (watts hour or kilowatt hours) during 24 hours of a day to Energy input (watt hours or kilowatt hours) during the same period of 24 hours of a day. The output and input energy should be measured in same units.

OR the all day efficiency can be written as

$$\% \text{ All day efficiency} = \frac{\text{Output energy in kWh during 24 hours of a day}}{\text{Energy put in kWh during 24 hours of a day}} \times 100$$

Transformers giving higher value of all day efficiency are selected for distribution purpose, because in such transformers the energy lost in losses is less in comparison to other transformers.

## 3.1.18 (a) O.C. and S.C. Test on Transformer

The open circuit and short circuit tests are the tests carried out on transformers without directly loading them, but are used to determine its performance such as regulation and efficiency at any desired load condition giving almost correct results, hence is called as indirect method of determining performance of transformer. This type of method is preferred due to the advantage that, the power loss in the conduction of above test is very small, hence the test is economical. Secondly, the direct loading method is not suitable for large capacity transformers, because it may not be possible to obtain large loads and power supply of such large capacity. And the results obtained by this method differ slightly or having negligible error.

**(1) O.C. Test**

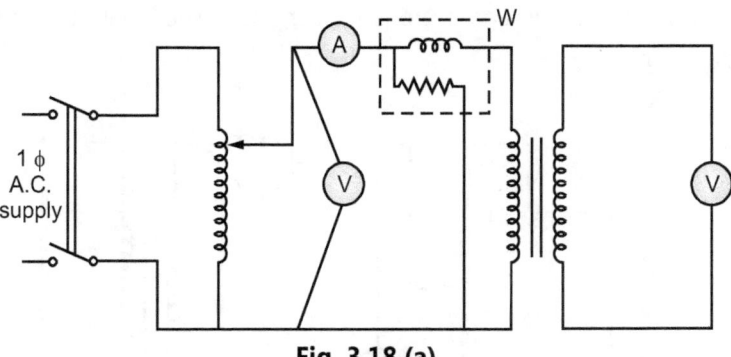

Fig. 3.18 (a)

In this test, generally the low voltage winding is connected to its rated voltage (adjusting with the help of auto transformer) at rated frequency. The secondary is kept open circuited, or a voltmeter is connected across secondary so that secondary current is nearly zero. (voltmeter being very high impedance instrument). The readings of wattmeter, ammeter and voltmeter are recorded in a observation table given below and are then used for calculation purpose. The reason of connecting supply to low voltage side is that it is available, the accidental risk is less and the high voltage may not be available in the laboratory for testing purpose.

## Observation Table

| Sr. No. | Primary Side | | Secondary Side | |
|---|---|---|---|---|
| | $V_1$ | $I_0$ | $W_0$ | $V_2$ |
| | | | | |
| | | | | |

**Calcualtions:**

(i) As the transformer is on no load condition, $V_2 = E_2$ and $V_1 \cong E_1$, hence $\frac{V_2}{V_1} = \frac{N_2}{N_1}$ i.e., the transformation ratio.

(ii) The no load current $I_0$ is having two components $I_\omega$ and $I_\mu$ being equal to $I_0 \cos \phi_0$ and supplies losses in transformer at no load, its value is equal to $\frac{W_0}{V_1}$ and $I_\mu = I_0 \sin \phi_0$ its value being equal to $\sqrt{I_0^2 - I_w^2}$, it is used to set up magnetic flux in the transformer core. For an equivalent circuit a shunt circuit consisting of resistance $R_0$ drawing the current $I_\omega$ and reactance $X_0$ drawing current $I_\mu$ can be determined as

$$R_0 = \frac{V_1}{I_w} \text{ and } X_0 = \frac{V_1}{I_\mu}$$

(iii) The reading of the wattmeter $W_0$ consists of iron loss (constant loss) of the transformer because primary no load current and resistance being very small primary copper loss is negligible and there is no current in secondary therefore there is no secondary copper loss.

## (2) Short Circuit Test

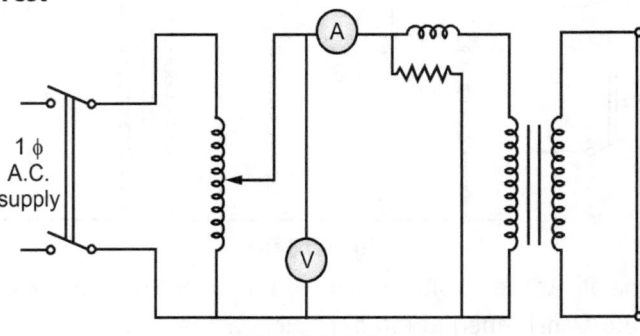

**Fig. 3.18 (b)**

Fig. 3.18 (b) represents the circuit diagram for conducting the short circuit test on a single phase transformer.

Generally, the H.V. winding of the transformer is connected to low voltage through an auto transformer, on the H.V. side are connected a wattmeter, ammeter and voltmeter to record the power supplied, current circulated and the voltage applied. The L.V. winding is short circuited by a thick copper link as shown in Fig. 3.18 (b) or a ammeter of suitable range is connected across L.V. terminals (because it is having very low resistance). With the help of Auto transformer the applied voltage is so adjusted that current circulated through both the windings is their full load current. The readings of the instruments under this condition are recorded in the observation table as shown below. The reason for applying low voltage to the H.V. winding and short circuiting L.V. winding is that, in short circuit test we need large (full load current at least) current to be circulated. The current required on H.V. side is small in comparison to L.V. side hence it is preferred to connect supply to H.V. side.

**Observation Table**

| Sr. No. | Primary Side | | |
|---|---|---|---|
| | $V_{SC}$ | $I_{SC}$ | $W_{SC}$ |
| | | | |

## Calculations:

As the current circulated through the windings is full load current, full load copper losses take place in both the windings, hence the wattmeter reading records full load copper losses of the transformer under test. The reading of the wattmeter also includes negligible core tosses, but they can be neglected due to the reason that voltage applied to the transformer being very low the flux set up in core is very small and iron losses (core loss) being almost proportional to square of flux, are negligible.

In the short circuit test, output voltage is zero (because of short circuit) hence the voltage $V_{SC}$ applied to the transformer is utilised as the impedance drop of the transformer. Hence, use of this test is made to determine the equivalent values of resistance, reactance, impedance referred to metering side.

$$W_{SC} = I_{SC}^2 R_1$$

where $R_1$ is equivalent resistance referred to primary side.

Also, $$V_{SC} = I_{SC} Z_1 \text{ or } Z_1 = \frac{V_{SC}}{I_{SC}}$$

where, $Z_1$ is equivalent impedance referred to primary.

$\therefore$ $$X_1 = \sqrt{Z_1^2 - R_1^2}$$ equivalent reactance referred to primary

If the metering would have been provided on secondary side and primary being short circuited, we will get parameters referred to secondary side such as

$$\frac{V_{SC}}{I_{SC}} = Z_2, \quad \frac{W_{SC}}{I_{SC}^2} = R_2$$

and $$\sqrt{Z_2^2 - R_2^2} = X_2$$

making use of O.C. and S.C. test we can draw now the equivalent circuit of the transformer.

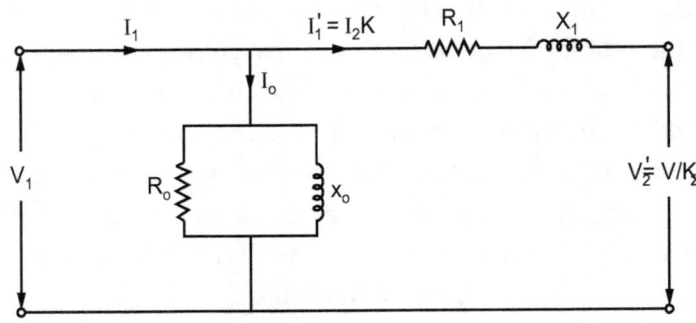

**Fig. 3.18 (c)**

## 3.1.18 (b) Calculations of Efficiency and Regulation at Desired Load Condition using Results of O.C. and S.C. test

As explained previously the reading of wattmeter ($W_0$) in the O.C. test carried at rated voltage and rated frequency gives the core loss or constant loss of the transformer.

The reading of the wattmeter used in S.C. test when full load current is circulated through its windings gives the full load copper losses in watts.

∴ Total losses at full load = $W_0 + W_{sc}$ and efficiency of the transformer at

$$\text{Full load} = \frac{\text{Output in watts}}{\text{Output in watts + Losses}}$$

$$= \frac{(kVA)\text{ Rating} \times 1000 \times p.f.}{(kVA)\text{ Rating} \times 1000 \times p.f. + W_i + W_{sc}}$$

If the efficiency at any desired load say a fraction x of the full load is to be calculated, then it will be calculated as follows :

Output at fraction X = x(kVA) × 1000 × p.f. and the copper losses will be equal to $x^2 W_{sc}$ or $x^2 P_c$, where $W_{sc} = P_c$ is full load copper loss

∴ Efficiency at fraction × of f.l. output

$$= \frac{X \times kVA \times 1000 \times p.f.}{X \times kVA \times 1000 \times p.f. + W_0 + x^2 P_c}$$

## 3.1.18 (c) Calculating Regulation of Transformer using Results of S.C. Test

If $I_1$ is full load current of primary side, $R_1$ and $X_1$ are its equivalent resistance and reactances referred to primary side then

$$\% \text{ Regulation} = \frac{I_1 R_1 \cos \phi_1 \pm I_1 X_1 \sin \phi_1}{V_1} \times 100$$

Where $I_1 R_1 \cos \phi_1 \pm I_1 X_1 \sin \phi_1$ represents the voltage drop. If the constants referred to secondary side are known, then

$$\% \text{ Regulation} = \frac{I_2 R_2 \cos \phi_2 \pm I_2 X_2 \sin \phi_2}{V_2} \times 100$$

Negative sign is used for capacitive loads.

The regulation can also be calculated using % Regulation

$$= \frac{E_2 - V_2}{E_2} \times 100$$

The value of $E_2$ for different p.f. load can be calculated using relation developed in Art. 3.1.14 (b2) (i), (ii) and (iii), i.e.

$$E_2 = \sqrt{(V_2 + I_2 R_2)^2 + (I_2 X_2)^2} \text{ for unity p.f. load}$$

$$E_2 = \sqrt{(V_2 \cos \phi_2 + I_2 R_2)^2 + (V_2 \sin \phi_2 + I_2 X_2)^2}$$

for lagging p.f. loads, and

$$E_2 = \sqrt{(V_2 \cos \phi_2 + I_2 R_2)^2 + (V_2 \sin \phi_2 - I_2 X_2)^2}$$

for leading p.f. loads.

## ILLUSTRATIVE EXAMPLES

**Example 3.1:** A single phase transformer has 300 turns on its primary and 750 turns on its secondary side. The maximum flux density produced in the core is 1 wb/m².

**Calculate:**

(i) The net cross-sectional area required for the core, and

(ii) The e.m.f. induced in the secondary side.

The primary of the transformer is connected to 440 volts 60 Hz supply.

**Solution:** Using Relation, $\frac{E_2}{E_1} = \frac{N_2}{N_1}$ taking $E_1 = V_1$

∴ $\quad \frac{E_2}{440} = \frac{750}{300}$ or $E_2 = 440 \times \frac{750}{300}$

or $\quad E_2 = 1100$ volts.

Now using the relation for induced e.m.f.

$$E = 4.44 \, B_m \cdot A_{inet} \, f \times N$$

For primary $\quad 440 = 4.44 \times 1 \times A_{inet} \times 60 \times 300$

or $\quad A_{inet} = \frac{40}{4.44 \times 1 \times 60 \times 300} = 0.0055 \text{ m}^2$

or $\quad A_{inet} = 0.0055 \times 10^4 = 55 \text{ cm}^2$.

**Example 3.2:** A 3300/230 V single phase 50 Hz core type transformer has a core area 400 cm². Permissible maximum flux density is 1.8 Wb/m². Calculate the number of turns required on the high and low voltages sides.

**Solution:** Using e.m.f. equation of transformer i.e., $E = 4.44\ B_m\ A_i\ f\ N$ volts

where,
$B_m$ = Maximum flux density
$f$ = Frequency in Hertz's
$N$ = Number of turns

For primary,
$E_1 = 4.44\ B_m\ A_i\ F\ N_1$ volts

or $3300 = 4.44 \times 1.8 \times (400 \times 10^{-4}) \times 50 \times N_1$

or $N_1 = \dfrac{3300}{4.44 \times 1.8 \times 400 \times 10^{-4} \times 50}$

$N_1$ = 206.45 say 207 turns

$N_2 = \dfrac{230}{4.44 \times 1.8 \times 400 \times 10^{-8} \times 50}$

$N_2$ = 14.389 say 15 turns

Once $N_1$ is calculated $N_2$ can also be calculated using relation.

$\dfrac{E_2}{E_1} = \dfrac{N_2}{N_1}$ or $\dfrac{230}{3300} = \dfrac{N_2}{207}$

or $N_2 = 207 \times \dfrac{230}{3300}$ = 14.42 say 15 turns.

**Example 3.3:** A 200 kVA $\dfrac{3300}{240}$ V 50 Hz, single phase transformer has 80 turns on the secondary winding. Assuming an ideal transformer calculate :

(1) The primary and secondary currents on full load.
(2) The maximum value of the flux.
(3) The number of primary turns.

**Solution:** (i) In case of ideal transformer

VA input = VA output

As output = 200 kVA = $200 \times 10^3$ VA

∴ $V_1 I_1 = V_2 I_2 = 200 \times 10^3$

$3300 \times I_1 = 200 \times 10^3$

∴ $I_1 = \dfrac{200 \times 10^3}{3300}$ = 60.60 Amps.

$I_2 = \dfrac{200 \times 10^3}{240}$ = 833.33 Amps.

(ii) Using relation, $E = 4.44\ \phi_m\ f\ N$ volts

For secondary $240 = 4.44\ \phi_m\ f\ N_2$

or $\quad\quad\quad\quad\quad 240 = 4.44 \times \phi_m \times 50 \times 80$

or $\quad\quad\quad\quad\quad \phi_m = \dfrac{240}{4.44 \times 50 \times 80} = 0.0135$ Wb

(iii) From $\quad\quad\quad\quad \dfrac{E_2}{E_1} = \dfrac{N_2}{N_1}$

$$\dfrac{240}{3300} = \dfrac{80}{N_1} \text{ or } N_1 = \dfrac{80 \times 3300}{240}$$

Primary turns, $\quad\quad N_1 = 1100$ turns

**Example 3.4:** The following data applies to a single phase transformer. Peak flux density in the core 1.41 Wb/m², Net core area 0.01 m². Current density in conductors 2.5 A/mm², conductor diameter 2 mm, primary supply (assume sinusoidal) 200 V, 50 Hz.

Calculate the kVA rating of the transformer and the number of turns on the primary winding.

**Solution:** As the diameter of conductor is 2 mm its area of cross-section

$$= \dfrac{\pi}{4} \times (d)^2$$

$$= \dfrac{\pi}{4} \times (2)^2 = 3.14 \text{ mm}^2$$

Total current flowing through primary = Current density × Area of cross-section

$$= 2.5 \times 3.14 = 7.85$$

As primary supply voltage = 200 volts

$\quad\quad\quad\quad\quad$ VA Rating $= 200 \times 7.85 = 1570$ VA

or $\quad\quad\quad\quad$ kVA Rating $= \dfrac{1570}{1000} = 1.57$ kVA

From $\quad\quad\quad\quad\quad$ E $= 4.44 \; B_m \; A_i \; f \; N_1$

or $\quad\quad\quad\quad\quad$ 200 $= 4.44 \times 1.41 \times 0.01 \times 50 \times N_1$

or $\quad\quad\quad\quad\quad N_1 = 63.89$ say 64 turns.

**Example 3.5:** The maximum flux density in core of a 240/3000 volts, 50 Hz transformer is 1.25 Wb/m². If the e.m.f. induced per turn is 8 volts. Find number of primary and secondary turns and the set cross-sectional area of core.

**Solution:** From E = 4.44 $B_m \; A_i \; f \; N$, E/N = 4.44 $B_m \; A_i \; f$ volts.

E/N is called as e.m.f. per turn.

∴ $\quad\quad\quad\quad\quad\quad\quad 8 = 4.44 \times 1.25 \times A_i \times 50 \text{ or } A_i = 0.028828 \text{ m}^2$

or $\quad\quad$ Net cross-sectional area $= 0.0288288 \times 10^4 = 288.288 \text{ cm}^2$

$$N_1 = \dfrac{V_1}{\text{e.m.f./turn}} \text{ or } \dfrac{V_1}{E_t}$$

or $\qquad N_1 = \dfrac{240}{8} = 30$ turns

and $\qquad N_1 = \dfrac{3000}{8} = 375$ turns.

**Example 3.6:** A transformer has same efficiency at 75% load and 125% load. Find ratio full load Cu loss to core loss. Assuming output of transformer at f.l. = let x be the full load copper losses and y be the core losses at rated voltage.

**Solution:** Then the efficiency at 3/4 f.l. can be calculated from

$$\eta = \dfrac{\text{Output}}{\text{Output + Copper loss + Iron loss}}$$

$\therefore \qquad \eta = \dfrac{1 \times 3/4}{1 \times 3/4 + (3/4)^2 x + y} \qquad \ldots (1)$

or $\qquad \eta = \dfrac{0.75}{0.75 + 0.5625 x + y}$

Similarly, at 1.25 f.l., $\qquad \eta = \dfrac{1 \times 1.25}{1.25 + 1.56 x + y} \qquad \ldots (2)$

Equations (1) and (2),

$$\dfrac{0.75}{0.75 + 0.5625 x + y} = \dfrac{1.25}{1.25 + 1.56 x + y}$$

or $\qquad 0.9375 + 1.17 x + 0.75 y = 0.9375 + 0.7031 x + 1.25 y$

or $\qquad 1.17 x - 0.7031 x = 1.25 y - 0.75 y$

$\qquad 0.4669 x = 0.5 y$

or $\qquad \dfrac{x}{y} = \dfrac{0.5}{0.4669} = 1.07$

i.e. ratio of full load copper loss to core loss will be 1.07.

**Example 3.7:** A 20 kVA transformer has a core loss of 180 watts. Its maximum efficiency is found to occur at 3/4 full load. Find its efficiency at full load unity p.f.

**Solution:** At maximum efficiency core loss (iron loss) = copper loss i.e. at 3/4 f.l. the copper loss is 180 watts.

We know that efficiency at any fraction x of the full load output is given by

$$\eta = \dfrac{x \cdot kVA \cdot \cos \phi}{x \cdot kVA \cdot \cos \phi + x^2 \cdot P_c + P_i}$$

Where $x^2 \cdot P_c$ is copper loss at fractional output x of f.l. kVA rating.

Here, $x = 0.75$ and $\cos \phi = 1$

$\therefore \qquad x^2 P_c = P_i$

or $\qquad (3/4)^2 P_c = 180$

$\therefore \qquad P_c = \dfrac{180}{(3/4)^2} = \dfrac{180 \times 16}{9}$

At f.l. unity p.f.

$$P_c = 320 \text{ watts; full load Cu loss}$$

$$\% \eta = \frac{20 \times 10^3 \times 1}{20 \times 10^3 \times 1 + 320 + 180} \times 100$$

% η at f.l. = 97.56%

**Example 3.8:** In a 20 kVA, 1000/400 V, single phase, 50 Hz transformer iron and full load copper losses are 300 watts and 500 watts respectively. Calculate the efficiency at :
(i) Full load and 0.8 lagging p.f., and
(ii) Half load and unity p.f.
At what load will the efficiency of the transformer be maximum ?

**Solution:** Efficiency of transformer $= \dfrac{x \times kVA \times 10^3 \times \cos \phi}{x \times kVA \times 10^3 \times \cos \phi + x^2 P_c + P_i}$

where,
$x$ = Fraction of the output
$P_c$ = Full load copper loss
$P_i$ = Iron loss at rated voltage

(i) Therefore, η at full load 0.8 p.f., for which x = 1

or $\quad$ Efficiency $= \dfrac{1 \times 20 \times 10^3 \times 0.8}{1 \times 20 \times 10^3 \times 0.8 + 500 + 300} = 0.9523$

(ii) At half load x = 0.5.

∴ $\quad$ η at half load $= \dfrac{0.5 \times 20 \times 10^3 \times 1}{0.5 \times 20 \times 10^3 \times 1 + (0.5)^2 \times 500 + 300}$

η at half load = 0.9592 or % efficiency = 95.92%

At maximum efficiency, $\quad x^2 P_c = P_i$

Where x is the fraction of the output at which maximum efficiency takes place

$$x^2 \times 500 = 300$$

∴ $\quad x^2 = \dfrac{300}{500}$

or $\quad x = \sqrt{\dfrac{300}{500}} = 0.7745$

∴ $\quad$ load on the transformer $= x \times kVA$
$= 0.7745 \times 20 = 16.49 \text{ kVA}$

**Example 3.9:** A 500/250 Volts, single phase transformer has iron losses of 150 watts when delivering an output of 8 kW to a load, the transformer takes 21 amperes at a p.f. of 0.8 from the 500 volts supply mains. Calculate the variable losses of the transformer at this load and maximum efficiency.

**Solution:** $\quad$ Output transformer = 8 kW
$= 8000$ watts

As it takes 21 amperes at 0.8 p.f. from 500 V mains its input

$$= 500 \times 21 \times 0.8 = 8400 \text{ watts}$$

∴ Total losses $= 8400 - 8000 = 400$ watts

i.e. Copper loss + Iron loss $= 400$ watts

∴ Copper loss or variable loss $= 400 - 150 = 250$ watts.

For maximum efficiency,

$$x^2 P_c = P_i$$
$$x^2 \, 250 = 150$$

∴ $x = 0.7745$

∴ Maximum efficiency $= \dfrac{X \times kVA \cos \phi \times 1000}{1000 \times x \cdot kVA \cdot \cos \phi + x^2 P_c + P_i}$

$$= \dfrac{0.7745 \times 8 \times 1000}{0.7745 \times 8 \times 1000 + 150 + 150}$$

$$= \dfrac{6196.77}{6496.77} = 0.9538$$

or $= 95.38\%$

**Example 3.10:** A 5 kVA, 500/250 V S.P. transformer gave the following readings :

When rated voltage at 50 Hz was applied to L.V. side and H.V. side kept open the watt meter reading was 64 watts. When H.V. side was short circuited and full load currents were circulated on both sides, the wattmeter reading was 100 watts. Calculate the efficiency of this transformer at 3 kVA 0.8 p.f. lagging.

**Solution:** From open circuit test, iron losses = 64 watts and from short circuit test, full load copper losses are = 100 watts.

Iron losses being constant, at 3 kVA their value will remain 64 watts only.

Copper loss at 3 kVA $= 100 \times \dfrac{(3)^2}{(5)^2}$ as they are proportional to square of output = 36 watts

∴ Efficiency at 3 kVA 0.8 p.f. load $= \dfrac{\text{Output in watts}}{\text{Output in watts + Iron loss + Cu loss}}$

$$= \dfrac{3 \times 1000 \times 0.8}{3 \times 1000 \times 0.8 + 64 + 36}$$

$$= \dfrac{2400}{2400 + 64 + 36} = 0.96 \text{ or } 96\%$$

**Example 3.11:** A single phase transformer with a ratio of 11000/440 V takes a no load current of 0.8 amps. at a p.f. of 0.5. If the secondary supplies a current of 100 amps. at a p.f. of 0.866 lagging. Calculate the current taken by the primary.

**Solution:** The vector diagram for this condition was drawn in Fig. 3.19 $I_0$ is no load current of 0.8 Amps. making an angle of 60° with $V_1$. $I_2$ is secondary current making an angle of 30° with $V_2$ or $E_2$. Its equivalent current $I_1'$.

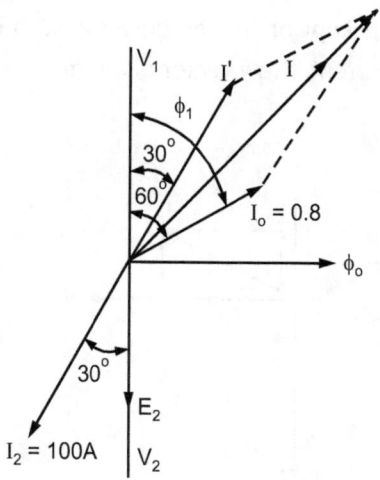

**Fig. 3.19**

$$= I_2 \times K = 100 \times \frac{440}{11000}$$

= 4 Amps. making angle of 30° with $V_1$.

$I_1$ is the vector of $I_0$ and $I_1'$ can be calculated using parallelogram law of forces as

$$I_1 = \sqrt{I_0^2 + I_1'^2 + 2I_0 I_1' \cos \phi}$$

where $\phi$ is the angle between two forces in this case it is 60° – 30 = 30°.

∴ 
$$I = \sqrt{(0.8)^2 + (4)^2 + 2 \times 4 \times 0.8 \times 0.866}$$
$$I_1 = \sqrt{22.1824} = 4.70 \text{ Amps.}$$

It can be solved by resolving component method also

$$I_1 \cos \phi_1 = I_0 \cos 30 + I_1' \cos 60°$$
$$= 0.8 \times 0.866 + 4 \times 0.5 = 2.6928$$
$$I_1 \sin \phi_1 = I_0 \sin 30 + I_1' \sin 60$$
$$= 0.8 \times 0.5 + 4 \times 0.866 = 3.864$$

∴ 
$$I_1 = \sqrt{(2.6928)^2 + (3.864)^2}$$
$$I_1 = \sqrt{7.25 + 14.93} = \sqrt{22.18}$$

or 
$$I_1 = 4.70 \text{ Amps.}$$

and 
$$\tan \phi_1 = \frac{14.93}{7.25}$$

and 
$$\phi_1 = 64°$$

**Example 3.12:** A transformer takes 0.75 amps. When its primary is connected to 200 V, 50 Hz supply. The secondary is kept open. The power absorb is 64 watts. Find the iron loss current and the magnetising current. Draw vector diagram.

**Solution:** At no load,

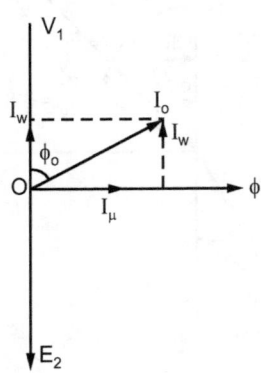

**Fig. 3.20**

$$W_0 = V_1 I_0 \cos\phi_0$$

or $$I_0 \cos\phi_0 = \frac{W_0}{V_1} = \frac{64}{200}$$

or $$I_0 \cos\phi_0 = 0.32$$

or Iron loss current = 0.32 A

Also, $$I_0 = \sqrt{I_w^2 + I_\mu^2}$$

$$I_\mu = \sqrt{I_0^2 + I_w^2}$$

or Magnetising current $$I_\mu = \sqrt{(0.75)^2 - (0.32)^2}$$

$$= \sqrt{0.5625 - 0.1024} = \sqrt{0.46}$$

or Magnetising current = 0.678 Amps.

**Example 3.13:** A transformer having rated output of 125 kVA has an efficiency of 96%, at full load 0.8 p.f. maximum efficiency occurs at half full load unity p.f.

Find : (i) Iron loss, (ii) The maximum efficiency.

**Solution:** Let,
$x$ = f.l. copper loss and
$y$ = Iron losses at rated voltage

∴ The output at f.l. = $1.25 \times 0.8$
= 100 kW

$$\text{Efficiency} = \frac{\text{Output}}{\text{Output} + \text{Iron losses} + \text{Cu loss}}$$

$$0.96 = \frac{100}{100 + y + x} \text{ where values of } x \text{ and } y \text{ are in kW}$$

$$96 + 0.96y + 0.96x = 100 \quad \ldots (1)$$

or $$0.96x + 0.96y = 4$$

Load at half full load u.p.f. = 62.5 kW
and copper losses at half full load i.e. at 62.5 kW i.e. 62.5 kVA at u.p.f.

$$= \frac{(62.5)^2}{(125)^2} \times \text{ or } \frac{1}{4} \times \text{kW}$$

Now as maximum efficiency takes place at 1.2 f.l., the iron and copper losses must be equal.

∴ $\qquad \frac{1}{4}x = y \qquad \ldots(2)$

Putting value of y in equation (1),

$\qquad 0.96x + 0.96 \times 0.25x = 4$

$\qquad 0.96x + 0.24x = 4$

or $\qquad x = \frac{4}{1.2} = 3.33 \text{ kW}$

and $\qquad y = 0.83 \text{ kW}$

∴ Maximum efficiency can be calculated as follows :

$\qquad$ Output = 62.5 kW

$\qquad$ Iron loss = 0.83 kW

$\qquad$ Copper loss = 0.83 kW

∴ $\qquad$ Maximum efficiency $= \dfrac{62.5}{62.5 + 0.83 + 0.83} = \dfrac{62.5}{64.16} = 0.9741$

or $\qquad = 97.41\%$

**Example 3.14:** The following results were obtained from a 250/125 V, 50 Hz, 2.5 kVA transformer no load test (L.T. open).

Voltage applied 250 V, current taken 0.8 A, power absorbed 60 W.

S.C. impedance test (L.T. open)

Voltage applied 15 volts, current taken 10 A, power absorbed 80 W.

Draw the equivalent circuit of the transformer and mark values of all elements in it.

**Solution:** From O.C. test data

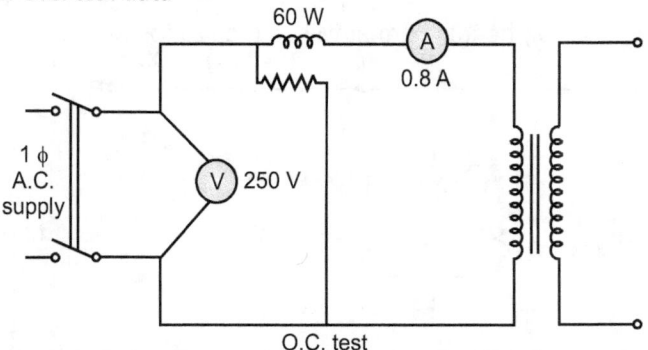

O.C. test

**Fig. 3.21 (a)**

$$I_w = I_0 \cos \phi_0 = \frac{W_0}{V_1}$$

$$= \frac{60}{250} = 0.24 \text{ A}$$

∴ Constants of shunt circuit, $R_0 = \dfrac{V_1}{I_0 \cos \phi_0} = \dfrac{250}{0.24} = 1041.66 \; \Omega$

$$X_0 = \frac{V_1}{I_0 \sin \phi_0} = 327.65 \; \Omega$$

**Fig. 3.21 (b)**

As L.V. is short circuited, we will get parameters of equivalent circuit referred to H.V. side, from the S.C. test.

From,
$$W_{se} = I_{sc}^2 R_1$$
$$80 = (10)^2 \times R_1$$

Equivalent resistance, $R_1 = \dfrac{80}{100} = 0.8 \; \Omega$

Similarly, equivalent impedance, $Z_1 = \dfrac{V_{sc}}{I_{sc}} = \dfrac{15}{10} = 1.5 \; \Omega$

and equivalent reactance referred to primary
$$X_1 = \sqrt{Z_1^2 - R_1^2} = \sqrt{(1.5)^2 - (0.8)^2} = 1.26 \; \Omega$$

The equivalent circuit of the transformer will be then as follows.

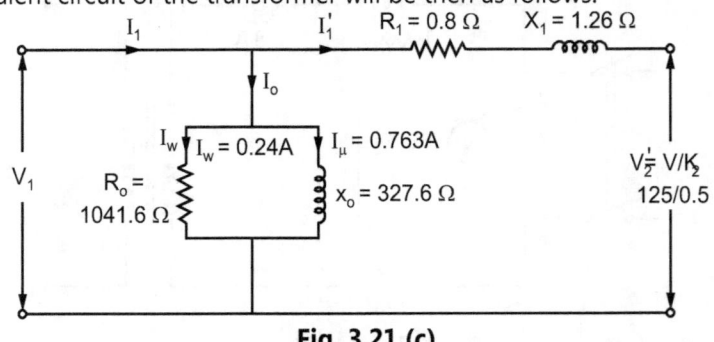

**Fig. 3.21 (c)**

**Example 3.15:** A 10 kVA 500/250 volts, 1 phase transformer gave the following results, with O.C. and S.C. O.C. test : 500 volts; 1 amp. 100 watts (H.V. side), S.C. test : 25 volts, 25 amps, 125 watts (H.V. side). Draw and write the values in the equivalent circuit referred to H.V. side, what is regulation and efficiency at full load 0.866 lagging p.f.

**Solution:** Fig. 3.22 for O.C. and S.C. test will be identical to those drawn for Example 3.12, except the values for O.C. test

$$I_\omega = \frac{W_0}{V_1} = \frac{100}{500} = 0.2 \text{ A}$$

$$\therefore R_0 = \frac{V_1}{I_\omega} = \frac{500}{0.2} = 2500 \text{ ohms.}$$

$$I_\mu = \sqrt{I_0^2 - I_\omega^2} = \sqrt{(1)^2 - (0.2)^2} = 0.9797 \text{ A}$$

$$\therefore X_0 = \frac{V_1}{I_\mu} = \frac{500}{0.9797} = 510.36 \text{ ohms.}$$

From S.C. test data : Equivalent resistance referred to primary

$$R_1 = \frac{W_{sc}}{(I_{sc})^2} = \frac{125}{(25)^2} = 0.2 \text{ ohms.}$$

$$Z_1 = \frac{V_{sc}}{I_{sc}} = \frac{25}{25} = 1 \, \Omega$$

$$\therefore X_1 = \sqrt{Z_1^2 - R_1^2} = \sqrt{(1)^2 - (0.2)^2} = 0.9797 \, \Omega$$

Equivalent reaction referred to primary.

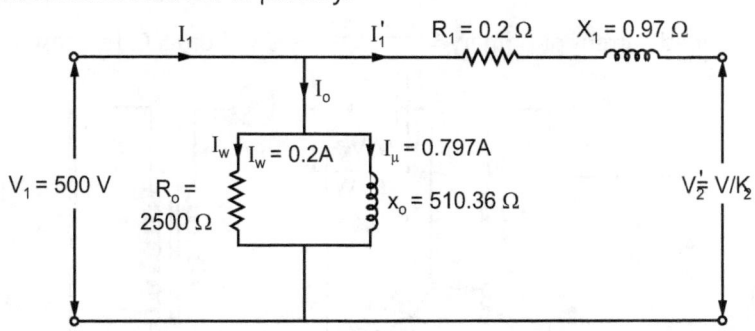

**Fig. 3.22**

% regulation can be calculated using the following relation.

$$\% \text{ Regulation} = \frac{I_1 R_1 \cos \phi_1 + I_1 X_1 \sin \phi_1}{V_1} \times 100$$

where,  $I_1$ = Full load primary current
$R_1$ = Equivalent resistance referred to primary
and  $X_1$ = Equivalent reactance referred to primary
$V_1$ = Rated voltage of primary

Rated full load current, $I_1 = \dfrac{10 \times 1000}{500} = 20$ A

% Regulation $= \dfrac{20 \times 0.2 \times 0.866 + 20 \times 0.97 \times 0.5}{500}$

% Regulation $= \dfrac{3.464 + 9.7}{500} \times 100 = 2.63\%$

Iron loss at rated voltage, from O.C. test = 100 W, copper loss at 25 Amps.
Primary current = 125 watts, but full load primary current 20 A.

∴ Cu loss at 20 A primary current $= 125 \times \dfrac{(20)^2}{(25)^2} = 80$ watts.

Output at full load 0.866 p.f. $= 10 \times 10^3 \times 0.866$ watts

∴ Efficiency at f.l. $= \dfrac{\text{Output}}{\text{Output} + P_i + P_c}$

$= \dfrac{10 \times 10^2 \times 0.866}{10 \times 10^2 \times 0.866 + 100 + 80}$

$= \dfrac{8660}{8840} = 0.9796$ OR $97.96\%$

**Example 3.16:** A 5 kVA, 200/400 volts, single phase transformer gave the following test results secondary short circuited 8 volts applied to primary circulated full load current in the secondary, power lost 80 watts.

Calculate the secondary terminal voltage at full load 0.8 p.f. leading and its regulation.

**Solution:** Full load current of primary $= \dfrac{5 \times 1000}{200} = 25$ A from S.C. test results

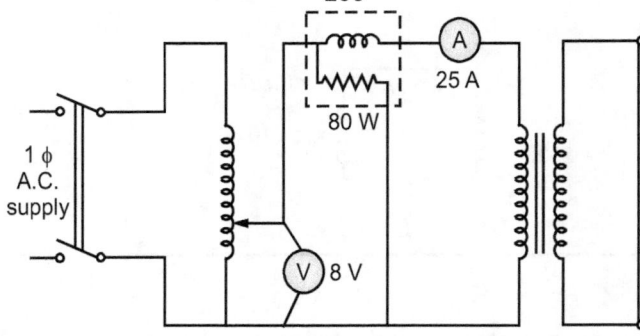

Fig. 3.23

We will calculate the parameters referred to primary, as metering is on primary side.

$R_1 = \dfrac{W_{sc}}{I_{sc}^2} = \dfrac{80}{(25)^2} = 0.128\ \Omega$

$Z_1 = \dfrac{V_{sc}}{I_{sc}} = \dfrac{8}{25} = 0.32\ \Omega$

# BASIC ELECTRICAL DRIVES & CONTROLS

## SINGLE PHASE & THREE PHASE ......

$$\therefore \quad X_1 = \sqrt{Z_1^2 - R_1^2} = \sqrt{(0.32)^2 - (0.128)^2}$$
$$= \sqrt{0.1024 - 0.016}$$
$$\therefore \quad X_1 = 0.29 \ \Omega$$

Assuming that at no load when 200 volts are applied to primary, secondary induced e.m.f. will be 400 volts, when the transformer is loaded its secondary voltage will reduce due to drop of voltage in its impedance, let the T.V. at full load on secondary side be $V_2$ volts.

The parameters transferred to secondary side

$$R_2 = R_1 \times K^2 = 0.128 \times (2)^2 = 0.512 \text{ ohm}$$
$$X_2 = X_1 \times K^2 = 0.29 \times (2)^2 = 1.16 \text{ ohm}$$

Now the equation for secondary induced e.m.f. for a leading p.f. will be used as

$$I_2 = \frac{5 \times 1000}{200} = 12.5 \text{ Amps.}$$

$$(E_2)^2 = \sqrt{(V_2 \cos\phi + I_2 R_2)^2 + (V_2 \sin\phi - I_2 X_2)^2}$$
$$(400)^2 = \sqrt{(V_2 \times 0.8 + 12.5 \times 0.512)^2 + (V_2 \times 0.6 - 12.5 \times 1.16)^2}$$
$$(400)^2 = \sqrt{(0.8 V_2 + 6.4)^2 + (0.6 V_2 - 14.5)^2}$$

OR
$$16000 = 0.64 V_2^2 + 10.24 V_2 + 40.96 + 0.36 V_2^2 - 17.4 V_2 + 210.25$$

or
$$0 = V_2^2 - 7.16 V_2 - 159748.79$$

Solving the quadratic equation using formula for $V_2$ as $\dfrac{-b \pm \sqrt{b^2 - 4ac}}{2}$

$$V_2 = \frac{7.16 \pm \sqrt{51.26 + 638995.16}}{2}$$

or
$$V_2 = \frac{7.16 \pm 799.4}{2}$$

Using positive sign $V_2 = 403.28$ and negative sign $V_2 = 395.12$. As the load is leading $V_2$ must be greater than $E_2$. Hence, secondary terminal voltage = 403.28 V.

Now, $\quad$ Regulation $= \dfrac{E_2 - V_2}{E_2} \times 100$

$$\% \text{ Regulation} = \frac{400 \pm 799.4}{400} \times 100$$

% Regulation = 0.82%, at full load, 0.8 p.f. lead.

**Example 3.17:** A 100 kVA, 2000/400 V, single phase transformer has a maximum efficiency of 94.5% which occurs at 70% of full load when the load p.f. is unity. The magnetising current at 2000 V is 90 amps. If O.C.T. is to be performed on this transformer, what will be the readings of the instruments connected ?

**Solution:** Output at 70% of full load, and unity p.f. condition
$$= 100 \times 0.7 = 70 \text{ kW at this output efficiency} = 94.5\%$$

∴ Input at 70% full load = $\frac{70}{0.945}$ = 74.07 kW

∴ Total losses at this load = 74.07 − 70 = 4.07 kW

As 4.07 kW are the total losses at maximum efficiency

$$\text{Iron loss} = \text{Copper loss} = \frac{4.07}{2} = 2.035 \text{ kW.}$$

i.e. Iron loss (constant loss) = 2.035 kW

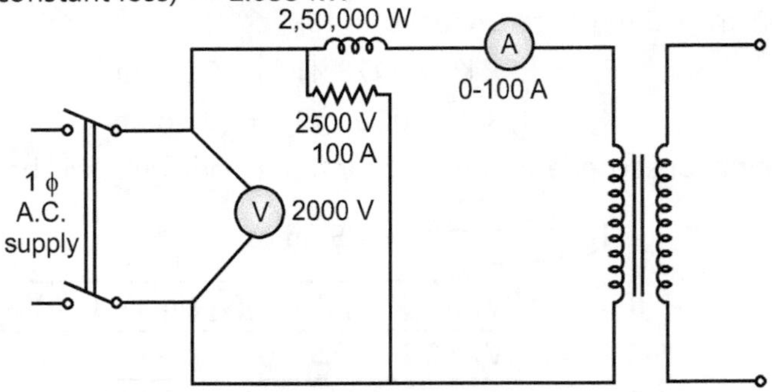

**Fig. 3.24**

The magnetising $I_\mu = I_0 \sin \phi_0$ = 90 A.

In O.C. test the transformer has to supply magnetising current $I_\mu$ and loss current (iron loss)

$$I_\omega = I_0 \cos \phi_0$$

∴ Iron loss, $W_0 = V_1 I_0 \cos \phi_0$

$$2.035 \times 10^3 = 2000 \times I_0 \cos \phi_0$$

∴ $$I_0 \cos \phi_0 = I_\omega = \frac{2.035 \times 10^3}{2000} = 1.0175$$

∴ $$I_0 = \sqrt{(1.0175)^2 + (90)^2} = \sqrt{1.035 + 8100}$$

or $$I_0 = 90.0075 \text{ A}$$

∴ Ammeter must be of 0 to 100 A range.

Voltmeter 0 − 2500

Wattmeter 2500 watts, 100 A range.

**Example 3.18:** A 50 kVA, 2200/2200 V, 60 Hz single phase transformer has an iron loss of 300 watts. The resistance of its low and high potential windings are 0.005 and 0.5 ohm respectively. Calculate the input to this transformer when it is delivering full load at 80% lagging p.f.

**Solution:** Primary full load current = $\frac{\text{kVA } 10^3}{V_1}$ amps.

$$= \frac{50 \times 1000}{2000} = 22.727 \text{ Amps.}$$

Secondary full load current = $\dfrac{50 \times 1000}{220}$ = 227.27 Amps.

∴ Primary full load Cu loss at full load = $(227.27)^2 \times 0.5$ = 258.258 W.
Secondary full load Cu loss = $(227.27)^2 \times 0.005$ = 258.258 W.

∴ Total copper losses at full load = 516.51 W

Output at full load 0.8 p.f. = $50 \times 10^3 \times 0.8$ = 40000 watts.

$$\text{Input} = \text{Output} + \text{Iron loss} + \text{Cu loss}$$
$$= 40000 + 300 + 516.51$$
$$= 40816.51 \text{ watts}$$

**Example 3.19:** A 20 kVA, 1000/250 V, 50 Hz single phase transformer have the following test results.

| | | | |
|---|---|---|---|
| O.C. test (H.V. side) : | 1000 V | 2 A | 250 W |
| S.C. test (L.V. side) : | 5 V | 50 A | 200 W |

Calculate the percentage regulation and efficiency at half full load 0.8 p.f. lagging.

**Solution:** As the metering is on L.V. (secondary) side, we will get parameters referred to secondary.

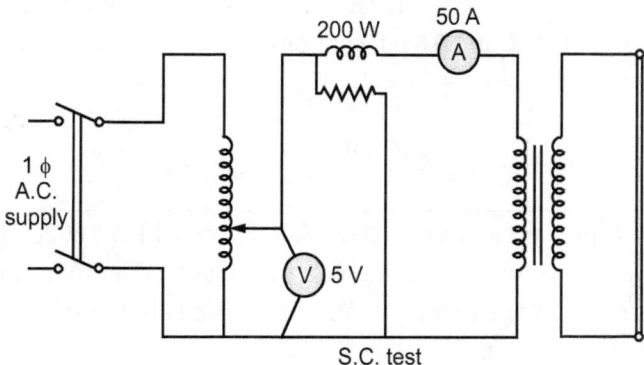

**Fig. 3.25**

Equivalent impedance referred to secondary,

$$Z_2 = \dfrac{V_{sc}}{I_{sc}} = \dfrac{5}{10} = 0.1 \text{ ohm}$$

and

$$R_2 = \dfrac{W_{sc}}{I_{sc}^2} = \dfrac{200}{(50)^2} = 0.08 \text{ ohm}$$

∴

$$X_2 = \sqrt{(0.1)^2 - (0.08)^2} = 0.06 \text{ ohm}$$

Current at half full load on secondary side

$$= \dfrac{10 \times 1000}{250} = 40 \text{ Amps.}$$

As the short circuit test is carried out at 50 Amps. wattmeter reading represents copper losses at 50 amps. secondary currents.

$$\therefore \text{ Copper loss at 1/2 f.l.} = 200 \times \left(\frac{40}{50}\right)^2 = 128 \text{ watts}$$

$$\text{While they will at full load} = 200 \times \left(\frac{80}{50}\right)^2 = 512 \text{ watts}$$

∴ Efficiency at 1/2 f.l. 0.8 p.f. lag

$$\text{kVA} = 0.5 \times 20 = 10$$

$$= \frac{\text{kVA} \cos \phi}{\text{kVA} \cos \phi + P_i + P_c}$$

$$= \frac{(10 \times 0.8) \times 10^3}{(10 \times 0.8) \times 10^3 + 250 = 128} = 0.9548$$

OR 95.48%, $P_i$ is taken from O.C. test.

For calculating regulation, using relation

$$E_2 = \sqrt{(V_2 \cos \phi + I_2 R_2) + (V_2 \sin \phi + I_2 X_2)^2}$$

$$E_2 = \sqrt{(250 \times 0.8 + 40 \times 0.08)^2 + (250 \times 0.6 + 40 \times 0.06)^2}$$

$$= \sqrt{(200 + 3.2)^2 + (150 + 2.4)^2}$$

$$= \sqrt{41290.24 + 23225.76} = 254 \text{ volts.}$$

∴ % Regulation at 1/2 f.l. and 0.8 p.f. lag from

$$= \frac{E_2 - V_2}{E_2} \times 100$$

$$= \frac{254 - 250}{254} \times 100 = 1.57\%$$

**Example 3.20:** A primary and secondary windings of 20 kVA, 6000/200 V, single phase transformer have resistance of 5 ohms and 0.01 respectively. The total leakage reactance of the transformer referred to the primary is 20 ohms. Calculate the percentage regulation of the transformer when supplying.

(i) Full load current at a p.f. of 0.8 lagging.
(ii) Half full load current at a p.f. 0.8 leading.

**Solution:** Primary full load current $= \frac{20 \times 10^3}{6000} = 3.33$ A

Transformation ratio, $K = \frac{200}{6000} = 0.0333$

Secondary resistance transferred to primary

$$r_2' = \frac{r_2}{K^2} = \frac{0.01}{(0.0333)^2} = 9.00 \, \Omega$$

∴ Equivalent resistance referred to primary

$$= r_1 + r_2' = 5 + 9 = 14 \text{ ohms}$$

Equivalent reactance referred to primary = 20 ohms.

$$\% \text{ Regulation} = \frac{I_1 R_1 \cos \phi_1 + I_1 X_1 \sin \phi_1}{V_1} \times 100$$

At full load 0.8 p.f. lag $= \dfrac{3.33 \times 14 \times 0.8 + 3.33 \times 20 \times 0.6}{6000} \times 100 = 1.28\%$

Primary current at half load = 1.665

∴ Regulation at 1/2 load 0.8 p.f. leading from

$$\frac{I_1 R_1 \cos \phi - I_1 X_1 \sin \phi}{V_1} \times 100 = \frac{1.665 \times 14 \times 0.8 - 1.665 \times 20 \times 0.6}{6000} \times 100$$

$$= \frac{18.64 - 19.98}{6000} \times 100 = 0.022\%$$

**Example 3.21:** A 6600/440 V, 1 phase transformer gave the following test results H.V. short circuited transformer took 80 amps. and 500 watts when 20 volts were applied to the L.V. side. What voltage must be applied to the primary winding, when the load is 150 amps. at 440 V at a p.f. 0.71 lagging ?

**Solution:** From S.C. test, we will obtain parameters referred to L.V. (secondary) side.

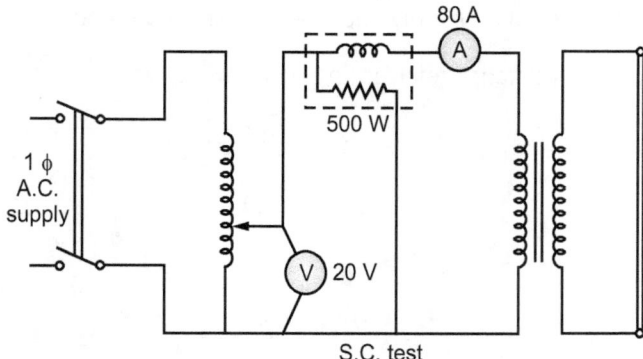

S.C. test

**Fig. 3.26**

$$R_2 = \frac{W_{SC}}{I_{SC}^2} = \frac{500}{(80)^2} = 0.078 \; \Omega$$

$$Z_2 = \frac{V_{SC}}{I_{SC}} = \frac{20}{80} = 0.25 \; \Omega$$

$$X_2 = \sqrt{(0.25)^2 - (0.078)^2} = \sqrt{0.06 - 0.006084}$$

$$X_2 = 0.237 \; \Omega$$

Transformation ratio $= \dfrac{440}{6600} = 0.0666$

Secondary current transferred to primary

$$I_1 = I_2 \times K = 150 \times 0.06666 = 10 \text{ amps.}$$

To supply 150 amps. at secondary voltage of 440 volts and 0.71 p.f. lagging, the primary voltage will be more than 6600 volts, because some voltage will drop, as impedance drop when the transformer delivers load, the primary applied voltage can be calculated using relation.

$$E_1 = \sqrt{(V_1 \cos\phi + I_1 R_1)^2 + (V_1 \sin\phi + I_1 X_1)^2}$$

or

$$E_1 = \sqrt{(6600 \times 0.71 + 10 \times R_1)^2 + (6600 \times 0.70 + 10 \times X_1)^2}$$

$$R_1 = \frac{R_2}{K^2} = \frac{0.078}{(0.0666)^2} = 17.55 \, \Omega$$

Now,

$$X_1 = \frac{X_2}{K^2} = \frac{0.237}{(0.0666)^2} = 53.33 \, \Omega$$

$$E_1 = \sqrt{(6600 \times 0.71 + 10 \times 17.55)^2 + (6600 \times 0.70 + 10 \times 53.3)^2}$$

$$E_1 = \sqrt{(4861.5)^2 + (5153)^2} = 7084.32 \, V$$

The voltage to be applied to primary = 7084.32 V

**Example 3.22:** The high and low voltage winding of a 6600/250 V, 50 Hz, 1 phase transformer have resistance of 0.21 $\Omega$, and $2.72 \times 10^{-4}$ $\Omega$ and reactances of 1 $\Omega$ and $1.3 \times 10^{-3}$ $\Omega$ respectively. Determine the current and power input when high voltage winding is connected to a 400 volts, 50 Hz supply, the low voltage winding being short circuited.

**Solution:** Equivalent resistance referred to H.V. (primary) side = $r_1 + \frac{r_2}{K^2}$

$$= 0.21 + \frac{2.72 \times 10^{-4}}{(0.03787)^2}$$

$$= 0.21 + 0.19$$

As

$$K = \frac{250}{6600}$$

or

$$R_1 = 0.4 \text{ ohm}$$

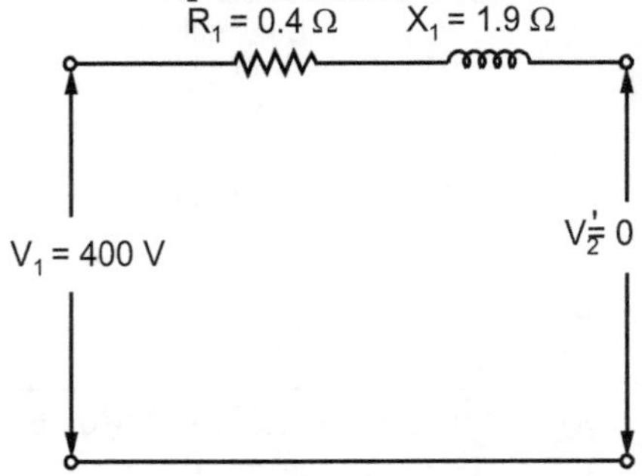

$R_1 = 0.4 \, \Omega$  $X_1 = 1.9 \, \Omega$

$V_1 = 400 \, V$  $V_2 = 0$

Fig. 3.27

Similarly,

$$X_1 = x_1 + \frac{X_2}{K^2}$$

$$= 1 + \frac{1.3 \times 10^{-3}}{(0.03787)^2}$$

or $\quad X_1 = 1 + 0.90 = 1.90\ \Omega$

Putting the values in approximate equivalent circuit, where
$$Z'_L = 0,\ V'_2 = 0$$

Impedance of the circuit, $\quad Z_1 = \sqrt{(0.4)^2 + (1.9)^2} = 1.94\ \Omega$

∴ Short circuit current $= \dfrac{V_1}{Z_1}$

$$= \dfrac{400}{1.94}$$

Power loss $= I_1^2 R_1$

$= (206.18)^2 \times 0.4 = 17004.99$ watts

or $\quad = 17.00499$ kW

**Example 3.23:** The diagram shows the equivalent circuit for a 1 phase transformer. Figures give resistances and reactances in ohms, in terms of the primary side. The ratio of the secondary to primary turns is 10 and the load is inductive. Find (a) the secondary terminal voltage, (b) the primary current, (c) the efficiency.

**Solution:** Load impedance transferred to primary side.

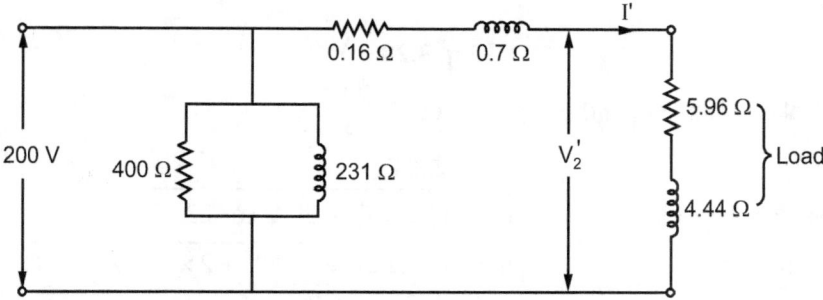

**Fig. 3.28 (a)**

$$Z'_L = \sqrt{(5.96)^2 + (4.44)^2} = 7.43\ \Omega$$

Total impedance of primary circuit $= \sqrt{(5.96 + 16)^2 + (4.44 + 0.7)^2} = 7.99\ \Omega$

∴ Secondary current transferred to primary side

$$I'_1 = \dfrac{V_1}{Z} = \dfrac{200}{7.99} = 25.23\ A$$

$$I_\mu = \dfrac{V_1}{X_0} = \dfrac{200}{231} = 0.86\ A$$

$$I_\omega = \dfrac{V_1}{R_0} = \dfrac{200}{400} = 0.5\ A$$

$$I_0 = \sqrt{(I_\omega)^2 + (I_\mu)^2} = \sqrt{(0.5)^2 + (0.86)^2}$$

or
$$I_0 = 0.99 \text{ A and } \phi_0 = \tan^{-1}\frac{I_\mu}{I_\omega} = 59.82°$$
$$V_2' = I_1' \times Z_L' = 25.03 \times 7.43 = 185.97 \text{ volts}$$

∴ Secondary voltage, $V_2 = V_2' \times k = 185.97 \times 10$
$$= 1859.7 \text{ volts}$$

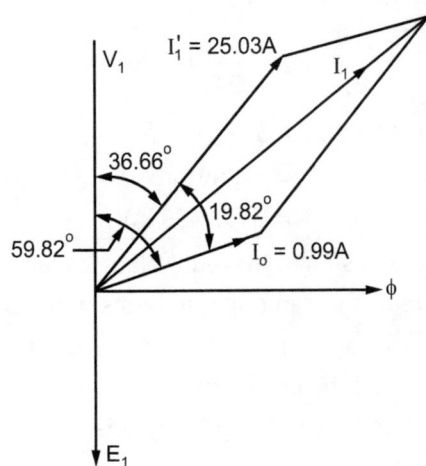

**Fig. 3.28 (b)**

$I_1'$ will make an angle $\phi_1'$ with $V_1$, $\phi_1' = \cos^{-1}\dfrac{5.96}{7.43}$

$$= 36.66°$$

From vector diagram, $I_1 = \sqrt{I_1'^2 + I_0'^2 + 2I_1' I_0 \cos 23.16}$

Putting the values, $I_1 = \sqrt{(25.03)^2 + (0.99)^2 + 2 \times 25.03 \times 0.99 \times 0.94}$

or $I_1 = \sqrt{626.5 + 0.98 + 45}$

$I_1 = \sqrt{672.48} = 25.93$ A

For determining efficiency, we will find out the output and losses separately as follows:

Secondary voltage, $V_2 = 1859.7$ volts.

Secondary current, $I_2 = \dfrac{I_1'}{k} = \dfrac{25.03}{10} = 2.503$ A

p.f. of load $= R/Z = \dfrac{5.96}{7.43} = 0.822$ lag

∴ Output power $= V_2 I_2 \cos \phi$
$$= 1859.7 \times 2.503 \times 0.802 = 3733.17$$

Copper losses $= I_2'^2 R_1$
$$= (25.03)^2 \times 0.16 = 100.24 \text{ watts}$$

$$I_\omega = I_0 \cos \phi_0 = \frac{V_1}{R_0} = \frac{200}{400} = 0.5 \text{ A}$$

Iron loss $= V_1 I_0 \cos \phi_0 = 200 \times 0.5 = 100$ watts

∴ Efficiency $= \dfrac{\text{Output}}{\text{Output + Iron loss + Cu loss}}$

$= \dfrac{3733.17}{3733.17 + 100 + 100.24} = 0.9490$

or % Efficiency $= 94.30\%$

**Example 3.24:** Calculate the regulation of a transformer in which the ohmic loss is 1% of output and reactance drop 5% of the voltage, when the power factor is (a) 0.8 lagging, (b) unity, (c) 0.8 leading.

**Solution:** When equivalent resistance is R and full load current is I the ohmic loss = $I^2R$ watts.

When V is applied voltage and I is current for u.p.f. condition

$$VI = \text{Output in watts}$$

As per given condition $\quad VI \times \dfrac{1}{100} = I^2R$

or $\quad \dfrac{I^2R}{VI} \times 100 = 1$

or $\quad \dfrac{IR}{V} \times 100 =$ i.e. % resistive drop $V_r = 1\%$

The % reactive drop = 5% (given)

Then using relation for regulation

as % Regulation $= V_r \cos \phi \pm V_x \sin \phi$

where, $\qquad V_r = \%$ resistive drop and

$\qquad V_x = \%$ reactive drop

(i) ∴ for 0.8 lagging condition regulation $= 1 \times 0.8 + 5 \times 0.6 = 3.8\%$

(ii) For unity p.f. condition, Regulation $= 1 \times 1 + 5 \times 0 = 1\%$

(iii) For 0.8 leading p.f. condition, Regulation $= 1 \times 0.8 - 5 \times 0.6 = -2.2\%$

**Example 3.25:** A 100 kVA transformer supplying lighting load has maximum efficiency at full load. The total losses at full load are 3 kW. During the day it operates on full load for 3 hours, on half load for 4 hours and 1/4 full load for remaining period. Find the all day efficiency.

| Load in kVA | p.f. | Load in kW | Hours | Copper loss in kW | Energy loss in kWh (In Cu loss) | Iron loss in kWh | Iron loss in kWh | Output kWh | Input kWh |
|---|---|---|---|---|---|---|---|---|---|
| 100 kVA | 1 | 100 | 3 | 1.5 | 1.5 × 3 = 4.5 | 1.5 | 1.5 × 3 = 4.5 | 100 × 3 = 300 | 300 + 4.5 + 4.5 = 309 |
| 50 kVA | 1 | 50 | 4 | $1.5 \times \frac{1}{4}$ = 0.375 | 0.375 × 4 = 1.5 | 1.5 | 1.5 × 4 = 6 | 50 × 4 = 200 | 207.5 |
| 25 kVA | 1 | 25 | 17 | $1.5 \times \frac{1}{16}$ = 0.09375 | 0.09375 × 17 = 1.59 | 1.5 | 1.5 × 17 = 25.5 | 425 | 452.09 |
| | | | | | Total 7.59 | | 36 | 925 | 968.59 |

**Solution:** As the efficiency is maximum at full load, losses of 3 kW at full load will be equally divided between iron loss and full load copper loss.

∴ Iron loss = 1.5 kW

Full load Cu loss = 1.5 kW

The calculations of energy output the energy input in kWh for different hours of the day are tabulated in the table given above.

$$\text{Now all day efficiency} = \frac{\text{kWh output in 24 hours}}{\text{kWh input in 24 hours}}$$

$$\frac{925}{968.49} = 0.9549 \text{ or } 95.49\%$$

**Example 3.26:** A 50 kVA transformer has core loss 400 watts and copper loss at rated current 600 watts. Determine the maximum efficiency corresponding to 0.8 p.f. load. Estimate also the all day efficiency from the following data.

| Duration | 6 Hours | 6 Hours | 6 Hours | 6 Hours |
|---|---|---|---|---|
| Loading | 100% | 80% | 50% | No load |
| Power factor | Unity | 0.8 | 0.5 | – |

**Solution:** For maximum efficiency $P_i = x^2 P_c$

where $P_i$ = Iron loss, $P_c$ = Full load Cu loss and x = Fraction of full load output at which maximum efficiency takes place.

∴ $400 = x^2 \times 600$ or $x = \sqrt{\frac{400}{600}}$

$x = 0.816$

∴ Output at maximum efficiency and 0.8 p.f. = 50 × 0.816 × 0.8 = 32.64 kW

∴ Maximum $\eta = \dfrac{\text{Output}}{\text{Output} + P_i + P_c} = \dfrac{32.64 \times 1000}{32.64 \times 1000 + 400 + 400}$

or Maximum $\eta$ = 0.976 or 07.6%

For calculating all day efficiency, we will prepare the table as in Example 3.25.

| Load in kVA | p.f. | Load in kW | Duration in kW | Copper loss in kW | Energy loss in kWh (In Cu loss) | Iron loss in kWh | Iron loss in kWh | Output kWh | Input kWh |
|---|---|---|---|---|---|---|---|---|---|
| 50 | 1 | 50 | 6 | $\dfrac{600}{1000}$ | 0.6 × 6 = 3.6 | $\dfrac{400}{1000}$ | 0.4 × 6 = 2.4 | 300 | 306 |
| 50 × 0.8 = 40 | 0.8 | 32 | 6 | $\dfrac{384}{1000}$ | 0.384 × 6 = 2.3 | $\dfrac{400}{1000}$ | 0.4 × 6 = 2.4 | 192 | 196.7 |
| 50 × 0.5 = 25 | 0.5 | 12.5 | 6 | $\dfrac{150}{1000}$ | 0.15 × 6 = 0.9 | $\dfrac{400}{1000}$ | 0.4 × 6 = 2.4 | 75 | 78.3 |
| 0 | – | – | 6 | – | – | $\dfrac{400}{1000}$ | 0.4 × 6 = 2.4 | – | 2.4 |
| | | | | | Total | | | 567 | 583.4 |

From the table, output energy in 24 hours of a day = 576 kWh and input energy in 24 hours of a day = 583.4 kWh.

∴ All day efficiency = $\dfrac{567}{583.4}$ = 0.97

or All day efficiency = 97%

**Example 3.27:** Find "All day efficiency" of a 500 kVA distribution transformer, whose copper and iron losses at full load are 4.5 kW and 3 kW respectively. During a day of 24 hours it is loaded as under :

| No. of hours | 6 | 6 | 8 | 4 |
|---|---|---|---|---|
| Load in kW | 450 | 300 | 150 | 0 |
| Power factor | 0.9 | 0.75 | unity | – |

**Solution:** From the given data load in kW is given as its p.f. is also known, we can find out the load in kVA for calculation of copper losses.

∴ First load of 450 kW at 0.9 p.f. = $\dfrac{450}{0.9}$ = 500 kVA

Second load = $\dfrac{300}{0.75}$ = 400 kVA

and Third load = $\dfrac{150}{1}$ = 150 kVA

A similar table is used for Example 3.24 or 3.23 will be used to determine kWh output in 24 hours and kWh input in 24 hours of a day.

| Load in kVA | p.f. | Load in kVA | Times in hours | Copper loss in kW | Energy loss in Cu loss | Iron loss in kWh | Iron loss in kWh | Output in kWh | Input in kWh |
|---|---|---|---|---|---|---|---|---|---|
| 450 | 0.9 | 500 | 6 | 4.5 | 27 | 3 | 18 | 2700 | 274.5 |
| 200 | 0.75 | 400 | 6 | $4.5 \times \left(\frac{400}{500}\right)^2$ = 2.88 | 17.28 | 3 | 18 | 1800 | 1835.28 |
| 150 | 1 | 150 | 8 | $4.5 \times \left(\frac{150}{500}\right)^2$ = 0.405 | 3.24 | 3 | 24 | 1200 | 1277.24 |
| – | – | – | 4 | – | – | 3 | 12 | – | 12 |
|  |  |  |  |  | Total |  |  | 5700 | 5819.52 |

$$\therefore \text{All day efficiency} = \frac{\text{Energy (kWh) output in 24 hours}}{\text{Energy (kWh) input in 24 hours}}$$

$$\therefore \text{All day efficiency} = \frac{5700}{5819.52} \times 100 = 97.94\%$$

**Example 3.28:** The maximum efficiency of a 500 kVA 3300/500 V, 50 Hz single phase transformer is 97% and occurs at 3/4 full load, unity p.f. If the impedance is 10%, calculate the regulation at full load, power factor 0.8 lagging.

**Solution:** Output at 3/4 f.l. unity p.f. = 500 × 3/4 × 1 = 375 kW

$$\text{Input at 3/4 full load} = \frac{\text{Output}}{\text{Efficiency}}$$

$$= \frac{375}{0.97} = 386.597 \text{ kW}$$

∴ Total loss at maximum efficiency = 386.597 − 375
= 11.597 kW

At maximum efficiency, Cu loss = Iron loss

∴ Iron loss = $\frac{11.597}{2}$ = 5.798 kW and Cu loss at

3/4 f.l. = 5.798 kW

Cu loss at full load = $5.798 \times \left(\frac{4}{3}\right)^2$ = 10.3 kW

Now, $\frac{I^2R}{VI} = \frac{\text{Cu loss}}{\text{VA output}} = \frac{IR}{V}$ i.e. unit

Resistive drop or $\dfrac{I^2 R}{VI} \times 100 = V_r$, % resistive drop

$$V_r = \dfrac{10.3 \times 10^3}{500 \times 10^3} \times 100 = 2.06\%$$

Now, Impedance = 10% i.e. $\dfrac{IZ}{V} \times 100$

But, $I_2 = \dfrac{500 \times 10^3}{500} = 1000 \text{ A}$

∴ $10 = \dfrac{1000 \times Z}{500} \times 100$

or $\dfrac{10 \times 500}{1000 \times 100} = 0.05 \text{ ohm}$

$I_2^2 R_2 = 10.3 \times 10^3$

$(1000)^2 R_2 = 10.3 \times 10^3$ or $R_2 = \dfrac{10.3 \times 10^3}{(1000)^2}$

$R_2 = 0.0103 \ \Omega$

∴ $X_2 = \sqrt{(0.05)^2 - (0.00103)^2} = 0.0489 \ \Omega$

∴ $\% V_x = \dfrac{I_2 X_2}{V_2} \times 100 = \dfrac{1000 \times 0.0489}{500} \times 100$

or $\% V_x = 9.78\%$

∴ Regulation at full load 0.8 p.f. lag, from

$\%$ Regulation = $V_r \cos \phi + V_x \sin \phi$

$= 2.06 \times 0.08 + 9.78 \times 0.6$

$= 1.648 + 5.87 = 7.518\%$

% Regulation = 7.518%

# THEORY QUESTIONS

**(I) Fill in the blanks with proper words:**

(A) Transformer works on the principal of _____ (Mutual Inductance)

(B) Transformer is a device (static machine) that change _____ without change of _____ (voltage, frequency)

(C) Transformer is having high efficiency in comparison to other electrical machines because it has no _____ losses. (Mechanical)

(D) The core of the transformer is made from _____ because it has high _____ and low _____ (silicon, resistivity, hysteresis loss)

(E) The core of transformer is laminated to reduce _____ losses. (eddy current)

(F) Hysteresis loss is reduced in case of transformers by using _____ having low _____ loop area.  (Grain oriented steel, Hysteresis loop)

(G) Cooling of transformer is necessary to _____  (Dissipate heat due to losses)

(H) The core flux leads by _____ to the induced e.m.f. in primary or secondary windings  (90°)

(I) There is phase shift of _____ between the input and secondary voltage at no load.  (180°)

(J) The wattmeter reading in an open circuit test can be taken as _____ losses because _____ losses at no load are negligible  (core, copper)

(K) The wattmeter reading in the short circuit test can be taken as _____ losses because _____ losses are negligible in short circuit test.  (core, iron)

(L) The efficiency of a transformer is maximum when _____ losses are equal to _____ losses.  (copper, iron)

(M) Transformer regulation is defined as the change in _____ when the load is thrown off.  (Terminal voltage)

(N) % Regulation is defined as the ratio of change in _____ when the load is thrown off to _____ voltage multiplied by 100.  (Terminal voltage, No load)

(O) Transformers having _____ value of regulation are preferred because they give _____ voltage on load.  (low, stable)

(P) All day efficiency of the transformer is a ratio of _____ in a day of 24 hrs. to _____ in a day of 24 hrs.  (Energy cut put in kWh, Energy in put in kWh)

(Q) Transformers having _____ value of all day efficiency are preferred because it has less loss of _____ in _____ losses.  (High, energy, iron)

(R) The approximate voltage drop in case of transformer is given by _____ (referred voltage primary side) ($I_1 R_1 \cos \phi_1 \pm I_1 X_1 \sin \phi_1$)

(S) When D.C. voltage of same rating is applied to the transformer winding it will draw _____ current because it has _____ resistance to D.C. and no reactance.  (Very high low, leakage)

(T) Transformer oil is provided in transformer tank to take way _____ from windings and core and provide _____ between parts of transformer.  (heat, insulation)

(U) In a transformer core flux is _____  (alternating)

(V) In a step down transformer secondary full load current is _____ than primary full load current.  (More)

(W) If in a transformer copper losses at full load are 100 watts, then at half full load are _____ watts.  (25 W)

(X) All day efficiency of a distribution transformer is _____ than its _____ efficiency.  (less, commercial)

## (II) Explain in Brief:

1. How the transformer works?
2. Compare the constructional difference between shell type and core type transformers.
3. Magnetic material is used for core, Why?
4. Grain oriented silicon steel is used for core construction of transformer, why?
5. Modern system of core assembly uses mitred joints, give its advantage.
6. Why a conservator tank is provided for transformers having rating above 25 kVA.
7. A breather is necessary for every transformer, why?
8. Derive the e.m.f equation of a transformer?
9. The e.m.f. induced is transformer windings lags the mutual flux by 90°, prove the statement?
10. Draw the vector diagram for an ideal transformer for no load condition and explain what do you mean by an ideal transformer.
11. Draw the vector diagram of an actual transformer for no load condition.
12. Explain what happens when a transformer is loaded, how the load taken on secondary side is transferred to primary?
13. What do you mean by leakage flux and leakage reactance ?
14. Draw a complete vector diagram of transformer working on load with lagging and leading p.f. load conditions?
15. Draw a neat diagram and explain how a no load test is conducted in laboratory? What is the use of it?
16. Draw a neat diagram and explain the laboratory method of conducting shot circuit test on transformer. What is the use of it?
17. Explain how will be make use of O.C. and S.C. test of transformer to determine its equivalent circuit parameters.
18. What do you mean by equivalent circuit of transformer, draw an exact equivalent circuit of transformer?
19. How an approximate equivalent circuit of the transformer is developed. Why it is called as approximate equivalent circuit?
20. What are types of losses taking place in transformer. Explain how they are developed.
21. Dervice the expression for maximum efficiency of a transformer.
22. What do you mean by regulation of transformer?
23. Derive the exact mathematical expression for regulation of transformer.
24. What is the meanings of per unit resistance, per unit reactance and % resistance and % reactance, state an expression for regulation in terms of these quantities.

25. What are the advantages of finding regulation and efficiency by O.C. and S.C. test over direct loading method.
26. Define all day efficiency. What is the use of determining all day efficiency of a distribution transformer?
27. How transformers are classified?
28. Transformer is rated in kVA and not in kW, why?
29. Why it is necessary to provide a cooling system for a transformer?
30. Explain the effect of power factor on the regulation of transformer.
31. Explain the properties of an ideal transformer, stating assumptions made for "Idealizing" the actual transformer.
32. Explain clearly the terms regulation up and regulation down as applied to a transformer.
33. Distinguish between no load primary current and magnetising current of a transformer.
34. Explain clearly the effect of primary and secondary leakage fluxes on the operation of a transformer.
35. Comment on the losses taking place in a transformer and suggest remedies to minimise them.
36. Compare between commercial efficiency and all day efficiency of a transformer.

## 3.2 THREE-PHASE TRANSFORMERS

Now-a-days for generation, transmission and utilization of electrical energy a three phase system is universally adopted due to its merits over other systems. It becomes very convenient by use of 3-phase voltage transformation system to adopt the suitable voltage for suitable purposes. The voltage transformation in a three phase system is obtained by using:

(i) Three single phase transformers connected to form a 3-phase bank.
(ii) A three phase transformer.

(1) A transformer bank used on 3 phase system consists of three independent single phase transformers with their primary and secondary windings connected either in start or in delta.

(2) The three phase transformation is also possible through the medium of one 3-phase transformer having a magnetic circuit common to all three phases. The three phase magnetic circuit for transformation of three phase voltages may be obtained by combining three individual single phase core or shell-type magnetic circuits into a common magnetic circuit with suitable changes in the configuration.

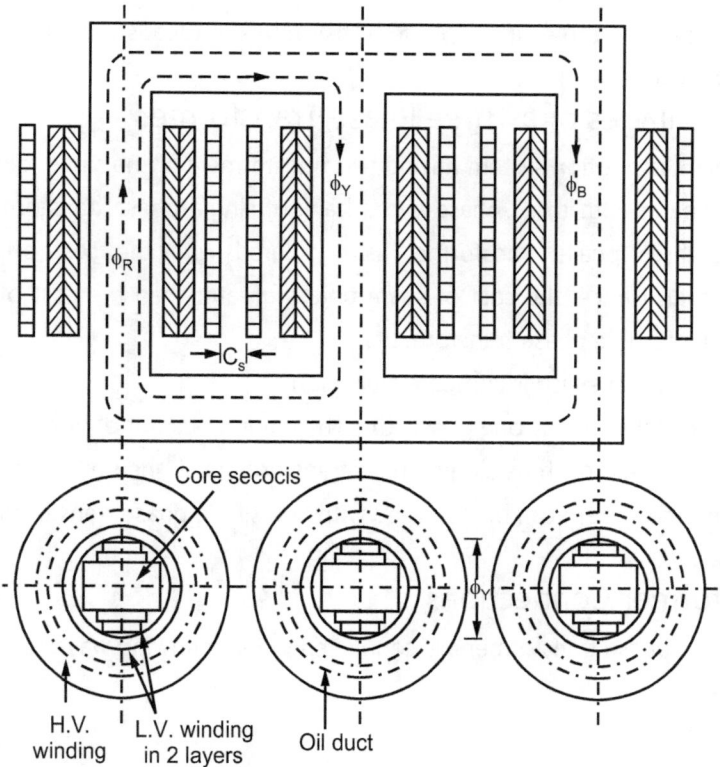

**Fig. 3.29: Core-type Transformer**

Fig. 3.29 shows a three phase core type transformer. The core consists of three legs with magnetic circuit completed through yokes. On each leg, the primary and secondary windings of one phase are wound. Flux flows up each leg in turn and down the other two legs in general. In Fig. 3.29 the instant for phase R developing flux up the leg is marked, it is maximum; while the flux in two legs of phase Y and B is down-ward and half that of flux produced by phase R. This is due to the fact that sum of currents in a three phase circuit at any time is zero; Hence, sum of the three fluxes at any time will be zero, or $\phi_R = \phi_Y + \phi_B$.

## 3.2.1 Advantages of a Three Phase Transformer

(1) A three phase transformer requires less material for a given output than a bank of three single phase transformers of equal capacity.
(2) A three phase transformer is lighter, costs less and requires less floor area than a bank of three single phase transformers of equal capacity.
(3) A three phase transformer has higher efficiency.
(4) The windings of a three-phase transformer can be connected in star or delta inside the containing tank. Thus, the number of high tension leads which have to be brought out through the tank, are reduced to three only.

In case of a bank of three single-phase transformers, six leads must be brought out for star or delta connections.

## 3.2.2 Disadvantages of a Three Phase Transformer

(1) In a small distribution system having few transformers of the same rating, the relative cost of spares with three-phase and a bank of single-phase transformers is the cost of one three phase transformer as compared with the cost one single-phase transformer. Hence, the cost of spare unit is greater than the cost of spare unit for the bank of single phase transformers.

(2) The cost of repairs also is comparatively high.

(3) In the even fault on any one phase, the whole unit goes out of operation.

In the case of a bank of three single phase transformers, if one unit develops fault, it can be removed, and the system can be operated with two single phase transformers, at 57.7% of its normal capacity.

## 3.2.3 Transformer Connections

Windings of 3-phase transformer are connected in the following ways:

(a) Star-star
(b) Delta-Delta
(c) Star-Delta
(d) Delta-Star

In case of three-phase transformers, designation star-star denotes that both the primary and secondary windings are connected in star. In general, the first word of designation refers to the interconnection of the primary windings and the second word refers to the interconnection of the secondary windings.

Fig. 3.30 (a), shows the connection diagram and Fig. 3.30 (b) shows the vector diagram for star-star connected three-phase transformer. In star connection, one end of each phase is connected to a common point - called the neutral point and the other ends are connected to the line wire. In three-phase core type transformer, the magnetic circuits of the three phases are not independent but interlinked with each other. For symmetrical three-phase supply, the line wires must be connected to the ends of the phases which have like polarity at successive instants. To fulfill this condition, in star-star connection, the neutral point on both the sides is formed by joining similar ends (either starting or finishing) of the phases together. In Fig. 3.30 (a), the neutral point on the primary side is formed by joining the similar ends $A_2$, $B_2$ and $C_2$ of the three phases together, and on the secondary side by joining $a_2$, $b_2$ and $c_2$ together.

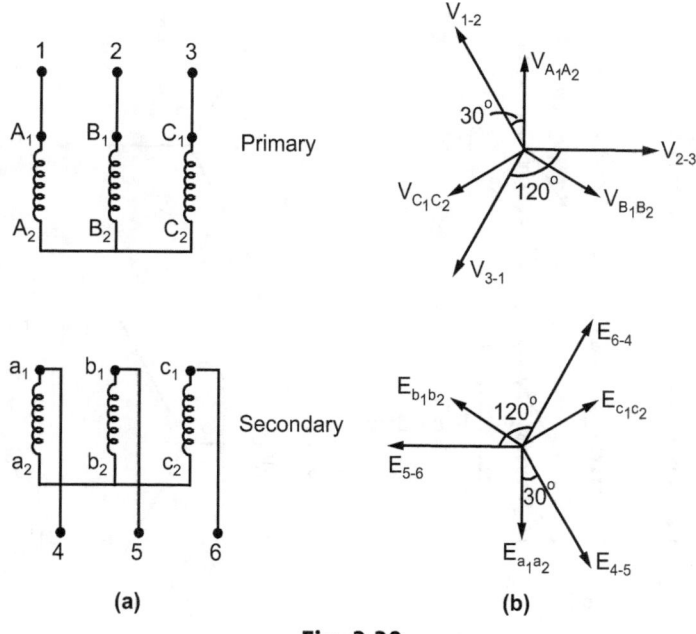

**Fig. 3.30**

The vector diagram can be developed on the following general principles.

The induced e.m.f.s in secondary windings are in phase opposition to the corresponding applied voltages to the primary windings, (applied voltage, $V_{A_1A_2}$ and induced e.m.f. $E_{a_1a_2}$ are in phase opposition). In star connection; applied voltage per phase is $\frac{V_L}{\sqrt{3}}$, and lags behind respective line voltage by 30°. The developed vector diagram for star-star connection is shown in Fig. 3.30 (b).

**Advantages of Star-Star Connection**

**(a) Star-Star:** Star-star connection is most economical for high voltage transformer. In a star connected system the line voltage is $\sqrt{3}$ times the phase voltage. Hence in star-star connection, the windings on each limb are designed for only 57.7 $\left(\frac{100}{\sqrt{3}}\right)$ per cent of the line voltage. Consequently, fewer turns and less insulation are required than if the windings are designed for the full line voltage. If the neutral point is earthed, the insulation on the high voltage side can be graded, and still further economy can be effected in construction.

Another advantage of star connected high voltage winding with earthed neutral, is that the transmission system is better protected against earth faults, and voltage to earth at all parts of the system is limited to phase voltage.

## (b) Delta-Delta Connection:

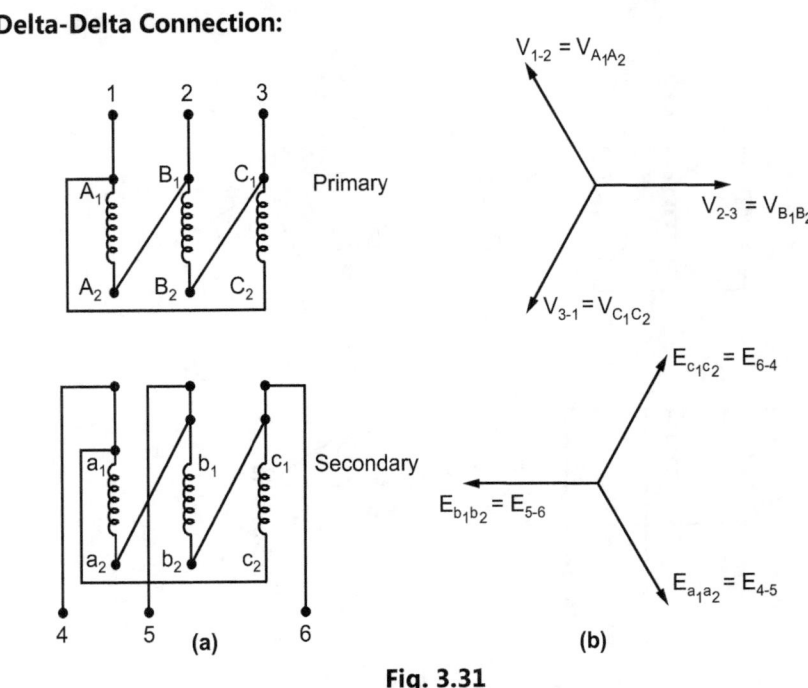

**Fig. 3.31**

Fig. 3.31 (a) shows the connection diagram and Fig. 3.31 (b) shows the vector diagram for Delta-Delta connected transformer. Delta-Delta connection is formed by connecting the windings in series to forma closed circuit. In a three phase core type transformer, the magnetic circuits of the phases being interlinked, dissimilar ends of the adjacent phases much be connected together to form a delta connected system. The resultant e.m.f. acting round the closed circuit is the vector sum of the phase e.m.fs. which is equal to zero in case of symmetrical system with sinusoidal e.m.fs. Hence no circulating current flows in a closed circuit. In Fig. 3.31 (a), $A_1$, $B_1$ and $C_1$ are the starting ends and $A_2$, $B_2$ and $C_2$ are the finishing ends of the phases A, B and C respectively on the primary side. The corresponding terminals on the secondary side are denoted by small letters ($a_1$ $b_1$ $c_1$ and $a_2$ $b_2$ $c_2$). Delta connection on the primary side is formed by joining $A_2B_1$, $B_3C_1$ and $C_2A_1$ on the secondary side, $a_2b_1$, $b_2c_1$ and $c_2a_1$. On primary side, three leads are taken from the junction points and are connected to supply lines. Similarly, three leads from the junction points on the secondary side are taken for the connection to the load.

Fig. 3.31 (b) shows the vector diagram. In delta connection applied voltage per phase is equal to the line voltage on the primary side. The induced e.m.f. on the secondary side is in phase opposition to the corresponding applied voltage. ($E_{a_1a_2}$ is in phase opposition to $V_{A_1A_2}$).

## Advantages of Delta-Delta Connection:

This is economical connection for large, low-voltage transformers when the line currents are large. The windings of the transformers are required to be designed to carry 57.7 $\left(\frac{I_L}{\sqrt{3}}\right)$ per cent of the line current. Thus, the cross-sectional area of the conductor reduces. Large unbalanced loads can be supplied without difficulty. If three identical single phase transformers are connected in delta-delta, and if one unit develops fault and is removed, the system can still be operated at 57.7 per cent of its normal capacity, as $V_{ee}$' connected transformers. This is however, not possible in case of three phase transformer.

The disadvantage is the lack of a neutral for grounding.

### (c) Star-Delta Connection:

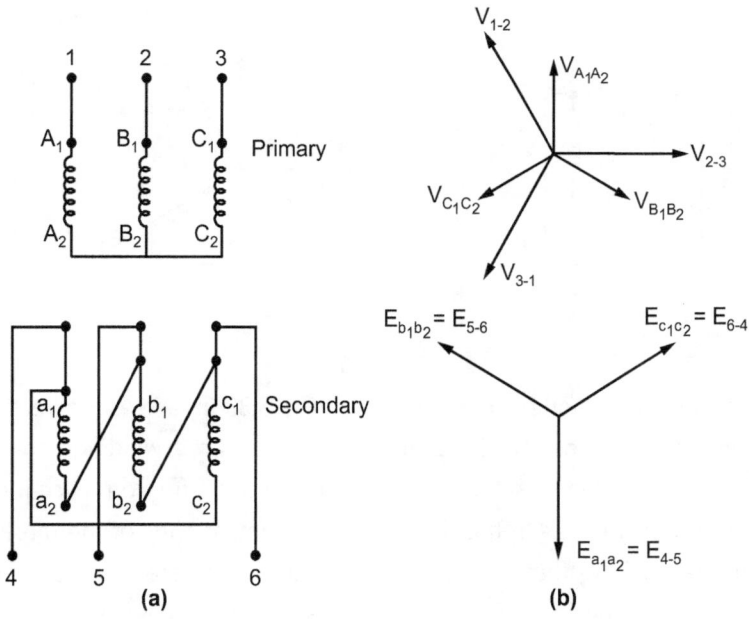

**Fig. 3.32**

Fig. 3.32 (a) shows the connection diagram and Fig. 3.32 (b) shows the vector diagram for the star-delta connected transformer. On the primary side, similar ends of the three windings are connected together to form the neutral point and the other ends are connected to line wires. On the secondary side, the three windings are connected in series to form a closed circuit, and from each junction a wire is taken out for the connection to the load. Vector diagram is developed on the same principles already explained.

The Star-Delta connection is commonly used at the receiving end of high voltage transmission lines. When the Star-Delta connection is used for transmission purposes, the neutral on the primary side can be earthed and the secondaries can be reconnected in star, if it is desired at any time to raise the transmission voltage to increase the capacity of the line.

**(d) Delta-Star Connection:**

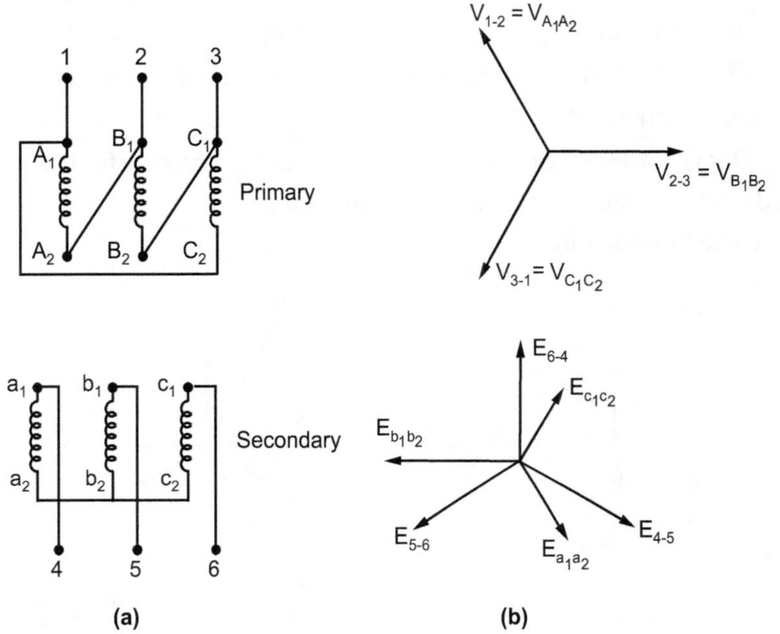

**Fig. 3.33**

Fig. 3.33 (a) shows the connection diagram and Fig. 3.33 (b) shows the vector diagram for Delta-Star connected transformer. On primary side, the three windings are connected in series to form a closed circuit, and three wires are taken out, one from each junction, for the connection to the supply lines. On the secondary side, similar ends of the three windings are connected together to form the neutral point and three wires are taken out from the other ends for connection to the load. The vector diagram is developed on the same principles already explained.

The Delta-star connection, which is commonly used at the generating end of the transmission line, gives higher secondary line voltage for transmission purposes, without increasing the strain on the insulation of the transformer.

The following table shows the open-circuit voltages for the four three phase transformer connections discussed above. It is assumed that the supply is symmetrical.

Turns per phase on primary side = $N_1$.
Turns per phase on secondary side = $N_2$.

| Connection | | Primary Voltage | | Secondary Voltage | |
|---|---|---|---|---|---|
| Primary | Secondary | Line | Phase | Phase | Line |
| Star | Star | $V_{L1}$ | $\dfrac{V_{L1}}{\sqrt{3}}$ | $\dfrac{V_{L1}}{\sqrt{3}} \dfrac{N_2}{N_1}$ | $V_{L1} \dfrac{N_2}{N_1}$ |
| Delta | Delta | $V_{L1}$ | $V_{L1}$ | $V_{L1} \dfrac{N_2}{N_1}$ | $V_{L1} \dfrac{N_2}{N_1}$ |
| Star | Delta | $V_{L1}$ | $\dfrac{V_{L1}}{\sqrt{3}}$ | $\dfrac{V_{L1}}{\sqrt{3}} \dfrac{N_2}{N_1}$ | $\dfrac{V_{L1}}{\sqrt{3}} \dfrac{N_2}{N_1}$ |
| Delta | Star | $V_{L1}$ | $V_{L1}$ | $V_{L1} \dfrac{N_2}{N_1}$ | $\sqrt{3}\, V_{L1} \dfrac{N_2}{N_1}$ |

## 3.2.4 Open-Delta or V-V Connection

Fig. 3.34 represents Δ/Δ connection of three single phase transformers.

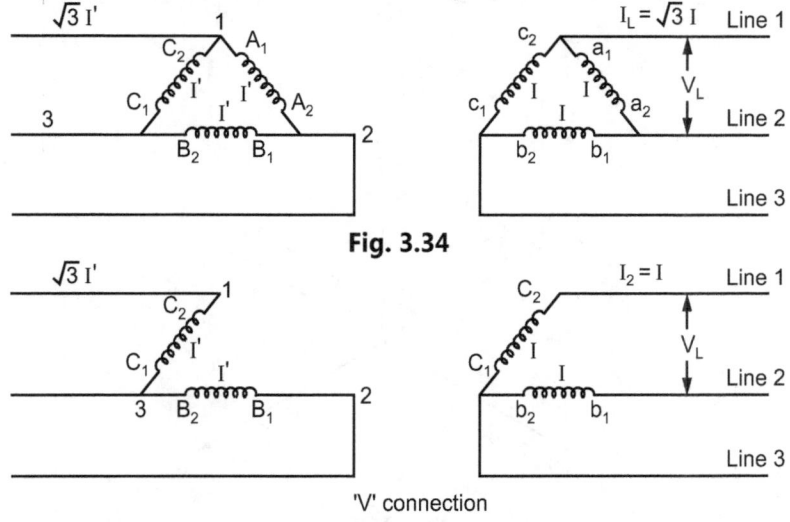

Fig. 3.34

'V' connection
Fig. 3.35

The 'Open-Delta' or 'Vee' connection is the same as delta connection with one transformer removed. When a small amount of three phase power is to be transformed from one voltage to another. 'Vee' connection is used. It requires only two identical single phase transformers.

Fig. 3.34 and 3.35 shows a Delta-Delta connection of three similar single phase transformers. If one transformer is removed 'Vee' connection will be formed. Fig. 3.34 shows the 'Vee' connection, in which transformer between lines 1 and 2 is removed. Fig. 3.35 shows the vector diagram for 'Vee' connections. The line voltages $V_{23}$ and $V_{31}$ are the phase voltages $V_{b_1 b_2}$ and $V_{c_1 c_2}$ respectively. There is no transformer between lines 1 and 2. The line voltage $V_{12}$ is the vector sum of $V_{c_3 c_1}$ and $V_{b_2 b_1}$. From the vector diagram shown in Fig. 3.35, it will be observed that $V_{12}$ has the same magnitude as $V_{23}$ and $V_{31}$ and the three line voltages are mutually displaced by 120°. Thus, it is possible to transform power from one symmetrical three phase system to another with the help of 'Vee' connection. The removal of transformer from delta connected system, does not affect the symmetry of the supply voltages.

Capacity of 'Vee' connected bank as compared with delta connected bank.

Let $V_L$ = Line voltage

$I$ = Maximum current per transformer

Consider first delta connected system Fig. 3.34.

The line current = $\sqrt{3}\, I$.

∴ kVA capacity of the delta connected bank.

$$\text{kVA (delta)} = \frac{\sqrt{3}\, V_L I_L}{1000}$$

$$= \frac{\sqrt{3}\, V_L \sqrt{3}\, I}{1000}$$

$$= \frac{3 V_L I}{1000}$$

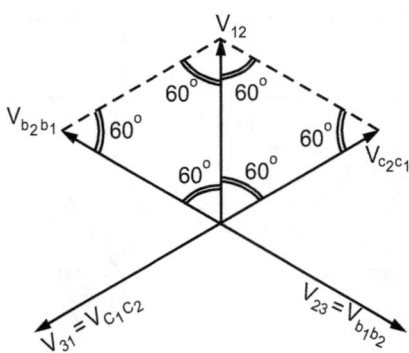

**Fig. 3.36**

Now consider 'Vee' connection, Fig. 3.35. It will be observed that $I_L = I$, while the line voltage is same as in the delta connected system.

∴ kVA capacity of the 'Vee'; connected bank.

$$\text{KVA (Vee)} = \frac{\sqrt{3}\, V_L I}{1000}\ \sqrt{3}\, V_L I$$

∴ $$\frac{\text{kVA (Vee)}}{\text{kVA (delta)}} = \frac{\sqrt{3}\, V_L I}{1000} \times \frac{1000}{3 V_L I}$$

$$= \frac{1}{\sqrt{3}}$$

$$= 0.578 \text{ or } 57.8\%$$

Hence the capacity of 'V$_{ee}$' connection is 57.8% that of delta connection. The reduction in capacity is 42.8% even though the rating of the bank is $\frac{2}{3}$ after removal of one transformer.

**Example:** Three-single phase transformers connected in delta supply 100 A per line to a three phase three-wire system.

(a) What is the current in each transformer ?

(b) What will be the % reduction in capacity, if one transformer is removed due to fault?

**Solution:** (a) Delta connected single phase transformers

$$\text{Line current} = 100 \text{ Amps.}$$

∴ Current in each transformer, I

$$I = \frac{I_L}{\sqrt{3}} = \frac{100}{\sqrt{3}} = 57.8 \text{ Amps.}$$

$$\text{kVA capacity of the delta bank} = \frac{\sqrt{3} \, V_L \, 100}{1000}$$

(b) When one transformer develops fault is removed, delta connection is converted into 'Vee' connection. In 'Vee' connection, the line current is equal to current in the transformer. For the same temperature rise the current in the transformer must be same as in delta connection i.e. 57.8 A.

$$\text{kVA capacity of 'Vee' bank} = \frac{\sqrt{3} \, V_L \, 57.8}{1000}$$

∴ $$\frac{\text{kVA (Vee)}}{\text{kVA (delta)}} = \frac{\sqrt{3} \, V_L \, 57.8}{1000} \times \frac{1000}{\sqrt{3} \, V_L \, 100} = 0.578 \text{ or } 57.8\%$$

∴ % reduction in capacity = 100 − 57.8 = 42.8%

## 3.2.5 Scott Connections

In some cases, a two phase supply is advantageous. It may be needed to supply low voltage electric furnaces. Sometimes it might be necessary to interlink two phase and three phase systems. At present, the bulk of the electric power is generated by three-phase systems, and the conversion from three-phase supply to two-phase supply, if required can be accomplished by 'Scott' connections of two single phase transformers.

The Scott connections requires two single phase transformers of different ratings, but from the point of view of provision of spares and interchangeability, the transformers may be identical with 50% and 86.66% tappings.

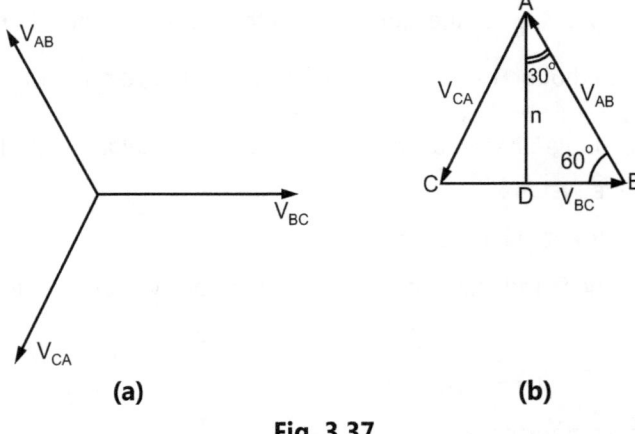

(a)                        (b)

**Fig. 3.37**

The line voltages of a symmetrical three phase system, $V_{AB}$, $V_{BC}$ and $V_{CA}$, shown in Fig. 3.37 (a) can be represented by an equilateral triangle as shown in Fig. 3.37 (b). Draw a perpendicular AD on BC. Then by geometry D is the midpoint of BC. Now the line voltage $V_{BC}$ and the voltage $V_{AD}$ are at right angles. If the line voltage of the symmetrical system is $V_L$ then

$$V_{AD} = V_{AB} \sin 60° \quad V_{AB} = V_{BC} = V_{CA} = V_L$$

$$= \frac{\sqrt{3}}{2} V_L = V_L \sin 60°$$

$$= 0.866 \, V_L$$

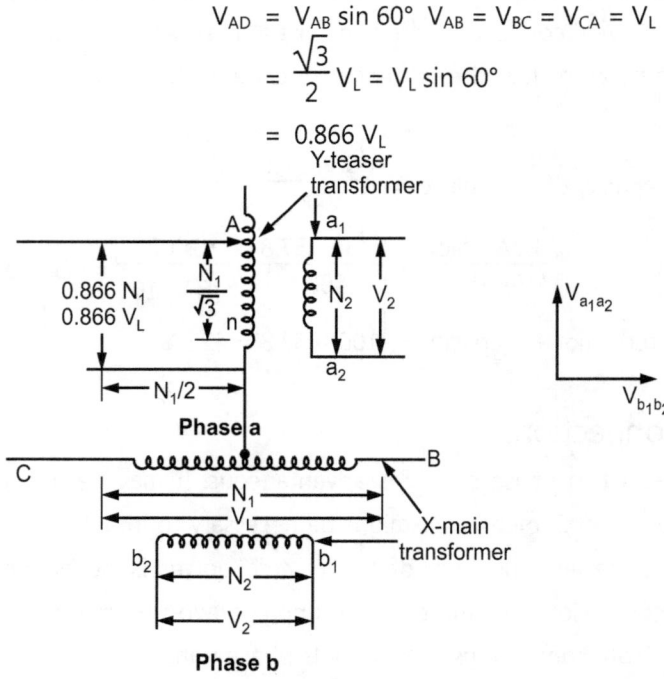

**Fig. 3.37 (c)**

If the primary of the transformer X, having $N_1$ turns, is connected between lines B and C, and the primary of the transformer Y having 0.866 $N_1$ turns, is connected between line A and the mid-point of transformer X, then the volts per turn for both the transformers will be the same. If the secondaries of the two transformers have the same number of turns $N_2$, then the two secondary voltages will be equal in magnitude, but will be in phase quadrature, since $V_{BC}$ and $V_{AD}$ are in phase quadrature. Thus, a 3-phase supply is converted to 2-phase supply. Transformer X, having $N_1$ turns and full line voltage $V_L$ across its primary is called the 'main' transformer and the transformer Y, having 0.866 $N_1$ turns and 0.866 $V_L$ voltage across its primary is called 'teaser' transformer.

If the Scott-connected transformers are fed from the two-phase side, a two-phase supply will be converted to a three-phase supply. For three-phase, 4-wire system, the neutral point can be located on the 'teaser' transformer. Line to neutral voltage must be $\frac{V_L}{\sqrt{3}}$.

$$\text{Now the volts per turn} = \frac{V_L}{N_1}$$

$$\text{Line to neutral voltage} = \frac{V_L}{\sqrt{3}}$$

∴ Number turns between supply end of the teaser transformer and the neutral point n.

$$= \frac{\frac{V_L}{\sqrt{3}}}{\frac{V_L}{N_1}} = \frac{N_1}{\sqrt{3}}$$

The neutral point n is as shown in Fig. 3.37 (b) and Fig. 3.37 (c).

**Determination of Line Currents on Three-phase Side:**

Let the load on the teaser transformer secondary be $P_1$ kW at p.f. cos $\phi_1$ lagging and the load on the main transformer secondary be $P_2$ kW at p.f. cos $\phi_2$ lagging.

Let $V_1$ be the voltage per phase on the two-phase side and $V_L$ be the line voltage on the three-phase side.

Let the teaser transformer be denoted by Y and the main transformer by X.

The current in the teaser transformer secondary, $I_{2Y}$.

$$I_{2Y} = \frac{P_1 \times 1000}{V_2 \times \cos \phi_1} \text{ Amps.}$$

and the current in the main transformer secondary, $I_{2X}$,

$$I_{2X} = \frac{P_2 \times 1000}{V_2 \times \cos \phi_2} \text{ Amps.}$$

Neglecting the magnetising current, the primary ampere turns must balance the secondary ampere turns, in both the transformers.

The number of turns on the teaser transformer primary are 0.866 times the number of turns on the primary of the main transformer. The number of turns on the secondary windings for both the transformers are same.

Let $N_1$ be the turns on the primary of the main transformer and $N_2$ be the turns on the secondary windings of both the transformer.

Then, for teaser transformer,

$$0.866\, N_1\, I_{1Y} = I_{2Y}\, N_2$$

∴ $I_{1Y}$, the balancing current in the teaser transformer primary,

$$I_{1Y} = \frac{I_{2Y}\, N_2}{0.866\, N_1}$$

$$= I_{2Y}\, \frac{V_2}{0.866\, V_L} \qquad \left[\text{Since } \frac{N_2}{N_1} = \frac{V_2}{V_L}\right]$$

$$I_{1Y} = 1.55\, I_{2Y}\, \frac{V_2}{V_L}$$

or

$$I_{1Y} = 1.155\, I_{2Y}\, \frac{N_2}{N_1}$$

For main transformer, $\quad I_{1X}\, N_1 = I_{2X}\, N_2$

∴ $I_{1X}$, the balancing current in the main transformer primary.

$$I_{1X} = I_{2X}\, \frac{N_2}{N_1}$$

$$= I_{2X}\, \frac{V_2}{V_L} \qquad \left[\text{Since } \frac{N_2}{N_1} = \frac{V_2}{V_L}\right]$$

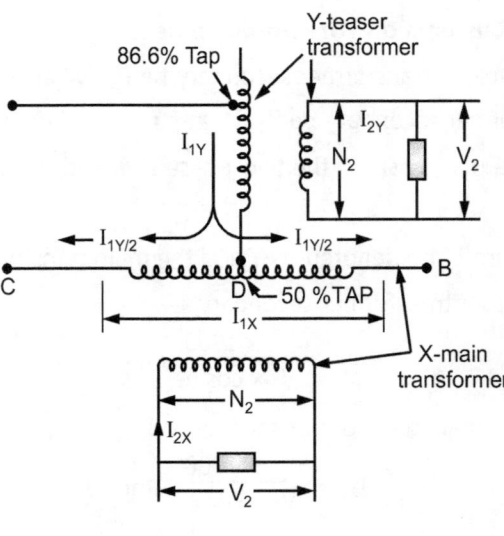

**Fig. 3.37 (d)**

Now refer to Fig. 3.37 (d), it would be observed that the main transformer primary provides a return path for the current in the primary of the teaser transformer. The primary current of the teaser transformer after reaching mid-point D, divides equally on either sides of D. Therefore, the total current in the primary winding of the main transformer is the vector sum of $I_{1X}$ and one-half of $I_{1Y}$ in either direction of mid-point D. The current with their directions are marked in Fig. 3.37 (e).

Line current $I_A = I_{1Y}$ (teaser primary)
Line current $I_B$ or current in section BD of the main transformer primary.

$$I_B = I_{BD} = I_{1X} - \frac{I_{1Y}}{2} \text{ (vectorially)}$$

and the line current $I_C$ or the current in CD section of the main transformer primary,

$$I_C = I_{CD} = -I_{1X} - \frac{I_{1Y}}{2} \text{ (vectorially)}$$

The vector diagram is shown in Fig. 3.37 (e)

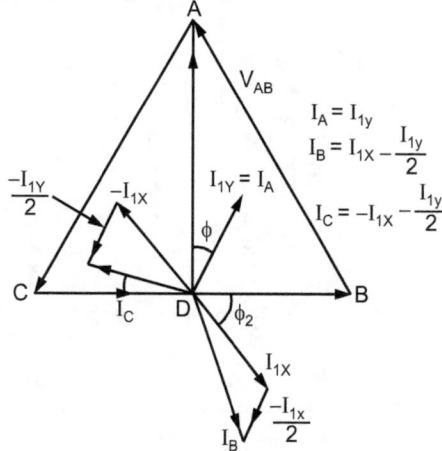

**Fig. 3.37 (e)**

### 3.2.5.1 Balanced Load Condition

To prove that when load on two phase side is balanced it is also balanced on three-phase side.

Let the load on two phase side be PkW at unity p.f.

Then $\quad I_{2Y} = \dfrac{P \times 1000}{V_2} \quad I_{2X} = \dfrac{P \times 1000}{V_2}$

Hence, under balanced conditions,

$$I_{2Y} = I_{2X} = I_2$$

Now, teaser transformer primary current, $I_{1Y}$,

$$I_{1Y} = \frac{I_2 N_2}{0.866 N_1} = 1.155 I_2 \frac{N_2}{N_1}$$

and the main transformer primary current $I_{1X}$

$$I_{1X} = I_2 \frac{N_2}{N_1}$$

$\therefore \qquad I_{1Y} = 1.155\, I_{1X}$

Refer to Fig. 3.38.

Line current $I_1 = I_{1Y}$ in phase with $V_{AN}$ (unity p.f.)

Line current $I_B = I_{1X} - \dfrac{I_{1Y}}{2}$ (vectorially)

$= \sqrt{I_{1X}^2 + (0.577\, I_{1X})^2}$

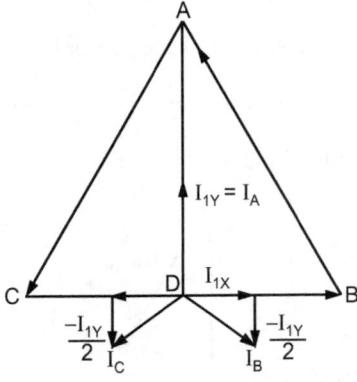

**Fig. 3.38**

$\therefore \qquad I_B = 1.155\, I_{1X}$

$= I_{1Y}$ in phase with $Y_{BN}$

Line current, $I_C = -I_{1X} - \dfrac{I_{1Y}}{2}$ (vectorially)

$= \sqrt{I_{1X}^2 + (0.577\, I_{1X})^2}$

$= 1.155\, I_{1X}$

$= I_{1Y}$ in phase with $V_{CN}$.

Hence, if the load on two phase side is balanced, the line currents on the three-phase side are equal in magnitude but have a phase difference of 120°. Therefore, the load on the three-phase side is also balanced.

## SOLVED EXAMPLES

**Example 3.29:** A Scott connected bank of single phase transformers connected to 6600 V, three-phase mains delivers a load of 400 kW at 80 volts, and unity p.f. to furnace loads on each phase of the two-phase side.

Calculate the voltage and current in all the transformer windings and mark them clearly on the schematic diagram of connections.

**Solution:** Line voltage on the three-phase side, $V_L = 6600$ V, voltage per phase on the two phase side, $V_2 = 80$ V. Load per phase on the two sides 400 kW at unity p.f.

Let the main transformer be denoted by X and the teaser transformer by Y.

Since the load the two-phase side is balanced, (same magnitude and p.f.)

$$I_{2X} = I_{2Y}$$

where, $I_{2X}$ and $I_{2Y}$ are the main and teaser transformer secondary currents.

$$I_{2X} = I_{2Y} = \frac{P \times 1000}{V_2 \cos \phi}$$

where P is the load in kW, $\cos \phi$ is the p.f. of the load, and $V_2$ is the voltage per phase on the two phase side.

$$\therefore \quad I_{2X} = I_{2Y} = \frac{400 \times 1000}{80 \times 1}$$

$$= 5000 \text{ Amps.}$$

$I_{1X}$, the balancing current in the main transformer primary

$$I_{1X} = I_{2X} \frac{N_2}{N_1}$$

$$= I_{2X} \frac{V_2}{V_L} \text{ since } \frac{V_2}{V_L} = \frac{N_2}{N_1}$$

$$= \frac{5000 \times 80}{6600}$$

$$= 60.6 \text{ Amps.}$$

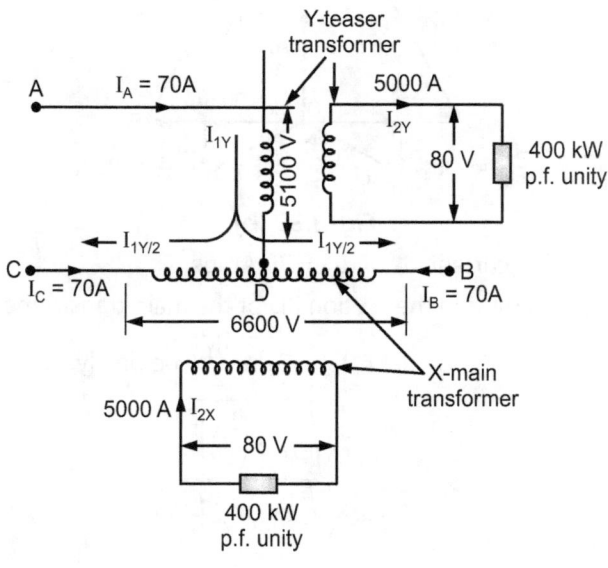

**Fig. 3.39 (a)**

$I_{1Y}$, the balancing current in the teaser transformer primary.

$$I_{1Y} = I_{2Y} \frac{N_2}{0.866 \, N_1}$$

$$= I_{2Y} \frac{V_2}{0.866 \, V_L}$$

Since the number of turns on the teaser transformer primary is 0.866 times the number of turns on the main transformer primary.

$$\therefore \quad I_{1Y} = \frac{5000 \times 80}{6600}$$

$$= 70 \text{ amp.}$$

Refer to Fig. 3.39 (a), it would be observed that the main transformer primary provides a return path for $I_{1Y}$, the primary current of the teaser transformer. $I_{1Y}$, after reaching mid-point D on the main transformer primary, divides equally on either side of D. Therefore, the total current in the primary winding is the vector sum of $I_{1X}$ and $\frac{1}{2} I_{1Y}$, in either direction of mid-point D. The currents with their directions are marked in Fig. 3.39 (a). The vector diagram is shown in Fig. 3.39 (b).

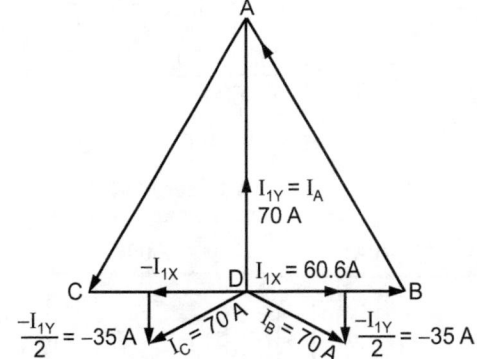

**Fig. 3.39 (b)**

Line current, $I_A = I_{1Y} = 70$ Amps.

Line current $I_B$ or the current in the section BD of the main transformer primary.

$$I_B = I_{BD} = I_{1X} - \frac{I_{1Y}}{2} \text{ (vectorially)}$$

$$= \sqrt{I_{1X}^2 + \left(\frac{I_{1Y}}{2}\right)^2}$$

$$= \sqrt{(60.6)^2 + \left(\frac{70}{2}\right)^2}$$

$$= 70 \text{ Amps.}$$

Line current $I_C$ or the current in section CD of the main transformer primary.

$$I_C = I_{CD} = -I_{1X} - \frac{I_{1Y}}{2} \text{ (vectorially)}$$

$$= \sqrt{I_{1X}^2 + \left(\frac{I_{1Y}}{2}\right)^2}$$

$$= \sqrt{(60.6)^2 + \left(\frac{70}{2}\right)^2}$$

$$= 70 \text{ Amps.}$$

The voltage across the main transformer primary winding is the line voltage $V_{BC}$ of the three-phase system, i.e. 6600 volts and the voltage across the teaser transformer primary is $V_{AD}$ 86.6% of the line voltage i.e. $6600 \times 0.866 = 5700$ volts.

**Example 3.30:** A group of transformers is Scott connected for transforming two-phase supply to three-phase supply. Each primary takes 20 Amps. at 6000 volts and the secondaries deliver power at 500 volts between lines. There are 1000 turns on each primary. How many turns are there on the secondaries and what is the current in each secondary. Neglect losses.

**Solution:** The Scott connection is used to convert two-phase supply to three-phase supply.

Fig. 3.40 shows the connection diagram.

Voltage per phase on two-phase or H.V. side = 6000 V.

Line voltage on the three-phase or L.V. side = 500 V.

Number of turns per phase on two phase or H.V. side = 1000.

Main transformer X

Voltage across the L.V. winding of the main transformer on three-phase side is $V_{BC}$ i.e. 500 V and the voltage across the H.V. winding of the main transformer on two-phase side is 6000 V.

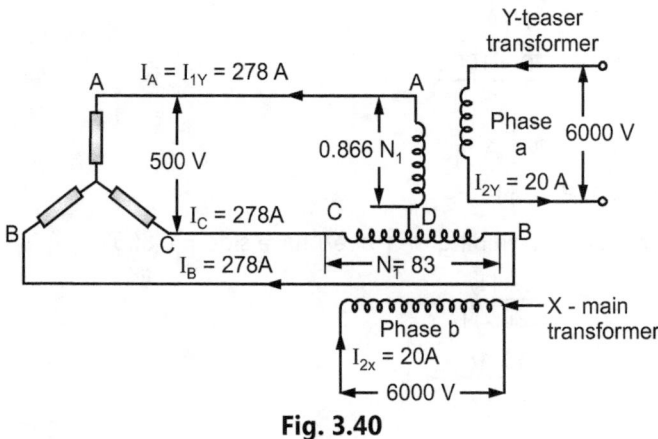

**Fig. 3.40**

Let $N_1$ = Turns on L.V. winding of the main transformer
and $N_2$ = Turns on H.V. winding of the main transformer

Then, $\dfrac{N_1}{N_2} = \dfrac{V_L}{V_2}$

Now, $V_L = 500$, $V_2 = 6000$, $N_2 = 1000$

$\therefore \quad \dfrac{N_1}{1000} = \dfrac{500}{6000}$

$\therefore \quad N_1 = \dfrac{500 \times 1000}{6000}$

$\quad\quad\quad = 83$ (whole number)

Now number of turns on the L.V. winding of teaser transformer on three-phase side

$\quad\quad\quad = 0.866 \times$ turns on the main transformer

$\quad\quad\quad = 0.866 \times 83$

$\quad\quad\quad = 72$

Now the ampere-turns in the H.V. and L.V. windings must balance each other in both the main and teaser transformers.

Let $I_{1X}$ = the balancing current in L.V. winding of the main transformer
$I_{2X}$ = current in H.V. winding of the main transformer
$I_{1Y}$ = the balancing current in L.V. winding of the teaser transformer
$I_{2Y}$ = current in H.V. winding of the teaser transformer

Now, $I_{2X} = I_{2Y} = 20$ Amp. current in H.V. windings on two-phase side.

Then, $I_{1X} N_1 = I_{2X} N_2$

$\therefore \quad I_{1X} = \dfrac{I_{2X} N_2}{N_1}$

$\quad\quad\quad = \dfrac{20 \times 1000}{83}$

$\quad\quad\quad = 241$ Amps.

and $I_{1Y} (0.866 \, N_1) = I_{2Y} N_2$

(Number of turns on L.V. winding on three-phase side = $0.866 \, N_1$)

$\therefore \quad I_{1Y} = \dfrac{I_{2Y} N_2}{0.866 \, N_1}$

$\quad\quad\quad = \dfrac{20 \times 1000}{0.866 \times 83}$

$I_{DA} = I_{1Y} = 278$ Amps. This is also line current $I_A$.

From Fig. 3.40, it is to be observed that the L.V. winding of the main transformer on three-phase side also carries one half the current of the teaser transformer on both sides of the mid-point D. Since the ampere turns due to this current balance each other, they do not affect the magnetisation of the core of the main transformer, but the magnitude of the current in the winding is affected.

$$\text{Line current } I_B \text{ or } I_{DB} = I_{1X} - \frac{I_{1Y}}{2} \text{ (vectorially)}$$

$$= \sqrt{I_{1X}^2 + \left(\frac{I_{1Y}}{2}\right)^2}$$

$$= \sqrt{241^2 + \left(\frac{278}{2}\right)^2}$$

$$= 278 \text{ Amps.}$$

$$\text{Line current } I_C \text{ or } I_{DC} = -I_{1X} - \frac{I_{1Y}}{2} \text{ (vectorially)}$$

$$= \sqrt{I_{1X}^2 + \left(\frac{I_{1Y}}{2}\right)^2}$$

$$= \sqrt{(241)^2 + \left(\frac{278}{2}\right)^2}$$

$$= 278 \text{ Amps.}$$

Hence the current in each secondary i.e. in L.V. winding, on three-phase side is 278 Amps.

**Example 3.31:** Two single phase Scott connected transformers supply a 3-phase 4 wire system with 400 volts between lines. The high voltage windings are connected to a 2-phase system with a phase voltage of 6600 V. If the number turns on each section of the high voltage winding is 825, determine the number of turns in the low voltage windings.

**Solution:** Scott connection is used to convert two-phase supply to three-phase four wire supply.

Voltage per phase on two-phase or H.V. side = 6600 V.

Line voltage on three-phase or L.V. side = 400 V.

Number of turns per phase on two phase or H.V. side = 825

Refer to Fig. 3.41.

Voltage across L.V. winding of the main transformer on three-phase side is $V_{BC}$ i.e. 400 V and the voltage across H.V. winding of the main transformer on two phase side is 6600 V.

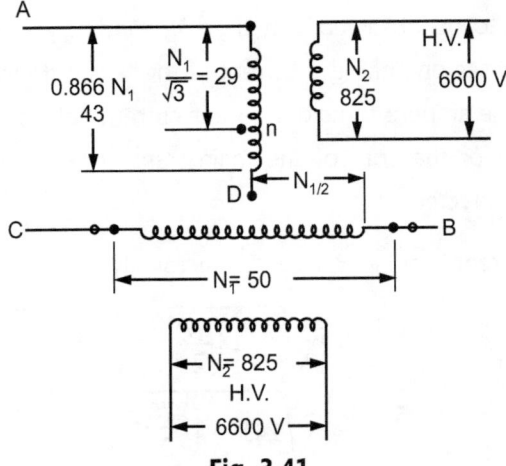

**Fig. 3.41**

Let $N_1$ be the number of turns on L.V. winding of the main transformer and $N_2$ number of turns on H.V. winding of the main transformer.

Then, $\dfrac{N_1}{N_2} = \dfrac{V_1}{V_2}$

Now, $V_1 = 400$, $V_2 = 6600$ and $N_2 = 825$

∴ $\dfrac{N_1}{825} = \dfrac{400}{6600}$

∴ $N_1 = \dfrac{400 \times 825}{6600}$

$= 50$

Now the number of turns on L.V. winding of the teaser transformer on three-phase side

$= 0.866 \times$ Number of turns on the main transformer on three phase side

$= 0.866 \times 50$

$= 43.3$ say $43$

The neutral point is located on L.V. winding of the teaser transformer for three-phase four wire supply.

Tapping for the neutral is taken at, $\dfrac{N_1}{\sqrt{3}}$ turns from the supply end of the teaser transformer.

∴ Turns to neutral $= \dfrac{N_1}{\sqrt{3}}$

$= \dfrac{50}{\sqrt{3}}$

$= 28.8$ say $29$.

## 3.2.6 Auto Transfer

It is a transformer with one winding only, part of this being common to both primary and secondary; hence in this transformer the primary and secondary are not electrically isolated from each other as is the case with a two winding transformer. This type of transformer works on same principle as that of a two winding transformer. As the copper required for such transformers is less its cost is low. It is mostly used where transformation ratio differs little from unity. It can be used as a step-down or stepup transformer.

In many cases, either an autotransformer or a two winding transformer may be used to accomplish the same transformation. Such two transformers are considered for the purpose of comparison. Hence the following assumptions are made with respect to ratings.
1. Both the transformers have the same primary and secondary voltage ratings.
2. Both the transformers have the same kVA ratings.

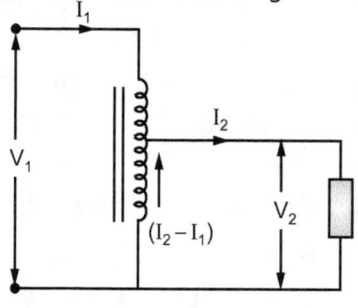

**Fig. 3.42**

3. From assumptions 1 and 2, it follows that both the transformers have the same rated values of primary and secondary currents.

   For the purpose of comparison, the following assumptions are made further with respect to the design of the autotransformer.
4. The core of the autotransformer is identical with that of a two-winding transformer.
5. Number of turns used in autotransformer is equal to that of the high voltage winding of the two winding transformer. The two transformers then would operate at the same flux density, and their core losses would be equal.
6. Current densities used is same as that used for the two-winding transformer.
7. The mean length of turn for the auto-transformer is the same as for the two-winding transformer.

On the basis of the above assumption the weight of copper required will be proportional to ampere-turns of the transformer.

    Let                 $N_1$ = Number of turns of the primary winding (high-voltage)

                         $N_2$ = Number of turns of the secondary (low-voltage)

$I_1$ = Primary rated current
$I_2$ = Secondary rated current

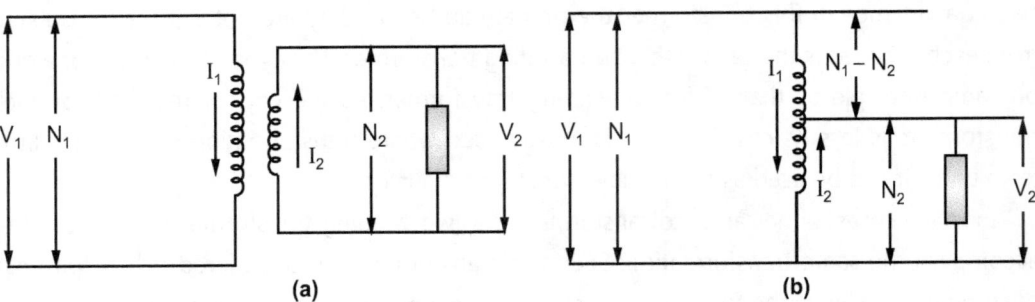

Fig. 3.43

Refer to Fig. 3.43 (a), weight of copper for the two winding transformer, $W_1$

$$W_1 = I_1 N_1 + I_2 N_2$$

In case of autotransformer, Fig. 3.43 (b) the uncommon part ($N_1 - N_2$ turns) carries primary current $I_1$, while the common part ($N_2$ turns) carries $I_2 - I_1$ (the primary and secondary currents are in phase opposition).

Therefore, the weight of copper required for autotransformer, $W_2$

$$W_2 = I_1 (N_1 - N_2) + N_2 (I_2 - I_1)$$
$$\approx I_1 N_1 + I_2 N_2 - 2 I_1 N_2$$

∴ The ratio of weight of copper required for the autotransformer to that for the two winding transformer.

$$\frac{W_2}{W_1} = \frac{I_1 N_1 + I_2 N_2 - 2 I_1 N_2}{I_1 N_1 + I_1 N_2}$$

$$= 1 - \frac{2 I_1 N_2}{I_1 N_1 + I_2 N_2}$$

Now, $I_1 N_1 = I_2 N_2$

∴ $$\frac{W_2}{W_1} = 1 - \frac{N_2}{N_1}$$

From the above equation it would be readily followed that an autotransformer requires less copper than that of a two-winding transformer of the same ratings. It should be noted that the saving in copper decreases as the transformation ratio, $\frac{N_2}{N_1}$ decreases.

The chief advantages of the autotransformer are better regulation and efficiency and lower cost. The main disadvantage is that its low voltage winding is electrically connected to high voltage winding and forms a part of it.

**Example 3.32:** A load of 20 kVA at 0.8 lagging power factor is supplied at 440 V from a 500 V supply through (a) an autotransformer, (b) a double wound transformer.

Calculate the currents in the transformer windings (or parts thereof) in each case. Explain your calculations.

**Solution:** Load = 20 kVA at 0.8 p.f. lagging
Secondary voltage, $V_2$ = 440 volts
Primary voltage, $V_1$ = 500 volts
Secondary current, $I_2 = \dfrac{kVA \times 1000}{V_2}$
$= \dfrac{20 \times 1000}{440}$
= 45.5 Amps.
Primary current, $I_1 = \dfrac{kVA \times 1000}{V_1}$
$= \dfrac{20 \times 1000}{500}$
= 40 Amps.

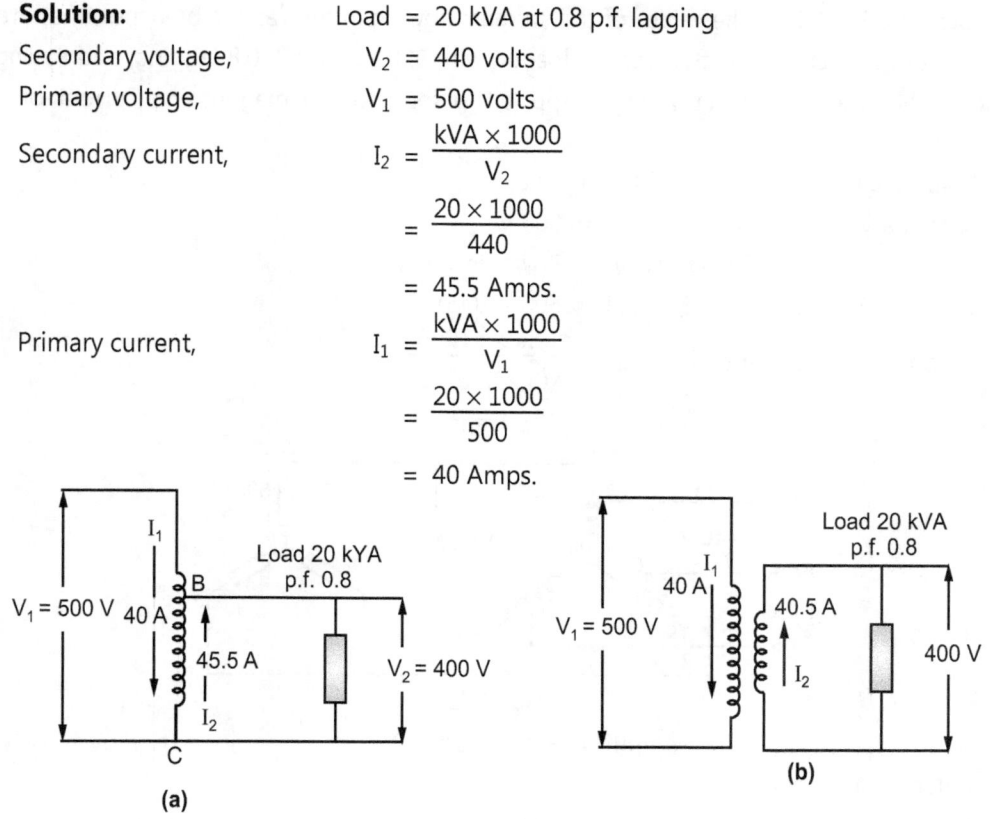

**Fig. 3.44**

Fig. 3.44 (a) shows the autotransformer connections, with the direction of currents marked therein.

The current in the uncommon part i.e. in section AB of the autotransformer is $I_1$.

$I_{AB} = I_1 = 40$ Amps.

It will be observed that, in the common part of the autotransformer, i.e. section BC, current $I_1$ and $I_2$ flow in opposite directions. Since $I_2$ is greater than $I_1$, resultant is $(I_2 - I_1)$.

= 45.5 − 40
= 5.5 Amps.

Current delivered to the load on the secondary side is 45.5 Amps.
Current taken from the supply on the primary side is 40 Amps.
The losses and magnetising currents are neglected.

Fig. 3.44 (b) shows a two winding transformer supplying the load. The magnitudes and the directions are marked.

Current in the secondary,     $I_2$ = 45.5 Amps.
Current in the primary,     $I_1$ = 40 Amps.

**Example 3.33:** Find the values of the currents flowing in the various branches of a three-phase star connected auto-transformer loaded with 500 kW at p.f. 0.8 lagging, and having a ratio of 440/500 V. Neglect voltage drop, all losses and the magnetising current of the transformer.

**Solution:** Load 500 kW at p.f. 0.8 lagging.

Secondary line voltage,     $V_{L2}$ = 500 V

∴     $\sqrt{3}\, V_{L2}\, I_{L2}\, \cos\phi$ = Power in watts

∴     $\sqrt{3} \times 500 \times I_{L2} \times 0.8 = 500 \times 1000$

Secondary line current,     $I_{L2} = \dfrac{500 \times 1000}{\sqrt{3} \times 500 \times 0.8}$

           = 721 Amps.

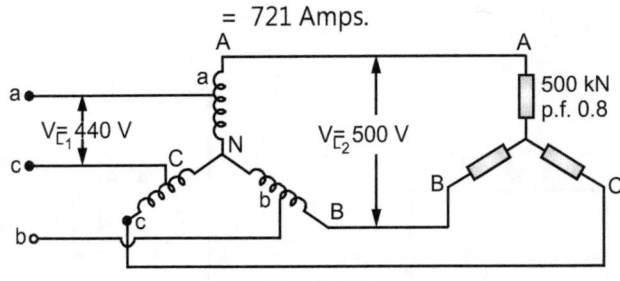

**Fig. 3.45**

Power input = Power output

When losses are neglected.

∴     $\sqrt{3}\, V_{L1}\, I_{L1}\, \cos\phi$ = Power input

∴     $\sqrt{3} \times 440 \times I_{L1} \times 0.8 = 500 \times 1000$

Primary line current,     $I_L = \dfrac{500 \times 1000}{\sqrt{3} \times 440 \times 0.8}$

           = 820 Amps.

Current in the uncommon parts of the autotransformer Aa, Bb and Cc is secondary line current i.e. 721 Amperes.

The direction of primary and secondary current being opposite, the difference of the two currents, i.e. $I_{L1} - I_{L2}$, will pass through the common parts of the autotransformers.

∴ Current in sections aN, bN and cN

           = 820 − 721
           = 99 Amps.

**Example 3.34:** An autotransformer has 200 volts applied to the full winding, the secondary circuit of which is supplied from 60 per cent of the turns. When a secondary current of 50 A is flowing, determine the current in each part of the winding, neglecting the losses and the no load current.

Primary applied voltage to the full winding = 220 V
Tapping for the secondary = 60%
∴ Secondary voltage = 200 × 0.6 = 120 volts
When the losses are neglected,
$$V_1 I_1 = V_2 I_2$$
∴ $$200 \times I_1 = 120 \times 50$$

Primary current, $$I_1 = \frac{120 \times 50}{200}$$
$$= 30 \text{ Amps.}$$

The current in the uncommon part of the autotransformer is 30 amperes.
Current in the common part i.e. through 60 per cent turns, is
$$= I_2 - I_1$$
$$= 50 - 30$$
$$= 20 \text{ amps.}$$

## 3.3 THREE-PHASE INDUCTION MOTORS

### 3.3.1 General

Electrical motors are the machines in which there takes place a conversion of electrical energy in to mechanical energy. In case of D.C. motor and commutator type A.C. motor the electrical power is conducted (fed) directly to the rotating part through brushes and the commutator, such motors can be called as conduction motors. In almost all type of A.C. motors (except commutator type) electrical power is not conducted to the rotor directly, the rotor receives its power inductively in exactly similar way as the secondary of the transformer receives its power. As the rotor receives its power by magnetic induction principle the motors operating on this principle are called as Induction Motors.

### 3.3.2 Construction

Three phase induction motors consist of main two parts.
(i) Stator
(ii) Rotor

The stator of the induction motor, is the stationary part which consist of stator core, stator frame, a distributed type of three phase winding carried in stator core, two end covers, bearing etc. The stator core is prepared by stacking, cylindrical silicon steel laminations, which are slotted along their inner periphery by application of suitable pressure by hydraulic compression machine. The laminations are insulated from each other to reduce eddy current loss in the slots is carried out a three phase distributed winding, providing proper slot insulation. The stator core fits closely in the cast iron stator frame. The two end cover, which are made from cast iron and the stator frame provide mechanical support to the stator core and the rotor and do not carry any flux.

The essential parts of the three-phase induction motor are illustrated in Fig. 3.46 (a) and (b).

**(1) Rotor:** There are two types of rotor construction.

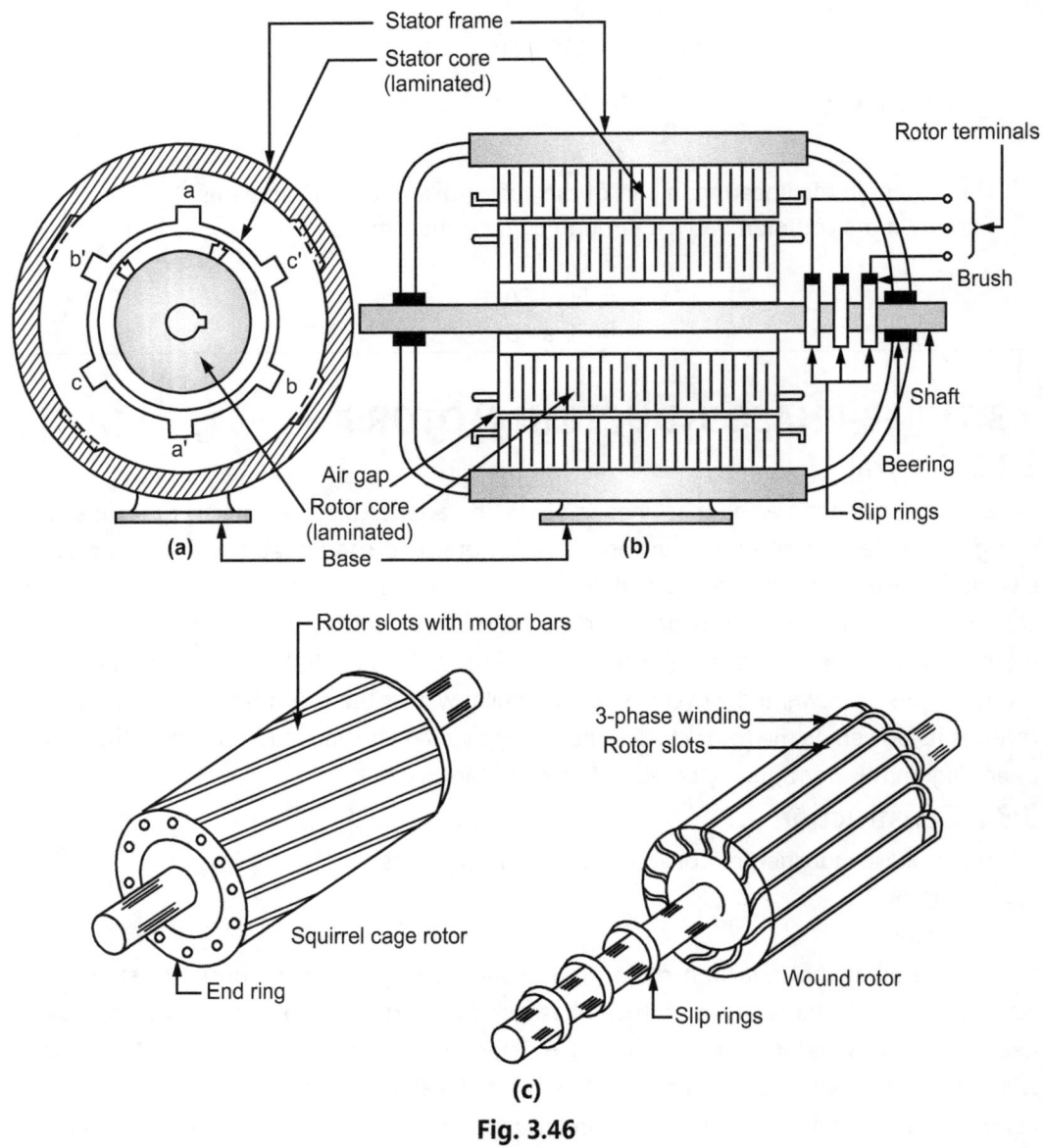

**Fig. 3.46**

**(i) Squirrel-Cage Rotor:** The motors which use this type of rotor are called as squirrel cage induction motors or cage motors.

**(ii) Phase wound or Wound rotor:** Motors employing this type of rotor are called as phase wound motors or slip-ring induction motors.

**(i) Squirel-Cage Rotors:**

Most of the induction motors are having rotors of this type, because it gives a most simplest and rugged construction and such motors operate almost without any trouble in rotor. The rotor consists of circular laminations with slots on the outer periphery, tightly assembled on the shaft or on the cast iron spider carried by the shaft. For squirrel-cage type rotor, the rotor winding is carried from un-insulated, copper or aluminium bars embedded in the semi-closed slots. These bars are then short circuited at both ends by end-rings of the same material. For good electrical connection riveted, brazed or welded with the two end rings [See Fig. 3.46 (c)] For small size machines, assembled rotor is placed in a mould and a molten aluminium is forced in to the slots (die cast rotor), which will cast the rotor bars, end rings and cooling fan, in one operation. Without the rotor cores the rotor bars and end rings look like a cage or squirrel. Hence, the name is squirrel cage induction motor. In this type of rotor, the rotor bars form a uniformly distributed winding in the rotor slots and as they are short-circuited at both ends permanently by two end rings no external resistance can be inserted in their circuit.

**(ii) Wound Rotor:**

In this type of rotor, the rotor slots accommodate an insulated distributed, three phase winding similar to that used on the stator, and is usually connected in star. The three lead from the star connected winding are connected to three slip-rings or collector rings mounted on the shaft but insulated from the shaft. Through carbon brushes which rest on the slip-rings external resistance can be inserted in the rotor circuit which is used for control of speed or for increasing the starting torque. As the rotor carries a winding and slip-rings. The motor using this type of rotor is called as wound rotor or slip-ring induction motor.

Squirrel cage type is simpler in construction more economical than slip-ring type. At the same it is more rugged and requires less maintenance than the slip-ring type as it does not require slip-rings and brushes. It is therefore possible to obtain uniform air gap between stator and rotor as small as is mechanically possible.

A three phase induction motor is singly excited machine. Its stator winding is directly connected to three phase A.C. supply while its rotor winding receives its energy from stator by means of induction action (transformer). When a balanced three phase supply is given to a three phase stator winding it produce constant magnitude rotating flux. The rotor induced current also setup a rotating magnetic flux in the air gap in same direction and rotating at same speed i.e. synchronous speed. These two fluxes are thus stationary w.r.t. each other. Consequently, the development of steady electromagnetic torque is possible at all speeds but not at synchronous speed. The stator and rotor m.m.f. waves combined to give the resultant air-gap flux density wave of constant amplitude and rotating at synchronous speed. Since, the induction motor cannot run at synchronous speed, it is called an asynchronous machine.

### 3.3.3 Induction Motor as a Transformer

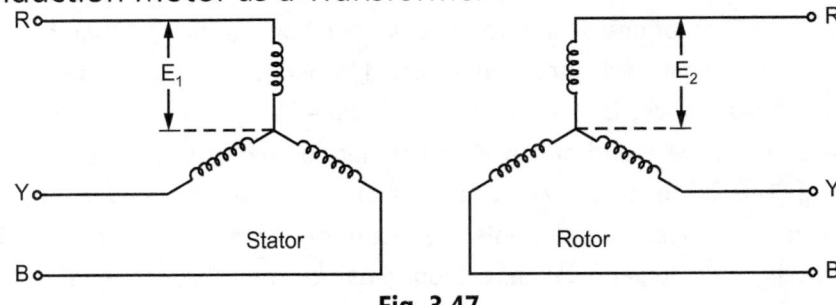

**Fig. 3.47**

For understanding this, consider a three phase induction motor with star connections both on stator and rotor. The rotor winding kept open, so that no current will flow through it and no torque will be produced then a balanced three phase supply is given to stator winding at frequency $f_1$ it will produce a rotating magnetic flux. The rotating flux cuts both stator and stationary rotor conductors at synchronous speed, which result in to production of induced e.m.f. in both stator and rotor at frequency $f_1$. The per phase induced e.m.f. in stator winding is given by

$$E_1 = 4.44 \, K_{W1} \, \phi \, f_1 \, N_1 \quad \ldots (1)$$

Similarly per phase value of e.m.f. $E_2$ induced in the rotor winding at stand still is given by

$$E_2 = 4.44 \, K_{W2} \, \phi \, f_1 \, N_2 \quad \ldots (2)$$

The e.m.f. or voltage ratio for induction motor

$$\frac{E_1}{E_2} = \frac{N_1 \, K_{W1}}{N_2 \, K_{W2}} = \frac{N_1}{N_2}$$

where, $N_1$ and $N_2$ are the effective turns/phase of stator and rotor winding. It is just similar to the voltage ratio of a transformer. Again the mutual flux in a transformer is due to combined action of primary and secondary m.m.f.s. Similarly in induction machines, the air gap flux is due to combined action of both stator and rotor m.m.f.s. In induction motor, the rotating flux causes a back e.m.f. $E_1$ in the stator winding similar to counter e.m.f. in primary winding of transformer. When transformer is loaded, the m.m.f.s of the secondary currents react on the primary in order to draw more power from A.C. supply. Similarly increase in shaft load, the rotor m.m.f.s reacts on the stator winding in order to draw more power from supply. In view of the above similarities induction motor is called as Generalized Transformer.

The voltage ratio of the induction motor includes winding factors $K_{W1}$ and $K_{W2}$ because the windings are distributed along the air gap periphery. In case of transformer, the windings are concentrated and hence need no winding factor.

Another difference between induction motors and transformer is that the no load current in case of induction motor varies from 30 to 50% of full load current, while in case of transformer it may be from 2 to 6% of full-load current. Usually, the no load p.f of the induction motor is nearly 0.15.

## 3.3.4 Production of Rotating Magnetic Field

When a balanced three phase supply is given to three phase stator windings displaced in space by 120° electrical, they produce a resultant magnetic flux of constant magnitude and changing position, represented by speed $N_S = 120\dfrac{f}{p}$, hence called as rotating magnetic field.

It will now be proved with the help of vectors, that a three phase supply when connected to a three phase winding produces rotating magnetic flux of constant magnitude.

The flux produced by each phase winding will be proportional to m.m.f. of that winding. As the currents flowing through each-phase winding are sinusoidal and displaced by 120° electrical, the fluxes produced by all the three phase windings will be sinusoidal in nature with a displacement of 120° electrical as shown in Fig. 3.48 (a). The assumed positive direction of flux due to each phase winding are represented in Fig. 3.48 (b).

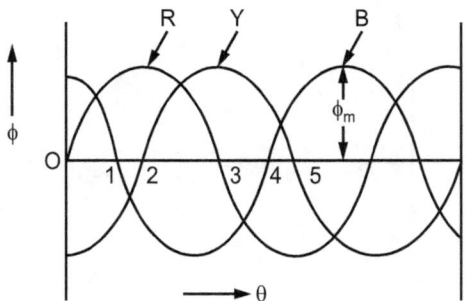

**Fig. 3.48 (a)**

Let the maximum value of flux produced by each phase winding be $\phi_m$, the resultant flux due to flow of current in all three-phase windings will be equal to vector, sum of instantaneous fluxes due to all the three phases. We will find out resultant flux at different instants as represented in Fig. 3.48 (a) by letters 1, 2, 3, 4 etc. which are taken at a displacement of 60° electrical.

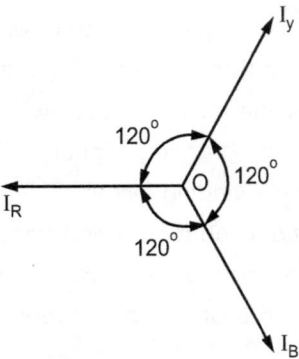

**Fig. 3.48 (b)**

i.e. Consider instant corresponding to point 0 i.e. when θ = 0°. From Fig. 3.48 (a), for 3-phase fluxes, we see that,

$$\phi_R = 0, \quad \phi_y = -\frac{\sqrt{3}}{2}\phi_m \text{ and } \phi_B = \frac{\sqrt{3}}{2}\phi_m$$

The vector for $\phi_y$ is drawn in direction opposite to the direction assumed positive Fig. 3.48 (b)

$$\therefore \phi_r = 2 \times \frac{\sqrt{3}}{2}\phi_m \cos\frac{60}{2} = \sqrt{3} \times \frac{\sqrt{3}}{2}\phi_m = \frac{3}{2}\phi_m$$

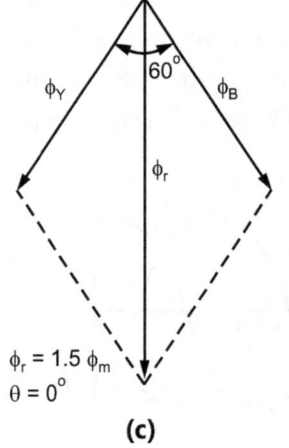
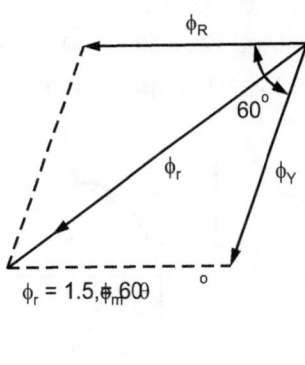

(c)  (d)

**Fig. 3.48**

**(ii)** When θ = 60° i.e. corresponding to point 1 in Fig. 3.48 (a).

$$\phi_R = \frac{\sqrt{3}}{2}\phi_m, \text{ in the direction of } OI_R$$

$$\phi_Y = \frac{\sqrt{3}}{2}\phi_m, \text{ in the opposite to } OI_Y$$

$$\phi_B = 0$$

$$\therefore \quad \phi_r = 2 \times \frac{\sqrt{3}}{2} \phi_m \times \cos 60° = \frac{3}{2} \phi_m$$

It is found that the resultant is again $\frac{3}{2}\phi_m$ but has rotated clockwise through an angle of 60°.

**(iii)** When $\theta = 120°$ i.e. corresponding to 2 in Fig. 3.48 (e)

$$\phi_r = \frac{\sqrt{3}}{2} \phi_m, \phi_y = 0, \phi_B = \frac{\sqrt{3}}{2} \phi_m$$

The resultant is again $= \frac{\sqrt{3}}{2} \phi_m$ i.e. the resultant is again same but has rotated clockwise through an angle of 60°, Fig. 3.48 (e).

**(iv)** When $\theta = 180°$ i.e. corresponding to point 3, $\phi_R = 0$, $\phi_Y = \frac{\sqrt{3}}{2} \phi_m$, $\phi_B = -\frac{\sqrt{3}}{2} \phi_m$ the resultant is again same $\frac{3}{2}\phi_m$, and has rotated clockwise through an angle of 60°, or through an angle of 180° from the start. Hence, it can be concluded that:

1. The resultant flux is of constant value = 1.5 $\phi_m$ i.e. 1.5 times maximum flux due to each phase.
2. The resultant flux rotates around the stator at synchronous speed given by
$$N_s = 120 \, f/p.$$

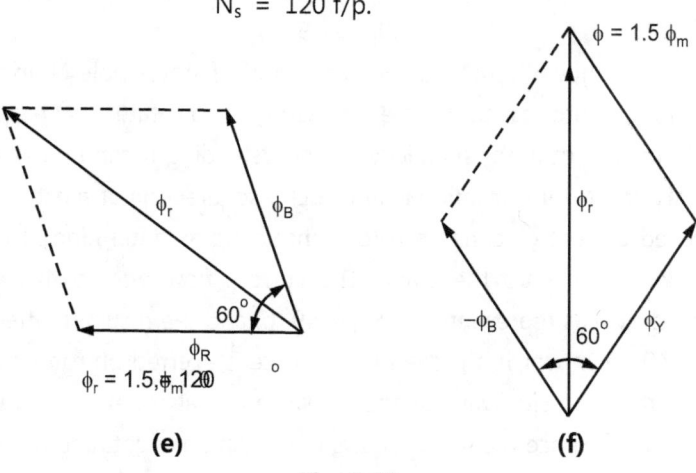

**Fig. 3.48**

### 3.3.5 Working Principle of 3φ, I.M.

As explained art 3.34, when a three phase supply is applied to three-phase winding on stator a magnetic flux of constant magnitude and rotating at constant speed is produced. This flux passes from the air gap and cuts the rotor conductors which are yet stationary. According to Faraday's law of electromagnetic induction, whenever conductors cut the magnetic flux there is induced e.m.f. in them, hence a e.m.f. is induced in the rotor conductors, as the conductors cut the flux at synchronous speed, the frequency of the induced e.m.f. at this stage is same as supply frequency and the magnitude being proportional to flux, relative speed and number of conductors/phase. As the rotor forms a closed electric circuit, there is set up a flow of current, the directions of this current will be such as to oppose the vary cause producing it, in case of induction motors it is the relative speed between the rotor conductors and rotating field which is responsible for this current, hence for this purpose the rotor will start to rotate in the same direction as the direction of rotating magnetic field to reduce the relative speed.

The torque developed on rotor conductors causing it to rotate can be explained with the help of the following figures.

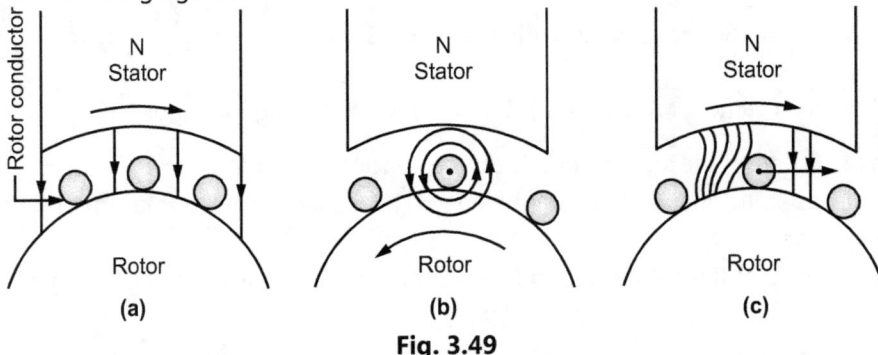

Fig. 3.49

In Fig. 3.49 (a) it is shown a instantaneous position of stator pole N and its direction of rotation w.r.t. stationary rotor as stator poles are assumed to rotate at syn-speed in clockwise direction w.r.t. stationary rotor, for simplicity of understanding it can be assumed that stator poles are stationary and rotor is rotating in anticlockwise direction at synchronous speed. The direction of induced current or e.m.f. in rotor conductors as determined by applications of Fleming's right hand rule is up the plane. The current flow due to this e.m.f. sets up a magnetic field of its own as represented in Fig. 3.49 (b) and the resultant effect of both fluxes is shown in Fig. 3.49 (c). In which it is seen that a force is exerted on rotor conductors which will make them to rotate in clockwise direction, which can also be checked with the help of Fleming's left hand rule. Hence the rotor follows the direction of rotating magnetic field.

## 3.3.6 Slip

We have seen that the rotor moves in the direction of rotating magnetic field to reduce the relative speed between the speed of rotating magnetic flux and the rotor conductors. If the rotor conductors, or rotor succeeds to attend the synchronous speed of rotating magnetic field, then there will be no relative speed between the rotor conductors and the rotating magnetic field, hence no induced e.m.f. in rotor conductors and no rotor current, which will set up a torque to make rotor to move i.e. rotor will stop moving. Hence in case of induction motors, the rotor will never attend a synchronous speed. The speed at which rotor moves is called the actual speed of induction motor and is represented by letter $N_a$, while the synchronous speed of rotating magnetic field is represented by $N_s$. The difference between $N_s$ and $N_a$ is called as slip speed,

i.e. $\qquad N_s - N_a$ = Slip speed in r.p.m.

while $\dfrac{N_s - N_a}{N_s}$ is called as fractional slip.

and $\dfrac{N_s - N_a}{N_s} \times 100$ is called as percentage slip.

It is to be understood that in an induction motor the stator field rotates at a speed $N_s$ w.r.t. stator. The rotor rotates at a speed $N_a$ w.r.t. stator. The magnetic field produced by rotor rotates at a speed $(N_s - N_a)$ w.r.t. rotor. In other word, the rotor field rotates at $N_a + (N_s - N_a)$ i.e. $N_s$ w.r.t. stator. As both the fields move at synchronous speed w.r.t. stator they are stationary w.r.t. each other. Due to this reason the induction motor can be considered as a transformer.

### 3.3.7 Frequency of Rotor e.m.f.

The relation between stator no poles, supply frequency and the synchronous speed of rotating magnetic field is $N_s = \dfrac{120\,f}{P}$ r.p.m. When the rotor rotates at a speed $N_a$ r.p.m., the rotor conductors will cut the rotating magnetic field at a speed $(N_s - N_a)$, hence the frequency of rotor induced e.m.f. can be written as,

$$f' = \dfrac{P(N_s - N_a)}{120}$$

from,
$$S = \dfrac{(N_s - N_a)}{N_s}; \quad N_s - N_a = SN_s$$

or
$$f' = \dfrac{PSN_s}{120} = S\dfrac{PN_s}{120}$$

$$f' = Sf \text{ as } f = \dfrac{PN_s}{120}$$

### 3.3.8 Stator and Rotor Induced e.m.f.

When the stator winding is connected to three-phase balance voltage, three-phase balanced currents flow through the stator winding, the m.m.f. due to these currents set up a rotating magnetic flux of constant magnitude, rotating at synchronous speed. At stand-still, the stationary rotor conductors cut this flux, the magnitude of induced e.m.f. in the rotor conductor will depend upon the magnitude of this flux and speed at which the flux is cut. Let $E_2$ be the induced e.m.f./phase in this case. This causes current to flow in closed rotor circuit developing a torque and causing the rotor to rotate; if $N_a$ is the speed attained by rotor, then the rotor conductors cut the flux at a speed $(N_s - N_a)$ i.e. $N_s S$ r.p.m.

As the induced e.m.f. in rotor at a speed $N_s$ of cutting, the flux is $E_2$.

The induced e.m.f. in rotor at a speed $SN_s$ of cutting the flux will be $SE_2$.

At start $\qquad S = I$

$\qquad E_2 = SE_2$ at start

Let
- $V_1$ = Voltage applied to stator winding/phase
- $T_1$ = Stator winding turns/phase
- $T_2$ = Rotor winding turns/phase
- $\phi$ = Flux/pole produced by stator amp. turns
- $E_2$ = Rotor e.m.f./phase at stand still
- $R_2$ = Rotor resistance/phase at stand still
- $X_2$ = Rotor leakage reactance/phase at stand still
- $K_p$ = Pitch factor of winding
- $K_d$ = Distribution factor of winding

At stand-still, the total flux cut by stator or rotor conductor will be $= P\phi$ webers if P is the number of poles for which winding is carried out, If $N_s$ = Synchronous speed in r.p.m., time for one revolution $= \dfrac{60}{N_s}$ seconds.

$$\text{Average induced e.m.f.} = \dfrac{\text{Flux cut}}{\text{Time}}$$

$$= \dfrac{P\phi}{60/N_s} = \dfrac{P\phi N_s}{60} \text{ volts}$$

$\therefore$ r.m.s. value of induced e.m.f. $= 1.1 \times \dfrac{P\phi N_s}{60}$ volts

Putting $\dfrac{PN_s}{120} = f$

Induced e.m.f./conductor $= 1.1\,\phi\,f \times 2$ volts

$\therefore$ Induced e.m.f./phase $= 2.2\,\phi\,f \times 2\,T_1$ in stator

where, $2T_1$ = Total number of stator conductors/phase

$\qquad = 4.44\,\phi\,f\,T_1$ volts.

When distributed and short pitch windings are used stator e.mf./phase

$$E_1 = 4.44\,K_p\,K_d\,\phi\,f\,T_1 \text{ V/phase} \qquad \ldots (3.32)$$

Neglecting very small voltage drop in stator winding at no load $E_1\,V_1$

$\therefore \qquad V_1 = 4.44\,K_p\,K_d\,\phi\,f\,T_1$ volts/phase $\qquad \ldots (3.33)$

OR $\qquad V_1 = 4.44\,K_{w1}\,\phi\,f\,T_1$ volts/phase

Similarly, rotor induced e.m.f./phase at stand still

$$E_2 = 4.44\ K_p\ K_d\ \phi\ f\ T_2\ \text{V/phase} \quad \ldots (3.34)$$

or
$$E_2 = 4.44\ K_{W2}\ \phi\ f\ T_2$$

Rotor e.m.f./phase in running condition will be

$$E_2' = SE_2 = 4.44\ K_p\ K_d\ \phi\ f'\ T_2\ \text{volts/phase} \quad \ldots (3.35)$$

As rotor current frequency in running condition $f' = Sf$

Similarly, leakage reactance of rotor,

$$X_2' = SX_2 = 2\pi f L_2 \times S$$

and Rotor current at stand still, $I_2 = \dfrac{E_2}{\sqrt{R_2^2 + X_2^2}} \quad \ldots (3.36)$

and in running condition, $I_2 = \dfrac{SE_2}{\sqrt{R_2^2 + (SX_2)^2}} \quad \ldots (3.37)$

If $\phi_2$ is the phase difference between rotor voltage $E_2$ and rotor current $I_2$ then rotor p.f.

$$\cos \phi_2 = \dfrac{R_2}{\sqrt{R_2^2 + (SX_2)^2}} \quad \ldots (3.38)$$

OR $\quad \dfrac{2\pi N_s T_g}{60} - \dfrac{2\pi N_a T_g}{60} = \text{Rotor I}^2\text{ R loss}$

or $\quad \text{Rotor I}^2\text{ R loss} = \dfrac{2\pi N_s T_g}{60} - \dfrac{2\pi N_a T_g}{60}$

$$= \dfrac{2\pi T_g}{60}(N_s - N_a)$$

or $\quad \dfrac{\text{Rotor I}^2\text{ R loss}}{\text{Rotor Input}} = \dfrac{2\pi T_g (N_s - N_a)}{60} \cdot \dfrac{1}{\dfrac{2\pi T_g N_s}{60}}$

$$\dfrac{\text{Rotor I}^2\text{ R loss}}{\text{Rotor Input}} = \dfrac{(N_s - N_a)}{N_s} = S \quad \ldots (3.39)$$

Rotor gross output = Input − Cu losses

$$= \text{Input} - S_x\ \text{input}$$

Rotor gross output = $(1 - S)$ input $\quad \ldots (3.40)$

∴ $\quad \dfrac{\text{Rotor gross output}}{\text{Rotor input}} = (1 - S) \quad \ldots (3.41)$

$$= 1 - \dfrac{(N_s - N_a)}{N_s} = \dfrac{N_a}{N_s}$$

OR $\quad \dfrac{\text{Rotor gross output}}{\text{Rotor input}} = \dfrac{N_a}{N_s} \quad \ldots (3.42)$

∴ $\quad \text{Rotor efficiency} = \dfrac{N_a}{N_s} \quad \ldots (3.43)$

And $\dfrac{\text{Rotor Cu loss}}{\text{Rotor gross output}} = \dfrac{S}{1-S}$ ... (3.44)

From equation (3.39) Rotor input $= \dfrac{\text{Rotor } I^2 R \text{ loss}}{S}$

Now, Rotor current, $I_2 = \dfrac{SE_2}{\sqrt{R_2^2 + (SX_2)^2}}$

∴ Total rotor Cu loss $(P_c) = 3 \times \dfrac{S^2 E_2^2}{R_2^2 + S^2 X_2^2} \times R_2$

And Rotor input $= \dfrac{3 S^2 E_2^2 R_2}{R_2^2 + S^2 X_2^2} \times \dfrac{1}{S}$ ... (3.45)

Mechanical power developed = Rotor input $(1 - S)$

$= \dfrac{3 S^2 E_2^2 R_2}{R_2^2 + (SX_2)^2} \times (1 - S)$ ... (3.46)

Gross torque developed by rotor $= \dfrac{1}{2\pi N_s/60} \times \dfrac{3 S^2 E_2^2 R_2}{R_2^2 + (SX_2)^2}$ Nm ... (3.47)

Power stages in I.M., $T_g \;\alpha\; \dfrac{SE_2^2 R_2}{R_2^2 + (SX_2)^2}$ ... (3.48)

as other factors are constant.

As $E_2 \;\alpha\; \phi$, $T_g \;\alpha\; \dfrac{S\phi^2 R_2}{R_2^2 + (SX_2)^2}$

For the given values rotor resistance, rotor reactance, slip

$T_g \;\alpha\; \phi^2$ As $\phi \;\alpha\; V_1$ ... (3.49)

$T_g \;\alpha\; V_1^2$ ... (3.50)

From expression (3.47), the shape of torque slip characteristic can be determined as follows.

As stator produces constant flux $\phi$.

$T \;\alpha\; \dfrac{SR_2}{R_2^2 + S^2 X_2^2}$

or $T = K \dfrac{SR_2}{R_2^2 + S^2 X_2^2}$ ... (3.51)

At stand still, reactance $X_2$ is greater than $R_2$. Assuming suitable values of $R_2$, $X_2$ and constant K, the value of T can be calculated for different values of slip, which varies from 1 to 0, and the torque slip characteristic can be drawn.

# BASIC ELECTRICAL DRIVES & CONTROLS

The nature of torque slip characteristic can be predicted without making actual calculations also. In equation (3.51) when S in very small the term $S^2 X_2^2$ can be neglected compared to $R_2^2$ i.e. torque.

$$T \alpha \frac{S}{R_2} \text{ or } T \alpha S \qquad \ldots (3.52)$$

For large values of S, say S = 0.1 to S = 1, $R_2^2$ becomes negligible as compared with $S^2 X_2^2$.

$$\therefore \quad T \alpha \frac{SR_2}{S^2 X_2^2} \alpha \frac{1}{S} \qquad \ldots (3.53)$$

Hence, the nature of the characteristic (torque versus slips) for small values of S will be straight line and for higher values of S will be a hyperbola as represented in Fig. 3.50 (a). While the nature of torque speed characteristic will be a straight line for higher value of speed and rectangular hyperbola for lower values of speed Fig. 3.50 (b).

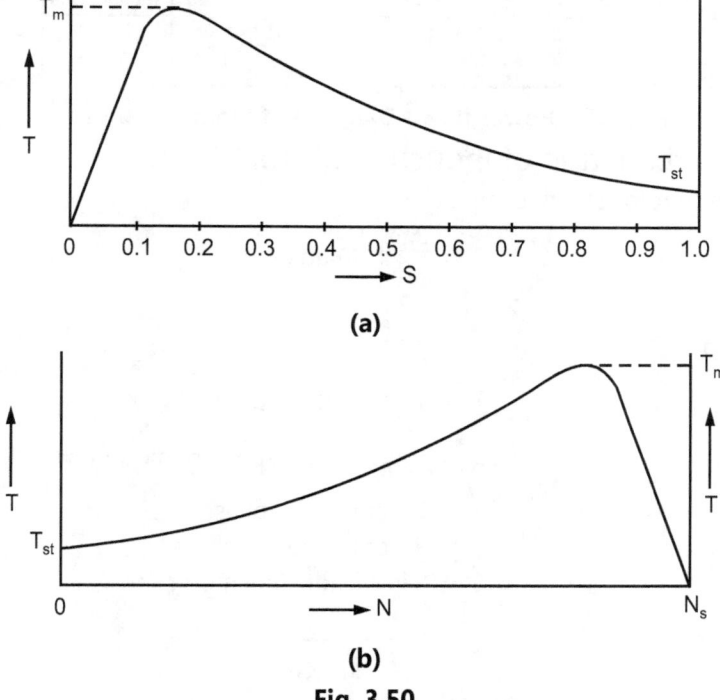

Fig. 3.50

## 3.3.9 Power Flow Diagram for Three-phase Induction Motor

The electrical power input to stator winding of an induction motor is transferred to rotor through the air gap between the stator and rotor by electromagnetic induction principle. This power is utilised to deliver the load at the shaft of motor and to supply $I^2 R$ loss in the rotor (Neglecting very small iron losses taking place in rotor).

Out of total power input to stator, stator Cu loss and iron loss, when subtracted, we get power input to rotor. If the gross torque developed by rotor is equal to TN m; and synchronous speed of rotating magnetic flux be $N_s$, which exerts this torque on rotor.

The power transferred from stator to rotor = $\dfrac{2\pi N_s T_g}{60}$ synchronous watts. When the rotor rotates at a speed $N_s$ r.p.m., Total mechanical power developed by the rotor

$$= \dfrac{2\pi N_a T_g}{60} \text{ watts}$$

Hence, power transferred from stator - mechanical power developed by rotor = rotor $I^2$ R loss.

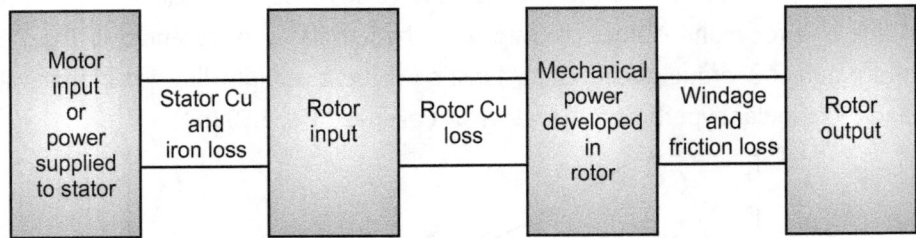

**Fig. 3.51: Power flow - Diagram of induction motor**

## 3.3.10 Torque Equation of Induction Motor

Power input to rotor of induction motor

$$= \dfrac{2\pi N_s T}{60} \text{ watts} \qquad \ldots (3.54)$$

which is also

$$= \dfrac{3 I_2^2 R_2}{S} \qquad \ldots (3.55)$$

where,     T = Torque developed

$N_s$ = Synchronous speed of motor given by $N_s = \dfrac{120 f}{P}$

$I_2$ = Rotor current/phase

$R_2$ = Rotor resistance/phase

and        S = Slip of induction motor

The rotor current,    $I_2 = \dfrac{S E_2}{\sqrt{R_2^2 + (S X_2)^2}}$

Substituting in equation (3.55) value of $I_2$,

$$\text{Power input} = 3 \times \left[ \dfrac{S E_2}{\sqrt{R_2^2 + (S X_2)^2}} \right]^2 \times \dfrac{R_2}{S} \qquad \ldots (3.56)$$

Equating equations (3.54) and (3.56)

$$\dfrac{2\pi N_s T}{60} = 3 \left[ \dfrac{S E_2}{\sqrt{R_2^2 + (S X_2)^2}} \right]^2 \times \dfrac{R_2}{S}$$

OR
$$\frac{S \times 2\pi N_s T}{60} = \frac{3 S^2 E_2^2 R_2}{R_2^2 + (SX_2)^2}$$

or
$$T = \frac{60 \times 3}{2\pi N_s} \times \frac{S E_2^2 R_2}{R_2^2 + (SX_2)^2}$$

or
$$T = K \times \frac{S E_2^2 R_2}{R_2^2 + (SX_2)^2} \qquad \ldots (3.57)$$

where,
$$K = \frac{60 \times 3}{2\pi N_s} = \frac{28.6624}{N_s} \text{ say.}$$

or
$$T \propto \frac{S E_2^2 R_2}{R_2^2 + (SX_2)^2} \qquad \ldots (3.58)$$

## 3.3.11 Effect of Variation of Rotor Resistance on the Torque - Slip Characteristic (Relation between Torque and Slip)

In case of slip ring induction motors it is possible to increase rotor circuit resistance by adding external resistance in rotor circuit through slip rings. For determining the effect of increased rotor resistance on torque of induction motor, we will substitute proper values of $R_2$, $X_2$, slip and constant K in equation.

$T = \dfrac{KSR_2}{R_2^2 + S^2 X_2^2}$ and plot the value to obtain the torque slip curve.

Let $R_2 = 1\,\Omega$, $X_2 = 10\,\Omega$, $K = 1000$ in first case and $R_2 = 5\,\Omega$, $X_2 = 10\,\Omega$, $K = 1000$ in second case, we will find out value of T for different values of slip.

**Calculate values of T for different slip and rotor circuit resistance $R_2$**

| Slip | Torque for $R_2 = 1$ and $X_2 = 10$ | Torque for $R_2 = 5$ and $X_2 = 10$ |
|---|---|---|
| 0.01 | 9.9 | 1.99 |
| 0.02 | 19.2 | 3.99 |
| 0.03 | 29.73 | 5.97 |
| 0.05 | 40.0 | 9.90 |
| 0.1 | 50.0 | 19.13 |
| 0.2 | 40.0 | 34.43 |
| 0.3 | 30.0 | 44.11 |
| 0.4 | 23.5 | 48.78 |
| 0.5 | 19.2 | 50.00 |
| 0.6 | 16.2 | 49.18 |
| 0.7 | 14.0 | 47.29 |
| 0.8 | 12.3 | 44.94 |
| 0.9 | 10.9 | 42.45 |
| 1.0 | 9.9 | 40.00 |

The nature of the torque slip curves is as shown in Fig. 3.52.

**From the curves it can be concluded:**
1. When $R_2$ is increased, torque at starting is increased, in this case from 9.9 to 4.0.
2. Maximum torque is same in both cases but the slip at which it takes place depends upon rotor resistance.
3. Maximum torque takes place at $R_2 = SX_2$.

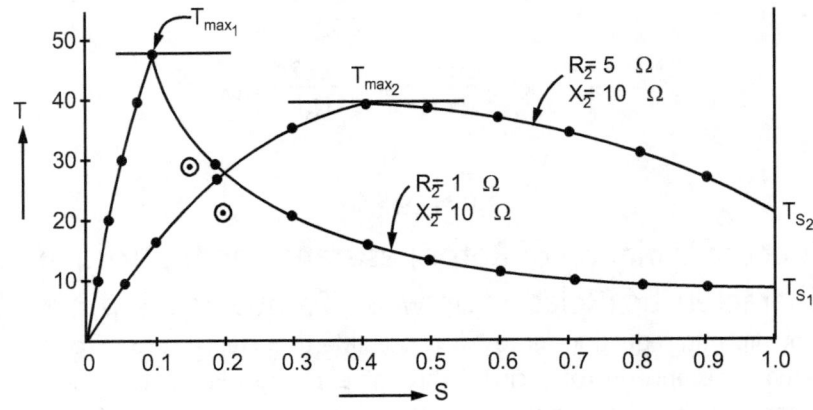

**Fig. 3.52**

## 3.3.12 Condition for Maximum Torque and its Value

As torque developed by the induction motor is represented by the following equation.

$$T \propto \frac{SE_2^2 R_2}{R_2^2 + (SX_2)^2}$$

or

$$T \propto \frac{SR_2}{R_2^2 + (SX_2)^2}$$

As $E_2$ is constant, if the torque developed by the motor is to be maximum $\frac{d}{ds}(T)$ must be equal to zero, hence differentiating the equation w.r.t. slip and equating it to zero.

$$\frac{d}{ds} \frac{SR_2}{R_2^2 + (SX_2)^2} = \frac{(R_2^2 + S^2 X_2^2) R_2 - SR_2 (2 SX_2^2)}{(R_2^2 + S^2 X_2^2)^2}$$

$$= \frac{R_2 (R_2^2 - S^2 X_2^2 - 2 S^2 X_2^2)}{(R_2^2 + S^2 X_2^2)^2}$$

$$= \frac{R_2 (R_2^2 - S^2 X_2^2)}{(R_2^2 + S^2 X_2^2)^2} = 0$$

or $\qquad R_2^2 = S^2 X_2^2$ or $R_2 = SX_2$

Hence, at maximum torque, $R_2 = SX_2$

Putting value in torque equation,

$$T \propto \frac{SE_2^2 R_2}{R_2^2 + S^2 X_2^2}$$

OR

$$T = \frac{KS E_2^2 R_2}{R_2^2 + S^2 X_2^2} \text{ but at maximum torque } R_2 = SX_2$$

Hence, maximum torque,

$$T_m = \frac{KS^2 X_2 E_2^2}{S^2 X_2^2 + S^2 X_2^2}$$

$$T_m = \frac{KE_2^2}{2X_2} \qquad \ldots (3.58)$$

or Maximum torque, $\qquad T_m = \frac{KSR_2}{R_2^2 + R_2^2} = \frac{KS}{2R_2} \qquad \ldots (3.59)$

## 3.3.13 Starting Torque

From $\qquad T \propto \dfrac{SE_2^2 R_2}{R_2^2 + S^2 X_2^2}$

$S = 1$ at starting.

$\therefore \qquad T_s \propto \dfrac{E_2^2 R_2}{R_2^2 + X_2^2}$

$$T_s = \frac{K_1 R_2}{R_2^2 + X_2^2} \text{ Nm}$$

## 3.3.14 Condition for Maximum Torque at Starting

From Article 3.3.13, $\qquad T_s = \dfrac{K_1 R_2}{R_2^2 + X_2^2}$

Differentiating w.r.t. $R_2$ and equating to zero.

$\therefore \qquad \dfrac{dT_s}{dR_2} = K_1 \left[ \dfrac{1}{R_2^2 + X_2^2} - \dfrac{R_2 (2R_2)}{(R_2^2 + X_2^2)^2} \right] = 0$

or $\qquad \dfrac{R_2^2 + X_2^2 - 2R_2^2}{R_2^2 + X_2^2} = 0$

or $\qquad R_2 = X_2$

## 3.3.15 Relation between Full Load Torque and Maximum Torque

We know that the torque developed by an induction motor is given as

$$T \propto \frac{\phi S E_2 R_2}{R_2^2 + (SX_2)^2} \text{ as } \phi \text{ is constant, } E_2 \text{ is also constant}$$

$$T \propto \frac{SR_2}{R_2^2 + (SX_2)^2}$$

Similarly, torque at full load, $T_f \propto \dfrac{S_f R_2}{R_2^2 + (S_f X_2)^2}$ ... (3.60)

and the maximum torque, $T_m \propto \dfrac{1}{2X_2}$

$$\therefore \frac{T_f}{T_m} = \frac{S_f R_2 \cdot 2X_2}{R_2^2 + (S_f X_2)^2}$$

dividing by $X_2^2$ to both denominator and numerator.

$$\frac{T_f}{T_m} = \frac{2S_f \cdot R_2 / X_2}{(R_2/X_2)^2 + S_f^2} = \frac{2 a S_f}{a^2 + S_f^2}$$

where, $a = \dfrac{R_2}{X_2}$

At any load when slip is equal to S, $\dfrac{T}{T_m} = \dfrac{2aS}{a^2 + S^2}$

## 3.3.16 Relation between Starting Torque and Maximum Torque

Torque at starting i.e. when S = 1, represented as

$$T_s \propto \frac{R_2}{R_2^2 + X_2^2} \qquad \text{... (3.61)}$$

and $T_m \propto \dfrac{1}{2X_2}$ ... (3.62)

$$\therefore \frac{T_s}{T_m} = \frac{2R_2 X_2}{R_2^2 + X_2^2}$$

dividing by $X_2^2$ to both sides numerator and denominator

$$\frac{T_s}{T_m} = \frac{2\dfrac{R_2}{X_2}}{\dfrac{R_2^2}{X_2^2} + 1}$$

where, $a = \dfrac{R_2}{X_2} = \dfrac{\text{Rotor resistance}}{\text{Stand still reactnace}}$ / Phase $\qquad \therefore \dfrac{T_s}{T_m} = \dfrac{2a}{a^2 + 1}$

## 3.3.17 Effect of P.F. and Torque

In case of D.C. motors torque developed is proportional to produce flux/pole and armature current i.e. $T \propto \phi I_a$.

In a similar way the torque developed by induction motor depends upon rotor current per phase and one more factor has to be taken into account and that is p.f. of rotor current which depends upon $R_2$ i.e. rotor resistance/phase and $X_2$ i.e. stand still leakage reactance/phase.

∴  $T_q \alpha \; \phi I_2 \cos \phi_2$
or  $T_q = K \phi I_2 \cos \phi_2$

where, $I_2$ = Rotor current/phase at stand still and $\cos \phi_2 = \dfrac{R_2}{X_2}$

As at stand still, rotor e.m.f./phase $E_2$ is directly proportional to flux $\phi$

$T_q \alpha \; E_2 I_2 \cos \phi_2$
or  $T_q = K_1 E_2 I_2 \cos \phi_2$, where $K_1$ is a constant

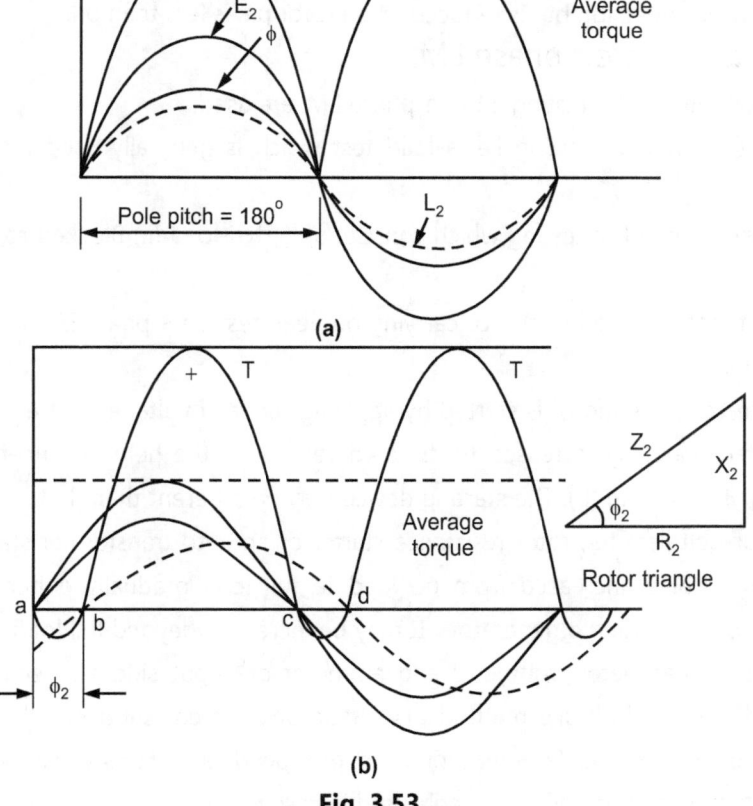

**Fig. 3.53**

The effect of rotor p.f. on torque developed by rotor is represented in 3.53 (a) and Fig. 3.53 (b).

When $E_2$ and $I_2$ are in phase, the nature of flux will be as shown in Fig. 3.53 (a) and the instantaneous value of torque will be as shown as the average value of torque during the cycle will be as represented by dotted line.

When $I_2$ lags $E_2$ by certain angle $\phi_2$ as represented in Fig. 3.53 (b), the flux will be in time phase with $E_2$ and the instantaneous torque developed will have values as represented in which for portion ab and cd the torque is negative i.e. reversed and for other position positive i.e. forward, the average torque is reduced.

From above Fig. 3.53 it is clear that as $\phi_2$ increases cos $\phi_2$ will decrease and the value of torque will reduce and vice-versa. As the stator flux is assumed sinusoidal the rotor e.m.f. will also be sinusoidal. When rotor p.f is unity the torque is positive and unidirectional but when rotor p.f. is less than one, the torque produced depends upon the angle between $E_2$ and $I_2$ or say on cos $\phi_2$. It is seen from Fig. 3.53 (b) the torque is negative in region ab and cd or is reverse, while it is positive during remaining portion or forward, the average torque is positive in forward direction but is reduced when rotor p.f. is less than one.

## 3.3.18 Tests on Three-phase I.M.

Following methods for testing a three-phase I.M. are used:

(a) Direct method of testing i.e. a load test which is generally used for testing small machines.

(b) Indirect method of testing which consists of: (i) No-load (ii) Blocked rotor test or S.C. test.

(c) Direct method (load test) : For carrying out load test on 3-phase I.M. following circuit diagram are used.

**(i) Brake test:** The motor is started by applying reduced voltage at rated frequency, the voltage is then gradually increased to its rated value with the help of auto-transformer as shown in Fig. 3.54 (a) and (b). The starting device may be different than that is shown in fig. It may be a star-delta starter, rotor resistance starter or an auto transformer starter. Then the load on the motor is increased from no load to full load gradually either by the brake arrangement or by loading a generators. It may be increased beyond full load also if desired. The readings of wattmeter, voltmeter and ammeter on input side are recorded, and the readings of $F_1$ and $F_2$ in brake method or voltage and current supplied by generators are recorded for the (ii) method. For measuring slip, the speed can be measured by a tachometer or a galvanometer method can be suitably used in case of three phase slip ring I.M.

# BASIC ELECTRICAL DRIVES & CONTROLS  SINGLE PHASE & THREE PHASE ......

The output of motor by a brake method is given by

$$\text{Output} = \frac{2\pi NT}{60 \times 75} \text{ when T is calculated in kg. m.}$$

or

$$\text{Output} = \frac{2\pi NT}{60} \text{ when T is calculated in Nm.}$$

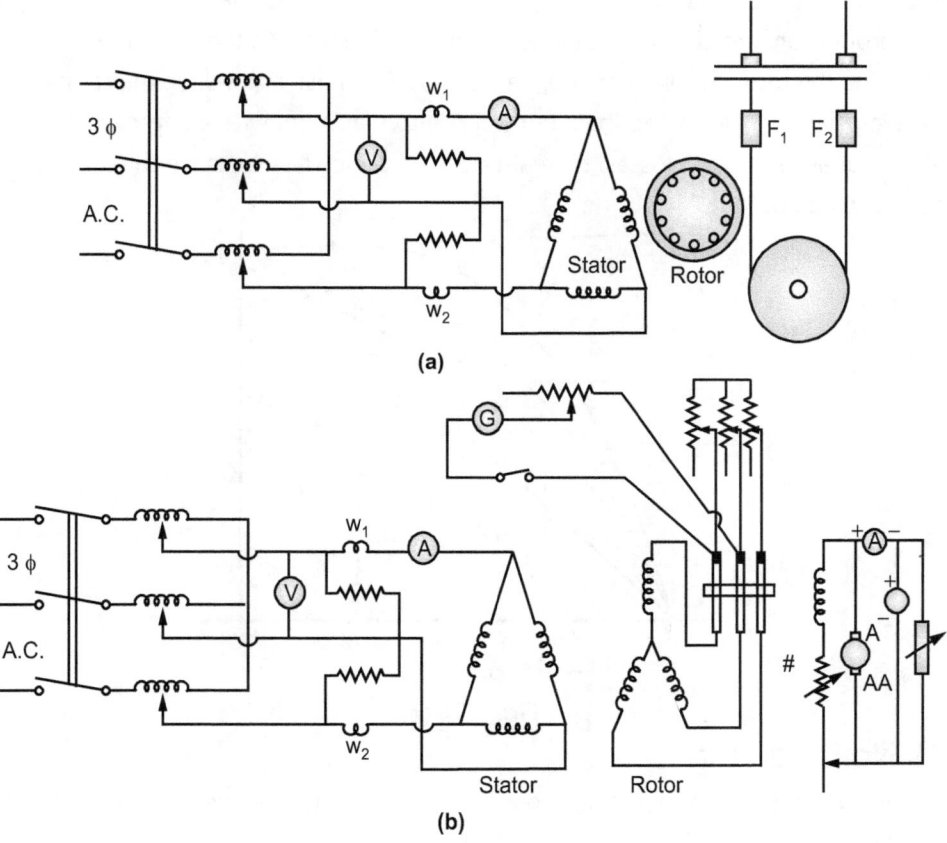

**Fig. 3.54**

The value of T is the torque in kg m or Nm which is equal to

$$T = (F_1 - F_2) \times r$$

$F_1$ and $F_2$ measured in kg.

While r is the radius of the brake pulley which is measured in metres.

$$T = (F_1 - F_2) \times r \text{ kg m}$$

or
$$T = (F_1 - F_2) \times r \times 9.81 \text{ Nm}$$

In case of (ii) method, the output of motor is equal to output of generator divided by generators efficiency at that load condition.

i.e. In this case motor output $= \dfrac{V_{dc} \times I_{dc}}{\eta_g}$

Input is recorded from the wattmeter reading, from the readings and calculations of load test, load characteristics as shown in Fig. 3.54 (c) are drawn, which represent the characteristics of speed p.f. efficiency h.p., torque and slip to a base of % normal full load output. The torque/current curve is nearly straight line, as flux remains constant torque will be proportional to rotor current or stator current. Also B.H.P. curve is nearly a straight line which is proportional to torque, speed being almost constant. As the current increases from no load value the rotor current increase, hence the p.f. will rise and will be maximum near full load. The efficiency is zero at no load, but will rise to maximum where approximately copper losses are equal to no-load losses, thereafter the efficiency falls because the losses increase more rapidly than output.

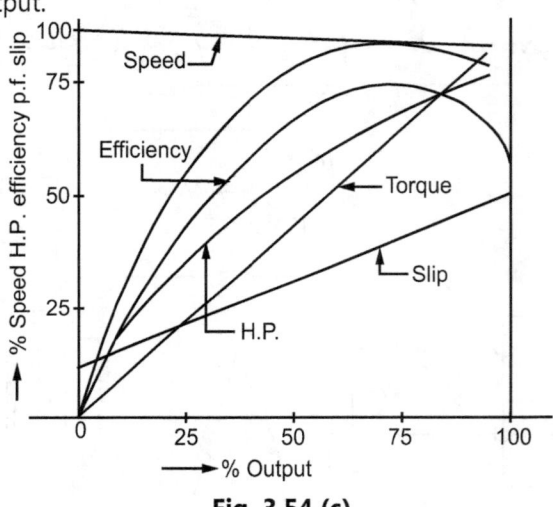

Fig. 3.54 (c)

## 3.3.19 No Load Test

The no load test of an induction motor is carried out to determine, the no load losses which consists of

  (i) Copper loss (no load) in stator winding.
  (ii) Core losses (Iron losses in stator and rotor).
  (iii) Friction and winding losses.

From the total input at no load when the $I^2 R$ loss taking place in stator is subtracted we get core-loss plus friction and windage loss. The copper loss taking place in rotor at no load being very small can be neglected as in no load condition, the rotor speed is nearly equal to synchronous speed, rotor e.m.f. being very small, rotor current is very small hence the copper losses are negligible. As these losses are nearly same at no load and full load they may be called as constant losses the reason being that the flux is constant and the speed is also almost constant from no load to full load.

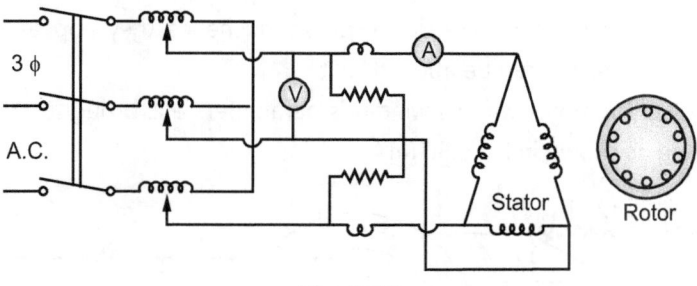

**Fig. 3.55**

Fig. 3.55 represents the circuit diagram for carrying out a no load test on 3-phase I.M. The motor is started by application of reduced voltage at rated frequency and then the voltage is increased to its rated value. At rated voltage and rated frequency, when the motor is running without any load, the readings of power drawn by the motor, recorded by two wattmeter in this case, voltage applied and current drawn by the motor are recorded, the speed may also be recorded if necessary.

The results of this test are used for computing efficiency using O.C., S.C. test results and also they are used to calculate constants of equivalent circuit and to plot a circle diagram in combination with S.C. test result.

## 3.3.20 Short Circuit Test (Block Rotor)

The circuit diagram for conducting above test is the same as shown in Fig. 3.55. The only difference will be instrument ranges, here we are supposed to use low voltage range wattmeter, high current range ammeter, and low voltage reading voltmeter.

In this test, the rotor of the I.M. is locked (Blocked) by suitable means, which can be by hands in case of small motors and the applied voltage from the autotransformer is gradually increased from zero, till the ammeter records full-load current. Under this condition the readings of wattmeter, voltmeter and ammeter are recorded. As voltage applied is low, flux is low hence iron losses which are almost proportional to square of flux will be negligible. As rotor is stationary, friction and windage losses are not present, hence the readings of wattmeters will record full load copper losses.

The readings of this test are used to determine efficiency of I.M. for a equivalent circuit and also to plot a circle diagram from which details about the working condition of I.M. can be calculated.

## 3.3.21 Approximate Equivalent Circuit and Phaser Diagram

### 3.3.21.1 Phaser diagram

The induction motor works on the principle of magnetic induction. As explained previously, though the rotor rotates at a speed less than the synchronous speed the magnetic flux produced by rotor and the magnetic field produced by stator both rotate with synchronous speed and in same direction w.r.t. stator, hence they appear to be stationary and the transformer principle can be applied to it.

Hence, an induction motor with its windings parameters etc. brought out of the machine can be represented as shown in Fig 3.56 (a).

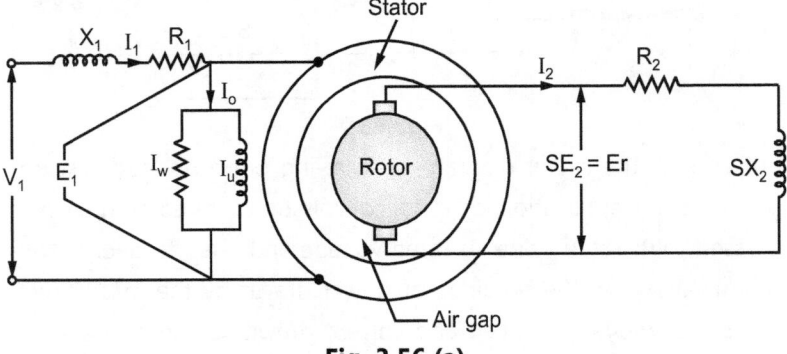

**Fig. 3.56 (a)**

$R_1$ and $X_1$ are stator resistance and leakage reactance/phase. The applied voltage $V_1$/phase will produce a magnetic flux which links both primary and secondary winding producing a back e.m.f. (counter e.m.f). $E_1$ is stator induced e.m.f. and a mutually induced e.m.f. $E_r = SE_2$ in the rotor. As the rotor is closed on itself, there will be no voltage across secondary.

Hence, we can write $\quad V_1 = E_1 + I_1 R_1 + JI_1 X_1$

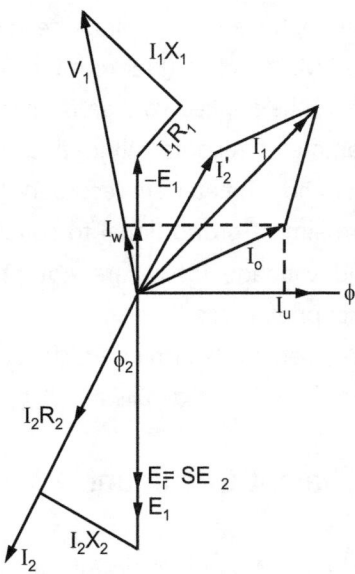

**Fig. 3.56 (b): Vector diagram of 3-phase I.M.**

The magnitude of $E_r$ depends upon voltage transformation ratio between stator and rotor and the slip at which rotor rotates. As no output voltage is available

$$SE_2 = E_r = I_2(R_2 + JSX_2)$$

Now the vector diagram can be drawn for 3-phase I.M. It represents the values per phase.

The motor draws a no load correct $I_0$ from supply, it has two components one in the direction of flux called $I_\mu$ i.e. $I_0 \sin \phi_0$ and is required to produce magnetic flux. Other $I_w$ at an angle of 90° with $I_0 \sin \phi_0$ and is used to supply, no load losses of the machine. The component $I_\mu$ is much more in case of I.M. as compared with transformer due to more leakage flux in air gap between stator and rotor, which increases no load current, and reduces p.f.

Let $I_2$ be the rotor current phase lagging $E_r$ at an angle $\phi_2$. Voltage drop in rotor resistance $IR_2$ will be in phase with $I_2$ and reactive drop $I_2 SX_2$ at an angle of 90° to $I_2$. Vector sum of $I_2 R_2 + J I_2 SX_2$ will be equal to $E_r$ or $SE_2$ as shown in Fig. 3.56 (b).

Let $I_2$ be the magnitude of rotor current transformed to stator by transformation ratio vector sum of $I_2$ and $I_0$ is equal to $I_1$, the stator current in amps./phase. Vector for counter e.m.f. in stator $E_1$ will be drawn in phase opposition to $E_r$. To this $E_1$ when $I_1 R_1$ and $I_1 X_1$ are added vectorially, we get applied voltage $V_1$ and the angle between $V_1$ and $I_1$ represents p.f. angle of the motor on load.

### 3.3.21.2 Equivalent Circuit of an Three-phase I.M.

Rotor current at any load condition is represented as

$$I_2 = \frac{SE_2}{\sqrt{R_2^2 + (SX_2)^2}} \qquad \ldots (3.63)$$

whereas the fractional slip at that instant and $E_2$, $R_2$ and $X_2$ have their usual meanings, or

$$I_2 = \frac{E_2}{\sqrt{R_2/S^2 + X_2^2}} \qquad \ldots (3.64)$$

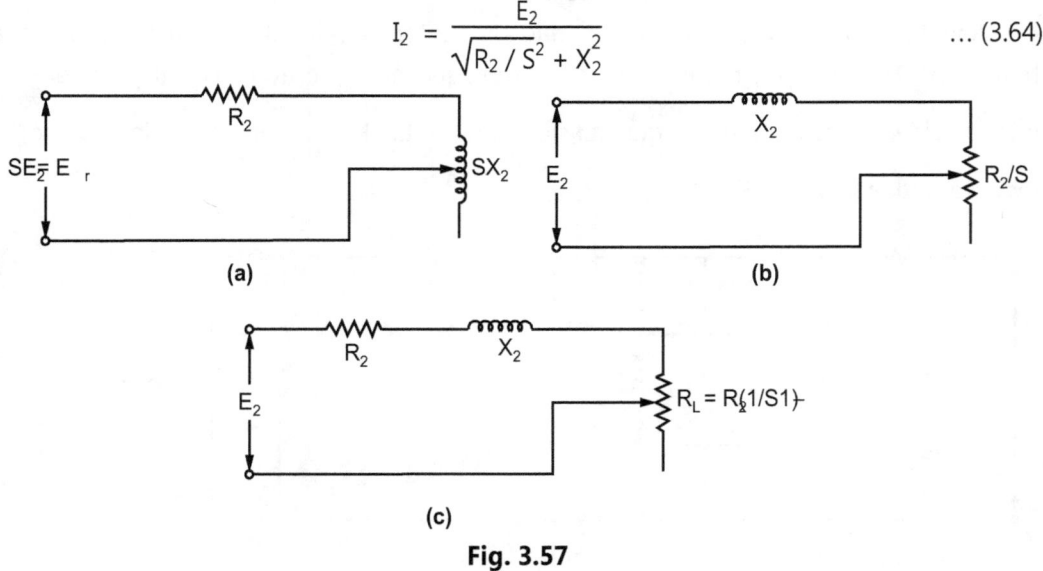

**Fig. 3.57**

From equation (1) it can be stated that the rotor consist of an impedance in which the resistance value $R_2$ is fixed and a variable reactance which is proportional to slip connected across a variable voltage $E_r$ equal to $SE_2$ as represented in Fig. 3.57 (c). Equation (1) when modified to equation (2) represents a rotor circuit connected across a fixed voltage $E_2$ and consisting of fixed reactance $X_2$ and a variable resistance equal to $\dfrac{R_2}{S}$ as represented in Fig. 3.57 (b).

The variable resistance $\dfrac{R_2}{S} = R_2 + R_2\left(\dfrac{1}{S} - 1\right)$ and the rotor circuit can further be simplified, such that it consists of a fixed resistance $R_2$, fixed reactance $X_2$ and a variable resistance $R_2\left(\dfrac{1}{S} - 1\right)$ which depends upon slip and is termed as load resistance. This circuit is represented in Fig. 3.57 (c).

The load resistance $R_L$ is the electrical equivalent of mechanical load of the motor.

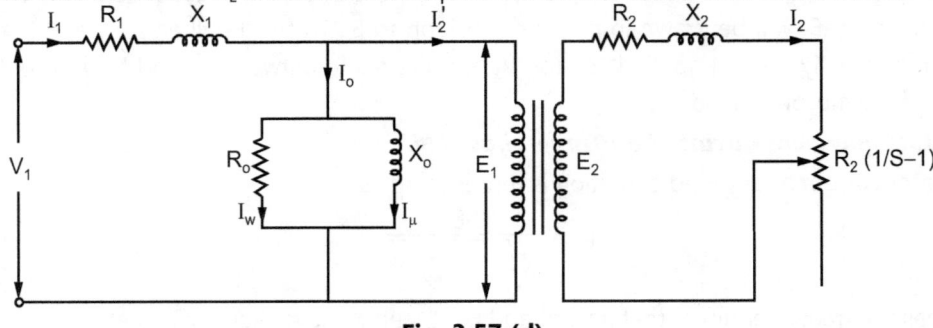

**Fig. 3.57 (d)**

Now the simplified circuit of an induction motor can be drawn, just similar to a transformer. Fig. 3.57 (d) represent it transferring secondary i.e. rotor circuit parameter to primary side, by suitably using the transformation ratio $K = \dfrac{E_2}{E_1}$ circuit in Fig. 3.57 (d) is reduced to that shown in Fig. 3.57 (e).

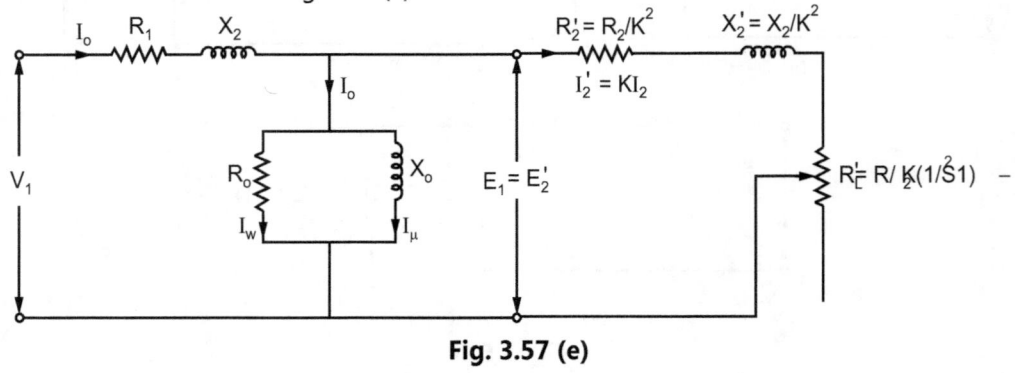

**Fig. 3.57 (e)**

The circuit represented in Fig. 3.57 (e) can be further simplified and represented as in Fig. 3.57 (f) by transferring the exciting parameter to the start of circuit, which causes a negligible error but the circuit is much more simplified for calculation purposes.

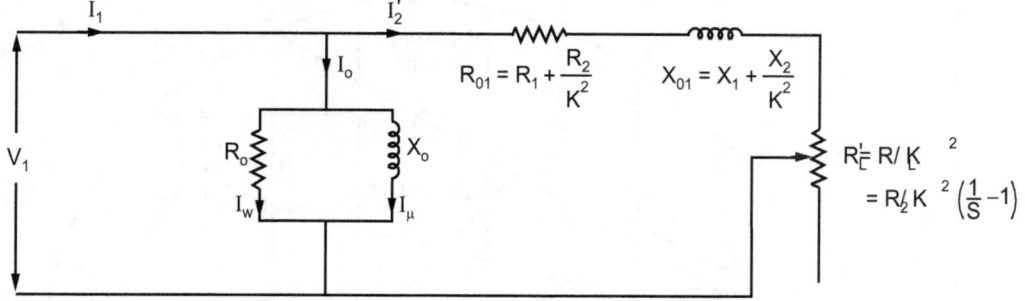

**Fig. 3.57 (f)**

**Approximate Equivalent Circuit of an Induction Motor:**

If the no load current drawn by the motor is very small in comparison to its full-load current. Neglecting the exciting circuit parameters, we get most simplified equivalent circuit for an induction motor as represented in Fig. 3.57 (g).

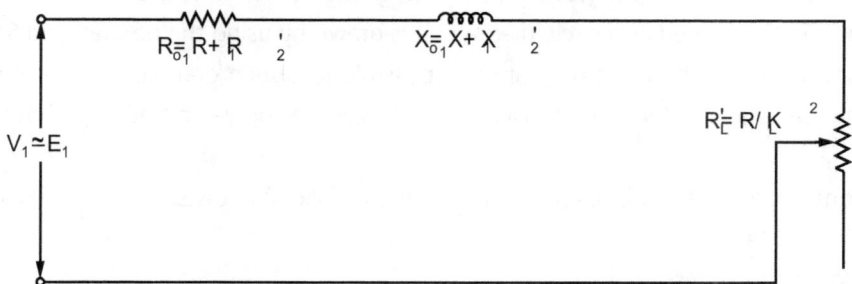

**Fig. 3.57 (g)**

## 3.3.22 Circle Diagram

Considering equivalent circuit of Fig. 3.57 (g), it can be stated that it is circuit connected across constant voltage and which consist of a fixed reactance and variable resistance and the locus of current flowing through such a circuit is a circle.

It can be proved thus current $I_2$ at any time will be given $I_2$

$$I_2' = \frac{V_1}{\sqrt{R_2^2 + X_2^2}}$$

or

$$I_2' = \frac{V_1}{X_2} \times \frac{X_2}{\sqrt{R_2^2 + X_2^2}}$$

$$= \frac{V_1}{X_2} \sin \phi$$

It represents a equation of the circle in polar form with diameter equal to $\frac{V_1}{X_1}$.

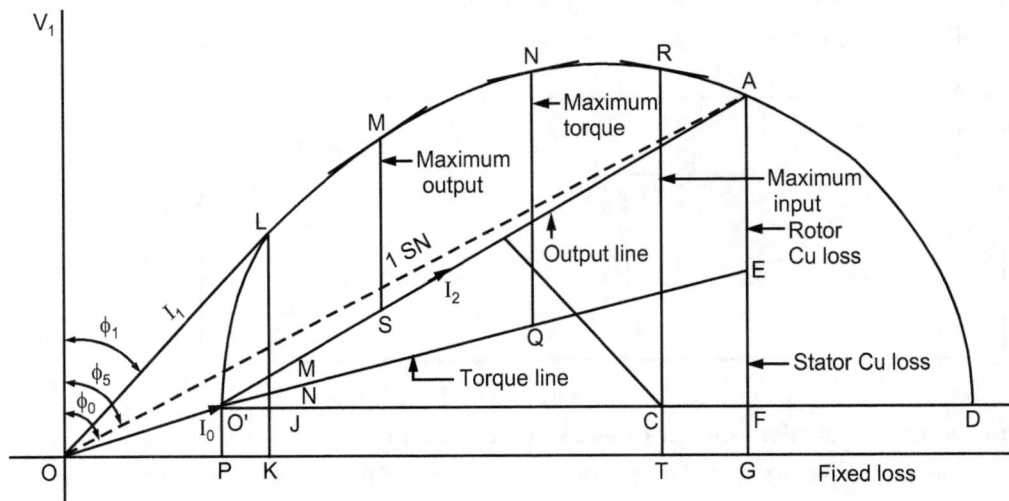

**Fig. 5.58 : Graph**

**Construction of Circle Diagram :** A diagram giving the locus of the current drawn by an induction motor is termed as a circle diagram. It is drawn by using the no load and S.C. (block rotor) test data. From the circle diagram it is possible to obtain graphically very large range of informations such as full load efficiency, p.f., maximum power output, maximum torque etc.

For constructing the circle diagram use is made of following tests.
1. No load test
2. Blocked rotor test.

**Step I :** First lay off the stators voltage vector $V_1$ along the Y axis using no load test data find out the p.f. angle of no load current.

i.e. $\phi_0 = \cos^{-1} \dfrac{W_0}{\sqrt{3}\, V_1\, I_0}$ where $W_0$ is the wattmeter reading in no load test, $V_1$ is the rated voltage applied to stator and $I_0$ is no load current,

Lay off vector for $I_0$, making angle $\phi_0$ with $V_1$ and lagging to $V_1$ to scale. Let it be OO'.

**Step II :** Then use of short circuit test is made to determine, the S.C. current when rated voltage will be applied across the motor terminals, assuming S.C. current when rated voltage will be applied across the motor terminals, assuming S.C. characteristic as a straight line.

$I_{SN}$ at rated voltage, $V_1 = I_{SC} \times \dfrac{V_1}{V_{SC}}$ amps.

and $\phi_s = \cos^{-1} \dfrac{W_{SC}}{\sqrt{3}\, V_{SC}\, I_{SC}}$

Then the vectors for $I_{SN}$ making angle of $\phi_{sy}$ with $V_1$ i.e. OA is drawn.

Now the two extremities i.e. O' of no load current and A of S.C. current line of the circle. Hence, O' A' is jointed and the bisector of O' A is drawn.

Then from O' perpendicular to voltage vector is drawn. The bisector of O' A will cut it at point C. O' C then represent radius of the circle, extend it upto D, so that O' C = CD means O' D will represent the diameter of the semi-circle. From point O also draw a perpendicular vector to $V_1$ and parallel to O'D equal to radius draw a semi-circle cutting a points O' and D. The line O' A is called as output line of I.M.

**Step III :** As the voltage vector is drawn vertical, all the components of current vector along this vector will represent the active components or power components. Hence, the vertical component O'P of no load current OO' will represent the no load input power, which supplies mainly the core loss and friction and winding loss as stator $I^2$ R loss at no load is very small. Similarly the vertical component AG of short circuit current OA represents input on short circuit. Hence, can be used to determine the power scale, equating FG equal to no load input.

Or AG equal to power input in S.C. test with normal voltage applied; the power scale is more accurately determined.

**Step IV :** The line which separates the stator and rotor Cu losses is termed as torque line. In the blocked rotor test the power supplied to the motor is utilised to meet the stator and rotor Cu losses. This power is proportional to AG out of this FG = O' P represents fixed losses.

Hence, AF is proportional to stator and rotor Cu losses, the point E such that

$$\frac{AE}{EF} = \frac{\text{Rotor Cu loss}}{\text{Stator Cu loss}}$$ and the line O' E is called as torque line

For locating point E, stator resistance per phase $R_1$ is determined and stator Cu-loss = $3 I_s^2 R_1$, where $I_s$ is stator current per phase, If $W_s$ = power loss in S.C. test.

Then $\dfrac{AE}{EF} = \dfrac{W_s - 3 I_s^2 R_1}{3 I_s^2 R_1}$ for cage motor, when a wound rotor motor is used.

In this case, the stator and rotor resistance/phase are determined if $R_1$ is stator resistance/ phase and $R_2$ is rotor resistance per phase.

Then $\dfrac{AE}{EF} = \dfrac{I_2^2 R_2}{I_2^2 R_1} = \dfrac{R_2}{R_1}\left(\dfrac{I_2}{I_1}\right)^2 = \dfrac{R_2}{R_1} \times \dfrac{1}{K^2}$

**Step V :** For determining performance at working condition, let the motor be drawing a current equal to OL on load.

Then the perpendicular LK be drawn to OG. Then JK will represent fixed losses, JN = stator Cu loss at that load, NL is rotor input, NM is rotor Cu losses.

ML is rotor output and LK is total motor input.
Now using the different relation we can find out.

(i) Efficiency = $\dfrac{ML}{LK}$

(ii) Slip (s) = $\dfrac{\text{Rotor Cu loss}}{\text{Rotator input}} = \dfrac{MN}{NL}$

(iii) $N_a/N_s = \dfrac{\text{Rotor output}}{\text{Rotor input}} = 1 - S = \dfrac{MN}{NL}$

(iv) $\cos\phi_1 = \dfrac{LK}{OL} = \text{p.f.}$

**Step VI :** To determine maximum quantities the following procedure is adopted.

**(a) Maximum torque or Rotor input :** A line parallel to torque line touching semi-circle at point N is drawn. Then length of vector NQ represents maximum torque.

**(b) Maximum output :** A line parallel to output line cutting the semi circle at point M represents maximum output line. Length MS represents maximum output.

**(c) Maximum input :** A tangent at the highest point of semicircle, cutting it at R will represent maximum input line and the length RT represents maximum input to motor.

**Example 3.35:** A 50 Hz, 3-phase induction motor has a full load speed of 460 r.p.m. estimate:

(i) Number of poles for which stator is wound.

(ii) Speed of r.m.f. relative to rotor surface.

(iii) Speed of r.m.f. relative to stator.

**Solution:** (i) As the actual speed is 460 r.p.m. synchronous speed using relation,

$$N_s = \dfrac{120 \times 50}{P}$$

when P = 12, $N_s$ = 500. Hence number of poles must be = 12.

(ii) Speed of rotating magnetic field = 500 r.p.m.

(iii) Speed of r.p.m. relative to rotor surface = slip – speed = 500 – 460 = 40 r.p.m.

(iv) Speed of r.m.f. relative to stator = 500 r.p.m.

**Example 3.36:** A three phase induction motor is wound for 4 poles and supplied from 50 Hz supply. Calculate :

(i) The synchronous speed.

(ii) Speed of rotor at 4% slip.

(iii) The rotor frequency when rotor runs at 1000 r.p.m.

**Solution:** (i) Synchronous speed,

$$N_s = \frac{120 \, f}{p} = \frac{120 \times 50}{4}$$

$$= 1500 \text{ r.p.m.}$$

(ii) From $S = \dfrac{N_s - N_a}{N_a}$   $S = \dfrac{4}{100} = 0.04$

$$0.04 = \frac{1500 - N_a}{1500} \text{ or } N_a = 1500 - 60$$

or   Rotor speed = 1440 r.p.m.

$$\text{Slip at 1000 r.p.m.} = \frac{1500 - 1000}{1500} = \frac{500}{1500} = 0.33$$

Rotor frequency = Sf

$$= 0.33 \times 50 = 16.5 \text{ Hz}$$

**Example 3.37:** A 4 pole, 3 phase, 50 Hz 400 volts induction motor runs at 1350 r.p.m. at some load. Its stator is delta connected and rotor star connected stator to rotor turns = 3; Rotor stand still impedance = 0.1 + j 0.8 ohm, Mechanical loss = 2000 watts. Estimate rotor loss and useful torque.

**Solution:** Stator voltage/phase = 400 volts

$$\text{Rotor voltage/phase} = \frac{400}{3} = 133.33 \text{ V at stand still.}$$

∴    Slip at load $= \dfrac{N_s - N_a}{N_s}$

$N_s$ for 4 pole, 50 Hz machine = 1500 r.p.m.

$$S = \frac{1500 - 1350}{1500} = 0.1$$

∴ Rotor e.m.f. under running condition

$$= SE_2 = 0.1 \times 133.33 = 13.333 \text{ Volts}$$

∴    Rotor current/phase $= \dfrac{SE_2}{Z_{r2}}$

Rotor impedance in running condition $= \sqrt{r_2^2 + S^2 X_2^2}$

where,   $Z_{r2} = \sqrt{(0.1)^2 + (0.1 \times 0.8)^2}$

$Z_{r2} = 0.128 \, \Omega$

∴    $I_{r2} = \dfrac{13.33}{0.128} = 104$ Amps.

Rotor loss $= 3 \, I_{r2}^2 \times R_2$

$$= 3 \times (104)^2 \times 0.1 = 3250.42 \text{ W}$$

Using relation $\dfrac{\text{Rotor Cu loss}}{\text{Rotor input}}$ = slip

$$\dfrac{3250.42}{\text{Rotor input}} = 0.1 \text{ or Rotor input} = 32504.2 \text{ watts}$$

Now rotor input − rotor Cu loss = Mechanical power developed

$$32504.2 - 3250.42 = 29253.78 \text{ watts}$$

Mechanical power developed − Friction and windage loss = output

$$29253.78 - 2000 = 27253.78 \text{ watts}$$

$$\text{Output} = \dfrac{2\pi NT}{60} \text{ watts where T is Nm}$$

$$27253.78 = \dfrac{2 \times 3.14 \times 13.50 \times T}{60}$$

or $\qquad T = 192.78$ Nm

**Example 3.38:** A 4 pole, 3 phase, 50 Hz, 400 volts induction motor develops an output of 5.5 kW at 1400 r.p.m. The mechanical torque lost is 2.5 Newton meters. Stator losses total to 314 watts. Calculate efficiency and current drawn at this output. Draw power flow diagram inserting values of this loading, power factor = 0.866.

**Solution:** Power in mechanical losses = $\dfrac{2\pi NT}{60}$ watts, where T is in Nm

$$\dfrac{2 \times 3.14 \times 1400 \times 2.4}{60} = 366.52 \text{ watts}$$

$$\dfrac{\text{Rotor gross output}}{\text{Rotor input}} = \dfrac{N_a}{N_s}$$

$$\dfrac{\text{Output + Mechanical loss}}{\text{Rotor input}} = \dfrac{1400}{1500} = \dfrac{5.5 \times 1000 + 366.52}{\text{Rotor input}}$$

∴ Rotor input = 6285.56 watts

Input to motor = Rotor input + Stator losses

= 6285.56 + 314 = 6599.56 watts

Rotor input − Mechanical power developed = Rotor Cu loss

6285.56 − 5866.52 = 419.04 watts

$$\%\eta = \dfrac{\text{Output}}{\text{Input}} \times 100$$

$$= \dfrac{5.5 \times 10^3}{6599.56} \times 100 = 83.33$$

From Input = $\sqrt{3}\, V_L I_L \cos\phi$

6599.56 = $\sqrt{3} \times 400 \times I_L \times 0.866$

∴ $\qquad I_L = 11$ amps.

**Power flow diagram**

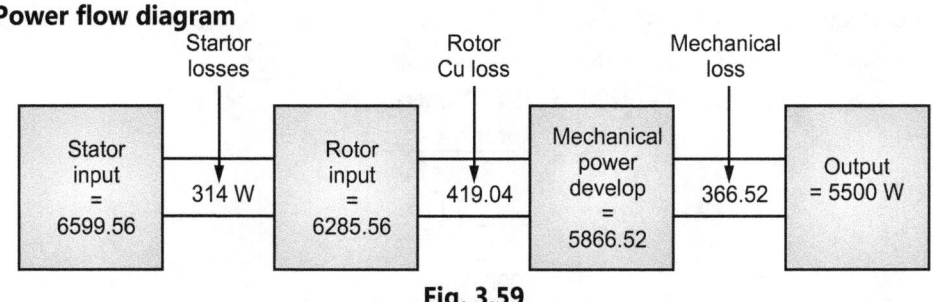

**Fig. 3.59**

**Example 3.39:** A 6 pole, 50 Hz, 3 phase induction motor has rotor resistance per phase of 0.125 ohm. The speed at which maximum torque occurs is 800 r.p.m. and full load speed is 970 r.p.m.

Find out the ratio $\dfrac{T_{max}}{T_{full\,load}}$

**Solution:** Slip at maximum torque = $\dfrac{1000 - 800}{1000} = 0.2$

$$N_s = 1000 \text{ r.p.m.}$$

Using relation at maximum torque, $R_2 = SX_2$

$$0.125 = 0.2\, X_2$$

∴ Stand still reactance/phase $X_2 = 0.625$ ohm

Slip at full load = $\dfrac{1000 - 970}{1000} = 0.03$

Now, $\dfrac{T_f}{T_m} = \dfrac{2\,a\,S_f}{a^2 + S_f^2}$ where, $a = \dfrac{R_2}{X_2}$

$$a = \dfrac{0.125}{0.625} = 0.2$$

∴ $\dfrac{T_m}{T_f} = \dfrac{a^2 + S_f^2}{2\,a\,S_f} = \dfrac{(0.2)^2 + (0.03)^2}{2 \times 0.2 \times 0.03}$

**Example 3.40:** The power input to the rotor of a 400 volt, 50 Hz, 6 pole induction motor is 80 kW. The rotor e.m.f. is observed to make 120 complete oscillations per minute, calculate the rotor speed and mechanical power developed.

**Solution:** Rotor e.m.f. frequency = $\dfrac{120}{60} = 2$ Hz

Now, from $f = S_f$, $2 = S \times 50$ or $S = \dfrac{2}{50} = 0.04$

$$\dfrac{\text{Rotor Cu loss}}{\text{Rotor input}} = S$$

or Rotor Cu loss = $0.04 \times 80 \times 10^2$ = 3200 watts
Rotor input − Rotor Cu loss = Rotor gross output
$$80,000 - 3200 = 76,800 \text{ watts}$$
$$\frac{N_a}{N_s} = \frac{\text{Rotor gross output}}{\text{Rotor input}}$$
$$N_a = \frac{120 \times 50}{6} = 1000$$
$$0.04 = \frac{1000 - N_a}{1000} = 960 \text{ r.p.m.}$$

**Example 3.41:** A 400 volts, 8 pole, 60 Hz, 3 phase slip ring induction motor has stand still impedance/phase of 0.05 + j 0.3 ohm estimate:
(i) Slip at maximum torque and corresponding speed.
(ii) The external resistance/phase to be inserted in the rotor circuit to obtain maximum torque at start.
(iii) What additional advantage is achieved by adding external resistance ?

**Solution:** At maximum torque,
$$R_2 = SX_2$$
$$0.05 = S \times 0.3$$
or
$$S = \frac{0.05}{0.3} = 0.167$$
$$N_s = \frac{120\,f}{p} = \frac{120 \times 60}{8}$$
$$= 900 \text{ r.p.m.}$$
$$S = \frac{N_s - N_a}{N_s} = \frac{900 - N_a}{900} = 0.167$$
or
$$N_a = 749.7 \text{ r.p.m.}$$

(ii)
$$\frac{T_s}{T_m} = \frac{2}{1 + a^2} \text{ where } a = \frac{R_2 + r}{X_2}$$

but
$$\frac{T_s}{T_m} = 1 \quad \therefore \quad 1 = \frac{2 \times a}{1 + a^2}$$
$$a^2 - 2a + 1 = 0 \quad \text{or } a = 1$$

or
$$1 = \frac{R_2 + r}{X_2} \quad \text{or } 1 = \frac{0.05 + r}{0.03}$$

∴ r = 0.25 ohm

(iii) In condition one if additional resistance is inserted in rotor circuit keeping constant the value of maximum torque, the slip will reduce and speed will increase, at the same time p.f. will improve.

**Example 3.42:** A 25 H.P., 6 pole, 50 cycles, 3 phase slip ring induction motor runs at 960 r.p.m. on full load with a rotor current/phase of 35 amps. Allowing 250 watts for the copper loss in short circuiting gears and 1000 watts for mechanical losses, find the resistance per phase of three phase rotor windings.

**Solution:** Synchronous speed $= \dfrac{120\, f}{p} = \dfrac{120 \times 50}{6} = 1000$ r.p.m.

$\therefore$ Slip at full load $= \dfrac{1000 - 960}{1000} = 0.04$

Output $= 25 \times 735.5 = 18387.5$ watts

Output + Mechanical losses = Mechanical power developed

$18387.5 + 1000 = 19387.5$ watts

$\dfrac{\text{Mechanical power developed}}{\text{Rotor input}} = \dfrac{N_a}{N_s}$

$\therefore$ Rotor input $= \dfrac{N_s}{N_a} \times$ Mechanical power developed

$= \dfrac{1000}{960} \times 19387.5 = 20195.31$ watts

Rotor input − Mechanical power developed = Rotor Cu loss

$20195.31 - 19387.5 = 807.81$ watts

Net rotor Cu loss = Total rotor Cu loss − Cu loss in rotor short

Circuiting gear $= 807.81 - 250 = 557.81$ watts

Rotor Cu loss $= 3\, I_2^2\, R_2$

$557.81 = 3 \times (35)^2 \times R_2$

$R_2 = 0.152\ \Omega$ Rotor Resistance/Phase

**Example 3.43:** The power input to the 50 Hz, 8 poles, 3-phase induction motor running at 720 r.p.m. is 49 kW. The stator loss is 1 kW and friction and windage loss is 2 kW, calculated slip rotor circuit loss efficiency and output H.P. Draw power flow diagram.

$N_s = \dfrac{120 \times 50}{8} = 750$ r.p.m.

$\therefore$ Slip at load $= \dfrac{750 - 720}{750} = 0.04$

Stator input − Stator loss = Rotor input

$40 \times 10^3 - 1 \times 10^3 = 39 \times 10^3$ watts

Rotor Cu loss = S × Rotor input

$= 0.04 \times 39000 = 1560$ watts

Gross mechanical power developed = Rotor input − Rotor Cu loss

$= 39000 - 1560 = 37440$ watts

$$\text{Net output} = \text{Mechanical power developed} - \text{Mechanical power losses}$$
$$= 37440 - 2000 = 35440 \text{ watts}$$

$$\therefore \quad \text{Efficiency} = \frac{\text{Output}}{\text{Input}} = \frac{35440}{40000} = 88\%$$

$$\text{H.P. Developed} = \frac{\text{Output}}{735.5} = \frac{35440}{735.5} = 48.18 \text{ H.P.}$$

**Example 3.44:** (a) A load test is to be performed on a 10 H.P., 2 pole, 3 phase, 50 Hz, 400 volts, star connected induction motor. The motor is coupled a precalibrated shunt generator 7.5 kW, 250 volts. Enlist the necessary meter (with ranges other equipments and suitable starting device).

(b) Load test as in (a) was performed calculate slip, power factor, efficiency, output H.P. and useful torque at the following observations set runs at 2850 r.p.m.

**Motor side:**

$$\text{Line voltage} = 400 \text{ volts}, \quad \text{Line current} = 14 \text{ amps.}$$
$$\text{Total input} = 8400 \text{ watts.}$$

**Generator side :**

250 votls, 23 amps. efficiency = 80%

Stator loss = 5% of input in (b) above, what is rotor Cu loss?

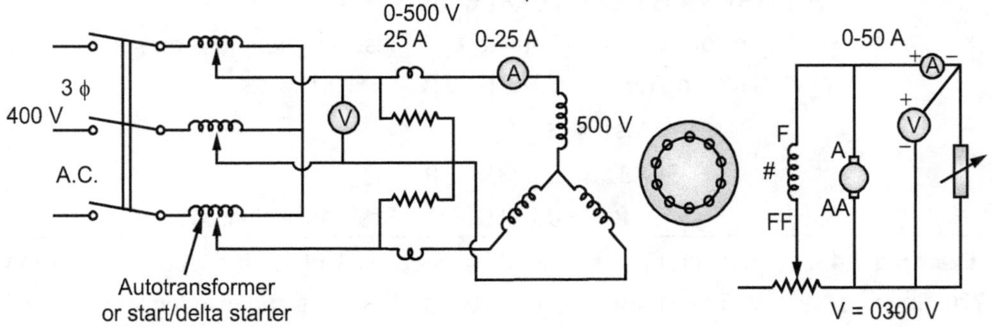

**Fig. 3.60**

**Solution:** 
$$\text{Synchronous speed} = \frac{120 \times 50}{2} = 3000 \text{ r.p.m.}$$

$$\text{Actual speed} = 2850$$

$$\therefore \quad \text{Slip} = \frac{3000 - 2850}{3000} = 0.05$$

$$\text{Generator input} = \frac{\text{Generator output}}{\text{Efficiency}}$$

$$= \frac{250 \times 23}{0.8} = 7187.5 \text{ watts}$$

Net motor output = 7187.5 watts

$$\text{Stator loss} = 8400 \times \frac{5}{100} = 420 \text{ watts}$$

$$\text{Motor efficiency} = \frac{7187.5}{8400} \times 100 = 85.56\%$$

$$\text{Input} = \sqrt{3}\, V_L I_L \cos\phi$$

$$8400 = \sqrt{3} \times 400 \times 14 \times \cos\phi$$

∴
$$\cos\phi = \frac{8400}{\sqrt{3} \times 400 \times 4} = 0.866$$

$$\text{Output H.P.} = \frac{7187.5}{735.5} = 9.77 \text{ H.P.}$$

$$\text{Output} = \frac{2\pi NT}{60}$$

or
$$T = \frac{7187.5 \times 60}{2\pi \times 2850} = 24.08 \text{ Nm}$$

**Example 3.45:** A three phase 415 volts, 5.5 kW induction motor tested for circle diagram give following results, Power was measured by two wattmeter method.

No Load Test : 415 volts, 4.6 amps,

$$W_1 = 1000 \text{ watts}$$
$$W_2 = -560 \text{ watts}$$

Blocked Rotor Test : 98 volts, 10 amps.,

$$W_1 = 770 \text{ watts}$$
$$W_2 = -160 \text{ watts}$$

Using scale 1 cm = 2 amps., find power scale.
Estimate efficiency and current (magnitude and p.f.) at full load, maximum output.

**Solution:**
$$\phi_o = \cos^{-1}\frac{W_o}{\sqrt{3}\, V_o I_o} = \cos^{-1}\frac{1000 - 560}{\sqrt{3} \times 415 \times 4.6} = 82.35°$$

$$\phi_{sc} = \cos^{-1}\frac{W_{ac}}{\sqrt{3}\, V_{sc} I_{sc}} = \cos^{-1}\frac{610}{\sqrt{3} \times 98 \times 10} = 68.94°$$

$$I_{SN} = I_{SC} \times \frac{V}{V_{sc}} = 10 \times \frac{415}{98} = 42.35 \text{ amps.}$$

$$W_{SN} = W_{sc} \times \left(\frac{I_{SN}}{I_{SC}}\right)^2 = 610 \times \left(\frac{42.35}{10}\right)^2 = 10940.49 \text{ watts}$$

Draw co-ordinate axes, to represents voltage axis, draw OO' = 2.3 cm, at 82.35° with V join O' A, which represent output line.

Draw a horizontal vector from O' parallel to X-axis.
Draw a perpendicular bisector of O' A cutting O' D at point C.
Draw a perpendicular from A on O' D cutting it at point F, extend it upto G on X-axis.

Then FG represents fixed losses, and AF represents copper losses.
Measure the length AF,

$$AF = 7.2 \text{ cm} = 10940.49$$

$$\therefore \quad \text{Power scale} = \frac{10940.49}{7.2} = 1519.51 \text{ watts/cm}$$

$$\text{Full load output} = 5.5 \text{ kW} = 5500 \text{ watts}$$

$$= \frac{5500}{1519.51} = 3.62 \text{ cm}$$

Extend GA by 3.62 cm and draw from it a line parallel to output line O' A, cutting semi-circle at point L. Joint OL, which represents motor current on f.l. it makes an angle $\phi$ with V, OL = 5 cm = 10 amps.

$$\phi = 37°, \quad \therefore \cos \phi = 0.99 \text{ lag}$$

$$\text{Input} = LK = 4 \text{ cm} = 4 \times 1519.51 = 6078.05 \text{ W}$$

$$\therefore \quad \text{Efficiency} = \frac{\text{Output}}{\text{Input}} = \frac{5500}{6078.05} = 90.49\%$$

Draw a tangent parallel to the output line cutting semicircle at point M, draw a vertical from M on output line, cutting it at S,

$$\text{Measure MS, MS} = 6.7 \text{ cm}$$

$$\therefore \quad \text{Maximum output} = 6.7 \times 1519.51 = 10180.73$$

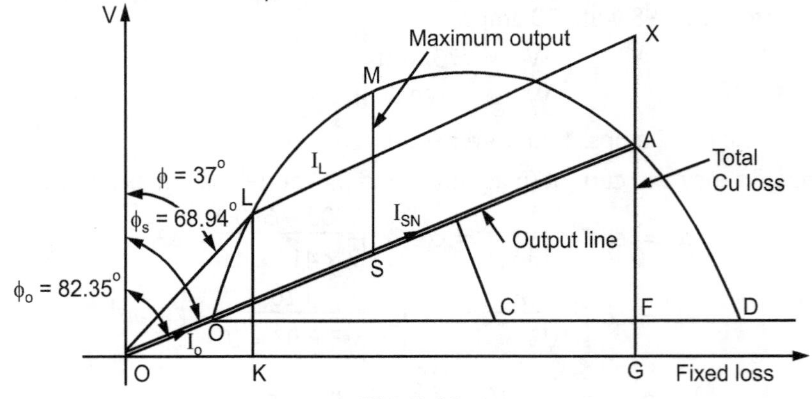

**Fig. 3.61**

**Example 3.46:** The following results were obtained from the test on a 3.5 kW, 3-phase, 220 volts, 50 Hz, 4 pole star connected introduction motor.

| Test | Line voltage | line current | Total input |
|---|---|---|---|
| No load | 220 | 5 A | 385 watts |
| Blocked rotor | 110 | 20 A | 1870 watts |

Assume stand still stator Cu losses to be 55% of total Cu losses.
Current scale 1 cm = 2 A

Draw the circle diagram and find out the following three from it:
(a) Full load current, power factor, efficiency and torque in Nm.
(b) Maximum torque in Nm and speed at which it occurs.
(c) The ratio $\dfrac{T_{maximum}}{T_{starting}}$.

**Solution:**

$$\phi_o = \cos^{-1}\dfrac{W_o}{\sqrt{3}\, V_o\, I_o} = \cos^{-1}\dfrac{385}{\sqrt{3} \times 220 \times 5} = 78.34°$$

$$\phi_{sc} = \cos^{-1}\dfrac{W_{sc}}{\sqrt{3}\, V_{sc}\, I_{sc}} = \cos^{-1}\dfrac{1870}{\sqrt{3} \times 110 \times 20} = 60.61°$$

$$I_{SN} = I_{SC} \times \dfrac{V}{V_{sc}} = 20 \times \dfrac{210}{110} = 40 \text{ Amps.}$$

$$W_{SN} = W_{SC} \times \left(\dfrac{I_{SN}}{I_{SC}}\right)^2 = 1870 \times \left(\dfrac{40}{20}\right)^2 = 7480.0 \text{ watts.}$$

Draw X and Y axis, Y axis representing voltage vector.
Draw OO' = 2.5 Amps., making 78.32° with OV.
Draw OA = $I_{SN}$ = 20 cm, making angle of 60.61° with OV.
Join O' A which represents output line and draw a perpendicular bisector of O' A, cutting O' D at point C.
Draw a perpendicular from A cutting O' D at point F, and X-axis at point G. AF represents total Cu loss, measure AF = 9.2 cm.

$$\therefore \quad \text{Power scale} = \dfrac{7480}{9.2} = 813.0.4 \text{ watts/cm}$$

Divide AF so that,   EF = 0.55 AF
5.06 × 813.04 = 4114.0 watts
Join O' E which represents torque line
  Full load output = 3.5 kW or 3500 watts
Extend point A upto X by $\dfrac{3500}{813.04}$ = 4.3 cm

and draw a line from X parallel to output line cutting semicircle at point L, which represents full load working condition.
  Measure OL, OL = 7 cm i.e. 7 × 2 = 14 Amps.
OL makes p.f. angle $\phi$ with V, $\phi$ = 34°,   $\therefore \cos\phi = 0.82$

$$\text{Efficiency} = \dfrac{\text{Output}}{\text{Input}} = \dfrac{3500}{5.7 \times 813.04} = 75.52\%$$

$$\dfrac{MN}{LN} = \dfrac{\text{Rotor Cu loss}}{\text{Rotor input}} = \text{Slip at full load} = \dfrac{0.4}{4.7}$$

$$\text{Synchronous speed} = \dfrac{120\, f}{p} = \dfrac{120 \times 50}{4} = 1500$$

∴  $N_a = 1372.5$ r.p.m.

$$\text{Output} = \frac{2\pi NT}{60}$$

or  $$3500 = \frac{2\pi \times 1372.5}{60} \times T$$

or  $T = 24.35$ Nm

(b) Draw a line parallel to torque line cutting semicircle at a point N. Draw NQ vertical cutting to torque line at Q.

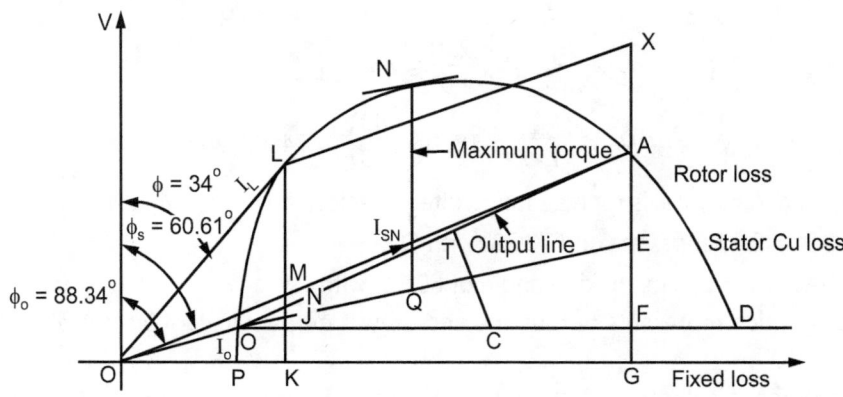

**Fig. 3.62**

$NQ = 7.2$ cm $= 7.2 \times 813.040 = 5853.89$ synchronous watts

$$T_{max} = \frac{\text{Maximum torque in watts}}{\omega}$$

$$T_{max} = \frac{5853.89 \times 60}{2 \times 3.14 \times 1500} \text{ Nm} = 37.27 \text{ Nm}$$

Slip for maximum torque $= \frac{TQ}{QN} = \frac{1.7}{7.2}$

∴ From  $$S = \frac{N_s - N_a}{N_a}$$

$$0.236 = \frac{1500 - N_a}{1500}$$

or  $1500 \times 0.236 = 1500 - N_a$

or  $N_a = 1500 - 354 = 1146$ r.p.m.

(c) Ratio of $\frac{T_{max}}{T_{starting}}$

Starting torque is proportional to AE or rotor Cu loss only.

∴  $$\frac{T_{max}}{T_{starts}} = \frac{7.2}{4} = 1.8$$

## 3.4 STARTERS FOR INDUCTION MOTORS AND METHODS OF STARTING

Following factors influence in selecting a particular method of starting for a squirrel cage motor:

(i) Voltage rating and size of motor.
(ii) The type of load it has to drive.
(iii) Capacity of supply lines to bear the jerks of starting current.
(a) Direct on line starting in case of cage motors having rating below 5 H.P.
(b) Reduced voltage method of starting.

**(a) Direct On Line Starting:** This is the most inexpensive and simplex method of starting cage motors. In this method, direct switching on of induction motor to the mains is used. At starting the motor being just similar to short circuited transformer it will draw nearly 6 to 10 times its full load current at very low p.f. such a high current does not harm to the motor as it is drawn for a short period but it has objectionable voltage drop in supply mains. In this method, of starting there are possibilities of damage of motor, as the rate of production of heat is large and if the starting period of motor is increased, which may take place due to

(i) Excessive load torque of the load connected to the shaft of motor.
(ii) Rotor resistance being low.
(iii) Low voltage being applied across motor terminals from the supply mains.

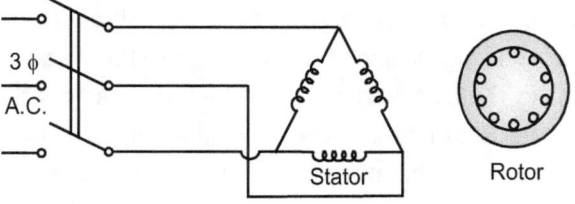

**Fig. 3.63**

For obtaining the relationship between starting torque and full load torque for this method of starting.

Let $I_{st}$, $I_{f.l.}$ be the currents drawn by motor at the time of starting and full load respectively.

Now, from
$$T \alpha \frac{I_2^2 R_2}{S}$$

S at start is one, and let $S_{f.l.}$ be the slip at load.

Then,
$$T_s \alpha\ I_2^2 R_2 \qquad \ldots (1)$$

and
$$T_{f.l.} \alpha\ \frac{I_2^2 R_2}{S_n} \qquad \ldots (2)$$

or
$$\frac{T_s}{T_{f.l.}} = \left(\frac{I_{2st}}{I_{2f.l.}}\right)^2 S_{f.l.} \qquad ...(3)$$

Neglecting small no load current,
$$\frac{I_{2st}}{I_{2f.l.}} = \frac{I_{st}}{I_{f.l.}}$$

where $I_{st}$ and $I_{f.l.}$ represent stator currents at start and at load

$$\therefore \quad \frac{T_s}{T_{f.l.}} = \left(\frac{I_{2st}}{I_{2f.l.}}\right)^2 \times S_{f.l.}$$

But $I_{st}$ is equal to short circuit current and can be represented as $I_{sc}$.

$$\therefore \quad \frac{T_s}{T_{f.l.}} = \left(\frac{I_{2sc}}{I_{2f.l.}}\right)^2 S_{f.l.} \qquad ...(4)$$

**(b) Reduced Voltage Starting :** As in cage motors there is no possibility of adding any resistance etc. In rotor circuit, the starting current can be reduced by application of reduced voltage at starting to the stator winding.

If we reduce the stator voltage from rated by a fraction, then the short circuit current will change in same proportion, and the magnetising current will also reduce the core losses will reduce at the same time the starting torque will reduce by $x^2$ times its normal value.

The reduced voltage can be applied by the following methods:
(i) Stator reactor (or resistance) method.
(ii) Auto transformer starting method.
(iii) Star delta starting.

**(i) Stator Reactor or Resistance Starting :** In this method, the applied voltage to the stator is reduced by connecting balanced resistors or reactors in series with stator winding terminals as shown in Fig. 3.64. At starting the voltage drop across the resistors or reactors reduces the voltage to the stator to a fraction x of the normal value, which will reduce the starting current of the motor. As the motor speeds up, the resistors or reactors are cut out in steps and finally short circuited when motor runs at normal speed.

Mostly, in this method reactors are preferred because the power loss in them is less, they are more effective in reducing the voltage and the current through them is nearly in phase with motor currents.

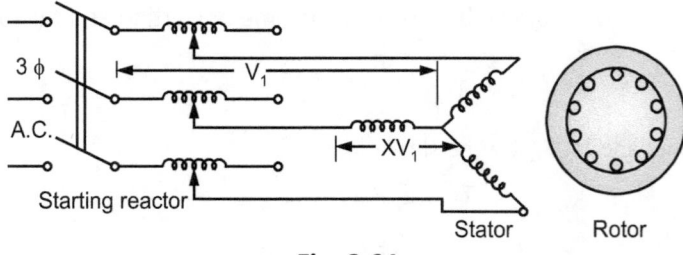

**Fig. 3.64**

Let $V_1$ – Normal voltage/phase applied to stator

$X V_1$ – Reduced voltage/phase applied to stator at the time of starting

$\therefore \qquad I_{st} = \dfrac{x V_1}{Z_{sc}}$

where, $Z_{sc}$ impedance of motor referred to stator

$\therefore \qquad I_{st} = \dfrac{V_1}{Z_{sc}} =$ S.C. current at rated voltage

$\therefore \qquad I_{st} = x I_{sc}$

and $\qquad \dfrac{T_{st}}{T_{f.l.}} = \left(\dfrac{I_{st}}{I_{f.l.}}\right)^2 S_{f.l.}$

or $\qquad \dfrac{T_{st}}{T_{f.l.}} = \left(\dfrac{x I_{sc}}{I_{f.l.}}\right)^2 \times S_n = x^2 \left(\dfrac{I_{sc}}{I_{f.l.}}\right)^2 \times S_{f.l.}$

and $\qquad \dfrac{\text{Starting torque with reactor starting}}{\text{Starting torque with D.O.L. starting}} = x^2$

**(ii) Auto Transfer Starting :** At the time of starting I.M. by this method fraction $x V_1$ of supply voltage $V_1$ is applied to the stator terminals with the help of auto transformer as shown in Fig. 3.65 (a). As the motor gets speed connections are so changed that auto transformers are cut out and full supply voltage is applied across motor terminals.

This change in connection is either achieved by an air-break switch or oil immersed switch, to reduce the sparking. In such starter there is also made a provision of no volt protection and over load protection. Generally, auto transformer starters are provided with three sets of taps so as to reduce voltage to 50%, 65% or 80% depending upon supply voltage conditions. Sometimes `V' connected auto transformer starters are used due to low cost, such starter produce an unbalance current during starting.

For determining relations for motor current, line current and torque developed we will take the following simple Fig. 3.65 (a) represents stator connected across rated voltage $V_1$/phase and stator winding being connected in star Fig. 3.65 (b) represents star connected stator winding being connected through auto transformer which connects voltage equal to $xV_1$ at starting across motor terminals at the time of starting, where x is ratio of auto - transformer used at the time of starting.

Now, starting current/phase in stator winding.

$$I_{st} = \dfrac{x V_i}{Z_{sc}} \times I_{sc} \qquad \ldots (1)$$

If we take phase values of voltage impedance etc.

If no load current of auto transformer is neglected VA input/phase to auto transformer equal to VA output of auto transformer.

i.e. $\qquad I_L V_1 = x V_1 I_{st}$

or $\qquad I_{st} = \dfrac{I_L}{x} \qquad \ldots (2)$

From equations (1) and (2),

$$\frac{I_L}{x} = x I_{sc}$$

or
$$I_L = x^2 I_s$$

In case of reactor starting, $I_{st} = x I_{sc}$

<u>Per phase starting current from supply with auto transformer starting</u>
Per phase current (starting) from supply with stator reactor starting

$$= \frac{x^2 I_{sc}}{x I_{sc}} = x$$

From
$$\frac{T_{st}}{T_{f.l.}} = \left(\frac{I_{st}}{I_{f.l.}}\right)^2 S_{f.l.}$$

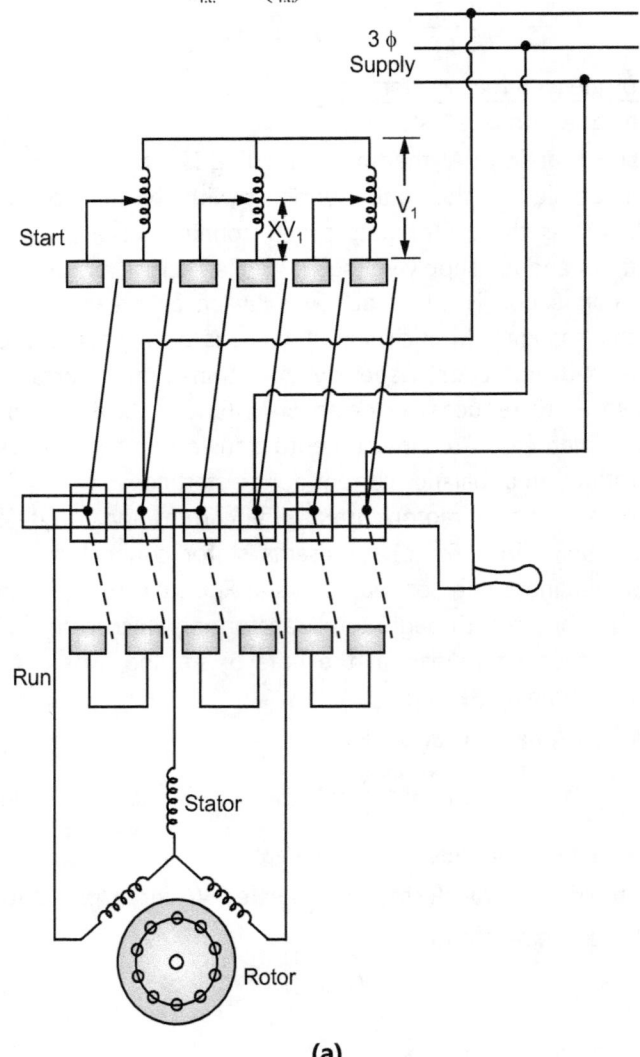

(a)

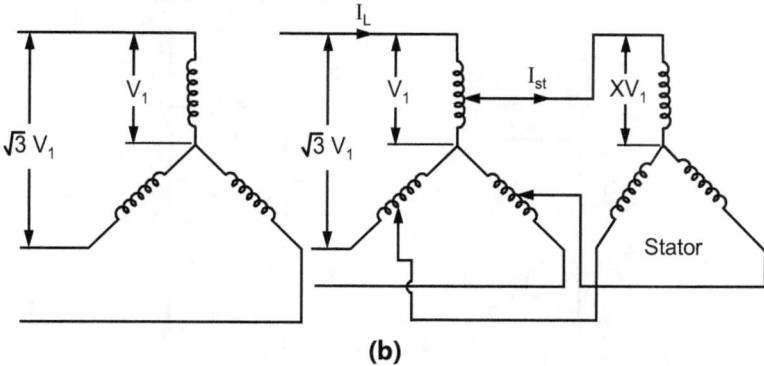

**Fig. 3.65**

$$\therefore \frac{\text{Starting torque with auto transformer starting}}{\text{Starting torque with D.O.L. starting}} = x^2$$

And starting torque with auto transformer starting = Starting torque with reactor starting

## 3.4.1 Star Delta Starting

This method is generally used in case of motors which are generally run in delta connection, but not permanently connect so. Connection diagram of a star delta starter is given in Fig. 3.65. Mostly this method is used for cage motors but can also be used in case of slip ring motor if required so. At starting the stator winding is connected in star connection when the triple pole change over switch is connected to position one. After the motor has reached nearly steady state speed, the change over switch is put in position 2, so the motor is connected in delta.

Let the line voltage be $V_L$, then the starting current per phase with stator winding in star is given by

$$I_y = \frac{V_L}{\sqrt{3}\, Z_{sc}} \qquad \ldots (3.65)$$

with delta connected winding the motor starting current/phase would have been

$$I_d = \frac{V_L}{Z_{sc}} \qquad \ldots (3.66)$$

as
$$V_L = V_{ph}$$

and the line current at starting

$$I_{L\delta} = \sqrt{3}\, I_d \qquad \ldots (3.67)$$

From the line current at starting with star connected winding $I_L$ star

$$I_y = \frac{V_L}{\sqrt{3}\, Z_{sc}} = \frac{I_d}{\sqrt{3}} \qquad \ldots (3.68)$$

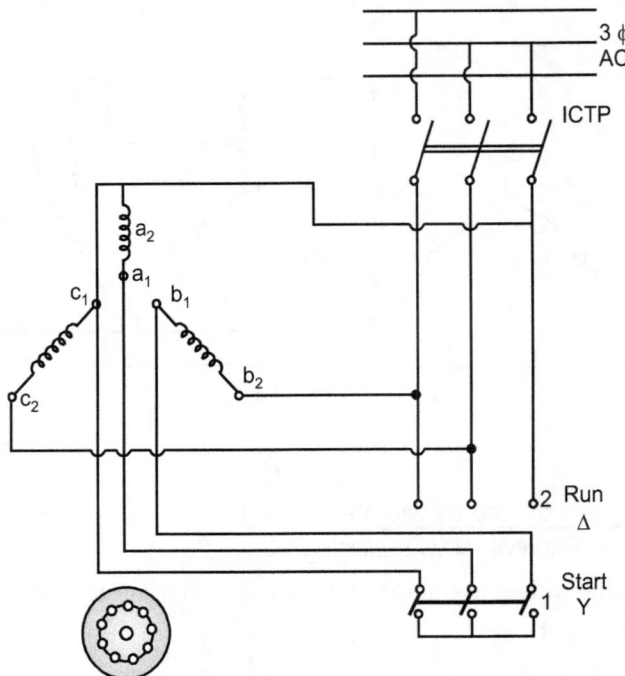

**Fig. 3.65 (c)**

Hence, from equations (3.67) and (3.68),

$$\frac{\text{Starting line current with stator in star}}{\text{Starting line current with stator in }\delta} = \frac{I_d/\sqrt{3}}{\sqrt{3}\, I_d}$$

Starting line current with stator in delta

Again, 
$$\frac{T_y}{T_{f.l.}} = \left(\frac{I_y}{I_{f.l.}}\right)^2 \times S_{f.l.}$$

and 
$$\frac{T_d}{T_{f.l.}} = \left(\frac{I_d}{I_{f.l.}}\right)^2 \times S_{f.l.} \qquad \ldots (3.69)$$

From equations (7) and (8),

$$\frac{T_y}{T_d} = \left(\frac{I_y}{I_d}\right)^2 = \left(\frac{I_d}{\sqrt{3}\, I_d}\right)^2 = \frac{1}{3}$$

Therefore, $\dfrac{\text{Starting torque with stator in star}}{\text{Starting torque with stator in }\delta} = \dfrac{1}{3}$

From equations (3.69) and (3.70) it is seen that with star delta connection starter a motor behaves as if it is started by auto transformer with a ratio $x = \dfrac{1}{\sqrt{3}} = 0.58$ i.e. with 58% tapping.

This method is cheap effective and is used extensively. This method is most suited for applications where starting torque not more than 50% of full load is required. This is not used beyond 3.3 kV due to limitations in design of motors above 3.3 kV.

## 3.4.2 Starting of Wound Rotor Motors

All methods used for starting of squirrel cage induction motor can be used for starting wound rotor I.M., but in general these methods are not used of wound rotor induction motor, because then we will loose the advantages of wound rotor.

The simplest and cheapest method of starting is by adding external resistance in rotor circuit and applying full rated voltage across stator terminals.

This method of starting has the following advantages :

(i) It reduces the starting current hence jerks on distribution or generating system are avoided.

(ii) It increases the starting torque, it is possible to obtain starting toque equal to pull out torque.

(iii) It improves the p.f. at the time of starting.

(iv) Energy loss at the time of starting is less.

In this method of starting, the rotor winding is star connected and the three ends are connected to three slip rings on the shaft. These slip rings are then connected to external resistances through brushes as shown in Fig. 3.66 (a).

At the time of starting the entire external resistance is placed in series with the rotor winding, as the motor accelerates, the external resistance is cut in steps so that the available electromagnetic torque remains maximum during accelerating period. Finally, under normal conditions the external resistance is fully cut off and the slip rings are short circuited, so that motor operates on its inherent character giving full load torque at low value of slip.

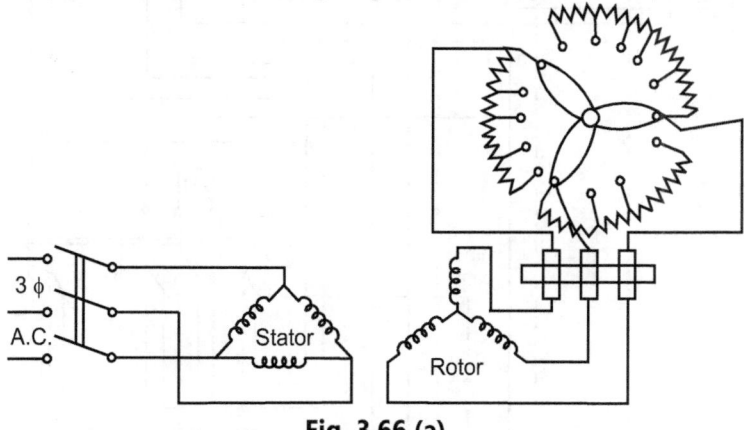

**Fig. 3.66 (a)**

**Circuits for Different Starters :**

Fig. 3.66 (b) represents the circuit diagram for a direct on line starter used for motor upto 5 H.P.

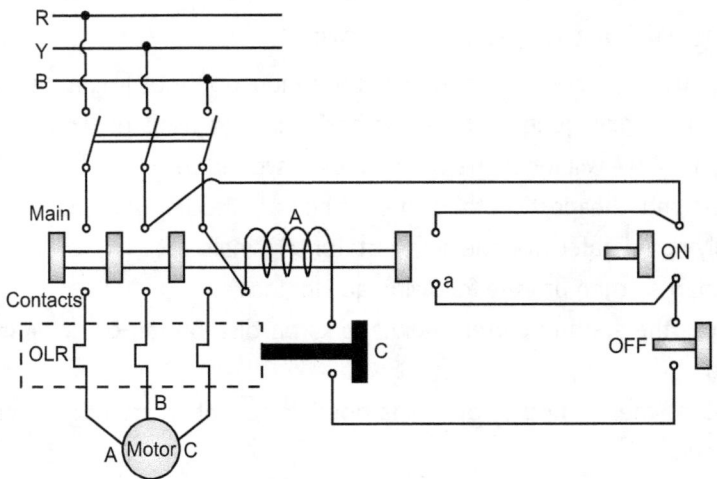

**Fig 3.66 (b)**

## 3.4.3 Star - Delta Starter

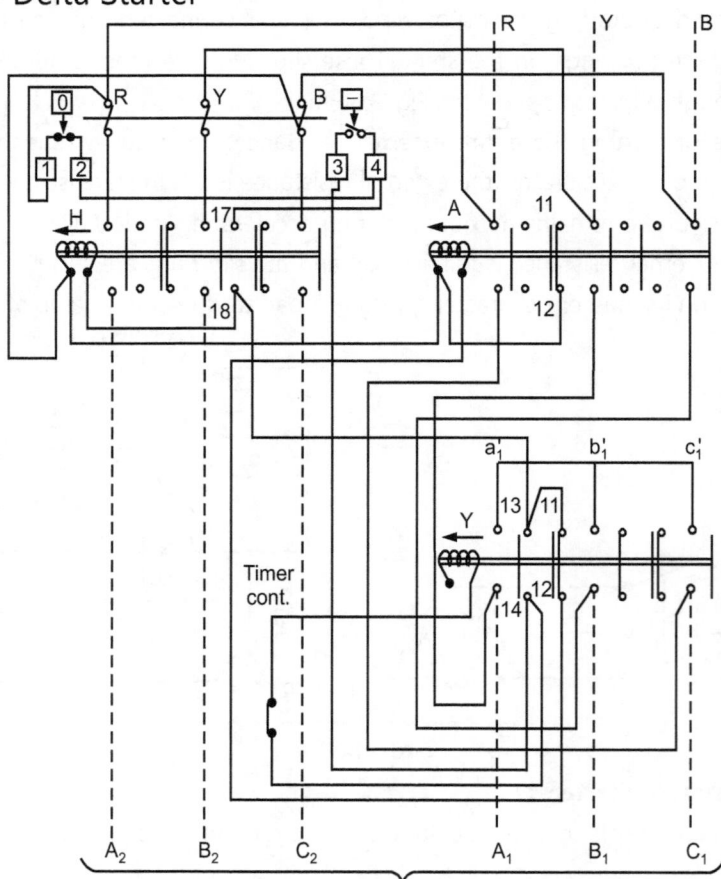

**Fig. 3.67: Fully automatic star - delta starter**

When push button ON is pushed, coil A is connected across line voltage, hence it will get energised, and closes the main contact. The motor will start. Now when ON button is released, the coil get current through auxiliary contact A when OFF button is pressed coil A will get de-energised and main contacts will open disconnecting motor from supply. In case of failure supply again. A will get de-energised and main contacts will open, hence coil A can be called as no volt coil also. When motor is over loaded, the bi-metallic strips on O.L.R. will bend, when this bend goes beyond set value, it opens contact C, disconnecting supply to coil A which will release main contacts opening the supply.

**Example 3.47:** Find the % tappling required on an auto transformer for starting a cage motor against 25% of full load torque, if directs switching current is 6 times full load current and full load slip is 5%.

**Solution:** In case of auto transformer stator

$$\frac{T_{st}}{T_{f.l.}} = x^2 \left(\frac{I_{sc}}{I_{f.l.}}\right)^2 S_{f.l.}$$

$$0.25 = x^2 (6)^2 \times 0.05$$

$$x^2 = 0.139 \text{ or } x = 0.373$$

or % tapping = 37.3%

**Example 3.48:** An induction motor with direct switching, draws 100 amps. Using auto transformer starter the current is to be reduced to 25 amps. Draw in detail the auto transformer connections, its exact tappings. What protections this starter can have.

**Solution:** Using relation, $I_L = x^2 I_{sc}$

$$25 = x^2 \, 100$$

or $x^2 = 0.25$

∴ $x = 0.5$

For other details see theory.

**Example 3.49:** The short circuit current of an induction motor is 7 times its full load current. The full load slip is 5%. Calculate the ratio of stating torque with star delta starter to full load torque.

**Solution:**

$$\frac{T_{st}}{T_{f.l.}} = \frac{1}{3} \times \left(\frac{I_{sc}}{I_{f.l.}}\right)^2 \times S_{f.l.}$$

$$= \frac{1}{3} (7)^2 \times 0.05$$

$$\frac{T_{st}}{T_{f.l.}} = 0.817$$

**Example 3.50:** Find out the starting torque of an induction motor in terms of full load torque when started by means of
(a) Star delta starter.
(b) An auto transformer stater with 60% tappings.

The short circuit current of motor at normal voltage is 5 times the full load current and full load slip is 4%.

**Solution:** (a) For star delta starter

$$\frac{T_{st}}{T_{f.l.}} = \frac{1}{3}\left(\frac{I_{sc}}{I_{f.l.}}\right)^2 \times S_{f.l.}$$

$$= \frac{1}{3} \times 5^2 \times 0.04$$

or

$$\frac{T_{st}}{T_{f.l.}} = 0.333$$

or $T_{st} = 0.33\ T_{f.l.}$ or 33.3% f.l. value.

(b) Here, $x = 0.6$

∴ $x^2 = 0.36$

Now,

$$x^2 = \frac{T_{st}}{T_{f.l.}} S_{f.l.} \left(\frac{I_{sc}}{I_{f.l.}}\right)^2$$

$$= 0.36 \times 5^2 \times 0.04 = 0.36$$

or $T_{st} = 36\%\ T_{f.l.}$

## 3.4.4 Speed Control of I.M.

In industrial applications, D.C. motors are preferred to a induction motor drive as they provide a very wide range and smooth variation of speeds. But use of D.C. drives requires to convert A.C. into D.C. which will cause certain loss of energy and also additional capital investment, due to above reasons preference is given to adjustable speed, induction motor drives, as they are cheaper, robust in construction and economical in operation and maintenance. A plain induction motor is essentially a constant speed motor and it has low operating p.f.

There are number of methods, for control of speed of induction motors, out of which some control the speed only while others will have a effect on p.f. also.

Some of the methods used for speed control of three phase induction motors may be as follows :
   (i) Variation of supply voltage
   (ii) Frequency variation
   (iii) Variation of number of poles
   (iv) Variation of motor resistance or reactance
   (v) Injected e.m.f. methods.

### 3.4.4.1 Variation of Supply Voltage

From the torque equation of an induction motor it is seen that, it is proportional to square of supply voltage and the slip at maximum torque is independent of supply voltage. Also variation of supply voltage does not change the synchronous speed of I.M. The speed characteristics for a three phase I.M. varying supply voltage are shown in Fig. 3.68 from which it is seen that for a given load the speed of the motor can be varied with small range by this method as this method having the following disadvantages is not generally used.

(a) Operation at high voltage result into magnetic saturation.

(b) Developed torque will reduce greatly by reducing of supply voltage.

(c) The range of speed control is very limited in the downward.

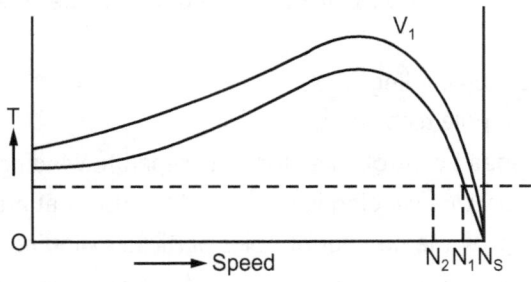

**Fig. 3.68**

### 3.4.4.2 Variation of Supply Frequency

Supply agency offers supply at constant frequency, hence change in supply frequency is not possible ordinarily. In case, electric propulsion of ships, where alternators are used to supply electricity to propelling motors on ships. It is possible to change the frequency of electric supply.

(i) by changing the speed of prime movers of alternators or

(ii) having two alternators which work at two different frequency, say for example 40 Hz and 60 Hz.

Since, the speed of the propeller is very low, a motor with say 36 Nos. of poles will drive the propeller motor to run at synchronous speed of 133 r.p.m. at 40 Hz supply. When the speed of the propeller motor is to be increased, it is connected to another alternator giving 60 Hz supply, so that propeller motor will run at a synchronous speed of 200 rpm. At the same time of going faster the propeller will require greater power. This increased power can be supplied by the 40 Hz alternator to another motor having 24 poles so that the synchronous speed of the second motor will be 200 rpm.

### 3.4.4.3 Variation of Poles

As we know that the synchronous speed of induction motor given by $N_s = \dfrac{120\,f}{p}$ where p is number of poles, and f is supply frequency will change if number of stator poles are changed.

A steady electromagnetic torque is produced when stator number of poles is equal to rotor number of poles. Hence only change in the stator number of poles must be accompanied by an equal change in the number of rotor poles. In case of wound rotor windings are wound for a given poles hence any change in stator number will not result a similar change in rotor. Hence this method is restricted to squirrel cage rotors as the squirrel rotors will always develop equal number as that of the stator by induction.

The variation of number of poles of stator winding can be effected by the following methods :

(a) use of multiple stator winding.

(b) use of consequent pole techniques.

**(a)** For this type of speed control, in stator slots separate windings for number, of poles are carried out, of that only one winding is connected to supply at a time, so that the motor runs at speed represented by the number of poles particular winding. The use of this system therefore limited to two speed motors change over from one speed to other may be made by a mechanical switch or by contractors. In order to avoid circulating currents and consequent heating the winding not in use is open circuited.

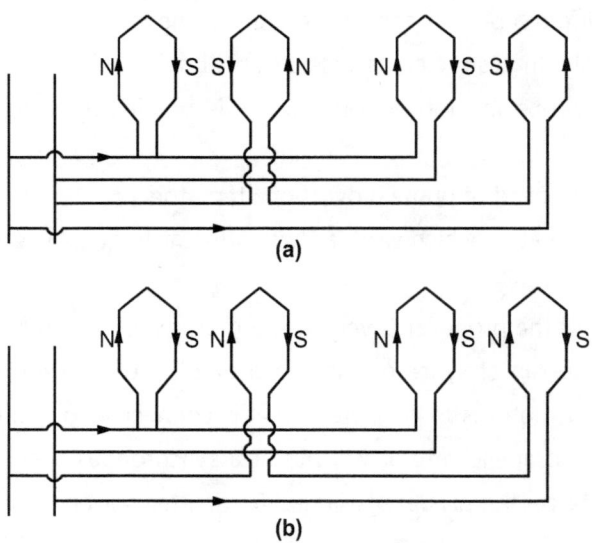

**Fig. 3.69**

**(b) Change of poles :** The change in number of stator winding poles is carried out by changing the stator winding connections with the help of suitable switching arrangement. When the desired speed ratio is 2 : 1, the consequent pole method is used there are two separate windings on the stator which produce same number of poles. Out of that one winding produces two N poles and the of other winding produces two south poles, the complete arrangement is as shown in Fig. 3.69 (a) producing four poles and a synchronous speed of 1500 r.p.m. If the connections of one of the windings is changed and made as shown in Fig. 3.69 (b). They will produce 4N poles and 4S poles, depending, upon which of the winding connection is revised.

### 3.4.4.4 Variation of Motor Resistance or Reactance Method

**(a) Variation of rotor resistance :** The variation of rotor resistance is possible only is case of wound rotor induction motors, as external resistance can be inserted in rotor circuit through slip rings. We know that at maximum torque $R_2 = SX_2$, but the value of maximum torque is independent of rotor resistance, but the slip for the maximum torque is proportional to rotor resistance. Fig. 3.70 represents the torque speed characteristics of an induction motor with varying rotor resistances. It is observed that motor speed decrease with the increase of rotor resistance. Hence by this method, speed control from rated speed in a downward direction is possible. Speed control by this method is stepped, but it can be made smooth if large number of sections of external resistance are provided.

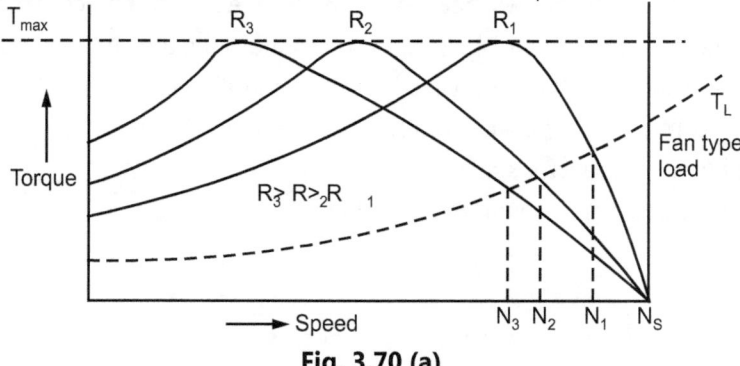

**Fig. 3.70 (a)**

This is a very simple method of speed control, with this method it is possible to have large starting torque, low starting current and large pull out torques at low values of slip. The circuit is as shown in Fig. 3.70 (b).

The main drawback of this method is the power loss in external resistance at low speeds, which are responsible for reducing the efficiency of motor at low speeds. Hence, such a method is not used for speed control at constant torque. But it is widely used where the load on the motor is having fan type torque characteristics as shown in Fig. 3.70, where it is seen that the power input will drop as the speed is reduced, which in term will reduce the rotor Cu losses as they are equal to S times rotor input. This method is not used for continuous speed control. It has another disadvantage that the speed regulation with change of load is poor.

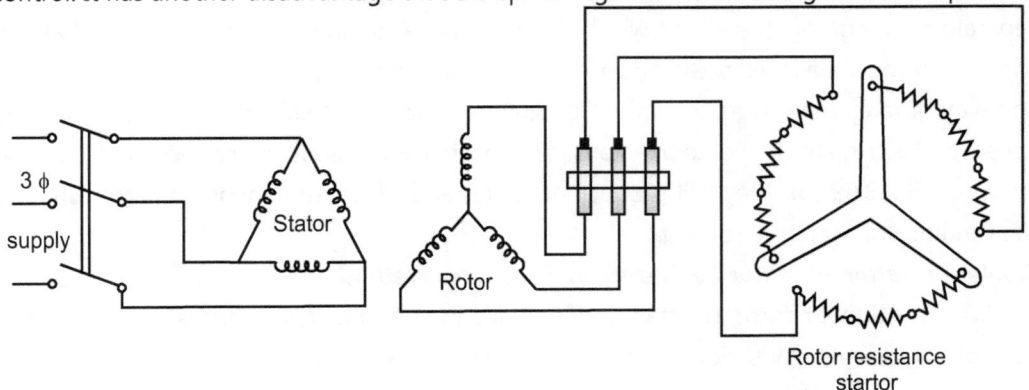

**Fig. 3.70 (b)**

**(b) Reactance Variation :** Stator reactance can be changed in both type of induction motors, while rotor reactance can only be changed in case of slip ring I.M. the speed control can be obtained by changing either the rotor reactance or stator reactance.

From the maximum torque condition it is seen that if equivalent reactance is increased by inserting external reactance in stator or rotor circuit, slip for maximum torque will decrease. The torque speed characteristics will decreased. The torque speed characteristics with varying equivalent reactance are shown in Fig. 3.70 (c), which indicates the speed control is achieved from rated lower speeds, in the downward direction and also the range of speed control is limited. Speed control is obtained in steps but smoother control can be obtained by increasing the number of reactor steps.

$X_1$, $X_2$, $X_3$ represents the equivalent reactance

$X_3 > X_2 > X_1$

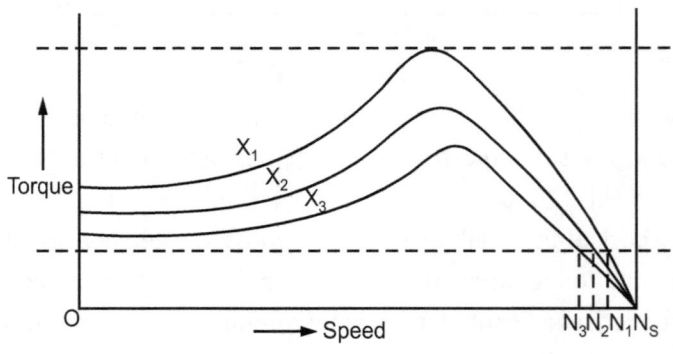

**Fig. 3.70 (c)**

# 3.4.5 (a) Tandem Speed Control or Speed control by Concatenation (Cascade)

In this method, the speed is changed by changing the slip of one motor, which changes the frequency supplied to the other motor. The two motors are connected rigidly together.

In this method, line frequency is supplied to the stator of motor no. 1. This motor should have a one to one ratio of transformation between stator and rotor, at stand still i.e. voltage across slip rings should be equal to line voltage. Let the two motors be similar and the rotors operate at slightly less than half the synchronous speed of the first motor. The rotor frequency of motor no. 1 is slightly greater than half line frequency. The synchronous speed of motor two therefore is about half that of motor no. 1. The rotors so adjust their speed that their combined torque is just sufficient to carry the load. Each rotor will operate at a speed which is slightly less than half the synchronous speed of the first motor. Various speeds for combinations in which the two motors have a different number of poles may be determined as follows.

Let N r.p.m. be the speed of combinations $f_1$ be the frequency for machine no. 1 and $f_2$ be the frequency for machine no. 2, $P_1$ and $P_2$ be their respective number of poles and $S_1$ and $S_2$ be the respective slips.

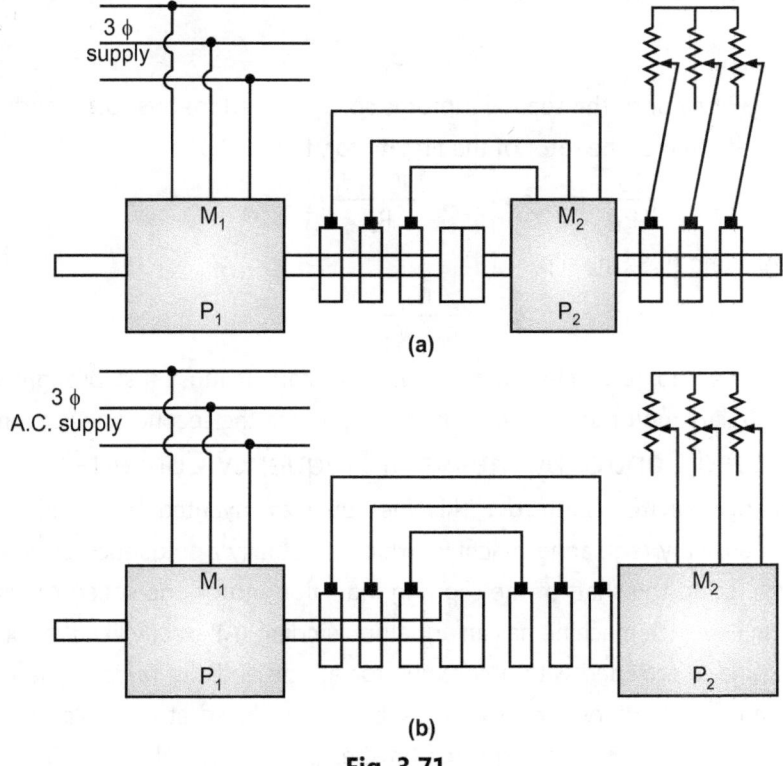

**Fig. 3.71**

Then the first machine will rotate at a speed

$$N_1 = \frac{120 f_1}{P_1} (1 - S_1) \qquad \ldots (3.70)$$

Speed of second machine, $\quad N_2 = \frac{120 f_2}{P_2} (1 - S_2) \qquad \ldots (3.71)$

But

$$\frac{120 f_2}{P_2} = \frac{120 S_1 f_1}{P_2}$$

$\therefore \qquad N_2 = \frac{120 S_1 f_1}{P_2} (1 - S_2)$

As the two motors are coupled mechanically,

$$N_1 = N_2$$

∴ Equation (1) and (2),

$$\frac{120 f_1}{P_1} (1 - S_1) = \frac{120 S_1 f_1}{P_2} (1 - S_2)$$

or

$$S_1 = \frac{P_2}{P_1 + P_2 - P_1 S_2} \qquad \ldots (3.72)$$

As $P_1 S_2$ is very small in comparison with $P_1 + P_2$ when the combination is operating near its synchronous speed, it can be neglected.

Hence, $\qquad S_1 = \frac{P_2}{P_2 + P_1} \qquad \ldots (3.73)$

If the stator or rotor of the second motor is so connected that its rotor tends to turn in a direction opposite that of the rotor of the first motor, then

$$\frac{120 f_1}{P_1} (1 - S_1) = - \frac{120 S_1 f_1}{P_2} (1 - S_2)$$

again neglecting $P_1 S_2$ the slip,

$$S_1 = \frac{P_2}{P_2 - P_1} \qquad \ldots (3.74)$$

When rotor are so connected, the set will not start. It must first brought upto speed either by an auxiliary motor or by one motor alone, before the second one is connected.

## 3.4.5 (b) Speed Control by Means of Frequency Converter

**The Leblance exciter method :** This method was invented by Maurise-Lablance. It consists of an auxiliary regulating machine, which is actually a frequency converter which is directly connected to the shaft of the slip ring induction motor, the speed of which is to be controlled. The Leblance machine has an armature winding (A) exactly like that of an ordinary D.C. machine and is provided with a commutator at one end slip rings at the other end, in the same manner as a rotary converter. Brushes are displaced at intervals of 120° elect. In case of three phase unit, there being three brushes per pair of poles and these brushes are connected to the slip rings of the main motor. The slip rings of the frequency converter are connected through tap changing transformers or other voltage regulating device, to main supply lines having frequency $f_1$. The stator frame of the frequency converter is a laminated cylindrical ring without any windings.

Fig. 3.72 represents diagrammatically a side view of frequency converter for a two pole machine. Current at frequency $f_1$ supplied from the lines through slip rings $SR_1$ will produce a magnetic field rotating at synchronous speed w.r.t. winding A. Let the magnetic field be moving in clockwise direction relative to A and that the latter be driven in anticlockwise direction, the motor M at a speed $N_2 = N_1 (1 - S)$, where $N_1$ is the synchronous speed of the magnetic field of M. If A and M both are wound for same number of poles, the magnetic field due to winding A will rotate in space at slip speed $N_1 S$.

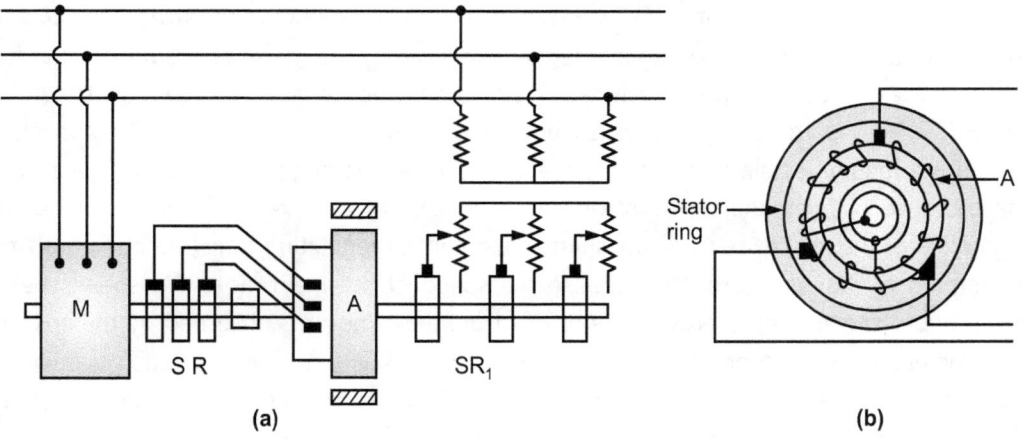

**Fig. 3.72**

The function of the stationary cylindrical smooth core stator winding A is simply to provide a path of low and uniform reluctance for this magnetic field, as it rotates slowly w.r.t. brushes on the commutator. It is then obvious that each of the sections of windings A lying between adjacent brushes always represents the same aspect to the magnetic field which is moving relative at slip speed, so that the frequency of the voltage generated in the turns between brushes is always slip frequency. Because of the fact that the brushes and the slip rings associated with winding A are physically related in the same manner as in a rotary converter the ratio of the brush voltage to the slip ring voltage is definitely fixed regardless of speed, but by rocking in brushes one way or the other, the phase of the brush voltage (of slip frequency) can be altered at voltage (of slip frequency) can be altered at will through any desired angle. Finally, by adjusting the ratio of transformation of the regulating transformer T, the magnitude of the brush voltage is likewise brought under control.

The Leblance A.C. exciter therefore makes it possible to inject into the rotor of the induction motor a voltage which may be adjusted over a considerable range, and which always has the proper frequency, mover over, its phase is adjustable by rocking the brushes. Variation of the magnitude of this voltage will then cause the speed of the induction motor to rise or fall as desired within the limits fixed by design. The control of the phase of the auxiliary voltage automatically controls the phase of the rotor current of the induction motor and therefore the phase of the stator current as well. Since, the m.m.f.s of the rotor and the stator currents are tied together by the requirement that their resultant shall yield the constant flux, in other wards, the p.f. of the induction motor can be adjusted as well as its speed.

## 3.4.6 The Kramer System

In case of steel rolling mills, it is necessary to supply large amount of power coupled with flexible control of speed. These requirements are fulfilled by the Kramer system.

It utilises a commutator machine, direct connected to main motor, as shown in Fig. 3.73. The slip frequency impressed upon the stator winding of the auxiliary machine develops a magnetic field rotating in space at the corresponding slip speed, and because of the presence of commutator the rotor e.m.f. and current will likewise have slip frequency regardless of the actual speed of the shaft adjustment of regulating transformer controls the magnitude of the rotor e.m.f., hence also the speed of the main motor. At speeds below synchronous the surplus energy in the rotor of the main motor is absorbed by the auxiliary machine acting as a motor, and there by causing the auxiliary machine to supply part of the mechanical load and to some extent relieve the load from main motor. The size of the auxiliary machine is determined by the amount of speed adjustment required.

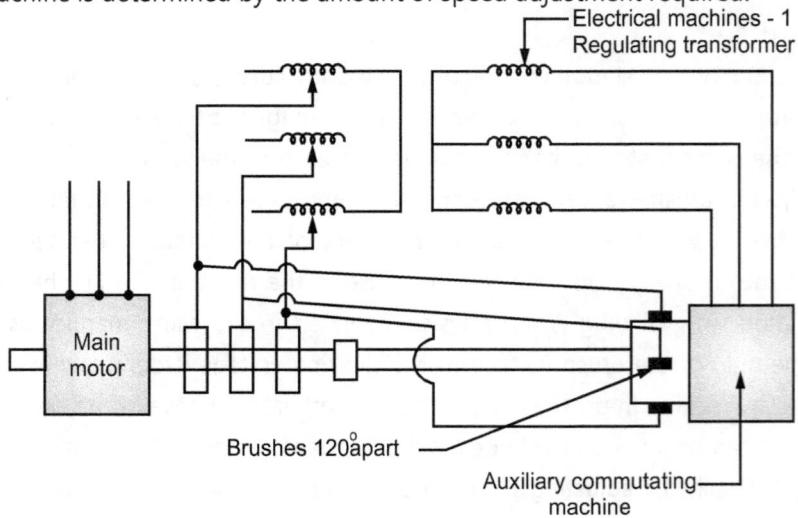

**Fig. 3.73**

Theoretically this arrangement permits p.f. control by shifting brushes of the commutating machine, but practically it is restricted by the circumstances that commutation difficulties limit the possible range of brush shift.

## 3.4.7 Squirrel Cage Motors with High Starting Torque

(i) Changing stator or rotor connections
(ii) Using composite rotor bars.
(iii) Double cage construction.

### 3.4.7.1 Changing Stator or Rotor Connections

One of the methods used to obtain a high starting toque in case of squirrel cage induction motors with change of connections is shown in Fig. 3.74 (a) and Fig. 3.74 (b). In this case, the stator and rotor are made in two parts. The polarities of the stator poles in the two parts are one pole pitch out of phase as shown in Fig. 3.74 (a). Rotor is also made in two parts each part has low resistance end ring and the two parts are connected together with a central high resistance ring as shown in Fig. 3.74 (a). Each part of the rotor is under the influence of the field of one of the stator parts. At starting the field from the two parts have a phase difference of one pole pitch hence the e.m.f. in the rotor bars of the two parts is in opposite direction, so that more current passes through high resistance ring. Hence, high torque is developed but for normal running condition, the connections of the stator are so changed of at the phase displacement of the stator poles in the two parts do not exist, as shown in Fig. 3.74 (b) and now practically zero current passes in the middle ring, and the machine behaves as an ordinary cage induction motor.

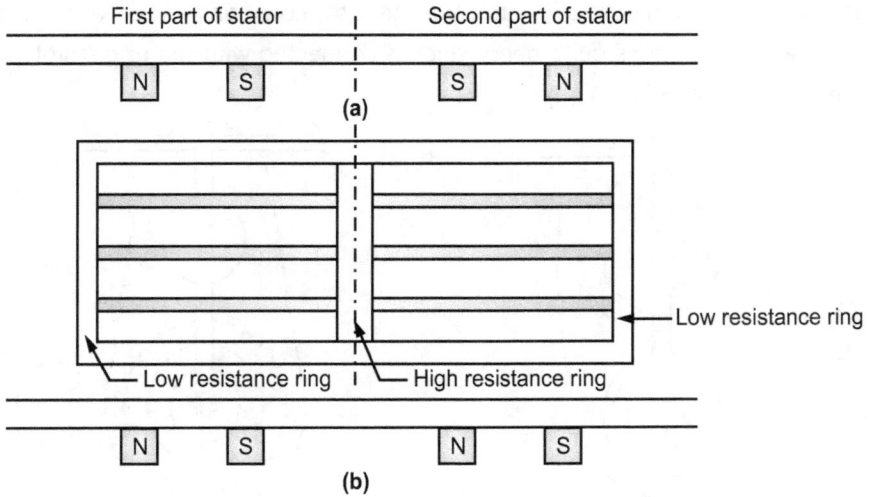

**Fig. 3.74**

### 3.4.7.2 Skin Effect OR Using Composite Rotor Bars

Composite conductor consists of a copper conductor at the centre over which is put up a seamless sheath of copper plated steel, only for the portion of the conductor within the slots. At the time of starting, frequency of rotor currents is equal to supply frequency hence due to steel sheath the skin effect is increased to a large extent, which results in increasing the A.C. resistance. At normal speeds of induction motor, the frequency of rotor current is much less, which will reduce the skin effect also, and the resistance of sheath is more compared with resistance of conductor, the current is confined to the inner copper core.

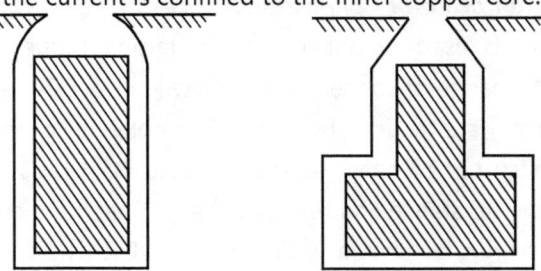

**Fig. 3.75**

Similar effect can also be obtained by using solid thick conductors in deep slots due to which the skin effect increases and there is also an increase in eddy currents which are proportional to the fourth power of the conductor depth such effect can also be developed by using the iron end rings.

### 3.4.7.3 Double Cage Rotors

The construction of stator for double cage type induction motor is just similar to that of the ordinary squirrel cage induction motor, but the rotor core consists of two slots, one near the periphery and the other is quite deep which is connected with the upper slot with a this slit as represented in Fig. 3.76 (a), (b).

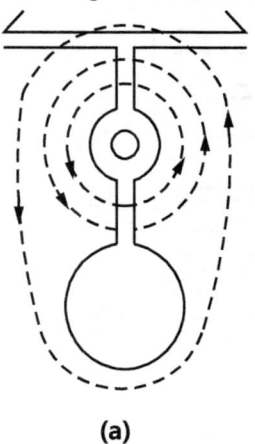
(a)

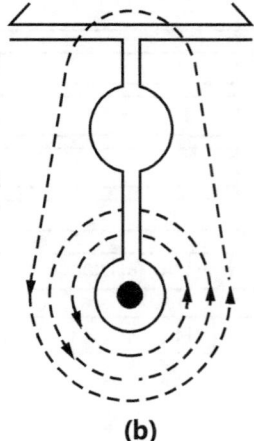
(b)

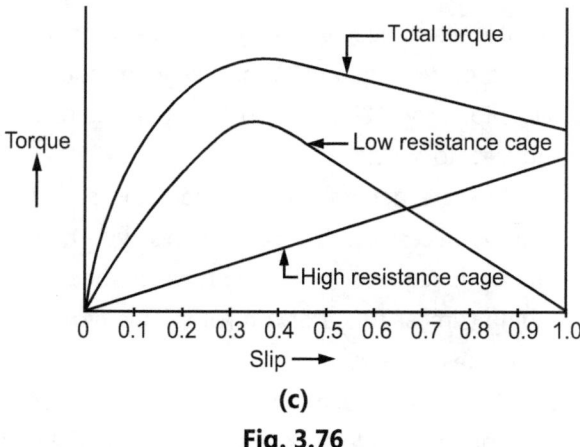

**Fig. 3.76**

The upper slot consists of conductors having low cross-sectional area, or having high resistance and into the bottom slots are placed conductors of very small resistance i.e. having more cross-sectional area but as they are embedded deep in the core portion they have large leakage reactance in comparison with conductors placed in outer periphery.

At starting frequency of rotor currents being same as that of supply, the reactance of the bottom conductors becomes very high which will not allow more current to flow through it, hence the rotor current is made to flow through the high resistance upper layer bars, which results in the high starting torque, but after the motor has gain speed, the frequency of the rotor currents becomes small hence the reactance of the lower layer conductors also reduces to a small value the effect being impedance of bottom conductors becomes much less than resistance at upper layer conductors, the result is rotor current shifts from top conductors to bottom conductors of low resistance, thus it maintains high torque at normal running too. Fig. 3.76 (a) represents slot when outer (top) conductor carries the current and Fig. 3.76 (b) when bottom conductor carries the current Fig. 3.76 (c) represents the torque slip curves due to individual cages and the combined effect.

## 3.4.8 Application of Induction Motors

Squirrel cage induction motors are simple and rugged in construction, the cost is low and they need negligible maintenance, hence they are used for the loads which require low starting torque and substantially constant speeds. Squirrel cage motors may be designed with low resistance or high rotor resistance. A high rotor resistance will give better starting conditions but it gives a poor running performance, while a squirrel cage motor having low rotor resistance will give poor starting conditions but better running performance.

Squirrel cage motors designed for low rotor resistance having a full load slip from 3 to 5% are used for fans, centrifugal pumps, machine tool, wood working tools etc. Cage motors having some what more rotor resistance i.e. giving full load slip nearly 3 to 7% are used for compressors, crushers, reciprocating pumps. While cage motors having still more rotor resistance giving full load slip 7 to 16% are used for intermittent loads such as punching presses, shears, hoists and elevators etc.

Slip-ring induction motors are generally used where the speed control is required or where high starting torque is necessary: The cost of this type of motor is much more in comparison to a cage motor, it requires more maintenance, because of brushes, slip rings and the three phase winding (similar to stator) on rotor. This type of motor car be used for hoists, cranes, elevators, compressors etc.

Comparison of cage and slip ring induction motor having same power rating :
1. A cage motor will require considerably less copper material to carry out its windings on stator and rotor in comparison with a slip ring induction motor hence its Cu losses will be less, cost will be low and efficiency will be more than a slip ring I.M.
2. In case of slip ring I.M., slip rings, brushes and short circuiting device for slip-rings is required. It will increase the cost of slipping I.M.
3. A squirrel cage I.M. has very small length of overhang leakage flux. Hence, leakage reactance of cage type of rotor is less in comparison with wound rotor; it results into cage motor having more pull out torque, greater maximum power output, and good operating p.f. as compared to wound rotor induction motor.
4. Squirrel cage motors are more rugged in construction, and does not consists slip-ring brushes etc. hence low maintenance and low maintenance cost.
5. Cooling effect in case of cage rotor is better because of their base and rings.

The disadvantages of cage motor in comparison to a slip-ring I.M. are as follows :
(i) Small starting torque.
(ii) Large starting current.
(iii) Poor starting p.f.
(iv) Energy loss during starting is more.

## 3.4.9 Operating Characteristics and Influence of Machine Parameters on the Performance of the Motor

**1. Power factor :** When the I.M. runs at no load, the stator current/phase $I_0$ of two comments i.e. $I_u$ and $I_w$ : $I_u$ being higher than the working component $I_w$, the no load current $I_0$ lags supply voltage $V_1$ by $\phi_0$, which is large so the p.f. if very low, which may be 0.2 to 0.3.

When the motor is loaded, the stator current is $I_1$ amps. which consists of vector sum of $I_0$ and $I_2^!$ (which is equivalent of rotor current $I_2$ reflected on stator side) and lags $V_1$ at an angle $\phi_1$ so that cos $\phi_1$ is more that cos $\phi_0$. When load is further increased it will increase the rotor current to $I_2'$ and reflected on stator as $I_2'$ giving a resultant of $I_1'$ making angle θ which is less than $φ_1$, hence cos φ is more than cos $φ_1$ i.e. p.f. is further improved. Actually if we go on increasing the load, the maximum p.f of about 0.8 to 0.9 is normally obtained at 80 to 90% of full load outputs.

When the motor is loaded beyond this load, p.f. reduces slightly due to increase in leakage reactance. The change is shown by vectors in Fig. 3.77 (a) and by graph in Fig. 3.77 (b).

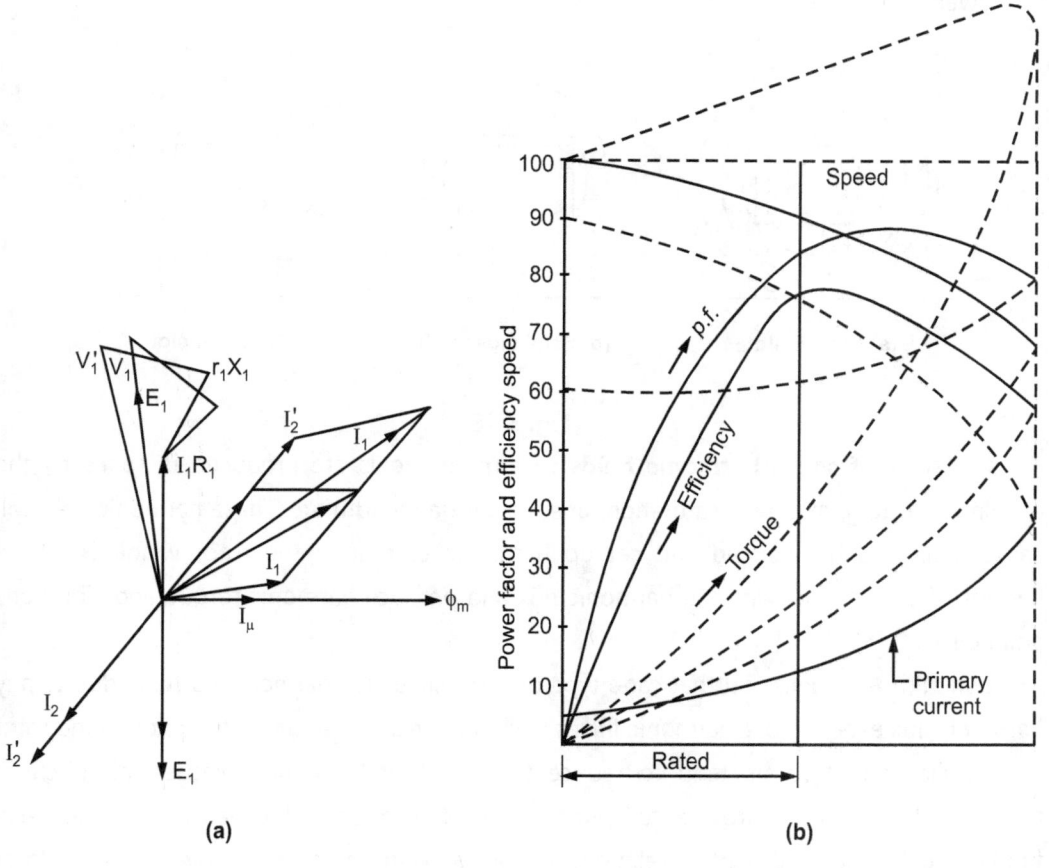

**Fig. 3.77**

**2. Air gap and stator slots :** In case of three phase induction motors, the flux in air gap will remain almost constant if the supply voltage remains constant. If we increase the air gap flux for the same we are required to supply more magnetising current, it will cause $I_0$ to lag $V_1$ by more angle, means it will reduce the no load p.f. as well as it will reduce the p.f. of the motor. Hence to make induction motor run at higher p.f. air gap length is reduced as much as possible.

The stator core can be built up by using either closed, semi-closed or open type of slots having the highest leakage reactance as shown in Fig. 3.78 while the semi-closed slots has less than the closed one and open type has the lowest, as open type of slots have less leakage flux or leakage reactance it has higher values of starting torque and pull-out torque. But due to low leakage reactance it will have high starting current again due to open slots the air gap length is increased, which will reduce the p.f. of the motor. While in case of semi-closed slots or closed slots having more leakage reactance will result in better operating p.f. and lower starting current and pull out torque.

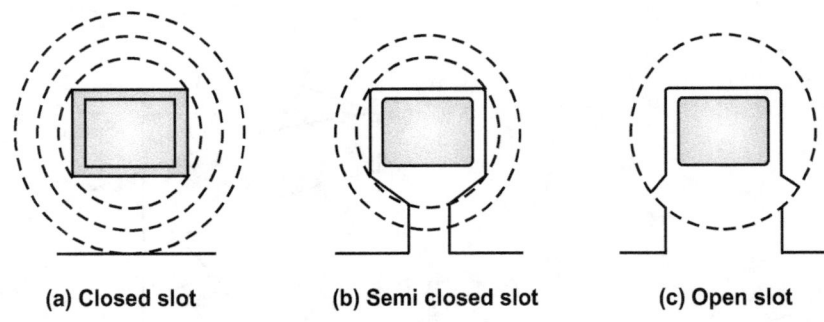

(a) Closed slot    (b) Semi closed slot    (c) Open slot

Fig. 3.78

**3. Effect of space harmonic fields :** Harmonic fields are produced in space by the windings, slotting, magnetic saturation, unequal air gap length etc. These harmonic field will cause e.m.fs. to be induced and set up harmonic current in the rotor windings. These harmonic current react with the harmonic flux and produce harmonic torque and vibrations and noise.

It should be understood that cage type of rotor circulates harmonic currents due to any harmonic flux except those harmonic fluxes having wavelength equal to the pitch of the rotor bars; while wound rotors tend to reduce the effect of harmonics whose pole-pitch or multiples there of differ from a coil pitch i.e. effect of most of the harmonics other than fundamentals. Thus with certain relationships between the number of poles and the stator and rotor slots in cage motors particular behavior may be observed.

**(a) Harmonic induction torque :** A three phase winding carrying sinusoidal current will produce harmonics given by

$$n_1 = 6k \pm 1 \quad \text{where, k is any integer.}$$

The direction of rotation of the harmonics fluxes is same or against the direction of rotation of the fundamental flux for positive or negative sings. The synchronous speed of the

$n^{th}$ harmonic is $n^{th}$ of the fundamental synchronous speed when k = 1, the three phase winding produces backward rotating $5^{th}$ harmonic rotating produces at $1/5^{th}$ of synchronous, $1/7^{th}$ of synchronous speed. It can be assumed that these harmonic fields are produced by sets of additional rotating poles super imposed on the fundamental poles. The interaction between these stator and rotor $7^{th}$ harmonic poles will produce a positive $7^{th}$ harmonic torque, with a synchronous speed equal to $1/7^{th}$ of that of fundamental. If the harmonic torques are sufficiently pronounced the $7^{th}$ harmonic may make the motor to crawl at about $1/7^{th}$ normal speed.

**(b) Harmonic synchronous torques :** The rotor slots produces separate harmonics given by

$$n_2 = 2Qr \pm 1$$

where 2 Qr = number of rotor slots/pair of poles here again the +ve sign gives direction of rotation as forward.

When the number of rotor slots is equal to number of stator slots, they produce same order harmonic which are very strong, all these harmonics are rotating at corresponding speeds in both stator and rotor. Thus, harmonics of every order would try to exert synchronous torques at their corresponding synchronous speed and the motor may refuse to start. The same thing will take place when number of rotor slots is an integral multiple of number of stator slots. This is called cogging of induction motors.

**(c) Vibration torques :** When the rotor of an induction motor rotates, periodical variation of flux density will take place in stator and rotor teeth when the rotor teeth move past stator teeth and stator slots periodically. It produces different noises. At a instant when the axes of stator and rotor teeth will co-inside a unidirectional pulling force is produced between the stator and rotor. This force moves around the air gap at a fixed speed with the rotating of the rotor and set up a force on the rotor so that it will vibrate. At a particular speed of the rotor these vibrations may get in resonance with the natural oscillations of the rotor which makes the operation of rotor impossible.

**4. Effect of skewed slots :** Induction motors are designed to have either skewed rotor slots or skewed stator slots; to eliminate the effect of cogging etc. Preferably rotor slots are skewed. It also reduces motor noise. It has a benefit to reduce the effect of space harmonics in the air gap flux. For example, consider a rotor bar skewed in such a way that one end of the bar under a north harmonic pole and the other end is also under a north harmonic pole, so that no current of that harmonic will flow in the bar. Also due to skewing has a effect to reduce the harmonic will flow in the bar. Also due to skewing has a effect to reduce the magnitude of induced e.m.f. It also slightly increases the rotor bar, which will result in to increasing the starting torque. It increases the leakage reactance of motor reducing there by the starting current; power p.f. and pull out torque.

## THEORY QUESTIONS

1. Derive the torque equation for a polyphase induction motor.
2. Develop equivalent circuit for one phase of a three-phase induction motor running on no load and draw its phasor diagram.
3. Draw a neat circuit diagram for a direct on line starter for 3-phase induction motor and explain its operation and protective feature. How could this starter be adopted for remote control.
4. Why a three phase induction motor is not suitable for wide speed variation ?
5. Describe the construction and operating characteristics of double cage rotor induction motor.
6. (a) What is single phasing? How does it affect the working of a three phase induction motor.
   (b) The air gap in an induction motor is kept as small as mechanically possible, why?
   (c) Describe a method to measure accurately the slip of wound rotor induction motor.
7. Draw sketch of star delta starter for three-phase induction motor. Explain its working.
8. How speed of induction motor is varied by inserting resistance in rotor circuit ?
9. How will you perform the experiment on circle diagram of induction motor, and how will you plot the circle diagram from it explain the method to obtain conditions at full load.
10. Explain why an induction motor can not run at synchronous speed.
11. Draw a power flow diagram and explain about the power stages of three phase induction motor.
12. Derive the following torque relations in case of 3-phase induction motor.
    (a) $\dfrac{T_{max}}{T_{start}}$      (b) $\dfrac{T_{max}}{T_{full\ load}}$
    
    in terms of rotor resistance standstill reactance and slip.

13. Fill in the gaps, selecting works from the bracket :
    (a) An induction motor with a direct start draws current of 50 amps. to limit the starting supply current to 20 amps. auto transform starter should have a tap of ..... (40, 16, 63.2)
    (b) An induction motor having starting with star delta starter will required at least ...... conductors between starter and motor. (3, 4, 6, 9)
    (c) In double cage induction motor the outer cage has ...... resistance and inner cage has ....... resistance. (high, low)
    (d) The maximum synchronous speed which can be obtained in India is ....... r.p.m. (3000, 4000, 6000)
    (e) $\dfrac{\text{Rotor Cu loss}}{\text{Rotor gross output}} = \ldots \left(\dfrac{S}{1-S}, \dfrac{1-S}{S}, \dfrac{S}{1}\right)$
    (f) Inschrage motor, the injected e.m.f. is of ...... frequency. (supply, slip)
14. Explain the pole changing method of speed control in case of three phase induction motor.
15. Explain any one modern method of speed control of three phase I.M.
16. Derive the proportional relations between the rotor input, rotor Cu loss and the gross mechanical power developed in terms of slip.
17. Compare the salient features of cage motor with wound rotor induction motor.
18. Describe the construction, working, characteristics and field of application of double cage rotor induction motor.
19. State the cause and remedy for magnetic locking of induction motors.
20. State whether the following statements are wrong or correct with reason in brief:
    (a) Three phase induction motor runs at synchronous speed.
    (b) The induced e.m.f. in the compensating winding of a charge motor is of slip frequency and hence it is useful to inject into the stator.
    (c) Three phase induction motor has higher p.f. on no load.
    (d) Single phase induction motor is self starting.
    (e) Double cage induction motors do not require stater.
21. Sketch and explain the shape of the torque speed characteristics of three phase induction motor for various values of rotor resistance.

22. Complete the following statements with reasonable backing. All statements are related to poly phase induction motors.

   (a) The projecting poles are not found in motor as ......

   (b) Rotor Cu loss and slip are related with relation ......

   (c) 10% fall in supply voltage reduces torque by ...... %

   (d) Power factor is maximum at one load, at lower loading it is less because ...... at higher loading it is less because ......

   (e) A 6 pole, 50 Hz wound rotor motor having per phase rotor resistance of 0.2 ohm runs at 950 r.p.m. to make speed of 800 r.p.m. at same torque, resistance at ...... ohms/phase should be added in rotor circuit.

   (f) Double cage motor do not required starter because ......

   (g) Motor employing star delta starter must have stator ...... connected for normal running.

# Chapter 4

# SINGLE PHASE INDUCTION MOTORS AND SYNCHRONOUS GENERATOR

## 4.1 SINGLE PHASE INDUCTION MOTOR

The construction of a single phase induction motor is similar to that of three phase induction motor. The stator structure completely surrounds the rotor, which is generally of the squirrel-cage type and the air gap is uniform. The simple physical theory for the reactions which take place in rotor is as follows:

### 4.1.1 Cross Field Theory

Fig. 4.1 (a) is a conventional diagram of a two pole motor with squirrel cage rotor in which the stator winding is shown as two oppositely placed coils for simplicity. The rotor conductors or bars are connected through the end rings so that corresponding bars may be considered to form a single short circuited turn of a coil, as shown by dotted lines in the Fig. 4.1 At the instant shown, the direction of the main flux, $\phi_s$, which is alternating in value,

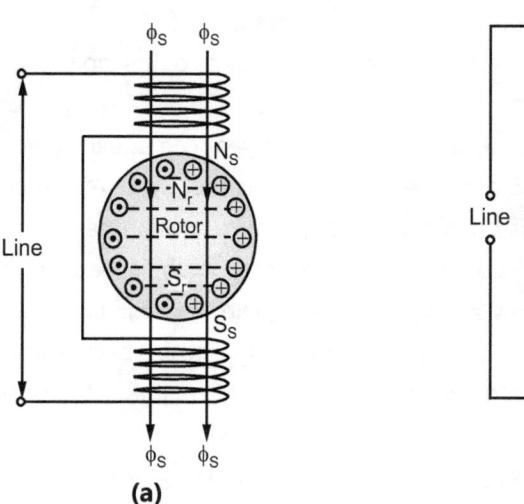

**Fig. 4.1**

is increasing and in a direction downward, as indicated. It links the rotor coils and induces e.m.f.s in them and currents due to transformer action. These are called transformer e.m.f.s and currents. These induced currents, must flow in such a direction as to oppose the flux, as per Lenz's law. The current in rotor conductors, at this instant, must therefore be flowing inward on the right hand side of the rotor and outward on the left hand side and the poles, $N_r$ and $S_r$ are formed in the rotor core. These poles are in line with stator poles $N_s$ and $S_s$ and it is evident that the reaction between these two sets of poles can produce no torque or turning effort.

Now assume that the rotor is made to move in a clockwise direction. There will be an e.m.f. induced in the rotor conductors, which is entirely due to their rate of cutting the flux $\phi_s$. This is called the speed e.m.f. or rotational e.m.f. It is alternating in value and is maximum when the flux is maximum and at any instant, in a direction in accordance with Fleming's right hand rule. Thus in Fig. 4.1 (a) the direction at this with respect to its resistance. So these current lag the speed e.m.f. by nearly 90°. The speed currents therefore, set up a flux $\phi_r$, at right angles to the flux $\phi_s$ Fig. 4.1 (a). This produces the poles $N'_r$ and $S'_r$ in the rotor core. This field which is called as the cross field, in turn sets up the corresponding opposite poles $N'_s$ and $S'_s$ in the stator core which completely surrounds the rotor.

It is already noted that speed e.m.f. is maximum when field flux $\phi_s$ phase with the stator poles $N_s$ and $S_s$. But the speed currents in the rotor lag practically 90° in time behind the speed e.m.fs. The flux $\phi_r$, and stator poles, $N'_s$ and $S'_s$ do not reach their maximum value, therefore, until one quarter cycle or 90 Electrical degrees after maximum value of the main field poles $N_s$ and $S_s$. Thus there are set up in space, two fields at right angles to each other and differing 90° in time, which results in to a rotating magnetic field.

When rotor rotates near synchronous speed, the flux and the poles, N's and S's are practically equal to those of the main field, and a so called 'Circular field' is produced. As the slip increases the rate of cutting the flux decreases. At reduced speed, then, two unequal fields at right angles exist, and a so called "elliptical field" is produced. At standstill, the flux $\phi_r$ is zero, and only a pulsating field is produced, which produces no torque.

If rotor in Fig. 4.1 is turned in a counter clockwise direction, the speed e.m.fs., current and flux $\phi_r$ are all reversed in direction w.r.t. $\phi_s$ of the main field. This will change the polarity of the poles $N'_s$ and $S'_s$. The combined field now rotates in the opposite direction and reverses the torque. Thus single phase induction motor will rotate in the direction in which it is started.

## 4.1.2 Double Revolving Field Theory of Single Phase Induction Motors

When a single phase supply is given to the stator winding of a single phase induction motor a pulsating magnetic field is produced as shown in Fig. 4.2 (a) and (b). It is seen from Fig. 4.2 (a) that due to A.C. voltage applied to the single phase winding in the stator, the flux produced is pulsating one with a maximum value equal to $\phi_m$. By Ferraris principle a single phase sinusoidal field, varying or pulsating sinusoidally with time along a field axis, can be resolved in to two equal sinusoidal fields.

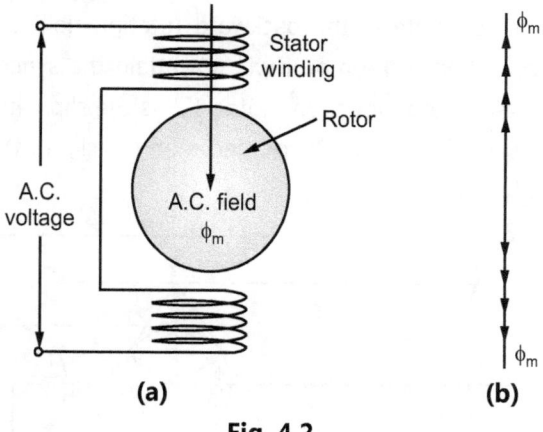

**Fig. 4.2**

Rotating in an opposite direction, each having a maximum value equal to one half that of Initial field.

Fig. 4.2 (c) shows a sinusoidally pulsating (varying) field wave. If the value of the flux at any instant is represented, will be seen that its projection varies along the vertical axis of the rotating phasor $\phi_m$ as shown in Fig. 4.2 (d).

The phasor $\phi_m$ is equal to the maximum value of the flux and its speed of rotation in revolutions per second is equal to the line frequency in cycles per second. Fig. 4.2 (e) and (f) shows the position of field $\phi_2$ and $\phi_3$. In each case, it is seen that the field will be sum of the two fields of strength $\dfrac{\phi_m}{2}$ rotating at line frequency in opposite directions one is forward rotating field and other is backward rotating field.

If the uniaxial flux with sinusoidal variation is expressed as, $\phi = \phi_m \cos \omega t$, this can be Expresses by Eular's equation

$$\phi_m \cos \omega t = \dfrac{\phi_m}{2} e^{j\omega t} - \dfrac{\phi_m}{2} e^{-j\omega t}$$

The right hand side of this equation represents two oppositely rotating phasors each of half the magnitude.

Fig. 4.2 (f) shows speed torque curve resulting from each rotating field similar to three phase rotating field, the exception being that this curve is extended into other quadrant. One due to forward rotating field and other due to backward rotating field, the resultant of these two gives the torque due to forward rotating field is equal and opposite to each other hence the resultant torque is zero, so the motor is not self starting. If the rotor is made to move in the direction of forward rotating field, the forward rotating torque will immediately exceed the backward torque and the rotor will begin to accelerate in the forward direction and reach near to synchronous speed. If the rotor is made to move in backward direction, when it is at standstill, it will continue to rotate in the backward rotating field direction. The torque at synchronous speed is zero, hence the motor will not attain the synchronous speed but will have slip as in case of three phase induction motor. If S is the slip with respect to the torque (Forward or backward) at which the rotor is rotating then the slip of the rotor with respect to the other torque will be (2 − s).

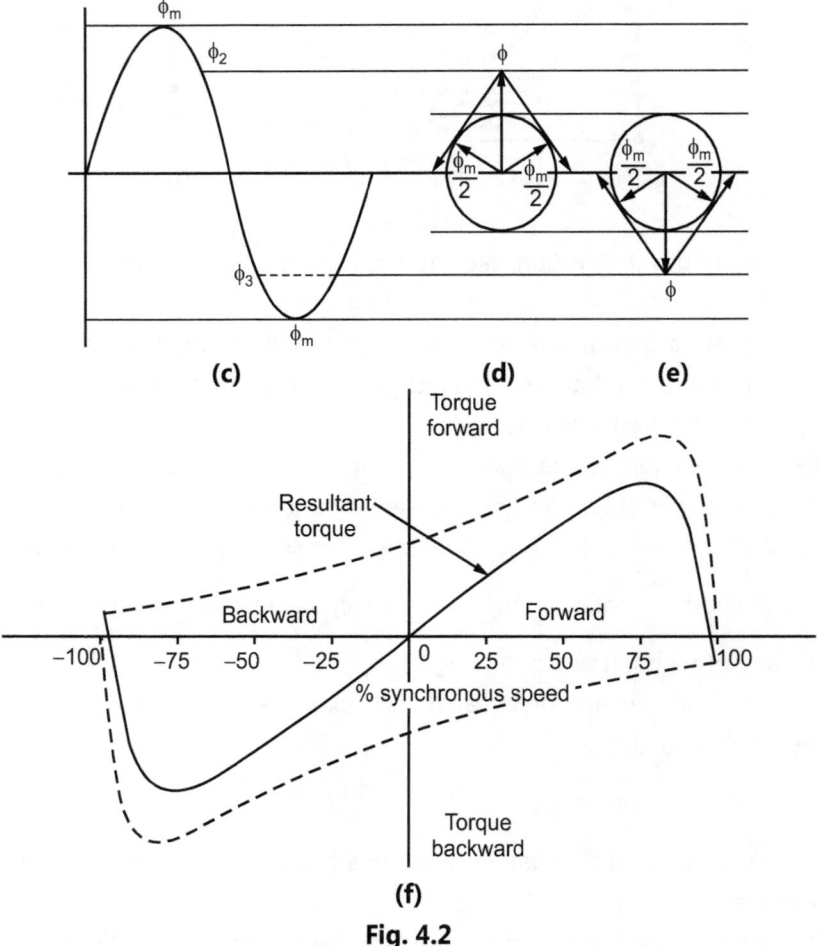

**Fig. 4.2**

The rotation of the rotor in the forward direction increases the forward flux above and decreases the backward flux below half the value. Hence, under running condition, the action of the single phase induction motor is not much inferior to that of three phase induction motor.

## 4.1.3 Methods of Obtaining Self Starting Torque

From the discussion of Article 4.1.2, we have seen that single phase motor at rest is not self starting. To make it self starting we required to make provision of either one more winding producing flux at nearly 90° to stator flux, or provide shedding rings which will produce a similar effect and make the motor to start from rest. Hence, the methods are known as.

(i) Split phase method.

(ii) Shaded pole method.

**(i) Split phase motor (Resistance splitting):** It is the most widely used type of single phase induction motor. It consists of squirrel cage rotor. It consists of two stator windings, a main or running winding and an auxiliary or starting winding. These windings produce a rotating field. The two windings are entirely separate and each consists of as many coil groups as there are poles. In most motors the windings are generally of two layer chain or concentric type. The starting winding is less bulky, occupies less space and generally has fewer turns than the main winding. This is to reduce its reactance and allow more current to flow, which tends to increase the flux set up by the winding. Also the starting winding is wound in place lastly and occupies the space in the top of the slots. The two windings are placed 90° electrical apart, and are connected in parallel across the line at starting, as shown in Fig. 4.3 (a). A starting switch mounted on the rotor and operated by centrifugal force, is connected in series with the starting winding. When the rotor accelerates to about 75% of synchronous speed, the starting switch opens the contacts disconnecting the starting (Auxiliary) winding from mains and the motor operates on the main winding only.

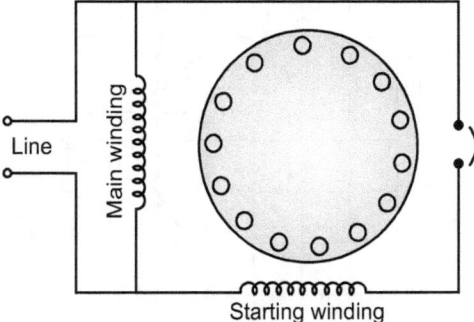

**Fig. 4.3 (a)**

The two windings set up the two fluxes and two sets of stator poles 90° electrical, as in a two-phase motor. But if the two stator windings of a two phase motor are connected across the same line, the current in these windings will be in phase. The two sets of stator poles will be in time phase and reach their maximum values at the same instant. The combined field will be pulsating in nature, hence no torque will be produced. To produce a rotating field and torque at starting there must be phase displacement of the currents in the two windings.

If additional resistance is placed in series with the starting winding of the motor, it will reduce the current in that winding, but will bring this current more nearly into phase with the impressed voltage. Additional resistance in the starting winding is generally obtained by using wire of smaller cross-section than in the main winding or by using wire of higher specific resistance than copper. In commercial motor, the phase difference of the currents in the two windings is nearly 30° as indicated in the vector diagram of Fig. 4.3 (b).

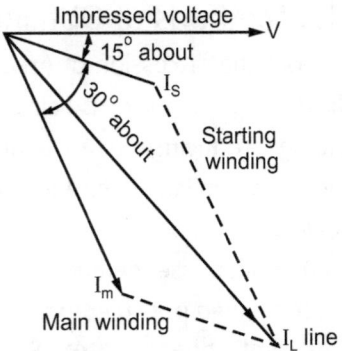

**Fig. 4.3 (b)**

In the diagram, $I_s$ is the current in the starting winding, $I_m$ is the current in the main winding and $I_L$ total motor current. The motor thus starts as an imperfect two phase motor. Fig. 4.3 (c) shows the typical speed torque curves for a split phase motor. It is seen that the starting torque developed by the main winding only is zero, while that developed by the combined windings is about 150 per cent of full-load value. It is to be noted also that the two curves cross at about 85% of synchronous speed, called the "Cross-over point" and above this, the main winding alone develops more torque, for a given slip, than both windings acting together. The motor accelerates on the two windings to approximately that speed at which the main winding torque is a maximum. At this speed, the centrifugal switch opens, cutting out the starting winding. The torque developed by the main winding when the centrifugal switch opens is called the "Pull-in-torque".

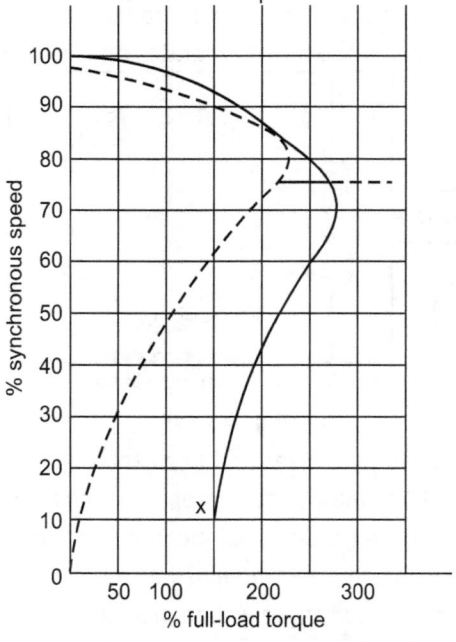

**Fig. 4.3 (c): Speed torque curves for split phase motor**

As the motor accelerates, the torque reaches a minimum value indicated by point X, on the combined curve. This is called the "Pull-up torque"

The direction of rotation of motor is reversed by reversing the connections of either starting winding or main winding.

Another form of split-phase motor is that in which a reactor (inductance) is placed in series with the main winding only while the motor accelerates. This is known as the reactor-start split-phase motor.

## 4.1.4 Capacitor Type Motor

A form of split-phase motor called the capacitor motor, has come into wide use during the past few years. This has been largely due to the development of electrolytic condenser, which costs low, is reliable and more compact than other types.

There are three general types of capacitor motor, which are
1. Capacitor start motor
2. Capacitor motor or Permanent-split capacitor motor, and
3. Two-value capacitor motor.

These motors, almost universally have squirrel-cage rotors.

## 4.1.4 (a) Capacitor Start Motor

It is similar to ordinary split phase type motor. It has a main winding and auxiliary winding, spaced 90° electrical degrees apart, as shown in conventional circuit-diagram of Fig. 4.4 (a). The electrolytic condenser or capacitor is connected in series with the auxiliary winding and a centrifugally operated starting switch. It is set to open when rotor reaches about 75% of synchronous speed as is the case of ordinary (resistance) split phase motor. The capacitor is generally cylindrical in shape and mounted on the motor frame. Their value for capacitor start motors vary from about 80 µF to 400 µF for motors having rating between 1/8 H.P. to one H.P.

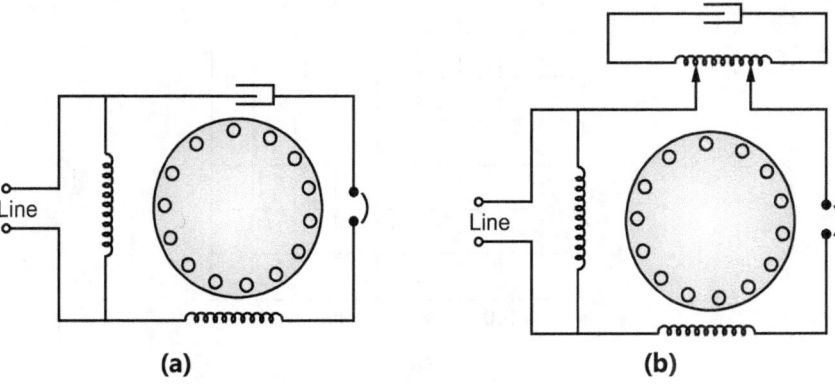

**Fig. 4.4**

The winding in the capacitor start motor differ some what from those in the ordinary split phase motor. The starting winding while consisting of smaller wire, has more turns than main winding. The increased reactance, due to the larger number of turns, is counteracted by that of the capacitor, so the current and flux of this winding is increased.

The effect of the capacitor caused the current in the starting winding to lead the impressed voltage, as indicated in Fig. 4.4 (c). The reactance of this winding and capacitance are so proportioned that the current in this circuit leads the voltage by nearly 40 to 45 degrees. This causes a phase difference between currents in the two windings which is nearly 90° as shown in vector diagram. The motor will thus start almost under the conditions of a two-phase motor i.e. they produce a rotating flux and the torque on rotor.

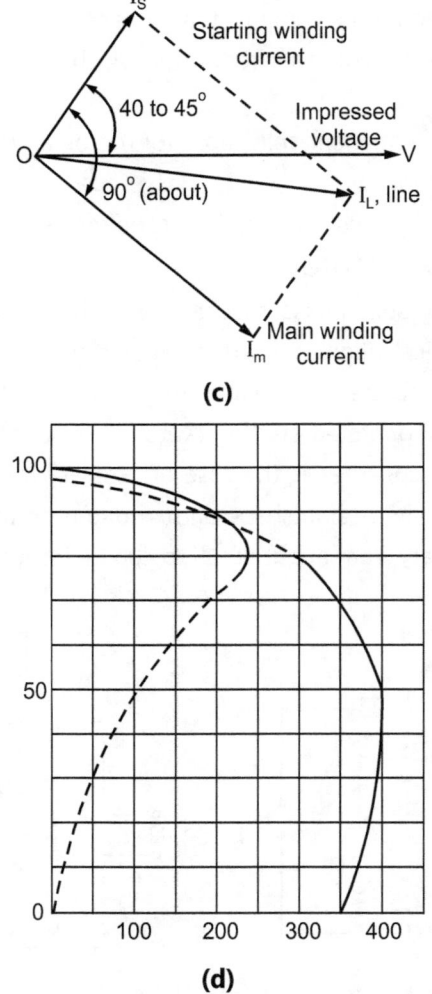

**Fig. 4.4: Speed torque curves for capacitor start motor**

The starting torque in a single phase induction motor, with two windings spaced 90 electrical degrees apart, is proportional to the sine of the angle of phase displacement between the two currents in these windings. Hence, the capacitor start motor, with practically 90° displacement of the currents, has much greater starting torque than the split-phase motor, with only 30° or so displacement.

Vector diagram of Fig. 4.4 (c) and Fig. 4.4 (d) are assumed to be for motors of same rating, for approximately the same currents in the corresponding windings of two motors, a comparison of two diagrams shows that the capacitor start motor takes less current from mains than split-phase (Resistance split) motor. The starting current in the capacitor start motor may be made close to unity power factor.

The condenser is some times connected in to the starting circuit through a small auto-transformer as shown in Fig. 4.4 (b).

Doubling the voltage on a condenser doubles current, so the volt-amperes change with the square of voltage. This gives the effect of four times the condenser capacity. The transformer thus permits the use of a higher voltage condenser of less capacitance.

Fig. 4.4 (d) shows the typical speed-torque curves for the motor. It clearly shows the increase in starting torque compared to that in Fig. 4.3 (c).

## 4.1.4 (b) Permanent Spilt Capacitor Motor

This type motor is having the windings same as for the capacitor start motor. It consists of both main and auxiliary windings. A capacitor is connected in series with the auxiliary winding and the centrifugal switch is omitted, as shown in conventional circuit diagram, Fig. 4.5 (a). In place of the electrolytic condenser which deteriorates and breaks down under continuous duty, an oil condenser is used. This type of capacitor of large capacity like electrolytic capacitors can not be used due to their increase volume, weight and cost. The capacitance of these condensers is about 2 to 3 µF for the smallest motor and may be about 20 µF for a 0.75 H.P. motor.

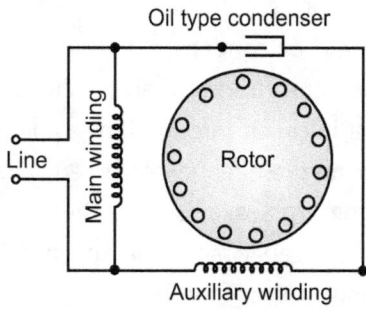

**Fig. 4.5 (a): Permanent split capacitor motor**

Due to less capacitance in auxiliary circuit, this motor gives lower starting torque than capacitor start motor. But the capacitor is capable of producing sufficient phase displacement in the winding currents to produce a cross field. Hence, the motor starts and runs as an imperfect two-phase machine (As phase shift is not 90°). Due to this it operates more quietly, at better efficiency, higher power factor greater pull-out torque with less pulsating effect in the torque.

It is generally used for oil burners, fans etc., where high starting torque is not required, and where silent operation is desirable.

**Two-value Capacitor Motor:**

The windings in the two-value capacitor motor are the same as in other type of capacitor motors. The difference from other type of motors is that it starts with one value of capacitance in series with the auxiliary winding and runs with other of smaller value. There are two general designs.

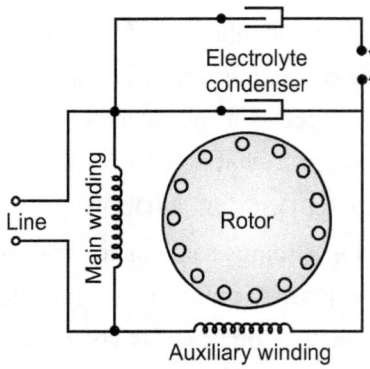

**Fig. 4.5 (b): Two-value capacitor motor**

One type uses two parallel connected condensers in series with the auxiliary winding as in Fig. 4.5 (b). One condenser of the oil type, is connected permanently in circuit for running. In the other, an electrolytic condenser of much higher capacitance, is used for starting only and is cut out automatically by a centrifugal switch, when motor attains about 75% of synchronous speed. In other type of condenser, an oil-filled condenser is connected into auxiliary circuit through a small auto-transformer, as shown in Fig. 4.5 (c). A centrifugal-switch connects the transformer in circuit through taps a and b. This steps up the voltage on the condenser, there by producing the effect of increased capacitance on starting. When the motor accelerates nearly to the cross-over speed, the switch closes the circuit through transformer tap c giving sufficient capacitance for running. The main disadvantage of this arrangement is the weight and size of container use for holding the transformer and condenser.

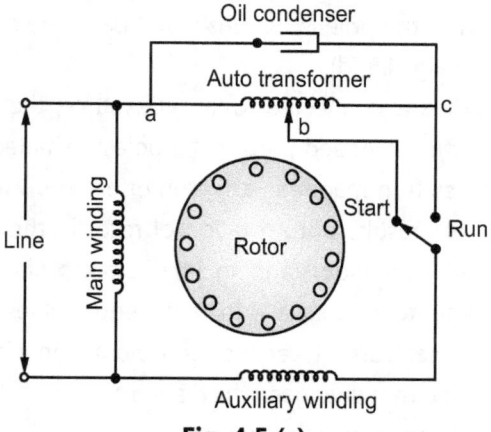

**Fig. 4.5 (c)**

The two value capacitor motor operates as a permanent-split motor with its desirable running characteristics and in addition, has the high starting torque.

## 4.1.4 (c) Shaded Pole Motor

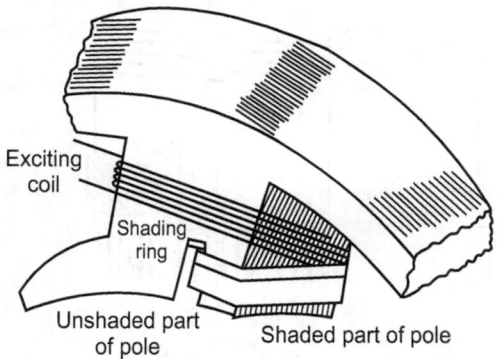

**Fig. 4.5 (d): Shaded pole construction**

One of the simplest and cheapest of manufactured motors is the shaded pole motor. It is actually an induction motor as its rotor receives power by electromagnetic induction. The difference in the induction motors (three phase or two phase) and the shaded pole motor lies in their magnetic fields. The three phase induction motor (two phase also) creates a true rotating field of constant magnitude, the magnetic field of shaded pole motor is not constant in magnitude and merely shifts from one side of the pole to the other, hence the torque produced by this motor is not uniform in magnitude.

Fig. 4.5 (d) represents the constructional details of one pole of a shaded pole motor. Each pole of stator are laminated and has a slot cut across the laminations about one-third the distance from one edge.

Around the smaller part is placed a heavy copper short-circuited coil (Ring) called as a shading coil. The iron around which the shading ring is placed is called the shaded part of the pole, while free portion of the pole is the unshaded part. The exciting coil surrounds the entire pole core as shown in Fig. 4.5 (d).

When the exciting winding is connected to an A.C. source, the magnetic axis of the flux produced by it shifts from the unshaded part of the pole to shaded part of the pole by the action of shading coil. This shift in magnetic axis is in effect equivalent to an actual physical movement of the pole, which results in to rotation of rotor in the direction from unshaded part of pole to shaded part. For understanding how it takes place, we will determine the positions of magnetic pole centers for several instantaneous values of current in the exciting winding. Here the base is that current varying sinusoidally. In Fig. 4.6 (a), the analysis is divided in to three parts for current changes, which are as:

(i) From zero to a nearly positive maximum.
(ii) In the region of maximum current.
(iii) From a nearly positive maximum to zero.

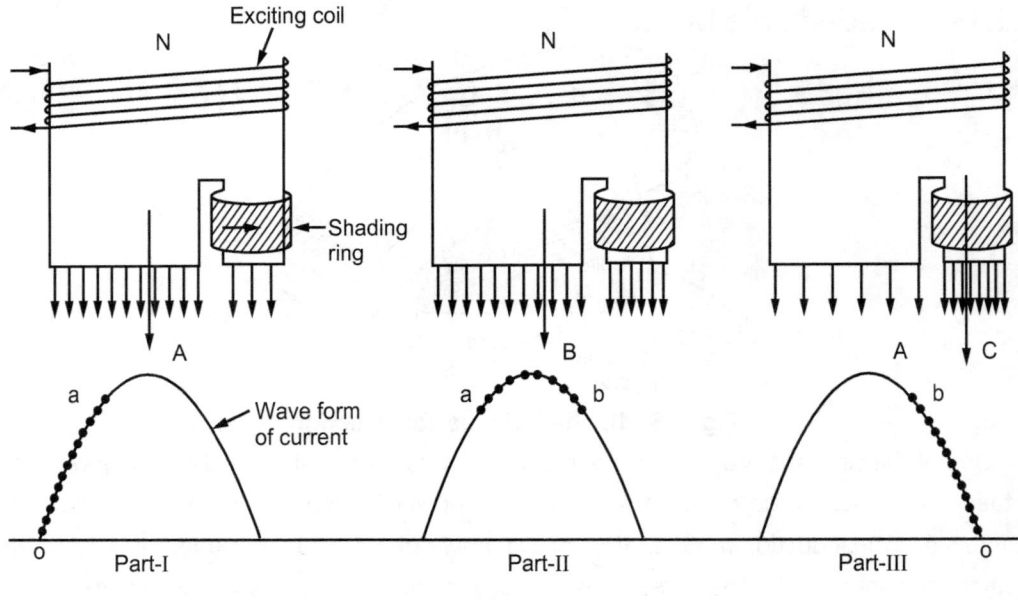

Fig. 4.6 (a)

**Part I: Considering Fig. 4.6 (a): The current changes from O to a:** The current increases at a very high rate along a sine curve, which sets up alternating flux causing the voltage to be induced in the shading ring by transformer action. As the resistance of the ring is very low, current through it will be high, and its direction will be such as to oppose the flux inducing it. Due to this the flux is shifted mostly to unshaded part of the pole, which sets up the magnetic axis along the large arrow A shown near the centre of unshaded part of the pole.

**Part II: Current changes from a to b:** The variation in the magnitude of current in this region i.e. from a to b is very small, along the top of the sine wave, under this condition, practically no voltage is induced in the shading coil i.e. no current flows through shading coil, hence it produces no flux. As the main exciting coil current is nearly maximum, the flux is maximum and is uniformly distributed over the entire pole face hence the magnetic axis will now shift to the centre of entire pole as shown by big arrow B.

**Part III: Current change from b to o:** The current drops (decreases) rapidly from b to o in this part. Under this condition voltage will be induced in the shading ring and will cause a comparatively large current through it. The direction of this current will be such as to create a flux so as to oppose the reducing flux in the shaded part of the pole, hence a strong field will be developed in the shaded part of pole while weak fields is in the remaining part of pole. Hence, the magnetic axis will get shifted to the centre of shaded part of pole as shown by dark arrow C.

It is to be noted that the magnetic axis shifts across the pole form A to C i.e. from unshaded part to shaded part of the pole. And as a negative half of the current wave flows in the exciting coil a south pole trails along. This effect is as though a set of real poles were sweeping across the space from left to right.

The direction of such motors, without constructional modification can not be changed. The shaft of such motors should be extended in a proper direction so that it can drive the load in correct direction. Specially, designed shaded pole motors have to be constructed for reversing the direction of rotation.

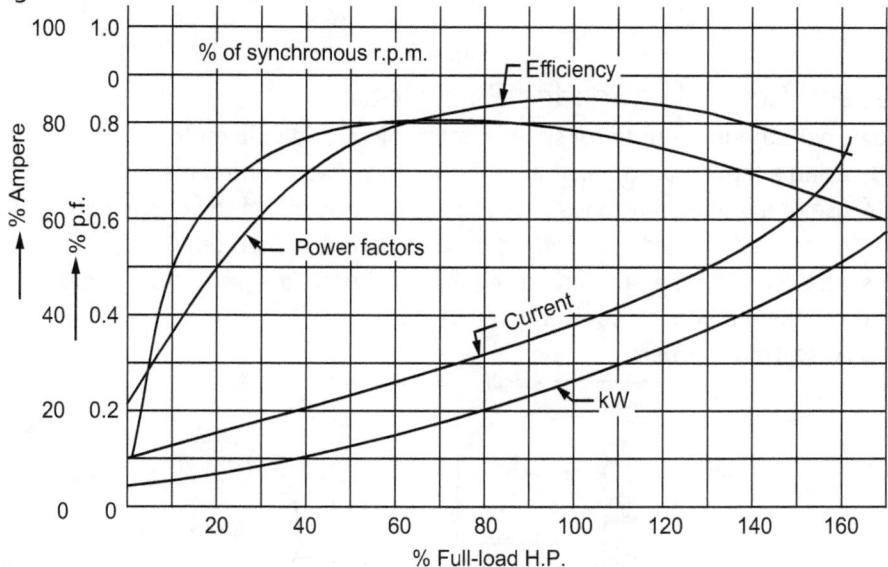

**Fig. 4.6 (b): Operating characteristics of 1ϕ induction motor**

It is simple in construction, and the cost is also low. But it gives low starting torque, very little overload capacity and used for animated signs, portable irons, photograph turn-bables etc. Fig. 4.6 represents typical characteristics of single phase motor.

## 4.1.5 Methods of Obtaining both Direction of Rotation in Shaded Pole Motor

It can be achieved by the following two methods:
(i) Double set of shading coil.
(ii) Double set of exciting windings method.

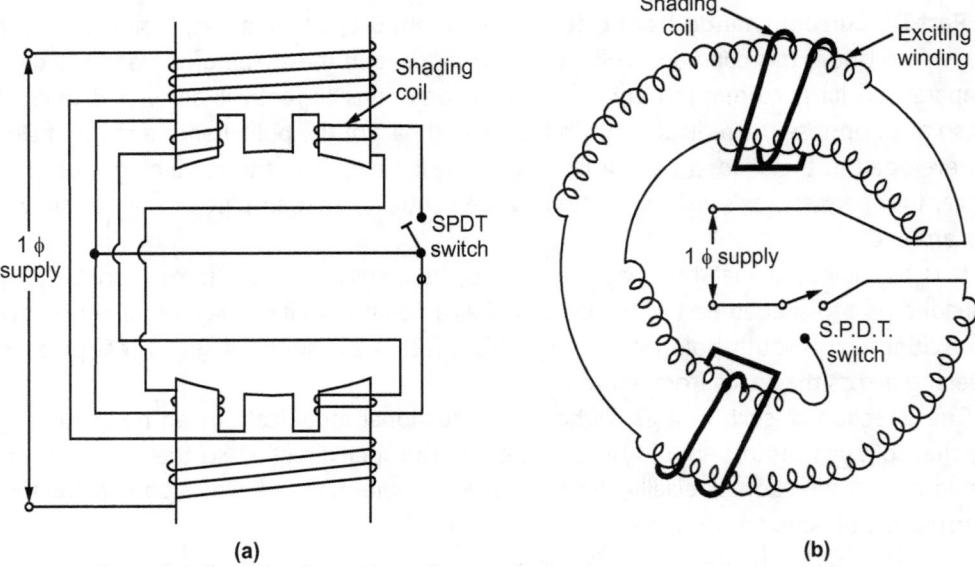

Fig. 4.7

## 4.1.6 Speed Control of Shaded Pole Motor

Following methods are used for speed control of shaded pole motors:
1. By using a tapped auto transformer i.e. using voltage control method.
2. By use of a tapped reactance or resistance method (it is also voltage control method).
3. Using tapped exciting coil method (it is a flux control method).

The simple circuit diagrams are given below, which are self explanatory, hence the explanation of the method is not given.

**(i) Using Auto-transformer:**

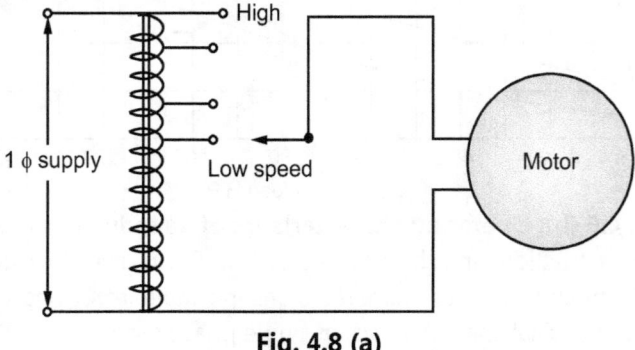

Fig. 4.8 (a)

## (ii) Using Tapped Reactance:

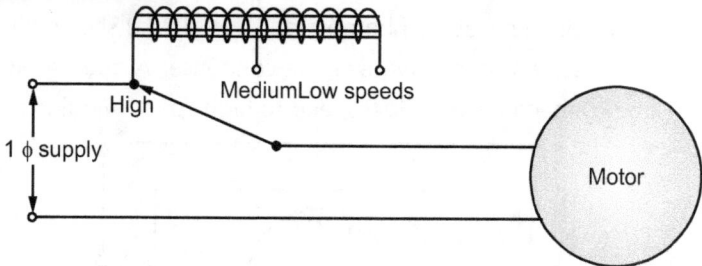

Fig. 4.8 (b)

## (iii) Using Tapped Excitation Coil:

In this case, lowest speed will be obtained when the entire winding is used and highest speed will be obtained when the smallest portion of winding is used. The reason for this action is that the volts per turn increases as the number of turn decreases. The flux produced by the exciting winding is directly proportioned to the volts per turn, which increase flux when lower turns are used, which reduces the speed.

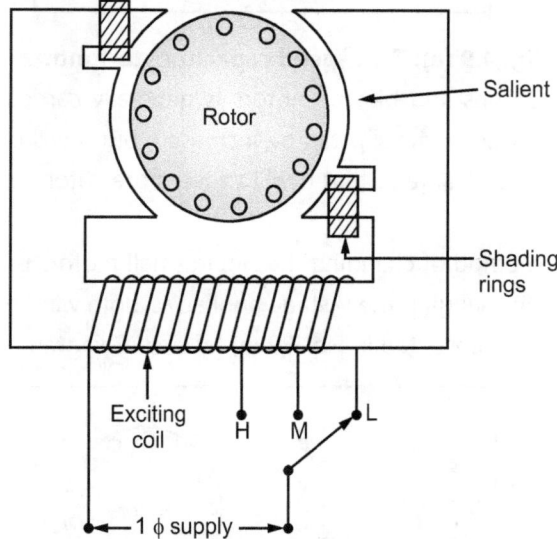

Fig. 4.8 (c): Tapped winding method

## 4.1.7 Speed Control of Single Phase Induction Motors

Similar to three phase I.M., single phase induction motors are approximately constant speed motors of which the slip increases gradually with the load. In this case, also the speed mainly depends on frequency of supply and number of poles for which motor is wound.

Multi-speed motors can be manufactured for two or three speeds with two or three sets of stator windings, each set consisting of a main and an auxiliary winding, would for a different number of poles. The two windings of each set are connected in parallel and the speed is changed by switching from one set of winding to another. The disadvantage of this scheme is that no intermediate speed can be obtained. Fig. 4.9 (a) shows the circuit diagram of a two-speed capacitor start motor, using a single condenser A double-pole double throw switch changes the line connections from low speed to high speed windings.

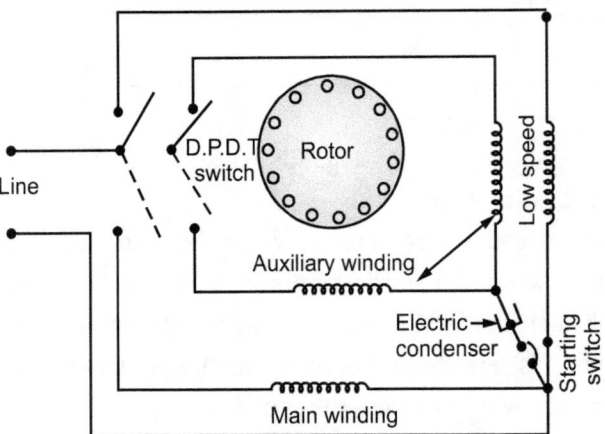

**Fig. 4.9 (a): Two speed capacitor start motor**

The speed control of fans and blower motors is generally carried out by changing the slip. Using high rotor resistance, the slip can be increased, but it will give only one speed on full-load. It has another disadvantage that it will cause more rotor copper loss and reduces efficiency of motor.

The most common method of changing the slip in small motors is by changing the value of flux. This is achieved by changing the voltage applied to both windings.

One of the method is represented in Fig. 4.9 (a) by circuit diagram.

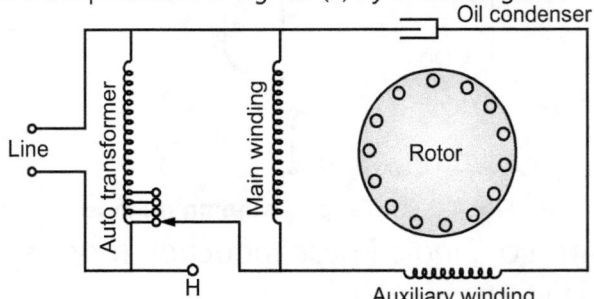

**Fig. 4.9 (b)**

We know that the torque developed for a given slip, is proportional to the square of the applied voltage. The applied voltage in this case is varied by means of auto-transformer. It is generally, mounted on the motor frame. The starting torque is reduced on the low-speed taps.

## 4.1.8 1 ϕ Synchronous Motors

### 4.1.8.1 Reluctance Motor

The split-phase motor when have properly designed for salient shaped poles, it will start- as an induction motor and attain the synchronous speed, and continue to run at a constant synchronous speed. When compared with physical dimensions of equal rating of other machine, it is some what larger than others, the rotor is usually constructed by assembling it from standard squirrel cage rotor parts, except-that some of the teeth are cut away as shown in Fig. 4.10 (a). An example can be given of a rotor-stamping using 48 slots in which following teeth can be kept as they are in normal rotor, 1, 2, 3, 4, 5, 6, 7 and 13, 14, 15, 16, 17, 18, 19 and 25, 26, 27, 28, 29, 30, 31 and 37, 38, 39, 40, 41, 42, 43 while following rotor slots will be cut of as shown in Fig. 4.10 (a) i.e. slot 8, 9, 10, 11, 12 and 20, 21, 22, 23, 24, 32, 33, 34, 35, 36 and 44, 45, 46, 47 and 48 respectively. Other things i.e. rotor bars and end rings etc. are installed in the same manner as they are used in usual rotors.

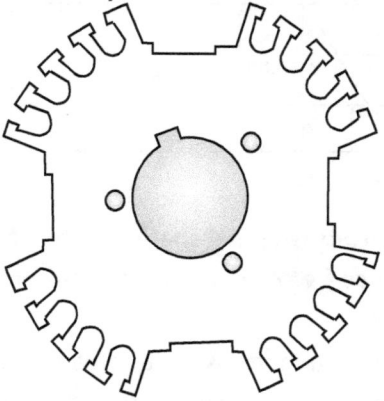

**Fig. 4.10 (a)**

At the time of working, the rotor comes up to nearly synchronous speed by the induction motor action, as the load on such machines is very low, the slip is negligibly small, the revolving field (Rotating field of stator) permanently magnetizes the projecting rotor poles. The rotor poles then "lock in step" with the revolving poles of opposite polarities and continue to rotate at synchronous speed i.e. the speed of the rotating field. The machine thus works as a synchronous motor without D.C. excitation. It is called a reluctance motor, it is called so as it works due to the variable magnetic reluctance of the air gap.

The reluctance motors are generally made in the fractional horse power sizes and use the conventional split phase stator and the centrifugal switch to open the auxiliary winding. When bigger size motor manufactured for heavier loads, permanent split capacitor construction with no centrifugal switch is used.

Due to constant speed characteristic, it is used for signaling devices, recording instruments, regulation and control equipments, many kinds of timers and phonographs.

The typical torque speed characteristic of reluctance motor is represented in Fig. 4.10 (b).

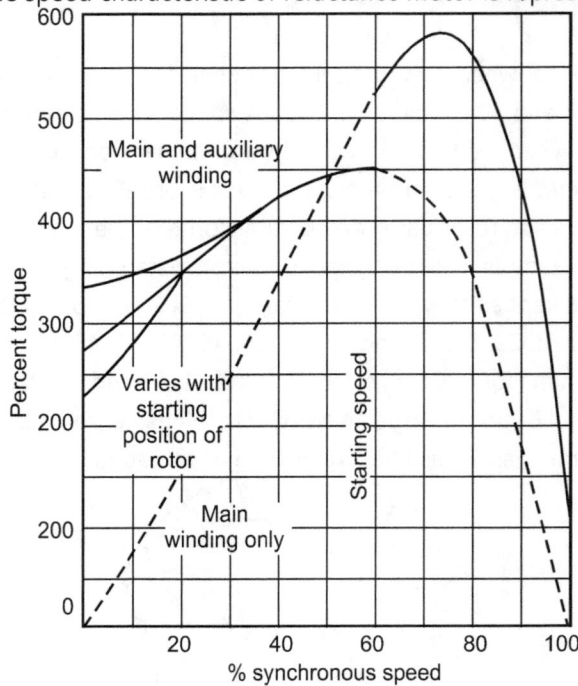

**Fig. 4.10 (b): Torque-speed characteristic of single phase, self starting reluctance motor**

### 4.1.8.2 Hystersis Motor

When the rotor of an induction motor is built up of a group of specially hardened steel rings instead of the usual silicon steel, laminations, the effect of hystersis is greatly magnified. As a result, the rotor will operate at synchronous speed because the Hystersis property of rotor steel strongly oppose any change in the magnetic properties once they are established. The stator of the motor can be either single or three phase. In case of a single phase motor the permanent capacitor is used with an auxiliary winding to provide as uniform magnetic field as possible. It will greatly reduce the losses of the motor.

Fig. 4.10 (b) shows the basis of operation of a hysteresis motor, when a single phase supply is applied to the stator (with main and auxiliary winding of the motor) a rotating magnetic field magnetises the metal of the rotor and induces poles in it.

When the motor is operating below synchronous speed, there are developed two torques within it, most of the torque is due to hysteresis, when the magnetic field of stator rotates around the surface of rotor, the rotor flux can not follow it exactly, because the metal of the rotor has large hysteresis loss. The greater the hysteresis loss of rotor material, the greater the angle by which the rotor magnetic field lags the stator magnetic field. As there is an angle between the two fields axis, a definite torque is produced in the motor. Also the stator magnetic field produces eddy currents in the rotor and they produce a magnetic field of their own which increases the torque which depends up on the relative motion between the stator and rotor magnetic fields.

When the motor reaches synchronous speed, the sweeping of the stator flux across the rotor stops and the rotor acts like a permanent magnet. The torque developed by the motor is then proportional to the angle between the rotor and stator magnetic field, up to a maximum angle set by the hysteresis in the rotor.

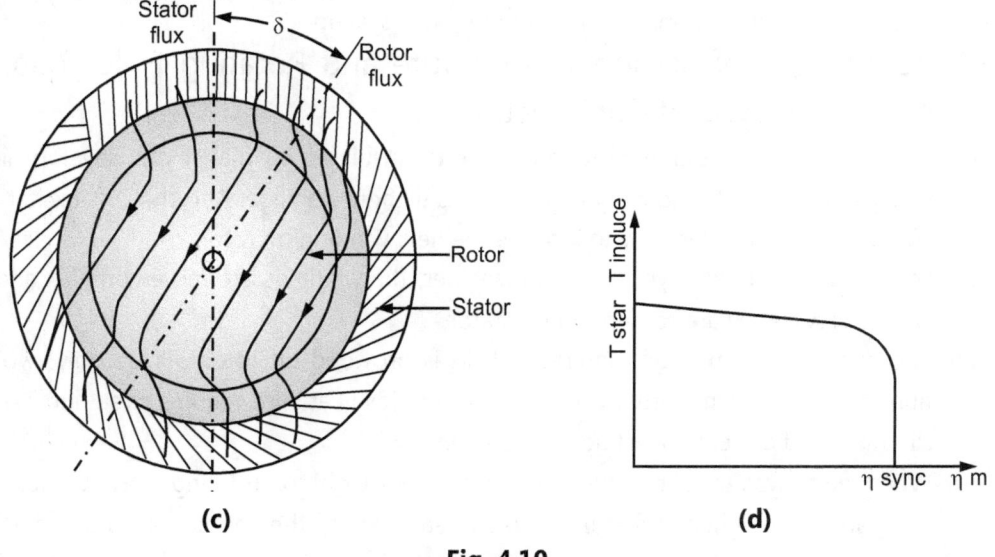

**Fig. 4.10**

The torque speed characteristic is shown in Fig. 4.10 (d). The hysteresis torque is nearly constant, the eddy current torque is approximately proportional to the slip of the motor. These two factors considered together gives the shape of hysteresis motor torque-speed characteristic.

A very small hysteresis motor can be built with shaded pole stator construction to create tiny, self starting, low power synchronous motor. It is commonly used as the driving mechanism in electric clocks.

# 4.2 ALTERNATOR

In an alternating current system, the A.C. generator is termed as alternator and as its prime mover always moves at a speed, corresponding to $N_s = \dfrac{120\,f}{p}$ which is called as a synchronous speed, the machine is also called as a synchronous generator.

A.C. generators are also having two main parts, similar to D.C. generators and they are:
1. The field system, for producing magnetic flux.
2. Armature, having conductors or winding to developed induced e.m.fs. A.C. generators can be constructed with rotating field system and stationary armature or with stationary field system and rotating armature.

As far as the principle of developing voltage is concerned it is immaterial whether the field is rotating or the armature is rotating; but if the armature is kept stationary and field is made to rotate it has certain advantages over the other type of construction hence it is preferred to have stationary armature and rotating field system.

## 4.2.1 Advantages of Stationary Armature and Rotating Field System over other Type of Construction

(a) If the armature is stationary it can be better insulated so that it can develop high voltages upto 33 kV and carry high currents without damage. And the D.C. excitation voltages being low it is easy to insulate the field winding on rotor.

(b) For large three phase synchronous machines, the windings are more complex and it will be easy if they are carried out on stator.

(c) The number of slip rings required if field is provided on rotor will be only two in numbers while if armature is provided on rotor it will at least require three number of slip rings and current collecting arrangements.

(d) When field system is provided on rotor the weight of rotating part will less in comparison to when armature is provided. Hence, the inertia of rotary part is reduced, which will reduce the vibrations due to unbalanced masses etc., and there will be less chances of winding conductor comming out due to centrifugal force.

(e) If stationary armature is used the arrangement for forced air cooling or hydrogen cooling can be easily made by enlarging the stator core and providing radial air ducts and ventilation holes.

(f) Current can be supplied to the load directly without involving the bus-bars etc.

## 4.2.2 Construction

### 4.2.2.1 Stator

The stator of the alternator is laminated for reducing the eddy current losses, as it will cut the flux due to field system. The rotating system has poles just similar to that of D.C. generators; they are separately excited. Generally a D.C. shunt generator is mounted on the same shaft of the alternator which develops D.C. voltage either at 110 or 250 volts as is required and is supplied to the field system. The alternator windings are wound in such a way that they will have large value of leakage reactance of alternator i.e. alternators will have poor regulation, it will have a advantage that at the time of external short circuit, it will keep the short circuit, current about three times the full load current since the protective relays are provided in the main circuit this current will not damage the insulation by the time the C.B. operates.

In case of high speed alternators generally force air cooling is adopted. In such alternators axial ducts are provided by punching holes in the stator armature stampings. If atmosphere surrounding the machine is dusty and moist closed ventilation system is adopted in which quantity of air is circulated continuously around an enclosed circuit. The hot air from machine is passed through air coolers, drying agents and fans and the some air is then made to enter the inlet passage of the machine. The machine is made completely air tight. So that no unpurified air enters the ventilating passages.

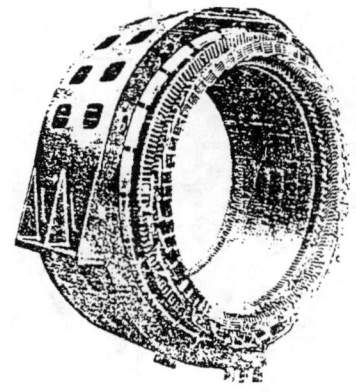

**Fig. 4.11 (a): Complete wound armature (Stator)**

For low speed alternators salient pole type rotors are used, in which case the diameter of the alternators is more and its length is less. While in case of high speed alternators cylindrical rotors are used because the limiting factor is the centrifugal force experienced by the field windings. In such machines the length of stator is more as compared with its diameter.

### 4.2.2.2 Rotor Construction

Rotors are generally manufactured in two ways:
(i) Salient Pole type
(ii) Smooth cylindrical type.

(i) In order to reduce pole face losses and at the same time to facilitate construction and mounting the cores of practically and salient poles are made of laminations riveted together, with slow speed these are either dovetailted or bolted to the rotor spider. The spider may be of cast iron or steel or it may be fabricated steel construction.

The field coils of smaller capacity machines are usually wound with wire of rectangular section cotton covered and thoroughly impregnated, with machines of larger ratings, edge-wise wound strap field coils are used.

In order to damp any pulsation or hunting, particularly when the alternator is driven by diesel engine cage dampers are built into pole faces.

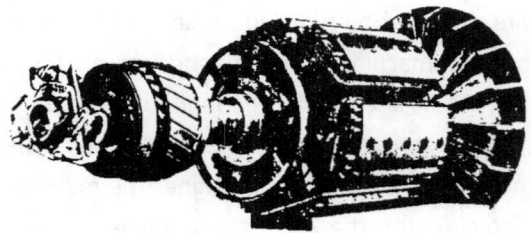

**Fig. 4.11 (b): Salient pole type rotor**

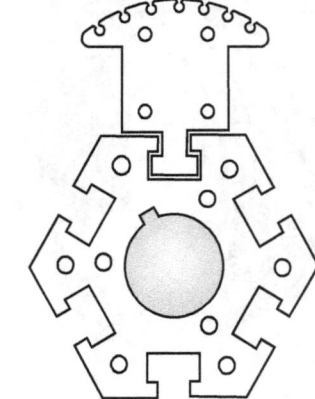

**Fig. 4.11 (c): Spider and pole punchings synchronous machine**

**Fig. 4.11 (d): Cylindrical forged steel rotor**

**Fig. 4.11 (e): Cylindrical rotor with winding**

(ii) Non-salient or cylindrical type of rotor is necessary for turbine or high speed alternators. The rotor is a cylindrical steel forging; in which longitudinal slots for holding the field windings are milled. The rotor shown in Fig. 4.11 (b) is for two poles.

The rotor is wound with copper strips. The copper end connections are supported by metallic end flanges to restrict centrifugal force.

## 4.2.3 Excition for Rotating System

The field windings of alternators are excited by direct current supply which can be obtained by the following ways:

(a) In case of small rating alternators it may be obtained by providing a small self excited D.C. shunt generator on the shaft of the same machine, called as exciter, while in case very large machine it can be obtained from the separately excited type of D.C. shunt generators which are excited by a pilot D.C. shunt generator mounted on the shaft of the same machine.

(b) In some case a small three phase alternators is mounted on the shaft of the main alternators and the output of which rectified with the help of rectifiers and then fed to field system of main alternators.

## 4.2.4 A.C. Armature Windings

The general principle which is used for D.C., windings also holds good for A.C. windings. In A.C. windings also the two sides of a coil should lie under the two adjacent poles so that the e.m.f. induced in the two sides, is in opposite direction or the resultant voltage is the addition in of two e.m.fs.

The general terms used in D.C. and A.C. windings are the same; still we will define some of the important terms used in A.C. windings.

(a) **Pole Pitch:** It can be defined as the distance measured between centres of two adjacent poles, equivalent to 180 electrical displacement.

It can also be defined as total number of armature slots/pole.

(b) **Full Pitch Coil:** When the two sides of a coil are one pole pitch apart, such a coil is known as full pitch coil, or the two coil sides of the coil will be 180 electrical apart; Such a winding is called as full pitch windings.

(c) **Fractional pitch:** If the span of the coil is less than full pitch, it is known as fractional pitch, and the winding may also be called as short pitch or short chorded winding.

## 4.2.5 Advantages of Using Short Pitched Windings

(i) The copper required for over hang portion of coil is reduced, hence cost is reduced and Cu losses are also reduced.

(ii) It improves the wave form of the generated e.m.f. and it can be made to approximate a sine wave.

(iii) The magnitude of the harmonic e.m.fs can be reduced due to short pitch windings.
(iv) As high frequency harmonics are eliminated or reduced, eddy current and hysteresis losses are reduced there by increasing the efficiency.

## 4.2.6 Single Layer Windings
These are the windings in which one coil side occupies on slot of armature.

## 4.2.7 Double Layer Windings
These are windings which are most commonly used, and in which there will be two coil sides in each and every slot. OR which will require total number of coils equal to armature slots.

## 4.2.8 Concentrated Winding
In this type of windings all the conductors required for producing one pole are concentrated in one slot only. In such type of windings, we can not make better use of the space available, hence not used.

## 4.2.9 Distributed Windings
When the conductors per pole are distributed as shown in Fig. 4.12. The effect is better utilisation of space but the e.m.f. induced in all the conductor/phase in this case will be equal to vector sum of e.m.f. induced in conductors or different slots/phase.

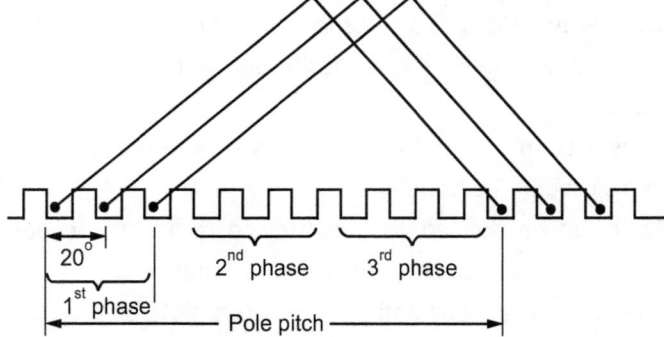

Fig. 4.12

## 4.2.10 Types of Single Layer Phase Distributed Windings
## 4.2.11 Lap Wound

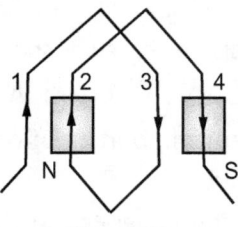

Fig. 4.13

## 4.2.12 Wave Wound

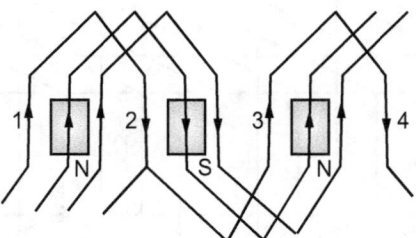

**Fig. 4.14**

## 4.2.13 Concentrated or Spiral Winding

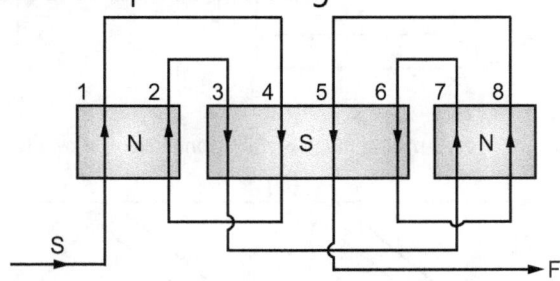

**Fig. 4.15**

## 4.2.14 Following Types of Windings are used in Case of 3-phase Alternators

(i) Three-phase single layer lap winding.
(ii) Three-phase single layer mush winding.
(iii) Three-phase double layer windings which are most commonly used.

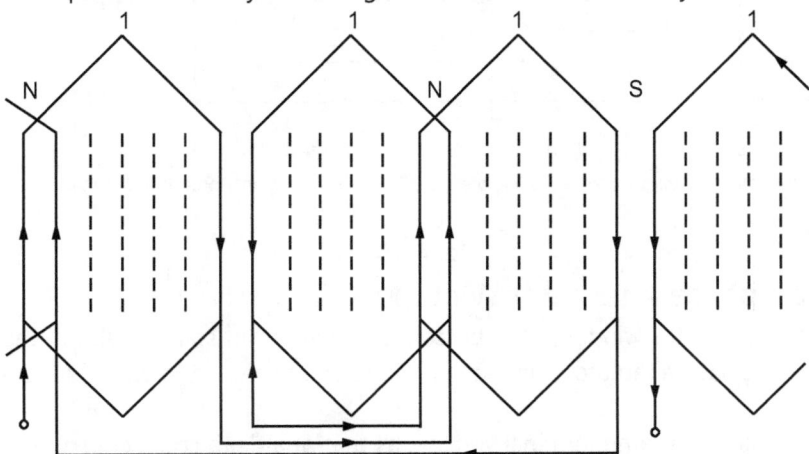

Single layer-3-phase, 4 pole, 24 slots full-pitch, lap-winding, only one-phase connections shown in figure

**(a)**

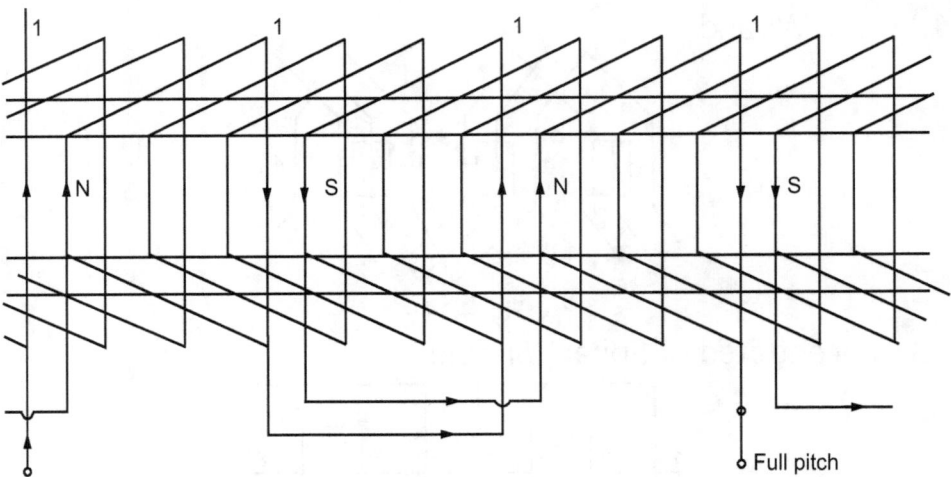

24 slots, 4 pole, Single layer -3-phase, mush winding connections shown for one phase only

**(b)**

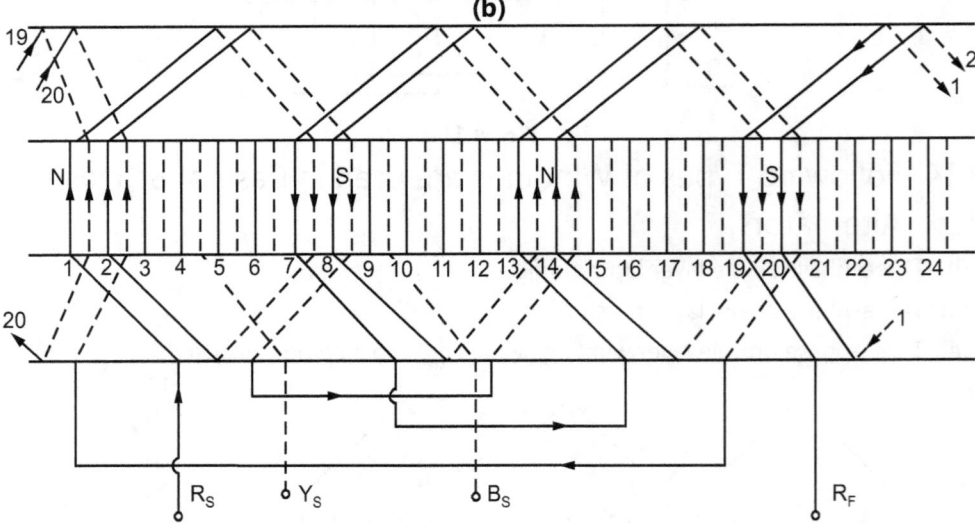

Double layer winding for 24 slots, 4 poles, 3-phase, full-pitch only one phase shown connected

**(c)**

**Fig. 4.16**

## 4.2.15 Three-phase Alternator Windings

Three-phase alternator windings can be connected either in star or delta formation, but majority of three-phase alternators have their windings connected in star, due to following advantages:

(i) For obtaining the same terminal voltage, as that of a delta connected alternator each phase winding of a star connected alternator requires only 58% of turns or its phase voltage is less, hence the cost of insulation required in case of star connection is less as compared with delta connection.

(ii) The star connected winding offers the advantage of a fourth or neutral lead making possible the advantages of a four wire system with or without ground neutral.

(iii) The wave shape of a star connected winding is improved owing to the elimination of third harmonies and all multiples of the third harmonics from terminal voltage.

## 4.2.16 Frequency of Alternating Currents

As a coil rotates between two magnetic poles one cycle is generated in the coil, i.e. in case of a two pole machine when the field coil completes one revaluation, one complete positive and negative pulse of current takes place in the armature conductor. Hence, the frequency in cycles per second will depend upon the number of pairs of poles and the revolution per second, made by the rotating field system. Hence in case of a multipolar machine, the frequency per revolution is equal to pair of poles and if the speed in N r.p.m. then the frequency will be given as

$$f = \frac{p}{2} \times \frac{rpm}{60} = \frac{pN}{120}$$

Where N is the speed in revolutions per minute.

Internal combustion engines have a low speed of say 200 r.p.m., hence for producing 50 Hz frequency the alternators should have 30 poles. Hydraulic turbines having medium speed of say 600 r.p.m. require alternators having 10 poles for producing 50 Hz frequency. While the steam turbines having high speed of 3000 r.p.m. require alternators of two poles for developing 50 Hz frequency of generated e.m.f.

## 4.3 DISTRIBUTION FACTOR OR BREADTH FACTOR

When the armature winding of an alternator is distributed as shown Fig. 4.17 the e.m.f. induced in the coil sides of one phase in the adjacent slots under one pole is not in phase, so the total e.m.f. is not an arithmetic sum, but is equal to a vector sum. Hence, the breadth factor or distribution factor may be defined as the ratio of vector sum of e.m.f. in all coils under one pole to the arithmetic sum had all the coils been concentrated in one slot.

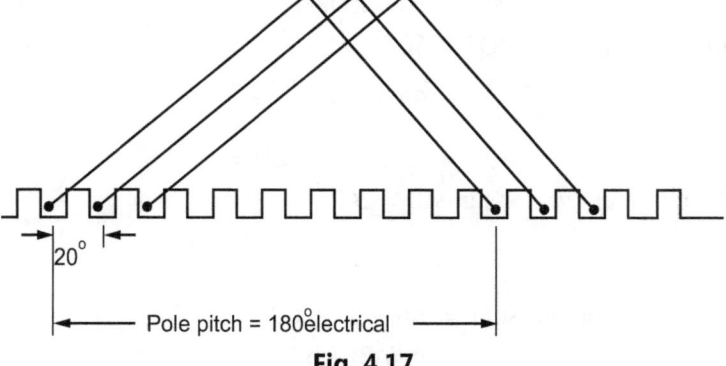

**Fig. 4.17**

Fig. 4.17 shows 9 slots per pole for a three-phase winding or 3 slots/pole/phase. The phase difference between e.m.fs. induced in adjacent conductors it two consecutive slots is 20. Fig. 4.17 shows a vector sum of 3 slots/pole per phase.

In general if there are N slots/pole, slot angle $\psi = \dfrac{180°}{N}$

$m$ = Number of slots per pole per phase
$N$ = Number of phases

If m is large then the vector diagram would be a semi-circle with resultant equal to its diameter Fig. 4.19.

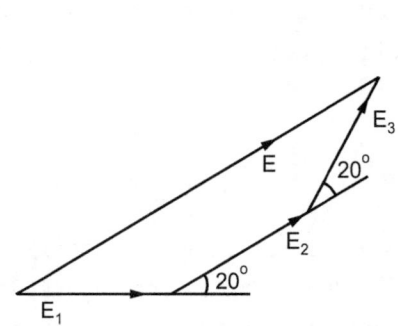
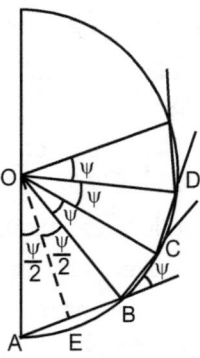
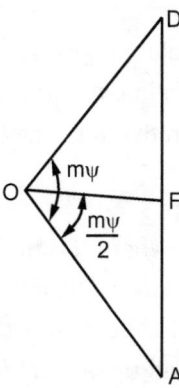

**Fig. 4.18**  **Fig. 4.19**  **Fig. 4.20**

AB = BC = CD = e.m.f. induced slot.
Draw OE perpendicular to AB

$$\angle OBA = \angle OBC$$

but $\quad \angle OBA + \angle OBC + \psi = 180$

∴ $\quad 2\angle = 180 - \psi$

or $\quad \angle OBA = 90 - \psi$ ... (1)

but from right angled triangle OBE

$$\angle OBE = 90 - \angle OBE$$ ... (2)

From equations (1) and (2), $\angle BOE = 90 - \angle OBE$

$$= 90 - \left(90 - \dfrac{\psi}{2}\right) = \dfrac{\psi}{2}$$

$$\angle AOB = \angle BOC = \angle COD = \psi$$

From Fig. 4.20 resultant vector sum AD = 2AF

$$= 2\,OA \sin \dfrac{m\psi}{2}$$

Arithmetic sum = AB + BC + CD + ...
$\qquad\qquad\qquad = m\,(AB) + m\,AE$

$$= m\, 2\, OA \sin \frac{\psi}{2}$$

$$\therefore \quad \text{Breadth factor} = \frac{\text{Vector } \Sigma}{\text{Arithmetic } \Sigma}$$

$$= \frac{2\, OA \sin m\, \psi/2}{2\, m\, OA \sin \psi/2}$$

where, $\psi$ = slot angle, and m = Number of slots/pole/phase

## 4.3.1 Coil Span Factor: Pitch Factor

When the two coil sides forming a coil are 180 apart, the coil is known as a full-pitch coil. In this case, the e.m.f. induced in the two sides of the coil is in series. When the coil span differs from the full pitch, the e.m.f. induced in each coil side is not in phase and the resultant e.m.f. of the coil is the vector sum of e.m.f.s induced in two coil sides. The coil span factor may be designed as the ratio of the vector sum to the arithmetic sum of induced e.m.fs. in the two sides of a coil.

Consider a coil short pitched by an angle from full pitch

$$AB = BC = \text{e.m.f. induced in each coil side.}$$

$$\therefore \quad \angle BAC = \angle BCA \text{ and } \angle CBA = 180 - \alpha$$

In $\triangle ABC$, $\angle BAC + BCA + \angle ABC = 180$

or
$$2 \angle BAC = 180 - \angle ABC$$

$$= 180 - (180 - \alpha) = \alpha$$

$$\angle BAC = \frac{\alpha}{2}$$

$$\therefore \quad \text{Vector sum, } AC = 2AD = 2AB \cos \frac{\alpha}{2}$$

$$\text{Arithmetic sum} = 2\, AB$$

$$\therefore \quad \text{Coil span factor} = \frac{2\, AB \cos \alpha/2}{2AB}$$

$$= \cos \frac{\alpha}{2}$$

where, $\alpha$ is the angle by which winding is short pitched.

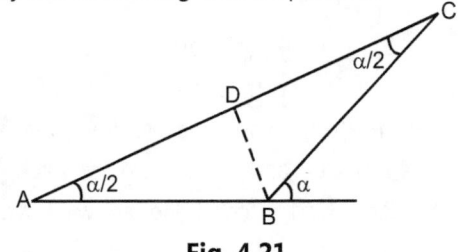

**Fig. 4.21**

## 4.3.2 E.M.F. Equation of Alternator

Consider a conductor on the stator of the alternator. Let the rotor of the alternators move through one revolution in t secs. If $\phi$ the flux emitted by each pole and P is the number of magnetic poles on the rotor. The total flux cut by the conductor in one revolution

$$= p\phi \text{ webers}$$

The average induced e.m.f./conductor will be found out by relation

$$e = \frac{d}{dt}(\text{flux}) \text{ volts} = \frac{p\phi}{t} \text{ volts}$$

If the rotor moves at a speed of N rpm, the time 't' for one revolution

$$= \frac{60}{N}$$

$\therefore$ Average e.m.f. $= \dfrac{P\phi N}{60}$ volt/conductor

**Fig. 4.22**

also, we know that, $\quad f = \dfrac{pN}{120} \text{ or } pN = 120f$

$$E_{av} = \frac{\phi\, 120\, f}{60} = 2\phi f \text{ volts/conductor}$$

where, f – frequency of induced e.m.f.

If the coil has T turns or 2T conductors.

The total e.m.f./coil = $4\phi fT$ volts

$\therefore \qquad E_{r.m.s.} = E_{av} \times \text{Form factor}$

For sine wave it is = 1.11

$$E_{r.m.s.} = 4k_1 \phi fT \text{ volts,}$$

where, $\qquad k_1$ = Form factor

The above equation will be true only when the winding is concentrated in one slot and full pitched, but practically it is not true as the winding for each phase, under each pole is distributed, as also usually they are short pitched. Hence, we have to take into account two factors $k_2$ and $k_3$, where,  $k_2$ = Breadth factor

and  $k_3$ = Pitch factor, hence the e.m.f. equation/phase is given as $E = 4k_1 k_2 k_3 \phi f T$ volts

where,  $\phi$ = Flux/pole in webers

$f$ = Frequency of induced e.m.f.

$T$ = Turns/phase

## ILLUSTRATIVE EXAMPLES

**Example 4.1:** A three-phase 16 pole, 60 Hz star connected alternator has 144 slots with 8 conductors/slot. The coil span $\frac{2}{3}$ of a pole pitch. Determine the phase and line e.m.f.s if the flux per pole is 0.062 weber.

**Solution:** Since the winding is short pitched,

$$\text{The pitched of winding} = 180 \times \frac{2}{3} = 120$$

∴ It is short pitched by 60.

Hence, Pitch factor $= \cos \frac{60}{2} = 0.866$

Total number of slots/pole/phase $= \frac{144}{16 \times 3} = 3$

∴ Number of slots/pole $= \frac{144}{16} = 9$ Nos.

∴ Slot angle $= \frac{180}{9} = 20$

The distribution or breadth factor $= \frac{\sin m\phi/2}{m \sin \phi/2}$

$$= \frac{\sin 3 \times 20/2}{3 \sin 20/2}$$

$$= \frac{0.5}{3 \times 0.1736}$$

$$= 0.961$$

Total number of slots/phase $= \frac{144}{3} = 48$

∴ Total number of conductors/phase $= 48 \times 8 = 384$

∴ Total number of turns/phase, $E = 4k_1 k_2 k_3 \phi f t$ volts

or  $E = 4$

or  Line voltage $= \sqrt{3} \times 2615$ volts

$= 4530$ volts

**Example 4.2:** A three-phase 1000 rpm delta connect alternator has double layer winding wound with 72 coils. Each coil has 40 turns and span of 150 electrical.

The flux/pole is 16.74 m. weber. Taking slot pitch as 15198 electrical. Calculate :

(i) conductor e.m.f.  (ii) turn e.m.f.
(iii) coil e.m.f.  (iv) line e.m.f. (frequency not to be assumed)

**Solution:** As total number of coils = 72 and the winding is double layer

Total number of slots = 72 Numbers

As slot pitch = 15 electrical total number of slots/pole = $\frac{180}{15}$ = 12 Nos.

∴ Total number of poles = $\frac{72}{12}$ = 6 Nos.

Now, from

$$f = \frac{pN}{120}$$

$$f = \frac{6 \times 1000}{120} = 50 \text{ Hz}$$

Now using the relation for average induced e.m.f./conductor

$$= 2 \phi f \text{ or r.m.s. value of e.m.f./conductor}$$

$$= 2 \times k_1 \phi f$$

where,

$k_1$ = Form factor = 1.11

(i) e.m.f./conductor = $2 \times 1.11 \times 16.74 \times 10^{-3} \times 50$

$$= 1.858$$

∴ e.m.f./turn = e.m.f./conductor

$$= 1.8585 \times 2 \times \cos \frac{30}{2}$$

$$= 3.589 \text{ volts}$$

(ii) coil e.m.f. = Turn e.m.f. × Number of turns per coil

$$= 3.589 \times 40 = 143.57 \text{ volts}$$

(iii) phase e.m.f. = line e.m.f.

= Coil e.m.f. × number of coils/phase × Distribution factor

$$= 1.43.57 \times \frac{72}{3} \times \frac{\sin m\phi/2}{m \sin \phi/2}$$

where, m = Number of slots/phase/pole = $\frac{72}{3 \times 6}$ = 4

and ψ = 15°

∴ line e.m.f. $= 143.57 \times 24 \times \dfrac{\sin 4\frac{15}{2}}{4 \sin \frac{15}{2}}$

$= 143.57 \times 24 \times \dfrac{0.5}{4 \times 0.13} = 3313.15$ volts.

## 4.4 ARMATURE REACTION IN CASE OF 3-PHASE ALTERNATORS

When the alternator runs at no load, there is induced e.m.f. developed in armature conductors if the field is excited, but there is no flow of current through armature conductors. When we connect the load across armature terminals, current flow through armature windings. In case of three phase alternators, this three phase current will produce a rotating magnetic field in the air gap. This flux will have certain effect on the flux produced by field system, which is called as Armature-reaction. This effect depends up on the nature of load p.f. Hence, we will find armature reaction effect of various p.f. loads.

### 4.4.1 When Alternator is Loaded with Unity p.f. Load

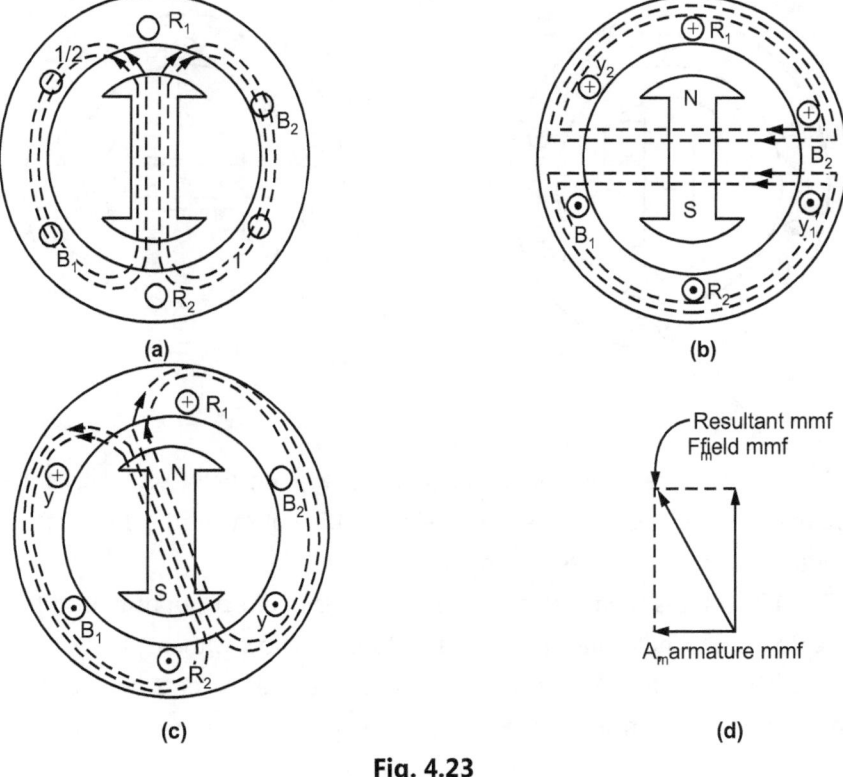

Fig. 4.23

We will consider a 3-phase 2 pole alternator having single layer concentrated winding, field being rotated in clock-wise direction, and resistive load being connected across armature terminals $R_1$, $R_2$, $Y_1$, $Y_2$ and $B_1$, $B_2$ represent the starting and finishing terminals of phases R, Y, B respectively. In Fig. 4.24 (a) a the flux due to field poles is represented in Fig. 4.24 (b) the flux due to induced currents only is represented, while in Fig. 4.24 (c), the combined effect of field flux and armature flux is shown; while representing armature flux, the direction of induced e.m.f. and direction of current flow is taken the same, as the p.f of load is unity.

The flux produced by field e.m.f. is rotated at synchronous speed. The flux produced by armature currents also rotates at synchronous speed. Thus, the two fluxes will be stationary with respect to each other. The two fluxes give rise to a resultant air-gap flux as shown in Fig. 4.23 (c) or represented by vector Fig. 4.23 (d). It is observed that the effect is a magnetic distortion or, it can be called as a cross magnetising effect.

## 4.4.2 Alternator Loaded with Lagging p.f. Load (Zero p.f. Lag)

When a purely inductive load is connected across the armature terminals, the armature current will lag the e.m.f. by 90°.

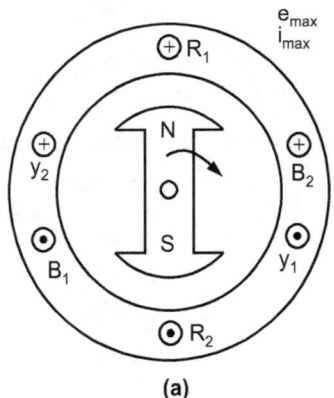
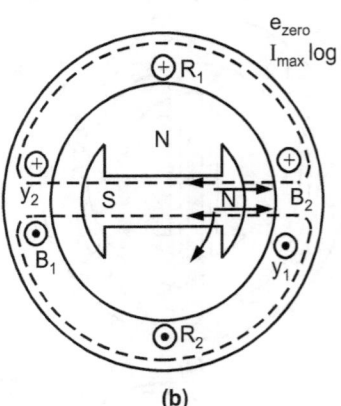

**Fig. 4.24**

Fig 4.24 (a) shows the condition of alternator delivering unity p.f load i.e. current and voltage are maximum at the same instant. While Fig. 4.24 (b) shows the condition when e.m.f. is zero in phase R, current in Phase R is maximum.

From Fig. 4.24 (b) it is seen that the armature flux is in direct opposition to the main flux or flux due to rotor. Thus, the effect of armature reaction with a purely inductive load connected across the armature terminals is to reduce the air gap flux i.e. the armature reaction effect is demagnetising. Hence Terminal Voltage will reduce on load, as e.m.f. will reduce.

## 4.4.3 Alternator Loaded with Zero p.f. Leading Load or Purely Capacitive Load

When we connect a purely capacitive load across the armature terminals, the current flowing through the armature windings will lead the induced e.m.f. by 90° i.e. the maximum e.m.f., phase R will take place after 90° the current in phase R. In this case, the position of rotor can be represented as in Fig. 4.25 (a) and (b) the position (a) again representing unity p.f. condition and Fig 4.25 (b) Zero p.f. lead.

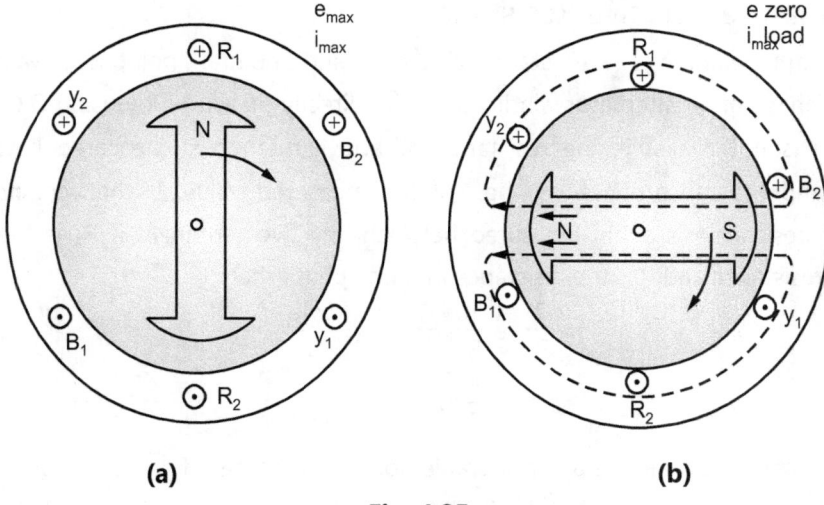

**Fig. 4.25**

It is seen from the Fig. 4.25 (a) and (b) that the armature flux acts in the same direction as that of the rotor flux i.e. the two fluxes help each other or the effect is strong magnetising. Hence, the Terminal Voltage will increase on load; as the e.m.f. will increased as load increases.

The effect of various load p.f. on the Terminal Voltage of alternator can be represented by the characteristics as shown in Fig. 4.26.

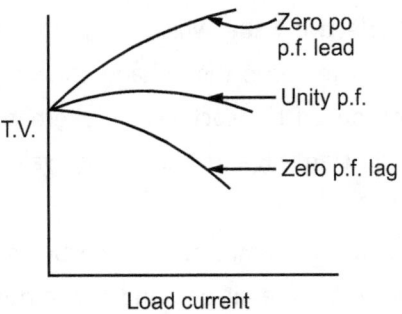

**Fig. 4.26**

It is observed from explanation that if the above magnitude the current is equal in all the above cases i.e. unity, lagging and leading p.f. the armature reaction is equal, However the effect on the flux produced by armature field is different i.e. cross magnetising D.C. magnetising, magnetising respectively.

In other words when power factor is lagging more field ampere turns are required i.e. main field system will require a larger field current to maintain a constant voltage on load, as angle of lag increases, and it will need reduced field current as angle of lead increase.

### 4.4.4 Armature Effective Resistance

If armature windings are star connected and neutral point is available, the resistance/phase of an alternator windings can be directly measured by using D.C. supply. If the neutral is not available, the resistance by above method is measured between two terminals and resistance/phase will be 1/2 the measured value. If the winding is delta connected, resistance is again measured between any two terminals, if $R_1$ is the value of measured resistance and R is the resistance in ohms/phase then

$$\frac{1}{R_1} = \frac{1}{R} + \frac{1}{2R}$$

or
$$R = \frac{3}{2} R_1$$

As the armature iron forms a considerable portion of the path for the flux which links the armature conductors alone, and as the flux is alternating in nature it will cause hysteresis and eddy current losses, in the iron immediately surrounding the slots. The power for these losses is supplied by the armature current. Also the slot leakage flux induces eddy currents in the armature conductors itself. At the same time due to the skin effect the A.C. current flows through the outer surface of conductor there by increasing the effective resistance. These factors increase the total loss when A.C. flows as compared with when same amount of D.C. flows through armature winding. Hence to obtain total loss with alternating current R must be increased to a suitable R effective value, which lies in the range of 1.25 to 1.75 times R, when calculating regulation of alternator, the voltage change due to resistance is small in comparison to the change produced by reactance of alternator. Therefore, it is sufficiently accurate to measure the D.C. resistance R and increase this value by nearly 50%.

### 4.4.5 Leakage Reactance

Load current flowing through the armature winding builts up magnetic flux of its own. Some portion of this does not cross the air-gap and hence does not an affect the field flux directly. It completes its parts in the stator core itself as shown in Fig. 4.27 conductors.

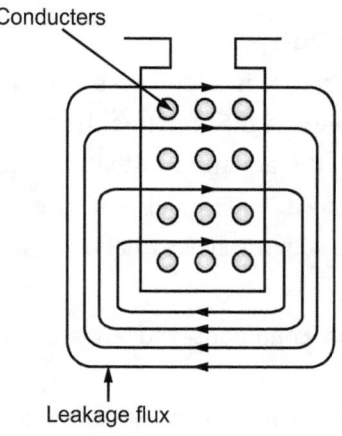

**Fig. 4.27**

This flux which links the armature coils but not the field coils, is called armature leakage flux, since the current in the armature conductors is alternating it produces e.m.f. due to self induction, which will act in opposition to e.m.f. in armature conductors; reducing its magnitude. Hence, it can be substituted by a leakage reactance $XL = 4\pi fL$, where L is the self inductance of armature per phase. Alternators having deeper and narrow slots will have higher self inductance.

## 4.4.6 Reactance Due to Armature Reaction

For different load conditions the magnitude of the air gap flux is different, because of the different effect of armature reaction; caused by different values of armature currents. The greater the value of armature current the greater will be the effect of armature reaction upon the air gap flux. This change in air gap flux with load will make the generated voltage different for different values of load. This effect of armature reaction up on generated voltage will depend not only on the magnitude of the armature current but also upon the load p.f. Since, the armature reaction results in a voltage effect in a circuit caused by change in flux produced by current in the same circuit its effect is some what of the nature of an inductive reactance. Therefore for a given load condition of the machine the effect of armature reaction can be replaced by a value of inductive reactance $X_a$, which would have the same effect on voltage relations.

Hence, when we add the two reactance i.e. $X_L$ the leakage reactance and $X_a$, the reactance replacing armature reaction effect we get $X_s = X_L + X_a$ where $X_s$ is called as synchronous reactance of the armature. It is a fictitious reactance that will produce an effect in armature equivalent to that produced by the actual armature leakage reactance $X_L$ and by the change in air gap flux caused by armature reaction. It is termed as synchronous reactance as it is due to the fluxes moving at synchronous speed.

## 4.4.7 Synchronous Impedance

When the synchronous reactance is added vectorially with the armature resistance; it is called the synchronous impedance of the armature. Thus, it is the fictitious impedance which wil produce the some effect in the armature as that produced by the actual resistance, the actual armature leakage reactance, and actual armature reaction. It is called synchronous impedance because it is related with machines rotating at synchronous speed.

## 4.4.8 Vector Diagrams

Representing different load conditions and armature reaction, leakage reactance and armature resistance drops :

Since the armature reaction results in a voltage effect in a circuit, caused by current in the same circuit its effect is some what of the nature of an inductive reactance. Hence, at the time of representing IX a drop is taken leading to current by 90°.

Vector diagram of alternator for different load conditions can be represented as follows.

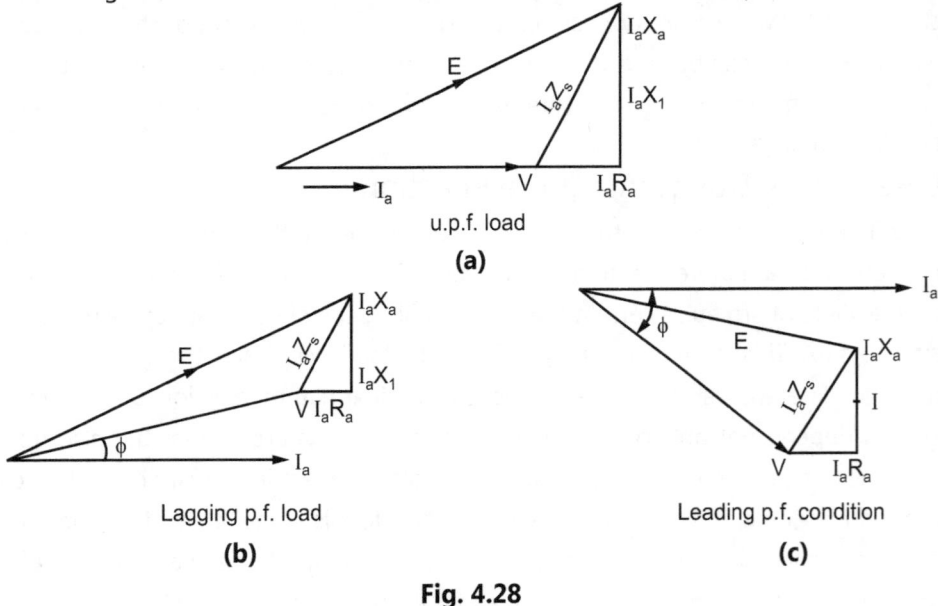

Fig. 4.28

# 4.5 REGULATION BY DIRECT LOADING METHOD

Regulation of alternator can be defined as the change in terminal voltage when its full load is thrown off, keeping excitation and constant.

Regulation by direct loading method is generally used for small rating machines as it will not be possible to conduct direct loading method, due to problems of heavy load, loss of energy etc. and availability of high power source in the testing laboratory.

## Circuit Diagram:

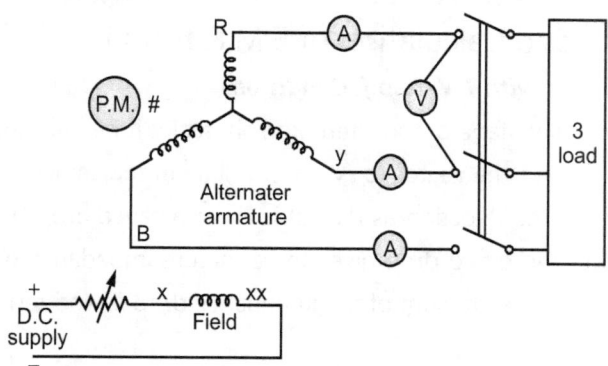

**Fig. 4.29**

First of all the prime mover of the alternator is started and its speed is brought upto its rated speed, or the speed represented by relation $N_s = \dfrac{120\,f}{p}$. Then the excitation of the alternator is increased so that its induced e.m.f. will increase the same is adjusted to its rated value. Then the load is taken on the alternator the speed is again adjusted to $N_s$ and the excitation increased so that T.V is rated T.V. on load rated frequency the load current is recorded. Then the load is suddenly thrown off excitation is kept constant, but the speed might have increased, which is brought to $N_s$ again and the value of no load voltage in this condition is recorded. This represents the induced e.m.f., corresponding to the load current recorded previously. The load is again connected across armature terminals, its value is increased now, the speed of P.M. is brought to $N_s$ again and excitation is adjust so that voltage across load is rated T.V. the value of load current is then recorded and the load thrown keeping excitation constant speed is adjusted to $N_s$ and value of induced e.m.f. is recorded. The process is repeated up to full load condition. Then the % regulation is calculated as follows:

$$\% \text{ regulation} = \dfrac{E - V}{V} \times 100$$

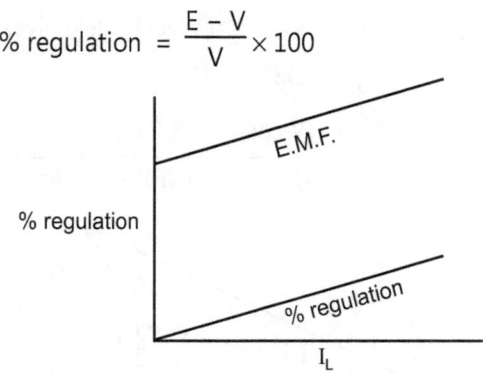

**Fig. 4.30**

where, E is the voltage at synchronous speed when load is thrown off, and V is the rated T.V. of alternator, If we plot % Regulation versus load current the characteristic will be as follows.

# 4.5.1 Representation of Vector Diagrams for Different Load Conditions and Calculation of E.M.F. from it

### 4.5.1.1 Current in Phase with T.V. (u.p.f. Condition)

Let V be the terminal voltage of the alternator/phase, let it be delivering a load current of I amps/phase at u.p.f. Then the vector for V and I will lie in the same direction. The resistive drop IR will act in the same direction as that of I. The reactance drop IX lead the current by 90°. The vector sum of these two drop gives the armature impedance drop IZ. The e.m.f. $E_o$ induced in the armature is vector sum of the impedance drop IZ and terminal voltage V from Fig. 4.31.

$$E_o^2 = (V + IR)^2 + (IX)^2$$

or

$$E_o = \sqrt{(V + IR)^2 + (IX)^2} \text{ volts}$$

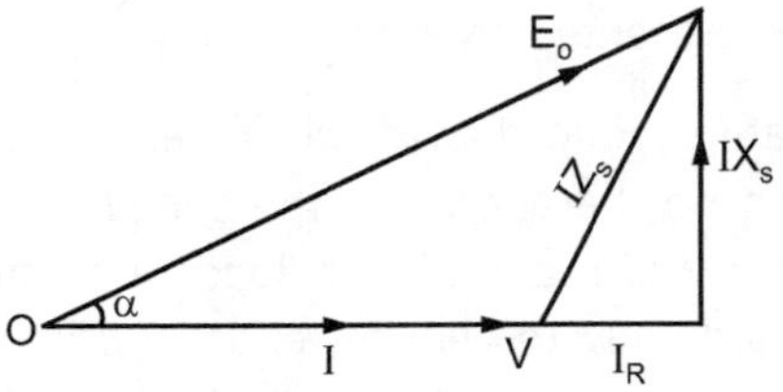

**Fig. 4.31**

It is seen from the vector diagram that with a load of u.p.f. the current is in the phase with T.V. but induced e.m.f. E by angle $\alpha$

### 4.5.1.2 For Lagging p.f. Loads

When current lags the T.V. by an angle. In Fig. 4.32, I is shown, lagging V, the T.V. by angle. The IR drop acts in the same direction as that of I, while I $X_a$ lead by 90°, and $IZ_s$ represents impedance drop; which when added to V vectorially gives the e.m.f. $E_o$

$$E_o^2 = (OB)^2 + (BF)^2$$

or

$$E_o^2 = (V \cos \phi + IR)^2 + (V \sin \phi + IX_s)^2$$

or

$$E_o = \sqrt{(V \cos \phi + IR)^2 + (V \sin \phi + IX_s)^2}$$

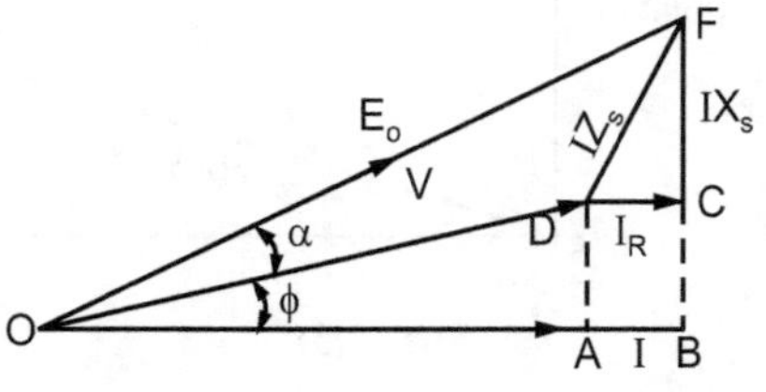

**Fig. 4.32**

## 4.5.1.3 For Leading p.f.

Fig. 4.33 shows the vector diagram when the alternator is connected to leading p.f. load. In this case, the load current leads the T.V. by an angle. In this case, also IR drop acts in the same direction as that of the current while $IX_s$ acts at an angle of 90° to I, in such a way that e.m.f. $E_0$ will be less than V.

From vector diagram, $\quad E_0 = OF$

or $\quad E_0^2 = (OD + DC)^2 + (CB - BF)^2$

or $\quad E_0^2 = (V \cos \phi + IR)^2 + (V \sin \phi \cdot IX_s)^2$

$\quad E = \sqrt{(V \cos \phi + IR)^2 + (V \sin \phi - IX_s)^2}$

When we known $E_0$, % regulation is calculated as

$$= \frac{E_0 - V}{V} \times 100$$

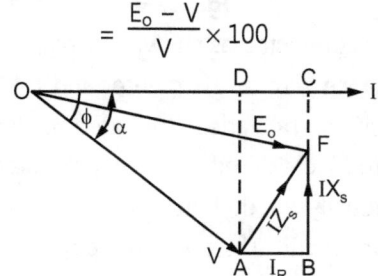

**Fig. 4.33**

## 4.5.2 O.C. and S.C. Test to Determine Synchronous Impedance

These test are conducted on the alternator to determine the data for calculating regulation of alternator.

### 4.5.2.1 Open Circuit Test

In this test, the alternators field is made to rotate at synchronous speed given by $\dfrac{120 f}{p}$ where f represents the frequency of induced e.m.f. and, p the number of poles for which armature winding is carried out. The field current is varied from zero in step and corresponding values of induced e.m.f. recorded. The graph representing relation between field current and induced e.m.f./per phase represent open circuit characteristic of the alternator and is similar in nature to magnetisation curve.

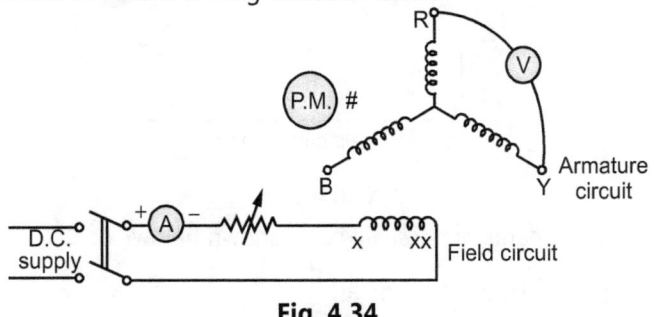

**Fig. 4.34**

### 4.5.2.2 Short Circuit Test

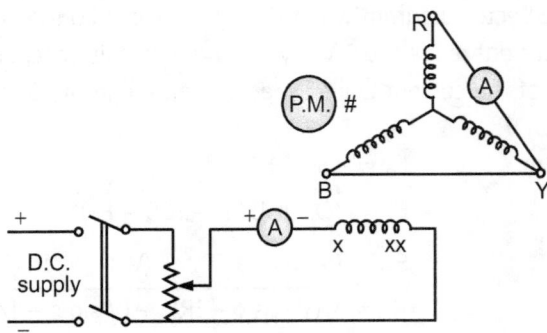

**Fig. 4.35**

In this test, the alternator is connected as shown in circuit diagram. The armature winding is short circuited by low resistance wire or a ammeter and the field circuit is connected to a D.C. supply so that field current can be varied from zero to desired value. The p.m. made to run at a speed required to produce desired frequency of alternator induced e.m.f. and the field current is increased gradually so that full load current of alternator is recorded by ammeter connected in armature circuit. The corresponding value of field current is recorded. As the armature terminals are short circuited, the terminal voltage is zero or the induced e.m.f. developed at this value of field current is utilised as impedance drop of armature winding. When a graph is plotted between field current and short circuit current and short circuit current it represent a straight line passing from field as at zero value of field current the S.C. current is also zero.

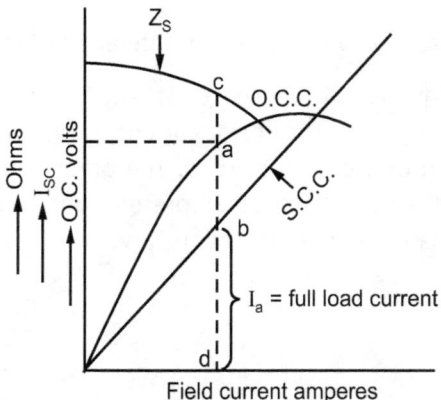

**Fig. 4.36**

The nature of the two characteristics will be as shown below.

$$\therefore \text{Synchronous impedance, } Z_s = \frac{E_a}{I_a} = \frac{ad}{bd}$$

### 4.5.3 Calculation of Synchronous Impedance

From the graphs it is clear that the field current required to produce full load armature current $I_a$ (bd) in the short circuit test is (od). When there is no armature current the e.m.f. $E_a$ produced in the armature for the same field current is (ad) volts. During short circuit test all this voltage $E_a$ is utilised in the impedance of the machine and hence T.V. is zero.

∴ Synchronous Impedance, $Z_s = \dfrac{E_a}{I_a} = \dfrac{ad}{bd}$

Generally, armature resistance $R_a$ is negligible as compared to its synchronous reactance, in this case $Z_s$, can be taken equal to $X_z$, but when $R_a$ is not negligible it can be measured by suitable methods and $X_s$ calculated as follows

$$X_s = \sqrt{Z_s^2 - R_a^2}$$

Knowing values of $R_a$, $X_s$, $I_a$ and terminal voltage, V regulation of alternator can be as explained before.

### 4.5.4 Error in Synchronous Impedance Method

In comparison to other methods of calculating regulation of alternator, this method gives results which are not so accurate. The regulation obtained by this method is too large; it is higher than actual, and hence is called as "Pessimistic method". The results are however more likely to be on safe side; and if we have some previous experience, allowance can be made for the amount of error in the method.

In this method, the value of Synchronous reactance particularly that part which replaces armature reaction is too large as it is determined at short circuit when the iron is not saturated. Also at short circuit the armature current lags the induced e.m.f. by nearly 90198 and armature m.m.f. is acting directly on the pole axis; where the effect of armature m.m.f. is much greater at short circuit, than the usual condition of load. These factors make $IX_s$ too large, so that the value of E is greater than under normal operating condition.

### 4.5.5 Alternator Regulation by m.m.f. Method

In synchronous impedance method of determining regulation, a voltage is substituted for armature reaction or for a m.m.f. In m.m.f. method, a m.m.f. is substituted for a voltage, this voltage being the $IX_s$ drop in the armature of the alternator. In other words armature leakage reactance is considered as being zero but armature reaction is increased by a sufficient amount to compensate for this.

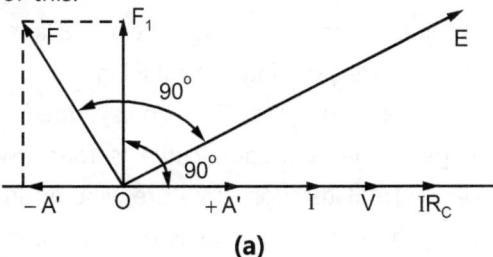

(a)

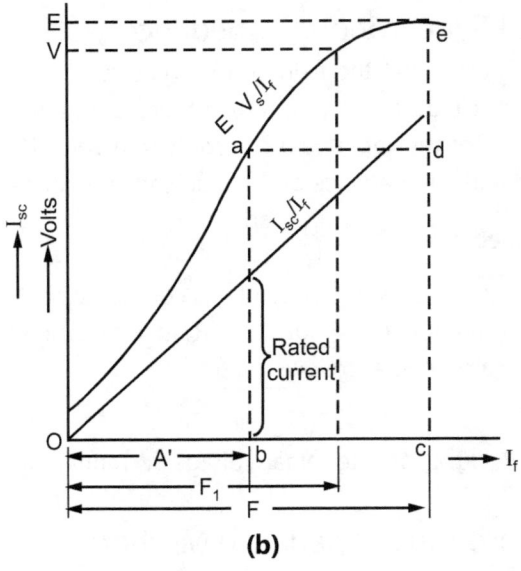

**Fig. 4.37**

This method also needs a short circuit and open circuit test on alternator Fig. 4.37 (a) represents the principle of the method. Fig. 4.37 (b) is constructed for unity p.f. load; in which V represents the T.V, to this added IR drop, which gives voltage $V_1$. A certain field current (m.m.f.) $F_1$ is required to produce this voltage $V_1$. The value of this m.m.f. in terms of field current (turns being constant) is found on the saturation current Fig. 4.37 corresponding to the value of $V_1$, the field current $F_1$ is found. $F_1$ is laid off at right angle to $V_1$ and leading it, as the m.m.f. leads by 90 the e.m.f. that its flux induces. In short circuit test field current is 'a' adjusted until the rated current flows through armature windings. The corresponding value of field current A' [Fig. 4.37 (a)] is then read. The m.m.f. represented by this field current is necessary to send rated current through the armature leakage reactance and at the same time over come the armature reaction. This m.m.f. A' replaces the combined effect of armature leakage reactance and armature reaction. It is laid off 180 from the current as shown at −A' Fig. 4.37 (b). Total m.m.f. that will produce total voltage drop in $X_s$ if $R_a$ is neglected as +A' the component that must balance this m.m.f. is −A'. The resultant m.m.f. is F; which at unity p.f. is the square root of the sum of squares of $F_1$ and $-A^1$. F is the m.m.f. exists at no load under assumptions made the no load e.m.f. E lags F by 90° Fig 4.37 (b) and is found on the saturation curve corresponding to field F Fig. 4.37.

To summarise the method at u.p.f. The IR drop is added to T.V and field current corresponding to this voltage $V_1$ on saturation curve is found which is $F_1$. Field current required to circulate full load current through armature winding in S.C. test is then marked square root sum of squares of these field currents is then found out. The value of e.m.f. on the saturation curve corresponding to this resultant field current is taken as no load e.m.f. of alternator and regulation is calculated in similar manner as

$$= \frac{E - V}{V} \times 100$$

## 4.5.6 Errors in m.m.f. Method

Because of low saturation on short circuit a given m.m.f. will produce greater increase of flux than an equal m.m.f. will produce under operating conditions; where the saturation of iron is greater. The e.m.f. corresponding to an increase in m.m.f. at short circuit will be much corresponding to an equal increase in m.m.f. taken higher up on the saturation curve. This is shown in Fig. 4.37 (a). On short circuit the e.m.f. ab corresponds to m.m.f. A'. The additional e.m.f. de corresponds to m.m.f. be equal to A' but taken higher up on the saturation curve. The e.m.f. de is obviously much less; than e.m.f. $ab_1$, hence that part of m.m.f. A' which replaces an e.m.f. is too small under load conditions. The no load e.m.f. E found on saturation curve is therefore too low, and the regulation as determined by this method is generally less then the actual regulation.

That part of m.m.f. A' which actually is armature reaction, is too high on short circuit, owing to low saturation and to the favourable position of the armature coils w.r.t. field poles. These two sources of error tend to off set each other in the m.m.f. method. The m.m.f. method therefore gives results closer to actual regulation than Synchronous Imp method. If the saturation curve is a straight line both methods will give nearly the same results.

## ILLUSTRATIVE EXAMPLES

**Example 4.3:** A 550 volts, 55 kVA single phase alternator has an effective resistance of 0.2 Ω. A field current of 10 Amps. produces an armature current of 200 Amps. on shorts circuit and an e.m.f. of 450 Volts oil open circuit calculate full load regulation with p.f. 0.8 lag. Draw vector diagram.

**Solution:** Full load current $= \frac{55 \times 10^3}{550} = 100$ amps.

Synchronous impedance, $Z_s = \frac{\text{O.C. voltage}}{\text{S.C. current}}$ at same field current

$$= \frac{450}{200} = 2.25 \; \Omega$$

∴ Synchronous reactance $= \sqrt{Z_s^2 - R_a^2}$

$$= \sqrt{(2.25)^2 - (0.2)^2} = 2.24 \; \Omega$$

From, $E = \sqrt{(V \cos \phi + I_a R_a)^2 + (V \sin \phi + I_a X_s)^2}$

$E = \sqrt{(550 \times 0.8 + 100 \times 0.2)^2 + (550 \times 0.6 + 100 \times 2.24)^2}$

or $E = 720.08$

$$\therefore \quad \% \text{ Regulation} = \frac{E - V}{V} \times 100$$

$$= \frac{720.08 - 550}{550} \times 100$$

$$= 30.92\%$$

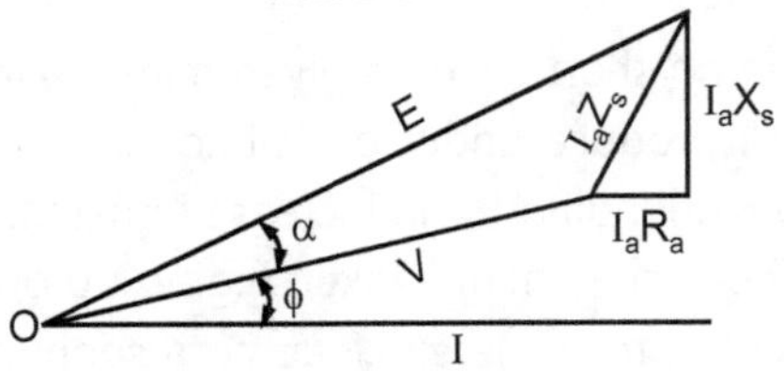

**Fig. 4.38**

**Example 4.4:** A 40 KVA, 400 V single phase A.C. generator gave the following test results.

**O.C. test:** A field current of 10 A produces an e.m.f. of 250 volts.

**S.C. test:** A field current of 10 Amps. caused a current of 150 A to flow in the short circuited armature.

Effective resistance of armature is 0.2 ohm. Calculate the synchronous impedance and reactance. If the A.C. generator is supplying full load current of 100 amps. of 0.8 p.f. lagging, find the regulation at this load.

**Solution:**

$$\text{Synchronous impedance} = \frac{\text{O.C. voltage}}{\text{S.C. voltage}} \text{ at same}$$

$$\text{Value of 10 amps. field current} = \frac{250}{150} = 1.666 \, \Omega$$

$$\therefore \quad \text{Synchronous reactance} = \sqrt{Z_s^2 - R_a^2}$$

$$= \sqrt{(1.166)^2 - (0.2)^2}$$

$$= 1.658 \, \Omega$$

$$\therefore \quad \text{Induced e.m.f. form} = \sqrt{(V \cos \phi + I_a R_a)^2 + (V \sin \phi + I_a X_s)^2}$$

$$= \sqrt{(400 \times 0.8 + 100 \times 0.2)^2 + (400 \times 0.6 + 100 + 1.658)^2}$$

$$E = 529.41$$

$$\therefore \quad \% \text{ Regulation form} \frac{E - V}{V} \times 100 = \frac{529.45 - 400}{400} \times 100 = 32.35\%$$

**Example 4.5:** A 2400 KVA, 800 (sqrt 3) volts, 3 phase star connected alternator, has synchronous impedance $Z_s = 0 + j\,30$ ohms per phase. Calculate the full load percentage regulation of 0.866 lagging p.f. Draw vector diagram.

**Solution:** Phase voltage $= \dfrac{800 \sqrt{3}}{\sqrt{3}} = 8000$ volts

as alternator is star connected

Full load current/phase = $\dfrac{2400 \times 10^3}{3 \times 8000}$

As 3-phase KVA = $3 V_P I_P \times 10^{-3}$ = 100 amps.

$R_a = 0, X_s = 30 \, \Omega$

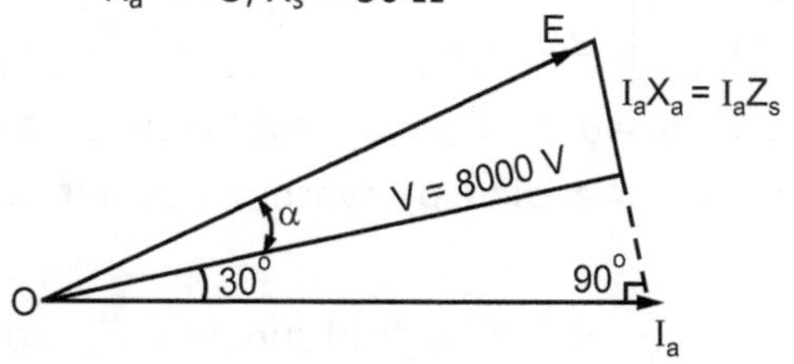

**Fig. 4.39**

∴ From,
$$E = \sqrt{(V \cos \phi + I_a R_a)^2 + (V \sin \phi + I_a X_a)^2}$$

or
$$E = \sqrt{(8000 \times 0.866 + 0)^2 + (8000 \times 0.5 + 100 \times 30)^2}$$

$E = 9848.71$

∴ % regulation from $\dfrac{E - V}{V} \times 100 = \dfrac{9848.7 - 8000}{8000} \times 1000 = 23.11\%$

**Example 4.6:** The test data for a 2000 V, single phase alternator is as below.

**Short circuit test:** Full load 100 A at $I_1$ = 2.5 amps.

**Open circuit test:** Terminal voltage of 500 V, at 2.5 amps.

(i) Find the value of synchronous impedance and synchronous reactance if $R_a$ = 0.8 ohm
(ii) Find the e.m.f. and % regulation when it carries a current of 25 amps. at zero p.f. leading.

**Solution:**
$$Z_s = \dfrac{\text{O.C. voltage}}{\text{S.C. current}} = \dfrac{500}{100} = 5\Omega$$

$$X_s = \sqrt{(5)^2 - (0.8)^2} = 4.935 \, \Omega$$

For leading p.f.,
$$E = \sqrt{(2000 \times 0 + 25 \times 0.8)^2 + (2000 \times 1 - 25 \times 4.93)^2}$$

$E = 1876.73$ volts

∴ % regulation from = $\dfrac{E - V}{V} \times 100$

$\dfrac{1876.73 - 2000}{2000} \times 100 = -6.163\%$

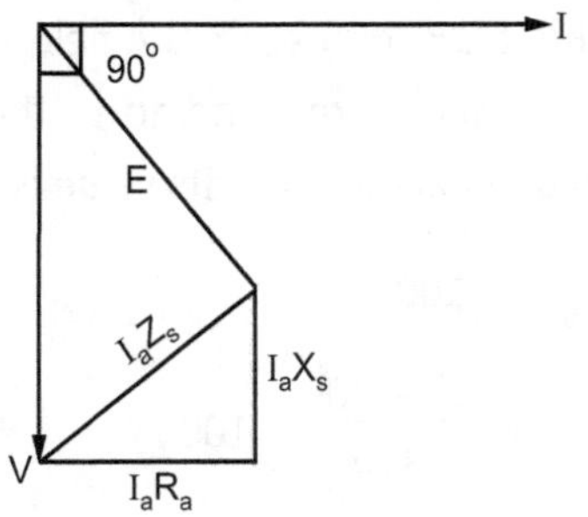

**Fig. 4.40**

**Example 4.7:** The magnetisation curve of 400 volts 50 Hz, alternator is given by the following readings.

| Open circuit volts  | 266 | 334 | 377 | 422 | 450 | 484 | 508 |
|---------------------|-----|-----|-----|-----|-----|-----|-----|
| Field current amps. | 2.0 | 2.5 | 3.0 | 3.5 | 4.0 | 4.5 | 5.0 |

Full load current was obtained by 2 amps. excitation on short circuit. Calculate the percentage regulation at 0.8 p.f. lagging by synchronous impedance method and m.m.f. method.

**Solution:** Open circuit voltage at 2 amps. field current = 226 volts.

Assuming full load current equal to 100 amps. as it is not given

$$\therefore \quad Z_s = \frac{266}{100} = 2.66 \text{ ohms}$$

As $R_a$ is not given

Taking, $\quad R_a = 0, X_s = Z_s$

$\therefore$ From,
$$E = \sqrt{(V \cos \phi + I_a R_a)^2 + (V \sin \phi + I_a X_s)^2}$$
$$= \sqrt{(400 \times 0.8 + 100 \times 0)^2 + (400 \times 0.6 + 100 \times 2.66)^2}$$
$$E = 598.69$$

$\therefore \quad$ % regulation from $= \dfrac{E - V}{V} \times 100$

$$= \frac{558.69 - 400}{400} \times 100$$

$$= 49.67\%$$

The method of calculating regulation by m.m.f. method is represented by the graph. Where OA represents the value of field current required to develop V + $I_a R_a$ drops, but $I_a R_a$ = zero i.e. it represent field current for V volts which is equal to 3.25 amps. To this added vectorially AB = field current required to circulate full load current in short circuit test, and lait at (90 + $\phi$)° to OA, where is p.f. angle, when p.f. is lagging at (90 − $\phi$)°.

When p.f. is unity. The resultant OB represents the field current required to maintain T.V. of 'V' volts on load. The induced e.m.f. corresponding to this field current is determined by projecting OB = OC on open circuit characteristic. Its value is 502 volts in this case.

Hence % regulation from $\dfrac{E - V}{V} \times 100$

$$= \frac{50 - 400}{400} \times 100$$

$$= 25.62\%$$

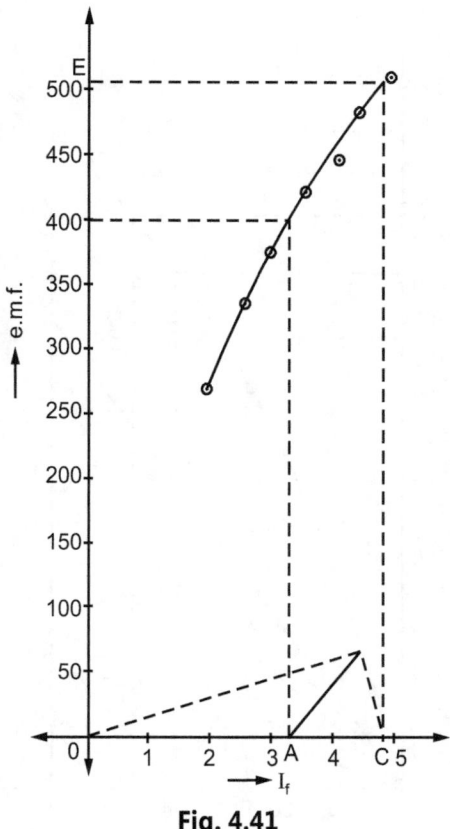

**Fig. 4.41**

**Example 4.8:** The open and short circuit test results for a three-phase star connected to 1000 KVA, 2200 volts, 50 Hz alternator are as follows:

**O.C. Test:**

| Field Current Amps. | 10 | 20 | 25 | 30 | 40 | 50 | 65 |
|---|---|---|---|---|---|---|---|
| O.C. Voltage (Terminal) | 800 | 1500 | 1760 | 2000 | 2350 | 2600 | 3000 |

**S.C. Test:**

| Field Current | 20A | 25 |
|---|---|---|
| Armature Current | 200 | 250 |

The armature effective resistance 0.25 ohm/phase. Determine regulation of the above alternator at full load, 0.8 p.f. lag, 0.8 p.f. lead and unity by m.m.f. method.

$$\text{Full load current/phase} = \frac{\text{Total volt amps.}}{3\,V_p}$$

$$= \frac{1000 \times 1000}{\sqrt{3} \times 2200}$$

$$= 262.44 \text{ Amps.}$$

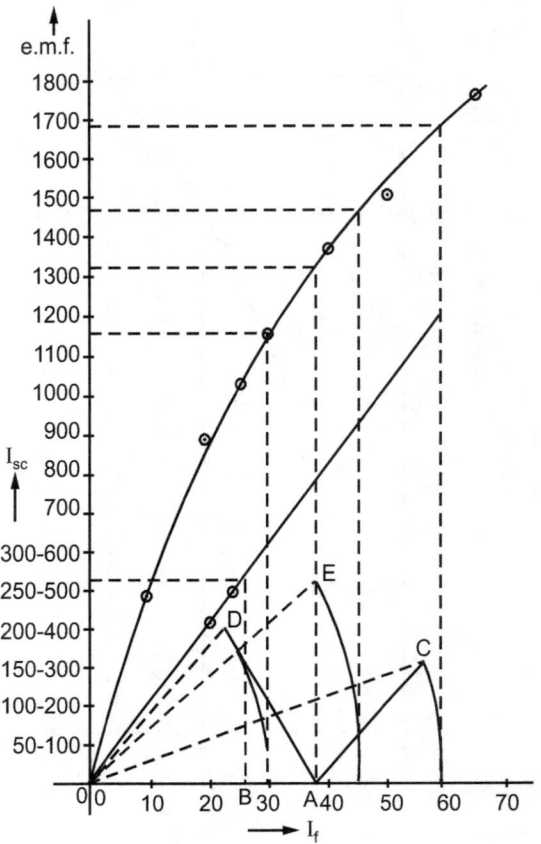

**Fig. 4.42**

The open circuit characteristic, between field current and O.C. voltage/phase will be as represented in the following table.

| Field Current Amps. | 10 | 20 | 25 | 30 | 40 | 50 | 65 |
|---|---|---|---|---|---|---|---|
| O.C. Voltage per Phase | 462 | 866 | 1016 | 1154.7 | 135.8 | 1501 | 1732 |

$$\text{Terminal voltage/phase} = \frac{2200}{\sqrt{3}} \text{ volts}$$

$$= 1270.17 \text{ volts}$$

$$V + I_a R_a \cos\phi = 1270.17 + 262.44 \times 0.25 \times 0.8$$

$$= 1322.65$$

Field current required to produced this e.m.f. from O.C. characteristic = 37.5 A.

Field current required to circulate full load current through armature winding in S.C. test, from S.C. characteristic = 26 amps. = Ob

Draw AC = OB at (90 + 36.86) to OA, then O.C. represents the field current required to maintain T.V. of 1270.17 volts at f.l. 0.8 p.f. lag.

e.m.f. corresponding to this field current (m.m.f.) = 1675 volts

∴ % regulation from $\dfrac{E-V}{V} \times 100$

at 0.8 p.f. lag $= \dfrac{1675 - 1270.17}{1270.17} \times 100$

$= 31.87\%$

Field current required to maintain T.V. of 1270.17 at f.l. and 0.8 p.f. lead is determined by laying AD at (90 – 36.86) to OA, and determining the value of AD.

e.m.f. corresponding to field current (m.m.f.) AD = 1160 volts

∴ % regulation at 0.8 p.f. lead, and full load from $\dfrac{E-V}{V} \times 100$

$= \dfrac{1160 - 1270.17}{1270.17} \times 100$

$= -8.67\%$

For finding regulation at unity p.f. the vector for field current of 26 amps. i.e. AE is laid 90 to OA, the total field current required to maintain rated T.V. of 1270.17 volts at unity p.f. is then equal = 45.75 amps.

e.m.f. corresponding to this field current is = 1470 volts

% regulation at f.l. unity p.f. condition from $\dfrac{E-V}{V} \times 100$ V

$= \dfrac{1470 - 1270.17}{1270.17} \times 100$

$= 15.73\%$

## 4.5.7 Ventilation

In case of slow speed salient pole alternators, the problem of ventilation is not difficult. The length of embedded conductors is not large as compared to that in case of turbo-generators hence the exposed dissipating surface is large, and the salient poles provide fan action to provide circulating air. While in case of large turbo generators the length of embedded conductor is very large, hence little ventilating, action is obtained from the smooth cylindrical rotor making it difficult a problem of proper ventilation. Also since ventilating ducts in the solid steel rotor are impracticable; all ventilating gas must flow in axially through the air gap or through axial ducts in this stator laminations. In the stator, special ventilating ducts must be provided, see Fig. 4.43. Totally enclosed systems of ventilation are now used. In addition to eliminating the accumulation of dirt, in the ventilating system, that wound result if outside air were circulated, this method minimizes fire hazard by eliminating the available supply of oxygen. Mains are also provided for releasing carbon dioxide if fire takes place.

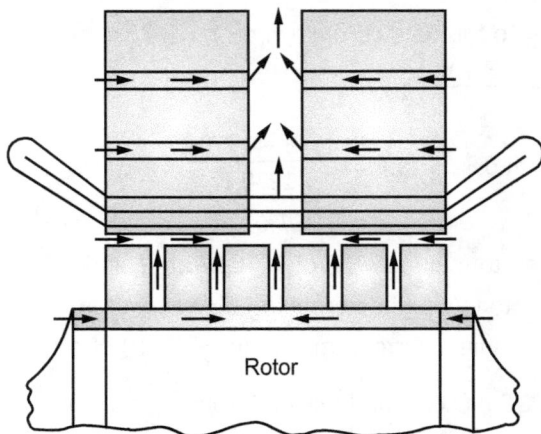

**Fig. 4.43: Passage of ventilating air through the ducts of a turbo alternator**

The cooling medium which may be either air or hydrogen, is cooled by passing over pipes through which cooling water is circulated; the cooling medium itself circulates continuously through; the alternator ventilating system.

Nearly all turbine driven alternators and large sized synchronous motors are now-a-day built with hydrogen cooling system. The main reasons for using hydrogen instead of air is to reduce the wind age loss. It reduces the value of windage loss to about one tenth the value when air is used for cooling, it results into increased efficiency at rated load; it also provides better cooling effect, which increases the rating of the machine by nearly 20%. Other advantages of hydrogen are the reduction of oxidation of the insulation and the reduction of fire hazard and of windage noise. The properties of hydrogen that make it more useful as a cooling medium are that its density is only 7 per cent that of air, hence the decreased windage loss, and it has 7.5 times the thermal conductivity of air and for a given temperature difference will transfer 30 per cent more heat from a given surface than air. Because of its explosive nature, it must be used in a gas light enclosure. In case of synchronous condensers, there is no extended shaft hence they were the first type of machine to employ hydrogen cooling. With alternators, a special oil seal in the bearings has been developed and the loss of hydrogen by leakage is made negligible. The danger of explosion is practically eliminated by maintaining the hydrogen pressure slightly above atmospheric. Also explosive range of hydrogen air mixtures is between 5 and 75 per cent hydrogen, and the normal percentage under operating hydrogen is 95 to 98 per cents. This mixture also will not support combustion.

In Fig. 4.43 is shown in simplified form the longitudinal system of ventilation. The cooling air flows longitudinally or axially through the air gap and the perforations in the laminations and is discharged radially through the ventilating ducts.

## 4.5.8 Losses in Synchronous Machines

The various losses taking place in a synchronous machine are as follows:
- **(i) Fixed losses or rotational losses :** These losses can further be divided as
    - (a) Friction and windage loss
    - (b) Open circuit core loss.
- **(ii) Field circuit loss :** It is actually the copper loss taking place in the field circuit and is equal to $I_f^2 R_f$ where $I_f$ represents field current in amps. and $R_f$ represents field circuit resistance in ohms.
- **(iii) Direct load loss :** It is the copper loss taking place in the armature winding. If I is the armature current per phase and R is the resistance of armature winding per phase then for a three phase synchronous machine, total Direct load losses = $3 I^2 R$ watts.
- **(iv) Stray load losses :** It consists of two components, namely:
    - (a) iron loss or core loss due to armature leakage flux, and
    - (b) armature copper loss due to skin effect and eddy currents in the armature conductors.

In iron parts, the stray load loss caused by the armature leakage flux, is due to the eddy current and hysteresis losses in the teeth, core end plates, end covers etc.

A part of the armature leakage flux links the armature conductors and consequently e.m.f.s are induced in them. These induced e.m.f.s set up circulating currents or eddy currents in the conductors and make the conductor current distribution no-uniform which gives rise to additional copper-loss. This additional copper loss forms a considerable percentage of stray load loss.

The combination of direct load-loss and stray load losses is referred to as

**Short Circuit Load Loss:**

Friction and windage loss can be measured by running the sychronous machine at rated speed with its field winding unexcited. The mechanical power input, $W_f$ required to drive the synchronous machine gives its friction and windage loss. If now the field winding is excited and the mechanical power input is measured it represents ($W_f + W_2$), where $W_f$ is friction and windage loss and $W_2$ represent open circuit core losses of synchronous machine, which consists of combination of eddy current and hysteresis losses, which are caused due to changing flux densities in the machine core, when only the field winding is excited. Since, the eddy current and hysteresis losses are approximately proportional to square of voltage, the open circuit core loss also varies approximately as the square of open circuit voltage, this variation is shown in Fig 4.44 (a). The variation of rotational losses or fixed losses with field current is shown in Fig. 4.44 (b). The intercept of rotational losses with the y-axis in

Fig. 4.44 (b) gives the constant friction and windage loss, because with zero field excitation open circuit core loss is zero.

The field circuit loss can be determined, if $V_f$ is the field voltage and $I_f$ is the field current as equal to $V_f I_f$ watts, or equal to $I_f^2 r_f$ where $r_f$ is field resistance at working temp.

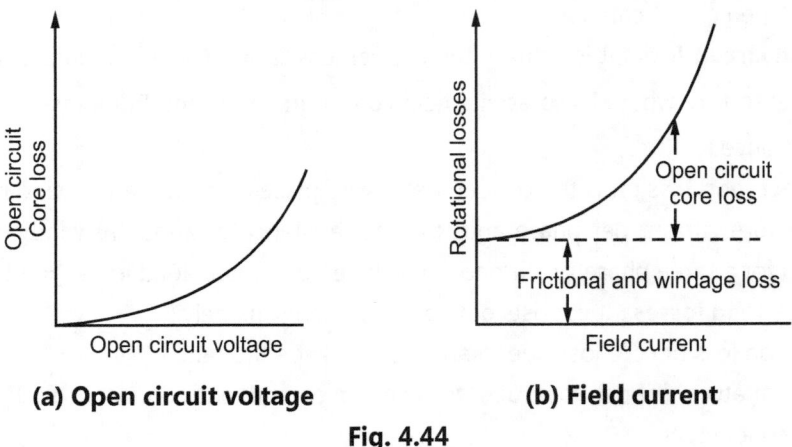

**(a) Open circuit voltage**  **(b) Field current**

**Fig. 4.44**

The short-circuit load loss is a combination of copper loss in the armature winding and the stray load loss. The stray load loss is obtained by the following relation:

Stray load loss = (Short circuit load loss) − (Armature copper loss at working temperature)

Fig. 4.44 (c) presents the variation of short circuit-load loss and stray load loss, with the armature current. It is seen that short-circuit load loss is approximately proportional to the square of armature current.

In A.C. electromagnetic devices, the short circuit-load loss divided by the square of the short-circuit armature current gives its effective resistance $r_{a.\ eff}$.

i.e.
$$r_{a.\ eff} = \frac{\text{S.C. load loss}}{(\text{S.C. armature current})^2}$$

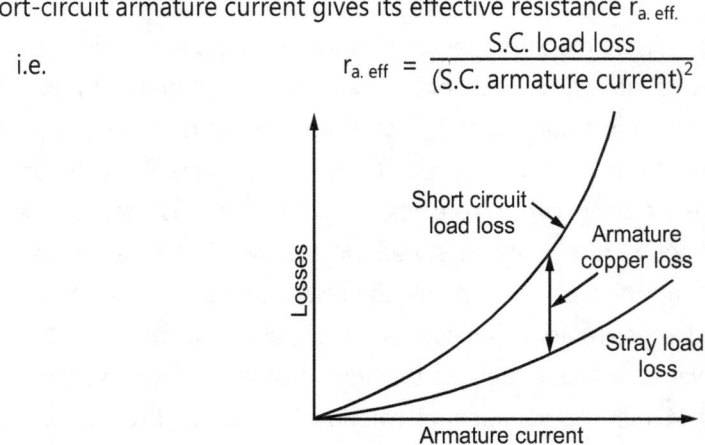

**Fig. 4.44 (c): Armature current**

The stray load loss and effective armature resistance once calculated at rated current are considered to remain constant under normal operating conditions.

Alternator efficiency in the laboratory can be determined by using D.C. shunt motor as its prime mover and performing the following tests.

(a) Uncouple the D.C. motor from alternator, and run it at synchronous speed of alternator, measure the applied voltage and armature current of motor. If armature resistance $r_a$ is known, then

$$VI_a = \text{Friction, windage and core loss of D.C. Motor (stray losses)} = W_1 + I_a^2 R_a$$

where $I_a^2 R_a$ represents very small no load armature copper loss and

$$W_1 = \text{Stray - Losses}$$

or

$$W_1 = VI_a - I_a^2 R_a$$

(b) Now couple the alternator with above D.C. shunt-motor, run it again at the synchronous speed of alternator, keeping field winding of alternator unexcited, and record, applied voltage and armature current of motor again, then

$$VI_{a1} = W_1 + I_{a1\,r_a}^2 + \text{Friction and windage loss of alternator, } W_f$$

or

$$W_f = VI_{a1} - (W_1 + I_{a1\,r_a}^2)$$

(c) Repeat (b) again, but exciting the alternator with normal field current and keeping armature terminals open.

Then,

$$VI_{a2} = W_1 + I_{a2\,r_a}^2 + W_f + \text{open circuit core loss of alternator, } W_2.$$

or

$$W + W = VI_2 - (W_1 + I_{a2\,r_a}^2)$$

or

$$W_2 = VI_{a2} - (W_1 + I_{a2\,r_a}^2 + W_f)$$

If $(W_2 + W_f)$ is plotted as a function of alternator field current then the curve will cut the y-axis, giving value of $W_f$ because when $I_f = 0$, $W_2 = 0$ and constant loss $W_f$ is obtained refer Fig 4.44 (b).

(d) Run the motor at synchronous speed of alternator, Perform 3 phase symmetrical short circuit test on alternator with short circuit current equal to rated current of alternator. Note down values of V, $I_{a3}$ for the motor now,

Then,

$$V I_{a3} = W_1 + E_{a3\,r_a}^2 + W_f + \text{Short circuit load loss } W_3$$

or

$$W_3 = V I_{a3} - (W_1 + I_{a3}^2 + W_f)$$

Since field current is small during short-circuit test, alternator core loss (being proportional to field current is neglected.

(e) Field circuit loss is equal to the product of applied voltage across the field and the field current or say

$$= VI_f \text{ watts}$$

where V is the applied voltage across field and $I_f$ is the current flowing through field winding.

∴ Total alternator losses = Friction and windage loss + Open circuit core less + Short-circuit load loss + Field circuit loss

$$= W_f + W_2 + W_3 + VI_f$$

And alternator efficiency $= 1 - \dfrac{\text{Total loss}}{\text{Total input}}$

**Example 4.9:** A 50 kVA, 400 volts, 3-phase, star-connected alternator has the following data:

(i) Friction and windage loss = 180 watts.
(ii) Open circuit core loss = 250 watts.
(iii) Field winding resistance at working temperature of 75°C = 200 Ω.
(iv) Effective armature resistance per phase = 0.03 Ω.

The field winding is excited at 200 volts.

Calculate the efficiency of alternator at 0.8 p.f. and at

(i) Half full load,   (ii) Full load.

**Solution:** Full load current/phase $= \dfrac{50 \times 1000}{\sqrt{3} \times 400}$

Short-circuit load loss at half-full load current = 72.17 amps.

$$= 3 \left(\dfrac{72.17}{2}\right)^2 \times r_a$$

$$= 3 \times (36.085)^2 \times 0.03 = 117.19 \text{ watts}$$

Short-circuit load loss at full-load current

$$= 3 \times (72.17)^2 \times 0.03 = 468.76 \text{ watts}$$

Field circuit loss $= \dfrac{V^2}{R_f} = \dfrac{(200)^2}{200}$

$$= 200 \text{ watts}$$

Total losses at half full-load $= W_f + W_2 + W_3 +$ field loss

$$= 180 + 250 + 117.19 + 200 = 747.19 \text{ W}$$

Output at half load, 0.8 p.f. $= 25 \times 1000 \times 0.8 = 20000$ watts

∴ $\eta$ at $\dfrac{1}{2}$ f.l., 0.8 p.f. $= \left(\dfrac{1 - \text{Total losses}}{\text{Output} + \text{Total losses}}\right)$

$$= \left(1 - \frac{747.19}{20000 + 747.19}\right) = 0.964$$

$$= 96.4\%$$

∴ $\eta$ at full load $= \dfrac{\text{Output}}{\text{Output + Losses}}$

$$= \frac{50 \times 1000 \times 0.8}{50 \times 1000 \times 0.8 + 180 + 250 + 468.76 + 200}$$

$$= 0.9732$$

or $= 97.32\%$

## 4.5.9 Hunting

If a reciprocating engine or a gas engine is used as prime mover for alternators, the torque developed by it is not uniform during a revolution; it varies from zero at dead centres to maximum at some intermediate position. For reducing this variation in torque a heavy fly-wheel is provided to such prime movers but even with a heavy fly-wheel, this variation of torque may impart impulses to the induced e.m.f. causing it to be ahead of its correct position at same instant and behind it at other instants. This will cause large currents to flow between alternators in parallel; and often causes their rotating members to oscillate about their average speed as they are rotating. The impulses often are communicated to the system. Causing synchronous motors to oscillate. These oscillations are called as hunting. It may become serious if the engine governors have a natural frequency of oscillation nearly the same as that of the machine rotors, the oscillations may then become cumulative and may even cause the alternators to go out of synchronous.

Remedies of hunting are to use heavy fly-wheel, to put dash pots on the engine governors, and to use squirrel cage (armature) windings around the field. Where several engine-driven units are used, they are often paralleled when their cranks occupy different angular positions.

## THEORY QUESTIONS

**(I) Fill in the gaps with suitable words:**
1. The maximum synchronous speed in India is ...... r.p.m.    (3,000, 4,000, 6,000)
2. The armature reaction in a 3 phase alternator at zero p.f. lagging is ...... and at zero p.f. leading is (demagnetising, magnetising)
3. The voltage regulation of an alternator is negative, when p.f is ...... (leading, lagging, unity)

4. Number of coil and number of slots are equal in ...... (single layer winding, double layer winding)
5. The effective armature resistance of alternator is ...... than D.C. resistance due to effect (greater, skin)
6. Synchronous reactance is the combined effect of ...... reactance and effect of ...... due to armature current when alternator is loaded. (leakage, reaction.)
7. ......, ......, ......, ...... are the factors affecting the regulation of the alternator. (load current, load p.f., armature resistance, synchronous reactance)

**(II) Answer the Following:**
1. Why is the synchronous impedance method treated as pessimistic method for regulation calculation of alternator ?
2. What is the effect of saliency on the performance of alternator.
3. Derive the e.m.f. equation per phase for alternator with distributed and short pitched coils.
4. The synchronous impedance method of determining regulation gives higher values than the values obtained in actual load condition. Explain.
5. Commercial alternators are built up with poles kept rotating. Explain the reasons in detail.
6. Explain armature reaction in alternator different p.f. conditions.
7. Modern trend is to build alternators with high regulation. "Explain".
8. In the case of alternators state briefly the effects of armature reaction and hence explain the term synchronous reactance.
9. Explain briefly the different factors affecting induced e.m.f. in a poly phase alternator and derive the usual expressions for them.
10. Describe briefly, the m.m.f. method for finding the regulation of alternator, and explain why this method is called as "optimistic method".
11. Discuss advantages of rotating field type alternators. Write briefly on constructional features of salient pole and cylindrical pole type alternators.
12. Define Regulation of alternator and explain laboratory method of finding regulation by direct loading method. Draw circuit diagram and indicate instrument ranges.
13. What will happen if the prime mover of the alternator is run faster/slower than the synchronous speed.
14. Alternator has steady armature and rotating field give reasons.

# BASIC ELECTRICAL DRIVES & CONTROLS

**SINGLE PHASE INDUCTION MOTORS .....**

## (III) Examples for Practices:

1. A 100 KVA, 3300 volts, 3 phase star connected alternator delivers full load current at rated voltage and 0.8 p.f. lagging. The resistance of the machine per phase in 0.5 ohm and reactance 6.5 ohms. Estimate the T.V. for the same excitation and load current at 0.8 p.f. leading.

2. An A.C. generate winding has per phase an effective resistance of 0.2 ohm and synchronous reactance of 2.2 ohms. Find the percentage regulation for the load of 50 A at terminal voltage or 500 volts at 0.87 lagging p.f. Draw vector diagram.

3. A 3-phase, 1000 rpm, delta connected alternate has double layer armature winding wound with 72 coils. Each coil has 40 turns and span of 150 electrical. The flux/pole is 16.74 mwb, sinusoidally distributed taking slot pitch as 15 electrical, calculate conductor e.m.f., turn e.m.f., hence coil e.m.f., hence phase e.m.f., and hence line e.m.f., (frequency not to be assumed.)

4. If a field current of 10 amps. in a certain alternator gives a current of 150 amps. on short circuit and a terminal voltage of 900 volts on open circuit, find the terminal voltage, drop with a load current of 60 amps. (IZ).

5. Determine from the following data on 17.3 KVA, 400 volts, 3-phase 50 H, star connected alternator, the percentage regulation on full load at 0.8 lagging p.f.
   (i) Effective resistance between the two terminals of an alternator is one ohm.
   (ii) In open circuit test on alternator the voltmeter between the line and neutral reads 35 volts, when the field current is 1.5 amps.
   (iii) In short circuit test on alternator the ammeter connected between two terminals reads 17 amps. for the same field current of 1.5 amps.
   
   (**Hint:** $R_a = \frac{1}{2}$ i.e. 0.5 Ω and $Z_s = \frac{35}{17}$ ohms)

6. The open circuit and short circuit test reading for a three phase, star connected 1000 KVA, 2000 V, 50 Hz synchronous generator are

| Field amperes | 10  | 20   | 25   | 30   | 40   | 50   |
|---------------|-----|------|------|------|------|------|
| O.C. Volts    | 800 | 1500 | 1760 | 2000 | 2350 | 2600 |
| S.C.C.        | 200 | 250  | 300  |      |      |      |

   $R_a$ = 0.2 ohm/phase, Draw O.C.C. and S.C.C and find regulation at full load 0.8 p.f. lagging and 0.8 p.f. leading from the graph.
   (**Hint:** Solve to Example No. 6)
   
   Laboratory experiments with real circuit diagram, instrument ranges, readings and method of calculations etc.
   (i) Regulation by direct loading method.
   (ii) Regulation by synchronous impedance method.

## Experiment No. 1: LOAD TEST ON 3-ALTERNATOR

**Aim:** To find out regulation of three phase 50 Hz alternator by loading it directly.

**Apparatus:** Voltmeter (0 – 300 V), Ammeter, Rheostar, Techometer, Lamp Load etc.

**Procedure:** Make the connections as shown in circuit. Adjust the speed of prime mover to rated speed. Adjust the no load voltage of alternator to its rated value. Note that alternator at its synchronous speed through out the test. Then put on some load with the help of lamp bank. It is observed that terminal voltage falls. Adjust it to its rated value by changing excitation. Keeping speed constant switch off the load suddenly and adjust the speed to synchronous speed. Take reading of volmeter. The readings of voltmeter is equal to no load speed. Take reading of volmeter. The readings of volmeter is equal to no load voltage of alternator i.e. its induced e.m.f.

**Specification of Alternator:** 230 V, 50 Hz, 3, 1500 rpm, 5 KVA, 12.5 Amps.

**Observation Table:**

| Sr. No. | Load Current | Terminal Voltage | Induced e.m.f. $E_o$, Volts | % Regulation |
|---|---|---|---|---|
| 1. | 0 | 220 | 220 | 0 |
| 2. | 1.1 | 220 | 228 | 3.636 |
| 3. | 2.2 | 220 | 236 | 7.27 |
| 4. | 5.8 | 220 | 240 | 9.09 |
| 5. | 5.3 | 220 | 250 | 13.63 |
| 6. | 6.5 | 220 | 252 | 14.54 |
| 7. | 7.8 | 220 | 262 | 19.09 |

**Calculation:** For reading no. 1

$$\% \text{ regulation} = \frac{E - V}{V} \times 100$$

$$= \frac{220 - 220}{220} \times 100$$

$$= 0\%$$

For reading no. 2, 

$$\% \text{ regulation} = \frac{E_o - V}{V} \times 100$$

$$= \frac{228 - 220}{220} \times 100$$

$$= 3.636\%$$

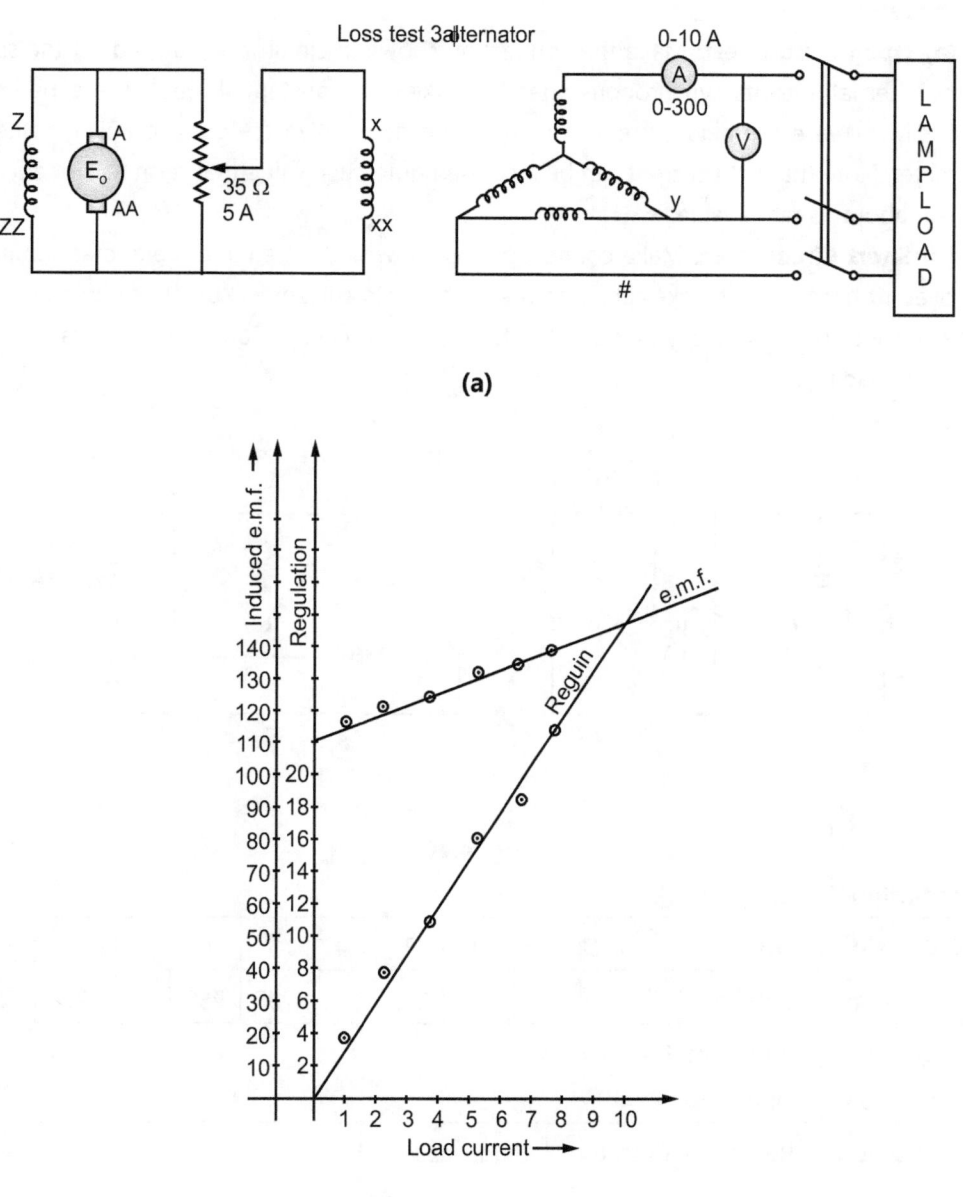

(a)

(b)

**Fig. 4.45**

## Experiment No. 2: SYNCHRONOUS IMPEDANCE METHOD

**Aim:** To calculate the synchronous impedance and find the regulation of the alternator at different power factor by synchronous impedance method.

**Apparatus:** Ammeter (0 - 10 A D.C.), Ammeter (0-10 A), Voltmeter (0-300 V), Rheostat

## Procedure:

**(a) Open Circuit Test:** Make the connection shown in circuit diagram. Adjust the speed of the alternator to its synchronous speed and keep it constant through the experiment. Gradually increase the field current from zero and note down the corresponding values of voltmeter. Note that field current can be increased upto such value that terminal voltage may be near about its rated value.

**(b) Short Circuit Test:** Make connections as shown in dotted line. Voltmeter should be removed from the circuit. Take care that at start the field current will be at its minimum value or zero value. Then gradually increase the field till short circuit. Current is at its rated value. Note the readings.

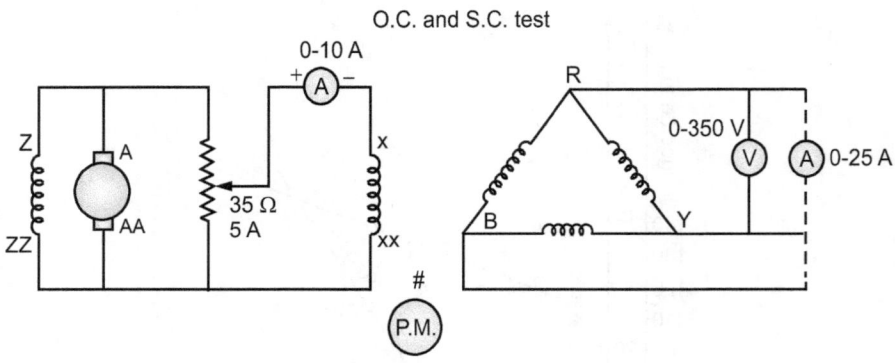

**Fig. 4.46**

## Observation Table:

| O.C. Field current ($I_f$) | 0 | 1 | 2 | 3 | 4 | 5 | 6 | 7 | 8 | 9 |
|---|---|---|---|---|---|---|---|---|---|---|
| Test Terminal Voltge | 18 | 52 | 114 | 162 | 198 | 232 | 250 | 266 | 276 | 284 |

S.C. Short Circuit Current ($I_{sc}$) = 7.16

Test Field Current ($I_f$)       = 3.7

**Calculations:** Resistance of stator winding/phase = 0.8 Ω

$$R_a = 0.8\, \Omega,\ I_{sc}/ph = \frac{12.4}{\sqrt{3}} = 7.16\ A,\ E_o = 190\ V\ (\text{from graph})$$

∴

$$Z_s = \frac{\text{O.C. e.m.f.}}{\text{S.C. current}} = \frac{190}{7.16} = 26.54\ \Omega$$

$$X_s = \sqrt{Z_s^2 - R_a^2}$$
$$= \sqrt{(26.54)^2 - (0.8)^2} = 26.53\ \Omega$$

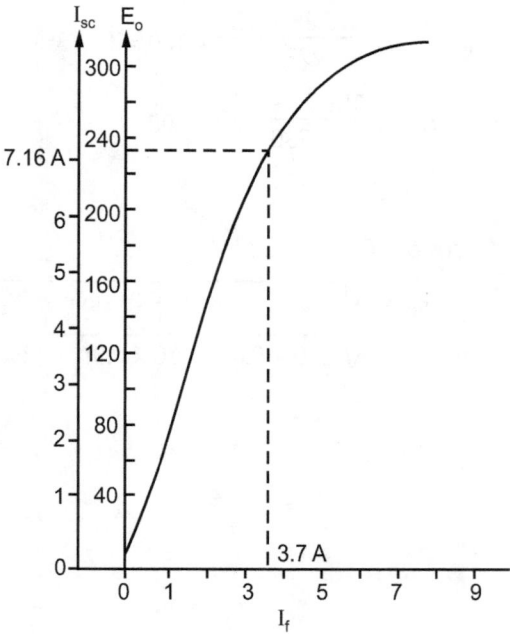

**Fig. 4.47**

(1) For unit p.f., $\quad V = 230 \text{ V}, \text{ I}$

$\quad = 7.16 \text{ A}$

$E_o = \sqrt{(V \cos \phi + IR_a)^2 + (V \sin \phi + IX_s)^2}$

$\quad = \sqrt{(230 \times 1 + 7.16 \times 0.8)^2 + (230 \times 0 + 7.16 \times 26.53)^2}$

$\quad = 302.73 \text{ V}$

% regulation $= \dfrac{E_o - V}{V} \times 100$

$\quad = \dfrac{302.73 - 230}{230} \times 100$

$\quad = 31.62\%$

(2) For 0.8 lagging p.f., $\cos \phi = 0.8$, $V = 230 \text{ V}$

$E_o = \sqrt{(V \cos \phi + IR_a)^2 + (V \sin \phi + IX_s)^2}$

$\quad = \sqrt{(230 \times 0.8 + 7.16 \times 0.8)^2 + (230 \times 0.6 + 7.16 \times 26.53)^2}$

$\quad = 378.88 \text{ V}$

$$\% \text{ regulation} = \frac{E_o - V}{V} \times 100$$

$$= \frac{378.88 - 230}{230} \times 100 = 64.73\%$$

$$\% \text{ regulation} = \frac{196.71 - 230}{230} \times 100$$

$$= -14.47\%$$

(3) For 0.8 leading p.f., $\cos \phi = 0.8$, $V = 230$ V

$$E_o = \sqrt{(V \cos \phi + IR_a)^2 + (V \sin \phi + IX_s)^2}$$

$$= \sqrt{(230 \times 0.8 + 7.16 \times 0.8)^2 + (230 \times 0.6 - 7.16 \times 26.537)^2}$$

$$= 196.71 \text{ V}$$

👌 👌 👌

# Chapter 5

# SENSORS, ROBOTICS, DAS AND RELAYS

## 5.1 SENSORS

Sensors are devices that are used to detect, and often to measure, the magnitude of something. They are a type of transducer used to convert mechanical, magnetic, thermal, optical and chemical variations into electrical voltages and currents. Sensors are usually categorised by what they measure and play an important role in modern manufacturing process control. They provide the equivalents of our eyes, ears, nose and tongue to microprocessor brain of industrial automation systems.

For example, optical sensor provide equivalents of eyes, microphone provides equivalents of ears, gas sensor provides equivalents of nose, and probe provides equivalents of tongue.

**Application of the sensor is, for example.**
1. Counting the number of products in factory.
2. Filling the bottle with the specified number of tablets in chemical industries.
3. Production control in a factory etc.

### 5.1.1 Proximity Sensor

Proximity sensors or switches are pilot devices that detect the pressure of an object without physical contact. They are solid state electronic devices that are completely encapsulated to protect against excessive vibration, liquids, chemicals and corrosive agents found in the industrial environment.

#### 5.1.1.1 Applications of Proximity Sensors
1. The object being detected is too small, too lightweight, or too soft to operate a mechanical switch.
2. Rapid response and high switching rates are required, as in counting or ejection control applications.
3. An object has to be sensed through non-metallic barriers such as glass, plastic and paper castons.
4. Hostile environments demand improved sealing properties, preventing proper operation of mechanical switches.

5. Long life and reliable service are required.
6. A fast electronic control system requires a bound-free input signal.

An inductive proximity sensor is a reusing device that is actuated by a metal object.

An oscillator is an electronic circuit for generating A.C. waveforms and frequencies from a D.C. energy source. When energy is supplied, the oscillator operates to generate a high-frequency field. At this moment, there must not be any conductive material in the high-frequency field. When a metal object enters the high-frequency field eddy currents are induced in the surface of the target. This results in a loss of energy in the oscillator circuit, consequently, this causes a smaller amplitude of oscillation. The detector circuit recognizes a specific changes in amplitude and generates a signal that will turn the solid- state output ON or OFF. When the metal object leaves the sensing area, the oscillator regenerates allowing the sensor to return to its normal state.

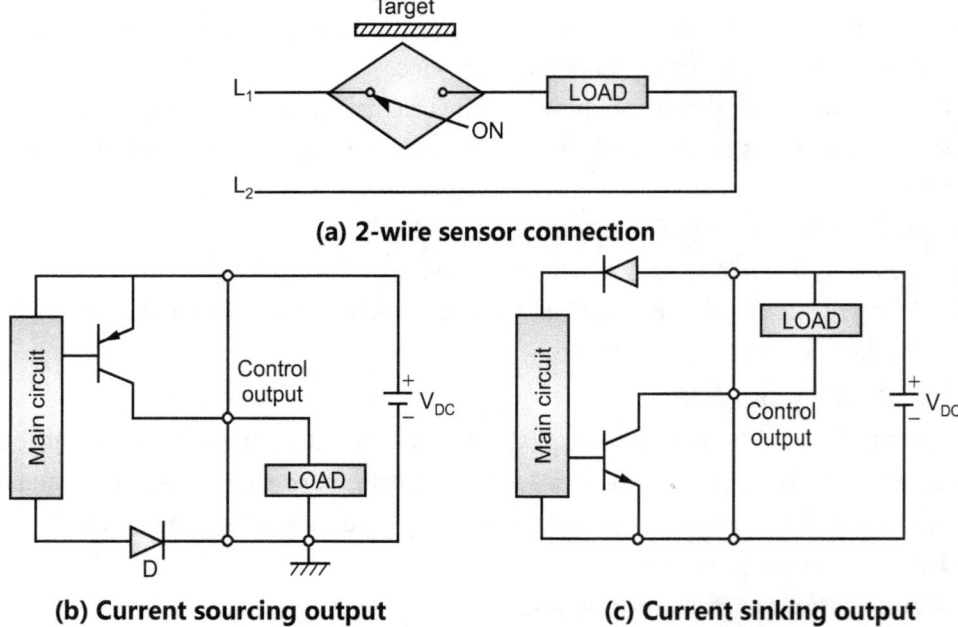

**Fig. 5.1: Proximity Sensor Connections**

The method of connecting and exciting a proximiting sensor will vary with the type of sensor and its application.

With current sourcing output the load is connected between the sensor and ground. Current flow from the sensor through the load to ground. With a current-sinking output the load connected between positive supply and sensor. Current flows from the load through the sensor to ground. Remember, these sensors are used as pilot devices for loads such as starters, contactors, solenoids, and so on.

As a result of solid-state switching of the output, a leakage current flows through the sensor even when the output is turned OFF. Similarly, when the sensor is ON, a small voltage drop is lost across its output terminals.

In order to operate properly, a proximity sensor should be powered continuously, the difference between the "operate' and "release" points of the sensor is called hysterisis or differential travel. Inductive sensors can be actuated in an axial or radial approach. It is important to maintain a minimum gap between the target and sensing face to prevent physically damaging the sensors.

A minimum amount of current must be allowed to continuously flow through the sensor in order to maintain operation. When load current is less than this minimum, a bleeder resistor is connected parallel to the load [See. Fig. 5.2 (a)]. In order to operate properly a proximity sensor should be powered continuously. A bypass can be added across the mechanical contact to keep the sensor ready for instantaneous operation. [See Fig. 5.2 (b)]. With the sensor ON, a small voltage is lost across its output. [See Fig. 5.2 (c)].

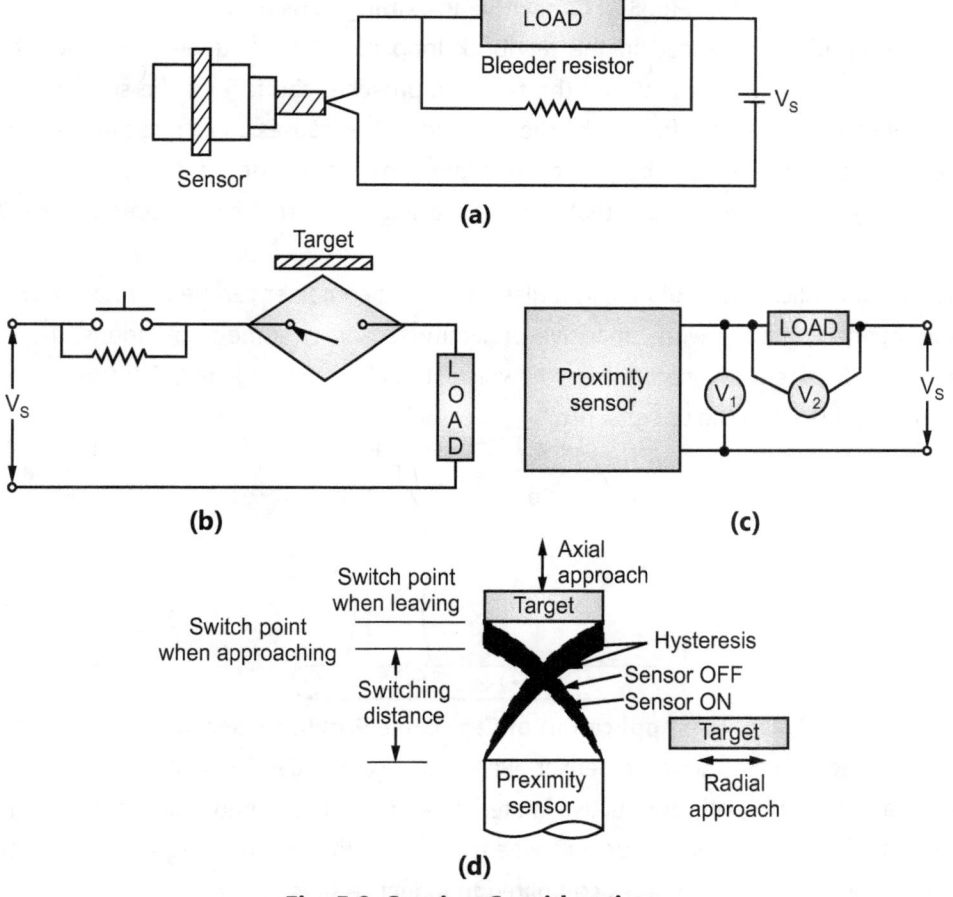

**Fig. 5.2: Sensing Considerations**

Hysteresis is the distance between the operating point when the target approaches the proximity sensor face and the release point. When the target is moving away from the sensor face. It is given as a percentage of the nominal sensing range. Hysteresis is needed to keep proximity sensors from chattering when subjected to shock and vibration, slow-moving target or minor disturbances such as electrical noise and temperature drift. [See Fig. 5.2 (d)].

A capacitive proximity sensor is a sensing device that is actuated by conductive and non-conductive materials. The operation of capacitive sensor is also based on the principle of an oscillator. Instead of a coil, however, the active face of a capacitive sensor is formed by two metallic electrodes rather like an "opened" capacitor. (See Fig. 5.3).

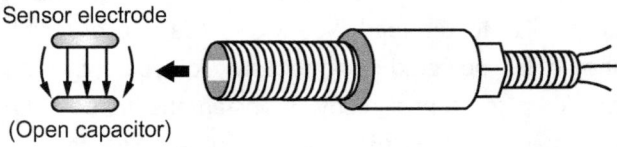

**Fig. 5.3: Capacitive Proximity Sensor**

The electrodes are placed in the feedback loop of a high-frequency oscillator that is inactive with "no target present". As the target approaches the face of the sensor, it enters the electrostatic field that is formed by the electrodes. This causes an increase in the coupling capacitance and the circuit begins to oscillate. The amplitude of these oscillations is measured by an evaluating circuit that generates a single to turn the solid state output ON or OFF.

A typical application, liquid filling a glass or plastic container can be monitored from the outside of the container with capacitive proximity sensor. In some applications, the empty container is detected by a second sensor, which starts the flow of liquid. The flow is shut off when the level reaches the upper sensor.

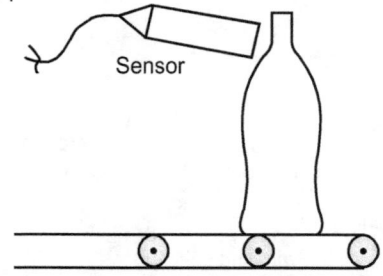

**Fig. 5.4: Application of Capacitive Proximity Sensor**

In order to actuate inductive sensor, we need a conductive material. Capacitive sensor may be actuated by both conductive materials and by non-conductive materials such as wood, plastics, liquid, sugar, flour and wheat. Along with this advantage of the capacitive sensor comes some disadvantages compared to inductive sensor.

| Inductive Proximity Switch | Capacitive Proximity Switch |
|---|---|
| These switches may actuated only by a metal and are insensitive to humidity, dust, drift and the like. | These switches can be actuated by any drift in their environment. For general applications, these switches are not really an alternative but a supplement to the inductive proximity switches. These are a supplement when there is no metal available for actuation. |

**Proximity Sensing:** The range sensors yield an estimate of the distance between a sensor and reflecting object. Proximity sensors, on other hand generally have a binary output which indicates the presence of an object within a specified distance interval. Typically, proximity sensors are used in robotics for near-field work in connection with object grasping or avoidance. In this section, we consider several fundamental approaches to proximity sensing and discuss the basic operational characteristics of these sensors.

### 5.1.1.2 Inductive Sensors

Sensors based on a change of inductance due to the presence of a metallic object are among the most widely used industrial proximity sensors. The principle of operation of these sensors can be explained with the aid of Figs. 5.5 and 5.6. Fig. 5.5 (a) shows a schematic diagram of an inductive sensor which basically consists of a wound coil located next to a permanent magnet packaged in a simple, rugged housing.

The effect of bringing the sensor in close proximity to a ferromagnetic material causes a change in the position of the flux lines of the permanent magnet, as shown in Fig. 5.5 (b) and (c). Under static conditions there is no movement of the flux lines and, therefore, no current is induced in the coil. However, as a ferromagnetic object enters or leaves the field of the magnet, the resulting change in the flux lines induces a current pulse whose amplitude and shape are proportional to the rate of change in the flux.

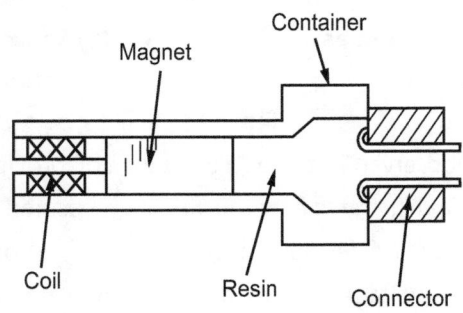

**(a) An inductive sensor**

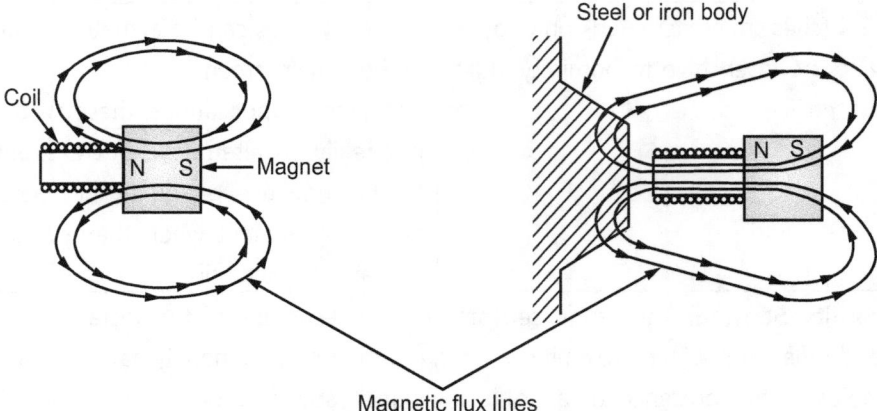

**(b) Shape of flux lines in the absence of a ferromagnetic body**

**(c) Shape of flux lines when a ferromagnetic body is brought close to the sensor.**

**Fig. 5.5**

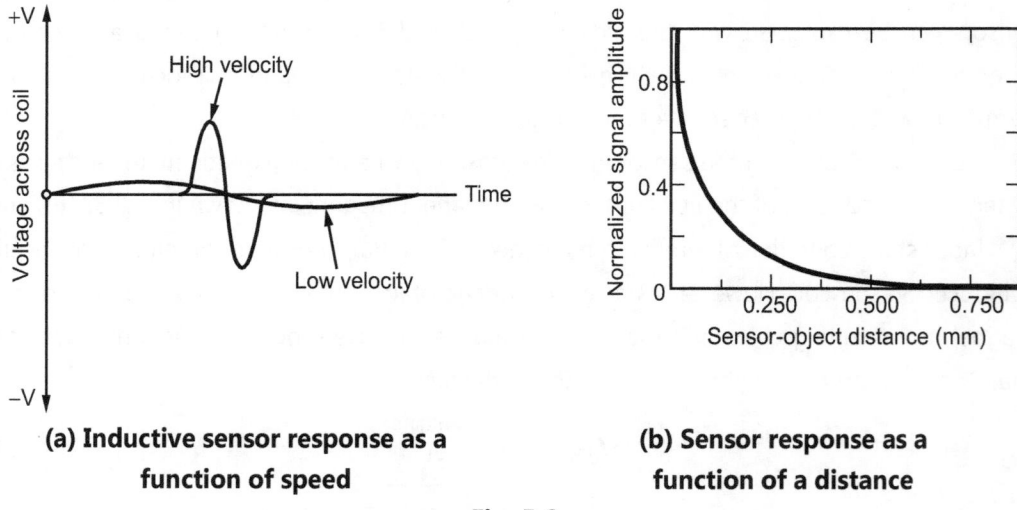

**(a) Inductive sensor response as a function of speed**

**(b) Sensor response as a function of a distance**

**Fig. 5.6**

The voltage waveform observed at the output of the coil provides an effective means for proximity sensing. Fig. 5.6 (a) illustrates how the voltage measured across the coil varies as a function of the speed at which a ferromagnetic material is introduced in the field of the magnet. The polarity of the voltage out of the sensor depends on whether the object is entering or leaving the field. Fig. 5.6 (b) illustrates the relationship between voltage amplitude and sensor-object distance. It is noted from this figure that sensitivity falls off rapidly with increasing distance, and that the sensor is effective only for fractions of a millimeter.

Since the sensor requires motion to produce an output waveform, one approach for generating a binary signal is to integrate this waveform. The binary output remains low as long as the integral value remains below a specified threshold, and then switches to high (indicating proximity of an object) when the threshold is exceeded.

## 5.2 HALL-EFFECT SENSORS

The reader will recall from elementary physics that the Hall-effect relates the voltage between two points in a conducting or semiconducting material to a magnetic field across the material. When used by themselves, Hall-effect sensors can only detect magnetized objects. However, when used in conjunction with a permanent magnet in a configuration such as the one shown in Fig. 5.7, they are capable of detecting all ferromagnetic materials. When used in this way, a Hall-effect device senses a strong magnetic field in the absence of a ferromagnetic metal in the near field (Fig. 5.7 (a)) When such a material is brought in close proximity with the device, the magnetic field weakens at the sensor due to bending of the field lines through the material, as shown in Fig. Fig. 5.7 (b).

Hall-effect sensors are based on the principle of a Lorentz force which acts on a charged particle traveling through a magnetic field. This force acts on an axis perpendicular to the plane established by the direction of motion of the charged particle and the direction of the field.

That is, the Lorentz force is given by

$$F = q(v \times B)$$

where, q is the charge, v is the velocity vector, B is the magnetic field vector, and "×" is the vector cross product. Suppose, for example, that a current flows through a doped, n-type semiconductor which is immersed in a magnetic field, as shown in Fig. 5.8 Recalling that electrons are the majority carriers in n-type materials, and that conventional current flows opposite to electron current, we would have that the force acting on the moving, negatively charged particles would have the direction shown in Fig. 5.8. This force would act on the electrons, which would tend to collect at the bottom of the material and thus produce a voltage across it which, in this case, would be positive at the top.

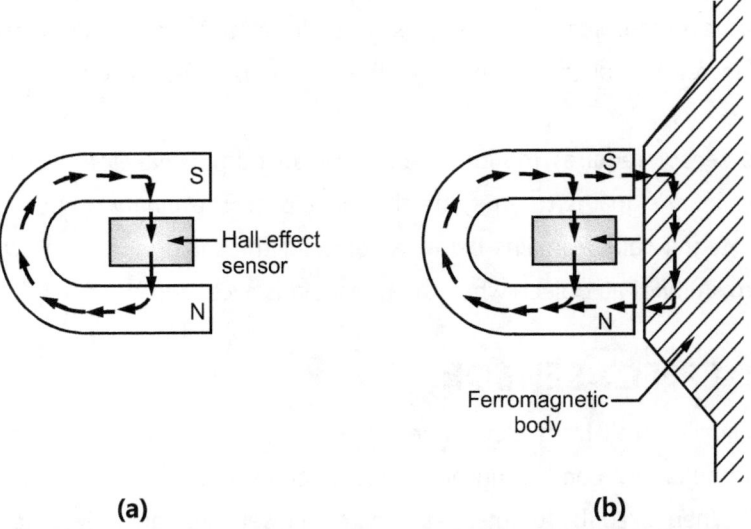

**Fig. 5.7: Operation of Hall-effect Sensor in Conjunction with a Permanent Magnet**

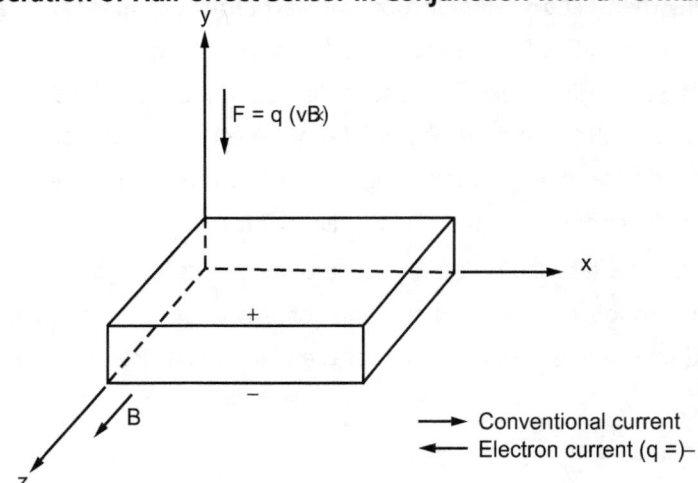

**Fig. 5.8: Generation of Hall Voltage**

Bringing a ferromagnetic material close to the semiconductor-magnet device would decrease the strength of the magnetic field, thus reducing the Lorentz force and, ultimately, the voltage across the semiconductor. This drop in voltage is the key for sensing proximity with Hall-effect sensors. Binary decisions regarding the presence of an object are made by thresholding the voltage out of the sensor.

It is of interest to note that using a semiconductor, such as silicon, has a number of advantages in terms of size, ruggedness, and immunity to electrical interference. In addition, the use of semi-conducting materials allows the construction of electronic circuitry for amplification and detection directly on the sensor itself, thus reducing sensor size and cost.

## 5.2.1 Capacitive Sensors

Unlike inductive and Hall-effect sensors which detect only ferromagnetic materials, capacitive sensors are potentially capable (with various degrees of sensitivity) of detecting all solid and liquid materials. As their name implies, these sensors are based on detecting a change in capacitance induced by a surface that is brought near the sensing element.

The basic components of a capacitive sensor are shown in Fig. 5.9. The sensing element is a capacitor composed of a sensitive electrode and a reference electrode. These can be, for example, a metallic disk and ring separated by a dielectric material. A cavity of dry air is usually placed behind the capacitive element to provide isolation. The rest of the sensor consists of electronic circuitry which can be included as an integral part of the unit, in which case it is normally embedded in a resin to provide sealing and mechanical support.

There are a number of electronic approaches for detecting proximity based on a change in capacitance. One of the simplest includes the capacitor as part of an oscillator circuit designed so that the oscillation starts only when the capacitance of the sensor exceeds a predefined threshold value. The start of oscillation is then translated into an output voltage which indicates the presence of an object. This method provides a binary output whose triggering sensitivity depends on the threshold value.

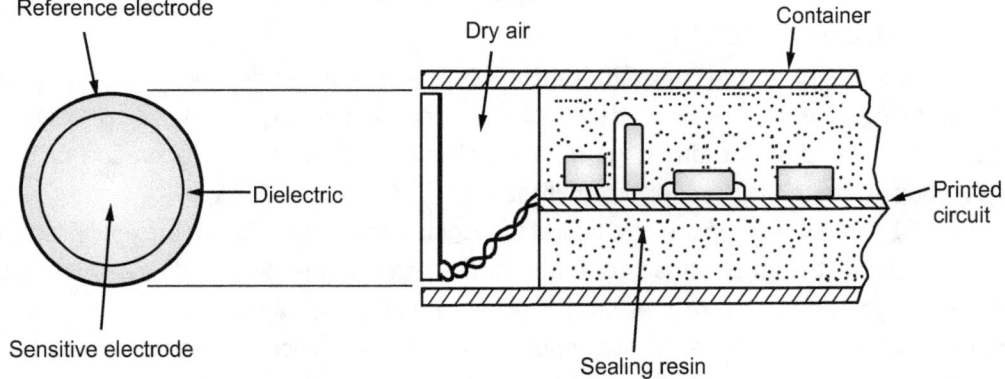

**Fig. 5.9**

A more complicated approach utilizes the capacitive element as part of a circuit which is continuously driven by a reference sinusoidal waveform. A change in capacitance produces a phase shift between the reference signal and a signal derived from the capacitive element. The phase shift is proportional to the change in capacitance and can thus be used as a basic mechanism for proximity detection.

Fig. 5.10 illustrates how capacitance varies as a function of distance for a proximity sensor based on the concepts just discussed. It is of interest to note that sensitivity decreases sharply past a few millimeters, and that the shape of the response curve depends on the material being sensed. Typically, these sensors are operated in a binary mode so that a change in the capacitance greater than a preset threshold T indicates the presence of an object, while changes below the threshold indicate the absence of an object with respect to detection limits established by the value of T.

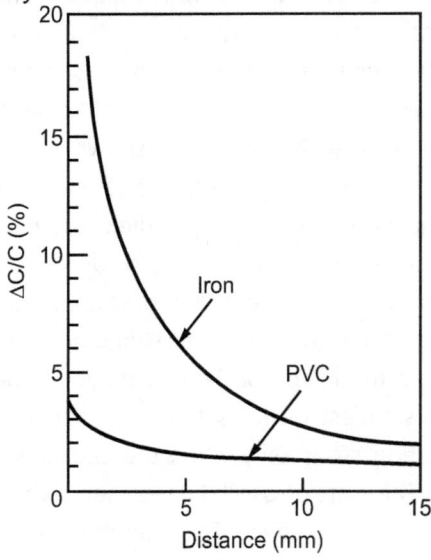

**Fig. 5.10**

## 5.2.2 Ultrasonic Sensors

The response of all the proximity sensors discussed thus far depends strongly on the material being sensed. This dependence can be reduced considerably by using ultrasonic sensors. In this section, we discuss in more detail the construction and operation of these sensors and illustrate their use for proximity sensing.

Fig. 5.11 shows the structure of a typical ultrasonic transducer used for proximity sensing. The basic element is an electroacoustic transducer, often of the piezoelectric ceramic type. The resin layer protects the transducer against humidity, dust, and other environmental factors; it also acts as an acoustical impedance matcher. Since the same transducer is generally used for both transmitting and receiving, fast damping of the acoustic energy is necessary to detect objects at close range. This is accomplished by providing acoustic absorbers, and by decoupling the transducer from its housing. The housing is designed so that it produces a narrow acoustic beam for efficient energy transfer and signal directionality.

The operation of an ultrasonic proximity sensor is best understood by analyzing the waveforms used for both transmission and detection of the acoustic energy signals. A typical set of waveforms is shown in Fig. 5.12. Waveform A is the gating signal used to control transmission. Waveform B shows the output signal as well as the resulting echo signal. The pulses shown in C result either upon transmission or reception. In order to differentiate between pulses corresponding to outgoing and returning energy, we intoroduce a time window (waveform D) which in essence establishes the detection capability of the sensor.

That is, time interval $\Delta t_1$ is the minimum detection time, and $\Delta t_1 + \Delta t_2$ the maximum. (It is noted that these time intervals are equivalent to specifying distances since the propagation velocity of an acoustic wave is known given the transmission medium.) An echo received while signal D is high produces the signal shown in E, which is reset to low at the end of a transmission pulse in signal A. Finally, signal F is set high on the positive edge of a pulse in E and is reset to low when E is low and a pulse occurs in A. In this manner, F will be high whenever an object is present in the distance interval specified by the parameters of waveform D. That is, F is the output of interest in an ultrasonic sensor operating in a binary mode.

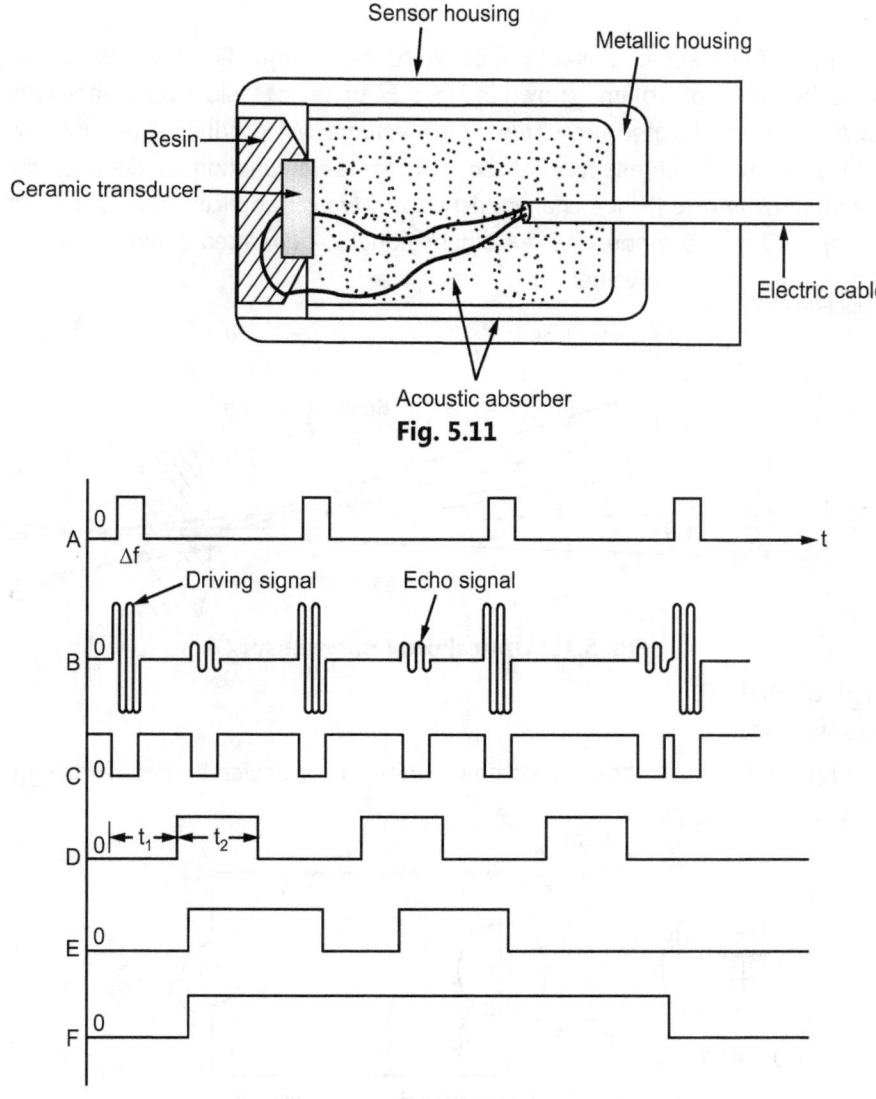

Fig. 5.11

Fig. 5.12

## 5.2.3 Optical Proximity Sensors

Optical proximity sensors are similar to ultrasonic sensors in the sense that they detect proximity of an object by its influence on a propagating wave as it travels from a transmitter to a receiver. One of the most common approaches for detecting proximity by optical means is shown in Fig. 5.13. This sensor consists of a solid-state light-emitting diode (LED), which acts as a transmitter of infrared light, and a solid-state photodiode which acts as the receiver. The cones of light formed by focusing the source and detector on the same plane intersect in a long, pencil-like volume. This volume defines the field of operation of the sensor since a reflective surface which intersects the volume is illuminated by the source and simultaneously "seen" by the receiver.

Although this approach is similar in principle to the triangulation method, it is important to note that the detection volume shown in Fig. 5.13 does not yield a point measurement. In other words, a surface located anywhere in the volume will produce a reading. While it is possible to calibrate the intensity of these readings as a function of distance for known object orientations and reflective characteristics, the typical application of the arrangement shown in Fig. 5.13 is in a mode where a binary signal is generated when the received light intensity exceeds a threshold value.

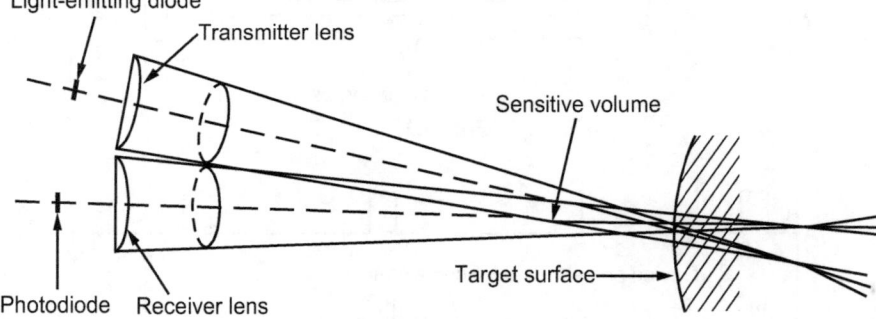

**Fig. 5.13: Optical proximity sensor**

## 5.2.4 Light Sensors

### (a) Photovoltaic Cell

The photovoltaic or solar cell, is a common light sensor device that converts light energy directly into electric energy.

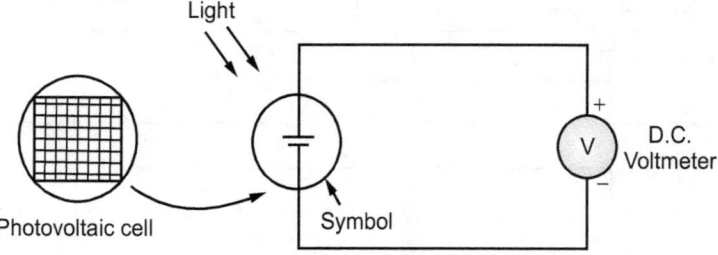

**Fig. 5.14: Photovoltaic or Solar Cell**

Modern silicon solar cells are basically PN junctions with a transparent P-layer. Shining light on the transparent p-layer causes a movement of electrons between P and N sections, thus producing a small D.C. voltage. Typically output voltage is about 0.5 V per cell in full sunlight.

**(b) Photoconductive Cell**

The photoconductive or photoresistive cell is another popular type of light transducer light energy falling on photoconductive cell will cause a change in resistance of the cell.

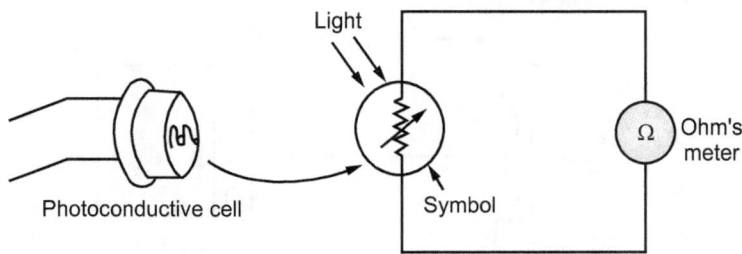

**Fig. 5.15: Photoconductive Cell**

One of the more popular types is the cadmium sulphide photocell. When the surface of this device is dark, the resistance of the device is high. When brightly lit, its resistance drops to a very low value.

**(c) Photoelectric Cell**

There are two main types of photoelectric sensors that are used to sense position. Each emits a light beam (visible, infrared or laser) from its light emitting element.

A reflective type photoelectric sensor is used to detect the light beam reflected from target. These sensors are classified in two types (i) Diffused-reflective and (ii) Ratio-reflective.

In diffused-reflective sensor, sensor emitted the light on the target, if target in the operating range. And receives light from the target by reflection. [See Fig. 5.16 (a)].

In Retro-reflective sensor, sensor emitted the light on the reflector and reflector reflect the light. If any interruptor comes, it will not receives the light. [See Fig. 5.16 (b)].

A trough-beam photoelectric sensor is used to measure the change in light-quantities caused by the targets crossing the optical axis. [See Fig. 5.16].

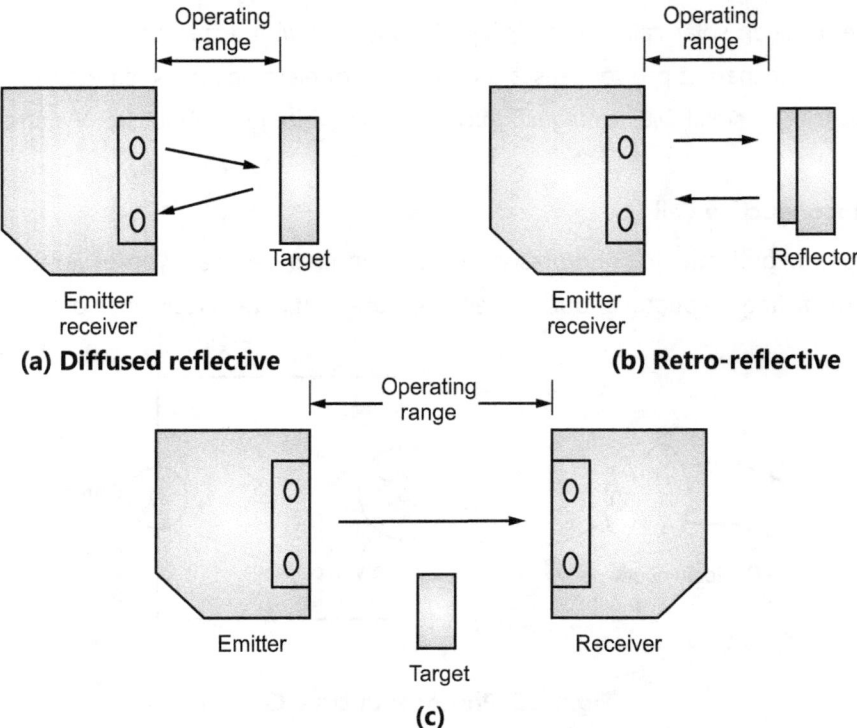

**Fig. 5.16: Trough Beam Type**

## 5.2.5 Features of the Sensor

1. **Non-contact detection :** Non-contact detection eliminates damage either to the target or sensor head, ensuring long service life and maintenance free operation.
2. **Detection of target of virtually any material :** Detection is based on the quantity of light received, or the change in the quantity of reflected light. This method allows detection of targets of device materials such as glass, metal, plastics, wood and liquid.
3. **Long detecting distance :** The reflective type photoelectric sensor has a detecting distance of 1 metre, and the through-beam type has a detecting distance of 10 metres.
4. **High response speed :** The photoelectric sensor is capable of a response speed as high as 50 μsec.
5. **Colour discrimination :** The sensor has the ability to detect light from an object based on the reflectance and absorptance of its colour, thus permitting colour detection and discrimination.
6. **Highly accurate detection :** A unique optical system and a precision electronic circuit allows highly accurate positioning and detection of minute objects.

## 5.2.6 Applications

1. A reflective-type photoelectric sensor used for the detection of the presence or object of the product is shown in Fig. 5.17.

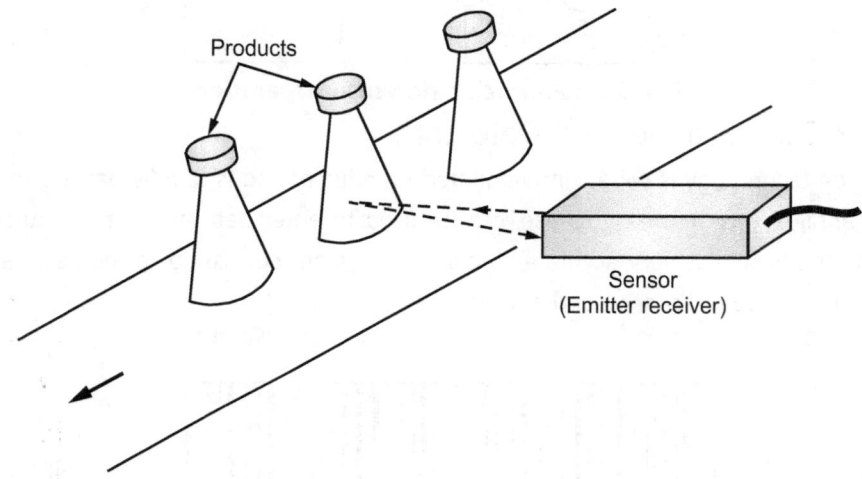

**Fig. 5.17: Reflective Type Photoelectric Sensor**

2. In trough beam photoelectric sensor heads, heads are positioned above and below the products travelling on a product line. (See Fig. 5.18).

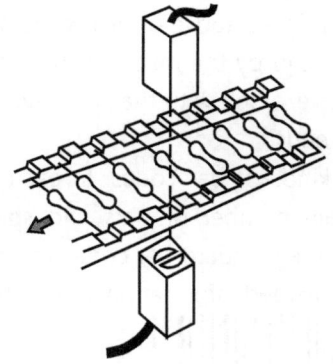

**Fig. 5.18: Trough Beam Photoelectric Sensor**

In most photoelectric sensors, a light-emitting diode (LED) is the light-transmitting source and a phototransistor is the receiving source. In operation, light from the LED falls on the input of the phototransistor and amount of conduction through the transistor changes. Analog outputs provide an output proportional to the quantity of light seen by the photodetector. (See Fig. 5.19)

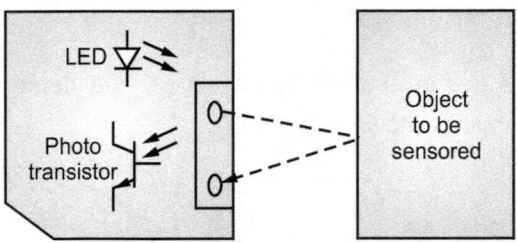

**Fig. 5.19: Photoelectric Sensor Operation**

## 5.2.7 Bar Code Scanner and Detector

Bar code technology is widely implemented in industry and is rapidly gaining in a broad range of applications. It is easy to use, can be used to enter data much more quickly than manual methods, and is very accurate. A bar code system consists of three basic elements the bar code, symbol, a scanner, and a decoder.

**Fig. 5.20: Bar Code Symbol**

The bar code symbol contains upto 30 characters that are encoded in a machine readable form. The characters are usually printed above or below the bar code, so data can be entered manually if a symbol cannot be read by the machine. The blank space on either side of bar code symbol, called the quiet zone, along with the start and stop characters, lets the scanner know where the data begin and ends.

There are several different kinds of bar codes. In each one, a number, letter or other character is formed by a certain number of bars and spaces. In the United States, the Universal Product Code (UPC) is the standard bar code symbol for retail food packaging. The UPC symbol contains all of the encoded information in one symbol.

**Fig. 5.21: UPC Bar Code Symbol**

It is strictly a numeric code containing:
1. UPC type (1 character)
2. UPT manufacturer or vendor, ID number (5 characters)
3. UPC item number (5 characters)
4. Check digit (1 character) used to mathematically check the accuracy of the read.

Bar code scanners are the eyes of the data collection system. A light source within the scanner illuminates the bar code symbol; those bars absorb light and space reflect light. A photo detector collects this light in the form of any electronic-signal pattern representing the printed symbol. The decoder receives the signal from the scanner and converts this data into the character data representation of the symbol's code. Although the scanner and decoder operate as a team, they can be integrated or separated depending on the application (See Fig. 5.22).

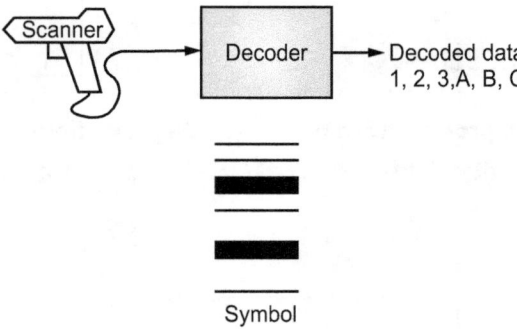

**Fig. 5.22: Bar Code Scanner and Decoder**

## 5.2.8 Hall-Effect Sensors

The hall-effect sensor is designed to sense the presence of a magnetic object, usually a permanent magnet. It is used to signal the position of a component. Because of its accuracy in sensing position, the hall-effect sensor is popular type of sensing device. Fig. 5.23 shows how a hall element operates. The hall element is a small, thin, flat slab of semiconductor material. When a current is passed through this slab and no magnetic field is present, zero output voltage is produced. When a magnet is brought close to the semiconductor material, the current path is distorted. This distortion causes electrons to be forced to the right side of the material, which produces a voltage across the sides of the device. Hall-effect devices use two terminals for excitation and two for output voltage.

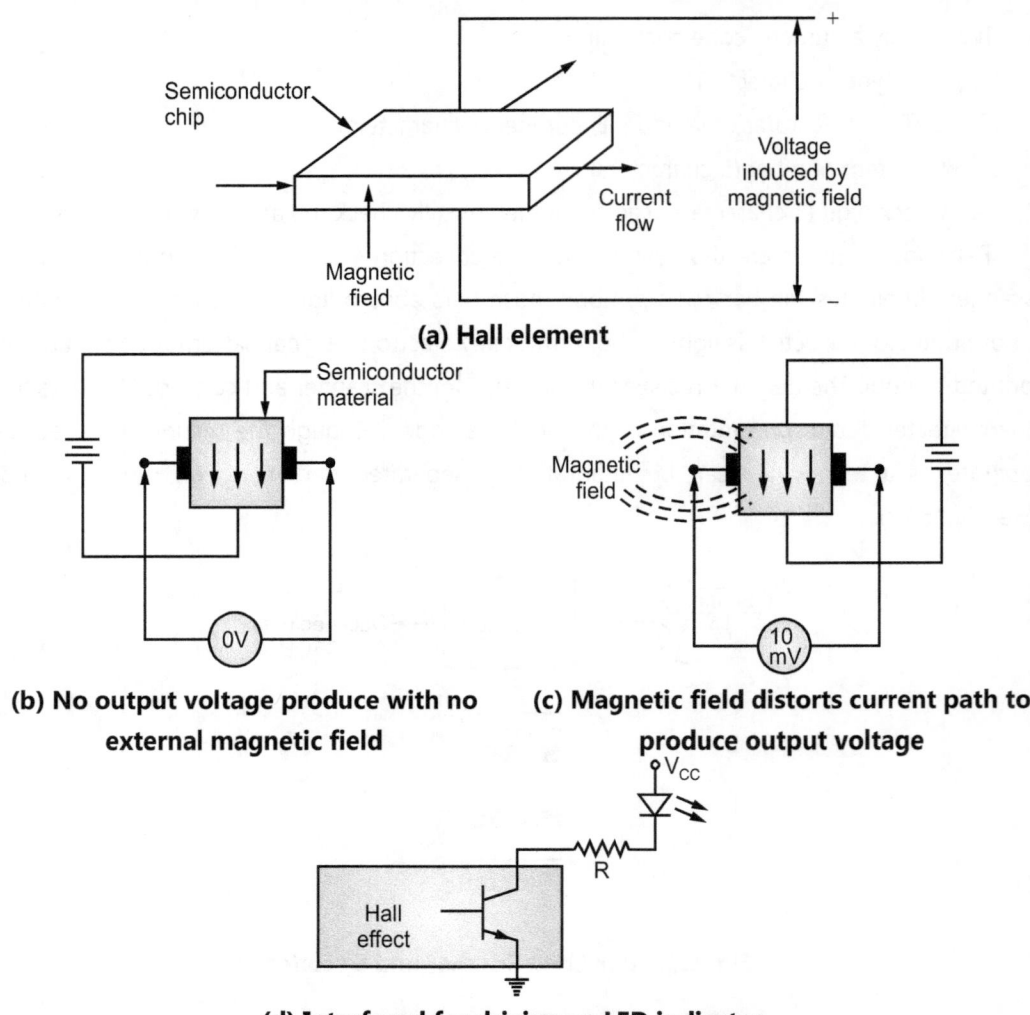

(a) Hall element

(b) No output voltage produce with no external magnetic field

(c) Magnetic field distorts current path to produce output voltage

(d) Interfaced for driving an LED indicator

**Fig. 5.23: Hall-effect Sensor**

Digital hall-effect integrated circuits, used in proximity switches, can be envisioned as a mechanical switch that allows current to flow when turned ON and blocks current when turned OFF. The digital hall-effect sensor can be used to measure speed. When the magnet passed the sensor, the hall switch activates, and a pulse is issued. By measuring the frequency of the pulses, the shaft speed can be determined. [See Fig. 5.24 (a)].

The analog hall-effect transducer puts out a continuous signal proportional to the sensed magnetic field. The analog hall-effect sensor can be used to sense position. As the magnet moves back and forth, the field seen by the sensor becomes negative as it approaches the north pole and positive as it approaches the south pole. [Fig. 5.24 (b)]

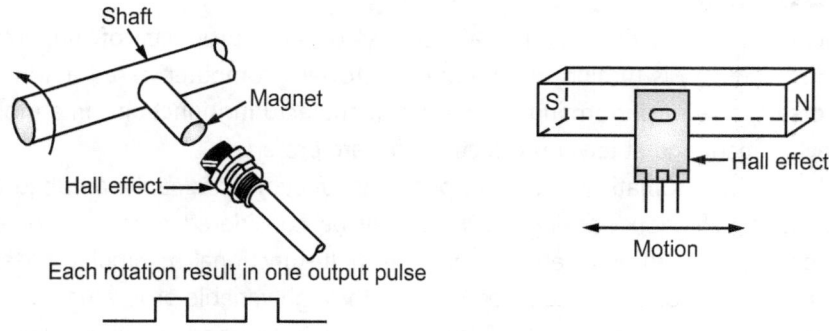

**Fig. 5.24: Digital and Linear Hall Effect Sensor**

## 5.2.9 Ultrasonic Sensors

An ultrasonic sensor operates by sending sound waves toward the target and measuring the time it takes for the pulse to bounce back. The time taken for this echo to return to the sensor is directly proportional to the distance or height of the object because sound has a constant velocity.

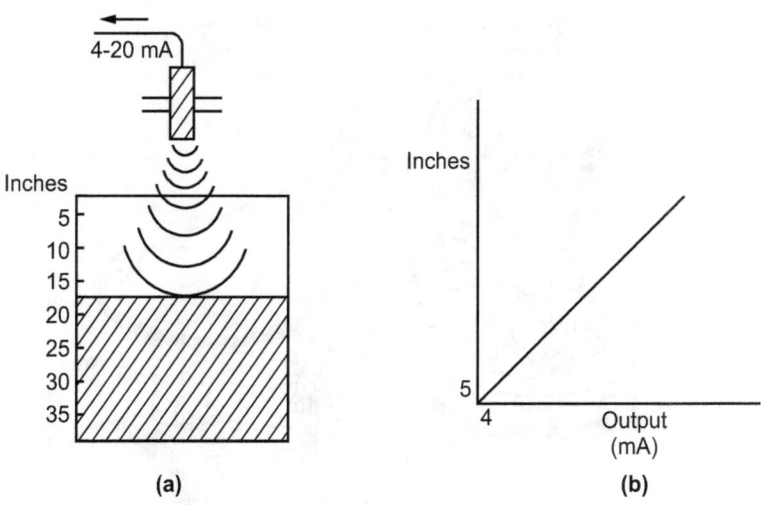

**Fig. 5.25: Ultrasonic Sensor**

In Fig. 5.25 the returning echo signal is electronically converted to a −20 mA output which supplies the monitored flow rate to external control devices. Solids, fluids, granular objects and textiles can be detected by an ultrasonic sensor. The sonic reflectivity of liquid surface is the same as solid objects. Textiles and foams absorb the sonic waves and reduce sensing range.

## 5.3 ROBOTICS

For increased productivity and the delivery of end products of uniform quality, manufacturing industry is turning more and more toward computer based automation. The use of robots capable of performing a variety of manufacturing functions, in a more flexible working environment and at lower production cost are preferred.

The robot is an automatic device that performs functions ordinarily, ascribed to human beings, with this definition washing machine may be considered robot. In now-a-days in general, it can be defined as a reprogrammable multi-functional manipulator, designed to move materials, parts, tools or specialized devices, through variable programmed motions for the performance of a variety of tasks. Thus, a robot is a reprogrammable general purpose manipulator with external sensors that can perform various assembly tasks. It possess intelligence, which is normally due to computer algorithms associated with its control and sensing systems.

An industrial robot is a general purpose, computer controlled manipulator consisting of several rigid links connected in series by revolute or prismatic joints. One end of the chain is attached to the supporting base, while other end is free and equipped with a tool to manipulate objects or perform assembly tasks. Mechanically, a robot is composed of an arm (mainframe) and a wrist sub-assembly plus a tool. It is designed to reach a workpiece located within its work volume i.e. a sphere of influence of a robot.

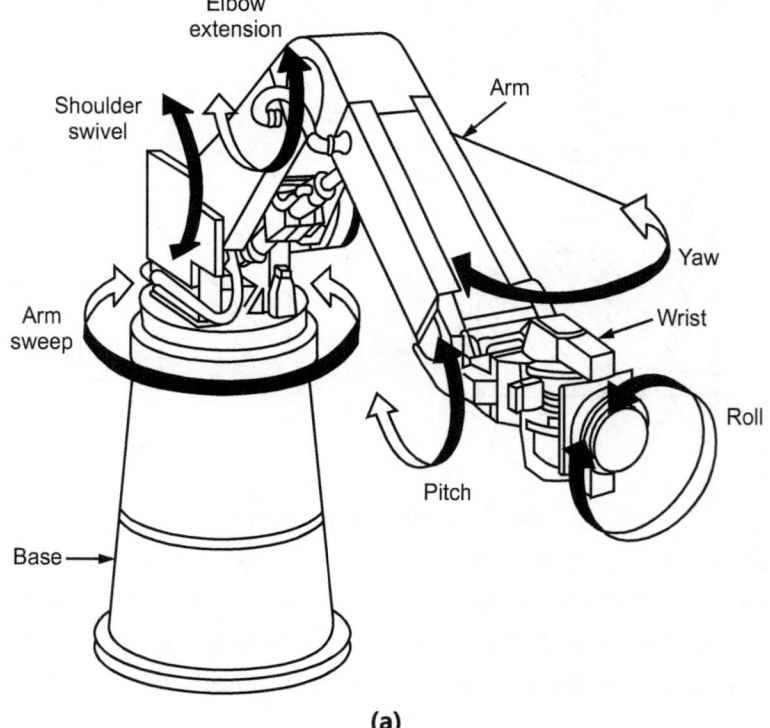

(a)

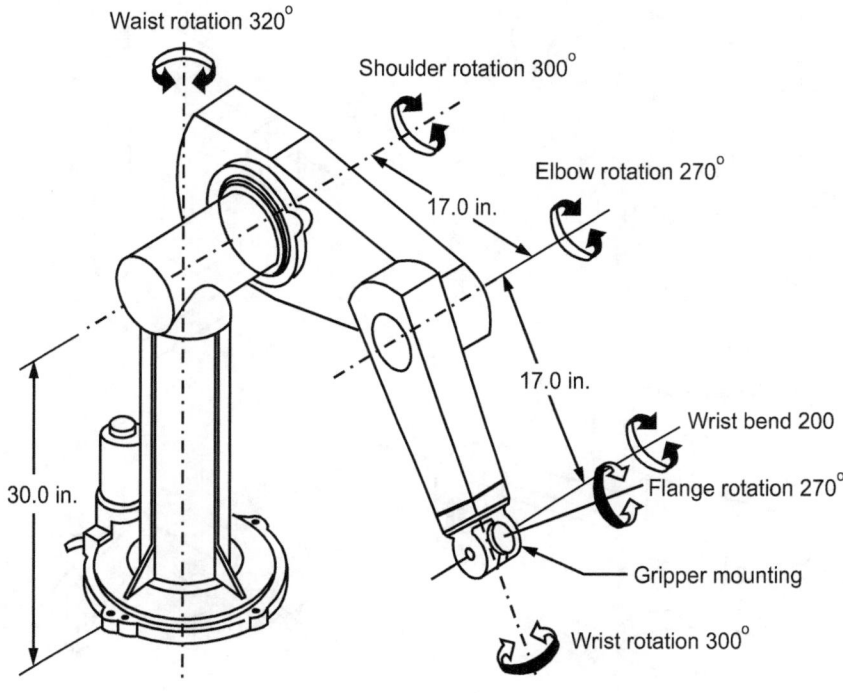

**(b)**
**Fig. 5.26**

Many commercially available industrial robots are widely used in manufacturing and assembly tasks, such as material handling, spot are welding, parts assembly, paint spraying, loading and unloading numerically controlled machines, space and under sea exploration, prosthetic arm research and in handling hazardous materials.

These robots fall into one of the four basic motion defining categories:

(i) Cartesian co-ordinates (three linear axes).

(ii) Cylindrical co-ordinates (two linear and one rotary axes).

(iii) Spherical co-ordinates (one linear and two rotary axes).

(iv) Revolute or articulated co-ordinates (three rotary axes).

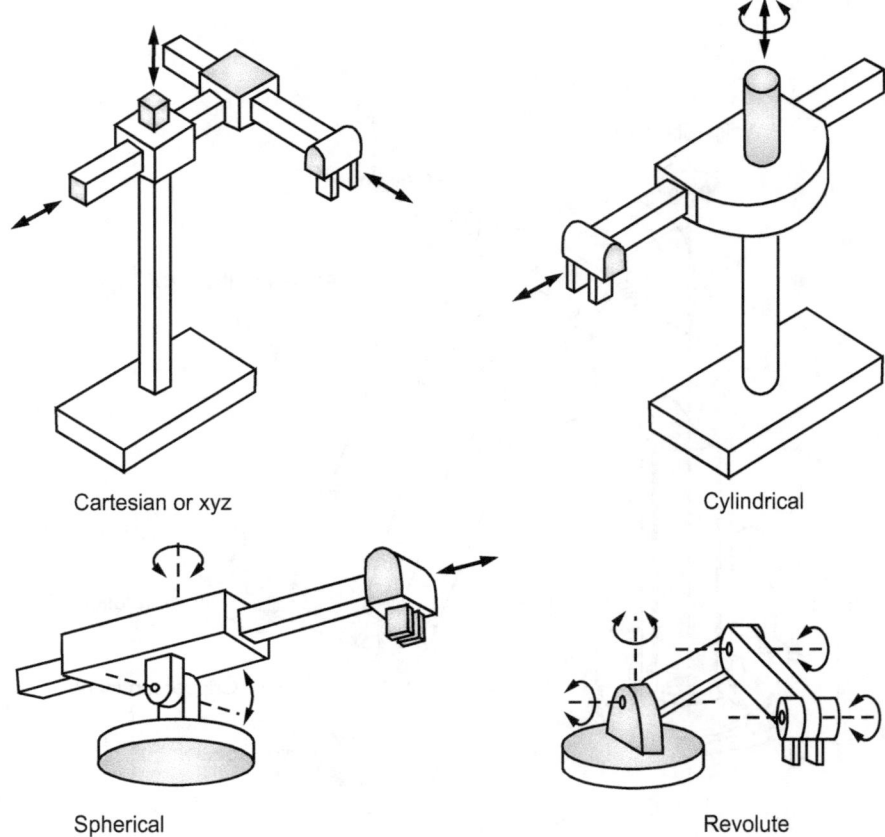

Cartesian or xyz

Cylindrical

Spherical

Revolute

**Fig. 5.27**

Most of today's industrial robots, though controlled by mini and micro-computers are basically simple positional machines. They execute a given task by playing back pre-recoded or pre-programmed sequences of motions that have been previously guided or taught by a user with a hand held control teach box. These robots are equipped with little or no external sensors for obtaining the information vital to its working environment. As a result, robots are used mainly in relatively simple, repetitive task.

The use of external sensing mechanisms allows a robot to interact with its environment in a flexible manner. This is in contrast to preprogrammed operations in which a robot is "taught" to perform repetitive tasks via a set of programmed functions.

The functions of robot sensors may be divided into two principal categories, internal state and external state. Internal state sensors deal with the detection of variables such as arm joint position which are used for robot control. External state sensors deal with the detection of variables such as range, proximity and tough. Although proximity, touch and force sensing play a significant role in the improvement of robot performance, vision is recognised as the most powerful of robot sensory capabilities. Robot vision may be defined as the process of extracting, characterising and interpreting information from images of a three dimensional world. This process commonly referred to as machine or computer vision may be sub-divided into six principal areas: (1) Sensing, (2) Preprocessing, (3) Segmentation, (4) Description, (5) Recognition, and (4) Interpretation.

These various areas of a vision are consider in three levels of processing: Low, medium, and high level vision.

One major obstacle in using manipulators is the lack of suitable and efficient communication between the user and the robotic system. There are several ways to communicate with a robot and the three major approaches to achieve it are discrete word recognition, teach and playback and high level programming languages. The usefulness of discrete word recognition to describe a task is limited and it requires a large memory space to store speech data. The teach and playback method involves in the following steps:

(i) Leading the robot in slow motion using manual control with joint and recorded in order to replay motion.
(ii) Editing and playing back the taught motion.
(iii) If taught motion is correct, then robot is run at an appropriate speed in a repetitive motion. This method is also known as guiding and is most commonly used approach in present days.

The human-robot communication problem is solved by use of high level programming. Robots are commonly used in areas such as arc welding, spot welding and paint spraying. These tasks requires no interaction between the robot and the environment and can be easily programmed by guiding. To perform assembly tasks generally requires high level programming techniques. This effort requires the manipulator controlled by a computer. The effective way for humans to communicate with computer is through a high level programming language. This increases the flexibility and versatility of the robot.

The basic problem in robotic is planning motion to solve some prescribed task and then controlling the robot as it executes the commands necessary to achieve those action.

In a typical formulation of a robot problem, we have a robot that is equipped with sensors and a set of primitive actions that it can perform in some easy to understand world. Robot actions change one state or configuration of the world into another.

Robots are computer controlled devices which perform tasks usually done by humans. The basic industrial robot is wide use today is an arm or manipulator which moves to perform industrial operations. Tasks are specialization and very tremendously. They includes:

1. **Handling :** Loading and unloading components on to machines.
2. **Processing :** Machining, drilling, painting and coating.
3. **Assembling :** Placing and locating a part in another compartment.

4. **Dismantling :** Breaking down an object into its component parts.
5. **Welding :** Assembling objects permanently by arc welding or spot welding.
6. **Transporting :** Moving materials and parts.
7. **Painting :** Spray painting parts.
8. **Hazardous tasks :** Operating under high levels of heat, dust, radioactivity, noise and noxious orders.

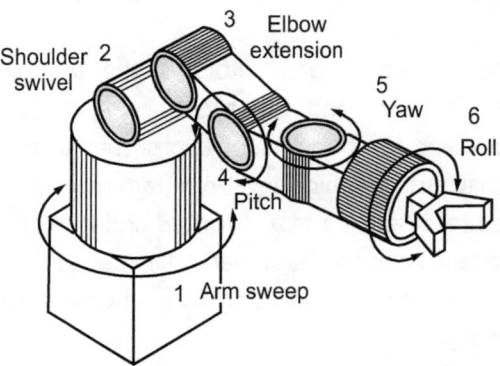

**Fig. 5.28: Six Axis Robot Arm**

A robot is simply a series of mechanical links driven by servomotors. The area at each junction between the links is called a joint or axis. The axis may be a straight line (linear), circular (rotational), or spherical. Fig. 5.28 shows a 6 axis robot arm. The wrist is name usually given to the last three joints on the robot's arm. Going out along the arm, these wrist joints are known as the pitch joint, you joint and roll joint. High-technology robots have from 6 to 9 axes. As the technology increases, the number of axes may increase to 16 or more. These robot's movements are meant to resemble human movements as closely as possible.

The reach of the robot is defined as the work envelope. All programmed points within the reach of the robot are parts of the work envelope. The shape of a work envelope is determined by the major (non-wrist) types of axes a robot has (Fig. 5.29).

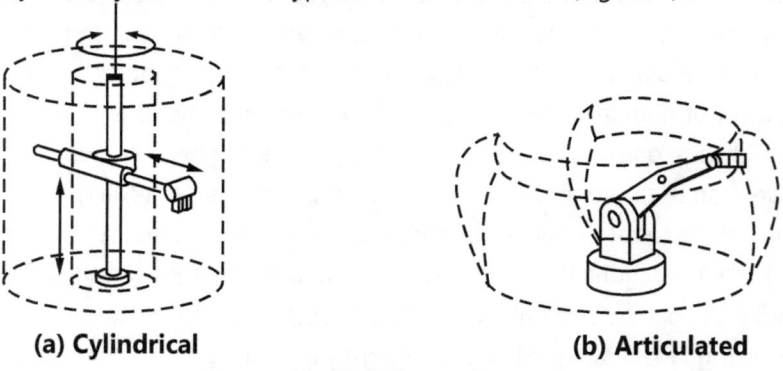

(a) **Cylindrical**            (b) **Articulated**

**Fig. 5.29: Robot Work Envelope**

A robot that has two linear major axes and one rotational major axis has cylindrically shaped work envelope. A robot has three rotational major axes has a work envelope very much like the motion range of a human body from waist to shoulder to elbow. Being familiar with the work envelope of the robot with which you work will help you avoid personal injury or potential damage to equipment.

Most applications require that additional tooling be attached to the robot. End of arm tooling depending on the type of work the robot does grippers or hands are used in material handling and assembly. Spot welding and arc welding require their own tooling, as do painting and dispensing (Fig. 5.30).

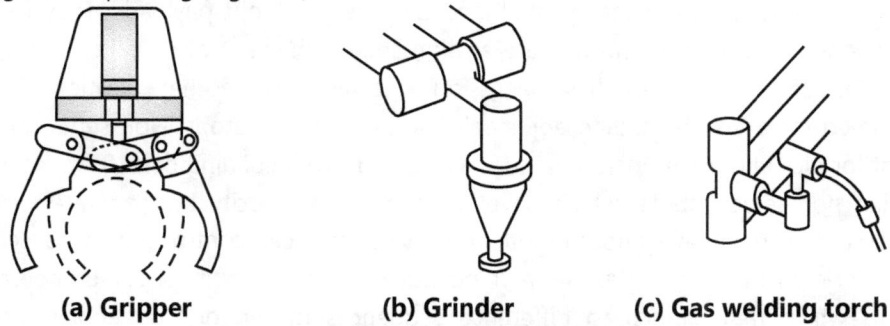

**(a) Gripper**      **(b) Grinder**      **(c) Gas welding torch**

**Fig. 5.30: End of arm tooling device**

Robots usually have one of the three possible sources of manipulator or muscle power: electric motors, hydraulic actuators or pneumatic actuators.

Robots powered by compressed air are lightweight, inexpensive and fast-moving but generally not strong. Robots powered by hydraulic fluid are stronger and more expensive but may lose accuracy if their hydraulic fluid changes temperature.

Originally, all robots used hydraulic servodrives. Driven mostly by the level of service required to maintain hydraulic servo systems in these early industrial robots, engineers developed the articulated robot with D.C. electric servo drive motors. The industrial robots has since evolved from D.C. electric to A.C. electric. The benefits of A.C. servomotors over D.C. motors were significant. The A.C. servomotor incorporated brushless, maintenance free designs and incremental encoders for servoposition feed-back.

There are two types of robot control systems : closed loop and open loop.

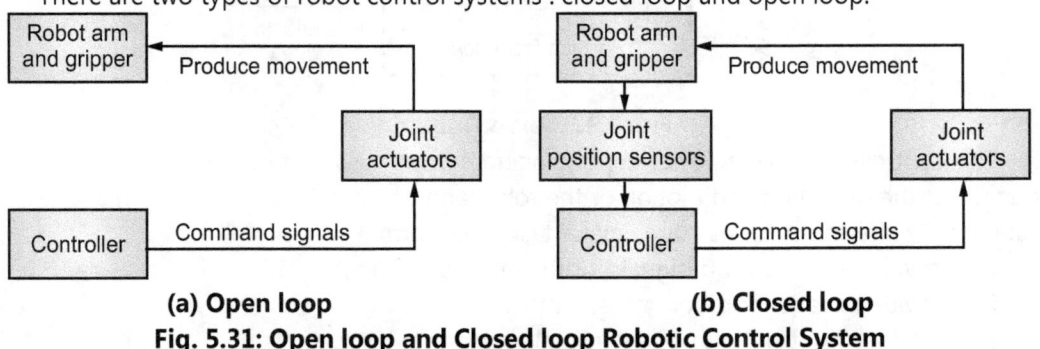

**(a) Open loop**      **(b) Closed loop**

**Fig. 5.31: Open loop and Closed loop Robotic Control System**

In the open loop system, there are no sensors or feedback signals that measure how the manipulator actually moved in response to the common signals.

The closed loop system uses feedback signals from joint position sensors. The controller compares the actual positions of the arm joints with the programmed positions. It then issues command signals which are designed to minimize or eliminate any discrepancies or errors.

The term servo robot is often used to refer to a closed loop system and the term non-servo robot to refer to an open loop system.

Non-servo robots are generally small and designed for light payloads. They have only two positions for each joint and operate at high speed. They are often called "bang-bang" robots because of the way they bang from position to another position. They are programmed for a task by setting adjustable mechanical limit stops. Non-servo robots are excellent for pick and place operations such as loading and unloading parts from machines.

Unlike non-servo robots, which have no control of velocity and operate with jerky motions, servo robots have smooth motions. Servo robots can control velocity, acceleration and deceleration of each link as the manipulator goes from point to point. They can use programs which may branch to difference sequences of motions depending on some condition that is measured at the time the robot is working.

Fundamentally each axis of a servo robot is close-loop servo control system. An example of a simple servo operation is illustrated in Fig. 5.32. In this example, the servo amplifier is responsible for amplifying the difference between the command voltage and the feedback voltage. The error signal produced is used to operate the servo motor, which is mechanically connected to the end effector and feedback potentiometer.

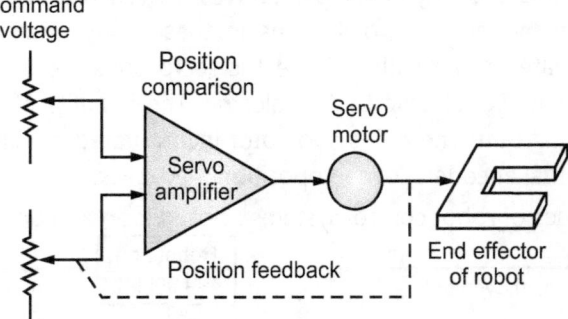

**Fig. 5.32: Servo Operation**

The controller contains power supply, operator controls, control circuitry and memory that direct the operation and motion of the robot and communication with external devices. Functionally, the controller has three major task to perform.

1. Provide motion control signals for the manipulator unit.
2. Provide storage for programmed events.
3. Interpret input/output signals, including operator instructions.

## 5.3.1 Robot Control System Configuration

Fig. 5.33 shows different controller configurations are used. In general, the controller includes the following devices that are used to operate the system.

**Operator Panel :** It comes equipped with lights, buttons and keyswitches. It performs tasks such as powering up and powering down the system. It calibrating the robot and resetting the controller after an error occurs. It holding robot motion, starting or resuming atomic operation and stopping the robot in an emergency.

**Teach Pendant :** Comes equipped with a keypad and liquid crystal display (LCD) screen and is connected to the controller by a cable that plugs into the computer RAM board inside the controller. It performs task such as jogging the robot. Teaching positional data. Testing program execution. Recovering from errors. It displaying user messages, error messages, prompts and menus, displaying and modifying positional data, program variables and inputs and outputs and performing some operations on computer file.

**CRT Screen and Keyboard :** Resembles a standard computer terminal. It performs task such as performing computer file operations. It displays status and diagnostic information and entering, translating and debugging programs.

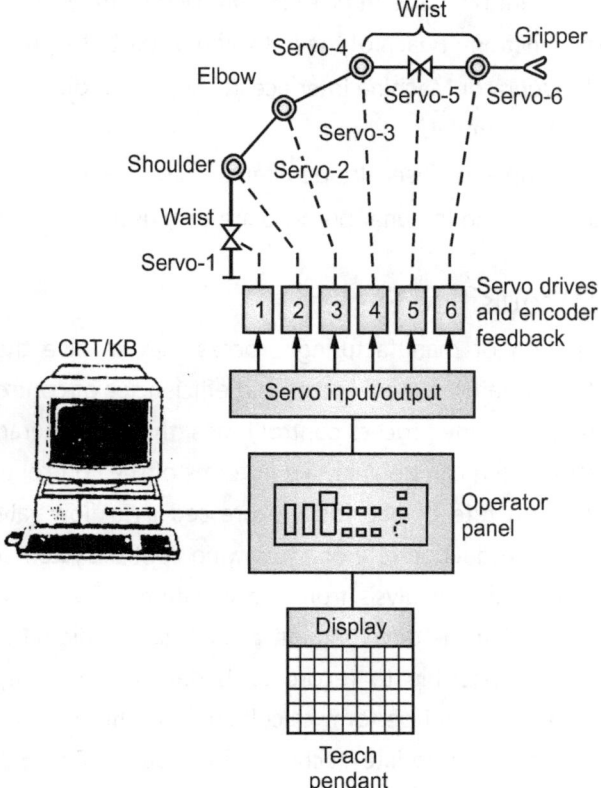

**Fig. 5.33: Robot Control System Configuration**

The robotic controller is a microprocessor based system that operates in conjunction with input and output cards or modules. With growing use of computers and PLCs in industry, the robot controller has become more important than the manipulator it controls. The robot controller is now required to communicate with devices outside itself such as PLCs and plant computer systems.

## THEORY QUESTIONS

1. List the three types of processes carried out in industries.
2. State the type of process used for each of the following applications:
   (a) Mixing ingredients to manufacture chemically based products.
   (b) Assembly of TV sets
   (c) Manufacturing of electronic chassis.
3. List three reasons why automatic machines and processes were developed.
4. Compare individual, centralized, and distributive control systems.
5. Define what is meant by the term process control system.
6. State the basic function of each of the following as part of a process control system:
   (a) Sensors, (b) Operator Machine Interface, (c) Signal conditioning,
   (d) Actuators, (e) Controller.
7. Compare open-loop and closed-loop systems.
8. What are regulators and for what purpose are they used?

## 5.3.2 Basic Data Acquisition System

The efficient operation of manufacturing process may involve the interplay of many factors, such as production rates, material costs and efficiencies of control. When the process requires implementation of many process control loops, then the interaction of one stage of the system with an other often can be analysed in terms of the control variables of the loops e.g. the rate of production rate of one loop, expressed as a flow rate, which serves as a determining factor in the production rate of a following control system. An understanding of this type of interaction requires analysis from the variations of various process parameters during a production run. With the development of high speed digital computers with mass digital storage, it become possible to record such data continuously and automatically, display the data on command and perform calculations on the data to reduce, it to a form suitable for evaluation by appropriate technical individuals. Fig. 5.34 shows the block schematic of data acquisition system.

## Block diagram of DAS

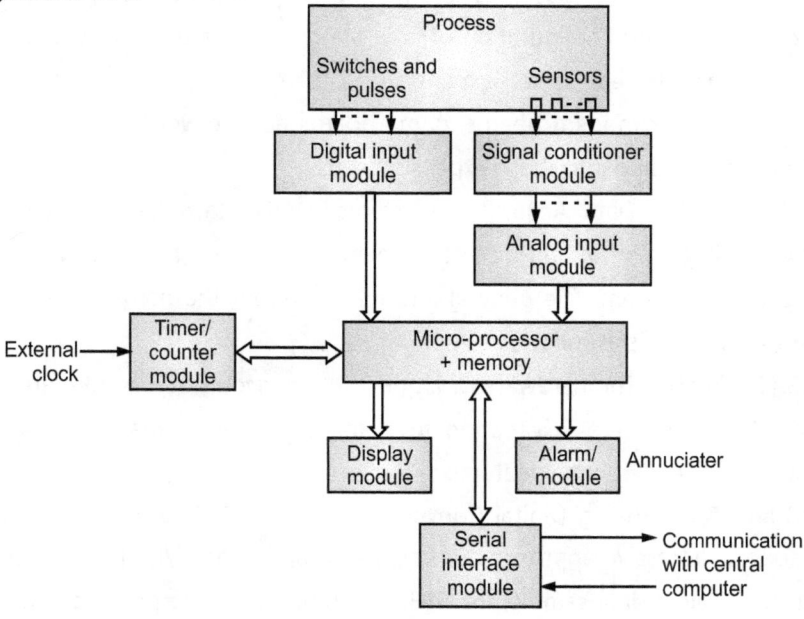

**Fig. 5.34**

## 5.3.3 Data-Acquisition Systems

Microprocessor based personal computers (PCs) are used extensively to implement direct digital control in the process industries. These familiar desktop computers are designed much like the system shown in Fig. 5.35 using a bus that consists of the data lines, address lines and control lines. All communication with the processor is via these bus lines. This includes essential equipment such as RAM, ROM, disc and CD-ROM.

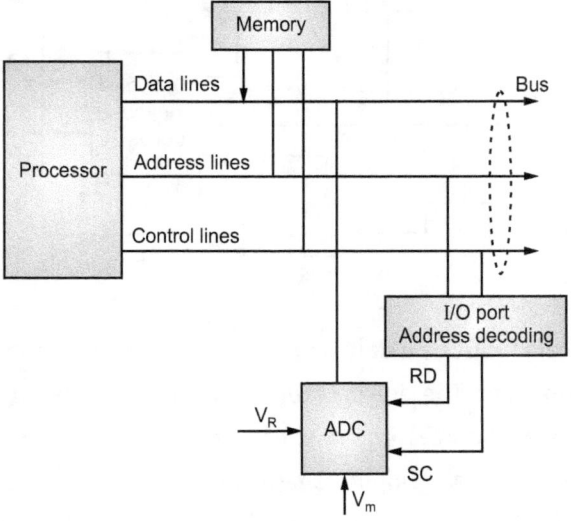

**Fig. 5.35 (a)**

The PCs also connects the bus lines to a number of printed circuit board. (PCB) sockets, using an industry standard configuration of how the bus lines are connected to the sockets. These sockets are referred to as expansion slots. Many special types of peripheral equipments such as Fax/modem boards, game boards and network connection boards are designed on PCBs that plug into these expansion slots.

Special PCBs called Data Acquisition Systems (DASs) have been developed for the purpose of providing for input and output of analog data. These are used when the PC is to be used in a control system. The general information about the hardware and software of data acquisition systems is as follows :

**(i) DAS Hardware :** The hardware of a general data acquisition system are as shown in Fig. 5.35 (b). Although there is variation from manufacturer to manufacture, the system shown demonstrates the essential features of DASs.

**(a) ADC and S/H:** Analog Digital Conversion and Sample and Hold: The DAS typically has a high speed, successive approximation type ADC and a fast S/H circuits. Whenever DAS is requested to obtain a data sample, the S/H is automatically incorporated into the process. The ADC conversion time constitutes the major part of the data sample acquisition time, but the S/H acquisition time must also be considered to establish maximum throughput.

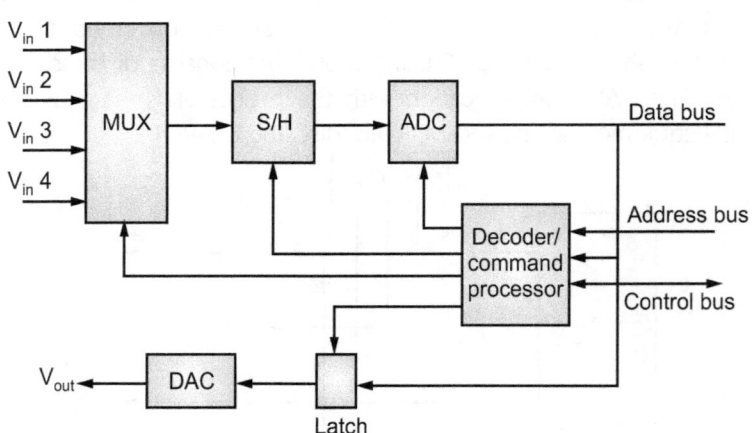

**Fig. 5.35 (b): Typical layout of a data acquisition board for use in PC expansion slot**

**(b) Analog Multiplexer:** The analog multiplexer (mux) allows the DAS to select data from a number of different sources. The mux has a number of input channels, each of which is connected to a different analog input voltage source. The mux acts like a multiple set of switches as shown in Fig. 5.35 (c).

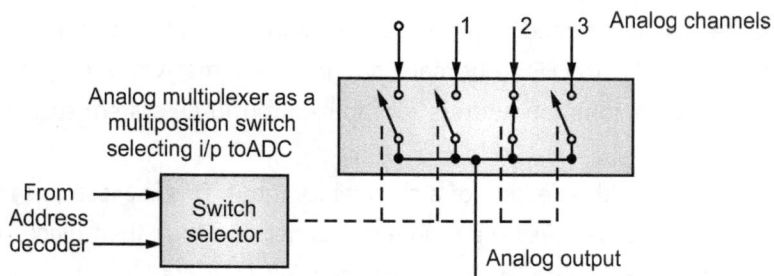

**Fig. 5.35 (c)**

They are arranged in such a fashion that any one of the input channels can be selected to provide its voltage to the S/H and ADC. In some cases, the DAS can be programmed to take channel samples sequentially.

**(c) Address Decoder/Command Processor:** The computer can select to input a sample from a given channel by sending an appropriate selection on the address lines and control lines of the computer bus. These are decided to initiate the proper sequence of commands to the mux, ADC and S/H. Another common feature is the ability to program the DAS to take number of samples from a channel with a specified time between samples. In this case, the computer is notified by interrupt when a sample is ready for input.

**(d) DAC and Latch:** For output purpose, the DAS often includes a latch and DAC (Digital Analog Conversion). The address decoder/command processor is used to latch data written to the DAS, which is then converted to an appropriate analog signal by the DAC.

**(ii) DAS Software:** The process of selecting a channel and initiating a data input from that channel involves some interface between the computer and the DAS. This interface is facilitated by software that the computer executes. The software can be written by the user; but is often also provided by the DAS manufacturer in the form of programs on disc. Fig. 5.35 (d) is a flow chart of the basic sequence of operation that must occur when a sample is required from the DAS. The each element of the sequence is as follows.

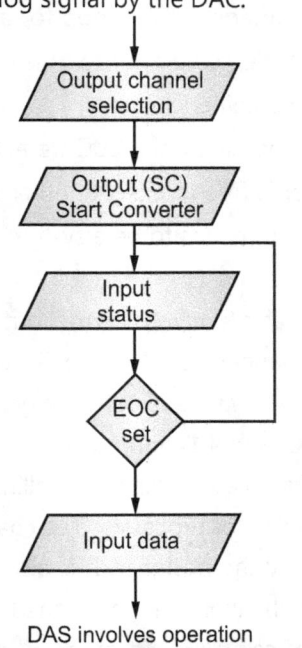

DAS involves operation
to startADC, test EOC and i/p the data

**Fig. 5.35 (d)**

Generally, the DAS is mapped into a base part address location in the PC system. This address can be from 000H to FFFH, but many addresses are reserved for use by the process and other peripherals. A common address for input/output (I/O) system such as the DAS is port 300H.

The sequence starts with selection of a channel for input. This is accomplished by a write to the DAS decoder that identifies the required channel. The mux then places that channel input voltage at the S/H input. The software then issues a start convert (SC) command according to the specification of the DAS. This is accomplished by a write to some base plus offset address. The DAS internally activates the hold mode of the S/H and start the converter.

The end of converter (EoC) is provided in a status registered in the DAS. The content of this status register can be read by the processor by a port input of a base plus offset address. The appropriate bit is then tested by the software to deduce whether the EoC has been issued.

Once the EoC has been issued, the software can input the data itself by a read of an appropriate address, again a base plus offset, which enable in states, placing the ADC output on the data bus.

There is one problem with operation described by Fig. 5.35 (d). If DAS fails, the computer will be locked in the loop waiting for the EoC to be issued. The one way to resolve this is to add an additional timer loop for a time greater than the conversion time of the ADC. If the EoC is not detected prior to time out, an error is announced, and the computer is returned to an error handling routine.

In some cases, the EoC detection is handled by an interrupt service routine. Thus, the computer is free to execute other software until the interrupt occurs. Then the data is input. Again, there needs to be a system to detect than an EoC was not provided to protect against DAS failure.

The basic functions carried out by DAS are :

(1) Channel scanning, (2) Conversion into engineering units, (3) Data processing.

The hardware and software general information of Das is as follows :

**(1) Channel Scanning:** The microprocessor scans the channels to read the data and this process is called "polling". In polling, the action of selecting a channel and addressing it is the responsibility of processor. The channel selection may be sequential or in any particular order decided by the designer. It is also possible to assign priority of some channels, over others, so some channels can be scanned more frequently than others. It is also possible to offer this facility of selecting the order of channel addressing and channel priorities to the operator level.

The channel scanning and reading of data requires the following actions to be taken :

(a) Sending channel address to the multiplexer, (b) Sending start convert pulse to ADC, (c) Reading the digital data.

For reading digital data at ADC output, the end of conversion signal of ADC chip can be read by processor and when it is "ON", the digital data can be read. Alternately, the microprocessor can execute a group of instructions for the times which are equal or greater than conversion time of ADC and then read ADC output. Another modification involves connecting the end of conversion line to one of the interrupt request-bins of the processor. In this case, the interrupt service routine reads the ADC output and stores at predetermined memory location. The channels can be polled sequential and may be scanned in some order, a channel scan array can be maintained in memory. If a channel number is repeated in the array, that particular channel will be scanned repeatedly. The processor may scan channels continuously in particular order indicated by the flowchart or may be scanned after every fixed time period, which requires a timer/counter circuit. The output of timer/counter is connected to interrupt request input. The scan routine for one channel is incorporated in "interrupt service routine". The scan array may be decided at the design stage itself and fused permanently in ROM.

Another way of scanning the channel may be provided some primitive facility after transducer to check for violation of limits. It sends interrupt request signal to processor when the analog signal from transducer is not within high and low limits boundary which is known as scanning by exception. Two analog comparators check whether the input signal is within high and low limits. The output is ORed and the final output is used as interrupt request to microprocessor.

**(2) Conversion of Engineering Units:** The data read from the output of ADC should be converted to the equivalent engineering units before any analysis is done or the data is sent for display or printing. An ADC output value will correspond to a particular engineering value based on the following parameter. (a) Calibration of transmitters, (b) ADC mode and digital output lines. The conversion of ADC output of engineering units, therefore involves multiplication by conversion factor. The conversion factor is based on the ADC type, mode and the transmitter range.

**(3) Data Processing:** The data read from the ADC output for various channels is processed by the microprocessor to carry out limit checking and performance analysis. For limits checking the 'Highest' and 'Lowest' limits for each channel are stored in an array. When any of the two limits is violated for any channel, appropriate action like alarm generation, printing etc. is limited. The limit array simplifies the limit checking routine. Through this, the facility to dynamically change the limits for any channel may also be provided on the lines similar to scan array.

In addition to limit checking, the system performance may also be analysed and report could be generated for the manager level. This report will enable the managers to visualise the problems in the system and to take decisions regarding system modification or alternate operational strategy to increase the system performance. The analysis may include histogram generation, standard deviation calculation, plotting one parameter with respect to another and so on. The software can be written depending on the type of analysis required. The analysis and report generation programs will be application dependent and will have to be written separately for different application.

## THEORY QUESTIONS

1. Name the three basic functions carried out by DAS.
2. Draw a block diagram of DAS and explain the operation.
3. Explain hardware and software of DAS.
4. Draw a layout of a DAS board.
5. Draw and explain the flow chart of basic sequence operation, when sample is required from DAS?

## 5.4 ELECTRO-MECHANICAL CONTROL RELAYS

Electromechanical relay is a magnetic switch. It makes a load on or off by energising an electromagnet, which opens or closes contacts in the electric circuit. These relays may be used in electric and electronic circuits. They are used for sequence. Operation of machines, such as drilling, boring, milling and grinding operations.

### 5.4.1 Construction

Electromechanical relays consists of stationary as well as moving contacts (Fig. 5.37). The moving contacts are attached to the plugger. The contacts are either normally closed type or normally open type. When current flows through the coil, if produces, magnetic field, which in turn causes the pluger to move through the coil, closing the normally open (NO) contacts and opening the normally closed (NC) contacts. Most machine control relays have some provision for changing contacts normally open to normally closed or vice versa.

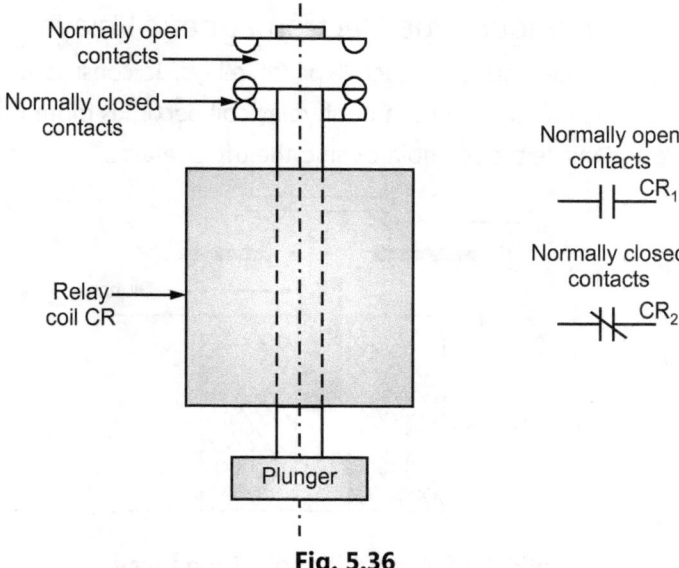

**Fig. 5.36**

Many electromagnetic relays consists of number of sets of contacts operated by a single coil.

They can be of the following type of construction.
(i) Hinged armature type electromagnetic relays.
(ii) Solenoid and plunger type electromagnetic relays.

## 5.4.2 (a) Hinged Armature Type Electromagnetic Relays

The constructional details of such type of relays is shown in Fig. 5.37. It consists of a magnetic coil, hinged armature and trip contacts. The coil is energised by the current from C.T. secondary of the system to be protected.

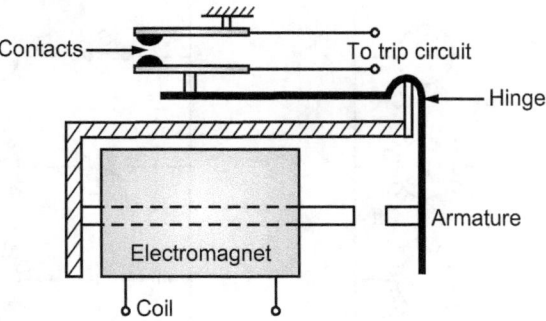

**Fig. 5.37: Hinged Armature Type Relay**

When the current or the actuating quantify applied to the coil, exceeds the pick-up value of the relay, the magnetic force of the coil insufficient to pull the armature inside it, and cause closing of contacts of trip circuit.

## 5.4.2 (b) Solenoid-plunger Type Electromagnetic Relays

Fig. 5.38 represents the details of such type of relays. It consists of a solenoid and movable iron plunger. When the current through relay coil becomes more than pick-up value the plunger is attracted inside the solenoid closing the trip contacts.

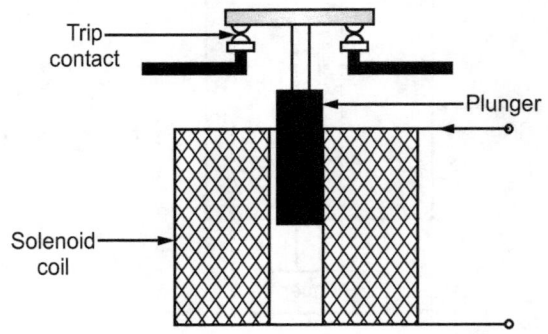

**Fig. 5.38: Solenoid Plunger Type Relay**

## 5.4.3 Control Circuit

Fig. 5.39 represents a simple circuit used to control two pilot lights using a EMR and NO and NC type of contacts.

With switch open, coil ICR is de-energised. The circuit of green light is completed through normally closed contact $ICR_2$, hence the green light will be lighted, while the circuit of red light is off through ICR, i.e. normally open contact. When the switch is closed, the coil ICR will get energised the (NO) contact will close, and (NC) will open, hence red light will be lighted.

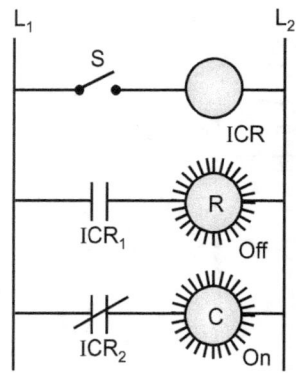 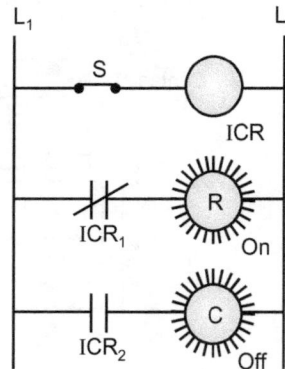

**(a) Switch open-coil de-energised**    **(b) Switch closed-coil energised**

**Fig. 5.39**

Generally, control relays are used as auxiliary devices to switch control-circuits and loads.

## 5.4.4 Applications

**(a) Control of High Voltage Circuit with Low Voltage Control Circuit:** Let it be required to control a 230 V motor circuit with a 24 volt control circuit. The motor is connected in series with the relay contacts to the 230 V source, Fig. 5.40 (a). The switch is connected in series with the relay coil, to a source of 24 volts. When the switch is operated, the relay coil is energised or de-energised. Which in turn, will close or open the contacts of EMR and will make the lamp either on or off. It is possible as the coil and contacts of the relay are electrically misulated.

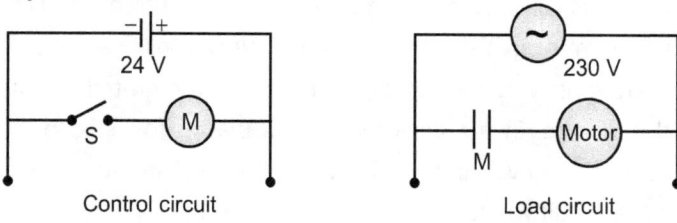

**Fig. 5.40 (a)**

**(b) Control of High Current Circuit with a Low Current Control Circuit:** Fig. 5.40 (b) represents such a circuit. In this circuit electronic control signal switches the transistor on or off, which in turn causes the relay coil to energise or de-energise. The current in the control circuit is quite small and the current in supply circuit, which consists of contacts and motor is much more in comparison to control circuit current.

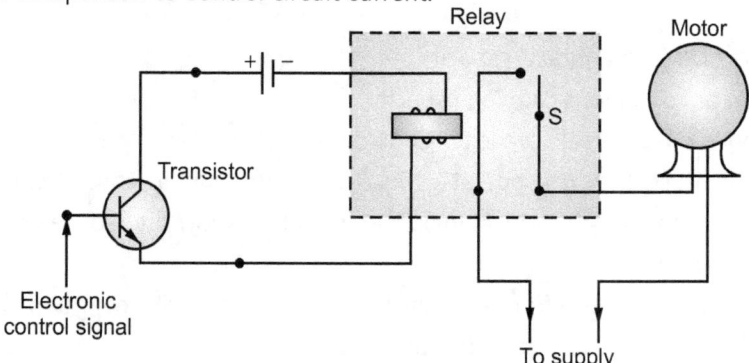

**Fig. 5.40 (b)**

This is possible because the current that can be handled by the contact can be much greater than what is required to operate the coil.

## 5.4.5 Terms Related with Relay Operation

- **(a) Pick-up Voltage:** The level of voltage at which the relay coil is energised, which results in contacts switching is called as pick up voltage.
- **(b) Drop-out Voltage:** Once the relay is energised, the level of voltage on the relay coil at which the relay contacts return to their up-operated condition is called the drop-out voltage.

**(c) In-rush Current:** When the coil is energised the plunger is in an out position, because of the open gap in the magnetic path (circuit) the initial current in the coil is high. The current level at this time is known as in rush current.

**(d) Sealed Current:** As the plunger moves into the coil, closing the gap, the current level (magnitude of current) drops to a lower value. This lower value is called sealed current of the relay.

## 5.4.6 Relay Ratings

The relay coils are usually rated for type of operating current i.e. D.C. or A.C., normal operating voltage or current, resistance and power. Very sensitive relay coils, rated in low milliampere range, are mostly operated from transistor or integrated circuits. They are either open type or enclosed type. In the enclosed type a plastic cover keeps the contacts from being exposed to corrosive environments. They are also plug in type, which can be changed without disturbing the circuit wiring.

The relays differ in number and arrangement of contacts. Although there are some single-break contacts used in industrial relays. For machine tool control double break contacts are used.

Relay contact specification is its current rating, which indicates the maximum amount of current the contacts are capable of handling. The current ratings generally as specified as follows.

(i) In-rush of "Make Contact" capacity.

(ii) Normal or continuous carrying capacity

(iii) The opening or break capacity. Contacts are also rated for maximum A.C. or D.C. voltage level at which they can operate. Most relays are used in control circuits, therefore their lower contact ratings. (0 to 15 A, maximum to 600 V) show the reduced current levels at which they operate.

Mostly contacts are made from silver instead of copper, as silver is good conductor, and its oxide which is formed on contacts is also a good conductor.

## 5.4.7 Solid-State Relays

The solid state relays are the semiconductor switching devices which may be bipolar transistors, silicon-controlled rectifiers (SCRS), MOSFET, or triacs. They have no moving parts or contacts. They are shock and vibration resistant and are sealed against dirt and moisture.

Similar to electromagnetic relays solid-state relays (SSR) are used to isolate a low voltage control circuit from a high power load circuit. Fig. 5.41 represents a block diagram of optically coupled solid-state relay, when the conditions in the circuit are correct to actuate the relay, a light emitting diode (LED) provided in the input circuit glows, as it shines on a photo-transistor it conducts, which causes trigger current to be applied to the triac. Thus, the output is isolated from the input by the LED and phototransistor arrangement. It is just similar to isolating the input from the switching contacts by the electromagnet in the electromechanical relay. As this relay uses light beam as control medium, no voltage spikes or electrical noise produced on the load side of the relay can be transmitted to the control side of the relay. Mostly the black-box approach is used to symbolize the SSR.

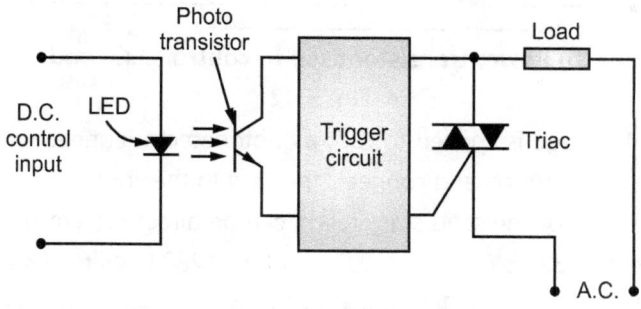

**(a) Internal circuit**

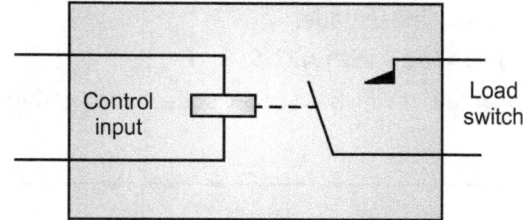

**(b) Schematic-symbol optically operated SSR**

**Fig. 5.41**

### 5.4.7.1 Control of A.C. or D.C. Loads with SSR

Fig. 5.42 (a) and (b) represents the use of SSR to control A.C. or D.C. loads.

When the relay is designed to control the A.C. load a triac is used in the load-circuit, to connect the load to the line. When such relays are used for D.C. loads, they have a power transistor connected in the load circuit instead of a triac.

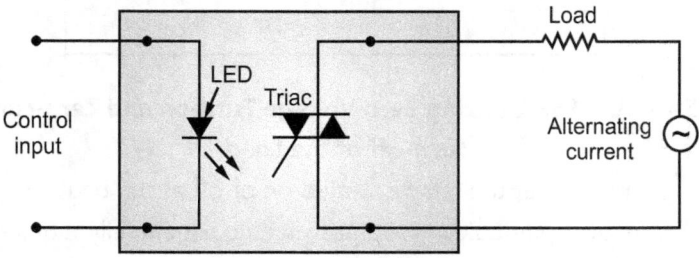

**(a) Triac used to control A.C. load**

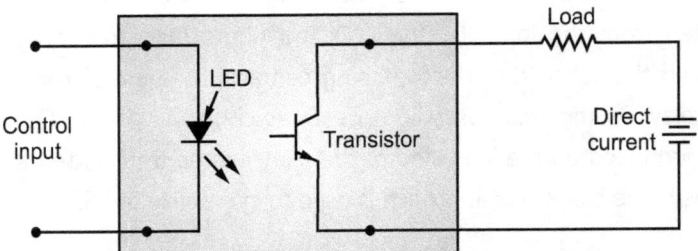

**(b) Power transistor used to control D.C. load**
**Fig. 5.42**

When the input voltage is applied to LED, a photodetector connected to the base of the transistor turns the transistor on and connects the load to the line.

The control voltage for the solid state relays can be direct current or alternating current and may vary from 3 to 32 volts, for the D.C. and 80 to 280 volts for A.C. versions. The load circuits may have a maximum load current up to 50 A at input voltage ratings of 120 V, 240 V, and 480 V, A.C. In most applications SSRs are used to interface between low voltage control circuit and a higher A.C. line voltage.

### 5.4.7.2 Zero-switching of the Load with A.C. SSR

Fig. 5.43 represents a circuit in which A.C. SSR utilizes zero voltage turn and zero current turn off of the load.

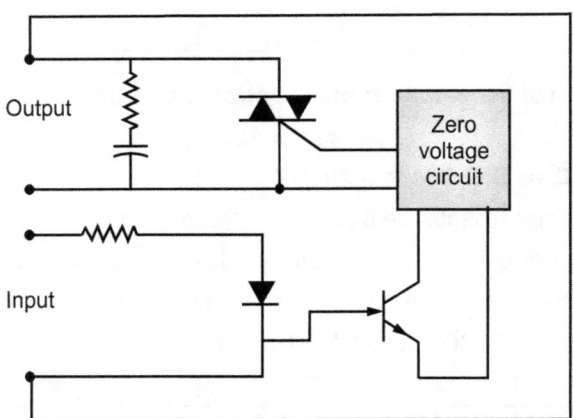

**Fig. 5.43: A.C. SSR Utilizing Zero Voltage Turn-on and Zero-current Turn-off of the Load**

Zero-switching ensures that the relay is turned on or off at the beginning of A.C. voltage Wave at the zero crossover point. Zero voltage switching is generally required to reduce the inrush current and radio frequency interference.

### 5.4.7.3 Hybrid Solid-state Relay

Fig. 5.44 represents a Hybrid solid-state which uses a small reed relay, which serve as the actuating device. A small set of reed contacts are connected to the gate by the triac. The control circuit (input) is connected to coil of the reed relay. When this coil is energised by the control current, it produces magnetic field around it, which will close the contacts of the reed relay, causing the triac to turn on. In this type of SSR, a magnetic field is used to isolate the control circuit from the load circuit, rather than a light beam.

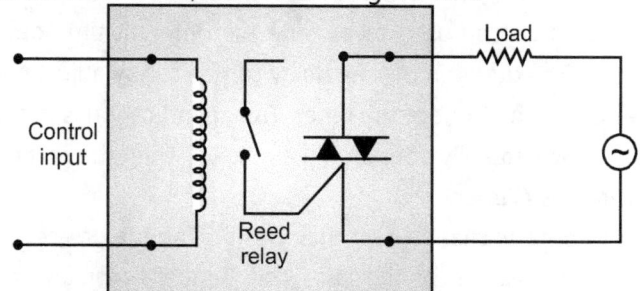

**Fig. 5.44: Hybrid solid-state relay incorporating reed relay**

### 5.4.7.4 Advantages and Disadvantages of SSRS

They are more reliable, have longer life due to absence of moving parts. It uses transistor and IC circuits hence does not produce much electromagnetic interference, they are more resistant to shack and vibrations have faster response time and does not exhibit contact bounce.

The semi-conductors used in SSR are susceptible to damage from voltage and current spikes. The switching semiconductor has a significant on-state resistance and off-state leakage current.

## 5.4.8 Timing Relays

In timing relay, the relay contacts change over their position after a pre-set delay from the time of energisation or de-energisation of the relay coil.

Timing relays are the conventional relays which are provided with an additional mechanism or circuitry to delay the opening or closing of load contacts. Timing relays are similar to other control relays in that they use a coil to control the operation of some number of contacts. The difference between the control relay and the timing relay is that the contacts of the timing relay delay changing their position when the coil is energised or de-energised.

There are four different types of timing relay utilizing different operating principles. These timers are :

    (i) Thermal timers,
    (ii) Pneumatic timers,

(iii) Electronic timers and

(iv) Synchronous motor driven timers.

A pneumatic timing relay uses mechanical linkage and an air-bellows system to achieve its timing cycle.

A solid state timing, relay uses electronic circuitry to achieve its timing cycle. Some of these timers use a resistor and capacitor (RC) time constant to obtain the time base, and others use quartz clocks as the time base. A RC oscillator network develops a highly stable and accurate pulse, which can be used to provide the different time delay increments and switch a contact output. The duration of time delay can be set by adjusting a control knob or potentiometer provided on the front of the timer. Timing indication is provided by a LED that flashes during timing, glows steadily after timing and is off when the timer is de-energised.

### 5.4.8.1 Time Delay Relays (Timer)

In time delay relay contacts change over their position after a pre-set delay from the time of energisation or de-energisation of the relay coil. Time delay relays are also commonly known as Timers. Timer can be of an ON-delay or an OFF-delay type. A timer is referred to as an ON-delay type if the contacts change over after a pre-set delay after energisation. On the other hand a timer is referred to as an OFF-delay type if the contacts change over after a pre-set delay from the instant of de-energisation. Besides the delayed contacts a timer can also have another set of contacts which operate as in an ordinary voltage relay. These are known as instantaneous contacts as they changeover their positions instantaneously when the timer is energised or de-energised. The representation of ON-delay and OFF-delay contacts of a timer in a control circuit is as shown in Fig. 5.45.

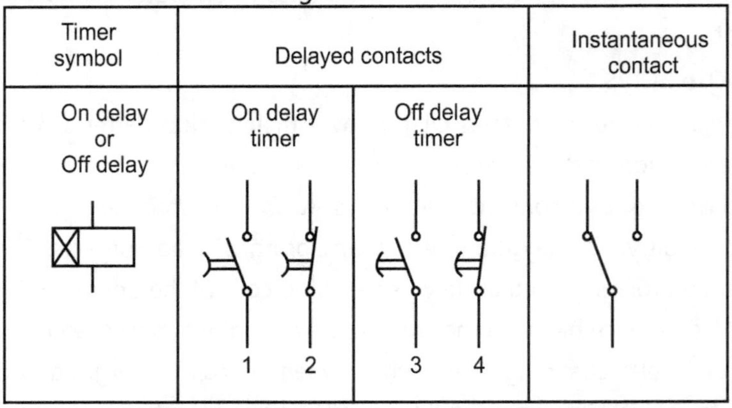

| Timer symbol | Delayed contacts | | Instantaneous contact |
|---|---|---|---|
| On delay or Off delay | On delay timer (1, 2) | Off delay timer (3, 4) | |

**Fig. 5.45: Symbols for a Timer and its Contacts**

We will represent the coil of the timer as the same for both ON and OFF-delay but delayed contacts will be represented differently. Normally, most circuits require ON-delay timers. Applications requiring OFF-delay timers can also be covered by ON-delay timers with suitable modifications in the circuitry. However, OFF-delay timers can, in few cases, simplify circuitry and thereby reduce the cost. Though the OFF-delay timer find limited applications, the reader should however thoroughly understand the contact operation of OFF-delay timer, to avoid confusion between the two types of timers. The difference of operation becomes clear from the following explanation.

ON-delay timer is normally in de-energised condition. The normal position of delayed contacts is as shown in Fig. 5.45. When the timer is energised, after a pre-set delay the contacts change over their positions. Contact 1 will become closed and contact 2 will open. However, when the timer is de-energised contacts change over almost instantaneously.

An OFF-delay timer is normally in energised condition. Thus, normally, contact 3 will be closed and contact 4 will be open. When the timer is de-energised the counting starts and after the pre-set delay, contacts 3 will open and contact 4 will close i.e., their positions will be as shown in Fig. 5.45. In the control circuits the changed over positions of the contacts are shown. As the time delay is only on one side (i.e. OFF-delay only), when timer is energised, contacts change over almost instantaneously.

Timers can also be classified as cyclic and non-cyclic timers. When a timer continues to repeat its sequence of operation till the supply is switched off, it is called a cycle timer. The change over contacts would continually switch ON and OFF at intervals as long as operating voltage is on. The non-cyclic timers operate only for one timing cycle when they are switched on. The change over contacts get switched over after the set time and stay in that state till they are reset either manually or by a knob or by switching ON or OFF an electrical signal.

Majority of applications require ON-delay, non-cyclic, non-manual reset type timers. There are four different types of timers utilizing different operating principles. These timers are thermal timers, pneumatic timers, electronic timers and motor driven (synchronous) timers.

### 5.4.8.2 Thermal Timer

Principle of working of a thermal timer is the same as that of a bimetallic overload relay discussed earlier. These are available with a limited delay range of 0-20 sec. The timing error can be very large of the order of ± 10 to 30%. By timing error it is meant that the time variation (plus or minus) between successive timing operations on the same timer represented as a percentage of maximum range of the timer. Due to higher timing error thermal timers are used only in star-delta starters where such error does not matter much.

Pneumatic and Electronic timers are suitable for delay range of 0-3 mins. For delays exceeding 3 minutes, synchronous timers are preferred. Pneumatic timers have a timing error of ± 10%, electronic timers, ± 5% and synchronous timers have timing error limited to ± 1%. The construction and working of these timers are discussed as follows.

### 5.4.8.3 Pneumatic Timer

It consists of solenoid coil, a plunger assembly and an air bleed unit consisting of an air chamber divided into upper chamber and lower chamber by a diaphragm. The diaphragm is attached to an operating rod and disc D as shown in Fig. 5.46 (a). There is a provision of air bleed (air flow) from upper chamber to lower chamber through a needle valve. Air flow rate can be changed by adjustment of the needle valve screw. Solenoid coil plunger assembly and air bleed unit are assembled together as shown in Fig. 5.46 (a) for ON-delay type operation. The contact block is mounted on the air bleed unit.

Before the coil is energised the diaphragm is in its down position as shown in the figure. A small orifice at the bottom of the lower air chamber is held closed by the diaphragm and does not allow airflow from upper air chamber to lower air chamber. Diaphragm is held in the down position as the plunger is pressing the disc and the operating rod down.

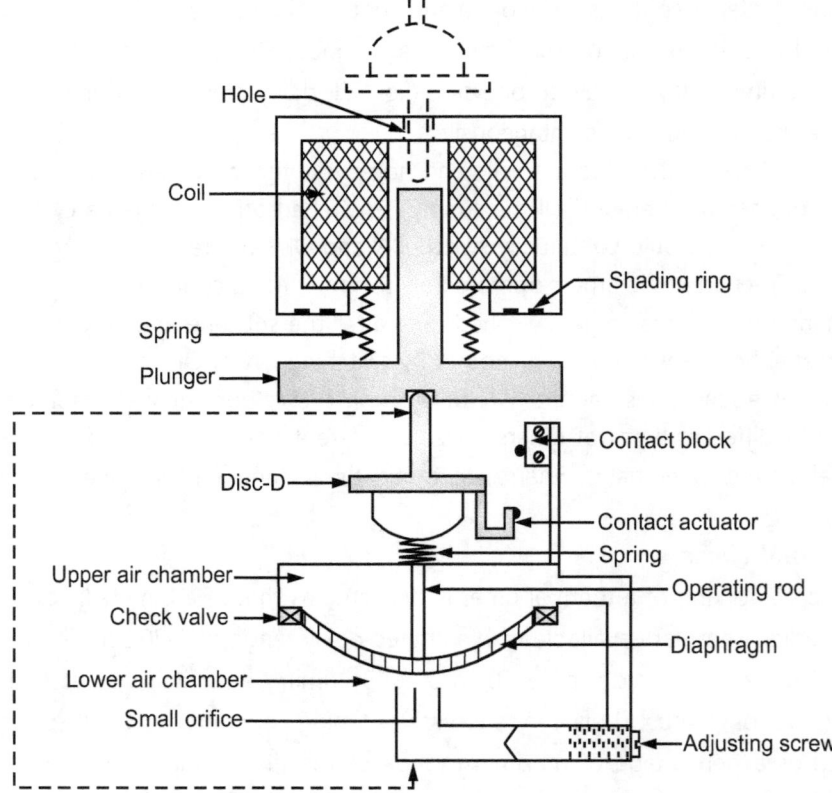

**Fig. 5.46: Pneumatic timer cross-sectional view**

When the solenoid coil is energised the plunger is attracted and thus pressure on the disc (D) and the operating rod is released. Now the diaphragm is free. Air from upper chamber leaks to the lower chamber through the needle valve. The rate of air flow can be adjusted by the screw of the needle valve. As pressure of air in the lower chamber starts increasing the diaphragm moves up slowly at a speed which depends upon the rate of air flow through the needle valve. The diaphragm in turn moves the operating rod and the disc upward. The diaphragm will move up till air pressure in both the chambers is equal. An actuating lever attached to the disc, which moves upwards, actuates the timer contacts.

The delay or time for actuation can be varied by adjustment of the needle valve. Operating rod, disc and diaphragm remain in up position as long as the coil is energised and therefore relay contacts remains closed.

When the coil is de-energised, plunger falls down which in turn presses the diaphragm down through the disc and the operating rod. The air in the lower chamber is pressurised and it flows to the upper chamber through the check valves. It may be understood here that check valves allow air flow only in one direction. In this case, this direction is from lower chamber to upper chamber and air flow is blocked in the reverse direction.

On de-energisation the same position from where we started is reached and the relay is ready for another ON-delay operation.

In the OFF-delay type of timer the air bleed unit and solenoid assembly are so arranged that, normally, when the coil is de-energised and the plunger is down the diaphgram is in the centre position and the contacts are in actuated condition. This is achieved if the whole of air bleed assembly is inverted and assembled over the solenoid coil assembly so that the rod of disc (D) enters the hole at the top of the coil assembly (shown dotted).

When the coil is energised, the diaphragm is pushed by the plunger through the disc and the operating rod to close the orifice. Therefore, the contacts also get de-actuated. When the coil is de-energised, diaphragm becomes free and starts moving towards the centre due to bleeding of air. Depending upon the speed of the operating rod and disc (D), the contacts are actuated after a delay.

### 5.4.8.4 Motor Driven Timers

This timer consists of a small motor, usually a synchronous motor, which is engaged with gear arrangement with the help of electrically operated clutch. Gear arrangement reduces the speed of motor to a desired low value. Motor thus rotates a contact actuating lever through gear arrangement. The actuating lever after travelling a pre-set distance operates the timer contacts. The time delay for actuation of contacts can be changed by a knob which varies the distance between the actuating lever and the contacts. If the distance between the actuating lever and the contacts is increased, the timer will take more time to actuate the contacts (as the motor speed is constant) and vice-versa. In ON-delay timers the motor starts counting time when the clutch coil is energised and in OFF-delay timers counting starts when the clutch coil is de-energised. Timer gets reset when the clutch is de-energised in an ON-delay timer and energised in case of an OFF-delay timer. In an ON-delay timer, the motor can be energised along with the clutch but in an OFF-delay timer the motor has to be kept running continuously.

Synchronous motor timers are also available in simple version without a clutch. In this case, the timer starts counting time when motor is energised and actuates contacts after the actuating lever moves through a pre-set distance. The timer gets reset when supply to motor is disconnected. Another version of motor driven timer makes or breaks a number of contacts during its timing period with the help of cams mounted on the motor shaft. A cam is a circular plastic material which is fitted on the motor shaft as shown in Fig. 5.47. Cams are shaped to produce protruding portions which actuate the contact blocks.

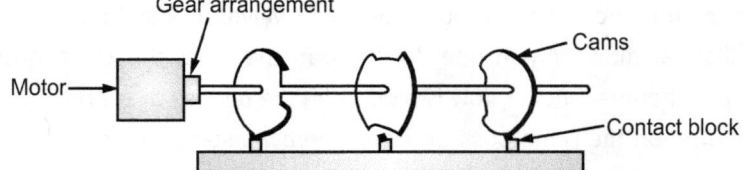

**Fig. 5.47: Simplified Representation of a Motor Driven Cam Timer**

When the motor is energised the cams start rotating. Protruding portion of the cam presses the knob of contact block and thus contacts remain actuated as long as the protruding portion of the cam passes over the contact knob. For the remaining position of the cam the contact gets de-actuated.

The time period required for actuation and de-actuation of a particular contact can be obtained by adjusting the shape of the cam as per requirement.

These timers are very useful for initiating different processes in sequence. Another important application is starting of motors in a conveyor system.

A time switch is another form of a motor driven timer. It offers independent control of the ON and OFF duration of the contacts. Any combination of ON-time and OFF-time can be selected as long as the total of ON-time and OFF-time does not exceed the maximum or full range time of the device.

An important application of time switch is for street lighting control where the full range-time is 24 hours. Time switch, for this purpose, is provided with battery supply also which can run the timer in case the main supply fails. Thus, interruptions due to supply failure does not effect the ON and OFF-time of the timer.

### 5.4.8.5 Electronic Timer

Electronic timers are widely used in industry for various applications due to their better accuracy and longer life than the pneumatic timers. They are less expensive than synchronous timers. Only critical processes which demand very high accuracy require synchronous timers.

Electronic timers achieve their timing action with an electronic circuit. Electronic timers are generally of the ON-delay type. When supply to the timer is given it starts counting and the contacts change over their positions after a pre-set delay. The length of time delay period is easily adjusted by a variable resistor placed in the electronic circuit. The timer gets reset when supply to the timer is cut off.

A very simple electronic timer circuit using a silicon controlled rectifier (SCR) is shown in Fig. 5.48. The SCR, also generally known as Thyristor, has three terminals Anode, Cathode and Gate. It conducts when a signal is applied between its Gate and Cathode and continues to conduct even if signal to the gate is removed after conduction starts. It conducts only when there is positive supply at the Anode and negative supply at the Cathode. The gate supply should be positive with respect to the Cathode to cause its conduction.

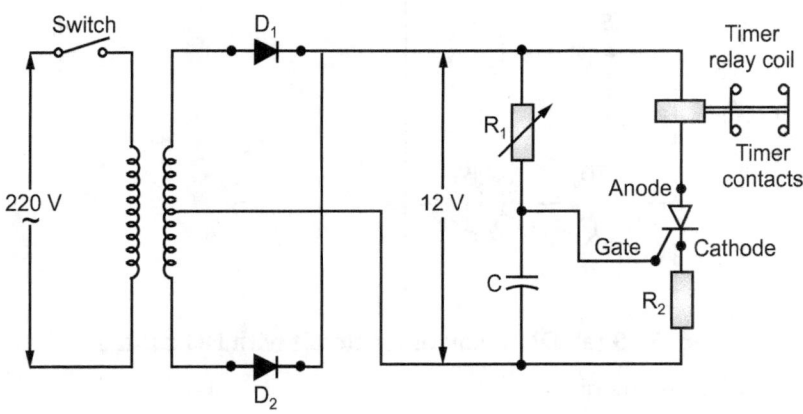

**Fig. 5.48: Simple Circuit of an Electronic Timer**

In the circuit of Fig. 5.48, control transformer (220/12 V centre tapped) and diodes $D_1$ and $D_2$ provide 12 V D.C. supply to the electronic circuit. When the timer switch is closed 12 V D.C. is available to the timer circuit. Resistance $R_1$ and capacitor C form the RC charging circuit. The coil of the timer relay is connected in series with the SCR as shown. The gate of SCR is connected to the capacitor terminal. When the timer switch is closed, the capacitor C starts charging. When the voltage of the capacitor is sufficient to send minimum gate current to trigger on the SCR, the SCR starts conducting. Resistance $R_2$ is there to limit the gate current. When the SCR starts conducting, relay coil picks up and closes its contacts. The required delay in closing the relay contacts may be obtained by changing the charging rate of capacitor (by varying the variable resistance $R_1$). A suitable time range of the timer can be designed by using required values of $R_1$ and C. The timer gets reset automatically when supply to the timer is cut off. The contacts of the timer then return to the normal position immediately.

### 5.4.8.6 Time Delay Relays

Time-delay relays are classified as :

(a) ON-delay

(b) OFF-delay

### (a) ON-delay Relays:

These relays are often called as DOE, which means 'Delay on Energise', when power is connected to the coil of an ON-delay timer, the contacts delay changing position for some period of time. Fig. 5.49 (a) represents a circuit for a such type of relay.

The sequence of operation is as follows :

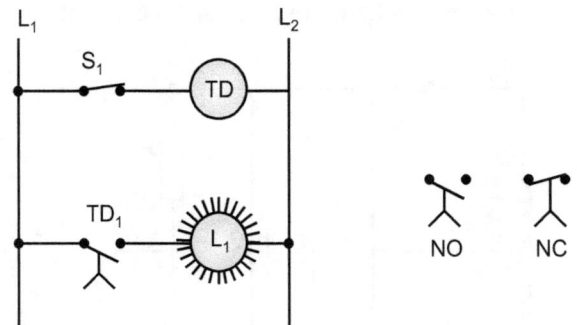

**Fig. 5.49 (a): ON-delay timer circuit with NO contact**

$S_1$ opens, TD de-energises,

TD, opens, $L_1$ is off.

$S_1$ closes, TD energises, timing period starts, $TD_1$ is still open, and $L_1$ is still OFF. After set time say 5 secs, $TD_1$ closes and $L_1$ is switched ON. $S_1$ opens, TD de-energises, $TD_1$ opens instantly, and $L_1$ is switched OFF.

Fig. 5.49 (b) represents ON delay timer circuit with NC contact.

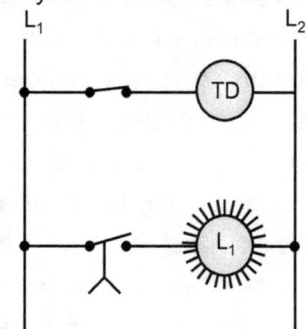

**Fig. 5.49 (b): ON-delay Timer Circuit with NC Contact**

The sequence of operation is as follows :

$S_1$ opens, TD de-energises, $TD_1$ closes, $L_1$ is ON.

$S_1$ closes, TD energies, timing period starts, $TD_1$ is still closed, and $L_1$ is still ON.

After set time of say 5 secs., $TD_1$ opens and $L_1$ is switched OFF.

$S_1$ opens, TD de-energies, $TD_1$ closes instantly and $L_1$ is switched ON.

### (b) OFF-delay Relay:

Fig. 5.49 (c) represents this type of relay, which is often referred to as DODE, which means, "delay on de-energise". The operation of the off delay timer is opposite of the operation of the ON-delay timer. When voltage is applied to the coil of the off delay timer, the contacts change position immediately, when the coil is de-energised, however there is a time delay before the contacts change to their normal positions.

NO    NC

**(c) OFF-delay NO and NC contacts**

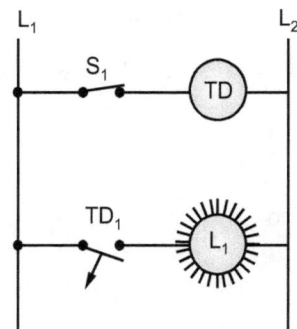

**(d) OFF-delay timer circuit with NO contacts**

**Fig. 5.49**

The sequence of operation is as follows :

$S_1$ Open, TD de-energises, $TD_1$ opens, and $L_1$ is OFF.

$S_1$ closes, TD energises, $TD_1$ closes instantly and $L_1$ is switched ON.

$S_1$ opens, TD de-energises, timing period starts, $TD_1$ is still closed, and $L_1$ is still ON.

After set time of say 5 secs., $TD_1$ opens and $L_1$ is switched OFF.

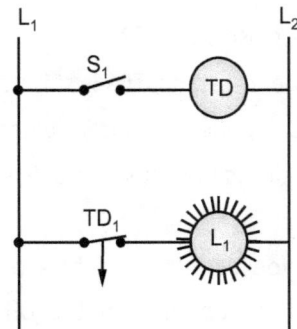

**Fig. 5.49 (e): OFF-delay Timer Circuit with NC Contact**

### 5.4.8.7 OFF-delay Timer Circuit with NC Contact

The sequence of operation for the above circuit is as follows:

$S_1$ Opens, TD de-energises, $TD_1$ closes, and $L_1$ is ON.

$S_1$ closes, TD de-energises, $TD_1$ opens instantly, and $L_1$ is switched OFF.

$S_1$ opens, TD de-energises, timing period starts, $TD_1$ is still open, and $L_1$ is still OFF.

After set time, say 5 secs, $TD_1$ closes and $L_1$ is switched ON.

Sometimes the abbreviations TO and TC are used with standard contact symbols, on some control schematics to indicate a time-operated contact.

TC stands for time closing

⊣⊢TC

and To stands for 'Time Opening'

⊣⊢TO

## 5.4.9 Latching Relays

Latching relays are those relays which hold the relay closed after power has been removed from the coil. They are used where it is necessary for contacts to remain open and, or closed even though the coil is energised only momentarily.

Fig. 5.50 represents, latching relay which uses two coils. When the latch coil is momentarily the latch coil is momentarily energised it will set the latch and will hold the relay in the latched position. When it is desired to disengage the mechanical latch the unlatch or release coil of the latching relay is momentarily energised; which disengage the mechanical latch and return the relay to the unlatched position.

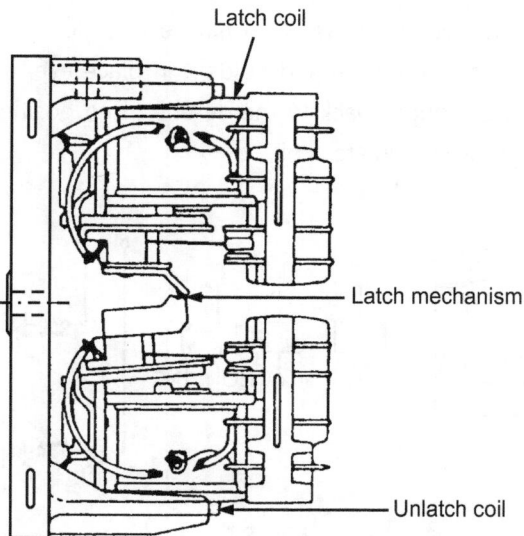

**Fig. 5.50: Mechanically held latching relay**

Fig. 5.50 represents a schematic diagram for an electromagnetic latching type relay circuit. In which the contact is shown which the relay in the unlatched position. Under this is shown with the relay in the unlatched position. Under this condition the circuit to pilot light (PL) is open, hence the light is OFF. When we actuate the 'ON' button momentarily, the latch coil will get energised, setting the relay to its latched position. Hence, the contacts will close, which completes the circuit to the pilot light, hence the light is switched on. It is not necessary that the relay coil be continuously energised to hold the contact closed to keep the light ON.

When it is desired to switch the lamp OFF, we have to operate the 'OFF' button, which energises the unlatch coil and return the contact to their open, i.e. unlatched condition.

The difference between a conventional voltage relay and latching relay is that the former drops to its de-energised position when the operating coil is de-energised, whereas a latching relay remains in energised position even when operating coil is de-energised.

Latching relay has two coils, an operating coil which is also referred to as latch coil and unlatch coil. When the latch coil is energised the relay operates and it held in the energised position either by a mechanical latch or a permanent magnet. The relay remains in the energised position even when the latch coil is de-energised. The relay can be brought back to the de-energised position only when the unlatch coil is energised. The relay construction can be of two types depending on how the relay is held in the energised position when the latch coil is de-energised. The construction and working of the two types of latching relays i.e. (i) Mechanically latched type and (ii) The permanent magnet type.

(a) In a mechanical latched relay, when armature is pulled by the operating coil, the mechanical latch engages the armature and holds it in place even when the coil voltage is removed. The relay can be brought back to the de-energised position when the mechanical latch is opened by energising the unlatch coil.

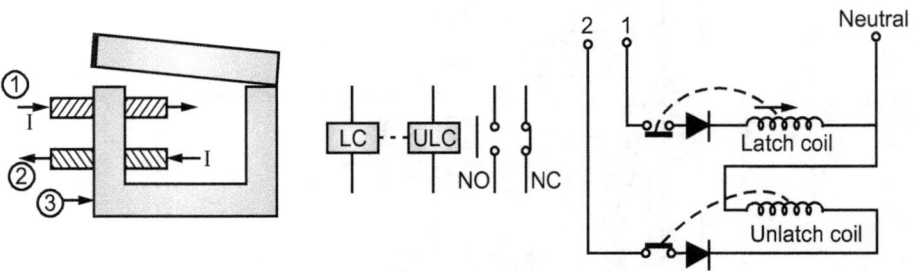

**Fig. 5.51**

In permanent magnet type latch relay, the magnetic circuit material gets permanently magnetised, when current flows through the operating coil (latch coil). Both the latch coil and unlatch coil are mounted on the same magnetic core.

When supply is given to terminal 1 and neutral, latch coil is energised and current flows in the direction shown. Relay is actuated and held closed due to magnetisation of the core even when supply is cut-off. The supply to latch coil can also be cut-off by using a normally closed contact of the relay in series with the coil. When relay closes, the contact opens and disconnects the coil, because the coil is not designed for continuous flow of current. Diodes are used to allow flow of D.C. current through the coil. When the relay is to be opened, supply is given between terminal 2 and neutral. Current in unlatch coil flows through the diode $D_2$ in direction so as to demagnetise the core. The current direction is opposite to that of the latch coil. When the core gets demagnetised the relay opens and supply to unlatch coil is also disconnected through a normally open contact of the relay.

Latching relays are often used as memory relays on machines or processes where the work on machine must start from where it is stopped when power had failed. When ordinary relays are used the machine cycle starts from the beginning when power is restored after a failure. Latching type relays can also be used where A.C. hum of the relay is objectionable. Here the relay coil is cut-ff once it is energised.

A simple application of latching relay can be to start a motor automatically when power is restored after a failure.

The control circuit is given in Fig. 5.52.

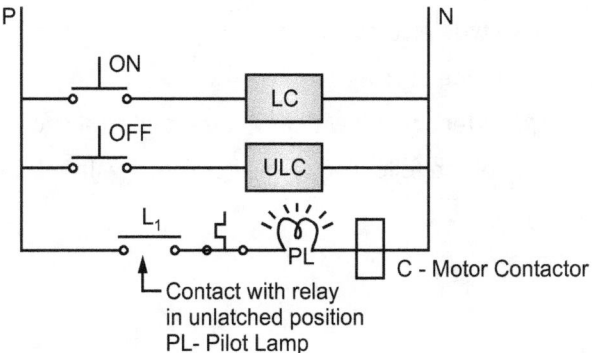

**Fig. 5.52**

When ON push button is pressed latching relay LR is energised and contact $L_1$ of motor closes and motor contractor C is energised, when power fails, relay does not drop and contact $L_1$ remains closed. Therefore, when power is restored, contractor C gets energised automatically and there is no need to push the ON push button. Whenever it is desired to stop the motor, the OFF push button is pressed which energises the unlatch relay coil ULC and thus contact $L_1$ opens. The pilot lamp is put in series with contact $L_1$ to indicate the ON and OFF position. Lamp lights when $L_1$ is closed and power is ON. Thus, latching relays are used for :

(1) It is used in control circuits to have to remember, when a particular event takes place, it is not allowed certain functions once this event occurs.

(2) Running out of a part on an assembly line may signal the shut down of the process, by momentarily energising the unlatch coil. The latch coil would then have to be momentarily energised before further operations could occur.

(3) Use of latching relay involves power failure circuit continuity during power failure. It is often important in automatic process equipment, where a sequence of operations must continue from the point of interruption after power is resumed rather than return to the beginning of the sequence.

(4) The relays are also used in machine tool control circuits. These relays can be latched and unlatched through the operation of pilot devices such as limit switches and push buttons.

## THEORY QUESTIONS

1. Draw sketches and explain in brief working principle of :
   (a) Hinged armature type electromagnetic relay.
   (b) Solenoid plunger type of relay.
   (c) Control of high current circuit with low current control circuit.
2. Explain the meaning of the following terms in relation with relay operation :
   (a) Pick-up voltage.
   (b) Drop-out voltage.
   (c) In-rush current.
   (d) Sealed current.
3. State how relays are rated ?
4. Draw the circuit in which A.C. S.S.R utilizes zero voltage turn and zero current turn-off of the load.
5. State advantages and disadvantages of SSR.
6. Draw a sketch and explain working of pneumatic timer.
7. Draw a circuit of a simple electronic timer and explain in brief.
8. What are latching relays ?

www.ingramcontent.com/pod-product-compliance
Lightning Source LLC
Chambersburg PA
CBHW060503300426
44112CB00017B/2535